Lecture Notes in Computer Science 14255

The series Lecture Notes in Computer Science (LNCS), including its subseries Lecture Notes in Artificial Intelligence (LNAI) and Lecture Notes in Bioinformatics (LNBI), has established itself as a medium for the publication of new developments in computer science and information technology research, teaching, and education.

LNCS enjoys close cooperation with the computer science R & D community, the series counts many renowned academics among its volume editors and paper authors, and collaborates with prestigious societies. Its mission is to serve this international community by providing an invaluable service, mainly focused on the publication of conference and workshop proceedings and postproceedings. LNCS commenced publication in 1973.

Lazaros Iliadis · Antonios Papaleonidas ·
Plamen Angelov · Chrisina Jayne
Editors

Artificial Neural Networks and Machine Learning – ICANN 2023

32nd International Conference on Artificial Neural Networks
Heraklion, Crete, Greece, September 26–29, 2023
Proceedings, Part II

Editors
Lazaros Iliadis
Democritus University of Thrace
Xanthi, Greece

Antonios Papaleonidas
Democritus University of Thrace
Xanthi, Greece

Plamen Angelov
Lancaster University
Lancaster, UK

Chrisina Jayne
Teesside University
Middlesbrough, UK

ISSN 0302-9743 ISSN 1611-3349 (electronic)
Lecture Notes in Computer Science
ISBN 978-3-031-44209-4 ISBN 978-3-031-44210-0 (eBook)
https://doi.org/10.1007/978-3-031-44210-0

This Springer imprint is published by the registered company Springer Nature Switzerland AG
The registered company address is: Gewerbestrasse 11, 6330 Cham, Switzerland

Paper in this product is recyclable.

Preface

The European Neural Network Society (ENNS) is an association of scientists, engineers and students, conducting research on the modelling of behavioral and brain processes, and on the development of neural algorithms. The core of these efforts is the application of neural modelling to several diverse domains. According to its mission statement ENNS is the European non-profit federation of professionals that aims at achieving a worldwide professional and socially responsible development and application of artificial neural technologies.

The flagship event of ENNS is ICANN (the International Conference on Artificial Neural Networks) at which contributed research papers are presented after passing through a rigorous review process. ICANN is a dual-track conference, featuring tracks in brain-inspired computing on the one hand, and machine learning on the other, with strong crossdisciplinary interactions and applications.

The response of the international scientific community to the ICANN 2023 call for papers was more than satisfactory. In total, 947 research papers on the aforementioned research areas were submitted and 426 (45%) of them were finally accepted as full papers after a peer review process. Additionally, 19 extended abstracts were submitted and 9 of them were selected to be included in the front matter of ICANN 2023 proceedings. Due to their high academic and scientific importance, 22 short papers were also accepted.

All papers were peer reviewed by at least two independent academic referees. Where needed, a third or a fourth referee was consulted to resolve any potential conflicts. Three workshops focusing on specific research areas, namely Advances in Spiking Neural Networks (ASNN), Neurorobotics (NRR), and the challenge of Errors, Stability, Robustness, and Accuracy in Deep Neural Networks (ESRA in DNN), were organized.

The 10-volume set of LNCS 14254, 14255, 14256, 14257, 14258, 14259, 14260, 14261, 14262 and 14263 constitutes the proceedings of the 32nd International Conference on Artificial Neural Networks, ICANN 2023, held in Heraklion city, Crete, Greece, on September 26–29, 2023.

The accepted papers are related to the following topics:

Machine Learning: Deep Learning; Neural Network Theory; Neural Network Models; Graphical Models; Bayesian Networks; Kernel Methods; Generative Models; Information Theoretic Learning; Reinforcement Learning; Relational Learning; Dynamical Models; Recurrent Networks; and Ethics of AI.

Brain-Inspired Computing: Cognitive Models; Computational Neuroscience; Self-Organization; Neural Control and Planning; Hybrid Neural-Symbolic Architectures; Neural Dynamics; Cognitive Neuroscience; Brain Informatics; Perception and Action; and Spiking Neural Networks.

Neural applications in Bioinformatics; Biomedicine; Intelligent Robotics; Neurorobotics; Language Processing; Speech Processing; Image Processing; Sensor Fusion; Pattern Recognition; Data Mining; Neural Agents; Brain-Computer Interaction; Neuromorphic Computing and Edge AI; and Evolutionary Neural Networks.

September 2023

Lazaros Iliadis
Antonios Papaleonidas
Plamen Angelov
Chrisina Jayne

Organization

General Chairs

Iliadis Lazaros	Democritus University of Thrace, Greece
Plamen Angelov	Lancaster University, UK

Program Chairs

Antonios Papaleonidas	Democritus University of Thrace, Greece
Elias Pimenidis	UWE Bristol, UK
Chrisina Jayne	Teesside University, UK

Honorary Chairs

Stefan Wermter	University of Hamburg, Germany
Vera Kurkova	Czech Academy of Sciences, Czech Republic
Nikola Kasabov	Auckland University of Technology, New Zealand

Organizing Chairs

Antonios Papaleonidas	Democritus University of Thrace, Greece
Anastasios Panagiotis Psathas	Democritus University of Thrace, Greece
George Magoulas	University of London, Birkbeck College, UK
Haralambos Mouratidis	University of Essex, UK

Award Chairs

Stefan Wermter	University of Hamburg, Germany
Chukiong Loo	University of Malaysia, Malaysia

Communication Chairs

Sebastian Otte	University of Tübingen, Germany
Anastasios Panagiotis Psathas	Democritus University of Thrace, Greece

Steering Committee

Stefan Wermter	University of Hamburg, Germany
Angelo Cangelosi	University of Manchester, UK
Igor Farkaš	Comenius University in Bratislava, Slovakia
Chrisina Jayne	Teesside University, UK
Matthias Kerzel	University of Hamburg, Germany
Alessandra Lintas	University of Lausanne, Switzerland
Kristína Malinovská (Rebrová)	Comenius University in Bratislava, Slovakia
Alessio Micheli	University of Pisa, Italy
Jaakko Peltonen	Tampere University, Finland
Brigitte Quenet	ESPCI Paris, France
Ausra Saudargiene	Lithuanian University of Health Sciences, Lithuania
Roseli Wedemann	Rio de Janeiro State University, Brazil

Local Organizing/Hybrid Facilitation Committee

Aggeliki Tsouka	Democritus University of Thrace, Greece
Anastasios Panagiotis Psathas	Democritus University of Thrace, Greece
Anna Karagianni	Democritus University of Thrace, Greece
Christina Gkizioti	Democritus University of Thrace, Greece
Ioanna-Maria Erentzi	Democritus University of Thrace, Greece
Ioannis Skopelitis	Democritus University of Thrace, Greece
Lambros Kazelis	Democritus University of Thrace, Greece
Leandros Tsatsaronis	Democritus University of Thrace, Greece
Nikiforos Mpotzoris	Democritus University of Thrace, Greece
Nikos Zervis	Democritus University of Thrace, Greece
Panagiotis Restos	Democritus University of Thrace, Greece
Tassos Giannakopoulos	Democritus University of Thrace, Greece

Program Committee

Abraham Yosipof	CLB, Israel
Adane Tarekegn	NTNU, Norway
Aditya Gilra	Centrum Wiskunde & Informatica, Netherlands
Adrien Durand-Petiteville	Federal University of Pernambuco, Brazil
Adrien Fois	LORIA, France
Alaa Marouf	Hosei University, Japan
Alessandra Sciutti	Istituto Italiano di Tecnologia, Italy
Alessandro Sperduti	University of Padua, Italy
Alessio Micheli	University of Pisa, Italy
Alex Shenfield	Sheffield Hallam University, UK
Alexander Kovalenko	Czech Technical University in Prague, Czech Republic
Alexander Krawczyk	Fulda University of Applied Sciences, Germany
Ali Minai	University of Cincinnati, USA
Aluizio Araujo	Universidade Federal de Pernambuco, Brazil
Amarda Shehu	George Mason University, USA
Amit Kumar Kundu	University of Maryland, USA
Anand Rangarajan	University of Florida, USA
Anastasios Panagiotis Psathas	Democritus University of Thrace, Greece
Andre de Carvalho	Universidade de São Paulo, Brazil
Andrej Lucny	Comenius University, Slovakia
Angel Villar-Corrales	University of Bonn, Germany
Angelo Cangelosi	University of Manchester, UK
Anna Jenul	Norwegian University of Life Sciences, Norway
Antonios Papaleonidas	Democritus University of Thrace, Greece
Arnaud Lewandowski	LISIC, ULCO, France
Arul Selvam Periyasamy	Universität Bonn, Germany
Asma Mekki	University of Sfax, Tunisia
Banafsheh Rekabdar	Portland State University, USA
Barbara Hammer	Universität Bielefeld, Germany
Baris Serhan	University of Manchester, UK
Benedikt Bagus	University of Applied Sciences Fulda, Germany
Benjamin Paaßen	Bielefeld University, Germany
Bernhard Pfahringer	University of Waikato, New Zealand
Bharath Sudharsan	NUI Galway, Ireland
Binyi Wu	Dresden University of Technology, Germany
Binyu Zhao	Harbin Institute of Technology, China
Björn Plüster	University of Hamburg, Germany
Bo Mei	Texas Christian University, USA

Brian Moser	Deutsches Forschungszentrum für künstliche Intelligenz, Germany
Carlo Mazzola	Istituto Italiano di Tecnologia, Italy
Carlos Moreno-Garcia	Robert Gordon University, UK
Chandresh Pravin	Reading University, UK
Chao Ma	Wuhan University, China
Chathura Wanigasekara	German Aerospace Centre, Germany
Cheng Shang	Shanghai Jiaotong University, China
Chengqiang Huang	Huawei Technologies, China
Chenhan Zhang	University of Technology, Sydney, Australia
Chenyang Lyu	Dublin City University, Ireland
Chihuang Liu	Meta, USA
Chrisina Jayne	Teesside University, UK
Christian Balkenius	Lund University, Sweden
Chrysoula Kosma	Ecole Polytechnique, Greece
Claudio Bellei	Elliptic, UK
Claudio Gallicchio	University of Pisa, Italy
Claudio Giorgio Giancaterino	Intesa SanPaolo Vita, Italy
Constantine Dovrolis	Cyprus Institute, USA
Coşku Horuz	University of Tübingen, Germany
Cunjian Chen	Monash, Australia
Cunyi Yin	Fuzhou University, Singapore
Damien Lolive	Université Rennes, CNRS, IRISA, France
Daniel Stamate	Goldsmiths, University of London, UK
Daniel Vašata	Czech Technical University in Prague, Czech Republic
Dario Pasquali	Istituto Italiano di Tecnologia, Italy
David Dembinsky	German Research Center for Artificial Intelligence, Germany
David Rotermund	University of Bremen, Germany
Davide Liberato Manna	University of Strathclyde, UK
Dehao Yuan	University of Maryland, USA
Denise Gorse	University College London, UK
Dennis Wong	Macao Polytechnic University, China
Des Higham	University of Edinburgh, UK
Devesh Jawla	TU Dublin, Ireland
Dimitrios Michail	Harokopio University of Athens, Greece
Dino Ienco	INRAE, France
Diptangshu Pandit	Teesside University, UK
Diyuan Lu	Helmholtz Center Munich, Germany
Domenico Tortorella	University of Pisa, Italy
Dominik Geissler	American Family Insurance, USA

DongNyeong Heo	Handong Global University, South Korea
Dongyang Zhang	University of Electronic Science and Technology of China, China
Doreen Jirak	Istituto Italiano di Tecnologia, Italy
Douglas McLelland	BrainChip, France
Douglas Nyabuga	Mount Kenya University, Rwanda
Dulani Meedeniya	University of Moratuwa, Sri Lanka
Dumitru-Clementin Cercel	University Politehnica of Bucharest, Romania
Dylan Muir	SynSense, Switzerland
Efe Bozkir	Uni Tübingen, Germany
Eleftherios Kouloumpris	Aristotle University of Thessaloniki, Greece
Elias Pimenidis	University of the West of England, UK
Eliska Kloberdanz	Iowa State University, USA
Emre Neftci	Foschungszentrum Juelich, Germany
Enzo Tartaglione	Telecom Paris, France
Erwin Lopez	University of Manchester, UK
Evgeny Mirkes	University of Leicester, UK
F. Boray Tek	Istanbul Technical University, Turkey
Federico Corradi	Eindhoven University of Technology, Netherlands
Federico Errica	NEC Labs Europe, Germany
Federico Manzi	Università Cattolica del Sacro Cuore, Italy
Federico Vozzi	CNR, Italy
Fedor Scholz	University of Tuebingen, Germany
Feifei Dai	Chinese Academy of Sciences, China
Feifei Xu	Shanghai University of Electric Power, China
Feixiang Zhou	University of Leicester, UK
Felipe Moreno	FGV, Peru
Feng Wei	York University, Canada
Fengying Li	Guilin University of Electronic Technology, China
Flora Ferreira	University of Minho, Portugal
Florian Mirus	Intel Labs, Germany
Francesco Semeraro	University of Manchester, UK
Franco Scarselli	University of Siena, Italy
François Blayo	IPSEITE, Switzerland
Frank Röder	Hamburg University of Technology, Germany
Frederic Alexandre	Inria, France
Fuchang Han	Central South University, China
Fuli Wang	University of Essex, UK
Gabriela Sejnova	Czech Technical University in Prague, Czech Republic
Gaetano Di Caterina	University of Strathclyde, UK
George Bebis	University of Nevada, USA

Gerrit Ecke	Mercedes-Benz, Germany
Giannis Nikolentzos	Ecole Polytechnique, France
Gilles Marcou	University of Strasbourg, France
Giorgio Gnecco	IMT School for Advanced Studies, Italy
Glauco Amigo	Baylor University, USA
Greg Lee	Acadia University, Canada
Grégory Bourguin	LISIC/ULCO, France
Guillermo Martín-Sánchez	Champalimaud Foundation, Portugal
Gulustan Dogan	UNCW, USA
Habib Khan	Islamia College University Peshawar, Pakistan
Haizhou Du	Shanghai University of Electric Power, China
Hanli Wang	Tongji University, China
Hanno Gottschalk	TU Berlin, Germany
Hao Tong	University of Birmingham, UK
Haobo Jiang	NJUST, China
Haopeng Chen	Shanghai Jiao Tong University, China
Hazrat Ali	Hamad Bin Khalifa University, Qatar
Hina Afridi	NTNU, Gjøvik, Norway
Hiroaki Aizawa	Hiroshima University, Japan
Hiromichi Suetani	Oita University, Japan
Hiroshi Kawaguchi	Kobe University, Japan
Hiroyasu Ando	Tohoku University, Japan
Hiroyoshi Ito	University of Tsukuba, Japan
Honggang Zhang	University of Massachusetts, Boston, USA
Hongqing Yu	Open University, UK
Hongye Cao	Northwestern Polytechnical University, China
Hugo Carneiro	University of Hamburg, Germany
Hugo Eduardo Camacho Cruz	Universidad Autónoma de Tamaulipas, Mexico
Huifang Ma	Northwest Normal University, China
Hyeyoung Park	Kyungpook National University, South Korea
Ian Nabney	University of Bristol, UK
Igor Farkas	Comenius University Bratislava, Slovakia
Ikuko Nishikawa	Ritsumeikan University, Japan
Ioannis Pierros	Aristotle University of Thessaloniki, Greece
Iraklis Varlamis	Harokopio University of Athens, Greece
Ivan Tyukin	King's College London, UK
Iveta Bečková	Comenius University in Bratislava, Slovakia
Jae Hee Lee	University of Hamburg, Germany
James Yu	Southern University of Science and Technology, China
Jan Faigl	Czech Technical University in Prague, Czech Republic

Jan Feber	Czech Technical University in Prague, Czech Republic
Jan-Gerrit Habekost	University of Hamburg, Germany
Jannik Thuemmel	University of Tübingen, Germany
Jeremie Cabessa	University Paris 2, France
Jérémie Sublime	ISEP, France
Jia Cai	Guangdong University of Finance & Economics, China
Jiaan Wang	Soochow University, China
Jialiang Tang	Nanjing University of Science and Technology, China
Jian Hu	YiduCloud, Cyprus
Jianhua Xu	Nanjing Normal University, China
Jianyong Chen	Shenzhen University, China
Jichao Bi	Zhejiang Institute of Industry and Information Technology, China
Jie Shao	University of Electronic Science and Technology of China, China
Jim Smith	University of the West of England, UK
Jing Yang	Hefei University of Technology, China
Jingyi Yuan	Arizona State University, USA
Jingyun Jia	Baidu, USA
Jinling Wang	Ulster University, UK
Jiri Sima	Czech Academy of Sciences, Czech Republic
Jitesh Dundas	Independent Researcher, USA
Joost Vennekens	KU Leuven, Belgium
Jordi Cosp	Universitat Politècnica de Catalunya, Spain
Josua Spisak	University of Hamburg, Germany
Jozef Kubík	Comenius University, Slovakia
Junpei Zhong	Hong Kong Polytechnic University, China
Jurgita Kapočiūtė-Dzikienė	Vytautas Magnus University, Lithuania
K. L. Eddie Law	Macao Polytechnic University, China
Kai Tang	Independent Researcher, China
Kamil Dedecius	Czech Academy of Sciences, Czech Republic
Kang Zhang	Kyushu University, Japan
Kantaro Fujiwara	University of Tokyo, Japan
Karlis Freivalds	Institute of Electronics and Computer Science, Latvia
Khoa Phung	University of the West of England, UK
Kiran Lekkala	University of Southern California, USA
Kleanthis Malialis	University of Cyprus, Cyprus
Kohulan Rajan	Friedrich Schiller University, Germany

Koichiro Yamauchi	Chubu University, Japan
Koloud Alkhamaiseh	Western Michigan University, USA
Konstantinos Demertzis	Democritus University of Thrace, Greece
Kostadin Cvejoski	Fraunhofer IAIS, Germany
Kristína Malinovská	Comenius University in Bratislava, Slovakia
Kun Zhang	Inria and École Polytechnique, France
Laurent Mertens	KU Leuven, Belgium
Laurent Perrinet	AMU CNRS, France
Lazaros Iliadis	Democritus University of Thrace, Greece
Leandro dos Santos Coelho	Pontifical Catholic University of Parana, Brazil
Leiping Jie	Hong Kong Baptist University, China
Lenka Tětková	Technical University of Denmark, Denmark
Lia Morra	Politecnico di Torino, Italy
Liang Ge	Chongqing University, China
Liang Zhao	Dalian University of Technology, China
Limengzi Yuan	Shihezi University, China
Ling Guo	Northwest University, China
Linlin Shen	Shenzhen University, China
Lixin Zou	Wuhan University, China
Lorenzo Vorabbi	University of Bologna, Italy
Lu Wang	Macao Polytechnic University, China
Luca Pasa	University of Padova, Italy
Ľudovít Malinovský	Independent Researcher, Slovakia
Luis Alexandre	Universidade da Beira Interior, Portugal
Luis Lago	Universidad Autonoma de Madrid, Spain
Lukáš Gajdošech Gajdošech	Comenius University Bratislava, Slovakia
Lyra Puspa	Vanaya NeuroLab, Indonesia
Madalina Erascu	West University of Timisoara, Romania
Magda Friedjungová	Czech Technical University in Prague, Czech Republic
Manuel Traub	University of Tübingen, Germany
Marcello Trovati	Edge Hill University, UK
Marcin Pietron	AGH-UST, Poland
Marco Bertolini	Pfizer, Germany
Marco Podda	University of Pisa, Italy
Markus Bayer	Technical University of Darmstadt, Germany
Markus Eisenbach	Ilmenau University of Technology, Germany
Martin Ferianc	University College London, Slovakia
Martin Holena	Czech Technical University, Czech Republic
Masanari Kimura	ZOZO Research, Japan
Masato Uchida	Waseda University, Japan
Masoud Daneshtalab	Mälardalen University, Sweden

Mats Leon Richter	University of Montreal, Germany
Matthew Evanusa	University of Maryland, USA
Matthias Karlbauer	University of Tübingen, Germany
Matthias Kerzel	University of Hamburg, Germany
Matthias Möller	Örebro University, Sweden
Matthias Müller-Brockhausen	Leiden University, Netherlands
Matus Tomko	Comenius University in Bratislava, Slovakia
Mayukh Maitra	Walmart, India
Md. Delwar Hossain	Nara Institute of Science and Technology, Japan
Mehmet Aydin	University of the West of England, UK
Michail Chatzianastasis	École Polytechnique, Greece
Michail-Antisthenis Tsompanas	University of the West of England, UK
Michel Salomon	Université de Franche-Comté, France
Miguel Matey-Sanz	Universitat Jaume I, Spain
Mikołaj Morzy	Poznan University of Technology, Poland
Minal Suresh Patil	Umea universitet, Sweden
Minh Tri Lê	Inria, France
Mircea Nicolescu	University of Nevada, Reno, USA
Mohamed Elleuch	ENSI, Tunisia
Mohammed Elmahdi Khennour	Kasdi Merbah University Ouargla, Algeria
Mohib Ullah	NTNU, Norway
Monika Schak	Fulda University of Applied Sciences, Germany
Moritz Wolter	University of Bonn, Germany
Mostafa Kotb	Hamburg University, Germany
Muhammad Burhan Hafez	University of Hamburg, Germany
Nabeel Khalid	German Research Centre for Artificial Intelligence, Germany
Nabil El Malki	IRIT, France
Narendhar Gugulothu	TCS Research, India
Naresh Balaji Ravichandran	KTH Stockholm, Sweden
Natalie Kiesler	DIPF Leibniz Institute for Research and Information in Education, Germany
Nathan Duran	UWE, UK
Nermeen Abou Baker	Ruhr West University of Applied Sciences, Germany
Nick Jhones	Dundee University, UK
Nicolangelo Iannella	University of Oslo, Norway
Nicolas Couellan	ENAC, France
Nicolas Rougier	University of Bordeaux, France
Nikolaos Ioannis Bountos	National Observatory of Athens, Greece
Nikolaos Polatidis	University of Brighton, UK
Norimichi Ukita	TTI-J, Japan

Oleg Bakhteev	EPFL, Switzerland
Olga Grebenkova	Moscow Institute of Physics and Technology, Russia
Oliver Sutton	King's College London, UK
Olivier Teste	Université de Toulouse, France
Or Elroy	CLB, Israel
Oscar Fontenla-Romero	University of A Coruña, Spain
Ozan Özdenizci	Graz University of Technology, Austria
Pablo Lanillos	Spanish National Research Council, Spain
Pascal Rost	Universität Hamburg, Germany
Paul Kainen	Georgetown, USA
Paulo Cortez	University of Minho, Portugal
Pavel Petrovic	Comenius University, Slovakia
Peipei Liu	School of Cyber Security, University of Chinese Academy of Sciences, China
Peng Qiao	NUDT, China
Peter Andras	Edinburgh Napier University, UK
Peter Steiner	Technische Universität Dresden, Germany
Peter Sutor	University of Maryland, USA
Petia Georgieva	University of Aveiro/IEETA, Portugal
Petia Koprinkova-Hristova	Bulgarian Academy of Sciences, Bulgaria
Petra Vidnerová	Czech Academy of Sciences, Czech Republic
Philipp Allgeuer	University of Hamburg, Germany
Pragathi Priyadharsini Balasubramani	Indian Institute of Technology Kanpur, India
Qian Wang	Durham University, UK
Qinghua Zhou	King's College London, UK
Qingquan Zhang	Southern University of Science and Technology, China
Quentin Jodelet	Tokyo Institute of Technology, Japan
Radoslav Škoviera	Czech Technical University in Prague, Czech Republic
Raoul Heese	Fraunhofer ITWM, Germany
Ricardo Marcacini	University of São Paulo, Brazil
Riccardo Renzulli	University of Turin, Italy
Richard Duro	Universidade da Coruña, Spain
Robert Legenstein	Graz University of Technology, Austria
Rodrigo Clemente Thom de Souza	Federal University of Parana, Brazil
Rohit Dwivedula	Independent Researcher, India
Romain Ferrand	IGI TU Graz, Austria
Roman Mouček	University of West Bohemia, Czech Republic
Roseli Wedemann	Universidade do Estado do Rio de Janeiro, Brazil

Rufin VanRullen	CNRS, France
Ruijun Feng	China Telecom Beijing Research Institute, China
Ruxandra Stoean	University of Craiova, Romania
Sanchit Hira	JHU, USA
Sander Bohte	CWI, Netherlands
Sandrine Mouysset	University of Toulouse/IRIT, France
Sanka Rasnayaka	National University of Singapore, Singapore
Sašo Karakatič	University of Maribor, Slovenia
Sebastian Nowak	University Bonn, Germany
Seiya Satoh	Tokyo Denki University, Japan
Senwei Liang	LBNL, USA
Shaolin Zhu	Tianjin University, China
Shayan Gharib	University of Helsinki, Finland
Sherif Eissa	Eindhoven University of Technology, Afghanistan
Shiyong Lan	Independent Researcher, China
Shoumeng Qiu	Fudan, China
Shu Eguchi	Aomori University, Japan
Shubai Chen	Southwest University, China
Shweta Singh	International Institute of Information Technology, Hyderabad, India
Simon Hakenes	Ruhr University Bochum, Germany
Simona Doboli	Hofstra University, USA
Song Guo	Xi'an University of Architecture and Technology, China
Stanislav Frolov	Deutsches Forschungszentrum für künstliche Intelligenz (DFKI), Germany
Štefan Pócoš	Comenius University in Bratislava, Slovakia
Steven (Zvi) Lapp	Bar Ilan University, Israel
Sujala Shetty	BITS Pilani Dubai Campus, United Arab Emirates
Sumio Watanabe	Tokyo Institute of Technology, Japan
Surabhi Sinha	Adobe, USA
Takafumi Amaba	Fukuoka University, Japan
Takaharu Yaguchi	Kobe University, Japan
Takeshi Abe	Yamaguchi University, Japan
Takuya Kitamura	National Institute of Technology, Toyama College, Japan
Tatiana Tyukina	University of Leicester, UK
Teng-Sheng Moh	San Jose State University, USA
Tetsuya Hoya	Independent Researcher, Japan
Thierry Viéville	Domicile, France
Thomas Nowotny	University of Sussex, UK
Tianlin Zhang	University of Manchester, UK

Tianyi Wang	University of Hong Kong, China
Tieke He	Nanjing University, China
Tiyu Fang	Shandong University, China
Tobias Uelwer	Technical University Dortmund, Germany
Tomasz Kapuscinski	Rzeszow University of Technology, Poland
Tomasz Szandala	Wroclaw University of Technology, Poland
Toshiharu Sugawara	Waseda University, Japan
Trond Arild Tjostheim	Lund University, Sweden
Umer Mushtaq	Université Paris-Panthéon-Assas, France
Uwe Handmann	Ruhr West University, Germany
V. Ramasubramanian	International Institute of Information Technology, Bangalore, India
Valeri Mladenov	Technical University of Sofia, Bulgaria
Valerie Vaquet	Bielefeld University, Germany
Vandana Ladwani	International Institute of Information Technology, Bangalore, India
Vangelis Metsis	Texas State University, USA
Vera Kurkova	Czech Academy of Sciences, Czech Republic
Verner Ferreira	Universidade do Estado da Bahia, Brazil
Viktor Kocur	Comenius University, Slovakia
Ville Tanskanen	University of Helsinki, Finland
Viviana Cocco Mariani	PUCPR, Brazil
Vladimír Boža	Comenius University, Slovakia
Vojtech Mrazek	Brno University of Technology, Czech Republic
Weifeng Liu	China University of Petroleum (East China), China
Wenxin Yu	Southwest University of Science and Technology, China
Wenxuan Liu	Wuhan University of Technology, China
Wu Ancheng	Pingan, China
Wuliang Huang	ICT, China
Xi Cheng	NUPT, Hong Kong, China
Xia Feng	Civil Aviation University of China, China
Xian Zhong	Wuhan University of Technology, China
Xiang Zhang	National University of Defense Technology, China
Xiaochen Yuan	Macao Polytechnic University, China
Xiaodong Gu	Fudan University, China
Xiaoqing Liu	Kyushu University, Japan
Xiaowei Zhou	Macquarie University, Australia
Xiaozhuang Song	Chinese University of Hong Kong, Shenzhen, China

Xingpeng Zhang	Southwest Petroleum University, China
Xuemei Jia	Wuhan University, China
Xuewen Wang	China University of Geosciences, China
Yahong Lian	Nankai University, China
Yan Zheng	China University of Political Science and Law, China
Yang Liu	Fudan University, China
Yang Shao	Hitachi, Japan
Yangguang Cui	East China Normal University, China
Yansong Chua	China Nanhu Academy of Electronics and Information Technology, Singapore
Yapeng Gao	Taiyuan University of Technology, China
Yasufumi Sakai	Fujitsu, Japan
Ye Wang	National University of Defense Technology, China
Yeh-Ching Chung	Chinese University of Hong Kong, Shenzhen, China
Yihao Luo	Yichang Testing Technique R&D Institute, China
Yikemaiti Sataer	Southeast University, China
Yipeng Yu	Tencent, China
Yongchao Ye	Southern University of Science and Technology, China
Yoshihiko Horio	Tohoku University, Japan
Youcef Djenouri	NORCE, Norway
Yuan Li	Military Academy of Sciences, China
Yuan Panli	Shihezi University, China
Yuan Yao	Tsinghua University, China
Yuanlun Xie	University of Electronic Science and Technology of China, China
Yuanshao Zhu	Southern University of Science and Technology, China
Yucan Zhou	Institute of Information Engineering, Chinese Academy of Sciences, China
Yuchen Zheng	Shihezi University, China
Yuchun Fang	Shanghai University, China
Yue Zhao	Minzu University of China, China
Yuesong Nan	National University of Singapore, Singapore
Zaneta Swiderska-Chadaj	Warsaw University of Technology, Poland
Zdenek Straka	Czech Technical University in Prague, Czech Republic
Zhao Yang	Leiden University, Netherlands
Zhaoyun Ding	NUDT, China
Zhengwei Yang	Wuhan University, China

Zhenjie Yao	Chinese Academy of Sciences, Singapore
Zhichao Lian	Nanjing University of Science and Technology, China
Zhiqiang Zhang	Hosei University, Japan
Zhixin Li	Guangxi Normal University, China
Zhongnan Zhang	Xiamen University, China
Zhongzhan Huang	Sun Yat-sen University, China
Zi Long	Shenzhen Technology University, China
Zilong Lin	Indiana University Bloomington, USA
Zuobin Xiong	Georgia State University, USA
Zuzana Cernekova	FMFI Comenius University, Slovakia

Invited Talks

Developmental Robotics for Language Learning, Trust and Theory of Mind

Angelo Cangelosi

University of Manchester and Alan Turing Institute, UK

Growing theoretical and experimental research on action and language processing and on number learning and gestures clearly demonstrates the role of embodiment in cognition and language processing. In psychology and neuroscience, this evidence constitutes the basis of embodied cognition, also known as grounded cognition (Pezzulo et al. 2012). In robotics and AI, these studies have important implications for the design of linguistic capabilities in cognitive agents and robots for human-robot collaboration, and have led to the new interdisciplinary approach of Developmental Robotics, as part of the wider Cognitive Robotics field (Cangelosi and Schlesinger 2015; Cangelosi and Asada 2022). During the talk we presented examples of developmental robotics models and experimental results from iCub experiments on the embodiment biases in early word acquisition and grammar learning (Morse et al. 2015; Morse and Cangelosi 2017) and experiments on pointing gestures and finger counting for number learning (De La Cruz et al. 2014). We then presented a novel developmental robotics model, and experiments, on Theory of Mind and its use for autonomous trust behavior in robots (Vinanzi et al. 2019, 2021). The implications for the use of such embodied approaches for embodied cognition in AI and cognitive sciences, and for robot companion applications, was also discussed.

Challenges of Incremental Learning

Barbara Hammer

CITEC Centre of Excellence, Bielefeld University, Germany

Smart products and AI components are increasingly available in industrial applications and everyday life. This offers great opportunities for cognitive automation and intelligent human-machine cooperation; yet it also poses significant challenges since a fundamental assumption of classical machine learning, an underlying stationary data distribution, might be easily violated. Unexpected events or outliers, sensor drift, or individual user behavior might cause changes of an underlying data distribution, typically referred to as concept drift or covariate shift. Concept drift requires a continuous adaptation of the underlying model and efficient incremental learning strategies. Within the presentation, I looked at recent developments in the context of incremental learning schemes for streaming data, putting a particular focus on the challenge of learning with drift and detecting and disentangling drift in possibly unsupervised setups and for unknown type and strength of drift. More precisely, I dealt with the following aspects: learning schemes for incremental model adaptation from streaming data in the presence of concept drift; various mathematical formalizations of concept drift and detection/quantification of drift based thereon; and decomposition and explanation of drift. I presented a couple of experimental results using benchmarks from the literature, and I offered a glimpse into mathematical guarantees which can be provided for some of the algorithms.

Reliable AI: From Mathematical Foundations to Quantum Computing

Gitta Kutyniok[1,2]

[1]Bavarian AI Chair for Mathematical Foundations of Artificial Intelligence, LMU Munich, Germany
[2]Adjunct Professor for Machine Learning, University of Tromsø, Norway

Artificial intelligence is currently leading to one breakthrough after the other, both in public life with, for instance, autonomous driving and speech recognition, and in the sciences in areas such as medical diagnostics or molecular dynamics. However, one current major drawback is the lack of reliability of such methodologies.

In this lecture we took a mathematical viewpoint towards this problem, showing the power of such approaches to reliability. We first provided an introduction into this vibrant research area, focussing specifically on deep neural networks. We then surveyed recent advances, in particular concerning generalization guarantees and explainability methods. Finally, we discussed fundamental limitations of deep neural networks and related approaches in terms of computability, which seriously affects their reliability, and we revealed a connection with quantum computing.

Intelligent Pervasive Applications for Holistic Health Management

Ilias Maglogiannis

University of Piraeus, Greece

The advancements in telemonitoring platforms, biosensors, and medical devices have paved the way for pervasive health management, allowing patients to be monitored remotely in real-time. The visual domain has become increasingly important for patient monitoring, with activity recognition and fall detection being key components. Computer vision techniques, such as deep learning, have been used to develop robust activity recognition and fall detection algorithms. These algorithms can analyze video streams from cameras, detecting and classifying various activities, and detecting falls in real time. Furthermore, wearable devices, such as smartwatches and fitness trackers, can also monitor a patient's daily activities, providing insights into their overall health and wellness, allowing for a comprehensive analysis of a patient's health. In this talk we discussed the state of the art in pervasive health management and biomedical data analytics and we presented the work done in the Computational Biomedicine Laboratory of the University of Piraeus in this domain. The talk also included Future Trends and Challenges.

Contents – Part II

A Data Augmentation Based ViT for Fine-Grained Visual Classification

Shuozhi Yuan[1,2](✉), Wenming Guo[1,2,3], and Fang Han[3]

[1] Beijing University of Posts and Telecommunications, Beijing, China
{ysz,guowenming}@bupt.edu.cn
[2] Key Laboratory of Trustworthy Distributed Computing and Service, Beijing, China
[3] Xinjiang Institute of Engineering, Urumqi, China

Abstract. Fine-grained visual classification (FGVC) is a fundamental and longstanding problem aiming to recognize objects belonging to different subclasses accurately. Unfortunately, since categories are often confused, this task is genuinely challenging. Most previous methods solve this problem in two main ways: adding more annotations or constructing more complex structures. These approaches, however, require expensive labels or sophisticated designs. To alleviate these constraints, in this work, we propose an easy but efficient method called **DA-ViT**, just using data augmentations to supervise the model. Specifically, we adopt a vision transformer as the backbone. Then, we introduce highly interpretable visual heatmaps to guide the targeted data augmentations, and three methods (local area enlargement, flipping, and cutout) are created based on the high-response areas. Furthermore, the margins among confusing classes can be increased by simply using label smoothing. Extensive experiments conducted on three popular fine-grained benchmarks demonstrate that we achieve **SOTA** performance. Meanwhile, during the inference, our method requires less computational burden.

Keywords: FGVC · Vision transformer · Data augmentation

1 Introduction

The task of FGVC attempts to recognize objects belonging to subordinate classes. However, subtle interclass differences make this a highly challenging problem. In addition, many images suffer from unconstrained poses, extreme lights, or other harmful conditions. Because of the difficulties mentioned above, the main idea to ease these problems is to focus on the critical detailed information and distinguish through the discriminative variations among similar samples.

This work is supported by the National Natural Science Foundation of China, Research on Key Technologies of Highly Reliable Nodes in Darknet Communication, no. 62162060.

L. Iliadis et al. (Eds.): ICANN 2023, LNCS 14255, pp. 1–12, 2023.
https://doi.org/10.1007/978-3-031-44210-0_1

To achieve this target, existing algorithms can be roughly divided into two types: strongly supervised methods [8,19,20] and weakly supervised methods [7,12,15,18]. The former relies on a large amount of additional information, forcing the model to pay more attention to details through artificially labeled bounding boxes, essential parts, etc. However, these annotations require labeled by experts, which are extremely expensive and bring in a significant number of subjective biases; thus, the performances are inferior. The latter methods only input image-level labels and gain the ability to capture subtle local differences by changing their structures, but usually require detailed design and complex additional models. In this case, we first propose a novel and easy weakly supervised method, just using data augmentations to help models focus on the information of interest without any auxiliary architecture or expensive labels.

Specifically, we adopt ViT [3] as the backbone, whose self-attention mechanism can capture more interconnections of detailed variations. Then, we introduce a highly interpretable method to generate visual heatmaps and locate the critical attention areas. As seen in Fig 1, based on the high-response regions, three data augmentation methods (local area enlarge, flip, and cutout) are established to guide the detailed features. Furthermore, label smoothing is proven helpful to weak the over-confidence and improve the margins among subclasses.

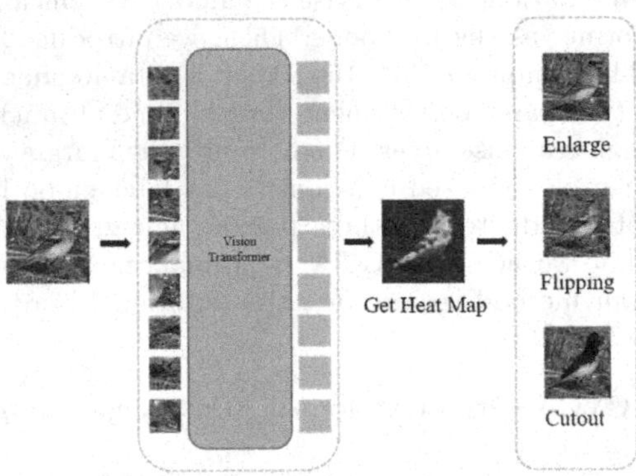

Fig. 1. Illustration of our DA-ViT. We adopt a ViT as the backbone, and three data augmentations are generated based on the high-response regions.

To evaluate our method, we conduct extensive experiments on three popular fine-grained benchmarks (CUB-200-2011 [17], NABirds [9], and Stanford Dogs [11]); the quantitative experimental results demonstrate that DA-ViT achieves SOTA performance. Meanwhile, during the inference, our proposed method is only 80% of the computational costs of the current best method TransFG [7]. In addition, DA-ViT has excellent interpretability, and some qualitative analyses are used to illustrate its effectiveness. In conclusion, our main contributions are as follows.

- To our best knowledge, we use targeted data augmentations to solve the FGVC for the first time. In the conducted experiments, our method achieves **SOTA** performance on three popular benchmarks without any additional labels or auxiliary architectures.
- We adopt greatly interpretable visual heatmaps of ViT to generate data augmentations, and three methods (local area enlargement, flipping, and cutout)are applied based on the high-response areas to guide the model to focus on the detailed information.
- Label smoothing is proven helpful for the FGVC tasks.
- During the inference, our method requires less computational burden.

2 Related Works

Many excellent approaches have developed to solve FGVC, and these methods can be roughly divided into two groups: strongly supervised and weakly supervised algorithms.

Strongly supervised methods guide the model to capture and fit subtle details by relying on additional information, such as bounding boxes, part annotations, etc. Zhang et al. [20] proposed Part R-CNN, which uses bounding boxes to generate multiple recommended regions and then merges the obtained features. We et al. [19] presented Mask-CNN, adopting additional part annotations and four-level convolutional vectors in parallel. Due to the labor-intensive acquisition processes of annotations, weakly supervised methods based on only image-level labels have become more popular. These algorithms commonly locate discriminative information via extra-designed module structures. Lin et al. [12] proposed the B-CNN, which uses two parallel convolution models to learn interacting features. Tap et al. [15] adopted a sophisticated bilinear attention pooling-based method. With the great breakthrough of transformers, the FGVC tasks are dominated by weakly supervised ViT-based methods. Compared with traditional CNNs, the self-attention mechanism is more powerful and can comprehensively consider detailed interconnections. Liu et al. [13] presented TPSKG to mine the practical information among fragmented discriminative clues. Hu et al. [10]created a recurrent transformer-based method with multiple image scales. He et al. [7] proposed the TransFG, which adopts the product of all self-attention scores to discriminate between attention regions.

These ViT-based methods have got some success. However, all of them require complex auxiliary modules, which result in more computational costs. By contrast, our DA-ViT keeps pure-ViT unchanged. To the best knowledge, we first use data augmentations to solve the problems, which are greatly interpretable. Based on three popular benchmarks, we achieve SOTA performance. During the inference, DA-ViT requires just 80% of the computational resources compared with the previous best method TransF

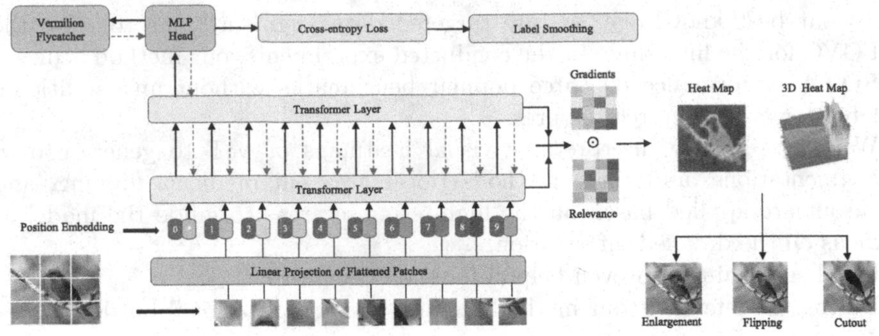

Fig. 2. The overview of our method. Starting from the results, we backpropagate the relevance levels and gradients to each layer (as shown by the red dashed lines). Then, we obtain visualization heatmaps. Based on the high-response areas, we adopt three data augmentation methods. The cross-entropy loss with label smoothing is used to supervise the model. (Color figure online)

3 Method

In this section, we first introduce the transformer visualization method [1]. Then, we elaborate on the three data augmentation techniques. Finally, the label smoothing strategy is described. The overall structure of our proposed method is shown in Fig. 2.

3.1 Visualization Method

Recently, vision transformer has achieved great success. The visualization method [1] makes it possible to explicitly indicate the main contributions and provide effective recommendations for subsequent processing steps. Through merging relevance levels and gradients, we can measure each self-attention layer's contributions and generate heatmaps for various classes.

The relevance satisfies the conservation rule. We backpropagate relevance starting from the predicted result, and the sum of each layer is equal:

$$\sum_j R_j^{(n)} = \sum_i R_i^{(n-1)} \tag{1}$$

where R represents relevance, index j corresponds to the elements in layer n, and index i corresponds to the elements in layer $n-1$. Initially, we assign the relevance as $R^{(0)} = \mathbb{1}_t$, and $\mathbb{1}_t$ is a one-hot vector denoting class t.

For a node j belonging to layer n, the relevance $R_j^{(n)}$ originates from all nodes connected to j in layer $n-1$. If j makes a major contribution to i in the upper layer, j occupies a large share of the $R_i^{(n-1)}$ values.

Following the above principles, we define the relevance levels of linear nodes as in Eq. 2:

$$R_j^{(n)} = \sum_i \frac{x_j w_{ji}}{\sum_{j'} x_{j'} w_{ji}} R_i^{(n-1)} \tag{2}$$

In this equation, j' represents the nodes in layer n that are related to the upper node i, and x_j and w_{ji} are two tensors that correspond to the input feature maps and weights.

Unlike linear elements, the nonlinear nodes cannot be simply expressed as linear combinations of weights and input features. Therefore, Eq. 2 is no longer suitable for relevance propagation. Formally, we denote the output of a specific nonlinear node i as follows:

$$Y_i = F_i(x_1, x_2, x_3, ..., x_j) \tag{3}$$

Based on the first-order Taylor expansion, Eq. 3 can be changed to Eq. 4:

$$Y_i = F_i(\tilde{x}_1, ..., \tilde{x}_j) + \sum_j \frac{\partial F_i}{\partial x_j}(\tilde{x}_1, ..., \tilde{x}_j)(x_j - \tilde{x}_j) + \varepsilon \tag{4}$$

Assuming that $F_i(\tilde{x}_1, ..., \tilde{x}_j) = 0$, ignoring the minimum value ε, the contribution $V_{i \leftarrow j}$ of a specific node j can be defined as Eq. 5:

$$V_{i \leftarrow j} = \frac{\partial F_i}{\partial x_j}(\tilde{x}_1, \tilde{x}_2, \tilde{x}_3, ..., \tilde{x}_j)(x_j - \tilde{x}_j) \tag{5}$$

In conclusion, we express the relevance of nonlinear elements as in Eq. 6:

$$R_j^{(n)} = \sum_i \frac{V_{i \leftarrow j}}{\sum_{j'} V_{i \leftarrow j'}} R_i^{(n-1)} \approx \sum_i x_j \frac{\partial F_i(\mathbf{X})}{\partial x_j} \frac{R_i^{(n-1)}}{F_i(\mathbf{X})} \tag{6}$$

Recalling the chain rule, the gradients $\nabla x_j^{(n)}$ of node j in layer n can be defined as follows:

$$\nabla x_j^{(n)} = \frac{\partial y_t}{\partial x_j^{(n)}} = \sum_i \frac{\partial y_t}{\partial x_i^{(n-1)}} \frac{\partial x_i^{(n-1)}}{\partial x_j^{(n)}} \tag{7}$$

According to the rules mentioned above, starting from the predicted result, each layer S of ViT obtains the corresponding relevance and gradients. Let $A^{(n)}$ be their fusion; we define this step as Eq. 8. $\odot$ is the Hadamard product, and E represents the mean result across obtained multiple dimensions.

$$A^{(n)} = E(\nabla S^{(n)} \odot R^{S^{(n)}}) \tag{8}$$

We multiply $A^{(n)}$ of each self-attention layer. After performing upsampling, we finally obtain heatmaps with the same sizes as those of the original images. In conclusion, the visualization approach is greatly interpretable and can be used in subsequent steps.

3.2 Data Augmentations

This subsection elaborates on three data augmentation strategies based on the high-response areas.

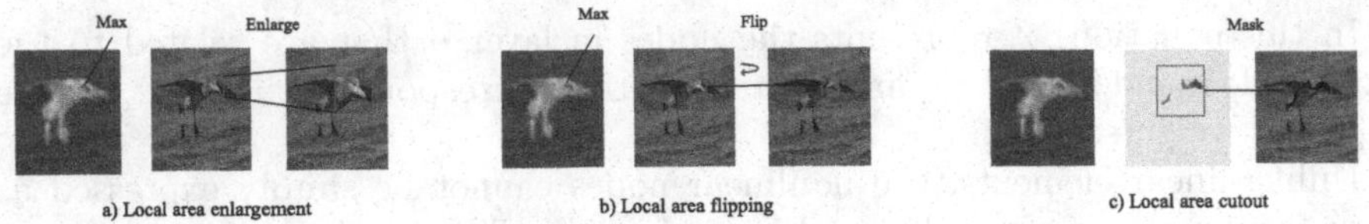

Fig. 3. Samples of three data augmentations, including local area enlargement, flipping and cutout.

Local Area Enlargement. We choose the pixel corresponding to the maximum value in the heatmap as the base point and then randomly generate a rectangular area as follows:

$$l = random(\alpha, \beta) \cdot L \tag{9}$$

$$w = random(\alpha, \beta) \cdot W \tag{10}$$

where l and w denote the length and width of the rectangular area, respectively, and L and W correspond to those of the original image. $\alpha, \beta \in (0,1)$ represent the upper and lower image size bounds. Specifically, we used grid search and best $\alpha = 0.05$ and $\beta = 0.15$. After that, we enlarge the rectangle area to twice its original size and pad it to the corresponding position of the original image. The method is shown in Fig 3(a).

Local Area Flipping. Similar to local area enlargement, following Eq. 9 and Eq. 10, we randomly select a rectangular region and flip it horizontally to replace the original pixels. The method is shown in Fig. 3(b).

Local Area Cutout. The above two methods make some progress based on the high-response areas. However, FGVC tasks should also consider information from other parts. Given this target, we propose a local area cutout strategy to force the model to learn more unnoticed fine-grained features.

As seen in Fig. 3(c), we design an image mask to eliminate some pixels with high responses as follows:

$$\text{mask}_k = \begin{cases} 1, if\ h_k > \eta \cdot h_{\max} \\ 0, otherwise \end{cases} \tag{11}$$

The h_k represents the pixels in the heatmap, $\eta \in (0,1)$ is the threshold. After controlled experiment, we randomly choose η from 0.4–0.6.

3.3 Label Smoothing

Recalling the cross-entropy loss:

$$loss = -\sum_{k=1}^{K} q_k \log(p_k) \tag{12}$$

In this equation, q_k represents the distribution of the ground truth, and p_k denotes the outputs. For a one-hot label y, only $q_y = 1$; the other $q_{k \neq y}$ are all 0.

Unfortunately, this loss may result in overconfidence. Specifically, the model is encouraged to maximize the distinctions between subclasses to the greatest extent possible. However, the interclass variations exhibited by fine-grained tasks are genuinely tiny; thus, the confusion samples should obtain similar scores. The ordinary cross-entropy loss may cause the model's results to be over-biased to a specific category. Label smoothing replaces the construction of ground truth with

$$q_k = \begin{cases} 1 - \varepsilon, if\ k = y \\ \varepsilon/(K-1), otherwise \end{cases} \tag{13}$$

where ε is a small constant, the method assigns a tiny value to classes $k \neq y$ and achieves the goal of preventing model over bias. From another aspect, soft labels provide a weak prior to prevent the model from directly fitting a 0–1 distribution to some extent, reducing the optimization difficulty. Moreover, label smoothing encourages samples from the same class to gather into a tight cluster around the correct templates while equally avoiding incorrect templates.

4 Experiments

In this section, we explain the conducted experiments and analyze the results in detail. First, we introduce the utilized datasets and implement procedures. Then, we compare our method's performance with that of the latest algorithms, and further ablation studies are presented to investigate how different components impact the model. Finally, we provide some qualitative results.

4.1 Datasets

To evaluate our proposed method, we conduct extensive experiments based on three popular FGVC benchmarks, including CUB-200-2011 [17], NABirds [9], and Stanford Dogs [11]. CUB-200-2011 consists of 200 categories of birds, with 5994 training samples and 5795 test samples. NABirds is more challenging, which has 555 subclasses with 23929 training and 24633 test samples. Similarly, Stanford Dogs consists of 120 kinds of dogs with 12000 training and 8580 test images.

Table 1. Comparison with the results of existing methods on CUB-200-2011.

Method	Backbone	Accuracy(%)	Method	Backbone	Accuracy(%)
Part R-CNN [20]	AlexNet	76.4	ViT [3]	ViT-B_16	90.6
Mask-CNN [19]	ResNet-50	87.3	TPSKG [13]	ViT-B_16	91.3
B-CNN [12]	VGG-19	84.1	RAMS-Trans [10]	ViT-B_16	91.3
DCL [2]	ResNet-50	87.8	FFVT [18]	ViT-B_16	91.6
WS-DAN [15]	Inception-V3	89.4	TransFG [7]	ViT-B_16	91.7
CIN [5]	ResNet-50	88.3	**DA-ViT**	ViT-B_16	**91.8**

Table 2. Comparison with the results of existing methods on NABirds.

Method	Backbone	Accuracy(%)	Method	Backbone	Accuracy(%)
MaxEnt [4]	DenseNet-161	83.0	ViT [3]	ViT-B_16	89.9
Cross-X [14]	ResNet-50	86.4	TPSKG [13]	ViT-B_16	90.1
PAIRS [6]	ResNet-50	87.9	TransFG [7]	ViT-B_16	90.8
FixSENet-154 [16]	SENet-154	89.2	**DA-ViT**	ViT-B_16	**91.2**

4.2 Implementation Details

Firstly, we resize the input images into 384×384. Then, we employ the pretrained ViT-B-16 as a backbone. The batch size is set to 8, and we apply SGD with a 0.1 learning rate, 0.8 momentum, and 5e-4 weight decay. After that, based on this initial model, we generate heatmaps and further obtain new samples. The three data augmentation techniques are randomly used with probabilities of 0.3 while loading data. The original model is finally fine-tuned. Most hyperparameters are set as above. Specifically, we adopt the differential learning rate. The classifier is initialized as 0.1, and the other parts are 0.02. The smoothing value is set to 0.4. StepLR, which decreases by 0.1 every 30 epochs, is employed as a scheduler of the optimizer. The training step early stops at about 80 epochs. We conducted all experiments based on RTX3090 with Pytorch.

4.3 Comparison with SOTA Methods

CUB-200-2011. The top-1 classification accuracy values are summarized in Table 1. Compared with the baseline ViT, we obtain a further **1.2%** increase. Compared with other ViT-based approaches, we achieve the **SOTA**.

NABirds. Due to a large number of confusing samples, NABirds is more challenging. ViT-based approaches achieve the desired breakthrough. As seen in Table 2, our method outperforms the pure ViT by **1.3%** and exceeds the SOTA approach by **0.4%**.

Table 3. Comparison with the results of existing methods on Stanford Dogs.

Method	Backbone	Accuracy(%)	Method	Backbone	Accuracy(%)
MaxEnt [4]	DenseNet-161	83.6	TransFG [7]	ViT-B_16	92.3
Cross-X [14]	ResNet-50	88.9	RAMS-Trans [10]	ViT-B_16	92.4
WS-DAN [15]	Inception-V3	92.2	TPSKG [13]	ViT-B_16	92.5
ViT [3]	ViT-B_16	91.7	**DA-ViT**	ViT-B_16	**93.2**

Stanford Dogs. Table 3 shows the comparison results obtained on the Stanford Dogs. Our method achieves the best performance. Specifically, it is **0.7%** higher than that of the current SOTA approach, and we obtain a **1.5%** improvement over baseline ViT.

4.4 Analysis of Computational Burden

The results of the above three FGVC benchmarks show that our proposed DA-ViT achieves SOTA performances. It is also worth noting that these methods create some complex auxiliary structures, whereas we keep the ViT unchanged, which results in less computational costs during the inference. As can be seen in Table 4, the number of calculations required by our model is just **80%** of the TransFG and **73%** of the FFVT with even better performance.

Table 4. Comparison of the calculation costs during the inference process.

Method	Accuracy(%)	FLOPS(G)
TPSKG [13]	91.3	65.91
FFVT [18]	91.6	67.13
TransFG [7]	91.7	61.67
DA-ViT	**91.8**	**49.34**

4.5 Ablation Study

The Influence of Different Components. In this paper, we propose three data augmentation techniques and a label smoothing strategy is applied to supervise the training process. We design some controlled experiments on CUB-200-2011, and the specific results are shown in Table 5. We can find that both components are beneficial to the results, and the combination of the two methods achieves the best results. Moreover, we also extend the two tricks to CNNs to study their generalization abilities. We choose a simple ResNet-50 as the backbone, and our method boosts the performance from **85.3% to 88.7%**, which approves the powerful performance of our method.

The Influence of the Data Augmentation Methods. In this section, we compare the performance of several other popular augmentation methods on CUB-200-2011. As summarized in Table 6, the MixUp and CutMix exhibit poor improvements relative to the baseline. We think this may be because random mixtures destroy the detailed semantic information. Even worse, color jitter and random affine transformation cause a performance drop. In contrast, our method achieves varying degrees of improvement. Furthermore, to investigate whether approaches based on high-response regions are actually helpful, we conduct controlled experiments with random strategies. In conclusion, our method does take great advantage of the FGVC tasks.

Table 5. Ablation study on different components.

Method	Accuracy (%)
ViT [3]	90.6
ViT + Data Augmentations	91.4
ViT + Label Smoothing	91.1
ViT + Data Augmentations + Label Smoothing	**91.8**

Table 6. Ablation Study on several data augmentations.

Method	Accuracy (%)	Method	Accuracy(%)
None	91.1	random Flipping	91.2
color Jitter	90.9	random Cutout	91.3
mixup	91.3	our Enlargement	91.5
cutmix	91.1	our Flipping	91.6
random affine transformation	90.3	our Cutout	91.6
random Enlarge	91.2	**DA-ViT**	**91.8**

The Influence of Label Smoothing. A hyperparameter ε is contained in the label smoothing strategy. A comparison among different values of ε is shown in Table 7. We can observe and analyze that the label smoothing mechanism does improve the model performance, and 0.4 is the best ε choice.

Table 7. Ablation Study on label smoothing.

value of ε	Accuracy (%)	value of ε	Accuracy(%)
0	91.2	0.3	91.5
0.1	91.2	0.4	**91.8**
0.2	91.3	0.5	91.6

4.6 Qualitative Analysis

In this section, we provide some interpretable visual analysis. We visualize the distribution of the penultimate layers in Fig. 4. Specifically, randomly choose ten classes from every dataset, and map features into 2D figures through t-SNE. We can find that our method obviously increases the distance between each pair of subclasses. Therefore, it is easier to find the boundaries among confusing categories. As seen in Fig 5 (a), we compared the heatmap of the same images with baseline and DA-VTT. Our proposed method encourages the model to focus on more discriminative areas (e.g., wings, heads, and tails for birds), increasing the model's attention fields. We also display the confusion matrix of CUB-200-2011; only a few samples are miss-classified (as shown in the yellow rectangle).

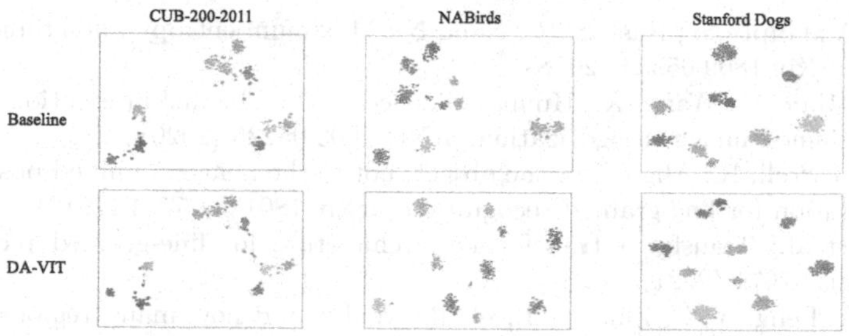

Fig. 4. The t-SNE visualization maps of the penultimate layer.

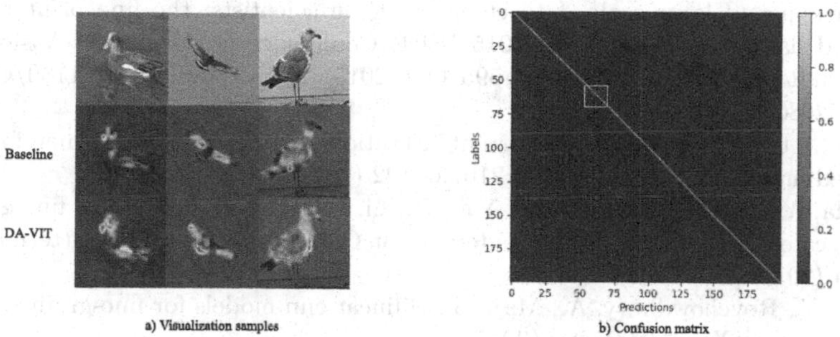

Fig. 5. Some visual analysis on CUB-200-2011. (Color figure online)

5 Conclusion

In this work, we propose a novel ViT-based method to tackle fine-grained tasks. Specifically, we offer three data augmentation techniques (enlargement, flipping, and cutout) based on high-response areas and apply the label smoothing strategy to enlarge the margins among confusing subclasses. Quantitative experiments demonstrate that we achieve **SOTA** performances with a lower computational burden. Ablation studies and qualitative results also show the effectiveness and great interpretability of our method.

References

1. Chefer, H., Gur, S., Wolf, L.: Transformer interpretability beyond attention visualization. arXiv:2012.09838 (2020)
2. Chen, Y., Bai, Y.L., Zhang, W., Mei, T.: Destruction and construction learning for fine-grained image recognition. In: 2019 IEEE/CVF Conference on Computer Vision and Pattern Recognition (CVPR), pp. 5152–5161 (2019). https://doi.org/10.1109/CVPR.2019.00530
3. Dosovitskiy, A., Beyer, L., Kolesnikov, A., Weissenborn, D., Houlsby, N.: An image is worth 16x16 words: Transformers for image recognition at scale. arXiv:2010.11929 (2021)

4. Dubey, A., Gupta, o., Raskar, R., Naik, N.: Maximum-entropy fine-grained classification. arXiv:1809.05934 (2018)
5. Gao, Y., Han, X., Wang, X., Huang, W., Scott, M.: Channel interaction networks for fine-grained image categorization. arXiv:2003.05235 (2020)
6. Guo, P., Farrell, R.: Aligned to the object, not to the image: a unified pose-aligned representation for fine-grained recognition. arXiv:1801.09057v4 (2018)
7. He, J., et al.: Transfg: a transformer architecture for fine-grained recognition. arXiv:2103.07976 (2021)
8. He, X.T., Peng, Y.X., Zhao, J.J., et al.: Which and how many regions to gaze: focus discriminative regions for fine-grained visual categorization. Int. J. Comput. Vision **127**(9), 1235–1255 (2019). https://doi.org/10.1007/s11263-019-01176-2
9. Horn, G.V., Branson, S., Farrell, R., Haber, S., Belongie, S.: Building a bird recognition app and large scale dataset with citizen scientists: the fine print in fine-grained dataset collection. In: 2015 IEEE Conference on Computer Vision and Pattern Recognition (CVPR), pp. 595–604 (2015). https://doi.org/10.1109/CVPR.2015.7298658
10. Hu, Y., et al.: Rams-trans: recurrent attention multi-scale transformer for fine-grained image recognition. arXiv:2107.08192 (2021)
11. Khosla, A., Jayadevaprakash, N., Yao, B., Li, F.F.: Novel dataset for fine-grained image categorization. In: IEEE Conference on Computer Vision and Pattern Recognition (2013)
12. Lin, T.Y., Roychowdhury, A., Maji, S.: Bilinear cnn models for fine-grained visual recognition. arXiv:1504.07889 (2015)
13. Liu, X., Wang, L., Han, X.: Transformer with peak suppression and knowledge guidance for fine-grained image recognition. arXiv:2107.06538 (2021)
14. Luo, W., et al.: Cross-x learning for fine-grained visual categorization. arXiv:1909.04412v1 (2019)
15. Tao, H., Qi, H.: See better before looking closer: weakly supervised data augmentation network for fine-grained visual classification. arXiv:1901.09891 (2019)
16. Touvron, H., Vedaldi, A., Douze, M., Jégou, H.: Fixing the train-test resolution discrepancy. arXiv:1906.06423v3 (2020)
17. Wah, C., Branson, S., Welinder, P., Perona, P., Belongie, S.: The caltech-ucsd birds- 200–2011 dataset. Tech. rep., california institute of technology (2011)
18. Wang, J., Yu, X., Gao, Y.: Feature fusion vision transformer for fine-grained visual categorizatio. arXiv:2107.02341 (2021)
19. Wei, X.S., Xie, C.W., Wu, J.X., Shen, C.H.: Mask-cnn: localizing parts and selecting descriptors for fine-grained bird species categorization. Pattern Recogn. **76**, 704–714 (2018). https://doi.org/10.1016/j.patcog.2017.10.002
20. Zhang, N., Donahue, J., Girshick, R., Darrell, T.: Part-based R-CNNs for fine-grained category detection. In: Fleet, D., Pajdla, T., Schiele, B., Tuytelaars, T. (eds.) ECCV 2014. LNCS, vol. 8689, pp. 834–849. Springer, Cham (2014). https://doi.org/10.1007/978-3-319-10590-1_54

A Detail Geometry Learning Network for High-Fidelity Face Reconstruction

Kehua Ma, Xitie Zhang, Suping Wu(✉), Boyang Zhang, Leyang Yang, and Zhixiang Yuan

School of Information Engineering, Ningxia University, Yinchuan 750021, China
pswuu@nxu.edu.cn

Abstract. In this paper, we propose a Detail Geometry Learning Network (DGLN) approach to investigate the problem of self-supervised high-fidelity face reconstruction from monocular images. Unlike existing methods that rely on detail generators to generate "pseudo-details" where most of the reconstructed detail geometries are inconsistent with real faces. Our DGLN can ensure face personalization and also correctly learn more local face details. Specifically, our method includes two stages: the personalization stage and the detailization stage. In the personalization stage, we design a multi-perception interaction module (MPIM) to adaptively calibrate the weighted responses by interacting with information from different receptive fields to extract distinguishable and reliable features. To further enhance the geometric detail information, in the detailization stage, we develop a multi-resolution refinement network module (MrNet) to estimate the refined displacement map with features from different layers and different domains (i.e. coarse displacement images and RGB images). Finally, we design a novel normal smoothing loss that improves the reconstructed details and realisticity. Extensive experiments demonstrate the superiority of our method over previous work.

Keywords: Multi-granularity · Features interaction · Detailed 3d face reconstruction

1 Introduction

Image-based 3D high-fidelity face reconstruction is one of the most popular research areas at the intersection of computer vision and machine learning, which aims to reconstruct 3D faces with detailed information such as wrinkles, and currently has a wide range of applications in face animation, human-computer

This work was supported by National Natural Science Foundation of China under Grant 62062056, in part by the Ningxia Graduate Education and Teaching Reform Research and Practice Project 2021, and in part by the Ningxia Natural Science Foundation under Grant 2022AAC03327.

K. Ma and X. Zhang—Equal Contribution.

L. Iliadis et al. (Eds.): ICANN 2023, LNCS 14255, pp. 13–25, 2023.
https://doi.org/10.1007/978-3-031-44210-0_2

interaction, and film production. In the process of 3D high-fidelity face reconstruction, estimating the geometry and face detail information of 3D faces from images has become a challenging problem due to a variety of complex factors such as lighting, reflectivity, and the presence of partial occlusions in natural scenes. Most of the early methods are based on 3D deformable model (3DMM) [1]. It was proposed by Blanz and Vetter to represent a face as a low-dimensional latent variable and a corresponding basis vector. These methods [2,3] based on 3DMM [1] are simple, efficient, and robust, but due to their low-dimensional nature, the rich details of the image are lost, resulting in a reconstructed face that is too smooth and lacks information on the local details of the face.

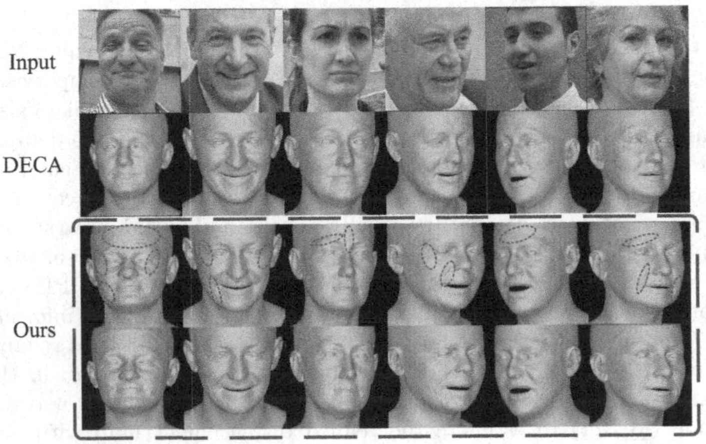

Fig. 1. Comparison with qualitative results of state-of-the-art method (DECA [4]). (row 1) Input images, (row 2) the DECA's detail shape, (row 3 ours detail) the DGLN's detail shape, (row 4 our) the DGLN's detail shape. The red ellipse area is the most obvious area. Compared with DECA, our method is unique in that our method can capture higher frequency details (such as wrinkles in the forehead, eye corners, mouth corners, etc.). However, since DECA [4] uses the generator to generate wrinkle details, it can be seen that the generated wrinkles are not real (column 1), and there will be cases where wrong wrinkle details are generated (column 5). Best viewed on-screen by zooming in.

Recently, with the development of deep learning, deep convolutional neural network (CNN)-based methods have achieved very good results in recovering 3D facial geometry. Several approaches [5,6] have utilized a coarse-to-fine CNN framework in an end-to-end manner, where the coarse CNN network mainly regresses 3DMM parameters representation to obtain the 3D face facial shape, and then the CNN refinement network applies a shadow-like shape refinement to capture fine facial details. Although these methods have recovered some detail, they are computationally too expensive. An end-to-end self-supervised network training framework was proposed by Feng et al [4], but the use of generators to generate details makes the reconstructed face detail information less realistic.

To address the above-mentioned problems in high-fidelity 3D face reconstruction, we propose a new self-supervised algorithm for high-fidelity face reconstruction. Our core idea is to make use of our proposed detailed geometric learning network, which allows the network to continuously learn the details of real faces. Specifically, it is divided into two phases. First, in the personalization stage, we use our designed multi-perceptual interaction module, which allows the network to fully learn global and local face shape information under the information interaction of different receptive fields. Then, in the detailization phase, our proposed multi-resolution refinement network model estimates detailed displacement maps from different layers and different fields. By combining these two modules, we achieve high-fidelity face reconstruction. Finally, we devise a novel normal smoothing loss that further enhances the detail and realism of our results. Our method is efficiently trained in a self-supervised manner and does not require additional 3D labels. Furthermore, to further visually demonstrate the performance of our method, we show the reconstruction results of DECA [4] and our method in Fig. 1. From the figure we can observe that the face mesh reconstructed by our method has more wrinkle details, especially in the mouth and eyes, and will not produce wrong details like DECA.

The core contributions of our work are summarized as follows.

1) We propose a multi-perceptual interaction module (MPIM). By interacting and adaptively weighting the fusion of information under different perceptual fields, it facilitates the network to better learn feature information, especially facial geometry information.
2) We present a multi-resolution refinement network (MrNet). It can extract finer facial detail information under the guidance of multi-scale input images.
3) We designed a normal smoothing loss. It can smooth the non-edge regions of the face normal map and improve the realism of the reconstructed face.
4) Experimental results on two different benchmarks both show that our method outperforms state-of-the-art methods.

2 Approach

The main goal of DGLN is to address an important limitation of existing methods in recovering realistic details and 3D facial shapes from a single image. Figure 2 shows an overview of the proposed method, which mainly consists of two stages: the personalization stage and the detailization stage. The following component is described in detail.

2.1 The Personalization Stage

In the personalization stage, the main goal is to solve the problem that complex scenes cannot accurately reconstruct the face shape. Further provide a more accurate face shape for the detailing stage, making the final output 3D face more realistic. Specifically, we are taking an image as input and feeding it into

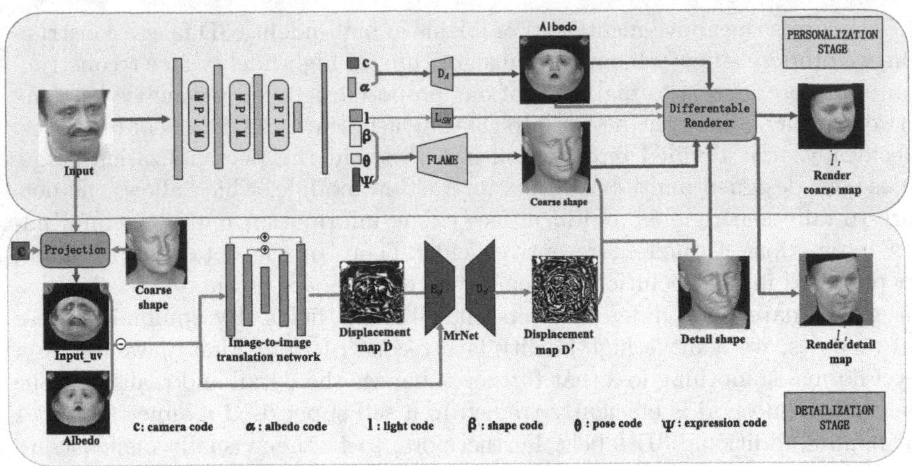

Fig. 2. The framework of the proposed DGLN. Our DGLN mainly consists of a personalization stage and a detailization stage. Specifically, in the personalization stage, we adopt the conventional method framework of learning a parametric model to obtain a coarse face model. We added the MPIM we designed to the first three blocks of the backbone network to screen the face features and select feature information that is beneficial to face shape reconstruction. In the detailization stage, we design a novel framework to obtain detailed face models. We take the difference between the input image and the albedo image as input to obtain high-frequency detail information. Then feed into MrNet to capture finer features. In the training phase, we use the normal smoothing loss L_{normal} to constrain to reduce the generation of artifacts.

an encoder to obtain a regression low-dimensional latent code such as FLAME [5] parameters: shape β, pose θ, expression Ψ, albedo coefficients α, camera c, and lighting parameters l. After a FLAME [5] decoder and a differentiable renderer a 3D face model with a shape consistent with the input image is obtained. The aforementioned encoder, which consists of a ResNet50 [7] and two fully connected layers.

Multi-perceptual Interaction Module. In order to enhance the encoder's ability to extract key features suitable for face reconstruction, We designed the multi-perceptual interaction module (MPIM). This module mainly solves the problem that the face shape cannot be accurately reconstructed under complex background conditions. Specifically, the structure of the MPIM is shown in Fig. 3. This module consists of two main parts. In the first part, in order to capture the global face shape features and local face shape features, we designed a 1×1 convolution and three 3×3 convolutions with different expansion rates, the expansion rates are 1, 3, and 5, respectively. Among them, 1×1 convolution mainly captures global face shape features, and 3×3 convolution captures local face shape features. We concatenate the different features and we obtain a dense feature with both global and local features. As the output of the previous step is dense features with high-level semantic information, the contribution of these features to the face reconstruction task varies greatly, Some of them are concentrated in background regions that are not suitable as candidate features for the face reconstruction task. In the second part of the MPIM module, we devise a cross-attention module to score the dense features output from the first part to extract the key features that contribute most to the face reconstruction task, thus enabling favorable feature selection. Specifically, we take the dense feature map output from the first part of MPIM and the input feature map as the input to the second part. The dense features are brought together after a weighted summation of the two CNN layers. The reason for using two different inputs for weighting is that we believe that the original input feature map and the dense feature map can interact with each other to extract key features. The attention module is implemented by generating a feature map and a dense feature map of the input image, using weighted summation pooling for feature dimensionality reduction, and then training a softmax classifier to obtain an attention score. Finally, attention features are obtained by multiplying the attention score with the dense feature map. Once the attention module is thoroughly trained, the relevant features are selected based on the weighted scores. The attention feature F is defined as:

$$F = \sum_{n} \alpha\left(f_n; \theta\right) \cdot f_n \tag{1}$$

where f_n is defined as the feature vector on the output feature map, the score function $\alpha(\cdot)$ is expressed as the score function of f_n, where θ is the parameter of $\alpha\left(f_n; \theta\right)$.

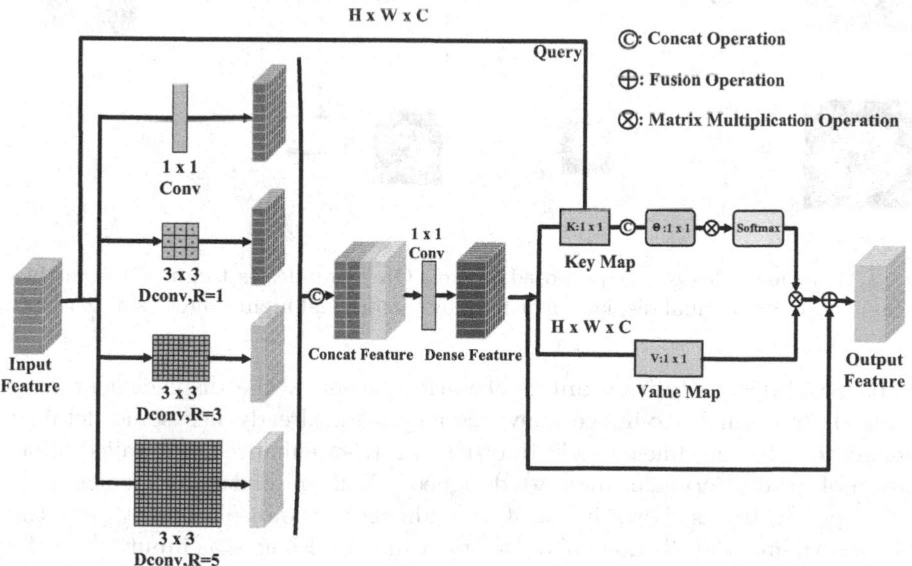

Fig. 3. The detailed structure of our MPIM. Our goal is to improve the model's ability to capture global and local face shapes.

Loss Function: The personalization stage is trained by minimizing:

$$L_{\text{person}} = L_{lmk} + L_{\text{eye}} + L_{pho} + L_{id} + L_{\text{reg}} \quad (2)$$

The loss function is consistent with [4]. Including landmark loss L_{lmk}, eye loss L_{eye}, photometric loss L_{pho}, identity loss L_{id}, and regularization L_{reg}.

2.2 The Detailization Stage

The detailization stage consists of two sub-networks. We adopt an image-to-image transformation network architecture similar to pix2pix and design a multi-resolution refinement network (MrNet).

Image-to-Image Translation Network Architecture. In order to preserve as much high-frequency detail information as possible, we employ an image-to-image translation network. First, we use the personalized face model results from the previous stage together with camera c to project the face image into UV space and then subtract the albedo map from it. We consider the face image to contain a large amount of high-frequency detail information. The albedo map reflects the skin color of the face and is smooth. We perform a subtraction operation to obtain high-frequency details. We then feed the results into an image-to-image conversion network to predict the displacement map in UV space.

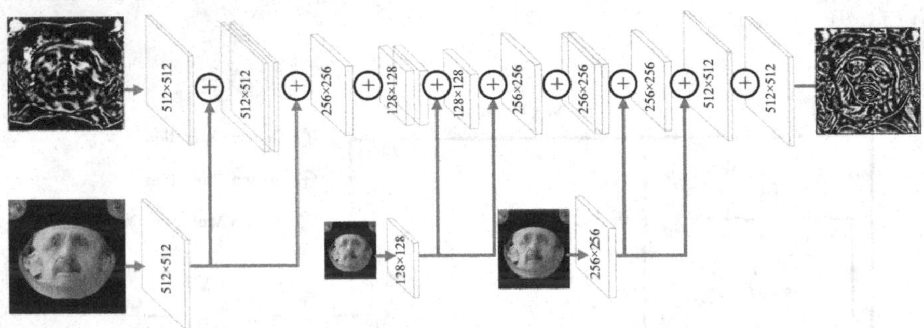

Fig. 4. The basic idea of our proposed MrNet. Our core idea is to guide the further refinement of the original displacement map by the original input image as a 'teacher'.

Multi-resolution Refinement Network. Although the displacement map output by the Image-to-image conversion network already has some detailed information, it is not fine enough. In order to further enhance the detailed information of the displacement map, we designed a Multi-resolution refinement network. Specifically, as shown in Fig. 4, in addition to the displacement map, the RGB map minus the albedo map of the input map is also used as input. After the CNN, the resolution of the feature maps is reduced to 1/4 and 1/2, and we scale the input according to the size of the feature maps to fuse the multi-resolution images. In this way, we can correct for local detail errors in different resolution backgrounds. Finally, we introduce a residual link in the input displacement map

d to the output displacement map d' to ensure that displacement information similar to that of the input displacement map is retained and further refined.

Loss Function: The detailization stage is trained by minimizing:

$$L_{detail} = L_{phoD} + L_{mrf} + L_{normal} + L_{regD} \tag{3}$$

The loss function is consistent with [4]. Including photometric detail loss L_{phoD}, ID-MRF loss L_{mrf} and detail regularization L_{regD}. To smooth artifact noise, we design a normal smoothing loss L_{normal}.

2.3 Normal Smoothing Loss

To address the artifact noise present in face reconstruction results, we design a normal smoothing loss. This loss smoothes out the non-edge regions of the normal map while preserving the edges. We use the neighborhood pixel values of the input image and the depth image in UV space to constrain the normal map smoothing of non-edge regions. The normal smoothing loss is defined as:

$$L_{normal}(I, D, N) = \frac{1}{|K|} \sum\nolimits_{x \in K} \left\| \sum\nolimits_{x_k \in N(x)} w_k^i w_k^d \left(N(x) - N\left(x_k\right) \right) \right\|^2 \tag{4}$$

where $N(x)$ is defined the neighbors of a pixel x, and K represents the set of all pixels, w_k^i is the input weighting term:

$$w_k^i = \exp\left(-\frac{\left\| I(x) - I\left(x_k\right) \right\|^2}{\sigma_i^2} \right) \tag{5}$$

and w_k^d is the depth weighting term:

$$w_k^d = \exp\left(-\frac{\left\| D(x) - D\left(x_k\right) \right\|^2}{\sigma_d^2} \right) \tag{6}$$

The weighting term enhances the information of edge regions and suppresses the information of non-edge regions. We use σ_i and σ_d to control the allowable pixel range of the input image and depth image.

3 Experiments

In this section, we conduct quantitative and qualitative experiments and ablation study on two different benchmarks (including NoW benchmark [8], Feng et al. [9] benchmark) to investigate the effectiveness of our proposed DGLN.

3.1 Datasets

DGLN is trained on three datasets including VGGFace2 [10], BUPT-Balancedface [11] and VoxCeleb2 [12].

VGGFace2: VGGFace2 [10] is a dataset containing face images of different poses, ages, lighting, and backgrounds. The data set is divided into a training set and an evaluation set, in which the training set contains 8631 classes, and the evaluation set contains 500 classes.

BUPT-Balancedface: BUPT-Balancedface [11] is a data set with a balanced distribution of the number of people of various skin colors, containing 1.3 million images of 28,000 people, which are divided into four skin color groups including white races, Indians, Asians, and Africans.

VoxCeleb2: VoxCeleb2 [12] is a video dataset containing 6,112 celebrity speakers extracted from videos uploaded to YouTube. The speakers cover different ages, genders, and accents. Voice scenes are also very rich, including red carpet catwalks, outdoor venues, indoor recording studios, etc. Overall, the VoxCeleb2 data representation is very rich.

3.2 Implementation Details

During the training process, for the parameters of the designed network, we empirically set the normal smoothing loss weights to 1. In addition, the weights of other loss functions are the same as DECA [4] to reflect the effectiveness of our method.

3.3 Evaluation

We compare our approach with the folds of state-of-the-art face reconstruction methods. The main goal of our method is to achieve high-fidelity 3D face reconstruction, but there is currently no fair standard for measuring detailed faces.

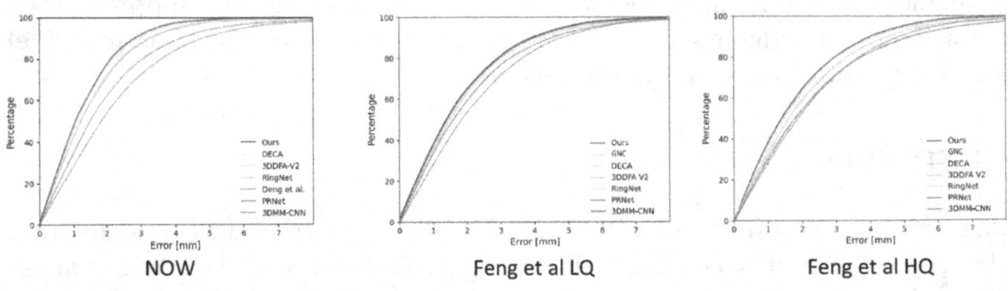

Fig. 5. The CED curves on two 3D face reconstruction benchmarks, namely the NoW [8] challenge (left) and the Feng et al. [9] benchmark for low-quality (middle) and high-quality (right) images.

Table 1. Feng et al. [9] benchmark performance.

Method	Median(mm) ↓		Mean(mm) ↓		Std(mm) ↓	
	LQ	HQ	LQ	HQ	LQ	HQ
3DMM-CNN [3]	1.88	1.85	2.32	2.29	1.89	1.88
Extreme3D [13]	2.40	2.37	3.49	3.58	6.15	6.75
3DDFA-V2 [14]	1.62	1.49	2.10	1.91	1.87	1.64
PRNet [6]	1.79	1.59	2.38	2.06	2.19	1.79
RingNet [8]	1.63	1.59	2.08	2.02	1.79	1.69
DECA [4]	1.48	1.45	1.91	1.89	1.66	1.68
GNC [15]	1.81	1.49	2.48	1.92	2.83	1.79
DGLN(ours)	**1.44**	**1.40**	**1.89**	**1.83**	**1.65**	**1.61**

Table 2. Reconstruction error on the NoW [8] benchmark.

Method	Median(mm) ↓	Mean(mm) ↓	Std(mm) ↓
3DMM-CNN [3]	1.84	2.33	2.05
PRNet [6]	1.50	1.98	1.88
3DDFA-V2 [14]	1.23	1.57	1.39
RingNet [8]	1.21	1.54	1.31
MGCNet [16]	1.31	1.87	2.63
Deng et al.19 [17]	1.23	1.54	1.29
DECA [4]	1.09	1.38	1.18
DGLN (ours)	**1.08**	**1.36**	**1.15**

Therefore, coarse faces are used in the quantitative evaluation part. The superiority of detailed faces is mainly evaluated in the qualitative evaluation part.

The Personalization Stage Evaluation: As shown in Table 1, we compare with the Feng et al. [9] benchmark. As shown in Table 1, our DGLN surpasses the performance in comparison to the previous methods. Moreover, it shows a large improvement in the high-resolution test set. We also evaluated our approach with the error accumulation curve in visual form. As shown in Fig. 5, It can be seen from the cumulative error curve that most of the errors of our method are within 3mm to 4mm. As shown in Table 2, we compare with the previous works on the NoW [8] benchmark, our DGLN is better than previous methods. Finally, our method is mainly aimed at the reconstruction of detailed shapes, but our method can still improve the accuracy of coarse face shapes, which further illustrates that our personalization stage can solve the problem of inaccurate face shape reconstruction in complex scenes.

The Detailization Stage Evaluation: Fig. 6 shows the qualitative results of 3D detailed face reconstruction. We compare our model with other state-of-

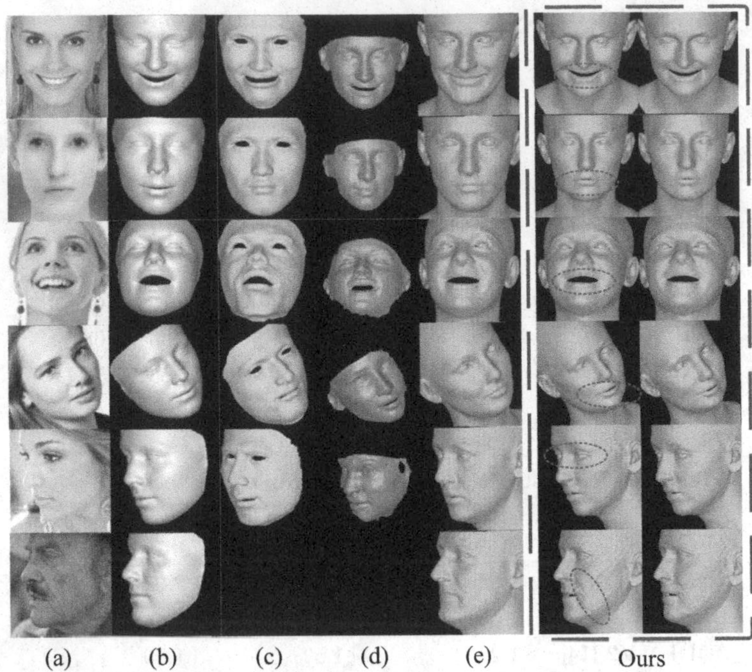

Fig. 6. Visual comparisons of 3D detailed face reconstruction from 2D images by different methods. from left to right: (a) Input, (b) 3DDFA-V2 [14], (c) FaceScape [18], (d) Extreme3D [13], (e) DECA [4], (Ours) DGLN detail reconstruction. Best viewed on-screen by zooming in.

the-art methods. Compared to these methods, DGLN better reconstructs the overall face shape with details like the nasolabial fold and forehead wrinkles(row 6). (c)FaceScape [18] and (d) Extreme3D [13] cannot reconstruct the face mesh of this image. In addition, there are also more realistic effects on mouth and nose shapes and expressions(rows 1, 2, 3, 5, 6).

Figure 1 shows the detailed face model comparison between our method and DECA. The details reconstructed by our method are more realistic, and the details of DECA are not real due to the use of generators to generate details (the forehead area in column 1, the details reconstructed by our method are closer to the real image), and there may even be cases where wrinkle details are incorrectly generated (the forehead area of the input image in column 5 has no wrinkles, while DECA reconstructs wrinkles. On the contrary, our method does not produce such errors). In addition, our method is more realistic in the corners of the eyes and mouth (columns 1, 2, 4, 6), and can even reconstruct details in the brow region (column 3). Therefore, the ability of our method to capture local details and more realistic details is further demonstrated.

3.4 Ablation Study

We performed ablation experiments on the NOW dataset to demonstrate the effectiveness of the different modules we designed.

The Effectiveness of MPIM. As Fig. 7 (row 1) shows, after we remove the MPIM module (column 2), for some face images, the face mesh structure such as lips cannot be accurately reconstructed. On the contrary, for the DGLN (column 2) with MPIM training added, the face shape can be accurately recovered.

The Effectiveness of MrNet. Fig. 7 (row 2) shows the effect of MrNet on the detail reconstruction. In the absence of MrNet (column 2), the wrinkle details (e.g. forehead, corners of the eyes, and sides of the mouth) are not sufficiently fine and the reconstruction is too smooth. With the addition of the MrNet module (row 3), DGLN is able to capture these details accurately.

The Validity of the Novel Normal Smoothing Loss. Figure 7 (row 3) shows the effect of L_{normal} (Eq. 4) on the DGLN reconstruction results. The results show that not adding this loss as a constraint during network training (row 2) leads to some reconstruction results with artifacts. It can be clearly seen that adding this loss (row 3) smoothes out the non-edge regions.

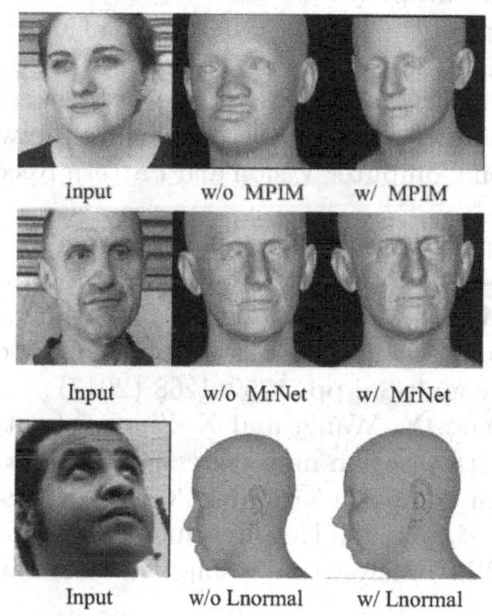

Fig. 7. Ablation study. We investigate the impact of our proposed different modules on the model. Row 1: Effect of MPIM on face shape. Row 2: Effect of MrNet on the detail reconstruction. Row 3: Effect of L_{normal} on the reconstructed details.

4 Conclusions

In this paper, we present a two-stage Detailed Geometric Learning Network (DGLN) approach for a self-supervised monocular image based high-fidelity 3D face reconstruction task. In the personalization phase, we design a Multi-Perceptual Interaction Module (MPIM) to fully extract the geometric features of the face by interacting with information from different sensory fields and adaptively calibrating the weighting. To further enhance the face detail information, in the detailization phase, we developed a multi-resolution refinement network module (MrNet). Finally, we devise a novel normal smoothing loss to further improve the detail and realism of the reconstruction. Extensive experiments demonstrate the advantages of our approach over previous methods. In future work, we plan to further investigate our method in the field of high-fidelity 3D face reconstruction with partial occlusion.

References

1. Blanz, V., Vetter, T.: A morphable model for the synthesis of 3d faces. In: Proceedings of the 26th Annual Conference on Computer Graphics and Interactive Techniques, pp. 187–194 (1999)
2. Zhu, X., Lei, Z., Liu, X., Shi, H., Li, S.Z.: Face alignment across large poses: a 3d solution. In: Proceedings of the IEEE Conference on Computer Vision and Pattern Recognition, pp. 146–155 (2016)
3. Tuan Tran, A., Hassner, T., Masi, I., Medioni, G.: Regressing robust and discriminative 3d morphable models with a very deep neural network. In: Proceedings of the IEEE Conference on Computer Vision and Pattern Recognition, pp. 5163–5172 (2017)
4. Feng, Y., Feng, H., Black, M.J., Bolkart, T.: Learning an animatable detailed 3d face model from in-the-wild images. ACM Trans. Graph (ToG) **40**(4), 1–13 (2021)
5. Richardson, E., Sela, M., Or-El, R., Kimmel, R.: Learning detailed face reconstruction from a single image. In: Proceedings of the IEEE Conference on Computer Vision and Pattern Recognition, pp. 1259–1268 (2017)
6. Y. Feng, F. Wu, X. Shao, Y. Wang, and X. Zhou, "Joint 3d face reconstruction and dense alignment with position map regression network," in Proceedings of the European conference on computer vision (ECCV), 2018, pp. 534–551
7. He, K., Zhang, X., Ren, S., Sun, J.: Deep residual learning for image recognition. In: Proceedings of the IEEE Conference on Computer Vision and Pattern Recognition, CVPR (2016)
8. Sanyal, S., Bolkart, T., Feng, H., Black, M.J.: Learning to regress 3d face shape and expression from an image without 3d supervision. In: Proceedings of the IEEE/CVF Conference on Computer Vision and Pattern Recognition, pp. 7763–7772 (2019)
9. Feng, Z.-H.: Evaluation of dense 3d reconstruction from 2d face images in the wild. In: 2018 13th IEEE International Conference on Automatic Face & Gesture Recognition (FG 2018), pp. 780–786. IEEE (2018)
10. Cao, Q., Shen, L., Xie, W., Parkhi, O.M., Zisserman, A.: Vggface2: a dataset for recognising faces across pose and age. In: 13th IEEE International Conference on Automatic Face & Gesture Recognition (FG 2018), vol. 2018, pp. 67–74. IEEE (2018)

11. Wang, M., Deng, W., Hu, J., Tao, X., Huang, Y.: Racial faces in the wild: reducing racial bias by information maximization adaptation network. In: Proceedings of the IEEE/CVF International Conference on Computer Vision, pp. 692–702 (2019)
12. Chung, J.S., Nagrani, A., Zisserman, A.: Voxceleb2: deep speaker recognition, arXiv preprint arXiv:1806.05622 (2018)
13. Trãn, A.T., Hassner, T., Masi, I., Paz, E., Nirkin, Y., Medioni, G.: Extreme 3d face reconstruction: seeing through occlusions. In: Proceedings of the IEEE Conference on Computer Vision and Pattern Recognition, pp. 3935–3944 (2018)
14. Guo, J., Zhu, X., Yang, Y., Yang, F., Lei, Z., Li, S.Z.: Towards fast, accurate and stable 3D dense face alignment. In: Vedaldi, A., Bischof, H., Brox, T., Frahm, J.-M. (eds.) ECCV 2020. LNCS, vol. 12364, pp. 152–168. Springer, Cham (2020). https://doi.org/10.1007/978-3-030-58529-7_10
15. Zheng, X., Cao, Y., Li, L., Zhou, Z., Jia, M., Wu, S.: Gnc: geometry normal consistency loss for 3d face reconstruction and dense alignment. In: 2022 IEEE International Conference on Multimedia and Expo (ICME), pp. 1–6. IEEE (2022)
16. Shang, J., et al.: Self-supervised monocular 3D face reconstruction by occlusion-aware multi-view geometry consistency. In: Vedaldi, A., Bischof, H., Brox, T., Frahm, J.-M. (eds.) ECCV 2020. LNCS, vol. 12360, pp. 53–70. Springer, Cham (2020). https://doi.org/10.1007/978-3-030-58555-6_4
17. Deng, Y., Yang, J., Xu, S., Chen, D., Jia, Y., Tong, X.: Accurate 3d face reconstruction with weakly-supervised learning: From single image to image set. In: Proceedings of the IEEE/CVF Conference on Computer Vision and Pattern Recognition Workshops (2019)
18. Yang, H.: Facescape: a large-scale high quality 3d face dataset and detailed riggable 3d face prediction. In: Proceedings of the IEEE/CVF Conference on Computer Vision and Pattern Recognition, pp. 601–610 (2020)

A Lightweight Multi-Scale Large Kernel Attention Hierarchical Network for Single Image Deraining

Xin Wang and Chen Lyu(✉)

Shandong Normal University, Jinan 250014, China
lvchen@sdnu.edu.cn

Abstract. Many current single image deraining methods focus on increasing network depth and width, which results in higher computational overhead and parameters. To address this issue, we propose a lightweight multi-scale large kernel attention hierarchical network(LMANet). Our approach combines multi-scale and Large Kernel Attention(LKA) to create Multi-Scale Large Kernel Attention (MSLKA), where large kernel decomposition can effectively decouple large kernel convolution operations to capture long-term dependencies at different granularity levels in a light weight. We then use the Channel Attention Feed-Forward Network (CAFN), which employs channel attention and gating mechanisms to correct channel information and reduce redundant features, thus further reducing the network size. Finally, we enhanced the inter-layer information learning of the feature maps by adding top-down Self Attention Distillation (SAD) to the network training process, thus accelerating the network training and alleviating 38% of the network parameters. Experimental results on benchmark datasets show that LMANet achieves satisfactory performance while significantly reducing the number of parameters.

Keywords: Single image deraining · Lightweight neural network · Large Kernel Attention · Multi-scale · Self attention distillation

1 Introduction

Single image deraining can be categorized as model-based and data-driven methods. Model-based methods rely on manual feature extraction based on a prior knowledge with poor robustness, such as image decomposition [1], Gaussian mixture models(GMM) [2], sparse coding [3], and low-rank representation [4]. There are two main data-driven methods. The first is the CNN-based method [5–8] to develop various network designs and functional modules, including multi-scale networks [7], multi-stage networks [8], recursive residual learning [9], dilated convolution [10], and attention mechanisms [11]. The network has been designed above to increase in depth and width, and to expand the perceptual field of rain streaks. The second is the Transformer-based method [12–15]. Transformer

L. Iliadis et al. (Eds.): ICANN 2023, LNCS 14255, pp. 26–37, 2023.
https://doi.org/10.1007/978-3-031-44210-0_3

demonstrates excellent SA [16] characterization capability due to its macro-level architecture display [17,18], and SA captures information at different positions in the sequence, which can perceive the whole picture information. It can be seen that the key to both methods is how to expand the perceptual field to improve the model performance. However, the massive stacking of convolutional layers leads to redundant deep networks and lack of global context information. Transformer, while effectively obtaining global context information, lacks convolutional induction bias leading to the destruction of the original 2D structure of the image, which results in partial loss of image spatial information [19]. The simplest idea is to combine the two methods and integrate the advantages of both to obtain better image deraining results. However, not only does the network need to be carefully designed to accommodate the two with very different feature extraction capabilities, but the introduction of Transformer inevitably causes a huge computational and parameter burden. Therefore, single image deraining awaits a better solution in improving the ability to model global contextual information while maintaining a grasp of the underlying details. We consider designing Transformer-like architectures and using simple convolution to obtain long-range dependencies.

Based on the above problems, we design a lightweight multi-scale large kernel attention hierarchical network for single image deraining(LMANet). The core idea of large kernel convolution is to expand the size of the convolution kernel so that the convolution can obtain a larger perceptual field. However, large kernel convolution also brings a large number of parameters and computational effort. Motivated by the convolutional decomposition mechanism, this paper decomposes large kernel convolutional blocks to replace the multi-head attention(MSHA) in Vits, which implements the remote dependency of simple convolution. We combine multi-scale with large kernel decomposition and design a Multi-Scale Large Kernel Attention Block (MSLKA) using three large kernel convolutions of different sizes to achieve coarse-to-fine acquisition of rich features with different granularity. In addition, the feed-forward module is redesigned to use the gating mechanism and the channel attention mechanism to propose the Channel Attention Feed-forward Network (CAFN), which corrects the channel information and eliminates the redundant information to refine the rain feature details. The combination of MSLKA and CAFN forms a Multi-Scale Attention Extraction Block (MAEB) of Transformer-like architecture to achieve efficient and low-overhead single image deraining. In addition, feature maps with rich semantic information can be extracted at different layers of the network. We reconsider the relationship between feature maps between different layers, and we propose Self Distillation Attention(SAD) in the training process of LMANet that allows the network itself to perform top-down and hierarchical self attention distillation for adaptive correction of different layer features.

Specifically, our contributions are as follows:

- We propose LMANet, an efficient Transformer-like convolutional architecture for single image deraining. LMANet uses fewer parameters and lower number of parameters than state-of-the-art methods.

- We designed a Multi-Scale Feature Extraction Block(MAEB), where MSLKA uses multi-scale and decomposed large kernel convolution to progressively extract rich features at different granularities, and CAFN combines channel attention and gating mechanisms to mitigate useless channel information, both of which work in concert to reduce network parameters and improve network representation.
- We reconsider the relationship between feature maps between different layers and propose Self Distillation Attention(SAD) in the network training process to reduce the network training burden and network parameters and enhance the information exchange between different layers.

2 Related Work

2.1 Single Image Deraining

Model-based methods mainly use handcrafted features and priors to describe rain patterns. Kang et al. [1] suggest decomposing the image into low and high frequency parts and removing rain patterns in the high frequency layers by dictionary learning. Li et al. [2] use a Gaussian mixture model (GMM) as a prior model for rain patterns and background for rain removal. Luo et al. [3] propose a discriminative sparse coding method for separating rain patterns from the background. Recently, many data-driven methods have been proposed for single image deraining and significant progress has been made in this area. Jiang et al. [7] proposed a multi-scale coarse-to-fine asymptotic fusion network to remove rain patterns. Zamir et al. [8] propose a multi-stage architecture that decomposes the recovery process into more manageable steps by injecting supervision at each stage to progressively improve the degraded inputs. Vision Transformer [16] has recently been introduced to image recovery tasks and has achieved remarkable performance due to its powerful modeling capabilities. Chen et al. [12] first applied the standard Transformer equipped with multiple heads and tails to several low-level vision tasks. Wang et al. [13] constructed a U-shaped Transformer for image recovery based on the Swin Transformer. Liang et al. [14] proposed a model based on the Swin Transformer by combining CNN and Transformer and achieved excellent performance while maintaining computational efficiency.

2.2 Knowledge and Attention Distillation

Knowledge distillation [20] is a technique that transfers knowledge from a pre-trained teacher model to a student model through distillation. Recent studies have extended knowledge distillation to attention distillation. Sergey et al. [21] introduced two types of attention distillation, namely activation-based attention distillation and gradient-based attention distillation. In both distillations, the student network is trained by learning attentional mappings derived from the teacher network. Self attention distillation that we propose in this paper differs from attention distillation in that our approach does not require a teacher network. Our main objective is to explore the feasibility of distilling hierarchical attention for self-learning.

3 Method

3.1 Network Architecture

As shown in Fig. 1, the proposed LMANet is constituted of three components: the shallow feature extraction module (head), the deep feature extraction module and the image reconstruction module (tail).

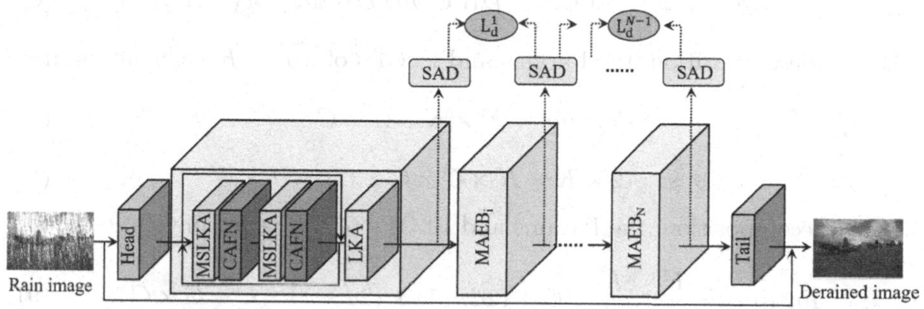

Fig. 1. The architecture of the proposed LMANet.

Given an input a rainy image $I \in \mathbb{R}^{H\times W\times C}$, the H_{SF} is first utilized to extract the shallow feature $F_0 \in \mathbb{R}^{H\times W\times C}$:

$$F_0 = H_{SF}(I) \tag{1}$$

where H_{SF} is the shallow feature extraction module, using a 3×3 Conv to extract low-level features to preserve texture details. Then, the deep feature extraction module extract deep feature $F_D \in \mathbb{R}^{H\times W\times C}$:

$$F_D = H_{DF}(F_0) \tag{2}$$

where H_{DF} consists of N cascaded Multi-Scale Feature Extraction Blocks (MAEBs), where MAEB contains two Multi-Scale Large Kernel Attention (MSLKA), two Channel Attention Feed-Forward Network(CAFN) and a 7-9-1 Large kernel Attention. The recursive structure shares weights among MAEBs, increasing the depth of the network while reducing the consumption of GPU memory and the size of the model parameters. Specifically, the intermediate features F^1_{MAEB}, F^2_{MAEB}, ..., F^N_{MAEB} are extracted by block as:

$$\begin{cases} F^1_{MAEB} = H_{MAEB}(F_0) \\ F^{i+1}_{MAEB} = H_{MAEB}(F^i_{MAEB}), \quad i = 1, 2, ..., N-1 \end{cases} \tag{3}$$

$$MAEB = LKA([CAFN_2(MSLKA_2(CAFN_1(MSLKA_1(X))))]^{\circlearrowleft}_{L}) \tag{4}$$

A 3×3 convolution is used in the image reconstruction module H_{IR} to obtain the final image:

$$\hat{I} = H_{IR}(F^N_{MAEB} + F_0) \tag{5}$$

3.2 Multi-scale Large Kernel Attention(MLKA)

Large Kernel Attention(LKA). Given the input feature maps $X \in \mathbb{R}^{H\times W\times C}$, the Large Kernel Attention(LKA) can decompose a $K \times K$ convolution into three components: a $(2d-1)\times(2d-1)$ depth-wise convolution, a $\lceil \frac{K}{d} \rceil \times \lceil \frac{K}{d} \rceil$ depth-wise dilation convolution and a point-wise convolution, which can be formulated as:

$$LKA(X) = PWConv(DWConv(DWDConv(X)) \tag{6}$$

Before decomposition, the Params and FLOPs of a $K \times K$ convolution are:

$$Params = K \times K \times C \times C \tag{7}$$

$$FLops = (2 \times K \times K \times C \times C - C) \times H \times W \tag{8}$$

After decomposition, the Params and FLOPs of a $K \times K$ convolution are:

$$Params = \frac{K}{d} \times \frac{K}{d} \times C + (2d-1) \times (2d-1) \times C + C \times C \tag{9}$$

$$FLops = \frac{K}{d} \times \frac{K}{d} \times C + (2d-1) \times (2d-1) \times C + C \times C \times H \times W \tag{10}$$

Multi-scale Large Kernel Attention(MSLKA). To learn feature maps with multi-scale information, we use group convolution to improve large kernel attention blocks. Suppose the input feature maps $X \in \mathbb{R}^{H\times W\times C}$ and X^* is first obtained by a convolution block. Next split X^* into three groups $X^* = [X_1^*, X_2^*, X_3^*]$, each of size $H \times W \times \lfloor \frac{C}{3} \rfloor$. For each group, a LKA decomposed by $\{K_i, d_i\}$ is utillzed to generate a homogeneous scale attention map LKA_i. In detail, we leverage three groups of LKA: $\{35, 4\}LKA_1$ implemented by 7-9-1, $\{21, 3\}LKA_2$ implemented by 5-7-1, and$\{7, 2\}LKA_3$ implemented by 3-5-1. The features of different groups are fed into their respective LKAs, and the features are extracted cumulatively in turn. Specifically, it can be expressed as:

$$X^* = GELU(PWConv(Norm(X)))) \tag{11}$$

$$X^* = [X_1^*, X_2^*, X_3^*] \tag{12}$$

$$X_1^{**} = LKA_1(X_1^*) \tag{13}$$

$$X_2^{**} = LKA_2(X_2^* + X_1^*) \tag{14}$$

$$X_3^{**} = LKA_3(X_3^* + X_3^*) \tag{15}$$

$$X = X + PWConv(X^* \bigotimes concat[X_1^{**}, X_2^{**}, X_3^{**}]) \tag{16}$$

Channel Attention Feed-Forward Network(CAFN). Different channel characteristics have different completely different weighting information, some channel characteristics are not particularly important in network optimization. Therefore, if we treat these channels equally, we will put resources on less critical information, which will affect the performance of the network. To reduce redundant information flow to the network, CAFN incorporates channel attention into the traditional feed-forward network, which allows the traditional feed-forward network to reweight different channel characteristics. For a given feature maps $X \in \mathbb{R}^{H \times W \times C}$, CAFN can be expressed as:

$$X = X + PWConv(CA(Norm(X)) \bigotimes GELU(DWConv(Pconv(Norm(X))))) \tag{17}$$

where the channel attention block can be denoted as:

$$CA(X') = sigmoid(DWConv(GELU(DWConv(GAP(X'))))) \tag{18}$$

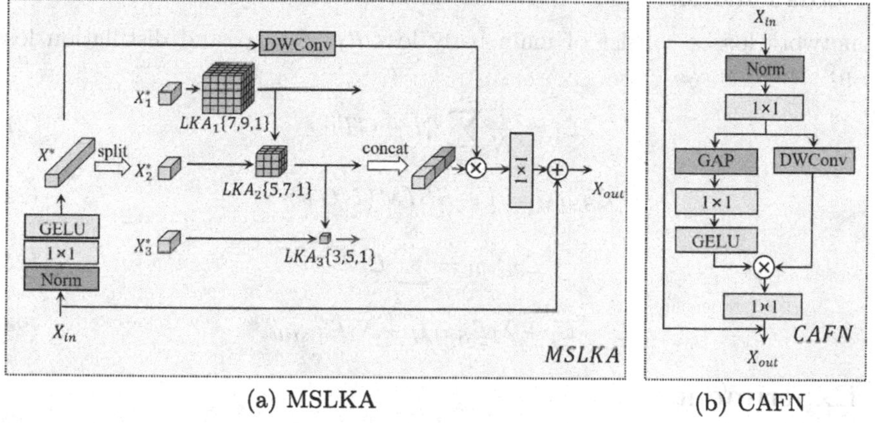

(a) MSLKA (b) CAFN

Fig. 2. Multi-Scale Attention Extraction Block(MAEB).

3.3 Self Attention Distillation(SAD)

For the output $F_i \in \mathbb{R}^{H_i \times W_i \times C_i}$ of layer i of the network, we use the mapping function f to obtain the attention graph $M_i \in \mathbb{R}^{H_i \times W_i}$ of the network output for that layer. The values in this attention graph represent the importance of that element in the feature, so we construct the mapping function f by computing the statistics of these values in the channel dimension:

$$f(F_i) = \frac{1}{C} \sum_{i=1}^{C} F_i^p \tag{19}$$

The corresponding attention maps are generated using the mapping function $f(F_i)$ for the feature map F_i at layer i and the feature map F_{i+1} at layer $i+1$, respectively. To enable learning between different multi-scale feature extraction blocks, the loss function between adjacent layers:

$$L_{i+1}(F_i, F_{i+1}) = MSE(f(F_i, F_{i+1})) \tag{20}$$

We suggests using a two-step strategy to train the network in this paper to guide the effective removal of rain streaks.

step1: LMANet is trained on the dataset using the loss function of the network subject, and the network is trained to a certain reasonable level to be able to perform the rain streak removal effectively.

step2: SAD is added to the feature extraction blocks of each layer of LMANet trained in step 1, at which time two loss functions are used in the network for continued training of LMANet, the loss functions are the loss function of the network body and the self-distillation loss function after adding SAD. The network is continuously trained until it is stable.

3.4 Loss Function

The network losses consist of main bady loss $\mathcal{L}_1$, $\mathcal{L}_{SSIM}$ and distillation loss $\mathcal{L}_{distill}$:

$$\mathcal{L}_1 = \frac{1}{N}\sum_{i=1}^{N} ||\hat{I} - GT|| \tag{21}$$

$$\mathcal{L}_{SSIM} = 1 - SSIM(\hat{I}, GT) \tag{22}$$

$$\mathcal{L}_{distill} = \sum_{i=2}^{N} \mathcal{L}_i \tag{23}$$

$$\mathcal{L} = \mathcal{L}_1 + \lambda_1 \mathcal{L}_{SSIM} + \lambda_2 \mathcal{L}_{distill} \tag{24}$$

4 Experiment

4.1 Implementation Details

Datasets. In our experiments, we use five synthetic datasets(Test100 [22], Rain100H [23], Rain100L [23], Test2800 [5], Test1200 [24]) and a real rain image dataset(SPA-DATA) to verify the effectiveness of our method.

Setting. In LMANet, we stack 6 MAEBs. To enhance the training data, we applied horizontal flip and randomly rotated the images by 90°, 180°, and 270°. The network is trained on 256×256 patches with a batchsize of 16 and a number of iterations of 4×10^{-5}. We used the Adam optimizer, the total number of iterations was 400K, the initial learning rate was 2×10^{-4}, and the cosine annealing strategy was used to learn at the initial 50K step 1. In the remaining 350K iterations, we add SAD, and the learning rate gradually decays from 2×10^{-4} to 1×10^{-6}. All experiments are conducted by Pytorch framework on 4 Nvidia RTX 3090 GPUs.

4.2 Comparision with the State-of-the-Art Methods

Qualitative Results. In Fig 3, we show the example of LMANet with state-of-the-art methods on Rain100H. Compared to other methods, LMANet can remove rain patterns and restore clean backgrounds more effectively. As shown in Fig 4, to further evaluate the generalizability of LMANet on real datasets, we give an example of rain removal on SPA-Data. Thus, our method can effectively remove the rain from synthetic and real scenes.

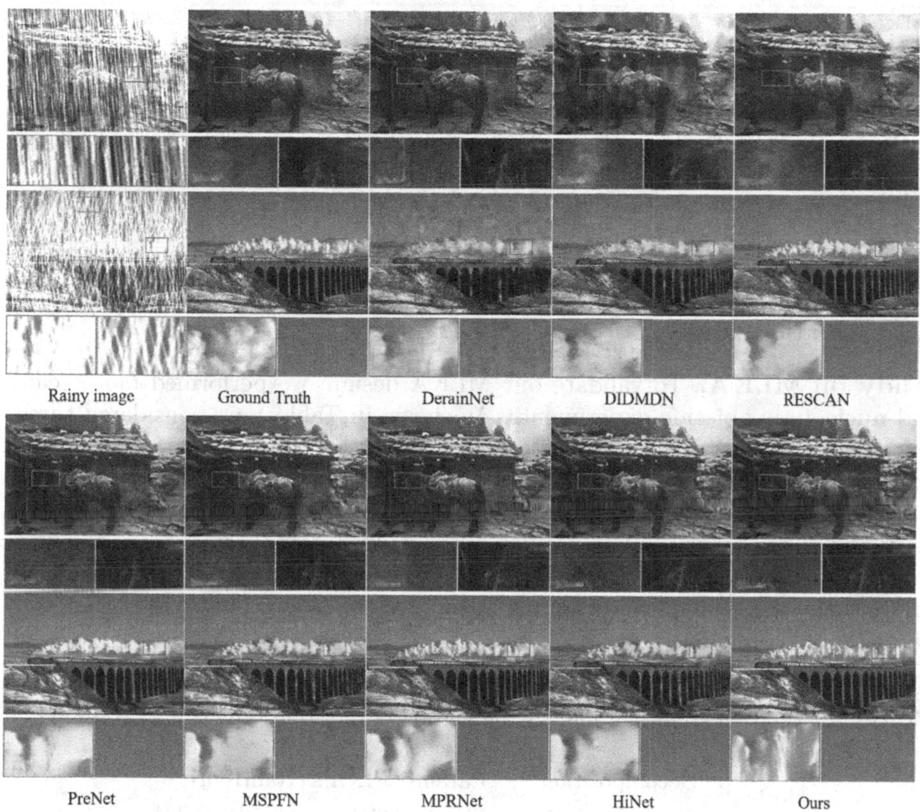

Fig. 3. Comparison with state-of-the-art methods on Rain100H.

Quantitative Results. To demonstrate the effectiveness of LMANet, we tested the deraining results on the synthetic datasets using PSNR and SSIM as shown in Table 1. LMANet improved PSNR by 0.05~0.75 dB and SSIM by 0.003~0.007 dB on the synthetic dataset.

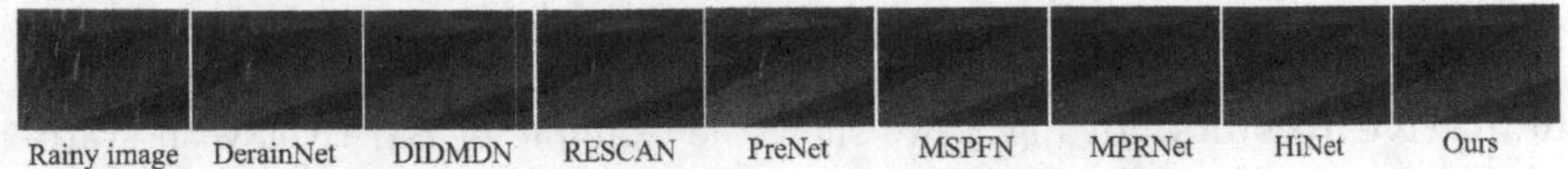

Fig. 4. Comparisons with state-of-the-art methods on SPA-Data images.

Table 1. Average PSNR and SSIM metrics on five synthetic datasets.

Methods	Test100		Rain100H		Rain100L		Test2800		Test1200	
	PSNR	SSIM	PSNR	SSIM	PSNR	SSIM	PSNR	SSIM	PSNR	SSIM
DerainNet [5]	22.77	0.810	14.92	0.592	27.03	0.884	24.31	0.861	23.38	0.835
DIDMDN [24]	22.56	0.818	17.35	0.524	25.23	0.741	28.13	0.867	29.65	0.901
RESCAN [6]	25.00	0.835	26.36	0.786	29.80	0.881	31.29	0.904	30.51	0.882
PreNet [25]	24.81	0.851	26.77	0.858	32.44	0.950	31.75	0.916	31.36	0.911
MSPFN [7]	27.50	0.876	28.66	0.860	32.40	0.933	32.82	0.930	32.39	0.916
MPRNet [8]	30.27	0.897	30.41	0.890	36.40	0.965	33.64	0.938	32.91	0.916
HiNet [26]	30.29	0.906	30.65	0.894	37.28	0.970	33.91	**0.941**	33.05	0.919
Ours	**31.04**	**0.913**	**30.73**	**0.898**	**37.81**	**0.973**	**33.96**	**0.941**	**33.23**	**0.921**

4.3 Ablation Study

Study on MLKA. To validate our MLKA design, we performed multi-scale and nucleolytic ablation experiments. As shown in Table 2, we considered three LKA and three MSLKA implementations. The results show that MLKA is superior to LKA, justifying our multiscale choice. The results show that the later the join time is, the faster the network converges and the PSNR increases accordingly, but the network consumes much more computational resources in the first stage of training than in the second stage. Therefore, in order to balance the computational resources and running speed, we choose to join SAD at the 50th iteration of the model.

Table 2. Ablation studies of multi-scale and decomposition type (LKA/MSLKA).

Methods	Decomposition			Params	FLOPs	Rain100H	
	3-5-1	5-7-1	7-9-1	MB	GB	PSNR	SSIM
LKA	✓			1.12	50.78	30.49	0.892
		✓		1.34	53.49	30.56	0.894
			✓	1.15	51.77	30.73	0.898
MSLKA	✓		✓	1.03	47.15	29.89	0.893
		✓	✓	1.09	49.77	29.93	0.896
	✓	✓	✓	1.16	52.78	**29.96**	**0.898**

Study on SAD. As shown in Table 3, We are adding SAD to a half-trained model, so we examine here the different points in time when SAD is added. We chose to add SAD in 50epoch, when the network parameters were reduced by 38%.

Table 3. Performance of the LMANet model with self-attentive distillation added at different time points on the Rain100L.

start epoch	convergence	Params(MB)	PSNR(dB)
10K	348K	1.05	34.26
20K	316K	1.09	35.34
50K	**264K**	**1.16**	**37.81**
100K	227K	1.40	37.82
no SAD	381K	1.87	37.62

Study on CAFN. We compare the proposed CFAN with the MLP, as the results in Table 4 show that we improve the performance of the feed-forward network while reducing the parameters.

Table 4. Ablation studies of MLP and CAFN.

Methods	Params	FLOPs	Rain100L	
	MB	GB	PSNR	SSIM
MLP	1.34	541.7	29.91	0.895
CAFN	**1.16**	**527.8**	**29.96**	**0.898**

Study on Lightweight Network. To further demonstrate the lightness of LMANet, we give HiNet, PreNet and LMANet a fixed input in Table 5. The results show that LMANet consumes the least amount of resources.

Table 5. Model size comparison of different methods.

Methods	Input Dim	Input size	FLOPs	Size
	C×H×W	MB	GB	MB
HiNet	3 × 336 × 336	1.29	293.79	2659.96
PreNet	3 × 336 × 336	1.29	114.13	417.96
Ours	3 × 336 × 336	1.29	**55.45**	**567.12**

5 Conclusion

In this paper, we propose a lightweight hierarchical deraining network that combines multi-scale and large kernel concerns to obtain long-term dependencies at different granularities, and uses channel attention and gating mechanisms to optimize channel information. In addition, we introduce a simple self attention distillation method to assist network learning in network training. We hope that the work in this paper can shed some light on the direction of lightweight image deraining, rather than shifting the focus of the work to more complex network architecture design.

References

1. Kang, L.-W., Lin, C.-W., Fu, Y.-H.: Automatic single-image-based rain streaks removal via image decomposition. IEEE Trans. Image Process. **21**(4), 1742–1755 (2011)
2. Li, Y., Tan, R.T., Guo, X., Lu, J., Brown, M.S.: Rain streak removal using layer priors. Proceedings of the IEEE Conference on Computer Vision and Pattern Recognition, pp. 2736–2744 (2016)
3. Luo, Y., Xu, Y., Ji, H.: Removing rain from a single image via discriminative sparse coding. In: Proceedings of the IEEE International Conference on Computer Vision, pp. 3397–3405 (2015)
4. Chen, Y.-L., Hsu, C.-T.: A generalized low-rank appearance model for spatio-temporally correlated rain streaks. Proceedings of the IEEE International Conference on Computer Vision, pp. 1968–1975 (2013)
5. Fu, X., Huang, J., Ding, X., Liao, Y., Paisley, J.: Clearing the skies: a deep network architecture for single-image rain removal. IEEE Trans. Image Process. **26**(6), 2944–2956 (2017)
6. Li, X., Wu, J., Lin, Z., Liu, H., Zha, H.: Recurrent squeeze-and-excitation context aggregation net for single image deraining. In: Ferrari, V., Hebert, M., Sminchisescu, C., Weiss, Y. (eds.) ECCV 2018. LNCS, vol. 11211, pp. 262–277. Springer, Cham (2018). https://doi.org/10.1007/978-3-030-01234-2_16
7. Jiang, K., et al.: Multi-scale progressive fusion network for single image deraining. In: Proceedings of the IEEE/CVF Conference on Computer Vision and Pattern Recognition, pp. 8346–8355 (2020)
8. Zamir, S.W., et al.: Multi-stage progressive image restoration. In: Proceedings of the IEEE/CVF Conference on Computer Vision and Pattern Recognition, pp. 14821–14831 (2021)
9. Anwar, S., Barnes, N.: Real image denoising with feature attention. In: Proceedings of the IEEE/CVF International Conference on Computer Vision, pp. 3155–3164 (2019)
10. Kupyn, O., Martyniuk, T., Wu, J., Wang, Z.: Deblurgan-v2: deblurring (orders-of-magnitude) faster and better. In: Proceedings of the IEEE/CVF International Conference on Computer Vision, pp. 8878–8887 (2019)
11. Zamir, S.W., et al.: Cycleisp: real image restoration via improved data synthesis. In: Proceedings of the IEEE/CVF Conference On Computer Vision And Pattern Recognition, pp. 2696–2705 (2020)

12. Chen, H., et al.: Pre-trained image processing transformer. In: Proceedings of the IEEE/CVF Conference on Computer Vision and Pattern Recognition, pp. 12299–12310 (2021)
13. Wang, Z., Cun, X., Bao, J., Zhou, W., Liu, J., Li, H.U.: A general u-shaped transformer for image restoration. Proceedings of the IEEE/CVF Conference on Computer Vision and Pattern Recognition, New Orleans, LA, USA, pp. 19–24 (2022)
14. Liang, J., Cao, J., Sun, G., Zhang, K., Van Gool, L., Timofte, R.: Swinir: image restoration using swin transformer. In: Proceedings of the IEEE/CVF International Conference on Computer Vision, pp. 1833–1844 (2021)
15. Zamir, S.W., Arora, A., Khan, S., Hayat, M., Khan, F.S., Yang, M.-H.: Restormer: efficient transformer for high-resolution image restoration. Proceedings of the IEEE/CVF Conference on Computer Vision and Pattern Recognition, pp. 5728–5739 (2022)
16. Dosovitskiy, A.,et al.: An image is worth 16x16 words: transformers for image recognition at scale, arXiv preprint arXiv:2010.11929 (2020)
17. Raghu, M., Unterthiner, T., Kornblith, S., Zhang, C., Dosovitskiy, A.: Do vision transformers see like convolutional neural networks? In: Advances in Neural Information Processing Systems, vol. 34(22), pp. 12116–12128 (2021)
18. Tolstikhin, I.O., et al.: Mlp-mixer: an all-mlp architecture for vision. In: Advances in Neural Information Processing Systems, vol. 34, pp. 24261–24272 (2021)
19. Pinto, F., Torr, P.H., Dokania, P.K.: An impartial take to the cnn vs transformer robustness contest. In: Computer Vision-ECCV,: 17th European Conference, Tel Aviv, Israel, 23–27 October 2022, Proceedings, Part XIII, pp. 466–480. Springer (2022). https://doi.org/10.1007/978-3-031-19778-9_27
20. Hinton, G., Vinyals, O., Dean, J.: Distilling the knowledge in a neural network, arXiv preprint arXiv:1503.02531 (2015)
21. Zagoruyko, S., Komodakis, N.: Paying more attention to attention: improving the performance of convolutional neural networks via attention transfer, arXiv preprint arXiv:1612.03928 (2016)
22. Zhang, H., Sindagi, V., Patel, V.M.: Image de-raining using a conditional generative adversarial network. IEEE Trans. Circuits Syst. Video Technol. **30**(11), 3943–3956 (2019)
23. Yang, W., Tan, R.T., Feng, J., Liu, J., Guo, Z., Yan, S.: Deep joint rain detection and removal from a single image. In: Proceedings of the IEEE Conference on Computer Vision and Pattern Recognition, pp. 1357–1366 (2017)
24. Zhang, H., Patel, V.M.: Density-aware single image de-raining using a multi-stream dense network. In: Proceedings of the IEEE Conference on Computer Vision and Pattern Recognition, pp. 695–704 (2018)
25. Ren, D., Zuo, W., Hu, Q., Zhu, P., Meng, D.: Progressive image deraining networks: a better and simpler baseline. In: Proceedings of the IEEE/CVF Conference on Computer Vision and Pattern Recognition, pp. 937–3946 (2019)
26. Chen, L., Lu, X., Zhang, J., Chu, X., Chen, C.: Hinet: half instance normalization network for image restoration. In: Proceedings of the IEEE/CVF Conference on Computer Vision and Pattern Recognition, pp. 182–192 (2021)

A Multi-scale Method for Cell Segmentation in Fluorescence Microscopy Images

Yating Fang and Baojiang Zhong(✉)

School of Computer Science and Technology, Soochow University, Suzhou, China
bjzhong@suda.edu.cn

Abstract. Accurate segmentation of cells in fluorescent microscopy images plays a key role in high-throughput applications such as the quantification of protein expression and the study of cell function. Existing cell segmentation methods have drawbacks in terms of inaccurate location of segmentation boundary, misidentification, and inaccurate segmentation of overlapping cells. To address these issues, a novel *multi-scale method for cell segmentation in fluorescence microscopy images* (MMCS) is proposed in this paper. Our motivation to adopt multi-scale image analysis in the cell segmentation task originates from the basic observation that cells on fluorescence microscope images are often composed of different structures at different scales. In our proposed MMCS, three scales are exploited. At the high scale, noise effects are sufficiently suppressed, and the cell contour is fully smoothed. Then, scale fusion is further performed, that is, the cell contours obtained by segmentation at high, medium, and low scales are averaged, to improve the location accuracy of contour segmentation. To solve the problems of misidentification and cell overlapping, an improved Bradley technique with constraints based on shape and intensity features and region-based fitting of overlapping ellipses technique are also developed and embedded in our multi-scale approach for extracting cell contours at each single scale. The experimental results obtained on a large number of fluorescence microscope images from two data sets show that the proposed MMCS can outperform state-of-the-art methods by a large margin.

Keywords: Cell segmentation · Ellipse fitting · Multi-scale · Fluorescence microscopy images

1 Introduction

Numerous areas of analysing and quantifying fluorescence microscopy images rely on quantitative cell nucleus image analysis [15]. For example, accurate

This work was supported in part by the Natural Science Foundation of the Jiangsu Higher Education Institutions of China under Grant 21KJA520007, in part by the Collaborative Innovation Center of Novel Software Technology and Industrialization, and in part by the Priority Academic Program Development of Jiangsu Higher Education Institutions.

L. Iliadis et al. (Eds.): ICANN 2023, LNCS 14255, pp. 38–50, 2023.
https://doi.org/10.1007/978-3-031-44210-0_4

cell segmentation in fluorescent microscope images plays a key role in high-throughput applications such as protein expression quantification and cell function research [22]. However, manual segmentation of cells from fluorescent microscope images is a time-consuming task. Thus, automatic cell segmentation using image processing technique has attracted considerable interest [4].

Over the past few decades, many technologies for cell segmentation have been proposed, including graph-based methods [16], ellipse fitting [13], intensity thresholding [19], watershed transform [18], morphological operations [25], deep-learning-based methods [7], etc. However, when used in the cell segmentation task of fluorescence microscope images, the influence of noise and the existence of overlapping cells could often cause inaccurate cell boundary segmentation positioning and wrong recognition [12]. In fact, these methods [13,16,18,19, 25] are all *single-scaled*, which employ only *one* fixed scale to identify cells. If the scale value of a single-scale method is set to be small, the noise may be mistaken as edges. On the other hand, if the scale value is set to be large, the useful contour information will be suppressed. Both of them will lead to poor edge location accuracy. It has been proposed to segment cells with multi-scale methods [3,21]. Ram *et al.* [21] used the multi-scale variance stabilizing transform as a preprocessing step to reduce the noise in the images. Al-Kofahi *et al.* [3] used the multi-scale Laplacian-of-Gaussian filtering in the seed detection step. However, these existing so-called "multi-scale" methods commonly adopt a multi-scale operation within *one* step of their developed algorithm *only* [3,21].

To overcome the above-mentioned problems and improve the cell segmentation performance, a novel *multi-scale method for cell segmentation in fluorescence microscope images* (MMCS) is proposed on the basis of region-based fitting of overlapping ellipse technique in this paper. Our motivation to adopt multi-scale image analysis in the cell segmentation task originates from the basic observation that cells on fluorescence microscope images are often composed of different structures at different scales. In computer vision, multi-scale image analysis has been widely adopted as a modern approach to address the limitations of single-scale methods, particularly in image feature extraction [1]. A typical multi-scale model—i.e., Gaussian scale space [23], performs image smoothing across multiple scales (that is, with multiple values of the standard deviation of the Gaussian kernel), and then conduct a multi-scale fusion of feature cues (e.g., detect the edge features at multiple given scale individually and then take the averaged results as the final output [17]) to obtain meaningful image features.

For our proposed MMCS, the input fluorescence microscope image is smoothed by Gaussian. The standard deviation of the Gaussian filter used here is used to upload our multi-scale setting to achieve a multi-scale segmentation of fluorescence microscope cells. In this paper, the fusion of multi-scale feature cues is modeled as a signal averaging process. This is to say, the given cell image will be smoothed with multiple standard deviations of the Gaussian filter, and at each scale a detected cell contour will be generated accordingly. These cell contours over multiple scales are processed by a multi-scale fusion operation, i.e., contour averaging, to produce the final cell segmentation result. Different from existing multi-scale methods [3,21], our proposed MMCS is a *true* or full-blown multi-scale method, as it has *multiple* branches that are obtained by performing *each* step of the cell segmentation method individually at each scale.

The main novel developments of our work are summarized as follows.

1) *A multi-scale approach of fluorescence microscope cell segmentation.* It overcomes the drawbacks of the existing single-scale methods and can segment the fluorescence microscope cells correctly with high accuracy. It is verified that the overall segmentation performance can thus be significantly improved.

2) *An improved Bradley segmentation technique.* Due to the existence of locally brighter background segments in the fluorescence microscopy cell images, the Bradley technique [6] identifies them as cells, resulting in false positive results. These false positives can be effectively rejected by adding shape- and intensity-based constraints.

3) *A region-based fitting of overlapping ellipse technique for identifying and extracting overlapping cells.* First, the skeleton of the cell's 2D shape is exploited to obtain important information on the parameters of the ellipses that could approximate the original shape. Then, combined with the Akaike Information Criterion (AIC) [12], an equal area constraint is used to automatically estimate an unknown number of ellipses. Finally, according to the detected ellipse and the boundary detected by the improved Bradley technique, the automatic segmentation of overlapping cells is realized.

2 The Proposed Method

Our cell segmentation approach, i.e., the MMCS, will be developed broadly following the method of Panagiotakis *et al.* [12]. In what follows, the motivation of adopting multi-scale image analysis in cell segmentation is clarified first, and then our approach is proposed.

2.1 Motivation

In the field of computer vision, the Gaussian scale space is a typical multi-scale model for image feature extraction [23]. Let $I(x, y)$ be the input image. To conduct a multi-scale analysis, the image is convolved with a 2D Gaussian kernel $g_\sigma(x, y)$ with varying standard deviation σ, i.e.,

$$I_\sigma(x, y) = I(x, y) * g_\sigma(x, y), \tag{1}$$

where the symbol $*$ denotes the convolution operator, and σ is treated as the scale parameter.

As the scale σ increases, the input image becomes more and more blurring. In this process, noise effects are gradually suppressed. In consequence, at a high scale, meaningful image features (e.g. smooth edges) can be easily identified. However, due to the effect of image blurring, image features (e.g. corners and edges) could have poor locations. Signal averaging is a signal processing technique applied in the time domain, intended to increase the strength of a signal

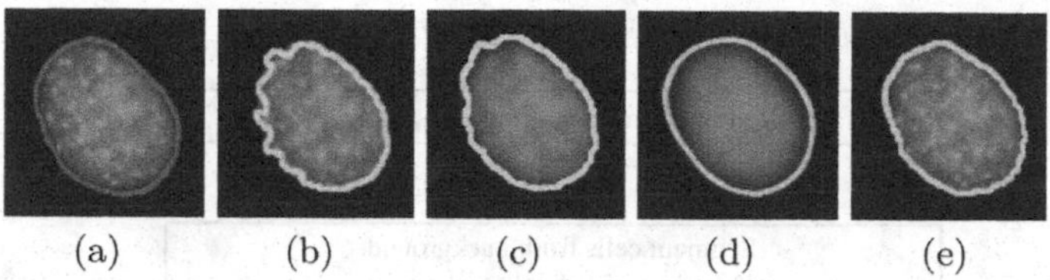

Fig. 1. Underlying idea of our proposed multi-scale approach: (a) the ground truth image; (b)–(d) cell segmenting performed at the low, medium, and high scales, respectively; (e) the cell contour produced by our approach through a multi-scale fusion.

relative to noise [14]. Thus, we combine the contour position information on the high, medium and low scales, and average them as the final result to weaken the influence of noise and improve its location accuracy. A multi-scale feature extraction method can be developed through this signal averaging strategy.

Figure 1 depicts the underlying idea of our proposed MMCS. The test image shown in Fig. 1(a) is cropped from a fluorescent microscopy image, which contains a single cell. The challenge to segmenting this cell lies in that the influence of noise, which makes the contour of the segmented cell far from its real shape, and thus greatly reduces the accuracy of cell segmentation. In our approach, three scales will be used. As a result, three cell contours are produced, as shown in Figs. 1(b) to 1(d), respectively. It is seen that at both the low and medium scales, the noise affects the smoothness of cell segmentation contours. At the high scale, due to sufficient amount of image blurring, the noise effect is suppressed and the resulting cell contours are closer to true shapes. On the other hand, at the high scale, the image blurring effect causes the cell contour to be expanded remarkably, leading to the accuracy of the segmentation results with low accuracy. By fusing the feature information (i.e. cell contours) on three scales and taking the average result as output, a multi-scale result is obtained, as shown in Fig. 1(e), which not only ensures that the segmentation result is closer to the real shape but also improves the accuracy of cell location.

2.2 Methodology

The outline of our MMCS is shown in Fig. 2. First, three steps are sequentially conducted over multiple scales, i.e. image smoothing, segmenting cells from their background, and identifying overlapping cells. A multi-scale fusion is then performed to produce the cell segmentation result. In what follows, we will start from the image smoothing step to describe our multi-scale approach.

Individual Image Smoothing over Multiple Scales: In the digital case, the image convolution process (1) is performed with a discrete sequence of scales. In this work, three scales are used: $\sigma_1 = 2/\sqrt{2}$, $\sigma_2 = 2$, and $\sigma_3 = 2\sqrt{2}$, respectively. Note that the medium scale σ_2 equals the default scale of the existing single-scale method [12]. The use of high scale σ_3 helps to smooth the contour of cell segmentation and the use of low scale σ_1 helps to improve cell location accuracy.

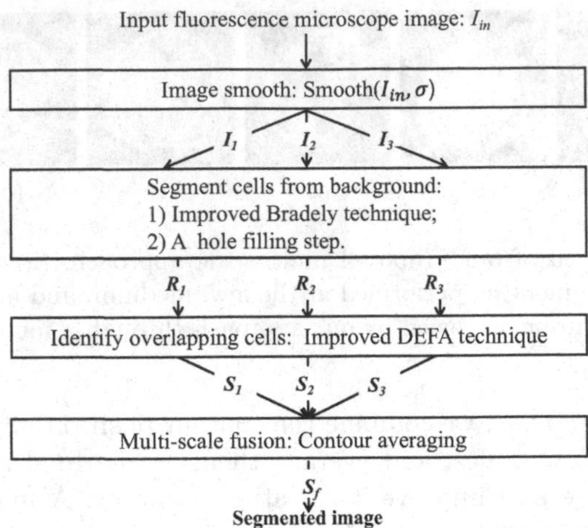

Fig. 2. Outline of the proposed multi-scale approach, where I_j, R_j, and S_j denote the fluorescence microscopic cell image by Gaussian smoothed, the connected region set generated by Bradley segmentation on each scale, and the cell contour set obtained at the jth scale, respectively, and S_f is the final produce set of cell contours for cell segmentation.

Assume that the input fluorescence microscope image is denoted as I_{in}. The image smoothing operation over the three specified scales can be expressed as:

$$I_i = \text{Smooth}\left(I_{in}, \sigma_i\right), \tag{2}$$

where I_i denotes the Gaussian blurred image yielded at the i-th scale for $i = 1, 2, 3$, respectively.

Segmenting Cells from Their Background: Fluorescence microscopy cell images contain many cells of various sizes with elliptic-like shapes, which may be touching each other. The brightness of these cells differs greatly from their background. Taking advantage of this feature, we apply the Bradley segmentation technique [6] and a hole filling step to segment cells from their background. However, a drawback of the Bradley technique is that segments of the background with locally higher brightness are identified erroneously as cells (see Fig. 3(b)). To reduce these false positives, we have introduced two shape-based constraints: *area constraint* and *roundness constraint*, and two intensity-based constraints: *local and global intensity constraint.*

In the *area constraint*, to avoid particularly small segments being considered as cells, the expected area of each cell should exceed a minimum threshold T_α. To avoid the rejection of partially visible cells that appear at image boundaries, the expected area is computed as the area of the circle that can be fitted best to the eight extrema points of their boundary [12]. In the *roundness constraint*, since cells are circular/elliptic-like objects, the roundness measure C [12] is used

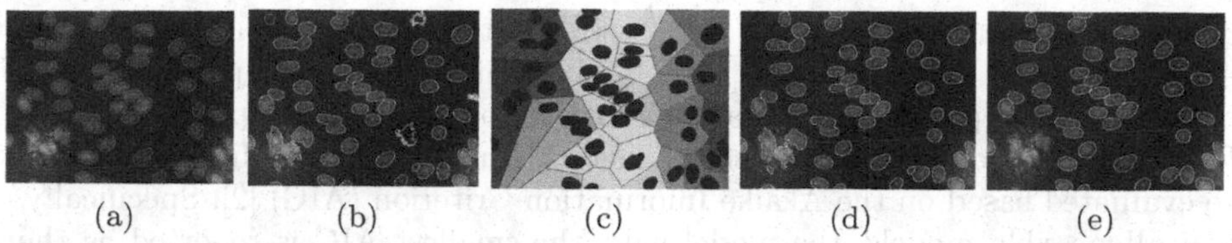

Fig. 3. (a) The ground truth image; (b) The boundaries of the detected cells according to the Bradley technique projected on the given image. The cell centroids according to the ground truth data are plotted with red "+"; (c) The local backgrounds of the detected cells according to the Voronoi diagram of their centroids. The detected cells are plotted in black; (d)–(e) The results of the RFOVE method and our MMCS method. (Color figure online)

to reject objects that deviate considerably from this shape. According to our experiments, $C > 0.2$ is required. The shape constraints can reject several false positives, such as the three on the right in Fig. 3(b).

In the *local intensity constraint*, the intensity distribution within a cell should be more similar to the intensity distribution within the rest of the cells, rather than to the intensity distribution of the local background. It can reject more false positives, such as the circular object on the top left of Fig. 3(b). Specifically, we first extract the local background of each detected object by computing the Voronoi diagram of the object centroid, and then remove the detected object from it (see Fig. 3(c)). Then we adopt the Bhattacharyya distance [10] to measure the distance between two intensity distributions.

There will be strong brightness ellipse-like background segments in fluorescence microscope images, with similar intensity cells nearby. In this case, they will still be mistaken for cells under the local intensity constraint (as shown in Fig. 3(d) lower left corner). To address this issue, we introduce a *global intensity constraint*. This constraint can be expressed intuitively by using OSTU [20] to determine the image's global threshold *level*, and resetting the segment whose intensity value is greater than the *level* in the image to the *level*.

Figure 3(b) shows the boundaries of the detected cells by the original Bradley segmentation technique [6], and the ground truth as in Fig. 3(a). These false positives are rejected by employing the proposed constraints (see Fig. 3(e)).

Identifying Overlapping Cells: The foreground cells from the background are discriminated by the aforementioned improved Bradley segmentation method, and a set of connected region $R = \{r_1, r_2, \dots\}$ can be obtained. However, it cannot discriminate between touching cells. Therefore, we improve the decreasing ellipse fitting method (DEFA) [11] and apply it to each connected region r_j, where $j = 1, 2, \cdots$.

The DEFA method approximates an arbitrary 2D shape with a number of ellipses to count the number of objects that make up the shape. In DEFA, the number and parameters of ellipses are automatically determined under the constraint that the total area $|E| = \sum_{i=1}^{k} |E_i|$ of the ellipses is equal to the area $|A| = |r_j|$ of the original shape. First, a skeleton of the 2D shape about r_j is computed, which provides information about the approximate ellipse parameters of r_j. Then, different models (i.e. solutions involving different numbers of ellipses) are evaluated based on the Akaike Information Criterion (AIC) [2]. Specifically, from all possible models, the model with the smallest AIC is reported as the optimal solution. To minimize the AIC criterion, we start with a custom set of initial size $|CC|$ and gradually reduce the number of considered ellipses until the set of all ellipses contains a single ellipse. In each iteration, a pair of adjacent ellipses is selected for merging. The pair that is finally merged is the one that results the lowest AIC. On the basis of DEFA, the improvements we made are as follows:

1) We redefine the area constraint in DEFA as the total area C_E covered by the ellipse is equal to A. Note that, $C_E \leq |E|$, because E counts the area of their intersection twice, while C_E does not.

2) DEFA considers the merging of adjacent ellipses, only. On the contrary, we consider any pair of ellipses as candidates for merging.

Finally, the object's pixels are clustered into groups according to the detected ellipses, while keeping the detected boundaries of the improved Bradley segmentation technique to complete the segmentation of overlapping cells. For convenience, the generated cell contours are denoted as $S = \{l_1, l_2, \ldots\}$, where l_i represents the contour of the ith cell and $i = 1, 2, \cdots$.

Multi-scale Fusion: To cope with cell features at different scales, the previous segmenting cells from their background and identifying overlapping cells steps are performed over three scales for conducting multi-scale cell segmentation. Denote a feature point of the i-th cell contour at the j-th scale as $p_{i_k}^{(j)}$, where $i, k = 1, 2, ...$ and $j = 1, 2, 3$. A multi-scale feature point $\bar{p_{i_k}}$ of the i-th cell contour is produced via performing the signal average calculation as follows:

$$\bar{p_{i_k}} = \left(\sum_{j=1}^{3} p_{i_k}{}^{(j)}\right)/3. \tag{3}$$

As a result, the final cell contour set $\bar{S}$ is obtained by combining all feature points, i.e.,

$$\bar{S} = \left\{\bar{l_i} : \bar{l_i} = \sum \bar{p_{i_k}}, i, k = 1, 2, \ldots\right\} \tag{4}$$

where $\bar{l_i}$ denotes the final i-th cell contour. In this way, each cell is segmented from the input image.

Specifically, cell contours appearing at the high scale will also appear at the low and middle scales, since the Gaussian kernel used in (1) for image smoothing has the nice property that it never introduces new features into the smoothed image [26]. In addition, the resulting cell contours at low scales are not smooth enough due to noise. As the scale increases, the noise influence gradually decreases, and the resulting cell contours at middle and high scales are closer to the true shape of the cell. However, the increase in scale can lead to less accurate

Table 1. Segmentation results on U20S and NIH3T3 datasets. The best performance in each comparison case is highlighted in bold. ↑ indicates that larger is better and ↓ shows that lower is better.

Dataset	Method	JSC ↑	MAD ↓	HD ↓	DiceFN ↓	DiceFP ↓
U20S	LSBR [8]	83.2	5.8	19.8	9.1	11.8
	Three-step [5]	88.4	4.7	13.4	5.2	5.3
	LLBWIP [15]	91.6	3.5	12.7	**3.9**	4.7
	OSTU [20]	83.5	4.5	11.5	16.7	3.0
	UCTransNet [24]	80.7	6.2	20.3	9.4	11.9
	Swin-Unet [7]	80.3	6.6	21.7	10.6	11.2
	RFOVE [12]	89.8	2.8	7.5	5.7	5.2
	Proposed	**92.9**	**2.3**	**6.6**	4.8	**2.6**
NIH3T3	LSBR [8]	64.2	7.2	19.8	20.4	21.2
	Three-step [5]	70.8	5.7	16.4	19.7	15.5
	LLBWIP [15]	75.9	4.1	14.3	12.2	12.7
	OSTU [20]	59.6	6.2	12.9	35.4	24.2
	UCTransNet [24]	73.8	5.1	14.8	14.5	15.6
	Swin-Unet [7]	69.9	6.4	17.2	20.3	15.2
	RFOVE [12]	81.0	3.5	**8.2**	8.1	13.3
	Proposed	**87.8**	**3.4**	**8.2**	**5.5**	**7.4**

positioning of cells. Therefore, the cell contours set yielded at each scale σ_j, i.e., S_j, is taken as the initial set of cell contour candidates. Then, the image features at each scale are fused, and the signal averaging result S_f is used as the final output result, thereby segmenting each cell from the input image.

3 Performance Evaluation

3.1 Experimental Setups

Datasets: Our proposed method is evaluated on two benchmark fluorescence microscopy cell datasets, including the U20S dataset, and the NIH3T3 dataset [9]. The NIH3T3 dataset is more challenging, since it contains cells/nuclei that vary greatly in brightness, and images often contain visible debris [9].

Objective Evaluation Metrics: In objective evaluation, we employed both region-based and contour-based metrics for evaluating the performance of cell segmentation, as in [15]. The region-based metrics include the Jaccard coefficient (JSC), Dice false positive (DiceFP), and Dice false negative (DiceFN). The contour-based metrics include the Hausdorff distance (HD) and mean absolute contour distance (MAD). In addition, the number of false positives (FP) and false negatives (FN) are used for evaluating cell splitting performance.

Table 2. Splitting results on the U20S and NIH3T3 datasets. The best performance in each comparison case is highlighted in bold. ↓ shows that lower is better.

Methods	U20S		NIH3T3	
	FP ↓	FN ↓	FP ↓	FN ↓
Three-step [5]	0.5	3.9	1.7	11.3
LLBWIP [15]	0.3	2.7	0.7	0.8
MSF [18]	1.9	4.6	1.8	1.7
UCTransNet [24]	1.3	3.3	1.6	4.1
Swin-Unet [7]	2.0	3.9	2.7	5.9
RFOVE [12]	1.9	0.3	**0.3**	0.8
Proposed	**0.2**	**0.2**	**0.3**	**0.5**

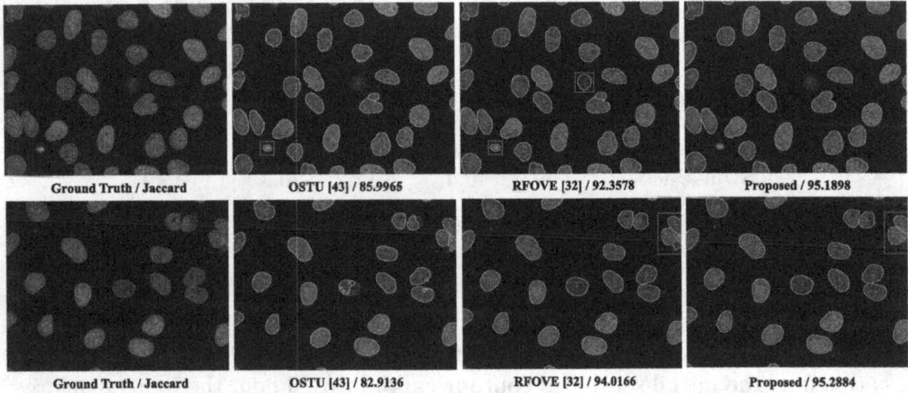

Fig. 4. Example of cell segmentation on the U20S dataset. The boundaries of the detected cells and the ground truth cell centroids are plotted with green curves and red "+", respectively. The first column shows the ground truth. The next few columns show the results of the OSTU, RFOVE and MMCS methods, respectively. (Color figure online)

3.2 Objective Evaluation

Comparison with Non-learning-based Existing Methods: In total five state-of-the-art non-learning-based methods are used for comparison, including the OSTU method [20], Three-step [5], LSBR [8], LLBWIP [15], MSF [18] and RFOVE [12]. Table 1 summarizes the segmentation results obtained on the U20S and NIH3T3 datasets, respectively. On the U20S dataset, our approach achieves the best MAD, HD, DiceFP, and JSC, and also delivers the second-best DiceFN. It is can be seen that the proposed MMCS produces the best performance for all the used evaluation metrics in the more challenging NIH3T3 dataset, due to our proposed MMCS giving high-performance results under variations in background and foreground brightness. Table 2 gives the evaluation of splitting results on the

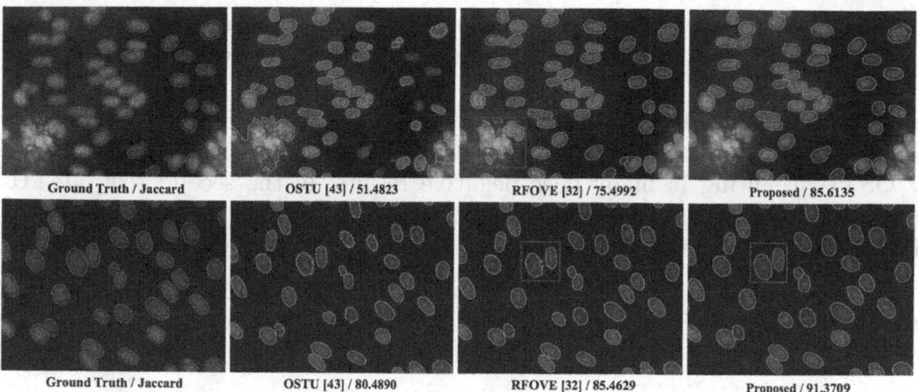

Fig. 5. Example of cell segmentation on the NIH3T3 dataset. The boundaries of the detected cells and the ground truth cell centroids are plotted with green curves and red "+", respectively. The first column shows the ground truth. The next few columns show the results of the OSTU, RFOVE and MMCS methods, respectively. (Color figure online)

U20S and NIH3T3 datasets. As can be seen from Table 2, the proposed MMCS works best on the division of U20S and NIH3T3 cells.

Comparison with Deep-Learning-Based Methods: Furthermore, the proposed MMCS is compared with two deep-learning-based methods, UCTransNet [24] and Swin-Unet [7], to demonstrate the proposed MMCS's superiority. According to [24], we divided the 49 images of NIH3T3 into three sets: 29 for training, 6 for validation, and 14 for testing, and the 48 U20S images into three sets: 28 for training, 6 for validation, and 14 for testing. As can be seen from Table 1 and Table 2, our MMCS is significantly better than the results of the UCTransNet [24] and the Swin-Unet [7].

3.3 Subjective Evaluation

Figure 4 shows a subjective comparison of our proposed and the existing methods by using test images from the U20S dataset. In the first row, the test image contains locally brighter background fragments, which RFOVE and OSTU misidentify as cells and yields false positives (such as the part circled by the red frame), while our multi-scale method can accurately reject them. In the second row, due to the influence of noise, cell edges generated by RFOVE segmentation are not smooth enough (such as the part circled by the red frame); most of the cell edges generated by OSTU segmentation are not smooth enough. However, our method can effectively reduce the influence of noise and produce smoother and more accurate cell edges.

Figure 5 shows a subjective comparison of our proposed and the existing methods by using test images from the NIH3T3 dataset, whose result analysis is similar to Fig. 4. It is worth reminding that the NIH3T3 dataset is more challenging, containing cells and background segments with widely varying brightness, which makes it difficult to segment cells using a single global threshold. Therefore, the segmentation performance of OSTU in Fig. 5 is relatively poor. For example, in the first row, a large number of cells are not accurately segmented by OSTU, resulting in many false negative results; in the second row, OSTU segmented out lots of cells with rough contours. In comparison, our proposed MMCS delivers the best subjective results with smooth and accurate segmented cell contours.

4 Conclusion

The existing cell segmentation methods have drawbacks in terms of inaccurate location of segmentation boundary, misidentification and inaccurate segmentation of overlapping cells. To address these challenging issues simultaneously, a novel *multi-scale method for cell segmentation in fluorescence microscope images* (MMCS) has been proposed. At each given scale, cells are first segmented from the background using an improved Bradley technique with two shape-based constraints and two intensity-based constraints. Then, a region-based fitting of overlapping ellipses technique is developed, which is applied to each connected region of the previous segmentation step to identify overlapping cells, keep the detected contours of the improved Bradley technique, and get the contour representation for each cell. To achieve multi-scale segmentation, the above-mentioned steps are conducted over three scales, and then the resulting multi-scale results are averaged to generate a final representation of the contour of each cell. Extensive experimental results obtained on three benchmark datasets have clearly shown that our MMCS can deliver superior performance over the state-of-the-art methods.

References

1. Ahmine, Y., Caron, G., Chouireb, F., Mouaddib, E.M.: Continuous scale-space direct image alignment for visual odometry from RGB-D images. IEEE Robot. Autom. Lett. **6**(2), 2264–2271 (2021)
2. Akaike, H.: A new look at the statistical model identification. IEEE Trans. Autom. Control **19**(6), 716–723 (1974)
3. Al-Kofahi, Y., Lassoued, W., Lee, W., Roysam, B.: Improved automatic detection and segmentation of cell nuclei in histopathology images. IEEE Trans. Biomed. Eng. **57**(4), 841–852 (2009)
4. Araújo, F.H.D., Silva, R.R.V., Medeiros, F.N.S., Neto, J.F.R., Oliveira, H.C.P.: Active contours for overlapping cervical cell segmentation. Biomed. Eng. Technol. **35**(1), 70–92 (2021)
5. Bergeest, J.P., Rohr, K.: Efficient globally optimal segmentation of cells in fluorescence microscopy images using level sets and convex energy functionals. Med. Image Anal. **16**(7), 1436–1444 (2012)

6. Bradley, D., Roth, G.: Adaptive thresholding using the integral image. Graph. Tools **12**(2), 13–21 (2007)
7. Cao, H., et al.: Swin-Unet: Unet-like pure transformer for medical image segmentation. In: Karlinsky, L., Michaeli, T., Nishino, K. (eds.) Computer Vision – ECCV 2022 Workshops. ECCV 2022. LNCS, vol. 13803, pp. 205–218. Springer, Cham (2023). https://doi.org/10.1007/978-3-031-25066-8_9
8. Chen, Y.T.: A level set method based on the Bayesian risk for medical image segmentation. Pattern Recogn. **43**(11), 3699–3711 (2010)
9. Coelho, L.P., Shariff, A., Murphy, R.F.: Nuclear segmentation in microscope cell images: a hand-segmented dataset and comparison of algorithms. In: International Symposium on Biomedical Imaging: From Nano to Macro (ISBI), pp. 518–521 (2009)
10. Coleman, G.B., Andrews, H.C.: Image segmentation by clustering. Proc. IEEE **67**(5), 773–785 (1979)
11. Panagiotakis, C., Argyros, A.: Parameter-free modelling of 2D shapes with ellipses. Pattern Recogn. **53**, 259–275 (2016)
12. Panagiotakis, C., Argyros, A.: Region-based fitting of overlapping ellipses and its application to cells segmentation. Image Vis. Comput. **93**, 103810 (2020)
13. Das, P.K., Meher, S., Panda, R., Abraham, A.: An efficient blood-cell segmentation for the detection of hematological disorders. IEEE Trans. Cybern. **52**(10), 10615–10626 (2022)
14. Drongelen, W.V.: Signal Processing for Neuroscientists. Academic Press, Cambridge (2018)
15. Gharipour, A., Liew, A.W.-C.: Segmentation of cell nuclei in fluorescence microscopy images: an integrated framework using level set segmentation and touching-cell splitting. Pattern Recogn. **58**, 1–11 (2016)
16. Hajdowska, K., Student, S., Borys, D.: Graph based method for cell segmentation and detection in live-cell fluorescence microscope imaging. Biomed. Signal Process. Control **71**, 103071 (2022)
17. Hallman, S., Fowlkes, C.C.: Oriented edge forests for boundary detection. In: Computer Vision and Pattern Recognition (CVPR), pp. 1732–1740 (2015)
18. Jia, D., Zhang, C., Wu, N., Guo, Z., Ge, H.: Multi-layer segmentation framework for cell nuclei using improved GVF Snake model, watershed, and ellipse fitting. Biomed. Signal Process. Control **67**, 102516 (2021)
19. Kostrykin, L., Schnörr, C., Rohr, K.: Segmentation of cell nuclei using intensity-based model fitting and sequential convex programming. In: International Symposium on Biomedical Imaging (ISBI), pp. 654–657 (2018)
20. Liao, M., Zhao, Y.-Q., Li, X.-H., Dai, P.-S., Xu, X.-W., et al.: Automatic segmentation for cell images based on bottleneck detection and ellipse fitting. Neurocomputing **173**, 615–622 (2016)
21. Ram, S., Rodriguez, J.J.: Size-invariant detection of cell nuclei in microscopy images. IEEE Trans. Med. Imaging **35**(7), 1753–1764 (2016)
22. Riccio, D., Brancati, N., Frucci, M., Gragnaniello, D.: A new unsupervised approach for segmenting and counting cells in high-throughput microscopy image sets. Biomed. Health Inform. **23**(1), 437–448 (2019)
23. Sporring, J., Nielsen, M., Florack, L., Johansen, P.: Gaussian Scale-space Theory. Springer, Cham (2013). https://doi.org/10.1007/978-94-015-8802-7
24. Wang, H., Cao, P., Wang, J., Zaiane, O.R.: UCTransNet: rethinking the skip connections in U-Net from a channel-wise perspective with transformer. In: Association for the Advancement of Artificial Intelligence (AAAI), vol. 36, pp. 2441–2449 (2022)

25. Wang, Z., Wang, Z.: Robust cell segmentation based on gradient detection, Gabor filtering and morphological erosion. Biomed. Signal Process. Control **65**, 102390 (2021)
26. Zhong, B., Ma, K.K.: On the convergence of planar curves under smoothing. IEEE Trans. Image Process. **19**(8), 2171–2189 (2010)

Adaptive Interaction-Based Multi-view 3D Object Reconstruction

Jun Miao[1(✉)], Yilin Zheng[1], Jie Yan[1], Lei Li[2], and Jun Chu[2]

[1] The School of Aeronautical Manufacturing Engineering, Nanchang Hangkong University, Nanchang, China
miaojun@nchu.edu.cn

[2] The Department of Key Laboratory of Jiangxi Province for Image Processing and Pattern Recognition, Nanchang Hangkong University, Nanchang, China

Abstract. This paper introduces an end-to-end deep learning framework for multi-view 3D object reconstruction. The algorithm constructs an adaptive multi-view combination module in the 2D encoding through calculating the feature correlation of pixel points of each view, allowing each view contains the feature information of other views. It addresses the issue of inconsistent object reconstruction resulting from input images being presented in different orders. Additionally, a voxel refinement loss is employed to produce a comprehensive 3D voxel and establishes an adaptive voxel discrimination module for 3D voxel calibration. This reduces the production of superfluous voxels in the 3D voxel and enhances the completeness of the reconstruction. Extensive validation using the ShapeNet synthetic dataset and the Pix3D real-world dataset demonstrates that the proposed algorithm outperforms existing methods.

Keywords: Deep Learning · Multi-view Combination · 3D Reconstruction · Adaptive Voxel Discrimination · Refinement Loss

1 Introduction

3D reconstruction based on multi-view images is widely studied in topics related to robot navigation, autonomous driving, and computer animation due to its advantages of complete observation structure and avoiding object polysemy. However, different orders of the input images can often affect the consistency of the reconstructed model. In traditional algorithms, such as Structure from Motion [1] and Multi-view Stereo Vision [2], the problem is solved by associatively matching features of the same name from different views based on multi-view geometry theory, however, traditional algorithms use manually produced feature extractors to extract features, which are affected by environmental changes and are not robust.

Recently, a number of deep learning approaches have been proposed to reconstruct 3D model from multiple images and have shown encouraging results. However, most of these algorithms are based on single images, and are trained or predicted individually; the target features lack correlation between multiple views. Some current studies have

L. Iliadis et al. (Eds.): ICANN 2023, LNCS 14255, pp. 51–64, 2023.
https://doi.org/10.1007/978-3-031-44210-0_5

adopted two association strategies: the first reconstructs a single viewpoint first, then fuses and associates the 3D models reconstructed from each viewpoint; the second one is to use a Transformer to divide the image into N patches and then associate them. For example, the Pix2Vox [15] method processes multiple views, using the proposed scoring mechanism to score the objects reconstructed from each view, retaining the highly scored parts and finally fusing the highly scored parts from each view. This method cannot rationalize the association between each pixel point of the same object between different views; each view does not combine the connection between the rest of the views, which can lead to the missing and empty structure of the object reconstruction; LegoFormer [23] uses Transformer to divide the image into multiple patches and associate each patch between multiple views using multi-headed attention. This association can directly lead to a lack of information between views. 3D-R2N2 [10] and LSM [11] use the temporal order of long-short-term-memory (LSTM) to address the reconstruction of complete and consistent objects, but due to the long-term dependency defect of LSTM, the input views must satisfy certain requirements. The order and angle of the views should not be different, otherwise it will directly lead to the failure of the reconstruction. Such methods also have certain requirements on the number of views, and a more complete object can only be reconstructed if the number of views is large. In addition, to make the prediction model approximate the real model, most of the current methods make use of binary cross-entropy loss [5] and dice loss [6], however, these losses can lead to a loss of perception of the object's voxel, resulting in a lack of detailed representation of the reconstructed object.

This paper presents an adaptive, interactive deep learning model for 3D reconstruction of multi-view objects. The model uses similarity judgments on pixel points of different views through the adaptive multi-view combination module to enable the association of homonymous features of different views, which reduces the influence of the disorder of the input images on the consistency of the reconstruction structure. In addition, voxel refinement loss, adaptive discrimination loss, and binary cross-entropy loss are used to train the model and improve the accuracy of the reconstruction. The main contributions of the present research include:

(1) An adaptive multi-view combination module is proposed, which adaptively associates multiple view features and selectively fuses related perspectives, addressing the inherent correlation between multi-view features and the influence of input view order on object reconstruction. Meanwhile, an attention enhancement module for viewpoint information is constructed to achieve the weighted fusion of global structural features and local details;
(2) A voxel refinement loss is proposed to mitigate the problem of missing detail structure during object reconstruction by assigning weights to the loss of voxels in the detailed parts of the object, addressing the balanced distribution of voxels in each object part; An adaptive voxel discrimination module is established to calibrate the generated rough voxel model and improve the integrity of the reconstruction by eliminating redundant voxels in the 3D object using adaptive discrimination loss.

2 Related Work

Traditional 3D reconstruction algorithms can be mainly divided into photometric and geometric methods. Some common single-view algorithms include contours [7], shadows [8], and other representations to recover 3D shapes, etc.; multi-view algorithms include Structure from Motion [1, 2], Multi-view Stereo Vision [3, 4], and simultaneous localization and map building, among others. These methods usually use inter-image feature matching to solve such problems, however, the accuracy of reconstruction is low when the view angle changes too much or the camera pose is violated. Therefore, traditional methods are less robust and cannot link implicit information between multiple views and have limitations in reconstructing the details and structural integrity of individual objects.

In recent years, with the rapid development of deep learning, single-view object-based reconstruction [9] has gained the attention of researchers. However, single-view methods reflect information from only one viewpoint, and the results of reconstructed objects suffer from polysemy, a typical pathological problem. Multi-view 3D object reconstruction is learning 3D shapes from multiple images. 3D-R2N2 [10] and LSM [11] use Recurrent Neural Networks for multi-view inference, which suffer from the drawbacks of being time-consuming and overly dependent on input sequences. The designers of 3DensiNet [12], Huang [13], Paschalidou [14], and others use max-pooling and tie-pooling methods to aggregate multiple image features and generate a 3D model of the object, which ignore other features of useful value. To address the reconstruction errors caused by the multi-view alignment problem, Pix2Vox [15] uses a context-aware fusion module to select high-quality reconstructions from the views. A dedicated fusion module [15, 16] is also used instead of the Recurrent Neural Network model solution, which improves performance by considering all views simultaneously and associating earlier views. However, as the views are mutually distinct, the correlation between multiple views cannot be addressed and may lead to undesirable reconstruction results. EVoIT [17] uses Transformer [18] to establish the relationship between views and argues that such an approach is more conducive to multi-view 3D fusion. However, this approach does not explicitly utilize the 3D feature structure, while not exploiting pixel-level detail, Bautista [19] used the differences between pixels to reconstruct objects. Although the aforementioned methods have improved the reconstruction results, they do not fully exploit the correlation between multiple views and do not find the corresponding features between different views. Based on these problems, an adaptive interaction algorithm for 3D reconstruction of multi-view objects is proposed.

3 Network Structure

In the 2D encoding network, after the image is input, a pre-trained VGG16 [21] model on ImageNet [20] is adopted to extract 2D underlying features, which are passed through different modules to generate a 2D feature map for multi-view association; then, the 3D voxel decoding network is employed to transform the 2D features into rough 3D voxel features of the corresponding target; finally, in the 3D voxel calibration network, the fused 3D voxels are further corrected to remove redundant voxels and refine the target object to generate the final 3D object. The overall structure of the network is illustrated in Fig. 1.

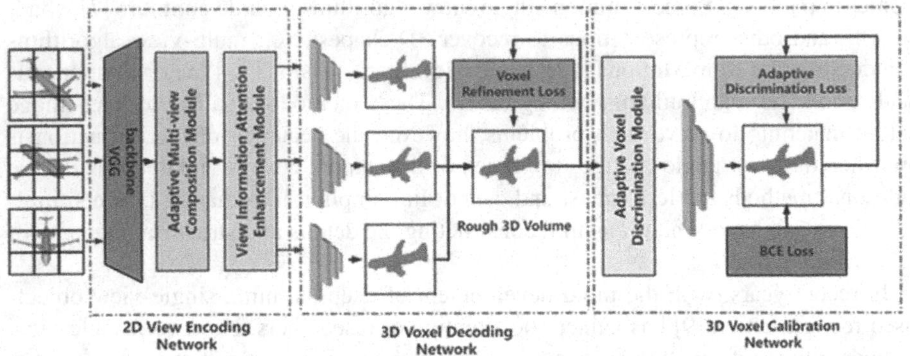

Fig. 1. Overall framework of the network

3.1 The 2D View Encoding Network

Adaptive Multi-view Combination Module (AMCM). The main structure of the adaptive multi-view combination module is shown in Fig. 2, whose input is the view button feature extracted by the feature encoder VGG16. Assuming the main view is View 1, the rest of the views are reference views. After inputting the underlying feature map of the main view 1, it is first convolved with a 1 × 1 convolution transform, followed by a normalization layer, a 3 × 3 convolution operation, then a ReLU layer. The features obtained from the 1 × 1 convolution block are then added to the features obtained from the 3 × 3 convolution block to obtain the fused feature map F_1. The two branches of the reference view 2 are operated in parallel. In the first branch, the underlying feature map F_2 is first globally pooled on average, followed by 1 × 1 convolution to obtain a feature map with global information $F_2\prime$. At this point the features $F_2\prime$ have been added to each pixel with the global information of the current channel. In the second branch, the features are adaptively pooled to remove redundant information and highlight the main features in the view, followed by 1 × 1 convolution to adjust their number of channels and obtain the corresponding features F_2''. The feature map is then $F_2\prime$ and the feature map F_2'' which is then subject to a reshaping operation, followed by multiplication, so that the pixels at each local position have a global association, and then a softmax normalization operation is used to obtain a weighting factor on the reference viewpoint W_k. Finally, the weight coefficients W_k with the feature map F_I and multiply the result by the feature map F_I to obtain the fused multi-view features. By analogy, the same steps are performed for the second viewpoint; the formula can be expressed as follows:

$$F_I = A\sum\nolimits_{\forall i} f(x_i, x_j)h(x_j) \tag{1}$$

where A is the normalization function and $f(x_i, x_j)$ is the function that calculates the correlation between pixels, and x_i represents the pixel of the primary view, x_j denotes the pixel of the reference view, and $h(x_j)$ refers to the feature computed for the reference view, and F_I is the feature after updating at position I.

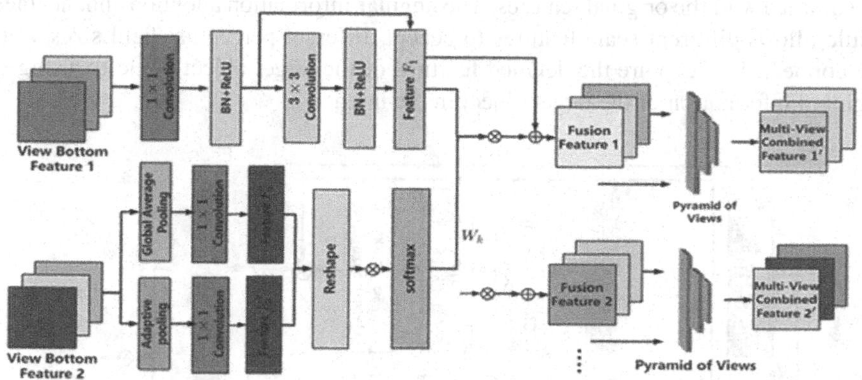

Fig. 2. Adaptive multi-view combination module.

To address the matching error where the two view angles are completely different, resulting in no correlation between the pixel points across the view, a view pyramid is adopted to solve the problem in Fig. 3. The main structure of the view pyramid is composed of 6 groups of different convolution blocks. When multiple view Angle features pass through each convolution block, there will be a normalization layer and ReLU non-linear activation layer. After processing multiple view angle features, there will be flat interaction processing. To determine the correlation between its pixels autonomously. If the correlation is small, the network adaptively retains the features of the main view and reduces the correlation to the reference view (other views).

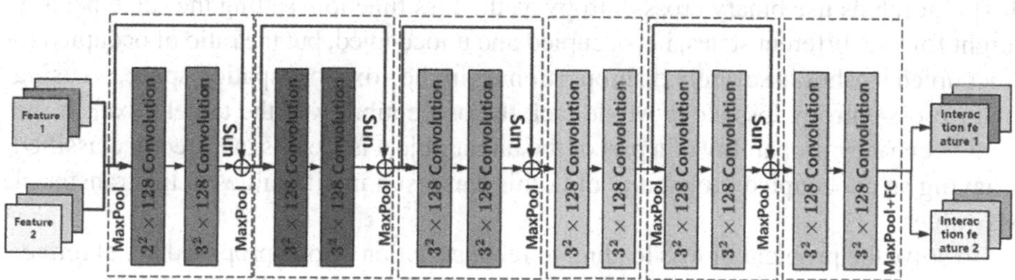

Fig. 3. View pyramid module.

View Information Attention Enhancement Module (VIAEM). The VIAEM is used to establish the link between local features of objects in the image and the overall features of the object as shown in Fig. 4. The model starts by constructing two different convolutions with 1×1 and 3×3 kernels, and we sum and fuse the multi-scale features obtained from these two convolutions, then use global average pooling to embed the global information and pass it through a fully connected layer to form a feature. Next, a softmax normalization operation is performed in each channel direction and the feature vectors obtained by multiplying the respective weights with the original features are then summed with the original features. The angular information attention enhancement module allows different scale features to accept different perceptual field sizes when fully connected, to capture the detailed features of the target object while focusing on the global information of the target object in the image.

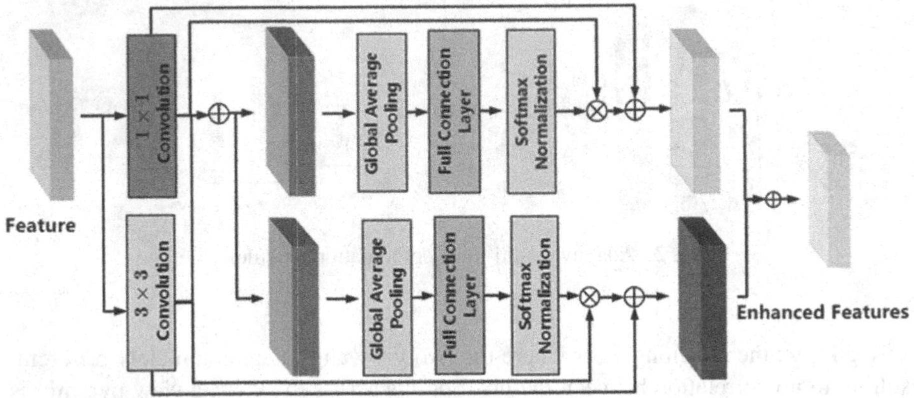

Fig. 4. View information attention enhancement module

3.2 The 3D Voxel Decoding Network

In the 3D voxel decoding process, the decoder decodes the fused features and then applies a penalty constraint to the fused multi-view results by means of a loss function. Most algorithms use binary cross-entropy as the loss function, setting the same penalty weight for two different states, i.e. occupied and unoccupied, but the ratio of occupied to unoccupied meshes is severely disproportionate in the voxel occupation space, so using binary cross-entropy loss alone would lack the perceptibility of the target voxel. If the voxel occupancy probability of a part of the target object is 1 but is incorrectly classified as having an unoccupied probability of 0, this can result in difficulties in the transfer of loss values.

To solve the problem of loss leading to reconstruction errors, proposed voxel refinement loss facilitates the generation of voxels, and assigning a weight to the loss of voxels in the detail part of the object to mitigate the problem of missing detail structure in the object reconstruction process, ensuring the integrity of the object. Its related formula can be expressed as follows:

$$L_{VR} = \begin{cases} -a(1 - p_{(i,j,k)})^b log p_{(i,j,k)} & X = 1 \\ -(1 - a)(p_{(i,j,k)})^b log(1 - p_{(i,j,k)}) & X = 0 \end{cases} \tag{2}$$

where $P_{(i,j,k)}$ denotes the probability of occupancy at (i,j,k) the predicted occupancy probability of the voxel at Eq. (2), by varying a to adjust the balance of voxel distribution for each object component. When $b > 0$, it makes the voxel generation in the local detail part of the object more of a concern. When $a = 1, b = 0$ when, the voxel refinement loss is the traditional binary cross-entropy loss. Experiments prove that by adjusting the parameters a and b, the weight of the voxel occupation probability of the object detail parts can be enhanced, the better to recover the realistic 3D model. Here, a takes the value of 0.6 and b takes the value of 1 in the algorithm.

3.3 The 3D Voxel Calibration Network

The 3D voxel decoding network can only generate rough 3D bodies with imperfect wholeness and details. To address this problem, an adaptive voxel discrimination module (AVDM) to eliminate the redundant voxels in the 3D model Fig. 5. The AVDM consists of four sets of 3D convolution blocks and two convolution layers, all with a convolution kernel size of 4^3 Each convolutional layer is followed by a batch normalization layer and a LeakyReLU activation layer, after which a cascaded sigmoid activation layer maps the 3D voxel model to a voxel occupancy probability value on the interval (0, 1), while this probability value is compared with ground-truth data for voxel adaptive discriminant loss (L_{AD}) for each component of the object to achieve the elimination of redundant voxels from the 3D model. Finally, the generated voxels are adaptively discriminated from the real voxels, and if the true value differs significantly from the generated 3D voxels, the parameters of the reconstruction network continue to be adjusted until the result reaches a state of equilibrium with the ground-truth value, so that a high-quality reconstructed object is generated. The voxel adaptive discriminant loss (L_{AD}) can be expressed as:

$$L_{AD} = log(A(gt_i)) + log(A(V)) \tag{3}$$

where gt_i is the true value of the voxel, and V denotes the network-generated voxel result.

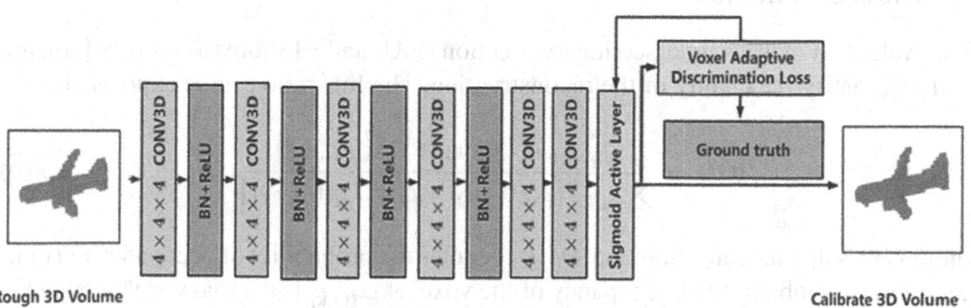

Fig. 5. Adaptive voxel discrimination module.

4 Experimental Results and Analysis

4.1 Loss Functions and Datasets

The loss function used in the present research has three main components: L_{VR}, L_{AD}, and binary cross entropy (BCE) L_{BCE} In the process of 3D object reconstruction, the binary cross entropy loss imposes a penalty constraint between the fused voxels and the true value, to generate the fused voxels more accurately and improve the integrity of the object reconstruction. The smaller the cross-entropy loss value, the closer the reconstruction result is to the true value. The loss function can be expressed as follows:

$$L_{BCE}(p, gt) = \left(1/r_v^3\right)\sum_{i=1}^{r_v^3}\left[gt_i\, log\,(p_i) + (1 - gt_i)\, log\,(1 - p_i)\right] \tag{4}$$

where r_v^3 denotes the number of voxels in the true value, and gt_i denotes the true value, and p_i denotes the final predicted voxel occupancy probability.

$$L = aL_{VR} + bL_{AD} + cL_{BCE} \tag{5}$$

where L_{VR} denotes voxel refinement loss, and L_{AD} denotes adaptive discriminant loss, and L_{BCE} denotes the binary cross-entropy loss.

The ShapeNet dataset: a subset of the ShapeNet dataset (ShapeNetCore) is used; this contains 55 common object classes with 13 categories such as aircraft, chairs and cars, including 43,783 3D models. Each 3D model is rendered with 12 images of different angles with a resolution of 128^2 while generating images with a resolution 32^3 of the real voxel occupancy. Approximately three-quarters of the images are used as the training set and one-quarter of the images are used as the test set. The Pix3D dataset: the real scene Pix3D dataset, with nine categories including 395 3D models such as aircraft, chairs, and tables is used.

4.2 Evaluation Indicators

Two evaluation metrics, Intersection over Union (IoU) and F1 score (F-Score@1%), are used to quantify the quality of the reconstruction. The IoU ratio can be expressed as:

$$IOU = \frac{\sum_{i,j,k} I\left(P_{(i,j,k)} > t\right) I\left(gt_{(i,j,k)}\right)}{\sum_{i,j,k} I\left[I\left(P_{(i,j,k)} > t\right) + I\left(gt_{(i,j,k)}\right)\right]} \tag{6}$$

where $I(x)$ is the indicator function, $P_{(i,j,k)}$ denotes the probability of occupancy at (i,j,k) the predicted probability of occupancy of the voxel at $gt_{(i,j,k)}$ is the true voxel occupancy probability at (i,j,k). t denotes the voxelization threshold, which is 0.3. The higher the value of IoU, the better the reconstruction effect.

The F1 score (F-Score@1%) is used as another indicator for the 3D reconstruction with the formula:

$$F\text{-}Score(d) = \frac{2P(d)R(d)}{P(d)+R(d)} \tag{7}$$

where P(d) and R(d) denote the precision and recall respectively, at the distance thresholds d P(d) and P(d) are respectively given by:

$$P(d) = \frac{1}{n_R}\sum\nolimits_{r\in R}\left[\min_{g\in G}\|g - r\| < d\right] \quad (8)$$

$$R(d) = \frac{1}{n_G}\sum\nolimits_{g\in G}\left[\min_{r\in R}\|g - r\| < d\right] \quad (9)$$

where R and G respectively represent the predicted truth voxel and the truth voxel; n_R and n_G are R and G in terms of the voxel points. The model is applied to the cubic algorithm [22] to generate voxels, and then 8192 voxel points are sampled from its surface to calculate the F-Score between the predicted voxel values and the true voxels, and the larger the value of F-Score@1%, the better the reconstruction effect.

4.3 Experimental Details

We use 224 × 224 RGB images as input, with a training batch of 64 and a final output of 32 × 32 × 32 as the voxel model. The network is built with PyTorch and trained end-to-end using the Adam optimizer, with $\beta_1$andβ_2 being 0.9 and 0.999 respectively, with a learning rate set to 0.0001 and a weight decay factor of 0.0005. Some 150 batches are used to train the multi-view network until convergence.

4.4 Analysis of Ablation Experiments

Experiments on the Ablation of Different Network Modules. To verify the effectiveness of the three network models of the proposed algorithm, ablation experiments are performed for the multi-view case. The values of the IOU ratio and the F1 score (F-Score@1%) are listed in Table 1 for the ShapeNet dataset.

Table 1. Quantitative comparison of the different modules under the ShapeNet dataset

Net	IOU	F-Score@1%
Baseline	0.696	0.430
Baseline + AMCM	0.721	0.441
Baseline + AMCM + VIAEM	0.725	0.445
Baseline + AVDM	0.726	0.449
Baseline + AMCM + VIAEM + AVDM	0.744	0.466

From Table 1, after constructing the AMCM in the base network IOU is improved by 0.25, F-Score@1% is shown to be increased by 0.11; after adding the VIAEM to strengthen the features among the target objects, IOU is improved by 0.29, F-Score@1% is increased by 0.15; after adding the AVDM in the base network alone module after which the IOU is improved by 0.30, F-Score@1% is increased by 0.19; cascading all the modules in the network. The IOU is improved by 0.48, F-Score@1% is increased by 0.36, thus it can be proved that the chosen algorithm improves object reconstruction.

Ablation Experiments with Different Loss Functions. To investigate the applicability of the voxel refinement loss proposed in this paper, a comparison test is performed in the underlying network, using BCE loss (L_{BCE}), or dice loss for comparison, while demonstrating in the network voxel refinement loss (L_{VR}), adaptive discriminant loss (L_{AD}) are deemed effective. As seen from Table 2, in the underlying network with L_{Dice} replacing L_{BCE}, the IOU value is improved by 0.04, F-Score@1% increased by 0.02, and the reconstruction effect is not significant, which can prove the correctness of the loss selection of the algorithm in this paper. The further to improve the reconstruction results, voxel refinement loss (L_{VR}) and adaptive discriminant loss (L_{AD}) are added, and after adding L_{VR} the IOU value is shown to be improved by 0.16 thereafter, the F-Score@1% is increased by 0.16; upon addition of L_{BCE} to the base L_{AD} loss, the IOU value is improved by 0.19, and the F-Score@1% is increased by 0.15; after addition of L_{BCE} to the base in L_{VR}, the L_{AD}, the IOU value is increased by 0.25, and the F-Score@1% is increased by 0.23.

Table 2. Comparison of different loss function ablation experiments

Net	IOU	F-Score@1%
Baseline + L_{BCE}	0.696	0.430
Baseline + L_{Dice}	0.700	0.432
Baseline + L_{BCE}+L_{VR}	0.712	0.446
Baseline + L_{BCE}+L_{AD}	0.715	0.445
Baseline + L_{BCE}+L_{VR}+L_{AD}	0.721	0.453

4.5 Comparative Experiments with Different Methods

Table 3 shows the quantitative comparison between the proposed algorithm and existing methods in cases involving different views. Compared with the state-of-the-art methods, there are different degrees of improvement in IOU, F-Score@1%, and at the eighth view, IOU is improved by 0.25 relative to the LegoFormer algorithm, F-Score@1% is increased by 0.05. It can also be seen that, as the number of views is increased, methods such as 3D-R2N2 and Pix2Vox fail to combine more view features, which leads to slightly poorer reconstruction results than the method described herein, thanks to the adaptive multi-view combination module used. Previous methods also need to obtain more relevant features when combining multiple view features with little difference in view angles, in contrast, the module described here does not discard features of any view and will adaptively retain useful features, solving the problem of inconsistent object reconstruction due to different orders of input images.

Table 3. Quantitative comparison of IOU, F-Score@1% values under different views

Net	1 view	2 views	3 views	4 views	5 views	6 views	8 views
Evaluation indicators (IOU)							
3D-R2N2 [10]	0.560	0.603	0.617	0.625	0.634	-	0.635
Pix2Vox [15]	0.670	0.695	0.704	0.708	0.711	-	0.715
LegoFormer [23]	0.617	0.674	0.689	0.695	0.699	-	0.704
Ours	0.671	0.699	0.701	0.710	0.728	0.728	0.729
Evaluation indicators (F-Score@1%)							
3D-R2N2	0.351	0.368	0.372	0.378	0.382	-	0.383
Pix2Vox	0.436	0.452	0.455	0.457	0.458	-	0.459
LegoFormer	0.364	0.422	0.438	0.445	0.449	-	0.455
Ours	0.437	0.454	0.454	0.456	0.460	0.461	0.460

As shown in Fig. 6, the visualization diagram of the proposed algorithm on the dataset ShapeNet for three perspectives, it can be seen that the 3D-R2N2 method suffers structural incompleteness in the reconstruction of the aircraft, electric light, and chair, the Pix2Vox method produces a hole in the backrest of the chair (not present in the actual object), and the LegoFormer method suffers from a lack of detail in the reconstruction part of each object. The proposed algorithm has a better overall, and more detailed, grasp of the reconstruction of the legs of the chair and the wings of the aircraft appear better (both overall and in detail).

Fig. 6. Visualization of reconstruction results from three views on the ShapeNet dataset. a indicates the input views from different views; b shows the 3D-R2N2 visualization; c represents the Pix2Vox visualization; d shows the LegoFormer visualization; e illustrates the result arising from use of the proposed method; f shows ground truth.

Figure 7 displays the visualization of a single-view on the ShapeNet dataset, where the table legs are more completely reconstructed compared to Pix2Vox and LegoFormer methods; in the chair, the backrest area is more realistic compared to that realized using the LegoFormer algorithm, and in the case of reconstruction of a lampshade, the structure reconstructed using the proposed method, evincing the superiority of our algorithm.

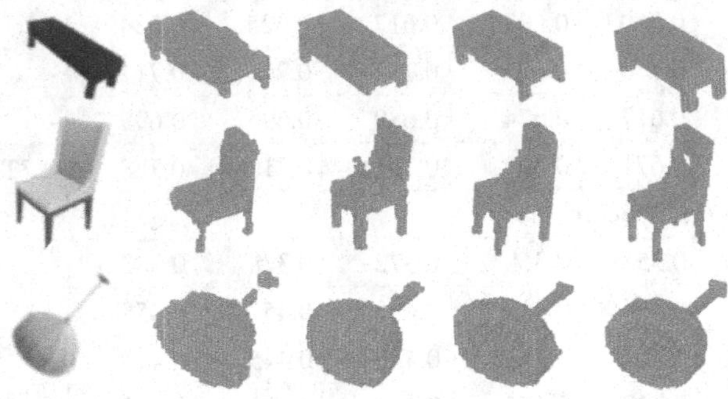

Fig. 7. Visualization of the results of single-view reconstruction on the ShapeNet dataset. a is a single input view; b is a Pix2Vox visualization; c represents a LegoFormer visualization; d present work; f is ground truth.

To verify the generalization of our algorithm, multi-view experiments on the real-world dataset Pix3D are conducted. Figure 8 shows the visualization results for three views of some objects. Our algorithm outperforms methods such as Pix2Vox and LegoFormer in the case of multiple views in terms of details such as chair legs, table legs, etc. The proposed algorithm can be used to reconstruct the complete object while ensuring that it retains accurate local details.

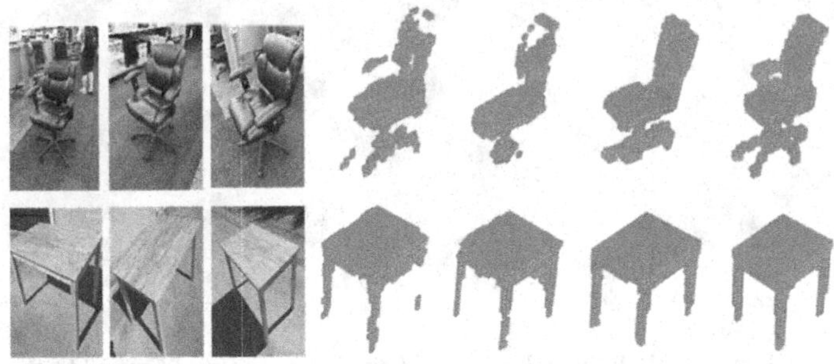

Fig. 8. Visualization of reconstruction results from three views on the Pix3D dataset; a shows the input view; b shows the Pix2Vox visualization; c shows the LegoFormer visualization; d present work; f ground truth.

5 Conclusion

An adaptive interactive 3D object reconstruction algorithm is proposed to address the inability of existing deep learning methods when linking feature correlations of multiple views and the inability to resolve the effect of multiple view input order on the inconsistent reconstruction results. The adaptive multi-view combination module is used to address the intrinsic correlation between multi-view features while eliminating the impact of input view order on object reconstruction; the proposed voxel refinement loss to facilitate voxel generation and generate complete 3D objects; and finally, the adaptive voxel discrimination module is constructed, which can eliminate redundant voxels in 3D objects and further improve the integrity of reconstruction.

References

1. Özyeşil, O., Voroninski, V., Basri, R., et al.: A survey of structure from motion. Acta Numer. **26**, 305–364 (2017)
2. Goesele, M., Snavely, N., Curless, B., et al.: Multi-view stereo for community photo collections. In: Proceedings of the IEEE International Conference on Computer Vision. Los Alamitos. IEEE Computer Society Press, pp. 1–8 (2007)
3. Hirschmuller, H.: Stereo processing by semiglobal matching and mutual information. IEEE Trans. Pattern Anal. Mach. Intell. **30**(2), 328–341 (2007)
4. Fuentes-Pacheco, J., Ruiz-Ascencio, J., Rendón-Mancha, J.M.: Visual simultaneous localization and mapping: a survey. Artif. Intell. Rev. **43**(1), 55–81 (2015). https://doi.org/10.1007/s10462-012-9365-8
5. Ma, Y.D., Liu, Q., Qian, Z.B.: Automated image segmentation using improved PCNN model based on cross-entropy. In: Proceedings of the International Symposium on Intelligent Multimedia, Video and Speech Processing. IEEE Computer Society Press, pp. 743–746 (2004)
6. Milletari, F., Navab, N., Ahmadi, S.A.: V-Net: fully convolutional neural networks for volumetric medical image segmentation. In: Proceedings of the 4th International Conference on 3D Vision. Los Alamitos: IEEE Computer Society Press, pp. 565–571 (2016)
7. Dibra, E., Jain, H., Oztireli, C., et al.: Human shape from silhouettes using generative HKS descriptors and cross-modal neural networks. In: Proceedings of the IEEE Conference on Computer vision and Pattern Recognition. IEEE Computer Society Press, pp. 4826–4836 (2017)
8. Richter, S.R., Roth, S.: Discriminative shape from shading in uncalibrated illumination. In: Proceedings of the IEEE Conference on Computer Vision and Pattern Recognition. Los Alamitos IEEE Computer Society Press, pp. 1128–1136 (2015)
9. Jia, C., Yu-Qi, Z., et al.: Application of deep learning to 3D object reconstruction from a single image. Acta Automatica Sinica **45**(4), 657–668 (2019). (in Chinese)
10. Choy, C.B., Xu ,D.F., Gwak, J., et al.: 3D-R2N2: a unified approach for single and multi-view 3D object reconstruction. In: Proceedings of the European Conference on Computer Vision. Heidelberg. Springer, pp. 628–644 (2016). https://doi.org/10.1007/978-3-319-46484-8_38
11. Kar, A., Häne, C., Malik, J.: Learning a multi-view stereo machine. Adv. Neural Inf. Proc. Syst. 30 (2017)
12. Wang, M., Wang, L., Fang, Y.: 3densinet: A robust neural network architecture towards 3d volumetric object prediction from 2d image. In: Proceedings of the 25th ACM International Conference on Multimedia. IEEE Computer Society Press, pp. 961–969 (2017)

13. Huang, P.H., Matzen, K., Kopf, J., et al.: Deepmvs: Learning multi-view stereopsis. In: Proceedings of the IEEE Conference on Computer Vision and Pattern Recognition. Los Alamitos: IEEE Computer Society Press, pp. 2821–2830 (2018)
14. Paschalidou, D., Ulusoy, O., Schmitt, C., et al.: Raynet: Learning volumetric 3d reconstruction with ray potentials. In: Proceedings of the IEEE Conference on Computer Vision and Pattern Recognition. Los Alamitos: IEEE Computer Society Press, pp. 3897–3906 (2018)
15. Xie, H.Z., Yao, H.X., Sun, X.S., et al.: Pix2Vox: context-aware 3D reconstruction from single and multi-view images. In: Proceedings of the IEEE/CVF International Conference on Computer Vision. Los Alamitos: IEEE Computer Society Press, pp. 2690–2698 (2019)
16. Xie, H.Z., Yao, H.X., Zhang, S.P., et al.: Pix2Vox++: multi-scale context-aware 3D object reconstruction from single and multiple images. Int. J. Comput. Vision **128**(12), 2919–2935 (2020). https://doi.org/10.1007/s10462-012-9365-8
17. Wang, D., Cui, X., Chen, X., et al.: Multi-view 3D reconstruction with transformers. In: Proceedings of the IEEE/CVF International Conference on Computer Vision. Los Alamitos: IEEE Computer Society Press, pp. 5722–5731 (2021)
18. Tomar, G.S., Duque, T., Täckström, O., et al.: Neural paraphrase identification of questions with noisy pretraining (2017). arXiv preprint arXiv:1704.04565
19. Bautista, M.A., Talbott, W., Zhai, S., et al.: On the generalization of learning-based 3d reconstruction. In: Proceedings of the IEEE/CVF Winter Conference on Applications of Computer Vision. Los Alamitos: IEEE Computer Society Press, pp. 2180–2189 (2021)
20. Deng, J., Dong, W., Socher, R., et al.: Imagenet: A large-scale hierarchical image database. In: Proceedings of the IEEE Conference on Computer Vision and Pattern Recognition. Los Alamitos: IEEE Computer Society Press, pp. 248–255 (2009)
21. Simonyan, K., Zisserman, A.: Very deep convolutional networks for large-scale image recognition. Comput. Sci. (2014). 1409.1556
22. Cubes, M.: A high resolution 3D surface construction algorithm. In: Proceedings of the 14th Annual Conference on Computer Graphics and Interactive Techniques. New York: Association for Computing Machinery, pp. 69–163 (1987)
23. Yagubbayli, F., Tonioni, A., Tombari, F.: LegoFormer: Transformers for Block-by-Block Multi-view 3D Reconstruction (2021)

An Auxiliary Modality Based Text-Image Matching Methodology for Fake News Detection

Ying Guo[1](✉), Bingxin Li[1], Hong Ge[1], and Chong Di[2]

[1] North China University of Technology, Beijing, China
guoying@ncut.edu.cn

[2] Shandong Artificial Intelligence Institute, Qilu University of Technology (Shandong Academy of Sciences), Jinan, China

Abstract. Owing to the national network "clearing up" action, it has become increasingly important to detect false information by the use of deep learning technology. As social networks gradually presents a multimodal property, many scholars have devoted to multimodal fake news detection. However, the current multimodal achievements mainly focus on the fusion modeling between texts and images, while their consistencies are still in their infancy. This paper concentrates on the issue of how to extract effective features from texts and images, how to match modes in a more precise way, and subsequently proposes a novel fake news detection method. Especially, the models of Bert, Vgg, and Optical Character Recognition (OCR) are respectively adopted to reflect the textual features, the visual counterparts, as well as the corresponding embedded contents in the attachment. The overall model framework consists of four components: one fusion module and three matching modules, where the former one joints text and image features, and the latter three computes the corresponding similarities among textual, visual, and auxiliary modalities. Aligning them with different weights, and connecting them with a classifier, whether the news is fake or real can thus emerge. Comparative experiments embody the effectiveness of our model, which can reach 88.1%'s accuracy on the Chinese Weibo dataset and 91.7%'s accuracy on the English Twitter dataset.

Keywords: multimodal fake news detection · feature extraction · feature fusion · feature matching

1 Introduction

With the continuous development and updating of information transmission methods, the dissemination of information has become more convenient and fast, simultaneously leading to the rapid transmission of fake news. Fake news refers to unverified or intentionally fabricated news to mislead people, which has the characteristics of rapid spread and severe social response. In most cases,

L. Iliadis et al. (Eds.): ICANN 2023, LNCS 14255, pp. 65–76, 2023.
https://doi.org/10.1007/978-3-031-44210-0_6

fake news is created to serve a specific objective by disseminating misleading information to fool the individuals involved. This has significant negative social consequences. Fake news is mostly brought on by the widespread usage of self-media, as news on social media is of far lower quality than news from traditional news sources. Everyone is allowed to voice their ideas in these circumstances, but there is no effective externally imposed regulation, which leads to fake news "flying all over the sky." As a result, there is a pressing demand for trustworthy techniques and tools to spot bogus news on social media.

Early fake news detection mainly focused on unimodal text perspective, modeling insulting or fraudulent text, and aggressive or leading text. Afterward, it is towards the single-modal image perspective, modeling image tampering, image forgery, etc [2]. Nowadays, as the rich contexts of social media, the research has inclined to the multimodal perspective, which includes two aspects: text-image fusion and text-image consistency. Text-image fusion starts earlier, which has achieved satisfying effects. Compared with it, text-image consistency is an emergency direction involving two stages: feature extraction and feature matching. In this field, the only pioneering and most representative work is SAFE [15]. The main innovation of SAFE is to convert the original image into text such that the similarity is measured between two texts. However, it usually loses the emotional factors during the direct conversion and there may be a certain content semantic gap, which is an essential component in feature extraction. And as for feature matching, the judgment between the original text and the converted text is insufficient as well. Foremost, the text-image consistency is limited to the main modalities, which neglects the textual parts embedded in images. Intuitively, the text in images can also supply profitable clues in both feature extraction and feature matching.

To solve the above problems, this paper builds a fake news detection model based on text-image matching. The proposed model consists of three parts: feature extraction part, feature matching part, and feature fusion part. Firstly, to excavate the textual clues in the attached images, a pre-trained OCR encoder is employed, to extract the auxiliary modality's features. For feature extraction, the Bert encoder and Vgg encoder are used for textual features and visual features respectively. For the feature matching part, the similarity between textual features and visual features, as well as the similarity between auxiliary features and textual or visual features, are determined individually. For the feature fusion part, textual features and visual features are concatenated as before. Based on it, different weights are assigned to all these components, which are followed by a decision classifier to get the predictive label of news. The contribution of this paper mainly includes three parts:

- This article presents a fake news detection model using text-image matching. It comprises four network branches: one fusion branch and three matching branches, with sufficient interaction between different modes.
- This article fully utilizes the multimodal features of news data, including text features, image features, and auxiliary feature which comes from the embedded content of the image. According to the research, more than 20% of

multimodal fake news is spread in the form of images, and the text embedded in these images usually provides a summary of the whole fake news story. This paper is the first work to use image-embedded content as a significant modality.
- Apply a more accurate method of calculating the similarity among different modalities in the model. This article fully measures the degree of correlation matching between modalities and assigns them the optimal weight. Experiments show that the proposed method can outperform the state-of-the-art baselines on two real-world datasets.

2 Related Work

2.1 Single-modal Text Angle

Early fake news detection based on unimodal text perspective is mainly a machine learning method combined with manual feature extraction. This stage requires complex feature engineering and is designed with the guidance of prior knowledge, lacking comprehensiveness and flexibility. Qazvinian, Vahed [8] uses Bayesian networks as classifiers to identify fake news by studying the thematic features of the text. Ma Jing [7] inputs each sentence of the news into Recurrent Neural Networks (RNN), and the hidden layer information of RNN represented the news information. Feng Yu [13] inputs news articles into Convolutional Neural Networks (CNN) for the first time. This work maps each post of a news event to a vector space and then concatenates each post vector to form a matrix, and CNN is used to extract textual features for detection. Mingxi Cheng [1] uses Variational Autoencoder (VAE) to model news text and achieves good results in the multi-task learning of text vectors.

2.2 Single-modal Image Angle

The early detection of fake news based on the unimodal image perspective mainly uses the traditional statistical method, but this method cannot get the semantic features of vision. Zhiwei Jin [4] analyzes the images between real news and fake news in terms of clarity and other aspects. The development of deep learning provides convenience for image modeling. Many scholars use CNN, Vgg, ResNet, and other models to extract features, but these alternative basic models can only extract shallow information from images, and are failure to identify whether images have been tampered or spliced. Peng Qi [9] proposes the MVNN model to identify fake news by extracting image spatial and frequency domain features to determine image tampering.

2.3 Multi-modal Text-Image Angle

The single-modal perspective detection method has a pioneering impetus, but the modeling is relatively simple and ignores the multimedia aggregation of news texts and images as well as their interaction. In the last few years, some scholars have paid attention to fake news detection methods based on multimodal texts and images. Shivangi Singhal [10] uses Bert and Vgg to extract the features of news, then combines semantic information into a classifier to identify fake news. Yaqing Wang [11] adds an event classifier based on feature splicing to better understand multimodal information. Yang Wu [12] uses co-attention to better fuse the semantic information of texts and images.

The above methods are all text-image fusion. In recent years, related work has begun to be carried out on text-image matching, and the most classic in this direction is SAFE [15]. The SAFE model proposed by Xinyi Zhou is a classic work of detecting fake news through the consistency of texts and images. However, it ignores the image-to-text semantic gap and does not fully exploit multimodal information. The model presented in this paper integrates four network branches and effectively captures the semantic features of texts and images as well as the similarity of various modal data in multimodal news data is aimed at solving these challenges.

3 Methodology

The goal of this work is to determine whether the news is true or fake, given the content of the text and image. The specific definition is as follows, give a piece of news $N = (t, i, e)$ contains text (t), image (i), and a large number of images contain embedded text (e). Our objective is to determine whether News N is fake news ($y = 1$) or real news ($y = 0$) using the correlations $s_1 = (t, i)$ between the text and the image, $s_2 = (t, e)$ between the original text and the image-embedded text, as well as $s_3 = (i, e)$ between the image and the image-embedded text, that is, the relationship between them can be defined as $(s_1, s_2, s_3, t, i, e) \Rightarrow y \in (0, 1)$. This model is called TIMAM, and the structure is shown in Fig. 1.

3.1 Multi-modal Feature Extraction

Textual Feature Extraction Module. For textual feature extraction, Bert, one of the most effective textual feature extractors currently recognized, is used to model news text. Specifically, given the text content T of a post, according to the length L determined during data preprocessing, after Bert embedding, the n-dimensional vectorized representation of each word in the sentence is obtained.

$$T = [T^0, T^1, ..., T^L] \tag{1}$$

For the Chinese dataset, we use the pre-trained Bert_base_Chinese, and for the English dataset, we use the pre-trained Bert_base_uncased to get a feature vector F_T^i of the given sentence as follows:

$$F_T^i = Bert(T^i), T = [T^0, T^1, ..., T^L] \tag{2}$$

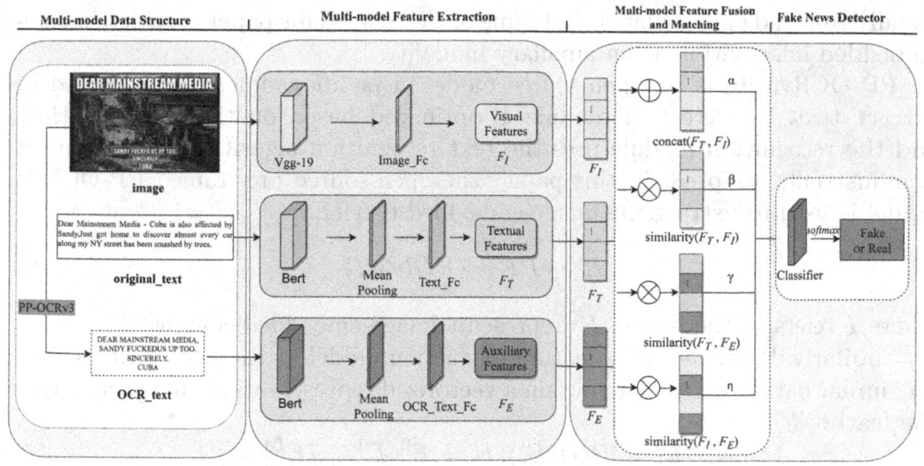

Fig. 1. TIMAM model structure, the overall model framework consists of four components: one fusion module and three matching modules.

The F_T^i is fed into an mean pooling layer to prevent overfitting and finally into a fully connected layer to ensure that the final output of the textual feature F_T has the same dimensionality as the visual features.

$$F_T = \sigma_t(W_t \cdot (mean(F_T^i)) + b_t) \tag{3}$$

where W_t refers the weight matrix of the fully connected layer, b_t represents the bias term, σ_t represents Leaky RELU activation function.

Visual Feature Extraction Module. For visual feature extraction, we employ Vgg-19, which has been pretrained on ImageNet, to extract visual features from the images attached in the posts. Specifically, given an image I, after preprocessing, input it into the Vgg network to obtain the semantic features of the image F_I^i:

$$F_I^i = Vgg - 19(I^i) \tag{4}$$

The F_I^i is fed into an mean pooling and a fully connected layer to get the visual feature F_I.

$$F_I = \sigma_i(W_i \cdot (mean(F_I^i)) + b_i) \tag{5}$$

where W_i refers the weight matrix of the fully connected layer, b_i represents the bias term, σ_i represents Leaky RELU activation function.

Auxiliary Feature Extraction Module. As is common knowledge, news stories' information is visually expressed through images and detailedly described in news texts. After observation, it is found that the images of many news articles contain a lot of embedded information. This embedded information is usually text and encapsulates the theme of the news. This paper considers image-embedded information as an auxiliary modality.

PP-OCRv3 [6] is an open-source model in paddlepaddle, which is used to extract text. Its detection module is optimized based on the DB algorithm, and the recognition module uses the text recognition algorithm SVTR, and it is industrially adapted. In this paper, the open-source pre-trained PP-OCRv3 model is used to extract the image-embedded text (E):

$$E^i = PP - OCRv3(I) \tag{6}$$

where I refers to the image, E^i represents image-embedded content.

Similarly, Bert, the same feature extraction model as the news text, is used for similar data processing to obtain a vectorized representation, and then obtain the feature F_E^i:

$$F_E^i = Bert(E^i), E = [E^0, E^1, ..., E^L] \tag{7}$$

where L is the maximum length.

The F_E^i is fed into an mean pooling layer and a fully connected layer to get the finally auxiliary feature F_E.

$$F_E = \sigma_e(W_e \cdot (mean(F_E^i)) + b_e) \tag{8}$$

where W_e refers the weight matrix of the fully connected layer, b_e represents the bias term, σ_e represents Leaky RELU activation function.

3.2 Multi-modal Feature Fusion

So far, text features and visual features have been obtained. Concatenate them in the final dimension after that, without considering their relationships, to accurately map to the possibility that the news is fraudulent and to further map to their right labels. Mathematically it can be defined as:

$$C = softmax(W_C(F_T \oplus F_I) + B_C) \tag{9}$$

where $\oplus$ is the symbol of splicing operation, C represents the probability of class prediction, W_C and B_C are weight parameters and offset items respectively.

To make the calculated possibility of falsification of a news article close to its true label y, a loss function based on cross-entropy is defined as:

$$\mathcal{L}_c(\theta_T, \theta_I, \theta_c) = -\mathbb{E}_{(a,y)\sim(A,Y)}[y \cdot \log C + (1-y) \cdot \log(1-C)] \tag{10}$$

3.3 Multi-modal Feature Matching

The relationship between texts and images of news can be used to evaluate the veracity of news stories. The creator of fake news may seek out irrelevant images on which to base misleading claims to grab readers' attention. News that does not match the sentences and visuals is more likely to be false information than the news that does. This study evaluates the agreement between the two modalities using a slightly modified cosine similarity for simplicity in calculation and accurate measurement. Firstly, consider the consistency of textual feature F_T and visual feature F_I, which can be defined mathematically as follows:

$$S\left(F_T, F_I\right)=\frac{F_T \cdot F_I+\| F_T \|\| F_I \|}{2 \| F_T \|\| F_I \|} \tag{11}$$

Through this calculation method, $S(F_T, F_I)$ can be guaranteed to be a positive number, and the value ranges between 0 and 1. If $S(T, I)$ is 0, it means that the text does not match the image. If $S(T, I)$ is 1, it means that the text semantics have the same probability as the image semantics. Similarly, considering the consistency of textual feature F_T and auxiliary feature F_E, it is mathematically defined as:

$$S\left(F_T, F_E\right)=\frac{F_T \cdot F_E+\| F_T \|\| F_E \|}{2 \| F_T \|\| F_E \|} \tag{12}$$

The treatment of $S(F_T, F_E)$ is the same as that of $S(T, I)$.

Finally, considering the consistency of visual feature F_I and auxiliary feature F_E, it is mathematically defined as:

$$S\left(F_I, F_E\right)=\frac{F_I \cdot F_E+\| F_I \|\| F_E \|}{2 \| F_I \|\| F_E \|} \tag{13}$$

The treatment of $S(F_I, F_E)$ is also the same as that of $S(T, I)$.

Then, define the following three cross-entropy loss functions to represent that from the perspective of similarity:

$$\begin{aligned}\mathcal{L}_s\left(\theta_T, \theta_I\right)= & -\mathbb{E}_{(a,y)\sim(A,Y)}\{y \cdot \log[1-S(F_T, F_I)] \\ & +(1-y) \cdot \log S(F_T, F_I)\}\end{aligned} \tag{14}$$

$$\begin{aligned}\mathcal{L}_s\left(\theta_T, \theta_E\right)= & -\mathbb{E}_{(a,y)\sim(A,Y)}\{y \cdot \log[1-S(F_T, F_E)] \\ & +(1-y) \cdot \log S(F_T, F_E)\}\end{aligned} \tag{15}$$

$$\begin{aligned}\mathcal{L}_s\left(\theta_I, \theta_E\right)= & -\mathbb{E}_{(a,y)\sim(A,Y)}\{y \cdot \log[1-S(F_I, F_E)] \\ & +(1-y) \cdot \log S(F_I, F_E)\}\end{aligned} \tag{16}$$

3.4 Multi-modal Model Learning

Finally, correct identification of fake news by news multimodal feature fusion and similarity of news multimodal data. α, β, γ, η mean the loss function weights of the four branch networks. For purpose of involving the validity of the four modes, have obtained the final loss function definition formula as follows:

$$\begin{aligned}\mathcal{L}\left(\theta_T, \theta_I, \theta_E, \theta_c\right)= & \alpha \mathcal{L}_c\left(\theta_T, \theta_I, \theta_c\right)+\beta \mathcal{L}_s\left(\theta_T, \theta_I\right)+ \\ & \gamma \mathcal{L}_s\left(\theta_T, \theta_E\right)+\eta \mathcal{L}_s\left(\theta_I, \theta_E\right)\end{aligned} \tag{17}$$

$$\left(\hat{\theta}_T, \hat{\theta}_I, \hat{\theta}_E, \hat{\theta}_c\right)=\underset{\theta_T, \theta_I, \theta_E, \theta_c}{\operatorname{argmin}} \mathcal{L}\left(\theta_T, \theta_I, \theta_E, \theta_c\right) \tag{18}$$

4 Experiments

4.1 Datasets

To fairly evaluate the performance of TIMAM, the experiments are established on two public datasets. According to preliminary statistics, over 70% of images in both datasets contain embedded text. The statistics of the datasets are shown in Table 1. The following is a description of the datasets:

1) Weibo dataset [4] comes from the Sina Weibo social platform. This dataset contains 4749 fake news data and 4779 real news data. Duplicate images and low-quality images are removed to ensure homogeneity across the dataset.

2) Twitter dataset [3] comes from the Twitter social platform. The dataset contains 7021 fake news data and 5924 real news data. As per the task requirements, news without texts or images are removed from the dataset.

Table 1. Dataset statistic.

Dataset	Label	Number	All
Weibo	fake	4749	9528
	real	4779	
Twitter	fake	7021	12945
	real	5924	

4.2 Settings

For the textual extractor, the dimensionality of textual features obtained from Bert is 768. For the visual extractor, images are first resized to $224 \times 224 \times 3$ and then fed to Vgg-19. The dimensionality of image features obtained from Vgg19 is 4,096. To avoid overfitting, the parameters of Bert_base and Vgg-19 are all frozen. The final features are input into the fully connected layer to obtain a common dimension of 32. The dropout rate is set to 0.5. In experiments, Adam is selected as the optimizer. The model is trained on a batch size of 32 and for 50 epochs. Weibo's learning rate is set to 0.01, whereas Twitter's learning rate is set to 0.0001. After comparing multiple sets of experiments, the weights of the four network branches in the model are finally set as $\alpha = 0.6$, $\beta = 0.2$, $\gamma = 0.1$, and $\eta = 0.1$. To prevent overfitting, early stopping is employed.

4.3 Baselines

- **EANN** [11]: EANN extracts textual and visual features from Text-CNN and Vgg respectively, acquires news features by concatenating texts and images, and detects fake news with the help of an event discriminator.

- **MVAE** [5]: MVAE extracts text features and visual features through bidirectional LSTM and Vgg, and splicing them to the autoencoder to reconstruct the correlation between feature learning modes.
- **Spotfake** [10]: Spotfake uses the Bert and Vgg-19, respectively, to obtain text and image features, and then concatenate them into the fake news detector for detection.
- **MKEMN** [14]: MKEMN regards to texts, images, and retrieved knowledge embeddings as stacked channels and makes a fusion via a convolutional operation.
- **SAFE** [15]: SAFE converts the image into text, and extracts textual features through Text-CNN. Finally, cosine similarity is used to detect the similarity between texts.

Table 2. Comparison of experimental results for methods.

Dataset	Method	Accuracy	Real Information			Fake Information		
			Precision	Recall	F1	Precision	Recall	F1
Weibo	EANN	0.816	0.810	0.810	0.810	0.820	0.820	0.820
	MVAE	0.824	0.802	**0.875**	0.837	0.854	0.769	0.809
	Spotfake	0.880	0.847	0.656	0.739	0.902	**0.964**	0.932
	MKEMN	0.824	0.823	0.799	0.812	0.723	0.819	0.798
	SAFE	0.816	0.695	0.811	0.748	0.831	0.724	0.774
	TIMAM	**0.881**	**0.883**	0.862	**0.873**	**0.912**	0.893	**0.935**
Twitter	EANN	0.719	0.771	0.870	0.817	0.642	0.474	0.545
	MVAE	0.745	0.686	0.777	0.730	0.801	0.719	0.758
	Spotfake	0.777	0.832	0.606	0.701	0.751	0.900	0.820
	MKEMN	0.714	0.814	0.756	0.708	0.634	0.814	0.831
	SAFE	0.762	0.831	0.724	0.774	0.831	0.822	0.823
	TIMAM	**0.917**	**0.937**	**0.911**	**0.953**	**0.862**	**0.931**	**0.904**

4.4 Performance Comparison

We compare TIMAM with representative methods introduced in Sect. 4.3. The results are presented in Table 2, from which we can draw the following observations: Firstly, the four branches of TIMAM jointly participate in decision-making based on their importance, and Table 2 shows that it outperforms the other five baseline models in both real-world datasets. Secondly, analyzed from the feature extraction perspective, TIMAM adds auxiliary features and extracts richer features compared to the other five models that use only text and image features. The image-embedded content contains the text of the news or the subject of the image, which provides more evidence for the decision of the truth or falsity of the news. Finally, analyzed from the perspective of feature matching, the SAFE model converts images into text with semantic bias, while TIMAM provides three network branches to calculate the semantic similarity between patterns, which fully emphasizes the multiple interactions between patterns and proves the effectiveness of the method proposed in this paper. Relevant training data are retained and visualized, as shown in Fig. 2. The *loss* in the figure represents the total loss, and the other four *loss* represent the losses of each of the four branch networks.

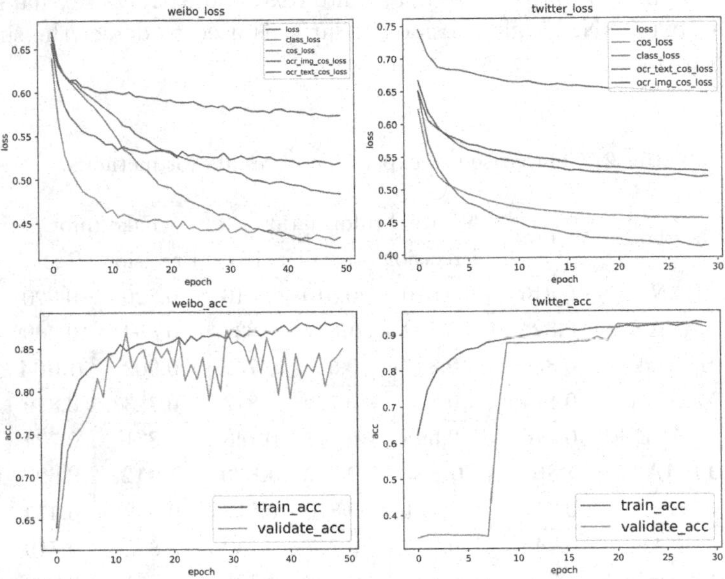

Fig. 2. Visualization Results of Experimental Data.

4.5 Architecture Ablation Analysis

In this section, to prove the effectiveness of each component of TIMAM, ablation experiments are carried out on the Weibo dataset and the Twitter dataset.

- TIMAM: α Experiments with text-image fusion only;
- TIMAM: β Experiments with text-image matching only;
- TIMAM: $\alpha+\beta$ Text-image fusion, text-image matching, experiments with weights of 0.6 and 0.4 respectively;
- TIMAM: $\alpha+\beta+\gamma$ Text-image fusion, text-image matching, text and image-embedded content matching, experiments with weights of 0.6, 0.2 and 0.2 respectively;

Table 3. Architecture ablation analysis of TIMAM.

Dataset	Method	Accuracy	Precision	Recall	F1
Weibo	TIMAM: α	0.812	0.822	0.801	0.821
	TIMAM: β	0.763	0.783	0.814	0.682
	TIMAM: $\alpha+\beta$	0.853	0.803	0.884	0.732
	TIMAM: $\alpha+\beta+\gamma$	0.874	0.821	0.913	0.861
	TIMAM: $\alpha+\beta+\eta$	0.872	0.872	0.882	0.881
	TIMAM	0.881	0.912	0.893	0.935
Twitter	TIMAM: α	0.831	0.830	0.931	0.884
	TIMAM: β	0.772	0.864	0.832	0.794
	TIMAM: $\alpha+\beta$	0.872	0.924	0.832	0.834
	TIMAM: $\alpha+\beta+\gamma$	0.901	0.851	0.901	0.883
	TIMAM: $\alpha+\beta+\eta$	0.897	0.862	0.905	0.884
	TIMAM	0.917	0.862	0.931	0.904

- TIMAM: $\alpha+\beta+\eta$ Text-image fusion, text-image matching, image and image-embedded content matching, experiments with weights of 0.6, 0.2 and 0.2 respectively;

According to Table 3, it can be seen that text-image fusion has the greatest impact on the detection of fake news. Only similarity does not achieve good results. In other words, similarity matching is very important for improving the performance of the model. Only text-image fusion and text-image matching cannot achieve the ideal effect, after adding image-embedded content, the indicator has been significantly improved, and the data information at this time has been fully mined. This proves that the detection method of text-image matching is effective, and it is very important to model the image-embedded content.

5 Conclusion

This study suggests a novel text-image matching-based fake news detection technique. The model of image-embedded material is added based on the model of texts and images. One fusion module and three matching modules constitute the four components of the entire model framework. Textual features and visual features are combined in the fusion module, while the matching modules determine the extent to which textual, visual, and auxiliary modalities match. Generally speaking, matching text-image news may be fake news, but unmatched text-image news must be fake news. Experiments show that our method outperforms existing baseline methods.

Acknowledgements. This research work was funded by the Beijing Social Science Foundation (21XCCC013).

References

1. Cheng, M., Nazarian, S., Bogdan, P.: VRoC: variational autoencoder-aided multi-task rumor classifier based on text. In: Proceedings of the web conference 2020. pp. 2892–2898 (2020)
2. Jawahar, G., Sagot, B., Seddah, D.: What does BERT learn about the structure of language? In: ACL 2019-57th Annual Meeting of the Association for Computational Linguistics (2019)
3. Jin, Z., Cao, J., Zhang, Y., Zhang, Y.: MCG-ICT at mediaeval 2015: Verifying multimedia use with a two-level classification model
4. Jin, Z., Cao, J., Zhang, Y., Zhou, J., Tian, Q.: Novel visual and statistical image features for microblogs news verification. IEEE Trans. Multimedia **19**(3), 598–608 (2016)
5. Khattar, D., Goud, J.S., Gupta, M., Varma, V.: MVAE: multimodal variational autoencoder for fake news detection. In: The world Wide Web Conference. pp. 2915–2921 (2019)
6. Li, C., et al.: Pp-ocrv3: more attempts for the improvement of ultra lightweight OCR system. arXiv preprint arXiv:2206.03001 (2022)
7. Ma, J., et al.: Detecting rumors from microblogs with recurrent neural networks (2016)
8. Qazvinian, V., Rosengren, E., Radev, D., Mei, Q.: Rumor has it: identifying misinformation in microblogs. In: Proceedings of the 2011 Conference on Empirical Methods in Natural Language Processing. pp. 1589–1599 (2011)
9. Qi, P., Cao, J., Yang, T., Guo, J., Li, J.: Exploiting multi-domain visual information for fake news detection. In: 2019 IEEE International Conference on Data Mining (ICDM). pp. 518–527. IEEE (2019)
10. Singhal, S., Shah, R.R., Chakraborty, T., Kumaraguru, P., Satoh, S.: Spotfake: A multi-modal framework for fake news detection. In: 2019 IEEE Fifth International Conference on Multimedia Big Data (BigMM). pp. 39–47. IEEE (2019)
11. Wang, Y., et al.: EANN: event adversarial neural networks for multi-modal fake news detection. In: Proceedings of the 24th ACM SIGKDD International Conference on Knowledge Discovery & Data Mining. pp. 849–857 (2018)
12. Wu, Y., Zhan, P., Zhang, Y., Wang, L., Xu, Z.: Multimodal fusion with co-attention networks for fake news detection. In: Findings of the Association for Computational Linguistics: ACL-IJCNLP 2021. pp. 2560–2569 (2021)
13. Yu, F., Liu, Q., Wu, S., Wang, L., Tan, T., et al.: A convolutional approach for misinformation identification. In: IJCAI. pp. 3901–3907 (2017)
14. Zhang, H., Fang, Q., Qian, S., Xu, C.: Multi-modal knowledge-aware event memory network for social media rumor detection. In: Proceedings of the 27th ACM International Conference on Multimedia. pp. 1942–1951 (2019)
15. Zhou, X., Wu, J., Zafarani, R.: Safe: similarity-aware multi-modal fake news detection. arXiv preprint arXiv:2003.04981 (2020)

An Improved Lightweight YOLOv5 for Remote Sensing Images

Shihao Hou[1], Linwei Fan[1], Fan Zhang[1], and Bingchen Liu[2](✉)

[1] School of Computer Science and Technology, Shandong University of Finance and Economics, Jinan, China

[2] School of Software, Shandong University, Jinan, China

lbcraf2018@126.com

Abstract. Achieving real-time accurate detection in remote sensing images, which exhibit features such as high resolution, small targets, and complex backgrounds, remains challenging due to the substantial computational demands of existing object detection models. In this paper, we propose an improved remote sensing image small object detection method based on YOLOv5. In order to preserve high-resolution features, we remove the Focus module from the YOLOv5 network structure and introduce RepGhostNet as a feature extraction network to enhance both accuracy and speed. We adopt the BiFormer prediction head for more flexible computational allocation and content perception, and employ the Normalized Wasserstein Distance (NWD) metric to alleviate IoU's sensitivity to small objects. Experimental results show that our proposed method achieves mAP scores of 75.54% and 75.65% on the publicly available VEDAI and DIOR remote sensing image datasets, respectively, with significantly fewer parameters and FLOPs. Our approach effectively balances accuracy and speed compared to other models.

Keywords: Remote sensing images · Small object detection · YOLOv5 · Normalized Wasserstein Distance

1 Introduction

Remote sensing technology has revolutionized the way we monitor and understand our environment. Utilizing sensors to collect data about objects or areas from a distance, remote sensing has become indispensable in a broad array of applications, from environmental studies to military surveillance. One such application, object detection, is particularly crucial for tasks such as shipwreck search and rescue [17], military intelligence reconnaissance [26], and geological disaster monitoring [24], highlighting the significance of remote sensing image analysis in these fields.

However, conventional deep learning-based object detection methods [4,9,15] are not directly applicable to remote sensing due to its unique characteristics, which distinguish it from traditional natural images. Firstly, remote sensing

L. Iliadis et al. (Eds.): ICANN 2023, LNCS 14255, pp. 77–89, 2023.
https://doi.org/10.1007/978-3-031-44210-0_7

images are often captured from varying heights and angles, resulting in a wide range of object scales. Depending on their distance from the imaging sensor, objects may appear significantly larger or smaller. Secondly, the backgrounds of remote sensing images are complex, and factors such as occlusions, shadows, and other environmental conditions can further impede the detection process. Thirdly, objects of interest are often quite small compared to the overall image size, and their low contrast with the background renders them difficult to discern. These three challenges make accurate object detection in remote sensing images a demanding task.

To overcome these challenges, various methods have been proposed, encompassing two-stage methods, one-stage methods, and more recently, Transformer-based methods. Despite their success, these methods still suffer from shortcomings, such as handling the drastic scale changes and complexities inherent in remote sensing images, which motivate the research presented in this paper. In this paper, we propose a novel YOLOv5 architecture tailored to the unique challenges of small object detection in remote sensing images. Our primary contributions can be summarized as follows:

- By eliminating the Focus module from the YOLOv5 network structure, we retain high-resolution features essential for detecting small objects in remote sensing images.
- We incorporate the lightweight RepGhostNet [5] as the feature extraction network within the backbone and neck, expediting the detection process without compromising performance.
- We substitute the original prediction head with the BiFormer [30] prediction head, enabling more flexible computational allocation and content perception to address the issue of drastic target scale changes.
- We introduce the novel NWD metric [25] to replace IoU, addressing its sensitivity to position offset and improving detection performance for small objects in complex backgrounds.

Our proposed method demonstrates superior performance on the widely recognized VEDAI [18] and DIOR [13] remote sensing image datasets. Compared to YOLOv5s, our approach achieves significant improvements in accuracy while reducing the number of parameters and FLOPs. This highlights the effectiveness of our model in balancing accuracy and computational efficiency in object detection tasks.

2 Related Work

In the field of computer vision, deep learning-based object detection methods have been extensively researched and demonstrated remarkable performance across various applications. These methods can be broadly categorized into two-stage methods, one-stage methods, and Transformer-based methods.

Two-stage methods involve a region proposal stage followed by a classification stage. The most notable models in this class are the R-CNN series, including R-CNN [9], Fast R-CNN [8], and Faster R-CNN [22]. These models have been instrumental in advancing the field of object detection, with each subsequent iteration improving upon the previous model's limitations. For instance, Mask R-CNN [11] added a segmentation branch for instance segmentation, while Cascade R-CNN [3] introduced a multi-stage detection pipeline to improve recall and precision. However, two-stage methods are often computationally expensive and slower compared to one-stage methods, which can be a limitation in real-time applications.

One-stage methods, also known as single-shot detectors, aim to predict object classes and bounding box coordinates in a single forward pass. Among the most representative models in this category are SSD [15] and the YOLO series [1,2,19–21]. SSD (Single Shot MultiBox Detector) extends the idea of predicting bounding boxes and class probabilities by utilizing multiple feature maps at different scales, effectively handling objects of varying sizes. The YOLO (You Only Look Once) series introduced the concept of dividing the input image into a grid and predicting bounding boxes and class probabilities for each grid cell, enabling real-time object detection due to its efficient processing pipeline. Although one-stage methods are well-known for their computational efficiency and real-time detection capabilities, they often exhibit lower detection accuracy and higher false positive rates when compared to two-stage methods. Despite these limitations, researchers have made significant strides in enhancing the performance of one-stage methods, with many achieving results that are competitive with two-stage methods.

Transformer-based methods treat object detection as a set prediction problem and employ an end-to-end approach. DETR [4] pioneered the use of Transformers in object detection, combining CNNs and the Transformer's encoder-decoder architecture. Following DETR, models like Deformable DETR [6] and Efficient DETR [27] were developed to address its limitations, such as convergence speed, resource consumption, and small object detection performance. More recent advancements, like DINO [28], have further enhanced performance by introducing improved denoising anchor boxes and contrastive loss.

3 Approach

In this section, we present our novel methodology designed to address the challenges of small object detection in remote sensing images. As depicted in Fig. 1, our approach incorporates a series of strategic enhancements to the YOLOv5 architecture, including the removal of the Focus module, introducing the RepGhostNet module, integrating the BiFormer module, and implementing a Receptive Field-Based Gaussian Regression Loss. Each of these advancements is discussed in depth in the following subsections, emphasizing the unique aspects of our work.

3.1 Preserving Resolution with a Conv Layer

The Focus module in the YOLOv5 backbone network is designed to aggregate information from adjacent pixels in the input image, directing the model's atten-

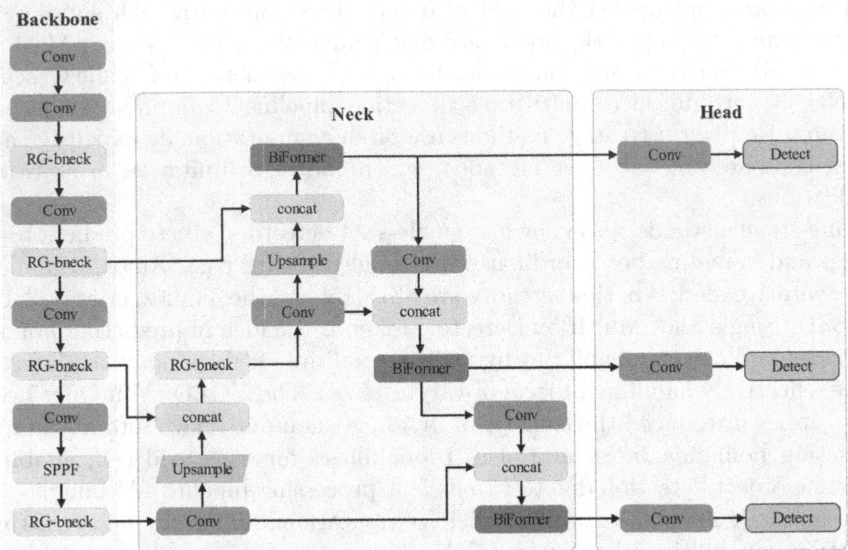

Fig. 1. The network architecture of the proposed model.

tion towards more relevant features. This is accomplished by dividing the input image into 2×2 windows and concatenating their values along the channel dimension. This process not only halves the spatial dimensions but also quadruples the channel depth, thus reducing computational complexity and enhancing spatial feature learning efficiency. However, this approach presents a drawback for small target detection; merging neighboring pixels leads to the loss of fine details and a reduction in spatial resolution [29]. Consequently, the model's ability to accurately detect and identify small objects within the input image is compromised. To tackle this issue, we replace the Focus module with a Convolutional Layer, which aids in preserving resolution.

3.2 RepGhost Module

The YOLOv5 C3 module uses CSPNet architecture and traditional convolution, resulting in resource-intensive computation and limited multi-scale object detection. We found that implementing the RepGhostNet module [5] effectively improves the C3 module's performance, addressing these limitations.

The RepGhost module, an extension of GhostNet [10], proposes a more efficient method for generating and fusing diverse feature maps via reparametrization. The RepGhost module eliminates the inefficient concatenation operations found in the Ghost module, significantly reducing inference time. Additionally, the information fusion process is executed by an add operator implicitly, rather than relying on other convolutional layers. The RepGhost module serves as the core of the RepGhostNet feature extractor, preserving the generation of diverse feature maps while substantially reducing the parameters and computational complexity of the network model compared to conventional convolutional neural networks.

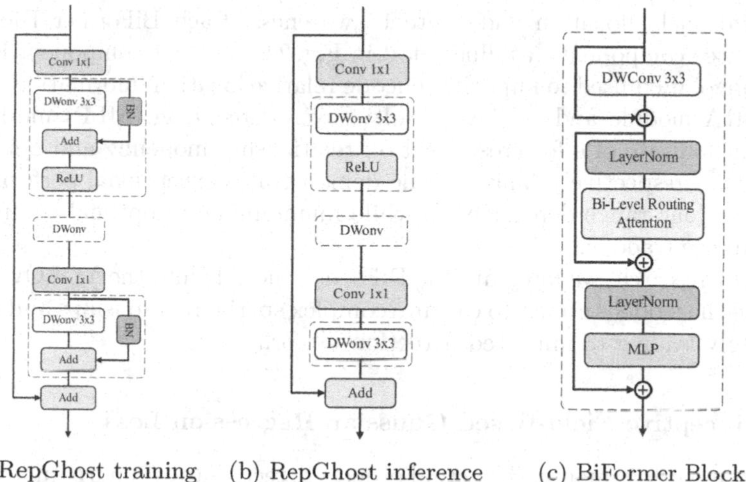

(a) RepGhost training (b) RepGhost inference (c) BiFormer Block

Fig. 2. Two important components of the feature extraction network.

Considering the advantages and features of the RepGhost module, the RepGhost bottleneck is constructed based on the RepGhost module, as shown in Fig. 2a. The RepGhost bottleneck comprises two RepGhost modules that perform different functions: the first RepGhost module increases the number of channels in the data, while the second RepGhost module decreases the number of channels. In the RepGhost bottleneck, a depthwise convolution layer is conditionally incorporated between the two RepGhost modules to facilitate downsampling when necessary. This design choice ensures that the RepGhost bottleneck retains the ability to adjust the input feature map size. The RepGhost bottleneck fuses the batch normalization layers and convolution layers into a single convolution layer with an adjusted kernel and bias during the inference process, making it more efficient in terms of memory cost and fast inference [7], as shown in Fig. 2b.

Currently, numerous lightweight neural networks are available, such as MobileNetV3 [12] and ShuffleNetV2 [16]. Distinct from these lightweight networks, RepGhostNet focuses more on addressing redundancy and correlation between feature maps. Consequently, employing RepGhostNet as the feature extraction network, which offers superior performance, can enhance detection accuracy and decrease the running time to a considerable extent.

3.3 BiFormer Integration

The original YOLOv5 head may not capture long-range contextual information. By integrating the BiFormer module [30], we aim to improve the model's contextual information processing.

To address these limitations and further enhance the performance of YOLOv5 for small target detection, we introduce BiFormer, a novel visual transformer. BiFormer introduces a new dynamic sparse attention mechanism using bi-level routing, which provides dynamic query-aware sparsity, allowing for more flexible computational allocation and content awareness. Each BiFormer Block comprises three components, as illustrated in Fig. 2c. The first component is a 3×3 deep convolution used to implicitly encode relative location information, followed by a BRA module and a 2-layer Multi-Layer Perceptron (MLP) module with an extension rate of e for cross-location relationship modeling and per-location embedding, respectively. This module demonstrates exceptional performance in capturing long-range dependencies while maintaining an optimal computation-performance tradeoff.

In our research, we integrate the BiFormer module into the YOLOv5 head to enhance the model's ability to capture complex spatial relationships and features, ultimately leading to improved detection performance.

3.4 Receptive Field-Based Gaussian Regression Loss

In remote sensing images, the actual objects detected are often irregular in shape and may include background pixels near their bounding boxes. To better describe the weights of different pixels within the bounding box, we can utilize a 2D Gaussian distribution [25] as a representation. Specifically, for a horizontal bounding box R = (cx, cy, w, h), where (cx, cy) represent the center coordinates, and (w, h) denote the width and height of the box, its inner tangent ellipse can be expressed as:

$$\frac{(x-\mu_x)^2}{\sigma_x^2} + \frac{(y-\mu_y)^2}{\sigma_y^2} = 1, \tag{1}$$

where (μ_x, μ_y) is the center coordinates of the ellipse, σ_x, σ_y are the lengths of semi-axes along x and y axes. Accordingly, $\mu_x = cx$, $\mu_y = cy$, $\sigma_x = \frac{w}{2}$, $\sigma_y = \frac{h}{2}$.

The probability density function of a 2D Gaussian distribution can be expressed as:

$$f(\mathbf{x}|\boldsymbol{\mu}, \boldsymbol{\Sigma}) = \frac{\exp\left(-\frac{1}{2}(\mathbf{x}-\boldsymbol{\mu})^\top \boldsymbol{\Sigma}^{-1}(\mathbf{x}-\boldsymbol{\mu})\right)}{2\pi|\boldsymbol{\Sigma}|^{\frac{1}{2}}}, \tag{2}$$

where x is the coordinate (x, y), μ is the mean vector, and $\boldsymbol{\Sigma}$ is the covariance matrix of the Gaussian distribution. When the covariance matrix $\boldsymbol{\Sigma}$ is a diagonal matrix, the ellipse in Eq. 2 can be regarded as a density contour of the Gaussian distribution.

Thus, the bounding box R = (cx, cy, w, h) can be modeled into a 2D Gaussian distribution $\mathcal{N}(\boldsymbol{\mu}, \boldsymbol{\Sigma})$ with

$$\boldsymbol{\mu} = \begin{bmatrix} c_x \\ c_y \end{bmatrix}, \quad \boldsymbol{\Sigma} = \begin{bmatrix} \frac{w^2}{4} & 0 \\ 0 & \frac{h^2}{4} \end{bmatrix}. \tag{3}$$

Consequently, the similarity between bounding boxes A and B can be translated into a distribution distance between two Gaussian distributions, replacing the original IoU measure.

We employ the Wasserstein distance from optimal transport theory to compute the distribution distance. Specifically, for a 2D Gaussian distribution of the predicted bounding box $\mathcal{N}_p(\boldsymbol{\mu}_p, \boldsymbol{\Sigma}_p)$ and the ground truth bounding box $\mathcal{N}_g(\boldsymbol{\mu}_g, \boldsymbol{\Sigma}_g)$, the 2nd order Wasserstein distance between $\mathcal{N}_p$ and $\mathcal{N}_g$ is defined as:

$$W_2^2(\mathcal{N}_p, \mathcal{N}_g) = \left\| \left(\left[cx_p, cy_p, \frac{w_p}{2}, \frac{h_p}{2} \right]^{\top}, \left[cx_g, cy_g, \frac{w_g}{2}, \frac{h_g}{2} \right]^{\top} \right) \right\|_2^2. \tag{4}$$

To obtain a new metric called Normalized Wasserstein Distance (NWD), we apply exponential normalization and incorporate it into our loss function

$$NWD(\mathcal{N}_a, \mathcal{N}_b) = \exp\left(-\frac{\sqrt{W_2^2(\mathcal{N}_a, \mathcal{N}_b)}}{C} \right), \tag{5}$$

where C is a constant closely related to the dataset. By exploiting the properties of Gaussian distributions, the NWD-loss can effectively capture the differences between predicted and true bounding boxes for small object.

In comparison to IoU, the NWD is more sensitive when detecting small objects, and it can measure the similarity between non-overlapping or mutually inclusive bounding boxes. As a result, the NWD significantly outperforms IoU in small object detection tasks.

4 Experimental

In our experiments, we employ the publicly available VEDAI dataset, specifically designed for multimodal remote sensing image object detection. To provide a comprehensive assessment of our proposed algorithm, we not only examine its performance on the multimodal object detection dataset but also utilize the single-modal dataset, DIOR, as a supplementary benchmark for evaluation.

4.1 Dataset Description

VEDAI. The Vehicle Detection in Aerial Imagery (VEDAI) dataset [18] encompasses vehicles presenting various challenges, including multiple orientations, illumination and shadow variations, specular reflections, and occlusions. It comprises 1,246 remote sensing images with dimensions of either 1024 × 1024 or 512 × 512, featuring two modalities: RGB and IR. The dataset includes diverse backgrounds such as grasslands, highways, mountains, and urban areas. Although VEDAI contains 11 vehicle classes, we focus on the eight categories with a sufficient number of instances, as presented in Table 1. Following [23], instances for each category are partitioned into ten groups. The testing process in this article uses a default image resolution of 512×512 for evaluation purposes.

Table 1. Class instances distribution in VEDAI dataset across 10 folds for cross-validation.

Table	Total Instances	Distribution Across 10 Folds
Car	1349	9 folds of 135; 1 fold of 134
Pickup	941	9 folds of 94; 1 fold of 95
Camping car	390	10 folds of 39
Truck	300	10 folds of 30
Other	200	10 folds of 20
Tractor	190	10 folds of 19
Boat	170	10 folds of 17
Van	100	10 folds of 10

DIOR. The DIOR dataset [13], designed for evaluating remote sensing target detectors, consists of 23,463 images and 192,472 instances across 20 object classes. Each instance has a horizontal bounding box label, with images sized at 800 × 800 pixels. For our experiments, we utilized 11,725 images as the training set and 11,738 images as the testing set.

4.2 Accuracy Metrics

The accuracy of target detection in remote sensing images depends on the combined calculation of localization and classification accuracy. In this paper, we primarily use the mean Average Precision (mAP) metric, which is commonly employed to evaluate the accuracy of predicted bounding boxes in terms of category and location. It is calculated based on precision (P) and recall (R), as follows:

$$P = \frac{TP}{TP + FP}, \quad R = \frac{TP}{TP + FN}. \tag{6}$$

True positive (TP) denotes correct prediction, while false positive (FP) and false negative (FN) indicate incorrect outcomes. Precision and recall are mutually influencing values; increasing one typically decreases the other. To consider both precision and recall, we introduce the Average Precision (AP):

$$AP = \int_0^1 p(r)dr, \tag{7}$$

where p denotes precision, and r denotes recall. In multi-class object detection, the AP value is calculated for each true target category and then averaged to obtain the mean Average Precision (mAP):

$$mAP = \frac{\sum_{i=1}^{N} AP_i}{N}, \tag{8}$$

where N is the number of categories. Additionally, we use the number of floating-point operations (FLOPs) and parameters to measure the compression performance.

4.3 Implementation Details

We implement our YOLOv5 using PyTorch 1.10.0 and train and test it on an NVIDIA RTX 3090. Upon examining the multimodal VEDAI dataset, we find that its instances consist exclusively of small objects. Consequently, we remove the PANet [14] structure and the two detection heads, responsible for enhancing large-scale target detection, when training on this dataset. This change significantly reduces the number of model parameters without substantially affecting accuracy. During the training phase, we train our proposed model from scratch since it shares only a few identical parts with YOLOv5, which prevents us from loading weights from YOLOv5s to train our proposed model. We employ various training strategies for different datasets, such as using an image size of 512, batch sizes of 2 and 16 for the VEDAI and DIOR datasets, respectively, a learning rate of 0.01, and 300 and 200 epochs for the VEDAI and DIOR datasets, respectively. Additionally, we apply data augmentation techniques like hue saturation value (HSV), multi-scale, translation, left-right flip, and mosaic. In the testing phase, we set the non-maximum suppression IoU threshold to 0.6 for the VEDAI dataset and 0.4 for the DIOR dataset.

4.4 Results and Analysis

To validate the superiority of the proposed improved model, we compare it not only with single-stage algorithms such as YOLOv3, YOLOv4, and YOLOv5 but also with the two-stage method Faster R-CNN and the YOLOrs [23] method, which is specifically improved for remote sensing images. As shown in Table 2 and 3, our model achieves the best mAP values on both remote sensing image datasets. The proposed model achieves accuracy improvements of 18.75% and 5.64% on the two datasets, respectively, compared to YOLOv5s, and its model parameters are much smaller than those of other detection methods. Although this modification increases the computational cost for inference (FLOPs), the RepGhost module accelerates inference by implicitly facilitating feature reuse through structural reparameterization. Furthermore, the FLOPs of our proposed improved model remain lower than those of YOLOv3 and YOLOv4. In practical applications, minimizing false positives is crucial. Overall, the improved method offers a more significant advantage in accuracy performance.

Table 2. Comparison of accuracy(%) on VEDAI testing set.

Method	Car	Pickup	Camping	Truck	Other	Tractor	Boat	Van	mAP	Params(M)	FLOPs(G)
Faster R-CNN	77.87	69.52	58.64	61.93	43.73	53.26	36.64	43.13	57.59	41.19	198.47
YOLOv3	83.62	71.81	65.33	67.64	43.14	66.72	37.91	60.29	62.16	61.54	49.68
YOLOv4	81.65	73.82	72.37	60.80	47.68	67.13	38.51	56.72	62.34	52.51	38.23
YOLOv5s	80.81	68.48	69.06	54.71	46.76	64.29	24.25	45.96	56.79	7.06	**5.32**
YOLOrs	83.03	76.51	67.78	52.91	47.48	70.48	20.67	46.42	58.16	–	–
Ours	**91.43**	**86.05**	**78.52**	**70.28**	**59.37**	**79.56**	**64.34**	**74.40**	**75.54**	**3.68**	11.83

Table 3. Comparison of accuracy(%) on DIOR testing set.

Method	mAP	Params(M)	FLOPs(G)
Faster R-CNN	61.72	41.19	198.47
YOLOv3	57.17	61.43	47.63
YOLOv4	72.69	52.51	38.17
YOLOv5s	70.01	7.0641	**5.11**
Ours	**75.65**	**5.7803**	15.20

Table 4. Ablation experiment.

Methods	a	b	c	d
Conv Layer	✓	✓	✓	✓
RepGhostNet		✓	✓	✓
BiFormer			✓	✓
NWD-Loss				✓
mAP(%)	62.76	76.69	79.60	82.13
Params(M)	4.7883M	3.6677M	3.6849M	3.6849M
FLOPs(G)	4.23G	11.56G	11.83G	11.83G

Furthermore, the visual detection results of the proposed method on the VEDAI and DIOR datasets are presented in Fig. 3. It can be seen that our proposed model can accurately detect some remote sensing small targets that are easy to miss, especially the pick-up trucks and cars in the VEDAI dataset, which are easily confused due to their similarity in the detection process. The proposed model with improved performance can better achieve this task.

4.5 Ablation Experiments

To evaluate the effectiveness of each improvement in our approach, we conducted ablation experiments on the VEDAI dataset. These experiments were performed using the first fold of the validation set, and, to ensure a fair assessment, we maintained consistent parameters across all variables. Detection results are presented in Table 4, which demonstrate the enhanced detection performance attributable to each module's improvement strategies.

In the ablation study, Method (a) highlights the impact of replacing the Focus module with a convolutional block, leading to a significant 5.97% mAP improvement. This result suggests the importance of preserving spatial interval information for small object detection. For Method (b), incorporating the RepGhostNet module reduces the parameter count and increases the mAP by a substantial 13.93%, underscoring the advantages of this module for remote sensing applications. In Method (c), the integration of the BiFormer detection head, based on Method (b), results in a 2.91% mAP increase, emphasizing the

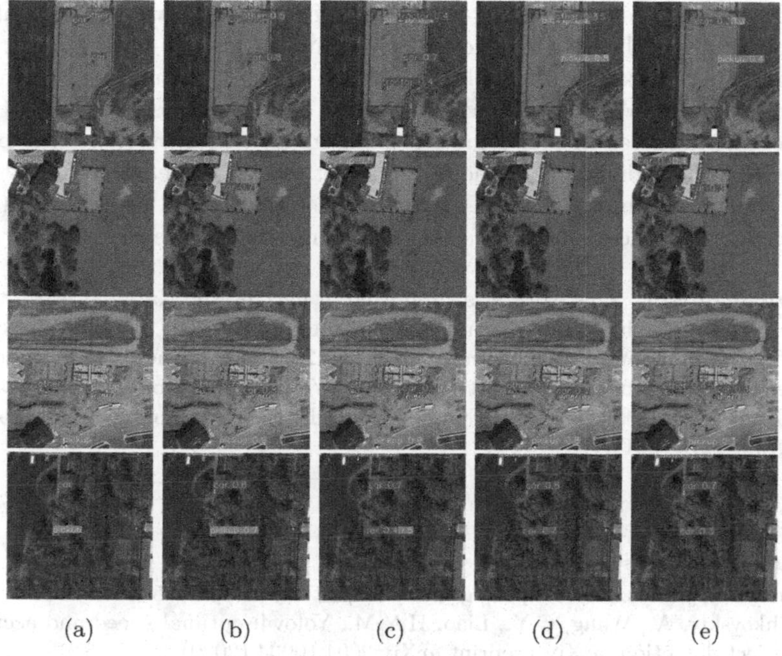

(a) (b) (c) (d) (e)

Fig. 3. Comparison of detection performance for different models: (a) Ground Truth; (b) Our Model; (c) YOLOv5s; (d) YOLOv4; (e) YOLOv3.

module's ability to effectively model long-range dependencies. Finally, Method (d) showcases the effectiveness of NWD-loss optimization, as it yields an mAP increase from 79.6% to 82.13%, illustrating its superiority over IoU for small object detection tasks.

5 Conclusion

In this paper, we analyze the challenges faced by current remote sensing image object detection algorithms and present a novel small target detection method for remote sensing images, considering the characteristics of high resolution, small targets, and complex backgrounds. Our approach preserves high-resolution features by eliminating the Focus module, incorporates the advanced RepGhostNet, and adopts the BiFormer prediction head to enhance both the accuracy and speed of target detection. Moreover, we employ a two-dimensional Gaussian distribution to represent the bounding box, offering a more refined description of the weights of different pixels within the bounding box. Our experimental results on the publicly available VEDAI and DIOR remote sensing image datasets demonstrate that our approach outperforms existing methods while utilizing significantly fewer parameters.

In comparison to other models, our method effectively balances accuracy and speed, showcasing its potential for practical applications in the field of small target detection in remote sensing images. For future work, we plan to continue our pursuit of simplicity and efficiency. We aim to further optimize our network structure by exploring simpler, yet more efficient, feature extraction and detection modules. We also aim to incorporate additional metrics that cater to the inherent characteristics of remote sensing images. Moreover, we will experiment with further lightweight model architectures to decrease computational cost while maintaining accuracy. Through these adjustments, we hope to further enhance the robustness and practicality of our method in the real world.

Acknowledgement. This work was supported in part by the National Natural Science Foundation of China under Grants 62002200 and 62202268, the Natural Science Foundation of Shandong Province under Grant ZR2020QF012, the Shandong Provincial Science and Technology Support Program of Youth Innovation Team in Colleges under Grant 2021KJ069, and the Shandong Social Science Planning Fund Program under Grant 22DGLJO11.

References

1. Ultralytics/yolov5:v5.0. https://github.com/ultralytics/yolov5 (2021).
2. Bochkovskiy, A., Wang, C.Y., Liao, H.Y.M.: Yolov4: optimal speed and accuracy of object detection. arXiv preprint arXiv:2004.10934 (2020)
3. Cai, Z., Vasconcelos, N.: Cascade r-cnn: delving into high quality object detection. In: Proceedings of the IEEE Conference on Computer Vision and Pattern Recognition, pp. 6154–6162 (2018)
4. Carion, N., Massa, F., Synnaeve, G., Usunier, N., Kirillov, A., Zagoruyko, S.: End-to-end object detection with transformers. In: Vedaldi, A., Bischof, H., Brox, T., Frahm, J.-M. (eds.) ECCV 2020. LNCS, vol. 12346, pp. 213–229. Springer, Cham (2020). https://doi.org/10.1007/978-3-030-58452-8_13
5. Chen, C., Guo, Z., Zeng, H., Xiong, P., Dong, J.: Repghost: a hardware-efficient ghost module via re-parameterization. arXiv preprint arXiv:2211.06088 (2022)
6. Dai, J., et al.: Deformable convolutional networks. In: Proceedings of the IEEE International Conference on Computer Vision, pp. 764–773 (2017)
7. Ding, X., Zhang, X., Ma, N., Han, J., Ding, G., Sun, J.: RepVGG: making VGG-style ConvNets great again. In: Proceedings of the IEEE/CVF Conference on Computer Vision and Pattern Recognition, pp. 13733–13742 (2021)
8. Girshick, R.: Fast R-CNN. In: Proceedings of the IEEE International Conference on Computer Vision, pp. 1440–1448 (2015)
9. Girshick, R., Donahue, J., Darrell, T., Malik, J.: Rich feature hierarchies for accurate object detection and semantic segmentation. In: Proceedings of the IEEE Conference on Computer Vision and Pattern Recognition, pp. 580–587 (2014)
10. Han, K., Wang, Y., Tian, Q., Guo, J., Xu, C., Xu, C.: Ghostnet: more features from cheap operations. In: Proceedings of the IEEE/CVF Conference on Computer Vision and Pattern Recognition, pp. 1580–1589 (2020)
11. He, K., Gkioxari, G., Dollár, P., Girshick, R.: Mask R-CNN. In: Proceedings of the IEEE International Conference on Computer Vision, pp. 2961–2969 (2017)
12. Howard, A., et al.: Searching for mobilenetv3. In: Proceedings of the IEEE/CVF International Conference on Computer Vision, pp. 1314–1324 (2019)

13. Li, K., Wan, G., Cheng, G., Meng, L., Han, J.: Object detection in optical remote sensing images: a survey and a new benchmark. ISPRS J. Photogrammetry Remote Sens. **159**, 296–307 (2020)
14. Liu, S., Qi, L., Qin, H., Shi, J., Jia, J.: Path aggregation network for instance segmentation. In: Proceedings of the IEEE Conference on Computer Vision and Pattern Recognition, pp. 8759–8768 (2018)
15. Liu, W., et al.: SSD: single shot multibox detector. In: Leibe, B., Matas, J., Sebe, N., Welling, M. (eds.) ECCV 2016. LNCS, vol. 9905, pp. 21–37. Springer, Cham (2016). https://doi.org/10.1007/978-3-319-46448-0_2
16. Ma, N., Zhang, X., Zheng, H.T., Sun, J.: Shufflenet v2: practical guidelines for efficient CNN Architecture Design. In: Proceedings of the European Conference on Computer Vision (ECCV), pp. 116–131 (2018)
17. Peng, J., Shi, C.: Remote sensing application in the maritime search and rescue. In: Remote Sensing-Applications. IntechOpen (2012)
18. Razakarivony, S., Jurie, F.: Vehicle detection in aerial imagery: a small target detection benchmark. J. Vis. Commun. Image Representation **34**, 187–203 (2016)
19. Redmon, J., Divvala, S., Girshick, R., Farhadi, A.: You only look once: Unified, real-time object detection. In: Proceedings of the IEEE Conference on Computer Vision and Pattern Recognition, pp. 779–788 (2016)
20. Redmon, J., Farhadi, A.: Yolo9000: better, faster, stronger. In: Proceedings of the IEEE Conference on Computer Vision and Pattern Recognition, pp. 7263–7271 (2017)
21. Redmon, J., Farhadi, A.: Yolov3: an incremental improvement. arXiv preprint arXiv:1804.02767 (2018)
22. Ren, S., He, K., Girshick, R., Sun, J.: Faster R-CNN: towards real-time object detection with region proposal networks. In: Advances in Neural Information Processing Systems, vol. 28 (2015)
23. Sharma, M., et al.: Yolors: object detection in multimodal remote sensing imagery. IEEE J. Sel. Top. Appl. Earth Obser. Remote Sens. **14**, 1497–1508 (2020)
24. Van Westen, C.: Remote sensing for natural disaster management. Int. Arch. Photogrammetry Remote Sens. **33**(B7/4; PART 7), 1609–1617 (2000)
25. Wang, J., Xu, C., Yang, W., Yu, L.: A normalized gaussian wasserstein distance for tiny object detection. arXiv preprint arXiv:2110.13389 (2021)
26. Watts, A.C., Ambrosia, V.G., Hinkley, E.A.: Unmanned aircraft systems in remote sensing and scientific research: classification and considerations of use. Remote Sens. **4**(6), 1671–1692 (2012)
27. Yao, Z., Ai, J., Li, B., Zhang, C.: Efficient detr: improving end-to-end object detector with dense prior. arXiv preprint arXiv:2104.01318 (2021)
28. Zhang, H., et al.: DINO: DETR with improved denoising anchor boxes for end-to-end object detection. arXiv preprint arXiv:2203.03605 (2022)
29. Zhang, J., Lei, J., Xie, W., Fang, Z., Li, Y., Du, Q.: Superyolo: super resolution assisted object detection in multimodal remote sensing imagery. IEEE Trans. Geosci. Remote Sens. **61**, 1–15 (2023)
30. Zhu, L., Wang, X., Ke, Z., Zhang, W., Lau, R.: Biformer: vision transformer with bi-level routing attention. arXiv preprint arXiv:2303.08810 (2023)

An Improved YOLOv5 with Structural Reparameterization for Surface Defect Detection

Yixuan Han and Liying Zheng(✉)

School of Computer Science and Technology, Harbin Engineering University, Harbin 150001, China

zhengliying@hrbeu.edu.cn

Abstract. Surface defects produced by the manufacturing process directly degrades the quality of industrial materials such as hot-rolled steel. However, existing methods for detecting surface defects cannot meet the requirements in terms of speed and accuracy. Based on structural re-parameterization, coordinate attention (CA) mechanism, and an additional detection head, we propose an improved YOLOv5 model for detecting surface defects of steel plates. Firstly, using the technique of structural re-parameterization in RepVGGBlock, the multi-channel structure of the training backbone network is converted to a single-channel structure of the inference network. This allows the network to speed up its inference while maintaining detection accuracy. Secondly, CA is integrated into the detection head to further improve detection accuracy. Finally, a layer of detection head is added at the end of the network to focus on detecting small targets. The experimental results on the Northeastern University (NEU) surface defect database show that, our model is superior to the state-of-the-art detectors, such as the original YOLOv5, Fast-RCNN in accuracy and speed.

Keywords: YOLOv5 · Re-parameterization · Coordinate Attention · Defect Detection

1 Introduction

Hot-rolled steel sheets are essential materials in the production of automobiles, bridges, ships, boilers, and pressure vessels. However, the surface defects of these steel sheets severely decrease the product strength, affect their service life, or even worse, cause mechanical failures such as jamming, resulting in safety accidents. Detecting surface defects in hot-rolled steel sheets is, therefore, crucial for ensuring product quality. However, the defect detections suffer from the variations of imaging illumination, material types, and defect shape and size. Moreover, the speed of existing detectors cannot meet the requirements on the present-day industrial intelligence.

Automatic surface defect detection methods fall into two categories: traditional visual detectors and deep learning-based ones. The former mainly use texture features [1, 2], color features [3], and shape features [4]. Such methods are restricted to feature extraction. The manual design and selection of features in traditional detectors make it

L. Iliadis et al. (Eds.): ICANN 2023, LNCS 14255, pp. 90–101, 2023.
https://doi.org/10.1007/978-3-031-44210-0_8

difficult to extend to a wider range of applications. In fact, traditional methods often struggle to handle changes in illumination, angle, or scale in scene images they process. Additionally, noise and interference often degrade the performance of traditional methods.

The deep learning-based defect detections can be further divided into two-stage detection and one-stage detection according to whether a Region Proposal Network (RPN) [5] is used initially. A two-stage detection first uses a region extraction network to find candidate boxes that may contain targets, then uses classifiers and regressors to finally outputs the category and location of the target. In 2014, Girshick et al. [6] proposed R-CNN which laid the foundation for the two-stage detections. R-CNN first generates 2000 candidate regions and performs feature extraction on them, then applies the obtained features to support vector machines (SVM) to determine the category, and finally the regressor finely corrects the position of the candidate regions. However, R-CNN is very time-consuming, and its resizing operation causes image distortion and affect the final result. In 2015, He et al. [7] proposed the SPP-Net to solve the above problems. The whole SPP-Net process, however, is still a multi-stage pipeline, and additional feature maps still need to be saved. Girshick et al. [8] proposed the Fast R-CNN algorithm in 2015. As an improved version of R-CNN, Fast R-CNN introduces VGG16 as the backbone network and separately sets up the Region of Interesting (ROI) pooling layer to solve the problem of weight updating. Shortly thereafter, Ren et al. [9] proposed Faster R-CNN with near-real-time performance,in 2015. They proposed RPN which greatly speed up the detection speed.

In view of the high-speed requirement of steel plate surface defect detection, Ren et al. constructed a lighter Faster R-CNN with depth separable convolution and center loss. Si et al. [10] used Feature pyramid network(FPN) [11] for feature fusion in the feature extraction layer of Faster R-CNN, replaced ROI Pooling with ROI Align in the pooling layer, and used the Softer-NMS connection layer in the final prediction. However, because the two-stage approaches require running two forward passes in the image, it is generally slower than single-stage ones.

A one-stage detection omits the RPN, and instead directly uses a classifier and regressor to classify and return each pixel in the entire image. The representatives are YOLO series and SSD series. In 2016, Redmon et al. [12] proposed YOLO, which considers the entire image as the network input, allowing the classification and regression analysis to be completed at the output layer. From then on, YOLOv2 ~ v5 [13–16] are successively proposed. Regarding steel surface defect detection, Kou et al. proposed an end-to-end strip steel surface defect detection model based on YOLOv3, which utilizes the free frame feature selection mechanism to replace the basic frame structure. S et al. [20] proposed the Attention-YOLOv5 algorithm, which replaces the original feature vector with the filtered weighted feature vector for residual fusion. However, the improved YOLO series algorithms remain inadequate for small target detection, and balancing detection speed and accuracy is challenging, too.

Aiming at detecting defects with high speed and high precision, this paper proposes an improved YOLOv5 model for detecting steel plate surface defects. We first introduce the structural re-parameterizing in RepVGGBlock to the backbone of the model. Structure re-parameterizing uses a high-performance multi-way branch structure during training, and switching to a single-way structure during inference to save time. Then, we apply Coordinate Attention (CA) to the detection neck, which can be improved with almost no computational overhead. Finally, we add an additional small target detection layer for detecting tiny flaws. We evaluate our model on the open-source Northeastern University steel belt surface public dataset and demonstrate better performance than the state-of-the-art models, including YOLOv3, YOLOv4, YOLOv5 and Fast-RCNN.

The rest of this paper is as follows: Sect. 2 introduces the benchmark model YOLOv5 for steel surface flaw detection used in this paper, Sect. 3 describes the proposed model in detail. Section 4 presents the experimental results and analysis, and Sect. 5 gives some Conclusions and future work.

2 Yolov5

YOLOv5 follows the one-stage strategy of the YOLO series, and achieves an efficient end-to-end target detector that takes into account both detection speed and accuracy. According to the depth and width of feature extraction, YOLOv5 expands the four structures of s, m, l, and x to adapt to target detection tasks at different scales. As shown in Fig. 1, YOLOv5 consist of uniformly composed input, backbone, neck, and output layers.

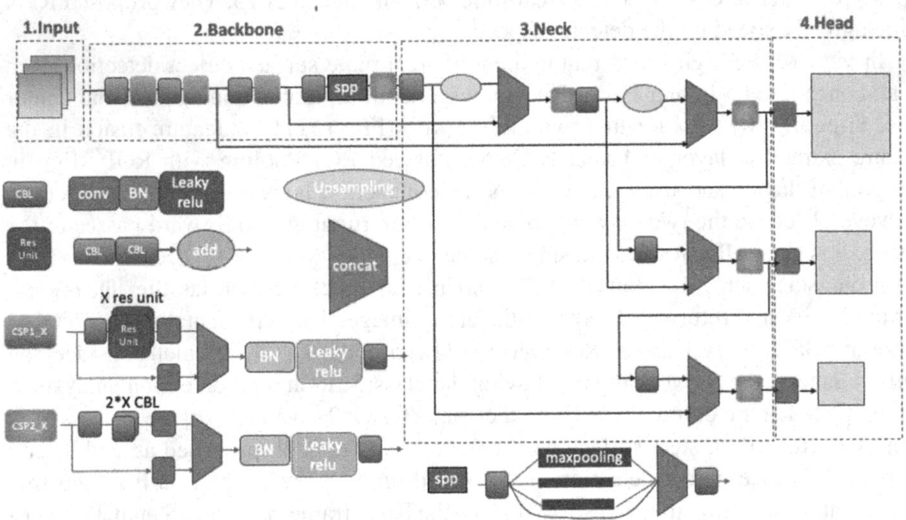

Fig. 1. YOLOv5

The input of Yolov5 employs the Mosaic technique to conduct a series of operations, including scaling and splicing, on the input image. Additionally, Yolov5 adopts the Adaptive Computationally Efficient Anchor Assignment (ACE) method to dynamically generate and adjust anchors for targets of various sizes and aspect ratios. Furthermore, Yolov5 utilizes adaptive scaling to adjust to the image sub-size, thus enhancing the model's robustness and reducing the time overhead of high-resolution image processing.

The backbone of Yolov5 is responsible for feature extraction, and it adopts the CSPNet [18] structure's cross stage partial connection method to connect deep and shallow feature maps. In the neck, Yolov5 employs Feature Pyramid Networks (FPN) to fuse multi-scale feature maps from bottom-up and top-down, and the Path Aggregation Network (PAN) [19] to further fuse multi-scale features.

The output of YOLOv5 adopts the Generalized Intersection over Union (GIoU) loss, which considers the overlap and difference between the predicted bounding box and the ground truth bounding box. As shown in Fig. 2, the Ground truth is denoted as A and the predicted bounding box is denoted as B, GIoU introduces the minimum circumscribed rectangle of the predicted bounding box and the actual bounding box, which is denoted as C. GIoU calculation formula is shown according to Eq. (1)–(2).

$$IoU = \frac{|A \cap B|}{|A \cup B|} \tag{1}$$

$$GIoU = IoU - \frac{|C(A \cup B)|}{C} \tag{2}$$

where | | represents taking the absolute value. Its purpose is to convert the result between the calculated intersection and union into a positive number, ensuring that the final IOU value is non-negative. ∪ is union, ∩ is intersection. *A* is Ground truth and *B* is predicted bounding box, *C* is the minimum circumscribed rectangle.

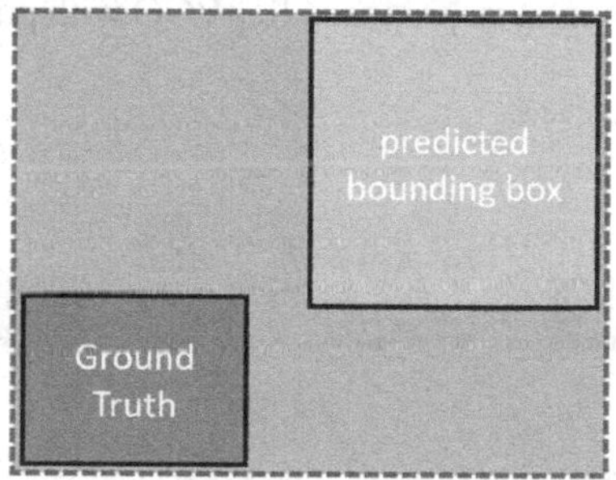

Fig. 2. GIoU

3 Our Improved YOLOv5

Although YOLOv5 has achieved better results than other algorithms in defect detection, there are still many challenges to address in scenarios with high detection speed and limited parameters or in application scenarios with higher detection accuracy and smaller targets. Therefore, as shown in Fig. 3, this paper proposes an improved YOLOv5 First, the backbone of our model is constructed based on the idea of structural re-parameterization in RepVGGBlock [17]. Moreover, the CA is applied to detection head to further enhance the detection accuracy. To well detect small defects, a small target detection branch is also added to the model. Finally, to well train our model, we continue to use the GIoU loss of the original YOLOv5.

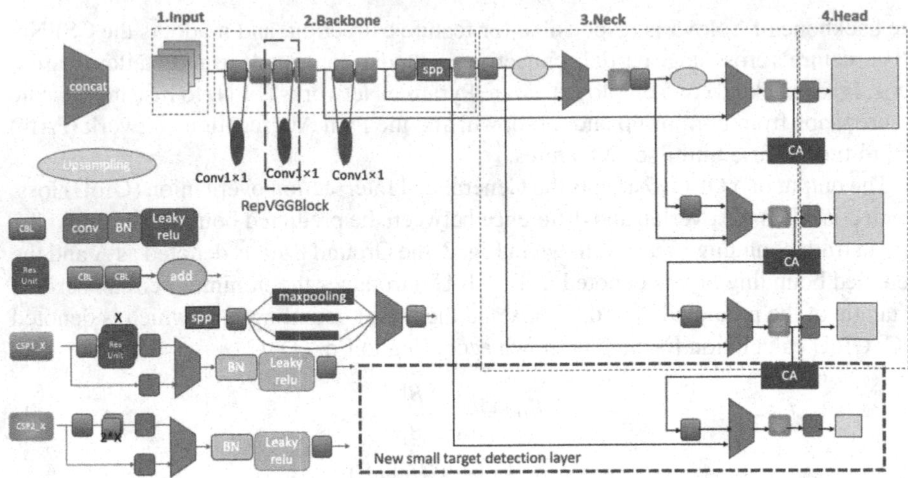

Fig. 3. Our improved YOLOv5

3.1 Structural Re-parameterization in RepVGGBlock

Considering the simple and regular architecture with good interpretability of the RepVGGBlock, we integrate of RepVGGBlock into the backbone network of YOLOv5, as shown in Fig. 3. In 2021, Ding et al. proposed RepVGG with powerful performance and simple structure.

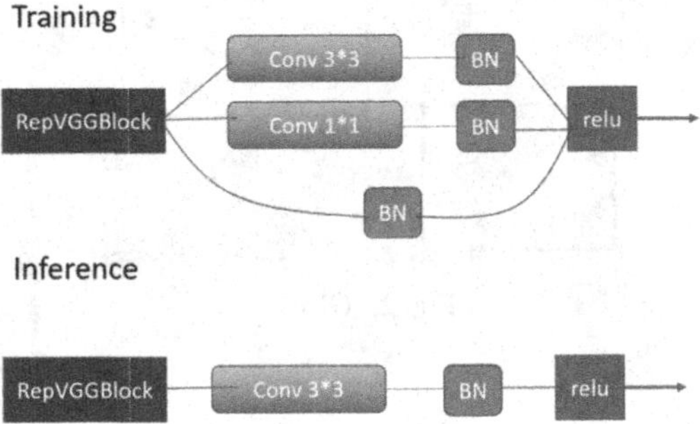

Fig. 4. RepVGGBlock in training and in inference

As shown in Fig. 4, to have the advantages of VGG's fast speed, memory saving and flexibility without affecting the network performance, the RepVGG uses a multi-way branch structure during training to ensure sufficient training and learning features. The basic RepVGGBlock is constructed by adding 1×1 convolution branches and identity maps separately at the parallel positions of each 3×3 convolutional layer. Inference stage is converted to a single-channel structure to reduce the occupation of video memory, resulting its RepVGGBlock contains only 3×3 convolutional layer, BN, and ReLU. The core part of RepVGGBlock is how to convert the multi-channel model into a single-channel model to achieve high performance during inference. As shown in Fig. 4, RepVGGBlock uses convolution and BN (Batch Normalization) multiple times. The two are connected to calculate Result as Eq. (3)–(5):

$$Conv(x) = W(x) + b \tag{3}$$

$$BN(x) = \gamma * \frac{x - mean}{\sqrt{var}} + \beta \tag{4}$$

$$BN(conv(x)) = \gamma^* \frac{W(x) + b - mean}{\sqrt{\text{var}}} + \beta \tag{5}$$

where x is the input variable, W() represents the convolution filter weight learned during training, b is the bias term; BN() is the operation of batch normalization of the input variable, where γ and β are each the optimal scale factor and displacement factor for normalized features; *mean* and *var* are the mean and variance of the current input samples, respectively.

Simplifying the formula further gives:

$$\begin{aligned} BN(conv(x)) &= \frac{\gamma^* W(x)}{\sqrt{var}} + \left(\frac{\gamma^*(b - mean)}{\sqrt{var}} + \beta\right) \\ &= W_{\text{fused}}(x) + B_{\text{fused}} \end{aligned} \tag{6}$$

From the above formula, it can be seen that the operation of convolution and BN serial can be simplified as a new convolution operation.

The fusion between the convolutional layer and the BN layer is completed through the aforementioned calculation steps. Afterward, the resulting fused layer is converted into a 3 × 3 convolutional structure. Regarding the Conv1 × 1 branch, the conversion involves moving the single value in the 1 × 1 convolution kernel to the center point of the 3 × 3 convolution kernel. This replaces the 1 × 1 convolution kernel with the 3 × 3 convolution kernel (Fig. 5 and Table 3).

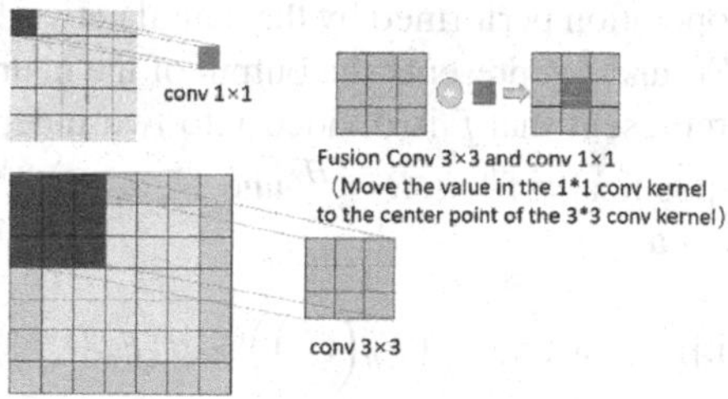

Fig. 5. Convolution fusion

For the BN branch at the bottom, there is no need to modify the value of the input feature map. Therefore, a convolution kernel with a weight value of 1 at 9 positions and a size of 3 × 3 is used to perform an element-wise multiplication with the input feature. This ensures that the original value remains unchanged. Finally, using the principle of convolution, the convolutional layers and biases of the three branches are combined through addition to form the final 3 × 3 convolutional structure.

3.2 Coordinate Attention

This paper proposes the Coordinate Attention (CA) to the detection head for highlighting important features. Hou et al. [21] propose Coordinate Attention in 2021, which embeds location information into the attention mechanism.

Using the condition of input x, the CA output of the c-th channel can be expressed as:

$$z_c = \frac{1}{H \times W} \sum_{i=1}^{H} \sum_{j=1}^{W} x_c(i,j) \tag{7}$$

where $x_c(i,j)$ is the value of the color of channel c at the i-th row and j-column pixel, H and W represent the height and width of the image, respectively.

CA encodes each channel along the horizontal or vertical coordinate using a pooling kernel of size (H, 1) or (1, W), respectively.

$$z_c^h(\mathrm{h}) = \frac{1}{W} \sum_{0 \le \mathrm{i} < W} x_c(\mathrm{h,i}). \tag{8}$$

$$z_c^w(\mathrm{w}) = \frac{1}{H} \sum_{0 \le j < H} x_c(\mathrm{j,w}) \tag{9}$$

Using the formula above, a pair of direction-aware feature maps can be obtained to provide more accurate position encoding information. This operation is known as position embedding. The next step is to generate Coordinate Attention, which involves concatenating the two spatial direction aggregation features and applying a convolutional transformation.

$$f = \delta\left(F_1\left(\left[z^h, z^w\right]\right)\right) \tag{10}$$

where F_1 represents the operation performed by the neural network layer, δ is the activation function acting on F_1, and f represents the output of the neural network layer. The f^{h} and f^{w} respectively represent that f is divided into two independent tensors along the spatial dimension, Specifically $\mathrm{f}^{\mathrm{h}} \in R^{\frac{C}{r} \times H}$ and $\mathrm{f}^{\mathrm{w}} \in R^{\frac{C}{r} \times W}$. Finally, the output through CA can be written as:

$$y_c(\mathrm{i,j}) = x_c(\mathrm{i,j}) \times \sigma\left(F_h\left(\mathrm{f}^h\right)\right) \times \sigma\left(F_w\left(\mathrm{f}^w\right)\right) \tag{11}$$

3.3 Small Target Detection Head

If the input image size is 640 × 640, the original YOLOv5 has a detection feature map size of 80 × 80 corresponding to P3/8, which is used to detect objects with a size above 8 × 8. Accordingly, P4/16 and P5/32 are respectively for objects above 16 × 16 and 32 × 32. However, due to the relatively large down-sampling multiple of YOLOv5, it is difficult to learn feature information for small targets from deep feature maps. As a result, the model often cannot achieve satisfactory results for fine target detection tasks with smaller sizes. To address this issue and capture tiny steel plate defects, we add a small target detection layer to the original three detection heads of YOLOv5. Figure 1 shows the details of the new added head. It has a detection feature map size of 160 × 160, enabling it to detect targets above 4 × 4. It is located in the low-feature layer and has strong position information but weak semantic feature information, making it suitable for small target detection. In our model, each detection head generates three prior frames, and with the addition of the new detection layer, the model generates a total of 12 prior frames.

4 Experiment Configuration and Result Analysis

4.1 Experimental Environment and Dataset

The steel surface defect detection model has been implemented in the Pytorch framework on Ubuntu20.04 with NVIDIA 2080Ti (11G memory), CUDA11, CUDNN6, and i7-8700K.The model was trained using the SGD optimizer with momentum of 0.937 and weight decay of 5e-4.

We utilize the NEU surface defect dataset [22], which contains six typical surface defects of hot-rolled steel strips: rolled-in scale (RS), patches (Pa), crazing (Cr), pitted surface (PS), inclusion (In), and scratches (Sc). For each category there are 300 annotated images with an original resolution of 200 × 200 pixels. The following experiments all use the complete NEU dataset.

The evaluation indicators selected in this paper include the number of model parameters, the mean average precision (mAP), and the number of floating-point operations (Flops) of the model.

4.2 Experimental Process and Results

Firstly, we use YOLOv5s to train on NEU data with a maximum epoch of 500 and use YOLOv5s as the baseline to compare with subsequent experiments. The initial momentum is 0.937 and weight decay is 5e-4. At the same time, set early-stopping to 100. The results in Table 1 shows that the mAP of the YOLOv5s with the small target detection head is significantly higher than that of the original model. Thus, in the following experiments, all test models are appended with the small target detection head, and referred to as YOLOv5h.

Table 1. The influence of the new added head on the model

	mAP/%	Para num/M	Flops/G
YOLOv5s(baseline)	82.1	6.9	16.0
YOLOv5 + new head	83.7	11.7	16.5

Then the RepVGGBlock is respectively added to the neck and the backbone of YOLOv5h. Sepcifically, YOLOv5h_rep_neck, YOLOv5h_rep_backbone, YOLOv5h_rep_all respectively mean to replace the components in neck, backbone, and neck + backbone of YOLOv5h at interval. YOLOv5h_rep_prune means the replacement is done for each component in backbone. Table 2 lists the experimental results from which one can see that the detection accuracy and mAP are not ideal for backbone + neck (all). Therefore, we choose to replacing the backbone components with RepVGGBlock at intervals.

Table 2. Evaluation on the position of RepVGGBlock

	mAP/%	Para num/M	Flops/G
YOLOv5h (baseline)	83.7	11.7	16.5
YOLOv5h_rep_neck	84.1	11.9	15.8
YOLOv5h_rep_all	81.3	12.3	16.9
YOLOv5h_rep_prune	81.1	13.3	16.8
YOLOv5h_rep_backbone	84.3	11.7	15.6

Table 3. Evaluation on different attention strategy

	mAP/%	Para num/M	Flops/G
YOLOv5h + new head (baseline)	83.7	11.7	16.5
YOLOv5h_SE	82.8	11.7	15.6
YOLOv5h_CBAM	83.3	12.3	16.9
YOLOv5h_CA	84.7	11.8	16.4

In this group of experiments, three attention mechanisms of SE [23], CBAM and CA were added to YOLOv5h for comparison. The results show that CA is superior to others.

Finally, we compare our proposed model that combines RepVGGBlock, CA, and an additional detection head to existing detectors. Here, YOLOv5s, YOLOv3, YOLOv4, and Fast R-CNN are chosen for comparison. Table 4 lists the comparison results. Moreover, Fig. 6 shows some visual results. From Table 4, one can see that the speed and parameter quantity of our improved model are significantly better than Fast-RCNN, and the accuracy of the model is also improved compared with YOLO series.

The visual results in Fig. 6 illustrate the performance of several algorithms. From the first column of Fig. 6, we can see that Our_model outperforms others in detecting small and densely packed targets. Moreover, from the second through the fourth columns where the inputs are with significant intra-class differences, we can see that Our_model demonstrates superior performance compared to others.

Table 4. Comparison to existing detectors

	mAP/%	Para num/M	Flops/G
YOLOv5s(baseline)	82.1	6.9	16.0
YOLOv3	80.2	58.6	132.7
YOLOv4	81.3	41.6	96.4
Fast-RCNN	86.1	229.6	232.7
our_model	85.3	12.1	16.8

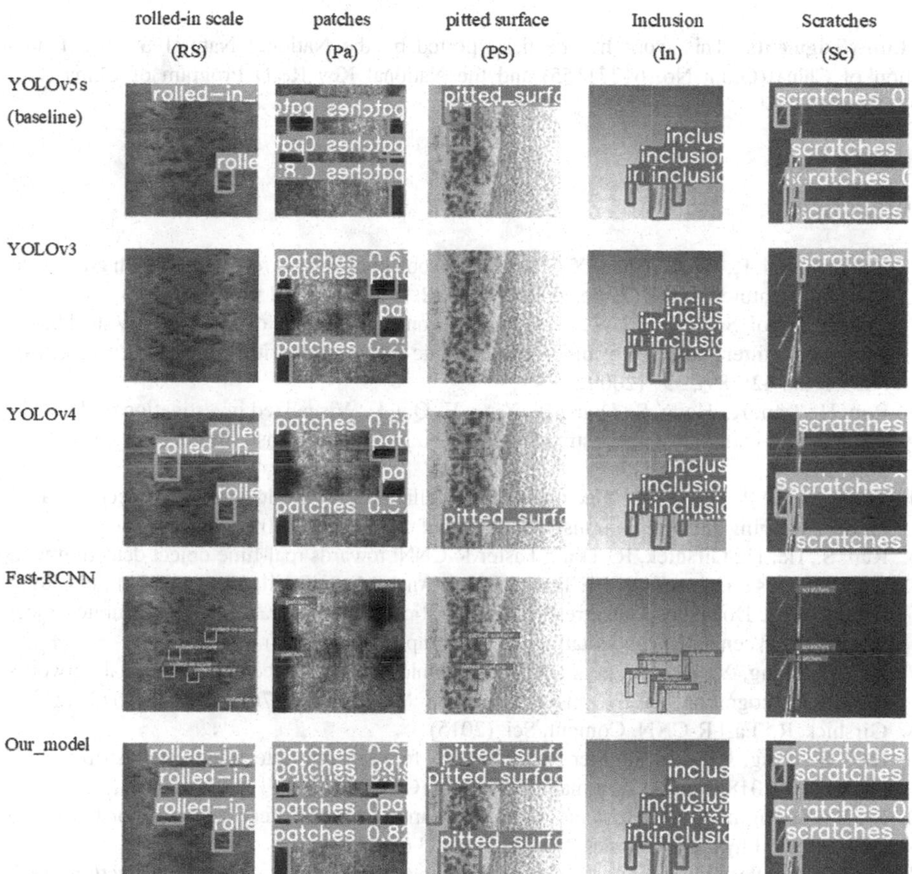

Fig. 6. Experimental results of flaw detection with different algorithms

5 Conclusions and Discussions

Based on the requirements for accuracy and speed in detecting surface defects on steel plates, and the difficulty in detecting small targets, this paper proposes an improved YOLOv5 model that introduces RepVGGBlock. The model applies the idea of structural re-parameterization to ensure speed, and adds a layer for detecting small targets to improve visibility. Additionally, the model utilizes CA to further enhance accuracy. Through experimental comparison, the accuracy and speed of existing target detection algorithms such as YOLOv5 and Fast-RCNN have been improved respectively. Deploying this algorithm for the challenging task of detecting surface defects on steel plates can further improve work efficiency.

Acknowledgments. This work has been supported by the National Natural Science Foundation of China (Grant No. 61771155) and the National Key R&D Program of China (No. 2021YFF0603904).

References

1. Song, X., Bai, F., Wu, J., Chen, X., Zhang, T.: Wood knot defects recognition with gray-scale histogram features. Laser Optoelectron. Prog. **52**, 20503904 (2015)
2. Yun, J.P., Choi, S.H., Kim, J.W., Kim, S.W.: Automatic detection of cracks in raw steel block using Gabor filter optimized by univariate dynamic encoding algorithm for searches (uDEAS). NDT E Int. **42**(389), 397 (2009)
3. Ren, H., Tian, K., Hong, S., Dong, B., Xing, F., Qin, L.: Visualized investigation of defect in cementitious materials with electrical resistance tomography. Constr. Build. Mater. **196**(428), 200 (2019)
4. Wang, J., Fu, P., Gao, R.X.: Machine vision intelligence for product defect inspection based on deep learning and Hough transform. J. Manuf. Syst. **51**, 52–60 (2019)
5. Ren, S., He, K., Girshick, R., et al.: Faster R-CNN: towards real-time object detection with region proposal networks. IEEE Trans. Pattern Anal. Mach. Intell. **39**(6), 1137–1149 (2017)
6. Girshick, R., Donahue, J., Darrell, T., et al.: Rich feature hierarchies for accurate object detection and semantic segmentation. IEEE Comput. Soc. (2014)
7. He, K., Zhang, X., Ren, S., et al.: Spatial pyramid pooling in deep convolutional networks for visual recognition. IEEE Trans. Pattern Anal. Mach. Intell. **37**(9), 1904–1916 (2015)
8. Girshick, R.: Fast R-CNN. Comput. Sci. (2015)
9. Ren, Q., Geng, J., Li, J.: Slighter Faster R-CNN for real-time detection of steel strip surface defects. In: 2018 Chinese AutomationCongress (CAC) 2018
10. Si, B., Yasengjiang, M., Huawen, W.: Deep learning-based defect detection for hot-rolled strip steel. J. Phys. Conf. Series **2246**(1), 012073 (2022)
11. Lin, T.Y., Dollar, P., Girshick, R., et al.: Feature pyramid networks for object detection. IEEE Comput. Soc. (2017). https://doi.org/10.1109/CVPR.2017.106
12. Redmon, J., Divvala, S., Girshick, R., et al.: You only look once: unified, real-time object detection. In: Computer Vision & Pattern Recognition. IEEE (2016)
13. Redmon, J., Farhadi, A.: YOLO9000: better, faster, stronger. In: IEEE Conference on Computer Vision & Pattern Recognition. IEEE, pp. 6517–6525 (2017)
14. Redmon, J., Farhadi, A.: YOLOv3: An Incremental Improvement. arXiv e-prints (2018)
15. Bochkovskiy, A., Wang, C.Y., Liao, H.: YOLOv4: Optimal Speed and Accuracy of Object Detection (2020)

16. Zhu, X., Lyu, S., Wang, X., et al.: TPH-YOLOv5: Improved YOLOv5 Based on Transformer Prediction Head for Object Detection on Drone-captured Scenarios (2021)
17. Woo, S., Park, J., Lee, J.Y., et al.: Cbam: convolutional block attention module. In: Proceedings of the European Conference on Computer Vision (ECCV), pp. 3–19 (2018)
18. Wang, C.Y., Liao, H.Y.M., Wu, Y.H., et al.: CSPNet: a new backbone that can enhance learning capability of CNN. In: 2020 IEEE/CVF Conference on Computer Vision and Pattern Recognition Workshops (CVPRW). IEEE (2020).https://doi.org/10.1109/CVPRW50498.2020.00203
19. Li, H., Xiong, P., An, J., et al.: Pyramid Attention Network for Semantic Segmentation (2018). https://doi.org/10.48550/arXiv.1805.10180
20. Ding, X., Zhang, X., Ma, N., et al.: RepVGG: making VGG-style convnets great again (2021)
21. Hou, Q., Zhou, D., Feng, J.: Coordinate Attention for Efficient Mobile Network Design (2021)
22. He, Y., Song, K., Meng, Q., Yan, Y.: An end-to-end steel surface defect detection approach via fusing multiple hierarchical features. IEEE Trans. Instrum. Meas. **69**(4), 1493–1504 (2020). https://doi.org/10.1109/TIM.2019.2915404
23. Hu, J., Shen, L., et al.: Squeeze-and-Excitation Networks. IEEE transactions on pattern analysis and machine intelligence (2019)

ASP Loss: Adaptive Sample-Level Prioritizing Loss for Mass Segmentation on Whole Mammography Images

Parvaneh Aliniya(✉), Mircea Nicolescu, Monica Nicolescu, and George Bebis

University of Nevada, Reno, NV 89557, USA
aliniya@nevada.unr.edu

Abstract. Alarming statistics on the mortality rate for breast cancer are a clear indicator of the significance of computer vision tasks related to cancer identification. In this study, we focus on mass segmentation, which is a crucial task for cancer identification as it preserves critical properties of the mass, such as shape and size, vital for identification tasks. While achieving promising results, existing approaches are mostly hindered by pixel class imbalance and various mass sizes that are inherent properties of masses in mammography images. We propose to alleviate this limitation on segmentation methods via a novel modification of the common hybrid loss, which is a weighted sum of the cross entropy and dice loss. The proposed loss, termed Adaptive Sample-Level Prioritizing (ASP) loss, leverages the higher-level information presented in the segmentation mask for customizing the loss for every sample, to prioritize the contribution of each loss term accordingly. As one of the variations of U-Net, AU-Net is selected as the baseline approach for the evaluation of the proposed loss. The ASP loss could be integrated with other existing mass segmentation approaches to enhance their performance by providing them with the ability to address the problems associated with the pixel class imbalance and diverse mass sizes specific to the domain of breast mass segmentation. We tested our method on two publicly available datasets, INbreast and CBIS-DDSM. The results of our experiments show a significant boost in the performance of the baseline method while outperforming state-of-the-art mass segmentation methods.

1 Introduction

Despite the significant progress in breast cancer screening in recent decades, breast cancer has been continuously one of the cancer types with the highest mortality rate among women [1]. Automated breast cancer detection could alleviate this problem in different ways - for example, when used to reduce the cost of a second reader [2,3], especially when developed for mammography input images, which are some of the most common screening tools with reported effectiveness in reducing mortality rate [4].

L. Iliadis et al. (Eds.): ICANN 2023, LNCS 14255, pp. 102–114, 2023.
https://doi.org/10.1007/978-3-031-44210-0_9

Recently there has been a significant increase in the accuracy of identifying different abnormalities in breast tissues, thanks to deploying and tailoring deep learning approaches for each task in this domain. However, the performance of these methods is restricted by one inherent data-specific challenge for the majority of approaches on the whole mammogram: pixel class imbalance in which one class is underrepresented [5]. This limitation, coupled with various sizes of masses constrains the performance of existing methods. In light of this, we propose customizing the hybrid loss function for each sample through the Adaptive Sample-Level Prioritizing (ASP) loss, which significantly outperforms the common setting for the hybrid loss used in the existing mass segmentation methods.

The ASP losses proposed in this paper are composed of two losses: cross entropy and dice losses [5]. Instead of fixed weights [6,7] for the loss terms, we propose to use the ratio of the mass to the image size as an indicator of the severity of pixel class imbalance and a differentiating factor for various mass sizes. This allows for balancing the contribution of each loss with respect to each sample. To achieve this goal, we propose three strategies for prioritizing one of the loss terms over another adaptively, based on the ratio of the mass, which is a relevant feature of each sample to the weighting of the loss terms.

In the first variation, we explore the idea of a quantile-based strategy that accentuates the contribution of one loss over the other based on the quantile to which the sample belongs. To take the distribution of the samples based on the ratio into consideration while prioritizing the loss terms, a second strategy is a cluster-based prioritizing approach which focuses on the proximity of the samples rather than the quantities for grouping. Lastly, we explore the idea of parameterizing the ASP loss based on learning the mapping from the real segmentation for each sample to weights for loss terms without explicitly incorporating the ratio into the ASP. The ASP losses have been tested on two benchmark datasets: INbreast [8], and CBIS-DDSM [9]. As the baseline method, AU-Net[6], which is a variation of U-Net [10] has been chosen. The results of our experiments illustrate that ASP has a significant effect on the performance of the method.

The contributions of this paper are the following:

- Proposing an adaptive sample-level prioritizing (ASP) loss function for mass segmentation on whole mammograms.
- Developing three different prioritizing strategies for the proposed ASP loss: quantile-based, cluster-based, and learning-based priority.
- Evaluating the proposed method with all its variations on two benchmark datasets, INbreast and CBIS-DDSM.
- Quantitatively analyzing and comparing the findings from our experimental results for the proposed method with state-of-the-art approaches.

In the following, first, the related work is presented, then the proposed method is delineated in detail, and finally, our experimental results (including the ablation study and the comparison with state-of-the-art methods) are analyzed from various perspectives.

2 Related Work

Recently, deep learning-based approaches have shown great promise in abnormality identification in medical images. In this section, we provide a brief review of related work in deep learning-based approaches for breast mass segmentation, categorized into two groups related to this study: breast mass segmentation on whole mammograms and loss functions mainly for binary segmentation.

2.1 Mass Segmentation on Whole Mammograms

In general, the input for breast mass segmentation methods could be categorized into two groups: region of interest (RoI), and whole mammograms. Approaches proposed for RoIs [11] have different challenges and strategies to address them compared to methods using whole mammogram images [6,7]. For instance, the severity of the pixel class imbalance and diverse mass sizes is less significant in RoIs. Therefore, we focus on the approaches using the whole mammogram.

Inspired by [12], which is among the pioneer deep learning-based approaches for semantic segmentation, U-Net [10] proposes a fully convolutional symmetric encoder-decoder architecture that is specifically useful for segmentation tasks with limited data. U-Net combines high-level semantic information from the decoder path with low-level location information from the encoder. [13] proposes a similar encoder-decoder architecture (with Dense Blocks), in which the authors introduced multiscale information to the network by leveraging the idea of using the results of atrous convolution [14] with various sample rates for the last encoder block, to enhance the performance of the segmentation network without additional parameters. [15] is another U-Net-based approach that uses a densely-connected network in the encoder, and for the decoder, CNN is used with attention gates. Another multi-scale approach is [16], where an adversarial framework incorporates the idea of using multiple networks for different scales for the discriminator, and an improved version of U-Net is used for segmentation (generator). In [17], the authors use the output error of intermediate layers in comparison with the ground truth labels as a supervision signal.

In [6], authors proposed an attention-guided dense-up-sampling asymmetric encoder-decoder network that has an intermediate up-sampling block with a channel-wise attention mechanism designed to use the useful information presented in both low and high-level features. With the goal of addressing the low performance of the U-Net on small-size masses, [7] proposes using a selective receptive field module which has two parts, one for generating several receptive fields with different sizes and one for selecting the appropriate size of the receptive fields. Our work is closely related to [6] and [7].

2.2 Loss for Segmentation in Medical Imaging

As the mathematical representation of the objective of a deep learning-based approach, the loss function has a significant impact on the performance of the method. Hence the choice of a loss function capable of appropriately reflecting the objective will lead to a large boost in the learning of the network in the segmentation task. This section aims to provide a concise summary of related loss functions for segmentation, specifically for medical imaging.

Binary Cross Entropy (BCE) [18] for the segmentation task (Eq. 1) is defined as the classification of pixels to the positive (foreground) and negative (background) classes. Weighted Binary Cross Entropy [19] and Balanced Cross Entropy [20] are variants of BCE that differentiate between the effect of false positive and false negative factors. The focal loss [21] could be considered as another variation of BCE in which the magnitude of the loss changes according to the hardness of the example based on the confidence of the model in false prediction. Dice loss is a commonly used loss function in the presence of pixel class imbalance [22], which is the ratio of the number of correctly classified pixels to the total number of real and predicted positive pixels (Eq. 2). Tversky loss [23] aims to accentuate the contribution of the false positive and the false negative terms in the dice loss via weighting these terms.

Combo loss [24] combines the dice and modified BCE in which the contribution of false positive and false negative has been controlled via a weighting strategy. Various compound losses have been proposed [21,23,24] to use the benefits of different losses. For instance, in the Combo loss [24], dice loss is beneficial for handling pixel class imbalance problems and the BCE for smoother training. Our proposed method is similar to this category in terms of using dice and BCE losses but differs in terms of the weighting strategy, in which the ratio of the positive class has been utilized as a weighting strategy between two loss terms. In addition, instead of directly using the ratio, we use it for grouping samples.

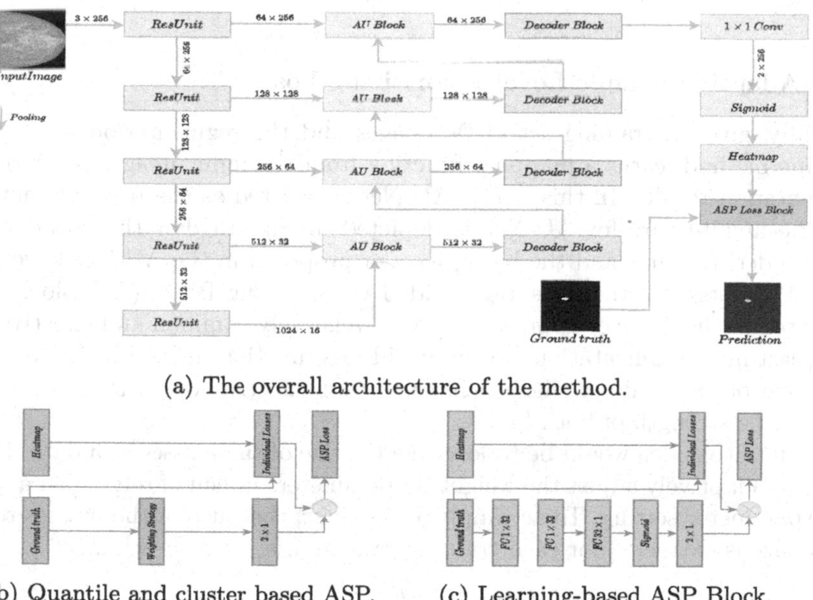

(a) The overall architecture of the method.

(b) Quantile and cluster based ASP. (c) Learning-based ASP Block.

Fig. 1. An overview of the proposed method.

3 Methodology

In this section, first, we provide an overview of hybrid loss which is one of the common loss functions for mass segmentation methods with mammography input type. The hybrid loss is defined as a weighted sum of BCE and dice loss, which are defined as follows:

$$L_{BCE} = -\Big(ylog(\hat{y}) + (1-y)log(1-\hat{y})\Big) \tag{1}$$

$$L_{Dice} = 1 - \frac{\sum_{j=1}^{H\times W} \hat{y}_j y_j + \epsilon}{\sum_{j=1}^{H\times W} \hat{y}_j + \sum_{j=1}^{H\times W} y_j + \epsilon} \tag{2}$$

$$L_H = \alpha L_{Dice} + \beta L_{BCE} \tag{3}$$

Here y and $\hat{y}$ are the ground truth and the predicted segmentation maps. α and β are the weighting parameters in the hybrid loss denoted as L_H in Eq. 3. While the BCE loss (Eq. 1) is defined to incorporate notions of false positive and negative in the learning process, dice loss (Eq. 2) specifically captures correctly classified, positive classes. Due to the pixel class imbalance problem, the combination (Eq. 3) of the two losses will provide a better learning signal. In addition, the BCE helps mitigate the unstable training of the dice loss when used alone [21,22]. While improving performance compared to using only one of them, we speculate that a constant weighting strategy for all the samples, regardless of the severity of the pixel class imbalance problem and mass size specific to each sample, restricts the performance of the hybrid loss (Eq. 3). We propose to incorporate the sample-specific signal for the hybrid loss weighting strategy.

3.1 Adaptive Sample-Level Prioritizing Loss

Formally, given a training set of N images and the segmentation masks, the baseline method learns a mapping function from the input images to predicted segmentation results. In this study, AU-Net is selected as the baseline method, and the architecture for AU-Net is depicted in Fig. 1a. For the encoder and the decoder, ResUnit and the basic decoder proposed in the AU-Net have been used. The details of the Attention-guided Up-sampling Block (AU Block) are presented in the AU-Net approach [6]. One relatively common and effective loss for breast mass segmentation is the hybrid loss function defined in Eq. 3. However, one of the main challenges is to use an effective weighting strategy to capture the strength of both losses.

An intuitive idea would be to leverage the size of the masses as a data-driven signal to adaptively adjust the weighting parameters in lieu of relying on a static hyperparameter setting. To accomplish this, first, the ratio of the masses to the image size is extracted for each training sample in a set $R = \{r^1, ..., r^N\}$.

$$r^i = \frac{\sum_{j=1}^{H\times W} y_j^i}{H \times W} \tag{4}$$

Here y is the ground truth label of the jth pixel in the ith sample. Now, the primary question is how to integrate this supplementary piece of information into the weighting scheme of the two loss functions. Based on the definition of BCE and the dice loss, the BCE is more favorable for larger mass sizes (as the size of the image is incorporated in the loss, BCE might penalize the mismatch between prediction and ground truth of the smaller masses less), while the dice loss is better suited for smaller masses. Therefore, we explore the idea of utilizing the correlation between mass size and loss type to define the weights for each loss term as defined in Eq. 5.

$$L^i_{ASP} = (I_{Dice} + (1 - p^i)\gamma)L^i_{Dice} + (I_{BCE} + (p^i)\gamma)L^i_{BCE} \tag{5}$$

Here I_{Dice} and I_{BCE} are the initial weights of each loss term, and γ and p are the magnitude parameter and prioritizing variable for the ASP loss. While p selects the more relevant loss term to prioritize for the ith sample, γ controls the amount of the effect of the loss term, which could be constant or sample-based. Also, γ could be different for both loss terms. It should be noted that I_{Dice} and I_{BCE} could correspond to α and β in the traditional weighting presented in Eq. 3. In addition, index i in Eq. 5 indicates that the proposed loss is a sample-level loss compared to the static loss in Eq. 3. There are various ways to define p, which is the main component of ASP loss. We explore three different variations.

Quantile-based Strategy. One basic idea would be to use the quantile of the values in R to divide the samples into two groups to prioritize different loss terms, as defined in Eq. 6:

$$p^i_Q = \begin{cases} 0 & r^i < Q_2 \\ 1 & \text{Otherwise} \end{cases} \tag{6}$$

Here Q_2 is the median of R and p^i_Q is the prioritizing variable for the ith sample using the quantile-based approach. It should be noted that the other quantiles could be used. The number of samples in the two groups will be equal.

Cluster-based Strategy. Due to the pixel class imbalance problem, as the distribution of the mass sizes is skewed toward smaller masses, the group with mass sizes above the median (in the second quantile) will still have diverse mass sizes. To alleviate this problem, K-means clustering with two centers has been used to cluster the masses based on the relative ratios, providing a more meaningful (in terms of relation with the mass size) division of the samples for the ASP loss. The definition of the cluster-based prioritizing variable is given in Eq. 7:

$$p^i_C = \begin{cases} 0 & r^i \in C_s \\ 1 & \text{Otherwise} \end{cases} \tag{7}$$

Here C_s is the center of the cluster for the smaller masses, and p_C^i denotes the prioritizing variable of the ASP loss using the cluster-based approach. Both quantile and cluster based strategies are defined in the way that they use the ratio as a guiding signal for learning. The ASP loss diagram for quantile and cluster based prioritizing variables has been shown in Fig. 1b.

Learning-based Strategy. In the last prioritizing strategy, the network learns the weights for the loss terms through the learning process. The ASP weight learning module is depicted in Fig. 1c and formulated in Eq. 8. This module (denoted as f in Eq. 8) takes the network prediction and the ground truth segmentation mask as inputs and generates the weights for the ASP loss. f consists of one convolution layer, two fully connected layers, and a sigmoid activation function. The indexes of 1 and 2 in the learning-based ASP loss (Eq. 8) indicate the output index as the output is a 2×1 matrix. The motivation behind the learning-based prioritizing strategy is to let the network learn the connection between the segmentation masks and the loss terms, which could capture different connections beyond the mass ratio.

$$L_{ASP}^i = f(y, w)_1 L_{Dice}^i + f(y, w)_2 L_{BCE}^i \tag{8}$$

Here w is the parameters matix for the ASP loss in Fig. 1c. In this study, AU-Net, as a new and broadly used variation of U-Net, has been chosen as the baseline architecture.

4 Experimental Results

Our findings on the two benchmark datasets suggest that the ASP strategies are effective in improving performance specifically for the varying size of the masses and handle the pixel class imbalance better than previous state-of-the-art methods, which is shown by boosted detection of highly imbalanced and diverse mass sizes. This section provides an overview of the selected datasets for evaluating the proposed method, along with definitions of evaluation metrics. Next, our findings through ablation studies and comparisons with previous state-the-art-methods are presented and analyzed in the following sections.

4.1 Datasets

For both datasets, images have been resized to 256×256 pixels. No data augmentation or pre-training was used. The validation set was utilized to prevent overfitting by hyperparameter tuning for the number of epochs. The number of epochs is set to a value between 170 and 240, and the batch size is four based on the setting of the baseline method. The learning rate is initially set to 10-e4, and the step decay policy with a decay factor of 0.5 has been used for experiments conducted on both datasets.

INbreast Dataset. A group of 150 cases with a total number of 410 images (some of the cases have several images for different views and follow-ups) are used in the INbreast dataset. 107 of the images containing masses have been used in this study. Image enhancement was not used for the INbreast dataset. For the validation, 5-fold cross-validation is used with the random division of 80%, 10%, and 10% for train, validation, and test sets, respectively.

CBIS-DDSM Dataset. CBIS-DDSM has a total of 1944 cases, 1591 of which contain masses. The standard split for train and test (1231 and 360 images for train and test sets, respectively) is used in this study. For the validation set 10% of the training set is randomly sampled. Before using the samples in CBIS-DDSM, the artifacts were removed, and images were cropped and resized.

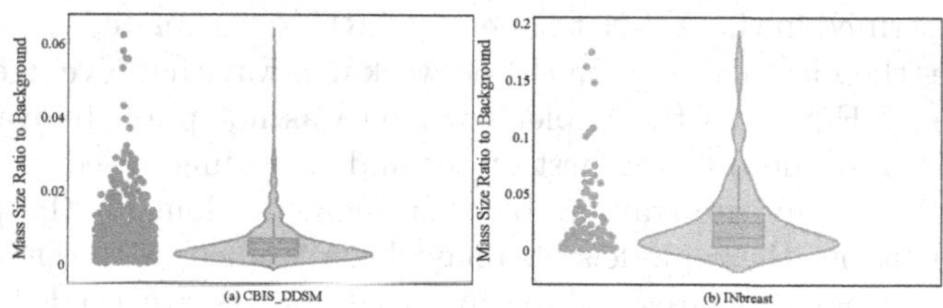

Fig. 2. Plots for the CBIS-DDSM (a) and INbreast (b) based on the mass ratio.

4.2 Evaluation Metrics

For evaluating the performance of the proposed method for mass segmentation, the Dice Similarity Coefficient (DSC), Relative Area Difference ΔA, Sensitivity, and Accuracy have been selected due to the complementary information that they provide. For the breast mass segmentation task, as the masses occupy a trivial portion of the image, using accuracy solely would not reflect the performance of the methods accurately. Hence, including metrics such as sensitivity, DSC, and ΔA will be helpful. sensitivity captures the percentage of the positive class in the ground truth that has been correctly predicted. DSC measures the ratio of the correctly predicted positive pixels over the number of positive areas in both ground truth and the prediction mask and considers the false positive rate in the calculations. ΔA measures the difference in the sizes of the actual and predicted masses (a smaller value for ΔA indicates closer sizes for masses).

4.3 Comparison of Dataset Characteristics

In this section, to analyze the difference in the mass ratios between the two datasets, the distributions of masses have been depicted in Fig. 2 using violin plots which are a combination of box and kernel density plots to capture both summary of statistics and the density of the variables. The length of the line above the box shows 4th quartile, the length of the box represents interquartile (2th *and* 3th quartiles), and the length of the line below the box represents the 1th quartile. The dashed line inside the box is the mean, and the solid line is the median. At one glance, it is clear that the CBIS-DDSM (Fig. 2a) has a smaller range compared to the INbreast dataset (Fig. 2b). Also, the length of the interquartile range is smaller for the CBIS-DDSM dataset, indicating less diversity in the ratio for the majority of the masses. Also, closer mean and median in the CBIS-DDSM dataset suggest less skewed data.

4.4 Comparison with State-of-the-Art Methods

For comparison purposes, two state-of-the-art methods, AU-Net (baseline) and ARF-Net have been selected. We used the official implementation of AU-Net, and the setting described in the AU-Net paper [6]. ARF-Net is related to our study as it incorporates the idea of designing the network in a way that leverages different sizes. For the ARF-Net, as the implementation was not publicly available, the method was implemented to the best of our understanding based on the paper. As we did not use any pre-training or data augmentation, for the purpose of a better comparison, these models also have been trained in the same manner. For the quantile-based strategy, three hyperparameters are needed. For I_{Dice} and I_{BCE}, 0.125 and 0.25 have been selected in this study for INbreast and CBIS-DDSM, respectively. For γ, a value between [0.25, 0,35] has been used with different values for dice and BCE terms. For the cluster-based strategy, the number of centers is a hyperparameter, for which 2 was selected. These hyperparameters have been selected experimentally.

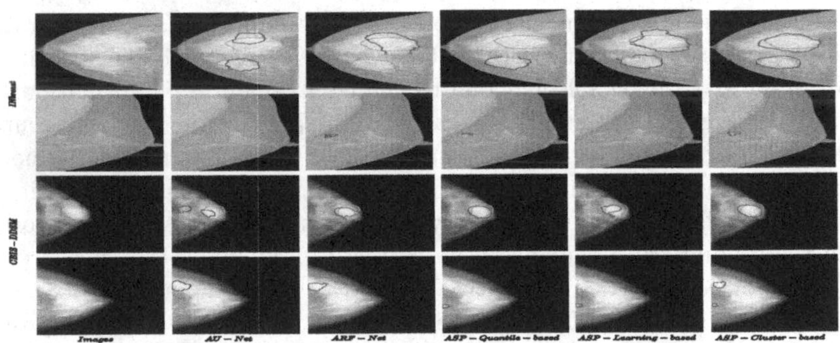

Fig. 3. Results for ASP, AU-Net, and ARF-Net approaches.

Experimental Results for INbreast Dataset. The results of the experiments of the trained model on INbreast are presented in Table 1. As shown in bold, the best results have been achieved by the proposed method. While showing a variety in the results for different prioritizing strategies in the ASP loss, all of them improved on the AU-Net (baseline) method and surpassed the ARF-Net. The largest improvement has been achieved using the cluster-based prioritizing strategy for the ASP loss (DSC: +8.86%, ΔA: −4.4%, Sensitivity: +9.26%, Accuracy:+0.32%), which is consistent and significant across all metrics. We attribute this to the fact that the cluster-based approach captures the distribution of the data in terms of the ratio better than other strategies. As shown in Fig. 2b, the smaller ratios are mostly in the same area in the interquartile range, and bigger ratios are at different ranges. This makes the cluster-based approach more appropriate for grouping the data as it represents the real distribution more accurately compared to the quantile-based approach, which uses the median as a factor of division. As for one of the groups (values above the median), there are a variety of sizes, from small sizes to larger ones. Some of the small masses will prioritize the loss terms in the same manner as the larger masses. We believe this might contribute to the smaller improvement in the quantile-based approach for the INbreast dataset.

The performance of the learning-based strategy is also superior compared to previous approaches. It confirms the idea that a learning-based strategy captures relevant properties of the mass in the ground truth for weighting the losses. Figure 3 shows that the learning-based ASP has superior performance in most of the cases compared to the previous methods.

Table 1. Comparison of ASP with state-of-the-art approaches for INbreast.

Method	DSC	ΔA	Sensitivity	Accuracy
ARF-Net	70.05	30.37	59.59	98.71
AU-Net	65.32	23.68	57.95	98.46
ASP-Quantile-based	68.03	25.04	63.12	98.54
ASP-Learning-based	71.92	22.31	64.56	98.71
ASP-Cluster-based	**74.18**	**19.28**	**67.21**	**98.78**

Figure 3 (first two rows) shows the results for some images in the test set for all ASP versions, AU-Net, and ARF-Net for INbreast dataset. The examples have been selected in such a way that they cover different sizes to showcase the prediction power of the methods on both types of masses according to the mass ratio. The green lines are the contours of the ground truth masks, and the blue lines are the contours of the prediction masks. As shown, all ASP variations predict masses in both sizes better than state-of-the-art methods. For masses with large sizes (larger ratio), the cluster-based and learning-based strategies outperform AU-Net and ARF-Net clearly, and the cluster-based approach has a more accurate contour. The quantile-based method has comparable performance. This might stem from the aforementioned argument that based on the distribution of the data in INbreast, the quantile-based approach does not capture the differences thoroughly like the cluster-based approach, which is the variation with the best overall performance. For the small ratio, the quantile-based and cluster-based methods have better performance compared to previous techniques.

Table 2. Comparison of ASP with state-of-the-art approaches for CBIS-DDSM.

Method	DSC	ΔA	Sensitivity	Accuracy
ARF-Net	48.82	11.47	47.27	99.43
AU-Net	49.05	09.94	51.49	99.38
ASP-Quantile-based	**51.48**	**02.05**	**52.00**	99.43
ASP-Learning-based	51.33	23.17	45.38	**99.50**
ASP-Cluster-based	51.04	04.47	49.90	99.45

Experimental Results for CBIS-DDSM Dataset. The ASP loss also has superior performance on the CBIS-DDSM dataset compared to AU-Net and ARF-Net approaches presented in Table 2. Quantile-based ASP has the best performance on CBIS-DDSM, which is different from the results in the INbreast dataset. We speculate that the reason stems from the difference between the distribution in the two datasets as CBIS-DDSM is less skewed regarding the ratios. While cluster-based ASP divides the data for INbreast better compared to quantile-based ASP, for the CBIS-DDSM dataset, as the data is mostly concentrated in the smaller mass size, the cluster-based strategy will place most of the data in one cluster. Therefore, the weighting strategy will not capture the differences accurately. On the other hand, quantile-based has a better data division as it uses the median. Even though there will be a range of small to large size masses in the second group, but as a small portion of the samples corresponds to large ratios, most of the samples will be weighted correctly compared to the cluster-based strategy, in which a large portion of the samples are in the same group which diminishes the effect of grouping. Figure 3 (last two rows) shows that all three ASP strategies have better performance on both large and small mass sizes when compared to the previous methods. Specifically, the quantile-based approach has the most accurate contours when compared to the two other variations and previous methods.

5 Conclusion

In this study, in order to use available additional information in the segmentation mask for mass segmentation in whole-view mammography images, we propose to modify the hybrid loss weighting strategy adaptively based on the mass size in each sample. Prioritizing loss terms in hybrid loss based on the property of the masses (size) in the sample-level is the main novel contribution of our work. Three different variations of the ASP loss based on different weighting strategies have been proposed in this study. The quantile-based strategy aims to group the data based on size while maintaining the same number of samples in both groups. The cluster-based approach takes the distribution of the data into consideration while dividing the data into groups. Finally, the learning-based strategy learns the prioritizing weights during the training process, so that in the beginning it is random, and during training, it will learn the appropriate weights, based on the segmentation mask. The main idea for this strategy is to generate the weights nonlinearly according to the segmentation mask, which will incorporate more information into the learning of the weights. Our experimental results demonstrate a substantial improvement based on commonly used evaluation metrics on benchmark datasets: INbreast and CBIS-DDSM.

References

1. Siegel, R.L., Miller, K.D., Fuchs, H.E., Jemal, A.: Cancer statistics, 2022. CA: Can. J. Clin. **72**(1), 7–33 (2022)
2. Batchu, S., Liu, F., Amireh, A., Waller, J., Umair, M.: A review of applications of machine learning in mammography and future challenges. Oncology **99**(8), 483–490 (2021)
3. McKinney, S.M., et al.: International evaluation of an AI system for breast cancer screening. Nature **577**(7788), 89–94 (2020)
4. Nyström, L., Andersson, I., Bjurstam, N., Frisell, J., Nordenskjöld, B., Rutqvist, L.E.: Long-term effects of mammography screening: updated overview of the Swedish randomised trials. Lancet **359**(9310), 909–919 (2002)
5. Malof, J.M., Mazurowski, M.A., Tourassi, G.D.: The effect of class imbalance on case selection for case-based classifiers: an empirical study in the context of medical decision support. Neural Netw. **25**, 141–145 (2012)
6. Sun, H., et al.: AUNet: attention-guided dense-upsampling networks for breast mass segmentation in whole mammograms. Phys. Med. Biol. **65**(5), 055005 (2020)
7. Xu, C., Qi, Y., Wang, Y., Lou, M., Pi, J., Ma, Y.: ARF-net: an adaptive receptive field network for breast mass segmentation in whole mammograms and ultrasound images. Biomed. Sig. Process. Control **71**, 103178 (2022)
8. Moreira, I.C., Amaral, I., Domingues, I., Cardoso, A., Cardoso, M.J., Cardoso, J.S.: Inbreast: toward a full-field digital mammographic database. Acad. Radiol. **19**(2), 236–248 (2012)
9. Lee, R.S., Gimenez, F., Hoogi, A., Miyake, K.K., Gorovoy, M., Rubin, D.L.: A curated mammography data set for use in computer-aided detection and diagnosis research. Sci. Data **4**(1), 1–9 (2017)
10. Ronneberger, O., Fischer, P., Brox, T.: U-net: convolutional networks for biomedical image segmentation. In: Navab, N., Hornegger, J., Wells, W.M., Frangi, A.F. (eds.) MICCAI 2015. LNCS, vol. 9351, pp. 234–241. Springer, Cham (2015). https://doi.org/10.1007/978-3-319-24574-4_28
11. Baccouche, A., Garcia-Zapirain, B., Castillo Olea, C., Elmaghraby, A.S.: Connected-UNets: a deep learning architecture for breast mass segmentation. NPJ Breast Cancer **7**(1), 151 (2021)

12. Long, J., Shelhamer, E., Darrell, T.: Fully convolutional networks for semantic segmentation. In: Proceedings of the IEEE Conference on Computer Vision and Pattern Recognition, pp. 3431–3440 (2015)
13. Hai, J., et al.: Fully convolutional densenet with multiscale context for automated breast tumor segmentation. J. Healthc. Eng. **2019** (2019). Hindawi
14. Chen, L.C., Papandreou, G., Kokkinos, I., Murphy, K., Yuille, A.L.: Deeplab: semantic image segmentation with deep convolutional nets, atrous convolution, and fully connected CRFs. IEEE Trans. Pattern Anal. Mach. Intell. **40**(4), 834–848 (2017)
15. Li, S., Dong, M., Du, G., Mu, X.: Attention dense-u-net for automatic breast mass segmentation in digital mammogram. IEEE Access **7**, 59037–59047 (2019)
16. Chen, J., Chen, L., Wang, S., Chen, P.: A novel multi-scale adversarial networks for precise segmentation of x-ray breast mass. IEEE Access **8**, 103772–103781 (2020)
17. Rajalakshmi, N.R., Vidhyapriya, R., Elango, N., Ramesh, N.: Deeply supervised u-net for mass segmentation in digital mammograms. Int. J. Imaging Syst. Technol. **31**(1), 59–71 (2021)
18. Yi-de, M., Qing, L., Zhi-Bai, Q.: Automated image segmentation using improved PCNN model based on cross-entropy. In: Proceedings of International Symposium on Intelligent Multimedia, Video and Speech Processing, pp. 743–746. IEEE (2004)
19. Pihur, V., Datta, S., Datta, S.: Weighted rank aggregation of cluster validation measures: a monte carlo cross-entropy approach. Bioinformatics **23**, 1607–1615 (2007)
20. Xie, S., Tu, Z.: Holistically-nested edge detection. In: Proceedings of the IEEE International Conference on Computer Vision, pp. 1395–1403 (2015)
21. Yeung, M., Sala, E., Schönlieb, C.B., Rundo, L.: Unified focal loss: generalising dice and cross entropy-based losses to handle class imbalanced medical image segmentation. Comput. Med. Imaging Graph. **95**, 102026 (2022)
22. Jadon, S.: A survey of loss functions for semantic segmentation. In: 2020 IEEE Conference on Computational Intelligence in Bioinformatics and Computational Biology (CIBCB), pp. 1–7. IEEE (2020)
23. Salehi, S.S.M., Erdogmus, D., Gholipour, A.: Tversky loss function for image segmentation using 3D fully convolutional deep networks. In: Wang, Q., Shi, Y., Suk, H.-I., Suzuki, K. (eds.) MLMI 2017. LNCS, vol. 10541, pp. 379–387. Springer, Cham (2017). https://doi.org/10.1007/978-3-319-67389-9_44
24. Taghanaki, S.A., et al.: Combo loss: handling input and output imbalance in multi-organ segmentation. Comput. Med. Imaging Graph. **75**, 24–33 (2019)

Cascaded Network-Based Single-View Bird 3D Reconstruction

Pei Su[1], Qijun Zhao[1,3](✉), Fan Pan[2], and Fei Gao[3]

[1] College of Computer Science, Sichuan University, Chengdu, China
{supei,qjzhao}@stu.scu.edu.cn
[2] College of Electronics and Information Engineering, Sichuan University, Chengdu, China
[3] School of Information Science and Technology, Tibet University, Lhasa, China

Abstract. Existing single-view bird 3D reconstruction methods mostly cannot well recover the local geometry such as feet and wing tips, and the resulting 3D models often appear to have poor appearance when viewed from a new perspective. We thus propose a new method that requires only images and their silhouettes to accurately predict the shape of birds, as well as to obtain reasonable appearance in new perspectives. The key to the method lies in the introduction of a cascaded structure in the shape reconstruction network. This allows for the gradual generation of the 3D shape of birds from coarse to fine, enabling better capturing of local geometric features. Meanwhile, we recover the texture, lighting and camera pose with attention-enhanced encoders. To further improve the plausibility of the reconstructed 3D bird in novel views, we introduce the Multi-view Cycle Consistency loss to train the proposed method. We compare our method with state-of-the-art methods and demonstrate its superiority both qualitatively and quantitatively.

Keywords: 3D birds reconstruction · cascaded network · attention mechanism · cycle consistency

1 Introduction

Birds play a significant ecological role in the natural world and are crucial for maintaining ecological balance and the health of ecosystems. Single-view bird three-dimensional (3D) reconstruction can provide valuable information about the 3D structure of birds in the real world, which can help researchers study bird behavior. For example, by reconstructing key parts of birds such as the head, wings, and legs, researchers can analyze posture, motion trajectory, and flight speed under different behavioral states, gaining a deeper understanding of bird behavior patterns, ecological roles, and adaptability. However, single-view bird 3D reconstruction is a formidable task in computer vision. Unlike humans who can effortlessly infer object shapes from a single view, even when objects are partially obscured or invisible, computers face significant challenges in performing

L. Iliadis et al. (Eds.): ICANN 2023, LNCS 14255, pp. 115–127, 2023.
https://doi.org/10.1007/978-3-031-44210-0_10

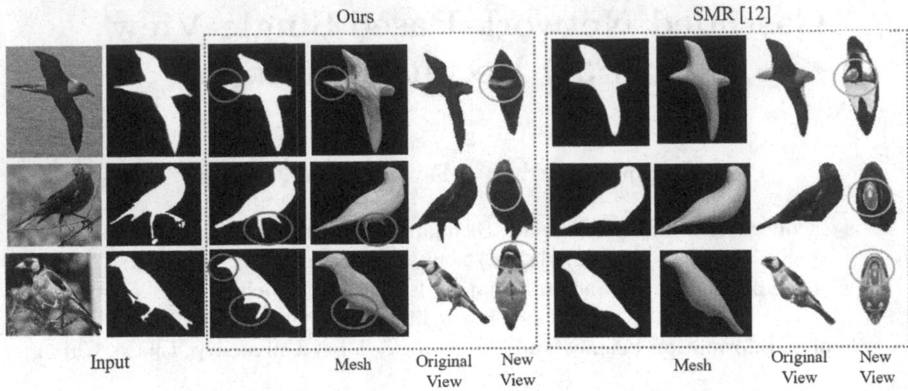

Fig. 1. Our method shows superiority over existing methods in reconstructing detailed shape and enhancing the realness of 3D models under various views.

such tasks. The advent of differentiable rendering techniques [1–4], which establish the correspondence between 3D model space and images, has enabled the reconstruction of 3D objects through image-level supervision. CMR [5] is one of the first single-view bird 3D reconstruction methods. It predicts 3D attributes from a single image and re-rendering the reconstructed 3D model back into the image space using a neural renderer [1]. The network is trained using 2D supervision such as image and mask reconstruction, and key point regression. Many research focus on further relaxing the 2D supervision, e.g., by eliminating the requirement for key points. But accordingly, other prior knowledge is introduced. For instance, CMR [5] and LSV [6] adopt a bird shape mesh template, UMR [7] introduces a semantic segmentation model, and SWR [8] incorporates background information. Despite the impressive reconstruction results obtained by existing methods, they are still limited in reconstructing some local geometry, e.g., beak and feet of birds, especially when key points are unavailable, and in recovering plausible shape and appearance under new views.

In this paper, we aim to improve the performance of reconstructing 3D birds from single-view images and their annotated silhouette masks, such that a reasonable shape and appearance even in new views can be obtained. To this end, we fulfill the reconstruction of shape and the reconstruction of texture, lighting and camera pose with respective networks, but train them jointly. For texture, lighting and camera pose, we use an encoder with attention mechanism to improve the realness of reconstruction results. For shape, we feed the mask into the cascaded network. By incorporating input mask information and leveraging the cascaded network's progressive refinement and adjustment mechanism, the network can better focus on local geometric features during the shape reconstruction process, thereby improving the accuracy of capturing local geometric features of birds. To train the method, we render the obtained 3D model from different views to create multi-view images, and apply the Multi-view Cycle Consistency loss to make the 3D model more realistic under various views.

2 Related Work

Deep learning-based single-view bird 3D reconstruction is one of the hot spots in the field of single-view 3D reconstruction research in recent years. The earliest approach is proposed by CMR [5], which trains a shared ResNet-18-based encoder by minimizing the losses of the predicted image, reconstructed mask, and regressed key points and uses three attribute prediction modules to predict shape, texture, and camera pose respectively. LSV [6] extends the CMR [5] to enhance the shape reconstruction by adding a multi-scale feature fusion module for images and applying side output mask constraint and edge constraints, which are shape-sensitive geometric constraints. To address the dependence on key points, U-CMR [9] uses a set of camera pose assumptions (camera-multiplex). UMR [7] proposes a self-supervised method to achieve 3D bird reconstruction by using semantic consistency. It introduces the semantic part information provided by an external SCOPS [10] model, to effectively capture the 3D features of birds by constructing semantic UV texture maps. However, its effectiveness is limited by the accuracy of the semantic segmentation results. TTP [11] regresses the coordinates of 2D points corresponding to the vertices of the 3D bird template mesh, and then uses predicted 2D points to drive the entire 3D reconstruction process, learning the 2D-3D relationship through end-to-end optimization. SMR [12] proposes a self-supervised 3D mesh reconstruction network that uses the obtained 3D model as a pseudo-3D groud truth model to supervise the training of the network. SMR achieves state of the arts for single-view bird 3D reconstruction. Recently, generative adversarial networks (GANs) are also introduced to 3D bird reconstruction. Instead of using Convolutional Neural Networks (CNNs) to predict the 3D properties of birds, GanIn [13] implements single-view bird 3D reconstruction by using a pre-trained textured 3D MeshGAN [4]. It minimizes the 2D reconstruction loss by searching for a latent code z and fine-tuning the pre-estimated camera pose through gradient descent.

Although these methods can accomplish the task of single-view bird 3D reconstruction, they either rely on external methods or require pre-estimated camera pose. What is more, the 3D shape obtained by existing methods is relatively rough, and the reconstructed texture often looks unreasonable from new views (especially the views invisible in the input image).

3 Method

Overview. The overall structure of our proposed method is shown in Fig. 2. Given the original image of a bird and its corresponding silhouette mask, we first crop out the foreground image. Then, we use three attribute encoders E_c, E_l, E_t, each followed by a Convolutional Block Attention Module (CBAM) [14], to encode the foreground features of the image, and three predictors to predict the camera pose, texture and lighting, respectively. For shape prediction, we take only the silhouette mask as the input of the shape encoder E_s, and propose a cascaded network (Cascaded Shape Predictor, or CSP) to gradually refine the

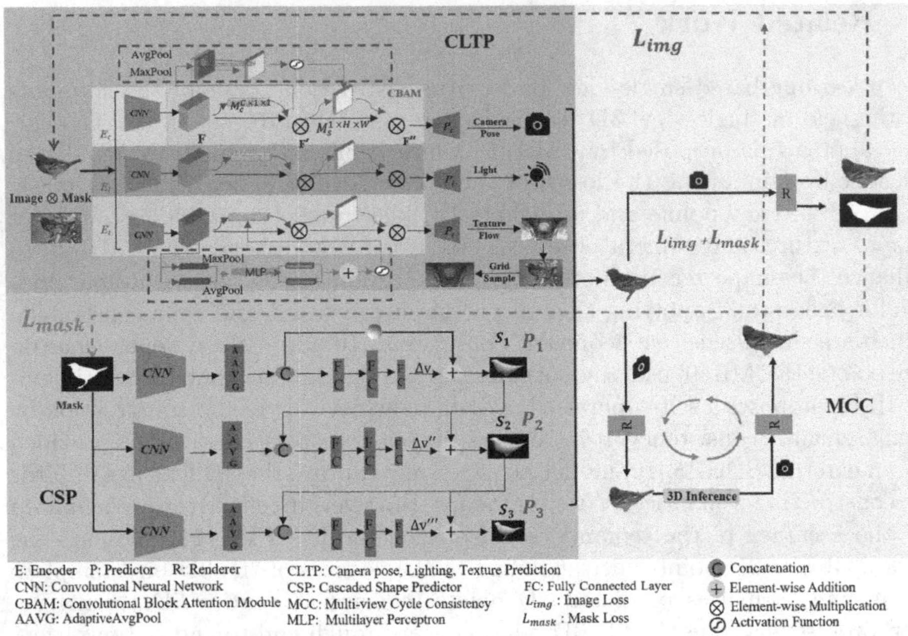

Fig. 2. Overview of our proposed single-view bird 3D reconstruction method.

reconstructed 3D bird model. We render the obtained 3D model to 2D space through a renderer R and then compare the resulting 2D images with the original input image and mask to supervise the training of the cascaded network with Multi-view Cycle Consistency (MCC) loss. By rendering multi-view images during training, our method allows the reconstruction of reasonable shapes and textures even from a new viewpoint.

Model Representation. We represent the 3D model as $X = [C, L, T, S]$, where C, L, T, S denote camera pose, lighting, texture, and shape, respectively. The camera pose $C \in R^3$ is represented as $C = [a, e, d]$, where a, e, d denote azimuth, elevation, and distance, respectively. The lighting $L \in R^9$ is represented by the spherical harmonics [15]. The texture $T \in R^{H\times W\times 3}$ is defined by the UV map, which has the same size as the input image. The shape $S \in R^{V\times 3}$ consists of 1280 faces and 642 vertices, same as those in [5,7,12].

3.1 Camera Pose, Lighting and Texture Prediction

It is crucial to capture the information regarding camera pose,lighting and texture from the input image. We employs three encoders that are similar in structure to extract texture, lighting, and camera pose features. Furthermore, we employ CBAM to effectively identify crucial features across channels and image regions, thereby maximizing the feature selection capability of the network. CBAM contains two sub-modules, Channel Attention Module (CAM) and

Spatial Attention Module (SAM), which perform attention on channel and space respectively. The channel attention is calculated as follows:

$$M_c = \sigma(\mathrm{MLP}(\mathrm{AvgPool}(F)) + \mathrm{MLP}(\mathrm{MaxPool}(F))) \tag{1}$$

$$F' = M_c(F) \otimes F \tag{2}$$

Specifically, we obtain two feature maps by Max Pooling and Average Pooling of the feature $F \in R^{C\times H\times W}$ extracted from the foreground. These two feature maps are fed into a Multilayer Perceptron (MLP), whose output is summed up by element-wise addition, and processed by an activation function σ to obtain the channel attention $M_c^{C\times 1\times 1}$. Finally, M_c and the input feature F are multiplied element by element to obtain F'. The spatial attention is computed as follows:

$$M_s = \sigma\left(f^{7\times 7}([\mathrm{AvgPool}(F'); \mathrm{MaxPool}(F')])\right) \tag{3}$$

$$F'' = M_s\left(F'\right) \otimes F' \tag{4}$$

We obtain two feature maps from F' by Max Pooling and Average Pooling and connect them. Then we pass them through a convolutional layer and an activation function to obtain spatial attention $M_s^{1\times H\times W}$.

For the camera pose and lighting prediction, we use Convolutional Neural Network (CNN) to extract the features F of the input foreground, and multiply F by the channel attention M_c and spatial attention M_s in turn to obtain feature F''. F'' is then subjected to Adaptive Average Pooling and four Fully Connected layers with the ReLu activation function, to predict the camera pose $C \in R^3$ and lighting $L \in R^9$. For texture prediction, the feature F'' is fed into five Convolutional and Up-Sampling layers after Adaptive Average Pooling and Fully Connected layers to obtain the texture flow $f \in R^{H\times W\times 2}$. Finally, we use the texture flow f to sample the original foreground image to get the texture $T \in R^{H\times W\times 3}$.

3.2 Cascaded Shape Predictor

Achieving an accurate reconstruction of the 3D shape of a bird from a single image is very challenging. In order to fully leverage the prior knowledge of silhouette without interference from other factors, we use shape encoder to extract the shape feature from the mask directly. Inspired by the application of cascade networks in tasks such as target detection [16], semantic segmentation [17], depth estimation [18], person re-identification [19], and point cloud reconstruction [20], we introduce the idea of cascaded networks to shape reconstruction.

The cascaded shape network is composed of multiple sub-networks, each of which is specialized in processing features at different levels of features. Lower-level sub-networks can capture category-level (bird) shape information, while higher-level sub-networks can capture more detailed shape information. Furthermore, the cascaded shape network employs an iterative approach for shape extraction and reconstruction, where each sub-network optimizes and refines the shape estimation based on the results from the previous stage. This iterative optimization process gradually improves the accuracy of shape reconstruction, leading to more precise shape estimation results. Specifically, in each stage of the cascaded shape network, an initial shape estimation is generated based on the input mask information. This initial shape estimation is then used as input for the next stage, combined with the input mask information, and passed to the subsequent sub-network. Through this iterative process, the cascaded network refines and adjusts the shape reconstruction based on the shape estimation results from previous stages and the input mask information, allowing for better capture of the local geometric characteristics of birds and progressively improving the accuracy of shape reconstruction.

As shown in Fig. 2, we extract the shape feature F directly from the silhouette mask. The extracted feature F is concatenated with the shape coordinates after the Adaptive Average Pooling, and then passed through three Fully Connected layers with the LeakyReLu activation function, to finally output offset of vertices ΔV. The shape is thus refined by $S = S_0 + \Delta V$. In the cascaded network, the predicted shape is iteratively refined as $S_i = P_i(S_{i-1}, F_{i,s}) + S_{i-1}$, where, S_i denotes the i_{th} 3D shape model, P_i denotes the i_{th} shape predictor, which takes the shape coordinates and shape features in the 3D shape model as input. It is worth highlighting that in our method the initial shape S_0 is simply a sphere, rather than a coarse 3D bird model. This makes our method easy to apply.

3.3 Multi-view Cycle Consistency

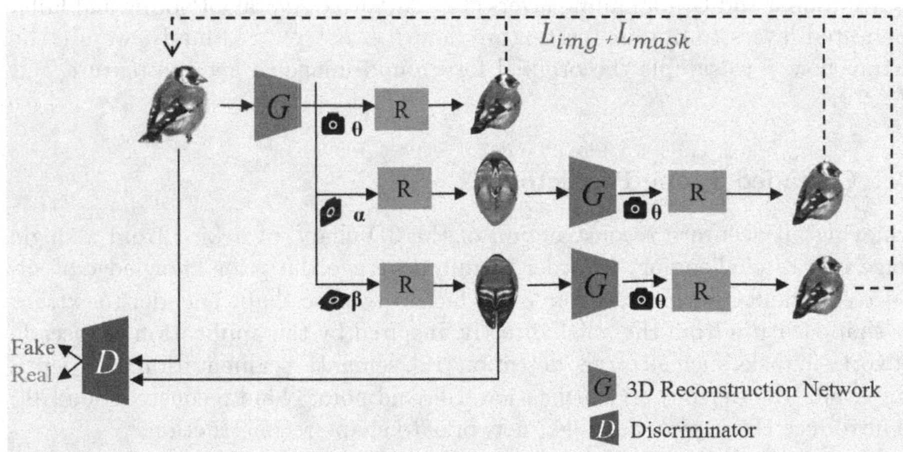

Fig. 3. The multi-view cycle consistency (MCC) loss.

One image provides only one view of the object, which contains limited information. When using a single view for 3D reconstruction, the reconstructed 3D model could be well fit to the view of the input image. However, without the supervision of other views, anomalous shapes and unrealistic textures can easily appear in new unseen views. To solve this problem, we propose MCC loss. Although there is only one image, we can obtain a multi-view image of the bird by rendering the reconstructed 3D model from new views. The obtained multi-view images are then used to supervise the reconstruction of the 3D model.

As shown in Fig. 3, the original foreground image I_i is fed through the 3D reconstruction network G to obtain the 3D model X_i. Suppose the predicted camera pose is θ. We render the obtained model X_i under new views α, β to obtain the 2D images I_i^α, I_i^β.

$$I_i^\alpha = R(G(I_i), \alpha)). \tag{5}$$

$$I_i^\beta = R(G(I_i), \beta)). \tag{6}$$

Subsequently, we use I_i^α, I_i^β as input to the reconstruction network G to obtain 3D models X_i^α, X_i^β. At this point, we render them using the original camera pose θ to obtain 2D images $I_i^{\alpha'}$, $I_i^{\beta'}$, respectively.

$$I_i^{\alpha'} = R(G(I_i^\alpha), \theta)). \tag{7}$$

$$I_i^{\beta'} = R(G(I_i^\beta), \theta)). \tag{8}$$

The proposed MCC loss aims to force $I_i^{\alpha'}$, $I_i^{\beta'}$ to fit to the original foreground image I_i as well as possible. The MCC implicitly obtains the information of invisible and occluded regions, which can significantly improve the reconstruction of the invisible views of the bird.

Adversarial Training. Furthermore, we incorporate adversarial training into our method. We train a discriminator D that feeds the original foreground image I_i and the image I_i^α obtained by rendering into the discriminator. By learning to distinguish the real image from the rendered image, the discriminator is able to learn shape and texture priors so that the 3D model generated by the reconstructed network G looks reasonable from other views as well.

$$L_{adv}(G, D) = G_{I_i}\left[\log D\left(I_i\right)\right] + G_{I_i^\alpha}\left[\log\left(1 - D\left(I_i^\alpha\right)\right)\right]. \tag{9}$$

3.4 Overall Loss

The original foreground image and mask are used as supervision for the generated 3D model. The input image is element-wise multiplied by the mask M_i to obtain the foreground image I_i. The image loss L_{img} is defined as the L1 distance between the I_i and the rendered image I_i^r. We use the Mask IoU loss to force the projected mask M_i^r to be consistent with the ground truth mask M_i. The mask loss is thus defined as:

$$L_{mask} = \frac{1}{N}\sum_{i=1}^{N}\left(1 - \frac{\|M_i \odot M_i^r\|_1}{\|M_i + M_i^r - M_i \odot M_i^r\|_1}\right). \tag{10}$$

We also inherit the SMR [12] 3D attribute interpolation consistency method. We feed the original foreground image I_i into the reconstruction network G to reconstruct the 3D model $X_i = G(I_i)$. Then we use X_i as pseudo-3D ground truth model and generate more pseudo-3D ground truth models by interpolation. Finally, we compute the L_1 distance between X_i and the 3D model obtained with the image $R(X_i, \theta)$ rendered with X_i to define the 3D loss as:

$$L_{3D} = \frac{1}{N}\sum_{i=1}^{N} \|G(R(X_i, \theta)) - G(I_i)\|_1 . \tag{11}$$

To ensure smoothness of mesh generation and to prevent arbitrarily large deformations, we employ $L_{smooth} = \|LV\|_2$ and $L_{def} = \|\Delta V\|_2$, where L is the discrete Laplace Beltrami operator and V denotes the mesh vertexs. To summarize, the overall loss we use to train our method is

$$\begin{aligned} L_{all} = \lambda_1 L_{img} + \lambda_2 L_{mask} + \lambda_3 L_{3D} + \lambda_4 L_{def} \\ + \lambda_5 L_{smooth} + \lambda_6 L_{MCC} + \lambda_7 L_{adv}. \end{aligned} \tag{12}$$

The loss weights are empirically set as $\lambda_1 = \lambda_2 = 10$, $\lambda_3 = 0.1$, $\lambda_4 = \lambda_5 = 0.001$, $\lambda_6 = 0.01, \lambda_7 = 0.001$.

4 Experiments

4.1 Dataset and Protocols

Dataset. We perform experiments on the CUB-200-2011 [21] dataset. It contains 11,788 bird images of 200 bird subcategories, among which 5,994 images are in the training data set and 5,794 images in the test set. Annotations are provided for each image, including the bird's key points, mask, bounding box, etc. In our approach, only mask annotations are needed. We use the same training set and test set as SMR [12].

Protocols. In our study, the 3D reconstruction accuracy is assessed using the commonly utilized metrics of Mask Intersection over Union (IoU) and Structural Similarity (SSIM). To evaluate the appearance quality of the reconstructed models, we employ the Image Synthesis Metric Fréchet Inception Distance (FID) [22], which compares the distribution of the test images with that of the images rendered from the reconstructed models.

4.2 Model Analysis

Baseline Model. We use three encoders to extract foreground features, and then predict camera pose, lighting, and texture with respective predictors. The mask is used as input to the shape encoder to directly predict the shape. That is, our baseline model does not contain CBAM, MCC, CSP.

Table 1. Effect of different attention mechanisms.

Methods	Mask IoU (%,↑)	SSIM (%,↑)	FID (%,↓)
Baseline	82.3	79.7	49.5
Baseline + CAM	82.0	79.8	47.3
Baseline + SAM	82.4	79.6	48.8
Baseline + CBAM	**82.8**	**80.5**	**45.3**

Impact of Attentional Mechanism Settings. In this experiment, we implement and compare three different attentional mechanisms, i.e., CAM, SAM and CBAM. The results, presented in Table 1, show that SAM and CAM lead to improved reconstruction compared to the baseline, but the improvement is not consistent and very marginal. In contrast, CBAM obtains a more significant improvement in both shape reconstruction and texture prediction. This suggests that, depending on the task, the combination of spatial and channel attention mechanisms can emphasize or suppress content and location in features to effectively refine features.

Effect of the Number of Cascaded Shape Prediction Networks. Table 2 summarizes the performance of our method when different numbers of shape prediction networks are used. In the following experiments, we adopt the use of three shape predictors, resulting in a 2.6% improvement in Mask IoU and a 2% improvement in SSIM. Figure 4 shows the prediction outcomes of each of the three cascaded shape predictors. As can be seen, the reconstructed shape is does gradually improved in its detail geometry.

Table 2. Impact of the number of cascaded shape prediction networks on the reconstruction results. P_2 and P_3 denote the use of two and three cascaded shape prediction networks respectively.

Methods	Mask IoU (%,↑)	SSIM (%,↑)	FID (%,↓)
Baseline	82.3	79.7	49.5
Baseline + P_2	83.8	80.5	49.3
Baseline + P_3	**84.9**	**81.7**	**48.9**

Table 3. Results of ablation experiments.

Methods	Mask IoU (%,↑)	SSIM (%,↑)	FID (%,↓)
Baseline	82.3	79.7	49.5
Baseline + CBAM	82.8	80.5	45.3
Baseline + CBAM + CSP	85.1	83.2	40.9
Baseline+CBAM+CSP+MCC	**85.3**	**84.2**	**38.3**

4.3 Ablation Study

The ablation study results are summarized in Table 3. Obviously, the utilization of cascaded networks effectively enhances the accuracy of shape reconstruction. The implementation of the Multi-view Cycle Consistency loss significantly reduces the FID, indicating an improvement in view generalization ability. This results not only in the generation of geometrically consistent shapes for invisible views, but also in the production of realistic textures. Figure 5 shows some example reconstruction results for visual inspection. It can be observed that CSP significantly improves the local shape reconstruction (feet). With only one viewpoint, the texture on the bird's belly and back may be erroneously reconstructed as the background (blue sky or green leaves). By introducing MCC loss, reasonable textures can be generated even from invisible perspectives.

4.4 Comparison to Existing Methods

Quantitative Results. In this experiment, we evaluate the performance of our method in comparison to recent state-of-the-art methods. The results, presented in Table 4, demonstrate the superiority of our method in terms of both Mask IoU and SSIM metrics. Moreover, our method also performs comparable to the best counterpart method on FID. Our approach attains a high level of accuracy in shape reconstruction and also produces a visually convincing texture representation, even when the viewpoint is not visible in the original input image.

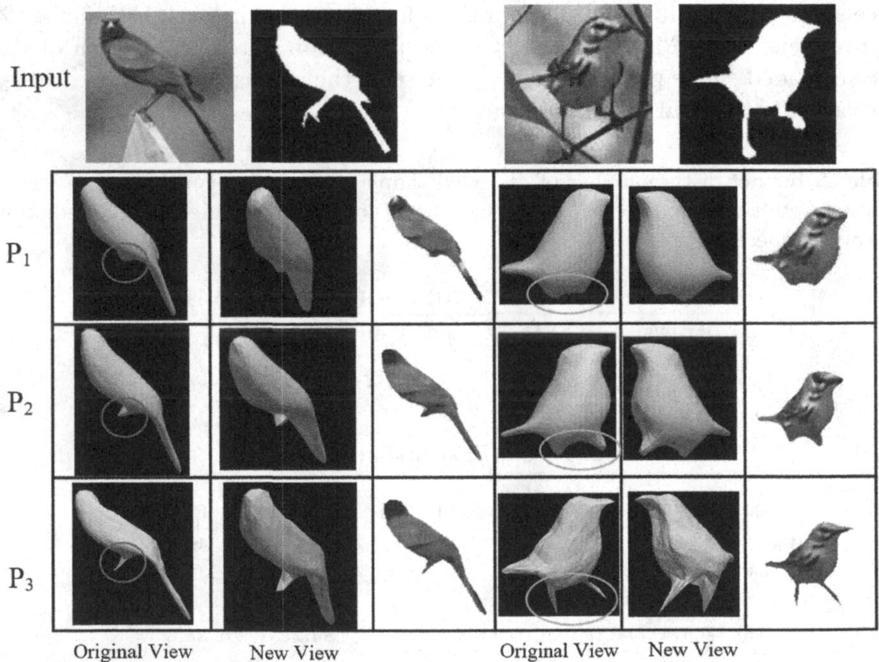

Fig. 4. Reconstruction results when different numbers of cascaded shape prediction networks are used.

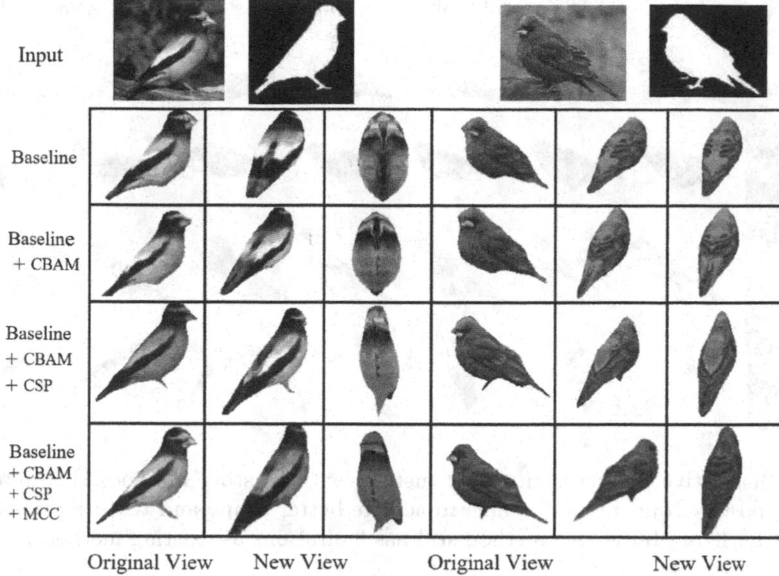

Fig. 5. Reconstruction results of different models in ablation experiments. (Color figure online)

Qualitative Results. Figure 6 shows a qualitative comparison of our method with existing methods. Compared with the counterpart methods, our method is able to reconstruct the shape of the bird's feet and beak tip, as well as to obtain good texture reconstruction. Yet, it is still challenging for all methods to reconstruct 3D models for flying birds.

Table 4. Comparison of our method with existing single-view bird-based 3D reconstruction methods.

Methods	Mask IoU (%,↑)	SSIM (%,↑)	FID (%,↓)
CMR [5]	73.8	73.6	–
LSV [6]	75.7	76.5	–
U-CMR [9]	70.1	–	65.0
UMR [7]	73.4	71.3	40.0
SMR [12]	80.6	83.2	55.9
GANIn [13]	75.2	–	**37.4**
Ours	**85.3**	**84.2**	38.3

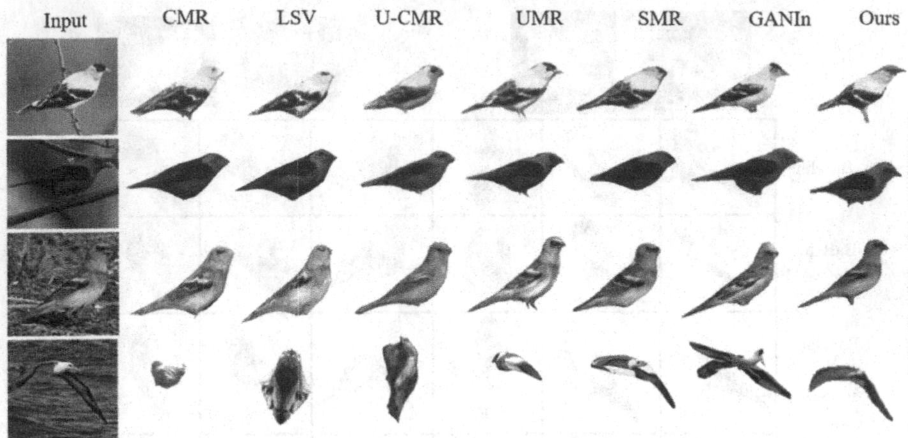

Fig. 6. Qualitative comparison of our method with existing methods. For birds in standing posture, our method is able to achieve better shape and texture reconstruction, but for flying birds, our method still has limitations as existing methods.

5 Conclusion

In this paper, we propose a new solution to the challenges faced by traditional single-view bird 3D reconstruction methods. By leveraging only image and silhouette, our method successfully predicts the shape of birds with improved accuracy and enhances the realness of the reconstructed model especially for unseen new views. Specifically, we adopt a cascaded shape prediction approach for shape reconstruction, and use three encoders with attention modules to extract texture, lighting, and camera pose features. Additionally, the MCC loss is introduced to enhance the realness of reconstructed 3D model. The results of our method demonstrate its superiority over state-of-the-art methods. Although our method has demonstrated its effectiveness, there are still some limitations, e.g., in dealing with flying birds.

Acknowledgements. This work is supported by the National Natural Science Foundation of China (Grant No. 62176170, 61971005). It is also supported in part by the key research and development program of Sichuan province under grant number 2022YFG0045; in part by Fundamental Research Funds for the Central Universities under grant number 2022SCU12008.

References

1. Kato, H., Ushiku, Y., Harada, T.: Neural 3d mesh renderer. In: CVPR (2018)
2. Chen, W., et al.: Learning to predict 3d objects with an interpolation-based differentiable renderer. In: NeurIPS (2019)
3. Liu, S., Li, T., Chen, W., Li, H.: Soft rasterizer: A differentiable renderer for image-based 3d reasoning. In: ICCV (2019)

4. Pavllo, D., Spinks, G., Hofmann, T., Moens, M.-F., Lucchi, A.: Convolutional generation of textured 3d meshes. In: NeurIPS (2020)
5. Kanazawa, A., Tulsiani, S., Efros, A.A., Malik, J.: Learning category-specific mesh reconstruction from image collections. In: ECCV (2018)
6. Sun, S., Zhu, Z., Dai, X., Zhao, Q., Li, J.: Weakly-supervised reconstruction of 3d objects with large shape variation from single in-the-wild images. In: ACCV (2020)
7. Li, X., et al.: Self-supervised single-view 3d reconstruction via semantic consistency. In: ECCV (2020)
8. Monnier, T., Fisher, M., Efros, A.A., Aubry, M.: Share with thy neighbors: single-view reconstruction by cross-instance consistency. In: ECCV (2022)
9. Goel, S., Kanazawa, A., Malik, J.: Shape and viewpoint without keypoints. In: ECCV (2020)
10. Hung, W.-C., et al.: Scops: self-supervised co-part segmentation. In: CVPR (2019)
11. Kokkinos, F., Kokkinos, I.: To the point: Correspondence-driven monocular 3d category reconstruction. In: NeurIPS (2021)
12. Hu, T., Wang, L., Xu, X., Liu, S., Jia, J.: Self-supervised 3d mesh reconstruction from single images. In: CVPR (2021)
13. Zhang, J., et al.: Monocular 3d object reconstruction with GAN inversion. In: ECCV (2022)
14. Woo, S., Park, J., Lee, J.Y., Kweon, I.S.: CBAM: convolutional block attention module. In: ECCV (2018)
15. Ramamoorthi, R., Hanrahan, P.: An efficient representation for irradiance environment maps. In: CGIT (2001)
16. Wang, T., Ma, C., Su, H., Wang, W.: CSPN: multi-scale cascade spatial pyramid network for object detection. In: ICASSP (2021)
17. Li, X., Zhang, G., Pan, H., Wang, Z.: CPGNET: cascade point-grid fusion network for real-time lidar semantic segmentation. In: ICRA (2022)
18. Shim, D., Kim, H.J.: Swindepth: unsupervised depth estimation using monocular sequences via swin transformer and densely cascaded network, arXiv (2023)
19. Chen, X., et al.: Salience-guided cascaded suppression network for person re-identification. In: CVPR (2020)
20. Li, Y., Zhao, Z., Fan, J., Li, W.: ADR-MVSNet: a cascade network for 3d point cloud reconstruction with pixel occlusion. In: PR (2022)
21. Wah, C., Branson, S., Welinder, P., Perona, P., Belongie, S.: The caltech-UCSD birds-200-2011 dataset. Technical Report (2011)
22. Heusel, M., Ramsauer, H., Unterthiner, T., Nessler, B., Hochreiter, S.: Gans trained by a two time-scale update rule converge to a local nash equilibrium. In: NeurIPS (2017)

CLASPPNet: A Cross-Layer Multi-class Lane Semantic Segmentation Model Fused with Lane Detection Module

Chao Huang[1,2], Zhiguang Wang[1,2](✉), Yongnian Fan[1,2], Kai Liu[1,2], and Qiang Lu[1,2]

[1] Beijing Key Laboratory of Petroleum Data Mining, China University of Petroleum, Beijing, China
cwangzg@cup.edu.cn

[2] Department of Computer Science and Technology, China University of Petroleum, Beijing, China

Abstract. Multi-class lane semantic segmentation is a crucial technology in the traffic violation detection system. However, the existing models for multi-classification lane semantic segmentation suffer from low segmentation accuracy for special lanes (e.g., ramp, emergency lane) and lane lines. To address this problem, we propose a cross-layer multi-class lane semantic segmentation model called CLASPPNet (Cross-Layer Atrous Spatial Pyramid Pooling Network) fused with lane detection module. We first design a Cross-Layer Atrous Spatial Pyramid Pooling (CLASPP) structure to integrate the deep and shallow features in the image and enhance the integrity of the lane segmentation. Additionally, we integrate the lane detection module during training in the cross-layer structure, which can improve the model's ability of extracting lane line features. We evaluate CLASPPNet on the expressway dataset based on aerial view, and the experimental results show that our model significantly improves the segmentation performance of special lanes and lane lines. Additionally, it achieves the highest mIoU (mean Intersection over Union) of 86.4% while having 28.9M parameters.

Keywords: Lane Semantic Segmentation · Lane Detection · ASPP

1 Introduction

The expressway traffic violation detection system is an important means to ensure the safety of expressway traffic. It detects illegal behaviors of vehicles in images, which relies on the acquisition and recognition of road information. Currently, there are two main methods used to detect and obtain road information: lane detection and multi-class lane semantic segmentation. Lane detection

This work is supported by National Natural Science Foundation of China (No. 61972414), National Key R&D Program of China (No.2019YFC0312003) and Beijing Natural Science Foundation (No. 4202066).

L. Iliadis et al. (Eds.): ICANN 2023, LNCS 14255, pp. 128–139, 2023.
https://doi.org/10.1007/978-3-031-44210-0_11

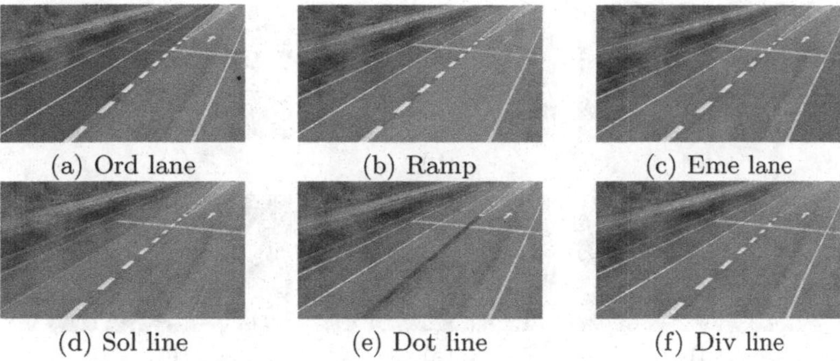

Fig. 1. Six-classification annotation examples of the expressway dataset based on aerial view. (a) Ord lane (Ordinary lane), the general driving area of vehicles; (b) Ramp, which changes the destinations of vehicles, and generally involves the merging and separation of lanes; (c) Eme lane (Emergency lane), the area where special vehicles are allowed to drive or stop; (d) Sol line (Solid line), which not allows vehicles to change lanes; (e) Dot line (Dotted line), which allows vehicles to change lanes between adjacent lanes; (f) Div line (Division line), which reminds the driver of the change in the number of lanes and prohibit driving in the area.

usually takes the lane lines as detections targets, and calculates the position of the lanes by detecting the position of the lane lines [5,18,23]. Therefore, it can specifically be called lane line detection. The method usually requires prior definitions of key points or anchor boxes, allowing for the effective utilization of prior information regarding the shape of the lane lines and providing the advantage of a fast detection speed. However, it cannot provide sufficient semantic information for traffic violation detection scenarios. Multi-class lane semantic segmentation usually categorizes lanes and lane lines into different classes, providing richer semantic information through semantic segmentation.

At present, generic semantic segmentation models still present some shortcomings when applied to multi-class lane semantic segmentation tasks on expressway. Specifically, when dividing lanes and lane lines into six different classes (see Fig. 1), models based on Convolutional Neural Network (CNN) [3,22] suffer from the following three problems in terms of segmentation performance (see Fig. 2): 1. They perform well in segmenting ordinary lanes, but poorly for special lanes (e.g., ramp, emergency lane); 2. They are effective in lane segmentation, but ineffective in lane line segmentation, especially dotted line. 3. They perform well in segmenting lanes and lane lines near the camera, but poorly at greater distances. On the other hand, models based on Transformer [12,13,19] have better segmentation effects in the above three scenarios, but their larger parameter size leads to higher computational complexity, making them unable to meet the requirements of traffic violation detection systems.

In this paper, we propose a lane semantic segmentation model based on CNN that improves the segmentation accuracy of special lanes and lane lines, as well as the segmentation performance in areas far from the camera. Building on DeepLab-ERFC [4], our model incorporates lane detection modules and

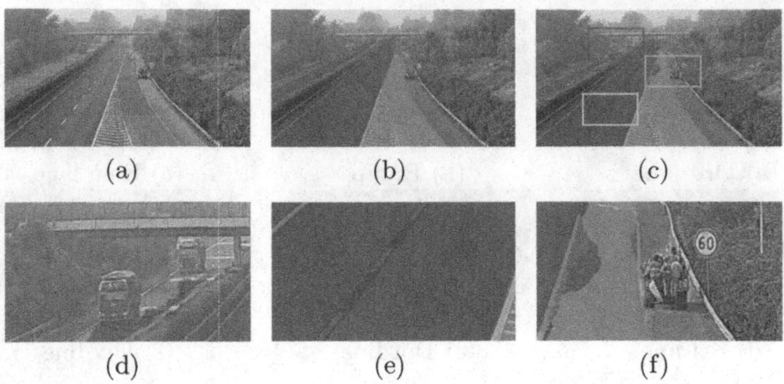

Fig. 2. Challenges in multi-class lane semantic segmentation. (a) Image from the expressway dataset based on aerial view, containing rich road information; (b) Corresponding semantic segmentation annotations for (a); (c) Segmentation results of existing multi-class lane semantic segmentation models on this dataset; (d) The red box in (c), showing an area with poor segmentation results due to distance from the camera; (e) The yellow box in (c), showing an irregular boundary in the dotted line area; (f) The green box in (c), showing significant errors in the special lanes (e.g., ramp, emergency lane). (Color figure online)

a Cross-Layer Atrous Spatial Pyramid Pooling structure. The CLASPP structure uses ASPP modules to extract features from adjacent layers' differently sized feature maps that are concatenated, fully fusing deep and shallow features to improve lane and lane line segmentation performance. Moreover, the structure incorporates the lane detection modules during training, fully utilizing the prior information, such as the shape of the lane lines, to enhance the ability of the model to extract lane line features. Finally, we conduct experiments on the expressway dataset based on aerial view. The results show that our model significantly improves the segmentation performance of special lanes and lane lines. Compared with other models, our model achieves the highest mIoU of 86.4%, while having 28.9M parameters and 82.1 GFLOPs (Giga Floating Point Operations).

2 Related Work

2.1 Lane Detection Methods

The goal of lane detection is to detect and distinguish the lane lines in an image. LaneATT [17] introduces an attention mechanism to gather global information. FOLOLane [16] uses local geometry construction manner to implement lane detection by treating it as a key point detection task. The CLRNet [21] uses a cross-layer structure to make full use of both high-level and low-level features, and introduces Line IoU to regress the lane lines as a whole unit, improving the detection accuracy. Lane detection typically does not distinguish the classes of lane lines. Therefore, it cannot be used in traffic violation detection systems.

2.2 Multi-class Lane Semantic Segmentation Methods

Multi-class lane semantic segmentation aims to use deep learning-based semantic segmentation models to perform pixel-level classification of the different classes in the road. Lo et al. [14] propose an improved multi-class lane semantic segmentation model, which can acquire more road information than a lane detection model. But it cannot provide more complete predictions for dotted lines and division lines. The DeepLab-ERFC [4] model proposes an expressway dataset based on aerial view and achieves better segmentation results on this dataset by introducing Erosion Loss (ER Loss) [8] and Fully-Connected Conditional Random Fields (Fully-Connected CRFs) [9] based on DeeplabV3+ [3]. However, the model's segmentation results for dotted lines are not very precise, and its segmentation performance for special lanes and distant areas of lanes and lane lines is not satisfactory.

2.3 Atrous Spatial Pyramid Pooling

Atrous convolution [20] is a powerful tool in image semantic segmentation that effectively arbitrarily enlarges the field-of-view of filters by introducing holes in standard convolution. Inspired by the Spatial Pyramid Pooling (SPP) [6,7,10], DeepLabV2 [1] designs an ASPP module that uses atrous convolutions with different dilation rates to capture multi-scale contextual information of the input image. DeepLabV3 [2] applies global average pooling to the final feature map of the ASPP module to help capture global context information.

3 Approach

We analyze the issues with existing multi-class lane semantic segmentation models mentioned in Sect. 1. Firstly, we find that pixel-level classification does not consider the lane line as a whole, resulting in the models' inability to fully utilize the prior information of lane lines. This shortcoming leads to unsatisfactory segmentation performance for special lanes and lane lines in traffic violation detection task. Secondly, we identify that deep features and shallow features in multi-class lane semantic segmentation models complement each other in terms of lane and lane line segmentation. However, traditional segmentation methods process these features hierarchically, failing to effectively integrate the two types of features. This shortcoming leads to the incomplete utilization of some features and unsatisfactory segmentation performance. To address these shortcomings, we propose a cross-layer multi-class lane semantic segmentation model fused with lane detection module, see Fig. 3. The model is divided into the CLLD structure and the CLASPP structure, and their specific designs will be discussed in Subsects. 3.2 and 3.3, respectively.

3.1 Lane Line Key Point Data Generation

Motivation. Although pixel-level annotations can provide rich semantic information, they cannot provide the key point information required for lane

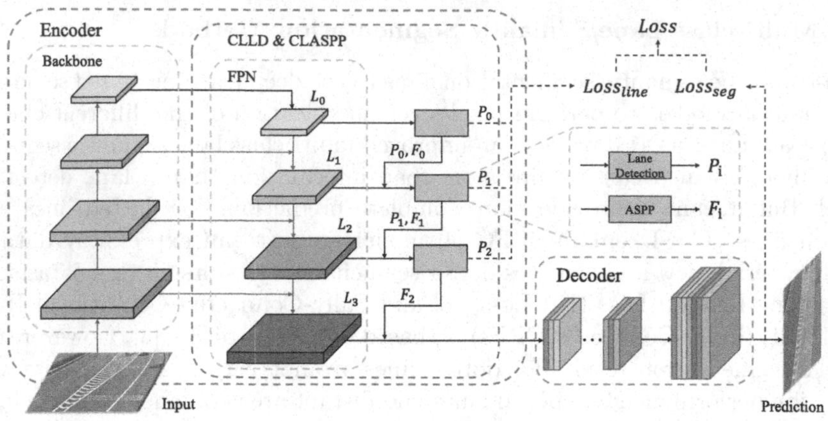

Fig. 3. The CLASPPNet model. In the figure, the model uses FPN [11] to generate four feature maps (e.g., $L_i(i \in [0,3])$) of varying sizes. The model comprises two structures: the CLLD structure, utilized during training to leverage the prior information of lane line, and the CLASPP structure, which includes three ASPP modules to perform effective feature fusion from concatenated feature maps of different sizes. Further information on the CLLD and CLASPP structures can be found in Fig. 5 and Fig. 6, respectively.

detection. Therefore, it is necessary to convert lane line pixel-level annotations into key point annotations to meet the labeling requirements of the lane detection branch in our proposed model, see Fig. 4.

Method. We propose a method to sample key points of lane lines from pixel-level annotations. To obtain key points for each lane line, we divide the image into rows with a spacing of δ, where $\frac{height}{\delta}$ denotes the number of resulting rows. These rows are defined as key rows. Subsequently, we perform a left-to-right pixel scan for each key row. When a boundary between the lane line and background appears between two adjacent pixels, we identify it as a boundary point. In row r, each lane line always has two boundary points, B_{r1} and B_{r2}. Finally, we calculate the key point K_r of the lane line using Eq. 1:

$$\begin{cases} K_r = \sum_{i=0}^{1} \frac{B_{ri}}{2} \\ 0 \leqq r < \frac{height}{\delta},\ r \in (0,1,2,...) \end{cases} \quad (1)$$

For the lane lines that are located at the image boundary, we also treat the image boundary as one of their boundary points. Finally, we remove the lane lines with only one key point, because such lane lines are too short in length and the lane detection branch cannot learn effective features from them. The setting of the row spacing δ is introduced in Subsect. 4.2.

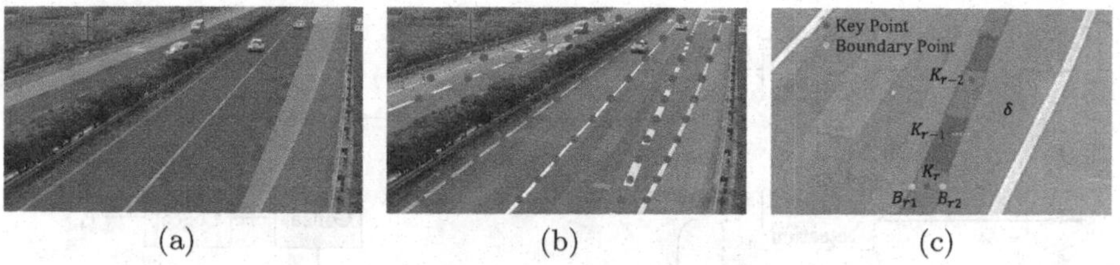

Fig. 4. Two types of data annotations used in CLASPPNet. (a) pixel-level annotations; (b) key point annotations; (c) key point calculation instructions.

3.2 Cross-Layer Lane Detection

Motivation. Lane detection usually calculates the position of the lanes by detecting the position of the lane lines, so the discussion below in this subsection will mainly focus on the lane lines. Lane lines in road images serve as boundaries of lanes and are also the dividing lines between different lanes. Lane lines provide more semantic information than lanes alone, and improving the accuracy of lane line segmentation (especially for dotted lines) can help obtain more complete lane information. We find that the lane detection methods mentioned in Subsect. 2.1 are highly flexible in using the prior information of lane lines. Among them, the methods based on key point can effectively use the prior shape information of lane lines. We believe that the methods based on lane detection and lane semantic segmentation can complement each other and can be integrated into one model.

Method. We design a Cross-Layer Lane Detection (CLLD) structure to improve the feature extraction ability for lane lines in our model. As shown in Fig. 5, CLLD incorporates the ROIGather from the CLRNet [21] as the Lane Detection module during training. To enable CLLD to extract lane line features effectively, it defines prior information for each lane line, denoted as P_i with $i \in [0, 2]$, which includes the coordinate offset values of 36 key points of each lane line. For each layer in the structure, CLLD defines a Lane Detection module that takes the output L_i of FPN and the upper-layer lane line prior information P_{i-1} (initialized through uniform distribution for layer 0) as input to obtain ROI features. Additionally, the module calculates the attention matrix to obtain the global contextual information, and finally produces the improved P_i as the output of the Lane Detection module for that layer. The CLLD structure is designed with three Lane Detection modules, each corresponding to a different layer in the network. The outputs of these modules and the lane line key point annotations are used to calculate the detection result loss, represented as $Loss_{line}$. This loss function improves the feature extraction ability of the backbone and FPN for lanes and lane lines. Importantly, the CLLD structure is only used during training and has no effect on the inference time.

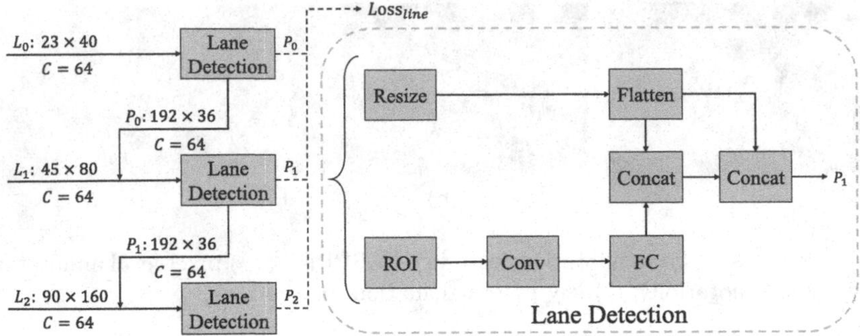

Fig. 5. Cross-Layer Lane Detection Architecture. In the figure, $L_i(i \in [0, 2])$ are the feature maps of different sizes output by the FPN, where C denotes *Channel*. The CLLD structure concatenates the prior features P_i among three layers and refines them layer by layer starting from the 0th layer.

3.3 Cross-Layer Atrous Spatial Pyramid Pooling

Motivation. During the feature extraction process of the neural network, deep features provide richer global information, whereas shallow features retain more local information. For the rough localization and segmentation of lanes and lane lines, it is often necessary to utilize deeper features. However, when segmenting the boundary, local information is essential. Therefore, the integration of deep and shallow features is crucial in multi-class lane semantic segmentation.

Method. We propose a method for integrating both types of features effectively, through a Cross-Layer Atrous Spatial Pyramid Pooling structure, which consists of three ASPP modules with different dilation rates, see Fig. 6. The dilation rates setting for each module is presented in Subsect. 4.2. The output of each layer ASPP module, denoted as F_i, is defined as follows:

$$F_i = ASPP_i\,(L_i \circ F_{i-1}) \tag{2}$$

where $i \in [0, 2]$ corresponds to the three layers in the structure from the top to the bottom in the figure, L_i represents the output of each FPN layer, $ASPP_i$ is the corresponding ASPP module, and $\circ$ denotes the concatenation operation. Specifically, for the 0th layer, we take the L_0 as the input of $ASPP_0$. For the i-th layer, where $i \in [1, 2]$, the output F_{i-1} from the previous $ASPP_{i-1}$ is first upsampled to the same size as the output L_i from the current FPN layer, followed by concatenation to form the input of the current layer $ASPP_i$. Then, through convolution with different dilation rates, the output F_i of $ASPP_i$ is obtained. Finally, the output F_2 of $ASPP_2$ is concatenated with the output L_3 from the 3rd FPN layer, serving as the input of the decoder. In the decoder, we use two convolutional layers to generate a feature map, which contains prediction information for each class. Finally, it is upsampled, and the segmentation loss $Loss_{seg}$ is computed by comparing it with pixel-level annotations.

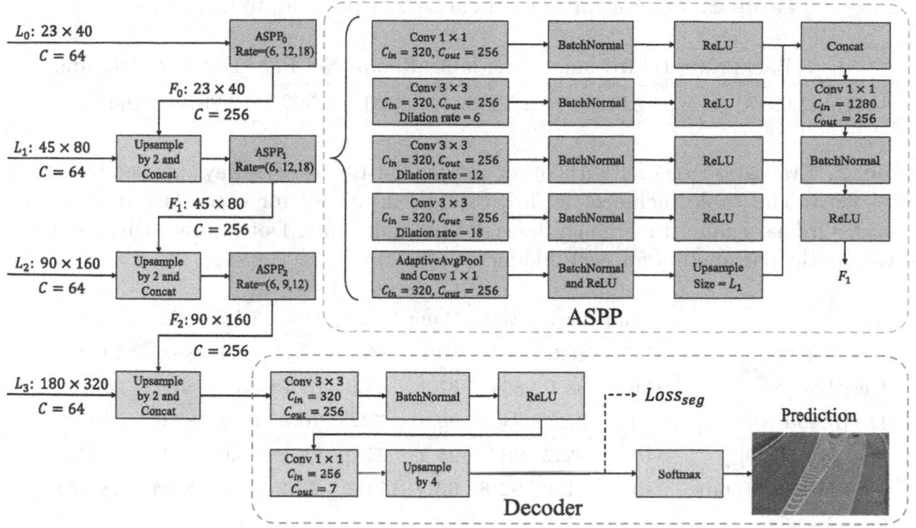

Fig. 6. Cross-Layer Atrous Spatial Pyramid Pooling Architecture. In the figure, L_i ($i \in [0, 3]$) are the feature maps of different sizes output by the FPN, where C denotes *Channel*. The green rectangular area represents the ASPP module, which consists of three atrous convolutions with different dilation rates to expand the model's receptive field. It also includes a 1×1 convolutional layer and a global average pooling operation to obtain the global context information of the input feature map. The red rectangular area signifies the Decoder, consisting of two convolutional layers and an upsampling operation, responsible for generating the final segmentation result. (Color figure online)

4 Experimental

4.1 Dataset

We conduct experiments on the expressway dataset based on aerial view [4], which comprises a total of 1510 images. This dataset was divided into two parts: a training set consisting of 1370 images, and a validation set consisting of 140 images. The dataset includes six classes of road objects (see Fig. 1, Page 2) and provides instance-level annotations for each class.

4.2 Experimental Details

In our experiments, we use the CULane dataset [15] to pre-train the lane detection module. For the formal training, we select AdamW as the optimizer of the model and set the initial learning rate to 4e-4. In the CLLD structure, we decrease the loss weights of each part by 50% based on CLRNet [21]. For the semantic segmentation branch, we choose the Cross-Entropy Loss (CE Loss) as the loss function and fine-tune the class weights w_c based on Deeplab-ERFC, with the specific settings listed in Table 1. The row spacing δ in Subsect. 3.1 is set to 15, and the dilation rates of the three ASPP modules in Subsect. 3.3 are set to (6, 12, 18), (6, 12, 18), and (6, 9, 12), respectively [4].

Table 1. The weight of each class corresponding to CE Loss.

	Background	Ord lane	Eme lane	Ramp	Sol line	Dot line	Div line
Weight	0.500	2.000	2.5000	3.000	2.5000	2.267	2.455

Table 2. Evaluation results with other models on the expressway dataset based on aerial view. The table includes the IoU(%) and mIoU(%) for each class (e.g., Background, Ordinary lane, Emergency lane, Ramp, Solid line, Dotted line, Division line) as well as the parameters for each model.

Model	Bkgnd	Ord	Eme	Ramp	Sol	Dot	Div	mIoU	Params
Unet++ [22]	**97.7**	86.6	82.3	80.1	66.7	67.7	83.4	80.6	29.1M
DeepLabv3+ [3]	94.6	88.1	85.0	87.2	64.3	63.7	83.7	80.9	58.8M
DeepLab-ERFC [4]	93.4	91.2	84.8	90.0	**72.1**	70.7	85.4	83.9	58.8M
SegFormer [19]	94.4	**92.2**	90.3	93.2	71.0	74.1	86.0	85.9	61.4M
CLASPPNet (Ours)	93.1	91.3	**92.8**	**93.7**	71.3	**76.2**	**86.6**	**86.4**	**28.9M**

4.3 Evaluation on the Expressway Dataset Based on Aerial View

We train four models on the expressway dataset based on aerial view and compare them with CLASPPNet (see Table 2 and Fig. 8). The results demonstrate that CLASPPNet exhibits superior segmentation capabilities on special lanes (e.g., ramp, emergency lane) and lane lines, and achieves higher mIoU than other models, with only 28.9M parameters. In addition, we test the mIoU and FLOPs of CLASPPNet using different backbones and compare them with several models with high mIoU (see Fig. 7). The results show that CLASPPNet achieves the highest mIoU of 86.4% when using ResNet34, with FLOPs only 58% of SegFormer using MiT-B4, a simple, efficient semantic segmentation framework based on Transformer with less paramcters. When CLASPPNet uses ResNet18, mIoU still reaches 86%, 1.1% higher than SegFormer using MiT-B2, which has similar FLOPs. Compared with the DeepLab-ERFC, CLASPPNet achieves significant improvements in accuracy and complexity. This demonstrates the powerful feature extraction capabilities of our designed model, which reduces the model's

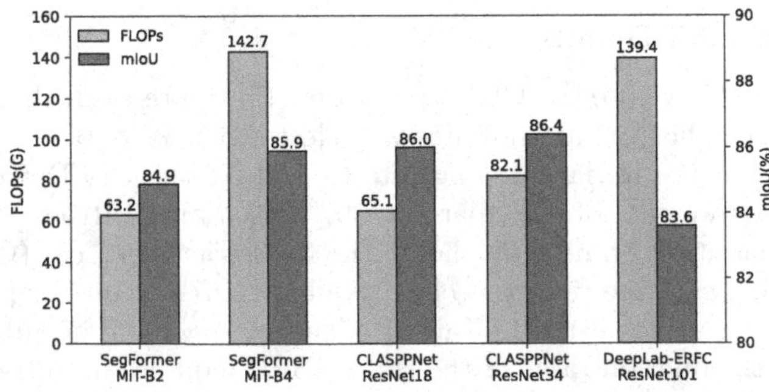

Fig. 7. Evaluation results with other models when using different backbones.

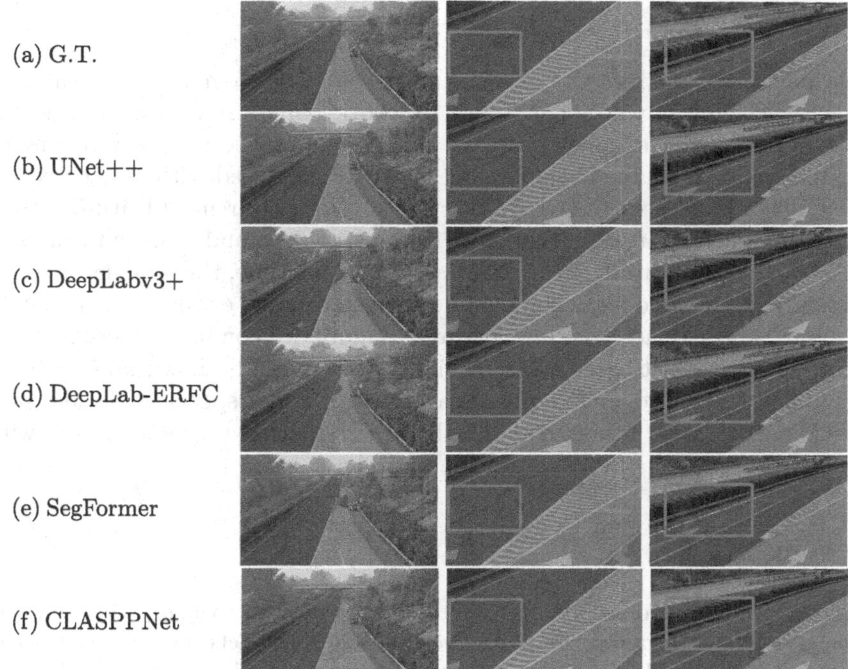

Fig. 8. Evaluation performance with other models on the expressway dataset based on aerial view.

requirement for backbone feature extraction and allows it to outperform other models even when using only ResNet18.

4.4 Ablation Study

We conduct experiments to evaluate the effectiveness of our proposed methods. Specifically, we use ResNet34 combined with an ASPP module as the baseline and test the effectiveness of the CLLD structure and the CLASPP structure (see Table 3). The results show that, in comparison with the baseline, the addition of CLLD and CLASPP greatly improves the model's segmentation performance, with a significant increase in mIoU. When combined, the model achieves a higher mIoU, demonstrating the effectiveness of our two proposed structures.

Table 3. Ablation study of CLASPPNet.

CLLD	CLASPP	Bkgnd	Ord lane	Eme lane	Ramp	Sol line	Dot line	Div line	mIoU
		93.0	88.6	91.8	89.8	71.0	72.0	86.0	84.6
✓		92.8	91.0	89.9	93.5	70.4	74.1	83.8	85.1
	✓	92.9	91.9	90.5	94.0	71.0	73.7	87.2	85.9
✓	✓	93.1	91.3	92.8	93.7	71.3	76.2	86.6	86.4

5 Conclusion

In this paper, we analyze the existing multi-class lane semantic segmentation models based on Convolutional Neural Network, which have low accuracy in segmentation of special lanes and lane lines. We propose a cross-layer multi-class lane semantic segmentation model CLASPPNet fused with lane detection module. The model uses the CLASPP structure for hierarchical feature extraction and cross-layer feature fusion, fully integrating deep and shallow features to improve lane segmentation performance. At the same time, the cross-layer structure integrates the lane detection module during training, enabling the model to better learn and extract lane line features. Finally, we conduct experiments on the expressway dataset based on aerial view, and the results show that CLASPP-Net significantly improves the segmentation accuracy of special lanes and lane lines. Compared with other models, CLASPPNet achieves higher mIoU with fewer parameters and FLOPs.

References

1. Chen, L.C., Papandreou, G., Kokkinos, I., Murphy, K., Yuille, A.L.: Deeplab: semantic image segmentation with deep convolutional nets, atrous convolution, and fully connected CRFs. IEEE Trans. Pattern Anal. Mach. Intell. **40**(4), 834–848 (2017)
2. Chen, L.C., Papandreou, G., Schroff, F., Adam, H.: Rethinking Atrous convolution for semantic image segmentation. arXiv preprint arXiv:1706.05587 (2017)
3. Chen, L.C., Zhu, Y., Papandreou, G., Schroff, F., Adam, H.: Encoder-decoder with Atrous separable convolution for semantic image segmentation. In: Proceedings of the European Conference on Computer Vision (ECCV), pp. 801–818 (2018)
4. Fan, Y., Wang, Z., Chen, C., Zhang, X., Lu, Q.: Multi-class lane semantic segmentation of expressway dataset based on aerial view. In: Pimenidis, E., Angelov, P., Jayne, C., Papaleonidas, A., Aydin, M. (eds.) Artificial Neural Networks and Machine Learning - ICANN 2022. ICANN 2022. LNCS, Part III, vol. 13531, pp. 200–211. Springer, Cham (2022). https://doi.org/10.1007/978-3-031-15934-3_17
5. Feng, Z., Guo, S., Tan, X., Xu, K., Wang, M., Ma, L.: Rethinking efficient lane detection via curve modeling. In: Proceedings of the IEEE/CVF Conference on Computer Vision and Pattern Recognition, pp. 17062–17070 (2022)
6. Grauman, K., Darrell, T.: The pyramid match kernel: discriminative classification with sets of image features. In: Tenth IEEE International Conference on Computer Vision (ICCV'05) Volume 1, vol. 2, pp. 1458–1465. IEEE (2005)
7. He, K., Zhang, X., Ren, S., Sun, J.: Spatial pyramid pooling in deep convolutional networks for visual recognition. IEEE Trans. Pattern Anal. Mach. Intell. **37**(9), 1904–1916 (2015)
8. Karimi, D., Salcudean, S.E.: Reducing the hausdorff distance in medical image segmentation with convolutional neural networks. IEEE Trans. Med. Imaging **39**(2), 499–513 (2019)
9. Krähenbühl, P., Koltun, V.: Efficient inference in fully connected CRFs with gaussian edge potentials. In: Advances in Neural Information Processing Systems, vol. 24 (2011)

10. Lazebnik, S., Schmid, C., Ponce, J.: Beyond bags of features: spatial pyramid matching for recognizing natural scene categories. In: 2006 IEEE Computer Society Conference on Computer Vision and Pattern Recognition (CVPR 2006), vol. 2, pp. 2169–2178. IEEE (2006)
11. Lin, T.Y., Dollár, P., Girshick, R., He, K., Hariharan, B., Belongie, S.: Feature pyramid networks for object detection. In: Proceedings of the IEEE Conference on Computer Vision and Pattern Recognition, pp. 2117–2125 (2017)
12. Liu, Z., et al.: Swin transformer v2: scaling up capacity and resolution. In: Proceedings of the IEEE/CVF Conference on Computer Vision and Pattern Recognition, pp. 12009–12019 (2022)
13. Liu, Z., et al.: Swin transformer: hierarchical vision transformer using shifted windows. In: Proceedings of the IEEE/CVF International Conference on Computer Vision, pp. 10012–10022 (2021)
14. Lo, S.Y., Hang, H.M., Chan, S.W., Lin, J.J.: Multi-class lane semantic segmentation using efficient convolutional networks. In: 2019 IEEE 21st International Workshop on Multimedia Signal Processing (MMSP), pp. 1–6. IEEE (2019)
15. Pan, X., Shi, J., Luo, P., Wang, X., Tang, X.: Spatial as deep: Spatial CNN for traffic scene understanding. In: Proceedings of the AAAI Conference on Artificial Intelligence, vol. 32 (2018)
16. Qu, Z., Jin, H., Zhou, Y., Yang, Z., Zhang, W.: Focus on local: Detecting lane marker from bottom up via key point. In: Proceedings of the IEEE/CVF Conference on Computer Vision and Pattern Recognition, pp. 14122–14130 (2021)
17. Tabelini, L., Berriel, R., Paixao, T.M., Badue, C., De Souza, A.F., Oliveira-Santos, T.: Keep your eyes on the lane: real-time attention-guided lane detection. In: Proceedings of the IEEE/CVF Conference on Computer Vision and Pattern Recognition, pp. 294–302 (2021)
18. Wang, J., et al.: A keypoint-based global association network for lane detection. In: Proceedings of the IEEE/CVF Conference on Computer Vision and Pattern Recognition, pp. 1392–1401 (2022)
19. Xie, E., Wang, W., Yu, Z., Anandkumar, A., Alvarez, J.M., Luo, P.: Segformer: simple and efficient design for semantic segmentation with transformers. Adv. Neural Inf. Process. Syst. **34**, 12077–12090 (2021)
20. Yu, F., Koltun, V.: Multi-scale context aggregation by dilated convolutions. arXiv preprint arXiv:1511.07122 (2015)
21. Zheng, T., et al.: CLRNet: Cross layer refinement network for lane detection. In: Proceedings of the IEEE/CVF Conference on Computer Vision and Pattern Recognition, pp. 898–907 (2022)
22. Zhou, Z., Siddiquee, M.M.R., Tajbakhsh, N., Liang, J.: Unet++: redesigning skip connections to exploit multiscale features in image segmentation. IEEE Trans. Med. Imaging **39**(6), 1856–1867 (2019)
23. Zoljodi, A., Loni, M., Abadijou, S., Alibeigi, M., Daneshtalab, M.: 3DLaneNAS: neural architecture search for accurate and light-weight 3D lane detection. In: Pimenidis, E., Angelov, P., Jayne, C., Papaleonidas, A., Aydin, M. (eds.) Artificial Neural Networks and Machine Learning - ICANN 2022. ICANN 2022. LNCS, Part I, vol. 13529, pp. 404–415. Springer, Cham (2022). https://doi.org/10.1007/978-3-031-15919-0_34

Classification-Based and Lightweight Networks for Fast Image Super Resolution

Xueliang Zhong and Jianping Luo(✉)

Guangdong Key Laboratory of Intelligent Information Processing, College of Electronic and Information Engineering, Shenzhen University, Shenzhen, China
ljp@szu.edu.cn

Abstract. Lightweight image super-resolution (SR) networks are of great significance for practical applications. Presently, there are several SR methods based on deep learning with excellent performance, but their memory and computation costs hinder practical applications. In this paper, we propose a down-up sampling continuous mutual affine super-resolution network (DUSCMAnet) to solve above problems. Moreover, we propose a classification-based SR algorithm based on image statistical features (TSClassSR-DUSCMAnet) for accelerating SR networks on large images (2K–8K). The proposed algorithm first decomposes the large images into small sub-images, then uses a Class-Module to classify sub-images into different classes according to the difficulty of reconstruction, then use a SR-Module to perform SR for different classes. The Class-Module is composed of a support vector machine (SVM) based on image statistical features, and the SR-Module is composed of our proposed DUSCMAnet, a lightweight SR network. After classifying, a majority of sub-images will pass through lighter networks, thus the computational cost can be significantly reduced. Experiments show that our DUSCMAnet is superior to the existing lightweight SR models in terms of time performance and also has competitive SR performance. Our TSClassSR-DUSCMAnet can help DUSCMAnet save up to 63% FLOPs on DIV8K datasets.

Keywords: Image Super-Resolution · Deep Learning · Machine Learning

1 Introduction

Single image super-resolution (SR) is to restore a high-resolution (HR) image from a given degraded low-resolution (LR) image. There are many ways [12, 14] to solve the SR problem. In recent years, researchers have focused on developing lightweight models for practical applications in super-resolution (SR), such as FSRCNN [4], CARN [2], IDN [6], RFDN [13], and BSRN [10]. In this paper, we not only design lightweight SR algorithms for normal size images but also explore how to accelerate SR algorithms for large image inputs, which typically have higher resolutions ranging from 2K to 8K. For SR algorithms based on deep learning, the memory, computational cost, and inference speed will grow drastically with input size. Therefore, it is necessary to design faster SR algorithms and divide large images into sets of sub-images to meet the real-time implementation requirements for real-world images.

L. Iliadis et al. (Eds.): ICANN 2023, LNCS 14255, pp. 140–152, 2023.
https://doi.org/10.1007/978-3-031-44210-0_12

Firstly, we propose a lightweight super-resolution network called DUSCMAnet that has faster speed, lower computational cost, and competitive super-resolution performance compared to existing lightweight networks. The DUSCMAnet is mainly composed of a pair of down-up sampling layers, a CMAB for the backbone, and a feature aggregation module in the CMAB. The down-sampling layer is to further reduce the spatial size of LR feature maps, which makes the FLOPs of the CMAB backbone decrease greatly and improves the inference speed by a large margin. The backbone of CMAB is a well-designed lightweight module, both the parameters and FLOPs of each mutual affine module are less than one of normal 3×3 convolution. Moreover, the CMAB utilizes lightweight feature aggregation modules to aggregate the hierarchical features, which is more helpful for image reconstruction.

To address the problems of insufficient GPU memory and high computational cost for large image inputs, we propose TSClassSR-DUSCMAnet, which decomposes the large image into a set of sub-images, uses sub-image statistical features to classify their difficulty level, and assigns simpler sub-images to a lighter network. The 'TS' means Three 's': simple, image statistic, and SVM. The framework consists of two modules, Class-Module and SR-Module. The Class-Module is an SVM (support vector machine) based on the image statistic features that classifies the input into a specific class according to the restoration difficulty, while the SR-Module is a network container that processes the classified input with the SR network of the corresponding class. We found that the simple sub-images perceived by human vision have smoother and fewer texture features. To represent them in computer vision, the spatial frequency of the sub-image's grayscale image and the mean and standard deviation of the sub-image's edge feature map can be used as features for SVM input. This method effectively classifies those simple and smoother sub-images, which can then be input into simpler networks to reduce computational complexity for our super-resolution task. Specifically, we compose three different difficulty super-resolution networks by reducing the number of channels of DUSCMAnet.

Overall, the main contributions of this work are summarized as follows:

- We propose a lightweight SR framework (DUSCMAnet), which is composed of down-up sampling layers, the CMAB, and a lightweight feature aggregation module. Due to the exquisite design of these modules, the running speed of this network is faster than other networks. Compared with the common 3×3 convolution layer, the CMAB module has fewer parameters and FLOPs. Moreover, the down-sampling layer helps us greatly reduce the number of FLOPs, while the feature aggregation module aggregates the hierarchical features. Therefore, our method can achieve competitive reconstruction accuracy in a short time.
- The proposed classification-based SR network based on image statistical features (TSClassSR-DUSCMAnet) can accelerate SR networks on large images (2K–8K). It uses the spatial frequency, mean, and standard deviation of sub-images as the basis for SVM classification, and classifies the difficulty of reconstructing sub-images into

three levels: simple level, medium level, and hard level. Then, these sub-images are assigned to the corresponding difficulty level super-resolution network, thereby significantly reducing the computational cost of our SR task, while maintaining comparable super-resolution performance.

2 Related Work

2.1 Lightweight SR Algorithm

Deep learning super-resolution models that have too many parameters have slow inference speeds, making them unsuitable for resource-constrained platforms like mobile devices. To address these drawbacks, researchers recently have explored lightweight image super-resolution models, such as FSRCNN [4], CARN [2], IDN [6], RFDN [13], and BSRN [10]. These models use different techniques to reduce the number of parameters and computation costs while maintaining good SR performance. FSRCNN simply reduces the number of layers or channels, which may sacrifice feature extraction ability and lead to reduced super-resolution quality. CARN improves the performance of the model by cascading multiple residual blocks while using group convolution and shared parameters to keep the model lightweight. IDN, RFDN, and BSRN redesign lightweight modules, called the information distillation module, to reduce parameters while preserving feature extraction ability, achieving faster speed without sacrificing much quality.

2.2 Classification-Based SR Algorithm

ClassSR [8] and ARM [3] are two deep learning-based algorithms that aim to accelerate the super-resolution (SR) process for large images (2K-8K). Both methods adopt a sub-images-based approach to handle large images SR tasks. ClassSR combines classification and SR into a unified framework by using a deep-learning-based Class-Module to classify the sub-images based on their restoration difficulty, followed by an SR-Module for each class. This method uses the Class-Loss and Average-Loss functions for joint training and constraining the convergence of the model. Afterwards, ARM employs a lookup table that maps edge scores to PSNR performance and calculates the computational cost of different sub-networks. During inference, sub-images are assigned to different sub-networks to balance computation performance.

3 Methods

3.1 DUSCMAnet

In this section, we first describe the proposed overall model architecture of DUSCMAnet. Then, the down-up sampling layers, the continuous mutual affine blocks (CMAB), and the feature aggregation module are discussed, which are the core of the proposed method.

Framework. As shown in Fig. 1, the proposed DUSCMAnet consists of five parts: a shadow feature extraction block, a pair of down-up sampling layers, a CMAB for the backbone, a finetune block, and a pixel-shuffle layer. Here, we denote $I_{LR} \in \mathcal{R}^{3\times H\times W}$ and $I_{SR} \in \mathcal{R}^{3\times dH\times dW}$ as the input and the output of DUSCMAnet, respectively, where H is the height of the LR image, W is the width of the LR image, and $d(d > 1)$ is the super-resolution scale factor. In the overall network structure, some residual connections are adopted to make the network learn the high-frequency part of the image, thus reducing the difficulty of network training.

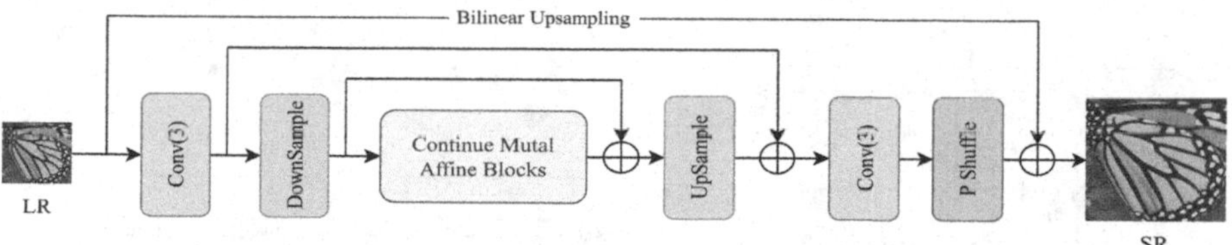

Fig. 1. The architecture of the DUSCMAnet. $Conv(3)$ means 3×3 convolution.

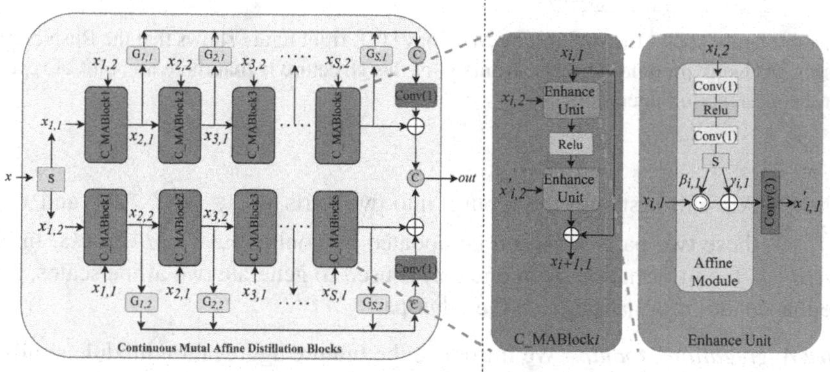

Fig. 2. Details of the Continuous Mutual Affine Blocks. The green s and pink c means channel split and concatenation operation respectively, $G_{i,j}$ means the group convolution, $Conv(1)$ means 1×1 convolution, and $Conv(3)$ means 3×3 convolution.

Down-Up Sampling Layer. In order to greatly reduce the number of FLOPs for the backbone of CMAB, we apply a down-sampling layer f_{down} before the backbone, as shown in Fig. 1. In other words, the feature maps will be down-sampled 2 times in spatial dimension to get the feature maps in $\mathcal{R}^{C\times\frac{H}{2}\times\frac{W}{2}}$ dimension. Compared to not using the down-sampling layer, it will save 4 times the computation costs theoretically. After extracting deep features by the backbone of CMAB, the feature maps will be up-sampled twice by an up-sampling layer to obtain feature maps of the same spatial size as the low-resolution input image I_{LR}.

Continuous Mutual Affine Blocks. Our backbone of CMAB consists of s C_MABlocks and s feature aggregation group convolutions, the details of CMAB are shown in Fig. 2.

C_MABlocks. The C_MABlock is an improved version of MAConv [11]. The structure of MAConv is shown in the left of Fig. 3. We do not stack our structure like ResNet as in MAConv, as shown in the right of Fig. 3, as this would contain too many channel concatenation and separation operations, which would slow down the inference speed. In our CMAB, as shown in Fig. 2, there is only one channel split operation and one concatenation operation. Continuous C_MABlocks are placed in the middle of CMAB to extract information. Finally, a feature aggregation module is adopted to aggregate the output of each C_MABlock.

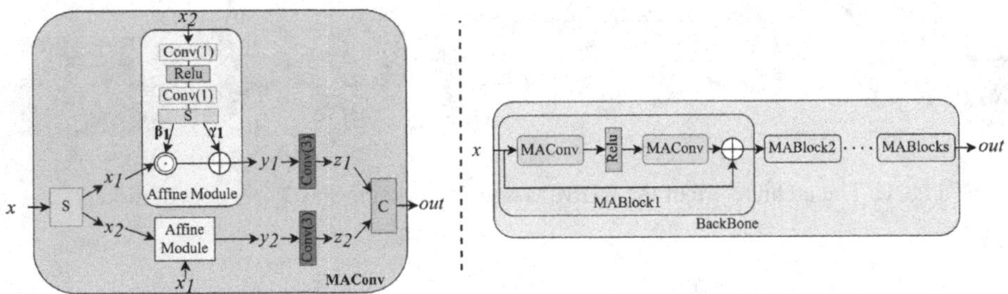

Fig. 3. Left figure shows the structure of MAConv [11], right figure shows that the ResNet structure using MAConv module. The disadvantage of this structure is that there are a lot of repeated split and concatenation operations.

The CMAB will first split the input x into two parts $x_{1,1} \in \mathcal{R}^{\frac{C}{2}\times\frac{H}{2}\times\frac{W}{2}}$ and $x_{1,2} \in \mathcal{R}^{\frac{C}{2}\times\frac{H}{2}\times\frac{W}{2}}$, these two parts will then be updated by continuous *C_MABlocks*. In each *C_MABlock*, the information from one part is used to generate two affine scales, β and γ, to enhance the information from the other part.

Feature Aggregation Module. We introduce the feature aggregation module similar to previous methods in BSRN [10], but our feature aggregation module is more lightweight and can maintain the representative hierarchical features, which is more helpful for the following image reconstruction.

Previous methods usually directly concatenate different hierarchical features and then use a fusion layer to reduce the channel number of concatenated hierarchical features, but this approach can result in a large number of network parameters. To address this issue, we propose a lightweight feature fusion module that uses group convolution and 1×1 convolution layer to adaptively aggregate hierarchical features. Firstly, we use group convolution to extract informative representations and then aggregate them via channel concatenation. The aggregated feature maps have the same channel number as the C_MABlock output. Then, we use 1×1 convolution layer to fuse the aggregated features and add the resulting output to the last C_MABlock output, obtaining the final aggregated feature maps. Finally, we concatenate the two parts of the aggregated feature maps to produce the final output of CMAB.

3.2 TSClassSR_DUSCMAnet

In this section, we will introduce the components of TSClassSR-DUSCAMnet, including the SVM classifier based on image statistical features and the SR networks with three levels of complexity.

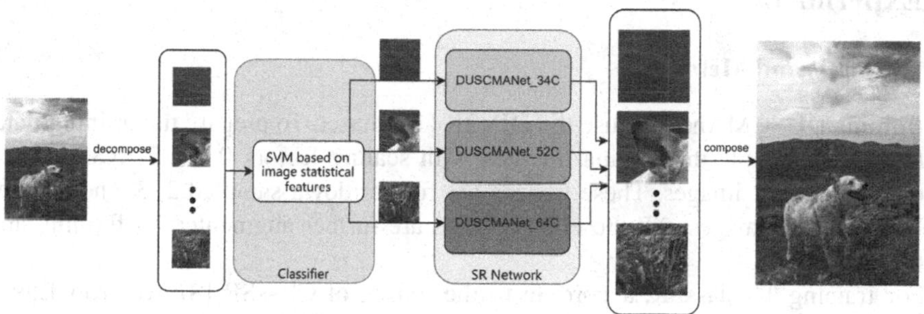

Fig. 4. The architecture of TSClassSR-DUSCMAnet.

Framework. As shown in Fig. 4, the TSClassSR-DUSCMAnet consists of an SVM classifier based on image statistical features and an SR module based on DUSCMAnet. The large image input is first decomposed into a set of sub-images, which are then fed into the classification module for feature extraction and difficulty classification. After classification, the classifier assigns the sub-images to different SR networks based on their respective difficulty levels for SR reconstruction. Finally, the SR sub-image sets are composed to form the final output.

SVM Classifier Based on Image Statistical Features. From the perspective of human vision, when an image has more texture features and edge features, it will contain more information, and the reconstruction will be more difficult. We find that several image statistical features can represent the difficulty of image reconstruction from the perspective of computer vision, such as the spatial frequency of the gray image, and the mean and standard deviation of the edge gray image. Using these three statistical features as the input of SVM, images of different reconstruction difficulties can be effectively classified.

SR Network. The SR network adopted by TSClassSR is our proposed lightweight super-resolution network, DUSCMAnet. We divide the SR networks into three different levels of complexity, called simple level, medium level, and hard level, by setting the number of channels. The simple SR network uses a small number of channels to perform super-resolution on small images with less texture and edge features, significantly reducing the computational cost. The hard SR network uses more channels and increases the complexity of the model to perform super-resolution on small images with complex textures and edge features, thereby improving the reconstruction quality of the images. The number of channels in the medium SR network is between that of the simple and hard SR networks, achieving a balance between speed and reconstruction performance.

By combining DUSCMAnet with an SVM classifier, TSClassSR not only has the advantage in speed but also can classify simple images to simple networks, greatly reducing the number of FLOPs and avoiding the problem of insufficient GPU memory and slow speed during inference.

4 Experiments

4.1 Datasets and Metrics

For training DUSCMAnet, we use the DIV2K [1] dataset. To prepare the training data, we first down-sample the original images with scaling factors 0.6, 0.7, 0.8, and 0.9 to generate the HR images. These images are further down-sampled 2, 3, and 4 times to obtain the LR images. All the HR-LR pairs are further augmented by flipping and rotation.

For training TSClassSR, according to the setting of ClassSR [8], we crop 1.59M sub-images with size 32×32 from LR images. After PSNR descending sorting through the MSRResNet [15] network, these sub-images are equally divided into three classes (0.53M for each). These three classes of datasets are used to pre-train our "simple, medium, hard" SR networks.

For testing DUSCMAnet, we use four standard benchmark datasets: Set5, Set14, BSD100, and Urban100. The SR results are evaluated with PSNR and SSIM on the Y channel of the transformed YCbCr space.

For testing TSClassSR, we use three high-resolution benchmark datasets: DIV2K, DIV4K, and DIV8K. The SR results are evaluated with PSNR and SSIM on the RGB channel.

4.2 Implementation Details

For training DUSCMAnet, we use Adam optimizer with β_1= 0.9 and β_2=0.999 to train our models with an initial learning rate 1×10^{-3}. The cosine annealing learning strategy is applied to adjust the learning rate, and the minimum learning rate is set to 1×10^{-7}. The period of cosine is 800K iterations. The L_1 loss function is adopted. The batch size is set to 64. The GT size is set to 192 for the 2 and 3 scale factors, and 384 only for the 4 scale factor. All models are built on the PyTorch framework and trained with NVIDIA 3090 GPUs.

Considering the trade-off between the execution time and the reconstruction performance, we construct our DUSCMAnet with 14 blocks of CMAB, and the channel of feature maps is set to 64.

For training TSClassSR-DUSCMAnet, we use the number of channels in each convolution layer to control the network complexity. We use the DUSCMAnet for our SR network. The number of channels for "simple, medium, hard" branches is 34, 52, and 64, where 64 is the channel number of the base network.

For training Class-Module, we use RBF Gaussian kernel function as SVM kernel function, penalty coefficient *C* is set to 1, *gamma* is set to 'scale', and *OVR* mode is used for three-class classification. All speed tests are performed on the NVIDIA GTX 1080 GPU.

Table 1. Average PSNR/SSIM for scale 2×, 3×, and 4×. The time cost is tested on 1080P image. Bold words indicate the best performance, and underline words indicate the second-best performance.

Scale	Method	Set5	Set14	BSD100	Urban100	Time Cost
		PSNR/SSIM	PSNR/SSIM	PSNR/SSIM	PSNR/SSIM	(ms)
X2	Bicubic	33.68/0.9304	30.24/0.8691	29.56/0.8435	26.88/0.8405	**9.41**
	VDSR [7]	37.53/0.9587	33.05/0.9127	31.90/0.8960	30.77/0.9141	834.72
	CARN-M [2]	37.53/0.9583	33.26/0.9141	31.92/0.8960	30.83/0.9233	300.91
	IDN [6]	37.83/0.9600	33.30/0.9148	32.08/0.8985	31.27/0.9196	247.29
	BSRN [10]	**38.10/0.9610**	**33.74/0.9193**	**32.24/0.9006**	**32.34/0.9303**	623.40
	DUSCMAnet (ours)	37.86/0.9601	33.47/0.9170	32.08/0.8987	31.72/0.9249	156.02
X3	Bicubic	30.40/0.8686	27.54/0.7741	27.21/0.7389	24.46/0.7349	**7.51**
	VDSR [7]	33.66/0.9213	29.78/0.8318	28.83/0.7976	27.14/0.8279	864.27
	CARN-M [2]	33.99/0.9236	30.08/0.8367	28.91/0.8000	26.86/0.8263	167.47
	IDN [6]	34.11/0.9253	29.99/0.8354	28.95/0.8013	27.42/0.8359	125.07
	BSRN [10]	**34.46/0.9277**	**30.47/0.8449**	**29.18/0.8068**	**28.39/0.8567**	274.50
	DUSCMAnet (ours)	34.15/0.9255	30.17/0.8394	28.99/0.8030	27.73/0.8441	76.06
X4	Bicubic	28.43/0.8109	26.00/0.7023	25.96/0.6678	23.14/0.6574	**7.01**
	VDSR [7]	31.35/0.8838	28.02/0.7678	27.29/0.7252	25.18/0.7525	840.20
	CARN-M [2]	31.92/0.8903	28.42/0.7762	27.44/0.7304	25.63/0.7688	112.54
	IDN [6]	31.82/0.8903	28.25/0.7730	27.41/0.7297	25.41/0.7632	74.43
	BSRN [10]	**32.35/0.8966**	**28.73/0.7847**	**27.65/0.7387**	**26.27/0.7908**	136.01
	DUSCMAnet (ours)	31.90/0.8901	28.39/0.7773	27.44/0.7317	25.68/0.7736	42.37

5 Result

We compare the proposed DUSCMAnet with other SR methods, including Bicubic, VDSR [7], CARN-M [2], and some recent lightweight SR methods, including IDN [6] and BSRN [10].

Table 1 shows that the proposed DUSCMAnet method achieves competitive SR performance and outperforms the IDN method by a large margin in Urban100 2× and 3× datasets, which means that our network can reconstruct clearer SR images for LR of large spatial size. Our down-sampling module plays a crucial role in enhancing the

Table 2. Comparison of the running time (ms) on 1080P image with scale factors 3 ×. Bold indicates the fastest algorithm. Our DUSCMAnet achieves the best time performance.

Network	Parameters(K)	FLOPs (G)	Time Cost(ms)
VSDR [7]	664.70	2761.70	864.272
LapSRN [9]	870.11	1461.14	704.963
CARN [2]	1500.00	536.68	173.764
CARN-M [2]	414.79	210.22	167.475
IDN [6]	590.91	477.54	125.072
SRMDNF [16]	1530.00	705.98	15981.471
DLSR [5]	**329.00**	136.68	331.23
BSRN [10]	340.28	150.00	274.500
DUSCMAnet(ours)	705.53	**105.98**	**76.060**

Table 3. The comparison of various methods and our TSClassSR on DIV2K to DIV8K.

Model	Par	DIV2K(dB)	FLOPs	DIV4K(dB)	FLOPs	DIV8K(dB)	FLOPs
DUSCMAnet (ours)	705.53K	26.07	880.1M (100%)	27.47	880.2M (100%)	33.41	879.99M (100%)
TSClassSR-DUSCMAnet (ours)	1.32M	25.95	388.9M (44.19%)	27.33	370.2M (42.06%)	33.24	323.47M (36.75%)
FSRCNN	25K	25.61	468M (100%)	26.90	468M (100%)	32.66	468M (100%)
ClassSR-FSRCNN	113K	25.61	311M (66.45%)	26.91	286M (61.11%)	32.73	238M (50.85%)
ARM-L-FSRCNN		25.64	366M (78.21%)	26.93	341M (72.86%)	32.75	290M (61.96%)
ARM-M-FSRCNN	25K	25.61	289M (61.75%)	26.90	282M (60.25%)	32.73	249M (53.20%)
ARM-S-FSRCNN		25.59	245M (52.35%)	26.87	230M (49.14%)	32.66	187M (39.95%)
CARN	295K	25.95	1.15G (100%)	27.34	1.15G (100%)	33.18	1.15G (100%)
ClassSR-CARN	645K	26.01	841M (73.13%)	27.42	742M (64.52%)	33.24	608M (52.87%)
ARM-L-CARN		26.04	945M (82.17%)	27.45	825M (71.73%)	33.31	784M (68.17%)
ARM-M-CARN	295K	26.02	831M (72.26%)	27.42	743M (64.60%)	32.27	612M (53.21%)
ARM-S-CARN		25.95	645M (56.08%)	27.34	593M (51.56%)	33.18	489M (42.52%)

performance of the CMAB backbone network by further reducing the spatial resolution of the feature map, it filters out the unnecessary information while retaining the

Table 4. The comparison of classification accuracy of various methods on DIV2K.

Network	Accuracy
TSClassSR-DUSCMAnet	72.28%
ClassSR-FSRCNN	63.59%
ClassSR-CARN	72.33%
ClassSR-SRResNet	70.40%
ClassSR-RCAN	66.17%

essential details required for effective reconstruction. This approach results in a significant reduction in the number of FLOPs and greatly improves the inference speed of our network.

Although the PSNR and SSIM of our model are not better than that of BSRN, we still have a great advantage in speed performance. In conclusion, the DUSCMAnet can achieve faster speed and competitive SR performance.

We made some comparisons with some lightweight models in terms of the number of parameters, FLOPs, and speed. As shown in Table 2, In particular, we compared DLSR [5], a lightweight super-resolution algorithm based on neural architecture search (NAS). Although the NAS technology can help DLSR search for the optimal structure and balance the number of parameters, FLOPs, and SR performance, the speed performance is not good enough due to the insufficient optimization of separable convolution and dilation convolution adopted by DLSR. Overall, our model has the fastest inference speed and the fewest FLOPs.

As listed in Table 3, we compare the proposed TSClassSR method with other classification-based SR methods with scale factor 4 ×, including ClassSR and ARM. Our TSClassSR achieves better results with less computation cost than those classification-based SR methods based on FSRCNN and CARN methods, and our classification method based on image statistical features can reduce the amount of computation to a greater extent. After applying our TSClassSR on DUSCMAnet, their computation costs on three test-datasets respectively accounted for 44.19%, 42.06%, and 36.75% of the original. The larger the image input resolution is, the more obvious the computational cost is reduced by our classification method.

Table 4 indicate that the classification accuracy of our TSClassSR method is not affected by the choice of super-resolution network, and our classification method based on image statistical features has better classification accuracy, therefore, our TSClassSR can reduce a large number of computation costs for large image SR task.

As shown in Fig. 5, to verify the validity of the three image statistical features of mean, standard deviation, and spatial frequency for our classification method, we counted the 3D data distribution maps of the three image statistical features of the sub-images with different difficulty levels under the DIV2K dataset. First of all, red data represents the simple image, green data represents the medium image, and blue data represents the hard image. As shown in the blue data, images with complex textures and more edge features usually have a larger mean, standard deviation, and spatial frequency. The premise of utilizing an SVM support vector machine for difficulty classification lies in the fact that datasets of varying difficulties exhibit distinct data distribution spaces. Therefore, combined with the three image statistical features of mean, standard deviation, and spatial frequency, the SVM can find a hyperplane in the high-dimensional space through the kernel function to distinguish different classes of data. At last, we conducted a subjective visual comparison of an image from the DIV8K test-set, using two classification-based super-resolution models, ClassSR-CARN and ARM-S-CARN. As shown in Fig. 6, our TSClassSR-DUSCAMnet model can achieve comparable SR results to the ClassSR-CARN model with less computational complexity. In addition, with slightly more computational complexity than ARM-S-CARN, our model can achieve a PSNR improvement of +0.07dB.

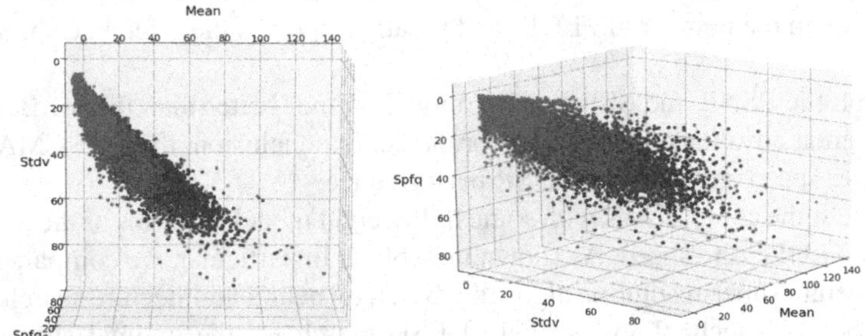

Fig. 5. 3D feature data distribution diagram of three classes datasets from two perspectives.

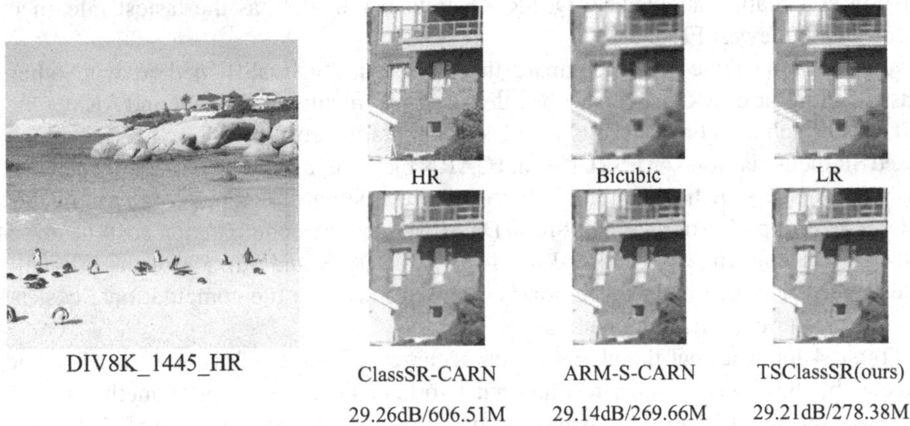

Fig. 6. Visual comparison for 4 × SR with other models on DIV8K dataset.

6 Conclusion

In this paper, we propose a novel SR framework called DUSCMAnet for fast super-resolution and a classification-based SR framework called TSClassSR. The proposed DUSCMAnet model adopts a pair of down-up sampling layers, a backbone of CMAB to reduce the number of FLOPs, and a feature aggregation module to aggregate the hierarchical features. The model has excellent inference speed and competitive SR performance. We show with several quantitative experiments that DUSCMAnet outperforms other existing lightweight models in terms of computational cost. The proposed TSClassSR adopts an SVM classification method based on image statistical features to accelerate the large image super-resolution task. Experimental results have shown that this method can effectively reduce the computational complexity of the large image super-resolution task compared to existing classification-based methods.

Acknowledgments. This work was supported by the National Natural Science Foundation of China under Grant 62176161, and the Scientific Research and Development Foundations of Shenzhen under Grant JCYJ20220818100005011 and 20200813144831001.

References

1. Agustsson, E., Timofte, R.: Ntire 2017 challenge on single image super-resolution: Dataset and study. In: Proceedings of the IEEE Conference on Computer Vision and Pattern Recognition Workshops, pp. 126–135 (2017)
2. Ahn, N., Kang, B., Sohn, K-A.: Fast, accurate, and lightweight super-resolution with cascading residual network. In: Proceedings of the European conference on Computer Vision (ECCV), pp. 252–268 (2018)
3. Chen, B., Lin, M., Sheng, K., Zhang, M., Chen, P., Li, K., et al.: Arm: Any-time super-resolution method. In: Computer Vision–ECCV 2022: 17th European Conference, Tel Aviv, Israel, October 23–27 2022, Proceedings, Part XIX, pp. 254–270 (2022). https://doi.org/10.1007/978-3-031-19800-7_15
4. Dong, C., Loy, C.C., Tang, X.: Accelerating the super-resolution convolutional neural network. In: European Conference on Computer Vision, pp. 391–407 (2016). https://doi.org/10.1007/978-3-319-46475-6_25
5. Huang, H., Shen, L., He, C., Dong, W., Liu, W.: Differentiable neural architecture search for extremely lightweight image super-resolution. IEEE Trans. Circ. Syst. Video Technol. (2022)
6. Hui, Z., Wang, X., Gao, X.: Fast and accurate single image super-resolution via information distillation network. In: Proceedings of the IEEE Conference on Computer Vision and Pattern Recognition, pp. 723–731 (2018)
7. Kim, J., Lee, J.K., Lee, K.M.: Accurate image super-resolution using very deep convolutional networks. In: Proceedings of the IEEE Conference on Computer Vision and Pattern Recognition, pp. 1646–1654 (2016)
8. Kong, X., Zhao, H., Qiao, Y., Dong, C.: Classsr: A general framework to accelerate super-resolution networks by data characteristic. In: Proceedings of the IEEE/CVF Conference on Computer Vision and Pattern Recognition, pp. 12016–12025 (2021)
9. Lai, W.-S., Huang, J.-B., Ahuja, N., Yang, M.-H.: Deep laplacian pyramid networks for fast and accurate super-resolution. In: Proceedings of the IEEE Conference on Computer Vision and Pattern Recognition, pp. 624–632 (2017)
10. Li, Z., Liu, Y., Chen, X., Cai, H., Gu, J., Qiao, Y., et al.: Blueprint separable residual network for efficient image super-resolution. In: Proceedings of the IEEE/CVF Conference on Computer Vision and Pattern Recognition, pp. 833–843 (2022)
11. Liang, J., Sun, G., Zhang, K., Van Gool, L., Timofte, R.: Mutual affine network for spatially variant kernel estimation in blind image super-resolution. In: Proceedings of the IEEE/CVF International Conference on Computer Vision, pp. 4096–4105 (2021)

12. Lim, B., Son, S., Kim, H., Nah, S., Lee, M.K.: Enhanced deep residual networks for single image super-resolution. In: Proceedings of the IEEE conference on Computer Vision and Pattern Recognition Workshops, pp. 136–144 (2017)
13. Liu, J., Tang, J., Wu, G.: Residual feature distillation network for lightweight image super-resolution. In: European Conference on Computer Vision, pp. 41–55 (2020). https://doi.org/10.1007/978-3-030-67070-2_2
14. Liu J, Zhang W, Tang Y, Tang J, Wu G.: Residual feature aggregation network for image super-resolution. In: Proceedings of the IEEE/CVF Conference on Computer Vision and Pattern Recognition, pp. 2359–2368 (2020)
15. Zhang, K., Danelljan, M., Li, Y., Timofte, R., Liu, J., Tang, J., et al.: Aim 2020 challenge on efficient super-resolution: Methods and results. In: Computer Vision–ECCV 2020 Workshops: Glasgow, UK, August 23–28 2020, Proceedings, Part III 16, pp. 5–40 (2020). https://doi.org/10.1007/978-3-030-67070-2_1
16. Zhang, K., Zuo, W., Zhang, L.: Learning a single convolutional super-resolution network for multiple degradations. In: Proceedings of the IEEE Conference on Computer Vision and Pattern Recognition, pp. 3262–3271 (2018)

CLN: Complementary Learning Network for 3D Face Reconstruction and Alignment

Kangbo Wu, Xitie Zhang, Xing Zheng, Suping Wu(✉), Yongrong Cao, Zhiyuan Zhou, and Kehua Ma

School of Information Engineering, Ningxia University, Yinchuan 750021, China
wuynlyxy@163.com, pswuu@nxu.edu.cn

Abstract. In the complex and changeable unconstrained state, the 3D Morphable Model (3DMM) parameters regression methods lack the ability to express local details and they are difficult to enrich geometric details. In this paper, we propose a complementary learning network (CLN), which aims to improve the ability to extract global discriminative features and capture local details through complementary learning between global and local information. Specifically, we first elaborately design a cross-domain self-shuffling data augmentation method to simulate the case of the inconspicuous or obscured face information under unconstrained conditions, thus increasing the sensitivity of the network to local information. Different from other methods, our augmented data contains global data that can guide the network in reasoning about the inconspicuous areas of the face in special lighting and partially obscured areas of the face in large poses. To better achieve the complementary between global information and local details, we design a complementary learning network in which one stream extracts global discriminative features from the original input image. Meanwhile, another stream extracts local detailed features from the shuffled image. Then, we adopt the coordinate attention transformer module to enforce our network's ability to capture the correlation between local information. Finally, we linearly fuse the global information that constrains the geometric shape of the face and the local information of the rich geometric details to improve the regression accuracy of the network. Extensive experiments on AFLW, AFLW2000-3D, and other datasets demonstrate that our method is superior to previous methods.

Keywords: Data augmentation · Dual-stream network · Attention mechanism · 3D face reconstruction and alignment

This work was supported by National Natural Science Foundation of China under Grant 62062056, in part by the Ningxia Graduate Education and Teaching Reform Research and Practice Project 2021, and in part by the Ningxia Natural Science Foundation under Grant 2022AAC03327.

Kangbo Wu and Xitie Zhang: Equal Contribution.

L. Iliadis et al. (Eds.): ICANN 2023, LNCS 14255, pp. 153–166, 2023.
https://doi.org/10.1007/978-3-031-44210-0_13

1 Introduction

The complexity and degree of freedom of faces make it a challenging problem to estimate the 3-dimensional face surface and other intrinsic components from a single image. The seminal work of Blanz and Vetter [2] showed that it is possible to reconstruct shape and texture by optimizing a linear statistical model. The proposed model in [2] which contained texture and shape is called 3DMM. The 3DMM and its variants were the preferred methods for 3D face reconstructio [3, 33] in recent years.

Recently, CNN-based methods [16,18,20,25,27] have superior performance in face reconstruction and face alignment, and have achieved significant successful results. For example, [31] introduced face parsing for 3D reconstruction to help the network learn facial geometry and multi-scale progressive rendering. But this method is hard to apply in a complex field environment because of the need for special input images. To more accurately predict the location of feature landmarks in face images with large poses and extreme expression by means of the 3D face model, Liu [6] adopted 6-layer cascaded convolutional neural networks. However, this method needs to calculate whether each feature point is visible or not, which is difficult to achieve for common face alignment methods. More recently, [10] adopted CNN directly to acquire the 3D face model by the regressing of 3DMM coefficients, and used the UV position map to clearly denote the 3D point cloud. Nevertheless, such a geometry representation (such as voxel, point cloud) in the texture space is difficult to further optimize the face reconstruction model.

Unconstrained states, such as extreme illumination and large pose faces where some local information is not visible or is obscured, prevent the network from performing accurate face alignment and reconstruction. To conquer the intrinsic limitation of existing methods, we design a complementary learning network (CLN) based on the cross-domain self-shuffling data augmentation, which aims to improve face reconstruction and alignment performance through complementary learning between the global discriminative features and local detailed features. Our core idea is to achieve complementary learning between global and local information. Specifically, our designed cross-domain self-shuffling data augmentation method incorporates the global and local domain information of the face, and achieves the mutual complementation of the two domain data, as shown in Fig. 1. Our complementary learning network includes two parts, where one stream network is adopted to extract global discriminative features from the original input image, and another stream network learns local detailed features under the constraints of global information from the image processed by our cross-domain self-shuffling data augmentation. Moreover, to improve the detection accuracy for fine face reconstruction, we adopt the coordinate attention transformer module to enforce our network's ability of capturing the correlation between local information. Finally, we linearly fuse the two results of the complementary learning network, i.e., the global information that constrains the geometric shape of the face and the local information of the rich geometric details. In this way, the global information and local details can complement each other well, i.e., global discriminative features can contain more detailed features and the network is able to better learn local detailed features under the constraints of global information. Therefore, the regression accuracy of the network can be further improved. Our key contributions are summarized as follows:

1. To achieve complementation between the shape constraint ability of global features and the capturing details ability of the local features, we design a complementary learning network to jointly learn the global and local features from 2D images.
2. In order that the network can capture global features while extracting local information, we elaborately design a cross-domain self-shuffling data augmentation method that randomly reorganizes local and global information.
3. We exploit the coordinate attention transformer to enhance the network's ability to learn detailed features. While retaining the spatial positional relationship between local features, it can also capture the positional dependence between local information.
4. Extensive experiments on AFLW2000-3D and AFLW demonstrate that our proposed CLN outperforms prior works.

2 Proposed Method

2.1 3D Morphable Model

For a unique face, we apply 3DMM to denote a 3D facial geometry. The 3D face geometry $S \in R^{3Q}$ which is rendered by 3DMM saves vertices' coordinates values of the mesh, and performs a linear combination on the basis of a set of PCA. Same as [33], the face geometry is determined by 40 bases that came from Basel Face Model [23], and the facial expression is composed of 10 bases generated by the Face Warehouse [5]. The formula for the 3D facial geometry is shown as:

$$S = \bar{S} + T_{geo}\alpha_{geo} + T_{exp}\alpha_{exp} \tag{1}$$

where S denotes a 3D face shape, and $\bar{S} \in R^{3Q}$ represents the mean geometry. $T_{geo} \in R^{3Q\times 40}$ is the shape principle, $\alpha_{geo} \in R^{40}$ denotes the shape coefficient. $T_{exp} \in R^{3Q\times 10}$ represents the basis of the facial expression and $T_{exp} \in R^{10}$ represents the corresponding expression coefficient. The goal of 3D face modeling from a single view is to estimate the 3D facial coefficients α_{geo} and α_{exp} from the input 2D image.

2.2 Network Architecture

For the regression of the 3D face attribute, the traditional methods are to regress parameters containing pose, identity, and expression from global features, which lacks strong constraints on local details. So the network is difficult to concentrate on learnable geometric details. To address the above problem, we propose a joint learning method of global and local features to regress the 3DMM parameters for different network branches. Our approach can make use of the dependence between local information and global information to enrich geometric details. Figure 1 shows the workflow of our network's architecture.

Specifically, we first get the mixed image after self-shuffling (we will elaborate on its specific process in the next section). Subsequently, the original image and the mixed image are fed into two RepVGG [9] networks to learn separately the holistic and local details from the face image. In particular, since the position information between the local features of the mixed image is more complicated, to retain the positional relationship between local structural features of the mixed image while capturing its dependence. We have carefully designed an attention mechanism. Under different experience fields, the network can find similar characteristic information. It helps to capture the correlation between disordered local blocks and global information. At the same time, it helps the entire model to be repositioned according to the spatial position. Finally, to obtain a strong regression model, we use a linear fusion method to estimate the pose, identity, and expression parameters of the 3D face model, which can be expressed as

$$y(x) = \sum_{i=1}^{2} \alpha_i * \theta_i(x) \qquad \text{s.t. } \alpha_i = f_\phi\left(\theta_i(x)\right) \tag{2}$$

where α_i represents the weight of the upper or lower part of the predicted sample. θ_i is the output of each granularity branch. $y(x)$ represents the output of the mixed prediction result for $\text{s.t. } \alpha_i = f_\phi\left(\theta_i(x)\right)$, $f_\phi()$ is the learned mapping function, which represents the network learning the weights α_i corresponding to the results $\theta_i(x)$ of the upper and lower branches that make the final fusion result best, based on the results# of the upper and lower branches, and the process from results to weights we can consider as a learnable mapping function.

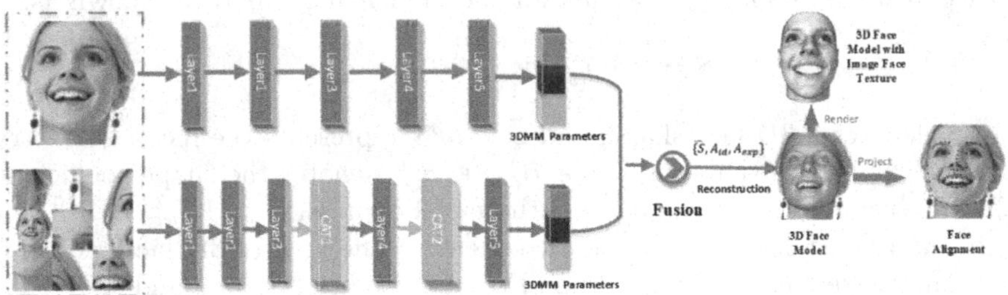

Fig. 1. The workflow of the proposed CLN framework. The upper part focuses on its global discriminative feature extraction, and the lower part focuses on the extraction of local details, focusing on its semantic details. Then, we use linear fusion to predict 3DMM parameters.

2.3 Data Augmentation Method of Self-shuffling

Data augmentation mainly generates virtual training sets near a given training dataset to enhance the generalization ability and robustness of the model. Because the face contains rich local detail information, the loss of local information will bring certain limitations to the face reconstruction task.

In this paper, we elaborately design a cross-domain self-shuffling data augmentation method. Different from traditional self-shuffling data augmentation methods, our cross-domain self-shuffling data augmentation integrates two kinds of domain information, i.e., global information and local information. The shuffled image achieves the mutual complementation of the two kinds of domain information, which contributes to the network learning global discriminative features and local detailed features more effectively. Specifically, we first get a thumbnail of a quarter of the original image, and paste it to the lower right corner of the original image to obtain a new image. Although a small amount of original image information is lost, the thumbnail in the new image still includes global information such as color and shape. To increase the diversity of the datasets, we subsequently cropped the new image in the form of a nine-square grid, shuffled, and reorganized them to obtain a mixed image in Fig. 1. In this way, the network strengthens the learning of local detailed features while paying attention to global information. Using the contained global information provides guidance for network training, which is more beneficial to face semantic feature extraction.

2.4 Coordinate Attention Transformer

The spatial position information in the feature map still plays an important role. Therefore, for complex and disordered partial image patches, it is particularly important to preserve the position messages and the position dependence in the space. Because the empirical receptive field is much smaller than the theoretical receptive field in deep networks [15,19], we merge the ASPP [8] module and the CA [11] module. We call this process a coordinate attention transformer module (CAT). The CAT is adopted to enhance the network to capture the local similarity facial structure information, as shown in Fig. 2.

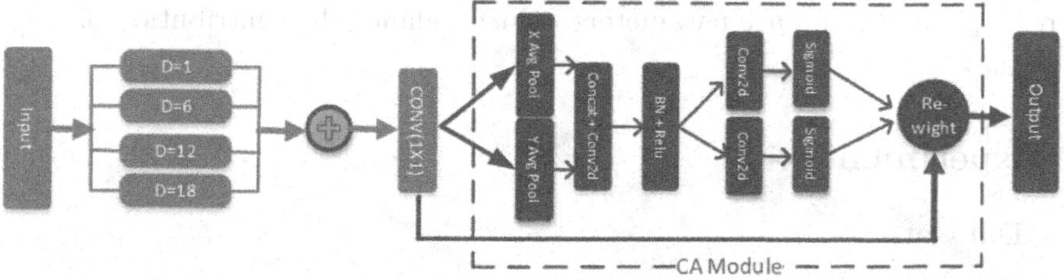

Fig. 2. The network architecture of the coordinate attention module.

The ASPP module provides different feature maps, each of which has a different scale receptive field. Afterward, multi-scale feature maps are generated by four parallel dilated convolution kernels with different dilated rates, (i.e., 1, 6, 12, 18). After that, the obtained feature maps are fused by one convolutional layer, the size of the convolution kernel is set to 1×1, and the stride is set to 1. We connect the ASPP module and the coordinate attention (CA) module effectively. The coordinate attention transforms the channel attention into two one-dimensional feature encoding processes, which perform feature aggregation along with two different spatial directions respectively. One of the one-dimensional features captures the spatial position dependence along the spatial direction, and the other one-dimensional feature retains the precise position information of its spatial direction. Therefore, it guides the network to capture the dependence of similar facial structural features under different receptive fields.

2.5 Objective Function

Same as [33], for the 3DMM parameters, we adopted the Weighted Parameter Distance Cost (WPDC) to optimize the learnable parameters. The key thought is to precisely learn the significance of each parameter:

$$L_{\text{wpdc}} = (P_{gt} - P_{pre})^T W (P_{gt} - P_{pre}) \tag{3}$$

where P_{pre} denotes the predicted value and P_{gt} represents the corresponding ground truth. W denotes the diagonal weights matrix. To accurately learn facial landmarks, we apply sparse 2D face landmarks to further constrain the 3D facial contour:

$$L_{\text{wing}}(\Delta V) = \begin{cases} \theta \ln\left(1 + \frac{|\Delta V|}{\zeta}\right), & \text{if } |\Delta V| < \theta \\ |\Delta V| - C, & \text{otherwise} \end{cases} \tag{4}$$

where $\Delta V = V_{gt} - V_{pre}$, V_{gt} represents the ground truth of the 3D facial landmarks. V_{pre} represents the 3D face landmarks learned through the network corresponding to the ground truth. θ and ζ denote hyperparameters of the loss. $C = \theta - \theta \ln(1 + \frac{\theta}{\zeta})$ denotes a constant that smoothly connects the linear and nonlinear parts. The final loss of our network is:

$$L = \lambda_{\text{wpdc}} L_{\text{wpdc}} + \lambda_{\text{wing}} L_{\text{wing}} \tag{5}$$

where λ_{wpdc} and λ_{wing} are parameters, which balance the contribution of L_{wpdc} and L_{wing}.

3 Experiments

3.1 Datasets

300W-LP [33]: 300W-LP [33] is an extended version of the 300W [24] across Large Poses. 300W [24] standardizes diverse alignment subsets with 68 annotated landmarks, which include AFW [32], IBUG [24], XM2VTS [21], etc. The challenging IBUG image set includes large poses, severe occlusion, and exaggerated expression images. Besides general dataset samples, we also investigate our CLN on challenging samples like IBUG.

AFLW: AFLW [13] means Annotated Facial Landmarks in the Wild. Due to the complete annotation dataset, it is well suited for evaluating facial alignment performance in large poses because it includes various large poses yaw from $-90°$ to $90°$. Nevertheless, since AFLW only has 21 landmarks annotation, we only use it for 3D landmarks alignment, not for 3D face reconstruction.

AFLW2000-3D: AFLW2000-3D [33] was first proposed because of the lack of paired 2D images and 3D models in unconstrained environments. The dataset [33] is used to evaluate challenging facial images in the wild for 3D face alignment. It is composed of the first 2000 facial images of AFLW, and increases the number of labeled landmarks to 68. Note that we use the 300W-LP [33] dataset as the training set, then we use AFLW [13] dataset and AFLW2000-3D [33] dataset for the evaluation of 3D landmarks alignment and 3D face reconstruction respectively. Finally, we test the generalization of our CLN on LFPW [1] and Helen [14] datasets.

3.2 Experimental Details

Our proposed CLN is designed based on Pytorch [22] framework. For each input image of the training dataset, We adopt a complementary learning network to extract features, one of which employs RepVGG to extract holistic information, and the other applies self-shuffling to extract local information. To balance the loss function, our method sets its weight to $\lambda_{\text{wpdc}} = 0.5$ and $\lambda_{\text{wing}} = 1$, respectively. During the experiment, the batch size and initial learning rate are set to 256 and 0.002, respectively. The input image resolution is 224×224. In our experiments, we train our CLN model by applying 2 NVIDIA RTX 2080Ti GPUs.

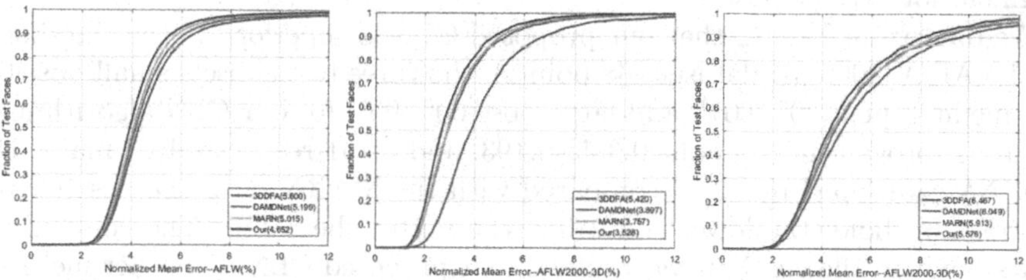

Fig. 3. The cumulative error distribution (CED) on AFLW and AFLW2000-3D.

3.3 Face Alignment and Reconstruction

For a fair comparison, we estimate the facial alignment effectiveness by employing the normalized mean error (NME) [33] like other methods. The Table 1 and 2 report the NME values for the angles of [0, 30], [30, 60], and [60, 90], namely, small pose, medium pose, and large pose, respectively. The values in bold in each column represent the best performance. The lower the value, the better the result.

Table 1. The NME(%) of face alignment results on AFLW Dataset (21pts).

Method	[0°, 30°]	[30°, 60°]	[60°, 90°]	Mean	Year
CDM [30]	8.150	13.020	16.170	12.440	2015
RCPR [4]	5.430	6.580	11.530	7.850	2013
ESR [7]	5.660	7.120	11.940	8.240	2014
SDM [28]	4.750	5.550	9.340	6.550	2013
3DDFA [33]	5.000	5.060	6.740	5.600	2016
Yu *et al.* [29]	5.940	6.480	7.960	–	2017
DAMDNet [12]	4.359	5.209	6.028	5.199	2019
GSRN [26]	4.253	5.144	5.816	5.073	2021
MARN [17]	4.306	4.965	5.775	5.015	2021
RADAN [34]	4.129	4.888	5.495	4.837	2023
CLN(Ours)	**3.998**	**4.650**	**5.309**	**4.652**	–

Comparison of Face Alignment on AFLW2000-3D and AFLW: Table 1 tabulates the NME's comparison for the state-of-the-art approaches and our CLN on AFLW datasets. Figure 3 is the corresponding CED curves. According to the results, the NME value of our CLN achieves 4.652 on the AFLW. Compared with MARN [17], our CLN decreases the error by 0.363 on AFLW. From the results in Table 1, our CLN has a conspicuous boost in the precision of face alignment for various poses.

We observe in Table 2 that our proposed CLN is superior to other methods. For the AFLW2000-3D dataset (68 points), the three test subsets small pose[0°, 30°], medium pose[30°, 60°], and large pose[60°, 90°] for our CLN algorithm all have an improvement of about 0.335, 0.193, and 0.151 respectively. Finally, the mean NME dropped by 0.229 compared with the MARN [17]. The best results are shown in bold, the lower the value, the better the result. The comparison results between the CED curve results of our proposed CLN and other methods are shown in Fig. 3 on AFLW2000-3D. Our CLN is prominently superior to 3DDFA [33], DAMDNet [12], and MARN [17] in the 3D face alignment. In order to compare the alignment results intuitively, we visualize the alignment results as shown in Fig. 4. It is clear that our face alignment results are significantly better than other methods in complex scenes with special lighting and large poses.

Table 2. The NME(%) of face alignment results on AFLW2000-3D Dataset (68pts).

Method	[0°, 30°]	[30°, 60°]	[60°, 90°]	Mean	Year
RCPR [4]	4.260	5.960	13.180	7.800	2013
ESR [7]	4.600	6.700	12.670	7.990	2014
SDM [28]	3.670	4.940	9.760	6.120	2013
DEFA [20]	4.500	5.560	7.330	5.803	2017
3DDFA [33]	3.780	4.540	7.930	5.420	2016
Yu *et al.* [29]	3.620	6.060	9.560	–	2017
Nonlinear [25]	–	–	–	4.700	2018
DAMDNet [12]	2.907	3.830	4.953	3.897	2019
GSRN [26]	2.842	3.789	4.804	3.912	2021
MARN [17]	2.989	3.670	4.613	3.757	2021
RADAN [34]	2.792	3.583	4.495	3.623	2023
CLN(Ours)	**2.645**	**3.477**	**4.462**	**3.528**	–

From the results of Table 1 and Table 2, we draw a conclusion that our CLN conquers the problem that the traditional CNN regression methods lack of detailed feature capturing ability in the process of learning large pose faces in the wild.

Comparison of 3D Face Reconstruction on AFLW2000-3D: We conducted experiments about face reconstruction and adopted the 3D NME metric to evaluate the comparison between our CLN and other methods for the 3D face reconstruction on AFLW2000-3D. The comparison is tabulated in Table 3, and the corresponding CED curve is shown in Fig. 3. Compared with other approaches, the experimental results prove that our CLN performs better in detail texture and contour. To better demonstrate the effectiveness of our CLN intuitively, Fig 5 shows the comparison of visualization between our CLN and other approaches. We observe that the reconstruction results of our method have more realistic contour details and more natural expressions for special lighting, large poses, and partial occlusions. In particular, it is clear from the first two rows of Fig 5 that our method corresponds to the most accurate texture mapping.

Table 3. Comparison of our method and other methods on NME(%) for 3D face reconstruction On AFLW2000-3D.

NME_{3D}^{68}	[0°, 30°]	[30°, 60°]	[60°, 90°]	Mean
3DDFA	4.877	6.086	8.437	6.467
DAMDNet	4.672	5.619	7.855	6.049
MARN	4.721	5.535	7.483	5.913
RADAN	4.497	5.196	7.140	5.611
CLN(Our)	**4.441**	**5.113**	**7.176**	**5.576**

For our tasks, face alignment assisted 3D face reconstruction. Since our CLN can capture the local and overall semantic information after self-shuffling processing while extracting the global features of the face, and our CAT modular enhances the network to capture the local similarity facial structure information. Our network alignment results are more accurate, as shown in Fig. 4. Therefore, the accurate alignment of the landmarks will lead the model to transform into a more accurate 3D face model.

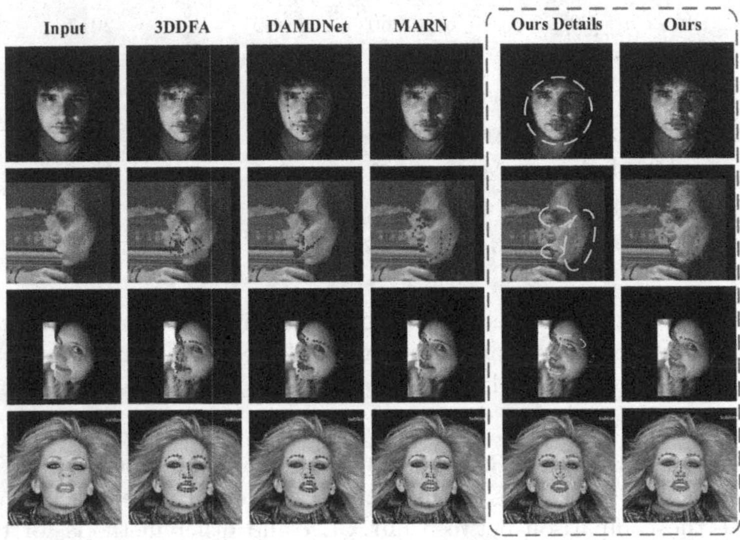

Fig. 4. Comparison of 3D face landmarks contours predicted by our network with 3DDFA [33], DAMDNet [12], MARN [17], and CLN(Ours) on AFLW2000-3D.

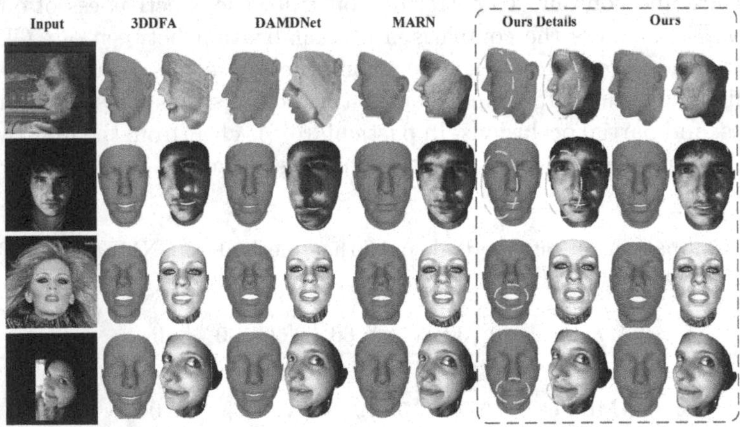

Fig. 5. Comparison of 3D face models predicted by our network with 3DDFA [33], DAMDNet [12], MARN [17] on AFLW2000-3D.

3.4 Ablation Study

In this subsection, to evaluate the effectiveness of our proposed CLN, we conducted several ablation experiments. We tested how various components affected the performance of the model, focusing on the effects of the cross-domain self-shuffling data augmentation (CDSDA), shuffled image with only local information (No-global), and coordinate attention transformer (CAT). Under various experimental settings, we adopted NME (%) to measure the effectiveness of the different modules on AFLW2000-3D and AFLW. Table 4 shows the effectiveness of various components of our CLN model. The CDSDA branch randomly shuffles and reorganizes the original pictures combined with a thumbnail for enhancing the learning ability of the network through data augmentation. The CAT module employs the captured position dependence of the spatial hierarchy and the precise position information of the spatial direction to help the entire model reposition. The global module uses smaller thumbnails to replace empty blocks. Even if some local information is covered, the information will not be lost due to the presence of global thumbnail information. At the same time, it can be better to retain contextual information during feature extraction. Global information enhances the network's ability to extract global features.

Table 4. Ablation experiments of our CLN.

Model Architecture	*AFLW2000-3D*	*AFLW*
CLN (w/o CDSDA, CAT)	3.763	4.992
CLN (w/o CDSDA)	3.728	4.942
CLN (w/o CAT, No-global)	3.646	4.857
CLN (w/o No-global)	3.624	4.868
CLN (w/o CAT)	3.628	4.845
CLN	**3.528**	**4.652**

3.5 Extended Experiment

To verify the robustness and generalization of our CLN in the wild and unconstrained scenes, we provide additional experiments on Helen [14] and LFPW [1] testing datasets with the trained CLN model. We explore experiments on Helen, and the qualitative outcomes are shown in Fig. 6, our models are superior to 3DDFA, DAMDNet, and MFIRRN in terms of contour and expression. Especially for special face shapes, such as the face of the child in the first row, the face models reconstructed by DAMDNet and MFIRRN are too average.

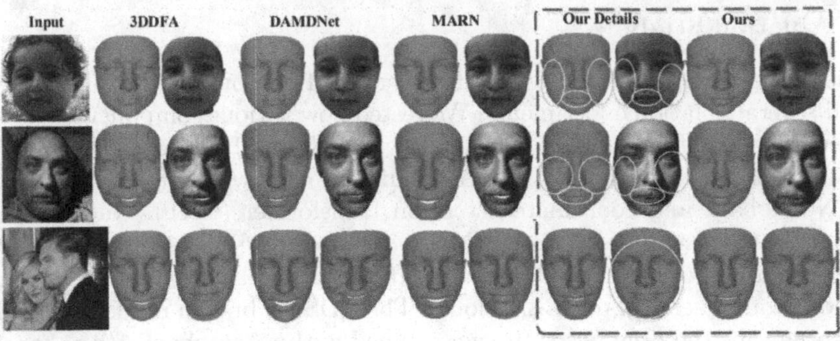

Fig. 6. Qualitative results of 3D face reconstruction on Helen [14] dataset are in the first two lines and LFPW [1] dataset is in the last line. The input image is shown in the first column, the other columns show the results for our method compared to various baselines.

4 Conclusion

In this paper, we propose a complementary learning network for 3D face reconstruction from unconstrained samples, which highlights the importance of complementary learning between global and local information. Specifically, we design a cross-domain self-shuffling data augmentation method and a complementary learning network, the former simulates the absence of face information under unconstrained conditions by self shuffling, thus increasing the network's sensitivity to local information and its ability to reason about the inconspicuous or obscured part of the face, while the latter realizes the mutual complementarity between global discriminative features and local detailed features. Moreover, we adopt the coordinate attention transformer module to enforce our network's ability to capture the correlation between local information. From the folds of experiments, we conclude that our CLN approach has achieved great boosting in both face alignment and 3D face reconstruction. In future work, we further explore the geometry to constraint face reconstruction task by fitting landmarks.

References

1. Belhumeur, P.N., Jacobs, D.W., Kriegman, D.J., Kumar, N.: Localizing parts of faces using a consensus of exemplars. IEEE Trans. Pattern Anal. Mach. Intell. **35**(12), 2930–2940 (2013)
2. Blanz, V., Vetter, T.: A morphable model for the synthesis of 3d faces, pp. 187–194 (1999)
3. Browatzki, B., Wallraven, C.: 3FabRec: fast few-shot face alignment by reconstruction, pp. 6110–6120 (2020)
4. Burgos-Artizzu, X.P., Perona, P., Dollár, P.: Robust face landmark estimation under occlusion, pp. 1513–1520 (2013)

5. Cao, C., Weng, Y., Zhou, S., Tong, Y., Zhou, K.: Facewarehouse: a 3d facial expression database for visual computing. IEEE Trans. Visual Comput. Graphics **20**(3), 413–425 (2013)
6. Jourabloo, A., Liu, X.: Large-pose face alignment via CNN-based 3d model fitting, pp. 4188–4196 (2016)
7. Cao, X., Wei, Y., Wen, F., Sun, J.: Face alignment by explicit shape regression. Int. J. Comput. Vision **107**(2), 177–190 (2014)
8. Chen, L.-C., Papandreou, G., Kokkinos, I., Murphy, K., Yuille, A.L.: DeepLab: Semantic image segmentation with deep convolutional nets, Atrous convolution, and fully connected CRFs. IEEE Trans. Pattern Anal. Mach. Intell. **40**(4), 834–848 (2017)
9. Ding, X., Zhang, X., Ma, N., Han, J., Ding, G., Sun, J.: RepVGG: Making VGG-style convnets great again, pp. 13733–13742 (2021)
10. Feng, Y., Wu, F., Shao, X., Wang, Y., Zhou, X.: Joint 3d face reconstruction and alignment with position map regression network, pp. 534–551 (2018)
11. Hou, Q., Zhou, D., Feng, J.: Coordinate attention for efficient mobile network design, pp. 13713–13722 (2021)
12. Jiang, L., Wu, X.-J., Kittler, J.: Dual attention MobDenseNet(DAMDNet) for robust 3d face alignment (2019)
13. Koestinger, M., Wohlhart, P., Roth, P.M., Bischof, H.: Annotated facial landmarks in the wild: a large-scale, real-world database for facial landmark localization, pp. 2144–2151 (2011)
14. Le, V., Brandt, J., Lin, Z., Bourdev, L., Huang, T.S.: Interactive facial feature localization. In: Fitzgibbon, A., Lazebnik, S., Perona, P., Sato, Y., Schmid, C. (eds.) ECCV 2012. LNCS, vol. 7574, pp. 679–692. Springer, Heidelberg (2012). https://doi.org/10.1007/978-3-642-33712-3_49
15. Lei, L., Hao, X., Su-Ping, W.: Fuzzy probability points reasoning for 3d reconstruction via deep deterministic policy gradient. Acta Automatica Sinica. 1–14 (2021)
16. Li, L., Wu, S.: Dmifnet: 3d shape reconstruction based on dynamic multi-branch information fusion, arXiv preprint arXiv:2011.10776 (2020)
17. Li, X., Wu, S.: Multi-attribute regression network for face reconstruction, pp. 7226–7233 (2021)
18. Liu, F., Zeng, D., Zhao, Q., Liu, X.: Joint face alignment and 3D face reconstruction. In: Leibe, B., Matas, J., Sebe, N., Welling, M. (eds.) ECCV 2016. LNCS, vol. 9909, pp. 545–560. Springer, Cham (2016). https://doi.org/10.1007/978-3-319-46454-1_33
19. Liu, W., Rabinovich, A., Berg, A.C.: Parsenet: looking wider to see better, arXiv preprint arXiv:1506.04579 (2015)
20. Liu, Y., Jourabloo, A., Ren, W., Liu, X.: Face alignment, pp. 1619–1628 (2017)
21. Messer, K., Matas, J., Kittler, J., Luettin, J., Maitre, G., et al.: Xm2vtsdb: the extended m2vts database. In: Second International Conference on Audio and Video-Based Biometric Person Authentication, vol. 964. Citeseer, pp. 965–966 (1999)
22. Paszke, A., et al.: Automatic differentiation in PyTorch (2017)
23. Paysan, P., Knothe, R., Amberg, B., Romdhani, S., Vetter, T.: A 3d face model for pose and illumination invariant face recognition, pp. 296–301 (2009)
24. Sagonas, C., Tzimiropoulos, G., Zafeiriou, S., Pantic, M.: 300 faces in-the-wild challenge: the first facial landmark localization challenge. In: Proceedings of the IEEE International Conference on Computer Vision Workshops, pp. 397–403 (2013)

25. Tran, L., Liu, X.: Nonlinear 3d face morphable model, pp. 7346–7355 (2018)
26. Wang, X., Li, X., Wu, S.: Graph structure reasoning network for face alignment and reconstruction. In: Lokoč, J., Skopal, T., Schoeffmann, K., Mezaris, V., Li, X., Vrochidis, S., Patras, I. (eds.) MMM 2021. LNCS, vol. 12572, pp. 493–505. Springer, Cham (2021). https://doi.org/10.1007/978-3-030-67832-6_40
27. Wu, F., et al.: MVF-net: multi-view 3d face morphable model regression, pp. 959–968 (2019)
28. Yan, J., Lei, Z., Yi, D., Li, S.: Learn to combine multiple hypotheses for accurate face alignment, pp. 392–396 (2013)
29. Yu, R., Saito, S., Li, H., Ceylan, D., Li, H.: Learning facial correspondences in unconstrained images, pp. 4723–4732 (2017)
30. Yu, X., Huang, J., Zhang, S., Metaxas, D.N.: Face landmark fitting via optimized part mixtures and cascaded deformable model. IEEE Trans. Pattern Anal. Mach. Intell. **38**(11), 2212–2226 (2015)
31. Zhu, W., Wu, H., Chen, Z., Vesdapunt, N., Wang, B.: Reda: reinforced differentiable attribute for 3d face reconstruction, pp. 4958–4967 (2020)
32. Zhu, X., Ramanan, D.: Face detection, pose estimation, and landmark localization in the wild. In: IEEE Conference on Computer Vision and Pattern Recognition, pp. 2879–2886. IEEE (2012)
33. Zhu, X., Lei, Z., Liu, X., Shi, H., Li, S.Z.: Face alignment across large poses: a 3d solution, pp. 146–155 (2016)
34. Zhou, Y., Li, L., Wu, P., Li, Y., Ma, H., Zhang, T.: Replay attention and data augmentation network for 3d face and object reconstruction. In: 2023 IEEE Transactions on Biometrics, Behavior, and Identity Science (2023)

Combining Edge-Guided Attention and Sparse-Connected U-Net for Detection of Image Splicing

Lin Wan, Lichao Su(✉), Huan Luo, and Xiaoyan Li

College of Computer and Data Science, Fuzhou University, Fuzhou 350116, China
fzu-slc@fzu.edu.cn

Abstract. The use of image-splicing technologies had detrimental effects on the security of multimedia information. Hence, it is necessary to develop effective methods for detecting and locating such tampering. Previous studies have mainly focused on the supervisory role of the mask on the model. The mask edges contain rich complementary signals, which help to fully understand the image and are usually ignored. In this paper, we propose a new network named EAU-Net to detect and locat the splicing regions in the image. The proposed network consists of two parts: Edge-guided SegFormer and Sparse-connected U-Net (SCU). Firstly, the feature extraction module captures local detailed cues and global environment information, which are used to deduce the initial location of the affected regions by SegFormer. Secondly, a Sobel-based edge-guided module (EGM) is proposed to guide the network to explore the complementary relationship between splicing regions and their boundaries. Thirdly, in order to achieve more precise positioning results, SCU is used as postprocessing for removing false alarm pixels outside the focusing regions. In addition, we propose an adaptive loss weight adjustment algorithm to supervise the network training, through which the weights of the mask and the mask edge can be automatically adjusted. Extensive experimental results show that the proposed method outperforms the state-of-the-art splicing detection and localization methods in terms of detection accuracy and robustness.

Keywords: Splicing detection · Image splicing forgery detection · Image manipulation Localization

1 Introduction

Due to the rapid development of smartphones, surveillance cameras, social media, and web services in the last decade, there has been tremendous growth in the amount of digital image data available [23]. At the same time, many powerful and easy-to-use image processing software packages have emerged, making it possible for nonexpert users to manipulate and modify image content with processes that produce more realistic changes that are difficult to detect. Processed images are may be used in a variety of data settings: scientific research,

L. Iliadis et al. (Eds.): ICANN 2023, LNCS 14255, pp. 167–179, 2023.
https://doi.org/10.1007/978-3-031-44210-0_14

social media, news media, political events, medical diagnostics, cultural media, evidence, finance, and the military. Thus, they can have serious negative impacts on all sectors of society.

Researchers usually classify methods for modifying images into 3 categories: copy and paste, splicing, and foreground deletion. Among them, splicing is the most common category. One instance is shown in Fig. 1. The image of a man cropped from the source image of Fig. 1B is copied and pasted into Fig. 1A (acceptor image), resulting in a manipulated image, as shown in Fig. 1C. Figure 1D (ground-truth image) reveals the location of the changed region in the final image. Since the changed region is similar to the background of the host image, it is difficult to rely on the naked eye to detect the change.

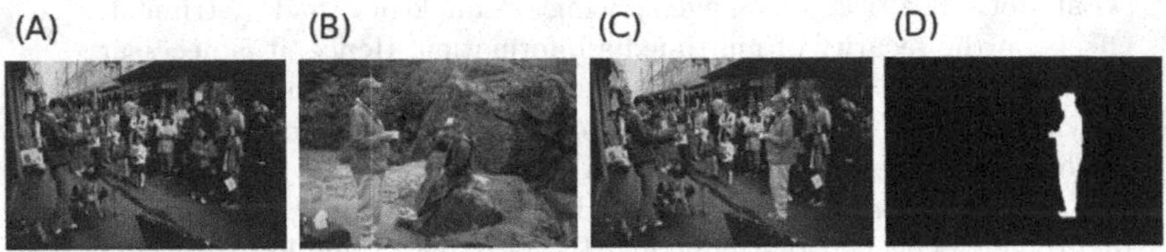

Fig. 1. One example of image splicing forgery: (A) source image, (B) acceptor image, (C) altered image, and (D) ground-truth image.

Deep learning has recently demonstrated promising performance in a variety of computer vision tasks, including object detection, semantic segmentation, and image classification. Because of its potent feature representation capability, the deep learning approach is more frequently used in image forgery forensics. The majority of the techniques in use [3,10,13,14,24,29,30] only define whether an image has been altered. In recent years, various techniques have been developed [4,12,28,31] that also support localization. However, the majority of models prioritize capturing the variability between tampered and non-tampered regions, which subsequently leads to inaccuracies near the boundaries, thereby affecting the accuracy of the models in those areas. Recently, some networks with multi-branch structures have been proposed to extract boundary information and detecting tampered regions [5,7,27]. However, the subtle traces around the boundaries may be lost due to the pooling operations in CNNs, resulting in inaccurate boundary detection. Moreover, there is a problem of gradient degradation in the process of backpropagation of CNNs. Therefore, the impact of edge learning on deeper CNN networks can be weak.

To address the problems mentioned above, we propose a new network called EAU-Net for image splicing detection. The network consists of two parts: a SegFormer feature extraction structure with boundary guidance and a sparsely connected U-Net fine mask generation network for image processing and positioning. First, the edges of the splicing areas are utilized as guides for label mask learning. Next, the low-level features generated from the shallow layer of the backbone network are fused with the high-level features. Then, the proposed sparse-connected

U-Net performs accurate pixel-level alteration localization. Finally, the weights of the mask and the mask edge are automatically adjusted by using the adaptive loss weight adjustment algorithm while training.

The contributions of this paper can be summarized as follows:

- Edge-guided SegFormer is proposed to fuse edge traces and image segmentation to identify manipulated regions faster and more accurately.
- A sparse-connected U-Net with multiscale feature fusion is proposed to eliminate false positives for more accurate localization results.
- An adaptive loss weight adjustment algorithm is proposed to adjust the loss weights of the mask and mask edges, which weigh multiple loss functions by considering the homomorphic uncertainty of each task.

2 Related Work

There are many past studies on image splicing detection with good results. De Carvalho, T.J et al. [6] proposed extracting texture-based and edge-based features, that are provided to a machine-learning approach for forgery detection. El-Alfy et al. [9] extracted and combined Markov features in spatial and discrete cosine transform domains to detect artifacts introduced by the tampering operation. Kaur, Mandeep et al. [17] proposed a passive-blind technique for detecting image splicing using discrete cosine transform and histograms of local binary patterns (LBPs). Wang, Jinwei et al. [26] combined YCbCr features, edge features and photo response nonuniformity (PRNU) features to distinguish splicing manipulation. Kanwal, N et al. [16] proposed using a new texture descriptor named the Otsu-based enhanced local ternary pattern (OELTP) for feature extraction from these blocks.

However, these methods do not meet the needs of practical applications because they do not provide clear information on the location of the alteration. Image splicing localization is a more challenging task than splicing detection because it requires determining whether each pixel in the image has been altered. Therefore, splicing localization can provide detailed contour information on the altered region. In recent years, image splicing localization techniques have made great progress. Specifically, Salloum, R et al. [25] utilized a fully convolutional network (FCN) to localize image-splicing attacks. Liu, Y et al. [22] proposed a novel adversarial learning framework to learn a deep matching network for CISDL. Liu, Y et al. [21] utilized a novel attention-aware encoder-decoder deep matching network for splicing detection. Liu, B et al. [20] proposed a novel neural network that concentrates on learning low-level forensic features. Bahrami, K et al. [2] proposed using blur type differences of the regions to trace the inconsistency for splicing localization. Although existing methods can roughly localize the spliced region, they mostly focus on learning the inconsistency between the affected region and the host image, while ignoring the edges of the spliced region, which are valuable for splice edge localization.

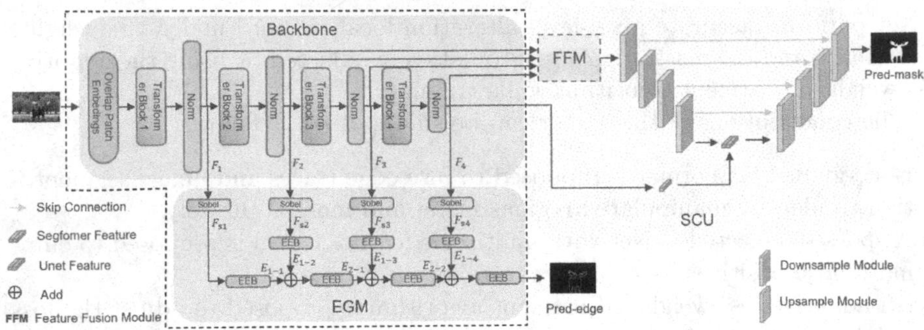

Fig. 2. Overview of the proposed network for image forgery detection (EAU-Net).

3 Proposed Method

The proposed framework of EAU-Net, which is shown in Fig. 2, consists of two parts: an edge-guided Segformer and a sparse-connected U-Net (SCU). The proposed method employs edge-guided Segformer to extract rough prediction masks. These masks are then refined using a U-Net with sparse connections, which processes the rough prediction masks obtained from the backbone network and generates the final, accurate tampering region prediction results (Pred Mask). To further optimize the performance of the model, we propose an adaptive loss function weighting algorithm that automatically adjusts the weights of the edge mask and mask.

3.1 Edge-Guided SegFormer

Backbone. SegFormer-encoder is utilized as the backbone in our network design. SegFormer is a self-attention network that includes a hierarchical Transformer encoder, which outputs multi-scale features including both high-resolution coarse features (F_n, where $n \in (0, 4)$) and low-resolution fine-grained features, as illustrated in Fig. 2. This design has been shown to improve the feature extraction performance of the network compared to other approaches. Additionally, SegFormer does not require positional encoding, which reduces the computational cost of interpolating positional encoding.

Edge-guided Module (EGM). The multi-scale features extracted from the Backbone contain lots of redundant information, which may lead to inaccurate extracted boundaries. Thus, a Sobel-based edge-guided module (EGM) is proposed to guide the network to extract more accurate boundaries. Rough boundaries are first extracted by the Sobel layer. Features from the n-th block first go through the Sobel layers. The Sobel edge calculation process can be represented by the following equations.

$$g_x = \begin{bmatrix} -1\,0\,1 \\ -2\,0\,2 \\ -1\,0\,1 \end{bmatrix}, g_y = \begin{bmatrix} 1 & 2 & 1 \\ 0 & 0 & 0 \\ -1 & -2 & -1 \end{bmatrix} \tag{1}$$

where g_x denotes the horizontal convolution kernel while g_y denotes the vertical convolution kernel. The gradient values on the x and y axes can be expressed as:

$$\begin{aligned} G(x) &= F_{ni} * g_x, \\ G(y) &= F_{ni} * g_y \end{aligned} \tag{2}$$

where F_{ni} ($F_{ni} \in F_n$) denotes the i-th channel of the stage-n features. $G(x)$ and $G(y)$ represent the gray gradients of F_{ni} on the x-axis, and the y-axis, respectively.

$$\begin{aligned} G(i,j) &= \sqrt{(G_x(i,j))^2 + (G_y(i,j))^2}, \\ G_x(i,j) &\in G(x), G_y(i,j) \in G(y) \end{aligned} \tag{3}$$

To calculate the Sobel features, we use the grayscale gradient G_x and G_y on the input image F_n. The values of G_x and G_y at coordinates (i,j) are denoted as $G_x(i,j)$ and $G_y(i,j)$, respectively. The resulting features are represented as a single-channel tensor F_s. After the Sobel calculation, we apply a batch normalization (BN) layer and a sigmoid layer to the features, and the output of the sigmoid layer is multiplied with the input Sobel features to produce the final Sobel features F_{sn}.

Then, F_{sn} is directly fed into edge-enhanced block (EEB) and produce a one-channel output E_{1-n}, as illustrated in Fig. 2. After two adjacent E_{1-n}s are combined, they are fed into another EEB so that interference from direct feature superposition can be avoided.

First, F_{sn} of EEB is first fed into a block of 1×1 convolution, producing E_s with one channel. Then, E_s go through a residual branch, which consists of a 3×3 convolution, a ReLU layer, two batch norm (BN) layers, and a 1×1 convolution, to obtain the output E_r. Finally, E_s and E_r are summed to get the final output. To prevent the effect of accumulation, the combined features go through another EEB before the next round of feature combinations.

3.2 Sparse-connected U-Net (SCU)

Feature Fusion Module (FFM). In order to fully utilize the multi-scale information of the backbone, we design a feature fusion module (FFM). Specifically, in SCU, multiscale features (i.e., F_1, F_2, F_3 and F_4) are first mixed in the FFM. This allows us to represent the FFM in pseudo-code as follows:

$$\begin{aligned} \hat{F_i} &= Upsample(W,W)(\hat{F_i}), \forall i \\ F &= Concat(\hat{F_i}), \forall i \\ M &= Conv(C,N)(F) \end{aligned} \tag{4}$$

where (W,W) is the resolution, set to $(512,512)$, C is the number of channels of F, N is the number of output channels, and we set it to 3.

U-Net. To address the problem of information loss during convolution in the traditional U-Net model, we propose an improved version called Sparse-Connected U-Net (SCU) which includes a feature fusion module (FFM) to connect multiscale features with U-Net. First, the MaxPool in U-Net is repalced by MaxBlurPool. Second, the features output from the encoder of U-Net are concatenated with the high-level features (F_4) obtained from the Backbone and then fed into the decoder.

3.3 Loss Function

The loss of the proposed framework consists of two parts: mask loss and edge mask loss. Among them, the mask loss improves the accuracy for detecting spliced regions, while the edge mask loss for learning spliced region edges.

Usually, the spliced region is only a small part of the whole image, which leads to an imbalance in the percentage of the image between the spliced region and the background. Because the class imbalance between manipulated and unmanipulated pixels can lead to reduced efficiency of training, we employ Dice loss to address this problem. The loss of the label mask, denoted by l_{mask} is written as:

$$l_{mask} = 1 - \frac{2 \cdot \sum_{i=1}^{W \times H} P(x_i) \cdot y_i}{2 \cdot \sum_{i=1}^{W \times H} P^2(x_i) + \sum_{i=1}^{W \times H} y_i^2} \tag{5}$$

where $P(x_i) \in (0, 1)$ denotes the spliced probability of the i-th pixel and $y_i \in (0, 1)$ is a binary label indicating whether the i-th pixel is manipulated $i = 1, ..., W \times H$. As for the loss of the mask edge, due to the relatively low percentage of edge pixels in the whole image, we still use dice loss for splicing region edge detection. The edge loss is calculated in the same way as the mask loss, and edge loss is computed at a much smaller size of $\frac{W}{4} \times \frac{H}{4}$. The loss of the mask edge, denoted as l_{edge}.

In multitask learning, homomorphic uncertainty can be considered task-dependent uncertainty, which can represent the difficulty between different tasks [18]. Therefore, an adaptive loss weight assignment strategy based on task-dependent uncertainty is proposed to dynamically adjust the loss weights for label mask and mask edge learning. In conclusion, the total loss of the proposed model for splicing detection and localization can be defined as:

$$Loss = \frac{1}{2\sigma_1^2} l_{mask} + \log(1 + \sigma_1^2) + \frac{1}{2\sigma_2^2} l_{edge} + \log(1 + \sigma_2^2) \tag{6}$$

where σ_1 and σ_2 are the learnable embeddings, which adaptively adjust the weights of l_{mask} and l_{edge}. $\log(1 + \sigma_i^2)$ is used to avoid negative values due to σ_i being less than 1.

4 Experiments

4.1 Experimental Settings

Data Preparation: We choose SF-Data [27] for the training data set, including 82,608 spliced images generated from CASIA v2.0 [8] and Forensics [1] data sets by SAN [27]. Besides, we evaluate the compared methods on four public datasets: CASIA1.0 [8], Columbia [11], In-The-Wild [15], and Realistic [19]. Among them, CASIA v1.0, Realistic and In-The-Wild contain splicing and copy-move images, and Columbia only contains splicing images. For convenience, images from all the datasets are resized into 512 × 512. The image formats and the number of forged images for each database are given in Table 1.

Table 1. The format and quantity of images on each data set.

Data set	Image format	All	Splicing images
CASIA1.0	TIFF, JPEG	921	462
Columbia	TIFF	180	180
In-The-Wild	JPEG	220	86
Realistic	TIFF	201	201
SF-Data	JPEG	82608	82608

We compare EAU-Net with six state-of-the-art deep learning-based detection methods: ManTra-Net [28], SPAN [12], RRU-Net [4], SATFL [31], and HDU-Net [27]. All the methods are trained on SF-Data and tested on other datasets. The experiments are performed on an NVIDIA RTX 3090 GPU. The EAU-Net is implemented with Pytorch. The input size is 512 × 512 with a batch size of 6. Adam optimizer with an initial learning rate of 1e-4 is set for training. Besides, we apply regular data augmentation for training, including flipping, and blurring.

Results of the Compared Methods. As shown in Table 2, the proposed EAU-Net achieves the highest F1 and AUC scores on all test datasets, significantly outperforming the other methods. Specifically, the performance on CASIA 1.0 and Columbia is better than on Realistic and In-The-Wild. Our method obtains the highest F1 score of 62.2% and the highest AUC score of 87.6% on Realistic, outperforming RRU-Net by 19.0% and 17.2%, respectively. This suggests that our method has a superior ability to capture tampering features and generalize well to high-quality manipulated image datasets. On In-The-Wild, our model achieves the best result of 52.2% in F1 and 78.4% in AUC, an improvement of 4.0% and 6.1% over HDU-Net, respectively. However, all detection algorithms perform worse on In-The-Wild than on other datasets. We attribute this to that the In-The-Wild dataset uses postprocessing and jpeg recompression, which may degrade the performance of the algorithms.

Visualization Results. We randomly selected seven groups of images from the test dataset as examples from CASIA1.0. As can be seen from Fig. 3, ManTra-Net hardly detected the splicing region and predicts most areas of the image as altered. SPAN and SATFL only predicted a fraction of the altered region. Although HDU-Net effectively located the altered area, their predictions were

Table 2. Detection results under the plain splicing forgery; the best results are shown in bold.

Methods	CASIA v1.0		Columbia		Realistic		In-The-Wild	
	F1	AUC	F1	AUC	F1	AUC	F1	AUC
ManTra-Net	0.207	0.574	0.234	0.475	0.147	0.634	0.244	0.561
SPAN	0.227	0.688	0.432	0.723	0.231	0.808	0.319	0.578
RRU-Net	0.652	0.810	0.524	0.701	0.432	0.749	0.301	0.621
SATFL	0.303	0.630	0.430	0.632	0.178	0.622	0.378	0.607
HDU-Net	0.734	0.845	0.588	0.717	0.387	0.704	0.482	0.723
OURS	**0.787**	**0.909**	**0.719**	**0.819**	**0.622**	**0.876**	**0.522**	**0.784**

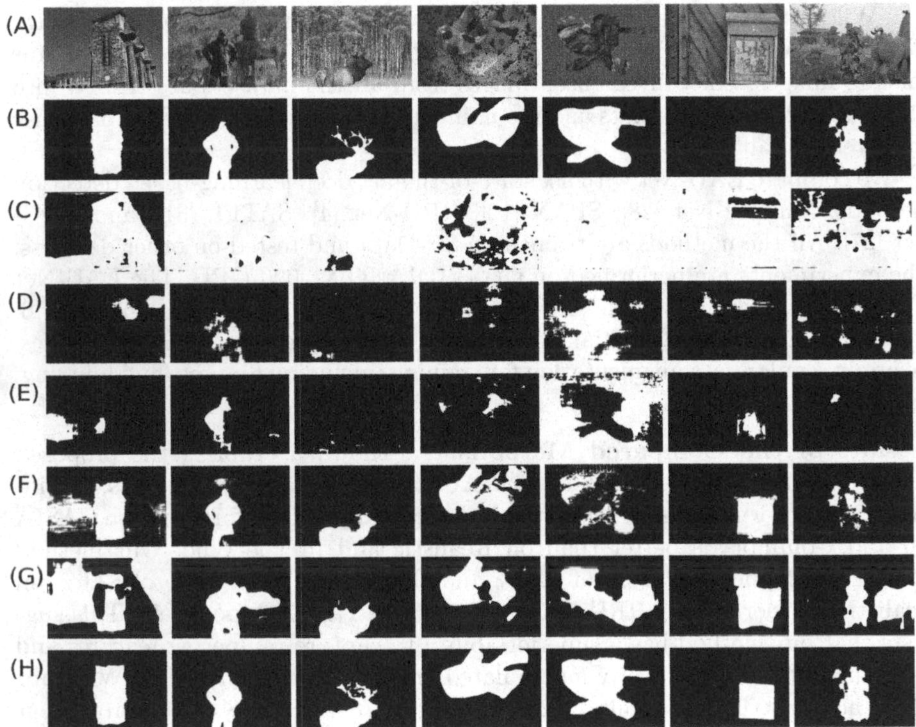

Fig. 3. The visual results of the diverse methods. (A) Tampered image, (B) Groundtruth, (C) ManTra-Net, (D) SPAN, (E) SATFL, (F) RRU-Net, (G) HDU-Net, and (H) EAU-Net.

inaccurate at the boundaries. RRU-Net exhibited better accuracy at the boundaries than the other methods, but the results were incomplete in the splicing region. In contrast, our method demonstrated superiority in Location accuracy.

4.2 Ablation Study

To reveal the influence of the individual components, we evaluated the performance of the proposed network in various settings with the components added progressively. We evaluated the splicing detection and localization performance on Columbia and In-The-Wild datasets.

Table 3. Ablation results on Columbia and In-The-Wild datasets by different variants of EAU-Net; the best results are shown in bold.

Components	Columbia		In-The-Wild	
	F1	AUC	F1	AUC
ResNet50+EGM+SCU	0.429	0.536	0.278	0.523
VGG16+EGM+SCU	0.472	0.629	0.315	0.609
backbone + SCU	0.609	0.746	0.434	0.715
backbone with EGM	0.668	0.780	0.481	0.725
backbone with EGM + SCU (No FFM)	0.679	0.788	0.492	0.732
backbone with EGM + SCU (With FFM)	**0.719**	**0.819**	**0.522**	**0.748**

As shown in Table 3, on Columbia, the F1 score of our model's backbone + SCU is 18.0% and 13.7% higher than those of Resnet50 with EGM + SCU and VGG16 with EGM + SCU, respectively. Similarly, the AUC score of our model's backbone + SCU is 21.0% and 11.7% higher than those of Resnet50 with EGM + SCU and VGG16 with EGM + SCU, on Columbia respectively. The addition of EGM (without FFM) resulted in a 5.9% increase in F1 and a 3.4% increase in AUC compared to the performance of the model's backbone + SCU on Columbia. The Incorporation of EGM (with FFM) and SCU resulted in a 4.0% increase in F1 and a 3.1% increase in AUC on Columbia than backbone with EGM + SCU (No FFM). This indicates that EGM and FFM enables the model to extract more accurate manipulated traces.

The experimental results in this section imply that the three components in the proposed network (EGM, FFM and SCU) can enhance the performance of splicing localization based on experiments results in this section.

To investigate the effect of the mask and mask edge losses on model performance, we set the loss function as:

$$Loss = \alpha \cdot l_{edge} + (1 - \alpha) \cdot l_{mask} \tag{7}$$

We then conducted experiments on Columbia and In-The-Wild datasets using different values of α. As shown in Fig. 4, when the value of α was less than 0.65, the F1 value decreased in both datasets as the value decreased. When α was between 0.85 and 0.65, both Columbia and In-The-Wild had higher F1 scores. This indicated that EGM assisted the backbone in extracting more manipulated features under the supervision of mask edges. However, it is difficult to find the optimal weights manually. In contrast, when adaptive loss weights were used, F1 reached 71.9% and 52.2% on Columbia and In-The-Wild, respectively, which was better than setting the weights manually. This demonstrated that the adaptive loss weights shown in Eq. 6 can automatically find the best weights to balance the mask extraction and mask edge extraction tasks to achieve the best results.

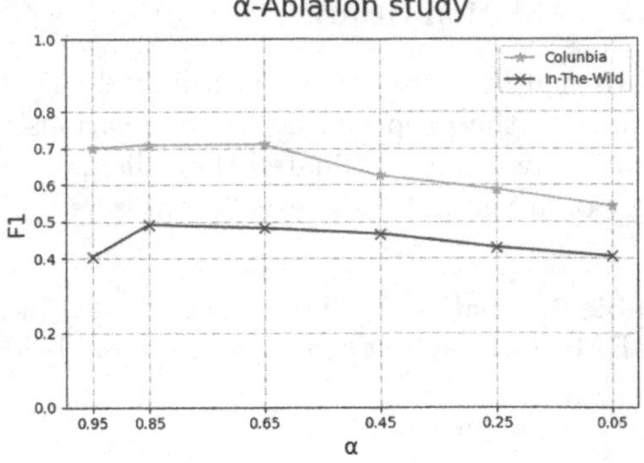

Fig. 4. The effect of different α values on the EASU-Net of F1 scores on Columbia and In-The-Wild datasets.

4.3 Robustness Evaluation

In this section, to evaluate the robustness of the proposed EAU-Net for different distortions, the following post-processing studies were performed on four datasets: (1) different types of Gaussian noise operations with variance, (2) different types of JPEG compression operations with quality factors, and (3) linear resize operations with resizing ratios.

Figure 5 shows the F1 curves of the pretrained EAU-Net and other methods, where each data point represents the performance under one fixed distortion. For Gaussian noise, as the disturbance increased, the performance of each model decreased slightly, but EAU-Net maintained the best results on the four datasets. In particular, our method was 24.1% higher than HDU-Net when the variance was 0.01 and 19.2% higher when the image-quality factor was 50 in terms of the F1 score on the Realistic dataset. For resizing, CASIA 1.0 incorporates multiple postprocessing operations, including texture obfuscation, blurring, and filtering. This led to a significant drop in F1 scores for various algorithms as scaling variance decreased, while it remained stable on other datasets. Image-quality factor variation also exhibited a similar result to resizing. Especially for Columbia, the conversion of images from TIF to JPEG format for disturbance experiments resulted in more obvious alterations, and the compared methods exhibited better localization performance. The results demonstrated that EAU-Net had better robustness against various distortion techniques.

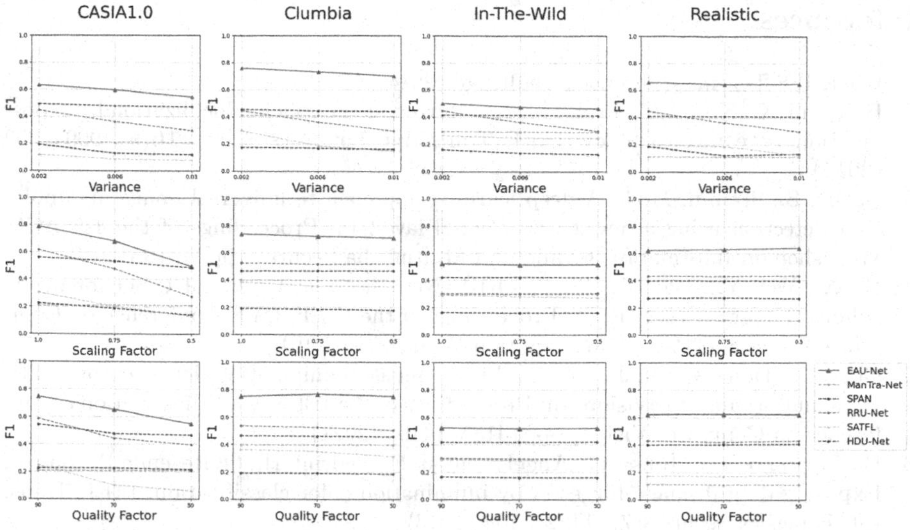

Fig. 5. Robustness tests under various distortions on the four public datasets, which include noise attacks with Gaussian, resizing attacks, and JPEG compression.

5 Conclusion

In this paper, we presented a new method, edge-guided attention and sparse-connected U-Net (EAU-Net), for image splicing forgery detection. In addition, we proposed the homoskedasticity uncertainty to learn the loss weights of the mask and mask edge. In our model, SegFormer encoder is utilized as the backbone network to extract multiscale features. Based on this, we designed an edge-guided module (EGM), in which rough boundaries are extracted using the Sobel layer, and then EGM uses a series of EEBs to refine the splicing region boundaries sequentially. As a result, EGM can supply abundant supervision in the spliced region. To eliminate false positives from the backbone network, we designed a sparse-connected U-Net (SCU) as a postprocessing module. Ablation studies verified the effectiveness of components of the network. We tested the robustness of the model by adding Gaussian noise, JPEG compression attacks, and resizing operations into the test images. The test results showed that the EAU-Net model had greater anti-noise, anti-compression, and anti-resizing attack capability than other detection methods.

Acknowledgements. The paper is supported by the National Natural Science Foundation of China (61902071 and 62002062), the Natural Science Foundation of Fujian province (2022J05028).

References

1. IEEE IFS-TC image forensics challenge (2014)
2. Bahrami, K., Kot, A.C., Li, L., Li, H.: Blurred image splicing localization by exposing blur type inconsistency. IEEE Trans. Inf. Forensics Secur. **10**(5), 999–1009 (2015)
3. Bayar, B., Stamm, M.C.: A deep learning approach to universal image manipulation detection using a new convolutional layer. In: Proceedings of the 4th ACM Workshop on Information Hiding and Multimedia Security, pp. 5–10 (2016)
4. Bi, X., Wei, Y., Xiao, B., Li, W.: RRU-Net: the ringed residual U-net for image splicing forgery detection. In: Proceedings of the IEEE/CVF Conference on Computer Vision and Pattern Recognition Workshops (2019)
5. Chen, X., Dong, C., Ji, J., Cao, J., Li, X.: Image manipulation detection by multiview multi-scale supervision. In: Proceedings of the IEEE/CVF International Conference on Computer Vision, pp. 14185–14193 (2021)
6. De Carvalho, T.J., Riess, C., Angelopoulou, E., Pedrini, H., de Rezende Rocha, A.: Exposing digital image forgeries by illumination color classification. IEEE Trans. Inf. Forensics Secur. **8**(7), 1182–1194 (2013)
7. Dong, C., Chen, X., Hu, R., Cao, J., Li, X.: MVSS-Net: multi-view multi-scale supervised networks for image manipulation detection. IEEE Trans. Pattern Anal. Mach. Intell. **45**(3), 3539–3553 (2022)
8. Dong, J., Wang, W., Tan, T.: CASIA image tampering detection evaluation database. In: 2013 IEEE China Summit and International Conference on Signal and Information Processing, pp. 422–426. IEEE (2013)
9. El-Alfy, E.-S.M., Qureshi, M.A.: Combining spatial and DCT based Markov features for enhanced blind detection of image splicing. Pattern Anal. Appl. **18**(3), 713–723 (2014). https://doi.org/10.1007/s10044-014-0396-4
10. Han, J.G., Park, T.H., Moon, Y.H., Eom, I.K.: Efficient Markov feature extraction method for image splicing detection using maximization and threshold expansion. J. Electron. Imaging **25**(2), 023031 (2016)
11. Hsu, Y.F., Chang, S.F.: Detecting image splicing using geometry invariants and camera characteristics consistency. In: 2006 IEEE International Conference on Multimedia and Expo, pp. 549–552. IEEE (2006)
12. Hu, X., Zhang, Z., Jiang, Z., Chaudhuri, S., Yang, Z., Nevatia, R.: SPAN: spatial pyramid attention network for image manipulation localization. In: Vedaldi, A., Bischof, H., Brox, T., Frahm, J.-M. (eds.) ECCV 2020. LNCS, vol. 12366, pp. 312–328. Springer, Cham (2020). https://doi.org/10.1007/978-3-030-58589-1_19
13. Huang, T., Chen, Y., Yao, B., Yang, B., Wang, X., Li, Y.: Adversarial attacks on deep-learning-based radar range profile target recognition. Inf. Sci. **531**, 159–176 (2020)
14. Huang, T., Zhang, Q., Liu, J., Hou, R., Wang, X., Li, Y.: Adversarial attacks on deep-learning-based SAR image target recognition. J. Netw. Comput. Appl. **162**, 102632 (2020)
15. Huh, M., Liu, A., Owens, A., Efros, A.A.: Fighting fake news: image splice detection via learned self-consistency. In: Proceedings of the European Conference on Computer Vision (ECCV), pp. 101–117 (2018)
16. Kanwal, N., Girdhar, A., Kaur, L., Bhullar, J.S.: Digital image splicing detection technique using optimal threshold based local ternary pattern. Multimedia Tools Appl. **79**(19), 12829–12846 (2020)

17. Kaur, M., Gupta, S.: A passive blind approach for image splicing detection based on DWT and LBP histograms. In: Mueller, P., Thampi, S.M., Alam Bhuiyan, M.Z., Ko, R., Doss, R., Alcaraz Calero, J.M. (eds.) SSCC 2016. CCIS, vol. 625, pp. 318–327. Springer, Singapore (2016). https://doi.org/10.1007/978-981-10-2738-3_27
18. Kendall, A., Gal, Y., Cipolla, R.: Multi-task learning using uncertainty to weigh losses for scene geometry and semantics. In: Proceedings of the IEEE Conference on Computer Vision and Pattern Recognition, pp. 7482–7491 (2018)
19. Korus, P., Huang, J.: Multi-scale analysis strategies in PRNU-based tampering localization. IEEE Trans. Inf. Forensics Secur. **12**(4), 809–824 (2016)
20. Liu, B., Pun, C.M.: Exposing splicing forgery in realistic scenes using deep fusion network. Inf. Sci. **526**, 133–150 (2020)
21. Liu, Y., Zhao, X.: Constrained image splicing detection and localization with attention-aware encoder-decoder and Atrous convolution. IEEE Access **8**, 6729–6741 (2020)
22. Liu, Y., Zhu, X., Zhao, X., Cao, Y.: Adversarial learning for constrained image splicing detection and localization based on Atrous convolution. IEEE Trans. Inf. Forensics Secur. **14**(10), 2551–2566 (2019)
23. Phan-Xuan, H., Le-Tien, T., Nguyen-Chinh, T., Do-Tieu, T., Nguyen-Van, Q., Nguyen-Thanh, T.: Preserving spatial information to enhance performance of image forgery classification. In: 2019 International Conference on Advanced Technologies for Communications (ATC), pp. 50–55. IEEE (2019)
24. Rao, Y., Ni, J.: A deep learning approach to detection of splicing and copy-move forgeries in images. In: 2016 IEEE International Workshop on Information Forensics and Security (WIFS), pp. 1–6. IEEE (2016)
25. Salloum, R., Ren, Y., Kuo, C.C.J.: Image splicing localization using a multi-task fully convolutional network (MFCN). J. Vis. Commun. Image Represent. **51**, 201–209 (2018)
26. Wang, J., Ni, Q., Liu, G., Luo, X., Jha, S.K.: Image splicing detection based on convolutional neural network with weight combination strategy. J. Inf. Secur. Appl. **54**, 102523 (2020)
27. Wei, Y., Ma, J., Wang, Z., Xiao, B., Zheng, W.: Image splicing forgery detection by combining synthetic adversarial networks and hybrid dense u-net based on multiple spaces. Int. J. Intell. Syst. **37**(11), 8291–8308 (2022)
28. Wu, Y., AbdAlmageed, W., Natarajan, P.: ManTra-net: manipulation tracing network for detection and localization of image forgeries with anomalous features. In: Proceedings of the IEEE/CVF Conference on Computer Vision and Pattern Recognition, pp. 9543–9552 (2019)
29. Yan, H., Hu, L., Xiang, X., Liu, Z., Yuan, X.: PPCL: privacy-preserving collaborative learning for mitigating indirect information leakage. Inf. Sci. **548**, 423–437 (2021)
30. Yang, Q., Peng, F., Li, J.T., Long, M.: Image tamper detection based on noise estimation and lacunarity texture. Multimedia Tools Appl. **75**(17), 10201–10211 (2016)
31. Zhuo, L., Tan, S., Li, B., Huang, J.: Self-adversarial training incorporating forgery attention for image forgery localization. IEEE Trans. Inf. Forensics Secur. **17**, 819–834 (2022)

Contour-Augmented Concept Prediction Network for Image Captioning

Ting Wang, Weidong Chen(✉), Jingyu Li, Yixing Peng, and Zhendong Mao

University of Science and Technology of China, Hefei, China
{wt1023,jingyuli,xk98}@mail.ustc.edu.cn, {chenweidong,zdmao}@ustc.edu.cn

Abstract. Semantic information in images is essential for image captioning. However, previous works leverage the pre-trained object detector to mine semantics in an image, making the model unable to accurately capture visual semantics, and further making the generated descriptions irrelevant to the content of the given image. Thus, in this paper, we propose a Contour-augmented Concept Prediction Network (CCP-Net), which leverages two additional aspects of visual information, including high-level features (concepts) and low-level features (contours) in an end-to-end manner, to encourage the contribution of visual content in description generation. Furthermore, we propose a contour-augmented visual feature extraction module and equip it with elegantly designed feature fusion. Utilizing homogeneous contour features can better enhance visual feature extraction and further promote visual concept prediction. Extensive experimental results on MS COCO dataset demonstrate the effectiveness of our method and each proposed module, which can obtain 40.6 BLEU-4 and 135.6 CIDEr scores. Code will be released in the final version of the paper.

Keywords: Contour-augmented Feature Extraction · Joint Prediction · Concept Prediction · Image Captioning

1 Introduction

Image captioning, which aims to generate descriptive sentences for images, has drawn extensive attention in recent years. It requires the model accurately capturing the semantic information of the main objects in the image and describing the relationship between objects, which helps the computer to better understand the image and thus generate natural language descriptions that fit the content of the image.

Inspired by the machine translation model, mainly previous works employed an encoder-decoder structure to address image caption task [1–4]. Xu et al. [5] proposed to use the attention mechanism in image caption task, that is, to selectively focus on some parts of the image when decoding, which pioneered the application of attention mechanism in image captioning. Anderson et al. [6] proposed the bottom-up method based on Faster R-CNN [7] to determine the

L. Iliadis et al. (Eds.): ICANN 2023, LNCS 14255, pp. 180–191, 2023.
https://doi.org/10.1007/978-3-031-44210-0_15

region of interest in the image, which greatly improves the efficiency and effect. Recently, the Transformer architecture has attracted extensive attention. As expected, it was introduced into the image captioning task. On the basis of traditional Transformer, Cornia et al. [8] adopted the method of multi-layer superposition in encoding and decoding, and made full use of visual features. Nguyue et al. [9]proposed a Transformer based structure that effectively integrates regional and grid visual features to provide object-level and contextual information necessary to describe images. Yang et al. [10] proposed the ReFormer based on the traditional Transformer structure, integrating scene graph generation and image captioning tasks, which can gradually learn the visual relationship features, so as to generate better descriptions.

As aforementioned, the encoder-decoder framework has been widely used in image captioning. For feature extraction, previous works leverage the pre-trained Region-based feature extractor [6,8,13] or Grid-based feature extractor [14]. The performance of image captioning continues to improve as more powerful feature extractors are developed. However, solely relying on the blossoming of powerful feature extractors is not enough to enhance the contribution of visual content. Some works [25] propose to leverage high-level concept features to enhance visual information. There are two technical problems. Firstly, image features are not enough to predict concept features of good quality as concept and image are heterogeneous. Secondly, high-level concept features cannot fuse with image features easily. There is a trade-off between fusion quality and complexity.

To this end, in this paper, we propose a Contour-augmented Concept Prediction Net (CCP-Net), which consists of contour-augmented image feature extraction module and a joint prediction module. The contour-augmented image feature extraction module leverages low-level contour information, which can be regarded as complementary view of image, to enhance image feature extraction. Unlike other low-level visual information such as segmentation, contours are more semantically and spatially aligned with the image because of easier availability, making fusion more straightforward and enhancing the visual contribution in prediction sentences. Besides, to the best of our knowledge, our paper is the first work to leverage contour to enhance the image feature extraction in image captioning. Furthermore, we equip the proposed contour-augmented image feature extraction with an elegantly designed feature fusion module, which further improves the performance. The proposed jointly prediction module firstly leverages the enhanced image feature to predict high-level visual feature (concept), and then leverages two aspect visual feature, including high-level concept features and low-level contour features along with the image feature to jointly predict languages. In this way, the proposed method strengthens the visual influence on determine the generated language rather than focusing only on the language itself.

There are another two benefits. First, our proposed network is trained in an end-to-end manner, which is kind to the training process and facilitates language prediction. Second, our progressive language prediction, which predicts concept (high-level visual information) according to the low level visual features first, makes the whole inference moderate and further improves the performance. The main contributions are summarized as follows:

- We propose a Contour-augmented Concept Prediction Network (CCP-Net) for image captioning, which leverages two additional aspects of visual information, including high-level features (concepts) and low-level features (contours) in an end-to-end manner, to jointly predict descriptive sentences of image.
- We propose a contour-augmented image feature extraction module, which treats contour as the complementary view of the image, promoting the concept prediction and increasing the visual contribution in language prediction.
- Competitive results on the popular MS COCO dataset demonstrate the effectiveness of our proposed method and each proposed module.

2 Related Work

2.1 Transformer-Based Image Captioning

Inspired by the transformer structure in NLP, the transformer-based encoder-decoder structure has recently become mainstream in the exploration of image captioning. It is hoped that in this structure, the interaction in visual information and text information is enhanced by self-attention or cross-attention. In [11], the standard transformer structure is used directly for image encoding and language decoding. Later, a kind of self-attention variant was designed specifically for Image Captioning [12,13], which integrate the relative geometry of regional objects into the self-attention module to consider the position information of the objects, which has a great effect on understanding the visual content. Huang L, et al. measure the correlation between attention results and queries to avoid misleading information about unrelated vectors. Specifically, the model can judge the relationship between different objects in an image in encoding and filter out irrelevant attention results and keeps only useful results in decoding. [16]. Cornia M, et al.use the proposed memory vector to utilize prior knowledge. And a mesh connection is established between the encoder and the decoder, considering the relationship between the low-level features and the high-level features [8]. Luo Y, et al. propose a Dual-Level Collaborative Transformer to realize the complementary advantages of region features and grid features [17].

2.2 Feature Fusion

Feature fusion is common in current neural network models, but most of the work is focused on building complex paths to combine features in different layers. Dai Y, et al. propose a simple, effective, universal, and uniform method for feature fusion [22]. Luo Y, et al. believe that only using region features is not enough, lack of contextual information and detail, so it introduces grid features to complement and provides a solution for achieving fusion interaction between the two features and avoiding semantic noise [17]. Wu M, et al. [20] takes the segmentation feature as a visual supplement to the grid feature, and proposes

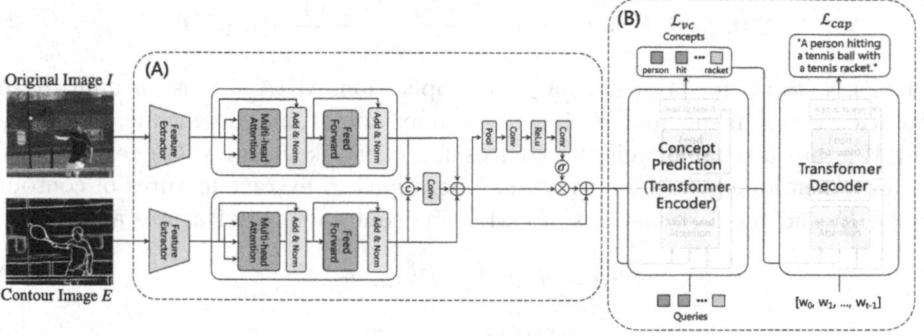

Fig. 1. The overall architecture of our proposed Contour-augmented Concept Prediction Network (CCP-Net), which includes (A) Contour-augmented Feature Extraction Module and (B) Joint Prediction Module.

an effective feature fusion module to maximize the use of these two information flows [20]. Dong B, et al. propose a fusion module for fusing edge features and area features, which is very helpful for making full use of visual information [23].

3 Method

The overall framework of our proposed CCP-Net is shown in the Fig. 1. As illustrated, our proposed method consists of two modules, a contour-augmented feature extraction module(Sect. 3.1), and a joint prediction module(Sect. 3.2).

3.1 Contour-Augmented Feature Extraction Module

The proposed module firstly encodes image and contour features separately, and then fuses these two features to get contour-augmented image features.

Feature Extraction. As we follow the same pipeline to extract features of original image and contour image. We take the original image as an example to illustrate our method.

Given an original image I, we firstly leverage the feature extractor,to encode their features. Then, the features of the original images are flattened and concatenated with the features of the whole image to consider both local and global visual information:

$$F_I = [F_{img}, F_I^1, F_I^2, ..., F_I^N], \tag{1}$$

where [,] is concatenate operation, F_I^i is i-th grid features obtained by the feature extractor, N is the total number of grid features, and F_{img} stands for the whole image features. Then, we leverage the Transformer encoder to further encode image features. The formulations of Transformer are:

$$\overline{F_I} = \text{LN}(\text{MHA}(F_I, F_I, F_I) + F_I), \tag{2}$$

$$\text{MHA}(Q, K, V) = \sigma_s[(\frac{(W_Q Q) \cdot (W_K K)^\top}{\sqrt{d}})(W_V V)], \tag{3}$$

where LN stands for layer normalization operation, MHA stands for multi-head attention mechanism, and σ_s is the softmax operation. Meanwhile, W_Q, W_K and W_V are learnable weight matrices for query, key and value respectively. As aforementioned, we take the same operations to extract features of contour image E, and the formulations of extracting contour image features are:

$$F_E = [F_{ctr}, F_E^1, F_E^2, ..., F_E^N], \tag{4}$$

$$\overline{F_E} = \text{LN}(\text{MHA}(F_E, F_E, F_E) + F_E), \tag{5}$$

where F_{ctr} is the contour image features, F_E^i is i-th grid features obtained by the feature extractor, and N is the total number of grid features.

Contour-Augmented Feature Extraction. The contour image and the original image have semantic consistency and spatial alignment [20]. Thus, a simple and lightweight fusion module is enough for fusing these two features. Inspired by [21,23], we propose an elegant feature fusion module.

Specifically, firstly, we concatenate the original image features and contour image features, and leverage the convolutional layer to encode fused features further. Then, we add image features and contour image features to the fused features in the form of residuals to avoid loss of visual information.

$$\overline{F_{fus}} = Conv[\overline{F_I}, \overline{F_E}] + \overline{F_I} + \overline{F_E}, \tag{6}$$

where [,] is the concatenate operation.

Afterwards, we leverage the global average pooling operation as well as squeeze and excitation to re-weight the fused features, which can be computed as:

$$F_{fus} = (1 + \alpha)\overline{F_{fus}}, \tag{7}$$

$$\alpha = \sigma_s(\text{MLP}(\sigma_{avg}(\overline{F_{fus}}))), \tag{8}$$

where MLP is a 2-layer convolution operation, σ_{avg} is the global average pooling, and σ_s is the softmax activation. F_{fus} is contour-augmented image features.

3.2 Joint Prediction Module

In this section, we first mine high-level visual cues (concept) based on the obtained final fused image features. Then, we utilize unified high-level visual features, low-level visual features, and original image features to jointly predict language.

Concept Prediction (Transformer Encoder). Following [24,25], we leverage a set of object queries to learn visual concept based on the contour-augmented image features guidance. Let $F_S = [F_S^1, F_S^2, ..., F_S^L]$ denote object queries.

The contour-augmented image features, which highlights visual concepts, along with L object queries are then fed into the Transformer decoder, pointing out the learning key-point of the object queries:

$$F_{vc} = \text{LN}(\text{MHA}(F_S, F_{fus}, F_{fus}) + F_S), \tag{9}$$

The visual semantic feature F_{vc} is fed into the prediction layer to predict visual concepts P_{vc}. Let Y_{vc} denote the visual concept of the ground-truth sentence that corresponds to the **concept vocabulary** (The details of building semantic vocabulary are introduced in 4.2). Thus, the concept prediction loss is:

$$\mathcal{L}_{vc} = \mathbf{asym}(P_{vc}, Y_{vc}), \tag{10}$$

where **asym** means asymmetric loss [26].

Language Prediction (Transformer Decoder). We follow the standard Transformer structure and employ enhanced visual features F_{fus} and concept features F_{vc} as inputs to generate reliable sentences sequentially.

$$H_i = \text{MHA}(w_i, F_{fus}, F_{fus}) + \text{MHA}(w_i, F_{vc}, F_{vc}), \tag{11}$$

$$w_{i+1} = \text{LN}(H_i + w_i), \tag{12}$$

where w_i is the i-th word of the predicted sentence, and H_i is the intermediate hidden state. Let Y denote the ground-truth sentence, and $W = [w_1, w_2, ..., w_T]$ is the predicted sentence. The loss function of captioning is defined as:

$$\mathcal{L}_{cap} = \sum_{t=1}^{T} \text{CE}(W, Y), \tag{13}$$

where CE is the cross-entropy loss.

Thus, the total loss is the combination of visual concept prediction loss and the language prediction loss:

$$\mathcal{L} = \mathcal{L}_{vc} + \mathcal{L}_{cap}. \tag{14}$$

To this end, our method can be trained in an end-to-end manner, which is kind to training and faster inference speed.

4 Experiment

4.1 Dataset and Metrics

Our experiments are conducted on the MS COCO [27], which contains 330,000 images, 2 million object instances, and 80 different object categories, and has

Table 1. Comparison with the state-of-the-art methods on COCO Karpathy test split. B-1, B-4, M, R, C and S in the table represent BLUE-1, BLUE-4, METEOR, ROUGR-, CIDEr and SPICE respectively.

Method	Cross Entropy						CIDEr Optimization					
	B-1	B-4	M	R	C	S	B-1	B-4	M	R	C	S
Up-Down [6]	77.2	36.2	27.0	56.4	113.5	20.3	79.8	36.3	27.7	56.9	120.1	21.4
GCN-LSTM [15]	77.3	36.8	27.9	57.0	116.3	20.9	80.5	38.2	28.5	58.3	127.6	22.0
AoANet [16]	77.4	37.2	28.4	57.5	119.8	21.3	80.2	38.9	29.2	58.8	129.8	22.4
M2 Transformer [8]	–	–	–	–	–	–	80.8	39.1	29.2	58.6	131.2	22.6
X-Transformer [18]	77.3	37.0	28.7	57.5	120.0	21.8	80.9	39.7	29.5	59.1	132.8	23.4
RSTNet [14]	–	–	–	–	–	–	81.1	39.3	29.4	58.8	133.3	23.0
A2 Transformer [19]	–	–	–	–	–	–	81.5	39.8	29.6	59.1	133.9	23.0
Ours	**78.5**	**38.9**	**29.3**	**58.6**	**124.8**	**22.2**	**81.9**	**40.6**	**29.8**	**59.7**	**135.6**	**23.9**

been the most popular image captioning benchmark dataset. For fair comparison with other techniques [6,8,14–16,18], we test on Karpathy splits [28]. We leverage five evaluation metrics(BLEU-N [31], METEOR [32], ROUGE-L [33], CIDEr [34], and SPICE [35]) to assess the quality of the generated descriptions.

4.2 Implementation Details

We use the pre-trained HED [29] network to obtain contour images. The feature encoder is CLIP (backbone: ResNet-101) [30]. Following [24], to build concept vocabulary, we filter out low-frequency words and convert all uppercase letters to lowercase letters. Thus, a concept vocabulary that containing 906 words is constructed. The Transformer block in the Feature Extraction Module, the Concept Prediction Module and the Language Prediction Module are 3 layers, 3 layers, and 6 layers, respectively. The hidden state size is set to 512. The query size is 17. The model is trained using a typical two-stage training method. In the first stage, we use the cross-entropy loss with the learning rate $3e^{-4}$. In the second stage, the self-critical sequence training strategy is used to further optimize the CIDEr scoring model, and the learning rate is set to $5e^{-5}$. In inference, the beam size is set to 3. All experiments are conducted on a single RTX 3090.

4.3 Main Results

Our main results are shown in Table 1. Compared with other representative methods, this method has strong competitiveness, especially in the CIDEr, we have improved 15.5 compared with the classic Up-Down method [6], and 2.3 compared with the recent popular RSTNet method [14]. This is due to the use of contour image to supplement effective information for image features, and the joint prediction module combines visual and textual features, high-level and low-level features together to enhance the impact of vision on language, thus avoiding only focusing on language.

4.4 Ablation Studies

As shown in Table 2, we conducted a series of ablation experiments to demonstrate the effectiveness of our method.

Table 2. The results of ablation studies (Cross Entropy)

Discussion	Method	B-1	B-4	M	R	C	S
The Proposed Modules	Baseline	77.4	37.1	28.8	57.4	121.5	22.1
	Baseline+CA	78.0	38.1	29.0	57.9	122.8	22.1
	Baseline+JP	78.2	38.0	29.0	58.0	123.4	22.1
	Baseline+CA+JP(**Ours**)	**78.5**	**38.9**	**29.3**	**58.6**	**124.8**	**22.2**
Different Contour Extractors	DoG	78.3	38.2	29.2	58.2	124.2	22.2
	Canny	78.5	38.3	29.0	58.3	124.1	22.2
	HED(**Ours**)	**78.5**	**38.9**	**29.3**	**58.6**	**124.8**	**22.2**
Feature Fusion Strategy	ADD	77.9	37.7	28.9	57.7	122.8	21.9
	iAFF [22]	77.8	37.9	28.9	57.8	123.0	22.2
	Ours	**78.5**	**38.9**	**29.3**	**58.6**	**124.8**	**22.2**
Number Of Layer	2-layers	78.4	38.1	28.9	58.0	123.5	22.2
	3-layers(**Ours**)	**78.5**	**38.9**	**29.3**	**58.6**	**124.8**	**22.2**
	6-layers	78.1	38.0	29.0	57.9	123.0	22.0

First, we explore the performance impact of each module. **Baseline** means solely leverage original image without predicting concept. **Baseline+CA** introduces contour information to enhance visual feature comparing to the baseline. **Baseline+JP** represents the use of joint prediction module under the condition that only the original image information is available. **Baseline+CA+JP** further integrates the Joint Prediction Module to assist in sentence generation, and the results of CIDEr were greatly improved.

Next, we demonstrate the universality of the idea of using contour diagrams to enhance visual semantics. We conduct experiments with different contour extractors, including traditional(**DoG, Canny**) and deep learning based methods(**Ours**). The results are slightly affected by different contour extractors, but not significantly. In addition, we want to clarify that HED is not the state-of-the-art contour feature extractor. We use it just want to prove that contour information is useful.

We also use other feature fusion strategies, such as direct addition (**ADD**) and **iAFF** [22]. However, the method of direct addition is too simple, and the method of iAFF is too jumbled, neither of them worked out well.

In addition, we try Transformer blocks with different layers when encoding features, and find that too few layers (**2-layers**) are not conducive to the interaction between features; Too many layers (**6-layers**) will over-encode features and make the model complex and difficult to train.

OURS: a zebra grazing in a field of grass.
GT: A zebra grazing on long dry grass in a field.

OURS: two people standing in a living room playing a video game.
GT: Two people are playing video games in a living room.

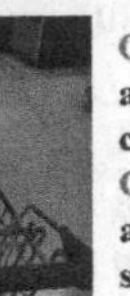

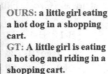

OURS: a little girl eating a hot dog in a shopping cart.
GT: A little girl is eating a hot dog and riding in a shopping cart.

OURS: a small blue and white airplane sitting in a field.
GT: A small blue plane sitting on top of a field.

OURS: a black dog standing in front of a plate of food.
GT: A small black dog standing over a plate of food.

OURS: a painting with fruit and a vase on a table.
GT: A painting of a table with fruit on top of it.

Fig. 2. Qualitative results of our method on the MS COCO – SOME SUCCESSFUL EXAMPLES.

GT:
① A very nice living room that is very clean.
② A big, open room with large windows and wooden floors.
③ A living room with a wooden floor filled with furniture.
④ THERE IS A LIVING ROOM WITH A TABLE AND TV
⑤ A living room with a couple of furniture.

OURS:
a living room with a couch and a table

GT:
① THERE IS A PERSON THAT IS SITTING IN THE BOAT ON THE WATER
② a woman in a red and white boat water and trees
③ A woman riding in a boat on a sunny day.
④ A women who is sitting on a boat.
⑤ a person riding inside of a boat on a body of water

OURS:
a woman sitting on a boat in the water

Fig. 3. Some failure cases of our method.

4.5 Caption Examples

To qualitatively illustrate the effectiveness of our method, we show some caption examples in Fig. 2. OURS represents the sentences generated by our model. GT represents the human-annotated ground-truth sentences. In general, because our CCP-Net not only absorbs the visual features of the original image and contour image, but also fully interacts with visual and language semantics. It achieves the same natural prediction results as humans in all examples. Moreover, our method pays more attention to detail than GT. We highlight the detail words in green.

Our method tends to generates satisfactory captions most of the time, but it occasionally falls short of perfection, as shown in Fig. 3. For the above image, our method generates a caption that fits the image content, but is not good enough. The model does not generate strongly perceived words like "nice" and "clean." There are a lot of objects in this picture. The model only "notices" unified and prominent objects, but cannot "see" all objects, especially "Windows" and "televisions" in the distance, and "floors" divided into many pieces. In the case of the image below, our model failed to recognize that it was a "sunny day" or that the long green things in the distance were trees, which humans could easily do with common sense.

5 Conclusion

In this paper, we propose a Contour-augmented Concept Prediction Network (CCP-Net), which consists of contour-augmented feature extraction module and joint prediction module. Contour-augmented feature extraction module treats contour as the complementary view of the image and leverages the contour to enhance image feature extraction, which promotes the concept prediction and increases the visual contribution in language prediction. Joint prediction module leverages two additional aspects of visual information, including high-level features (concepts) and low-level features (contours), to jointly predict descriptive sentences of image. The whole network is trained in an end-to-end manner. Extensive experiments demonstrate the effectiveness of our proposed method and each individual component.

Acknowledgement. This work was supported by the National Key Research and Development Program of China No.2021YFF0901601.

References

1. Vinyals, O., Toshev, A., Bengio, S., et al.: Show and tell: a neural image caption generator. In: Proceedings of the IEEE Conference on Computer Vision and Pattern Recognition, pp. 3156–3164 (2015)
2. Zeng, P., Zhang, H., Song, J., et al.: S2 transformer for image captioning. In: Proceedings of the International Joint Conferences on Artificial Intelligence, vol. 5 (2022)
3. Lian, Z., Wang, R., Li, H., Hu, X.: Context-assisted attention for image captioning. In: Pimenidis, E., Angelov, P., Jayne, C., Papaleonidas, A., Aydin, M. (eds.) Artificial Neural Networks and Machine Learning - ICANN 2022. ICANN 2022. Lecture Notes in Computer Science, vol. 13529, pp 722–733. Springer, Cham (2022). https://doi.org/10.1007/978-3-031-15919-0_60
4. Wang, X., Huang, J.: Say in human-like way: hierarchical cross-modal information abstraction and summarization for controllable captioning. In: Farkaš, I., Masulli, P., Otte, S., Wermter, S. (eds.) ICANN 2021. LNCS, vol. 12891, pp. 217–228. Springer, Cham (2021). https://doi.org/10.1007/978-3-030-86362-3_18

5. Xu, K., et al.: Show, attend and tell: neural image caption generation with visual attention. In: International Conference on Machine Learning, pp. 2048–2057. PMLR (2015)
6. Anderson, P., He, X., Buehler, C., et al.: Bottom-up and top-down attention for image captioning and visual question answering. In: Proceedings of the IEEE Conference on Computer Vision and Pattern Recognition, pp. 6077–6086 (2018)
7. Ren, S., He, K., Girshick, R., et al.: Faster R-CNN: towards real-time object detection with region proposal networks. In: Advances in Neural Information Processing Systems, vol. 28 (2015)
8. Cornia, M., Stefanini, M., Baraldi, L., et al.: Meshed-memory transformer for image captioning. In: Proceedings of the IEEE/CVF Conference on Computer Vision and Pattern Recognition, pp. 10578–10587 (2020)
9. Nguyen, V.Q., Suganuma, M., Okatani, T.: GRIT: faster and better image captioning transformer using dual visual features. In: Avidan, S., Brostow, G., Cissé, M., Farinella, G.M., Hassner, T. (eds.) Computer Vision - ECCV 2022. ECCV 2022. LNCS, vol. 13696, pp. 167–184 Springer, Cham (2022). https://doi.org/10.1007/978-3-031-20059-5_10
10. Yang, X., Liu, Y., Wang, X.: Reformer: the relational transformer for image captioning. In: Proceedings of the 30th ACM International Conference on Multimedia, pp. 5398–5406 (2022)
11. Dosovitskiy, A., Beyer, L., Kolesnikov, A., et al.: An image is worth 16x16 words: transformers for image recognition at scale. arXiv preprint arXiv:2010.11929 (2020)
12. Guo, L., Liu, J., Zhu, X., et al.: Normalized and geometry-aware self-attention network for image captioning. In: Proceedings of the IEEE/CVF Conference on Computer Vision and Pattern Recognition, pp. 10327–10336 (2020)
13. Herdade, S., Kappeler, A., Boakye, K., et al.: Image captioning: transforming objects into words. In: Advances in Neural Information Processing Systems, vol. 32 (2019)
14. Zhang, X., Sun, X., Luo, Y., et al.: Rstnet: captioning with adaptive attention on visual and non-visual words. In: Proceedings of the IEEE/CVF Conference on Computer Vision and Pattern Recognition, pp. 15465–15474 (2021)
15. Yao, T., Pan, Y., Li, Y., et al.: Exploring visual relationship for image captioning. In: Proceedings of the European Conference on Computer Vision (ECCV), pp. 684–699 (2018)
16. Huang, L., Wang, W., Chen, J., et al.: Attention on attention for image captioning. In: Proceedings of the IEEE/CVF International Conference on Computer Vision, pp. 4634–4643 (2019)
17. Luo, Y., Ji, J., Sun, X., et al.: Dual-level collaborative transformer for image captioning. In: Proceedings of the AAAI Conference on Artificial Intelligence, vol. 35, no. 3, pp. 2286–2293 (2021)
18. Pan, Y., Yao, T., Li, Y., et al.: X-linear attention networks for image captioning. In: Proceedings of the IEEE/CVF Conference on Computer Vision and Pattern Recognition, pp. 10971–10980 (2020)
19. Fei, Z.: Attention-aligned transformer for image captioning. In: Proceedings of the AAAI Conference on Artificial Intelligence, vol. 36, no. 1, pp. 607–615 (2022)
20. Wu, M., Zhang, X., Sun, X., et al.: DIFNet: boosting visual information flow for image captioning. In: Proceedings of the IEEE/CVF Conference on Computer Vision and Pattern Recognition, pp. 18020–18029 (2022)
21. Hu, J., Shen, L., Sun, G.: Squeeze-and-excitation networks. In: Proceedings of the IEEE Conference on Computer Vision and Pattern Recognition, pp. 7132–7141 (2018)

22. Dai, Y., Gieseke, F., Oehmcke, S., et al.: Attentional feature fusion. In: Proceedings of the IEEE/CVF Winter Conference on Applications of Computer Vision, pp. 3560–3569 (2021)
23. Dong, B., Zhou, Y., Hu, C., et al.: BCNet: Bidirectional collaboration network for edge-guided salient object detection. Neurocomputing **437**, 58–71 (2021)
24. Li, Y., Pan, Y., Yao, T., et al.: Comprehending and ordering semantics for image captioning. In: Proceedings of the IEEE/CVF Conference on Computer Vision and Pattern Recognition, pp. 17990–17999 (2022)
25. Fang, Z., Wang, J., Hu, X., et al.: Injecting semantic concepts into end-to-end image captioning. In: Proceedings of the IEEE/CVF Conference on Computer Vision and Pattern Recognition, pp. 18009–18019 (2022)
26. Ridnik, T., Ben-Baruch, E., Zamir, N., et al.: Asymmetric loss for multi-label classification. In: Proceedings of the IEEE/CVF International Conference on Computer Vision, pp. 82–91 (2021)
27. Lin, T.-Y., et al.: Microsoft coco: common objects in context. In: Fleet, D., Pajdla, T., Schiele, B., Tuytelaars, T. (eds.) ECCV 2014. LNCS, vol. 8693, pp. 740–755. Springer, Cham (2014). https://doi.org/10.1007/978-3-319-10602-1_48
28. Karpathy, A., Fei-Fei. L.: Deep visual-semantic alignments for generating image descriptions. In: Proceedings of the IEEE Conference on Computer Vision and Pattern Recognition, pp. 3128–3137 (2015)
29. Xie, S., Tu, Z.: Holistically-nested edge detection. In: Proceedings of the IEEE International Conference on Computer Vision, pp. 1395–1403 (2015)
30. Mokady, R., Hertz, A., Bermano, A.H.: Clipcap: Clip prefix for image captioning. arXiv preprint arXiv:2111.09734 (2021)
31. Papineni, K., Roukos, S., Ward, T., et al.: Bleu: a method for automatic evaluation of machine translation. In: Proceedings of the 40th Annual Meeting of the Association for Computational Linguistics, pp. 311–318 (2002)
32. Denkowski, M., Lavie, A.: Meteor universal: language specific translation evaluation for any target language. In: Proceedings of the Ninth Workshop on Statistical Machine Translation, pp. 376–380 (2014)
33. Lin, C.Y.: Rouge: a package for automatic evaluation of summaries. In: Text Summarization Branches Out, pp. 74–81 (2004)
34. Vedantam, R., Lawrence Zitnick, C., Parikh, D.: Cider: consensus-based image description evaluation. In: Proceedings of the IEEE Conference on Computer Vision and Pattern Recognition, pp. 4566–4575 (2015)
35. Anderson, P., Fernando, B., Johnson, M., Gould, S.: SPICE: semantic propositional image caption evaluation. In: Leibe, B., Matas, J., Sebe, N., Welling, M. (eds.) ECCV 2016. LNCS, vol. 9909, pp. 382–398. Springer, Cham (2016). https://doi.org/10.1007/978-3-319-46454-1_24

Contrastive Knowledge Amalgamation for Unsupervised Image Classification

Shangde Gao[1,2], Yichao Fu[1], Ke Liu[1], and Yuqiang Han[1,2(✉)]

[1] College of Computer Science and Technology, Zhejiang University, Hangzhou, Zhejiang, China
{fuyichao,lk2017}@zju.edu.cn
[2] ZJU-Hangzhou Global Scientific and Technological Innovation Center, Hangzhou, Zhejiang, China
{gaosde,hyq2015}@zju.edu.cn

Abstract. Knowledge amalgamation (KA) aims to learn a compact student model to handle the joint objective from multiple teacher models that are specialized for their own tasks respectively. Current methods focus on coarsely aligning teachers and students in the common representation space, making it difficult for the student to learn the proper decision boundaries from a set of heterogeneous teachers. Besides, the KL divergence in previous works only minimizes the probability distribution difference between teachers and the student, ignoring the intrinsic characteristics of teachers. Therefore, we propose a novel Contrastive Knowledge Amalgamation (CKA) framework, which introduces contrastive losses and an alignment loss to achieve intra-class cohesion and inter-class separation. Contrastive losses intra- and inter- models are designed to widen the distance between representations of different classes. The alignment loss is introduced to minimize the sample-level distribution differences of teacher-student models in the common representation space. Furthermore, the student learns heterogeneous unsupervised classification tasks through soft targets efficiently and flexibly in the task-level amalgamation. Extensive experiments on benchmarks demonstrate the generalization capability of CKA in the amalgamation of specific task as well as multiple tasks. Comprehensive ablation studies provide a further insight into our CKA.

Keywords: Knowledge amalgamation · Contrastive learning

1 Introduction

Reusing pre-trained models to get lite ones for reducing computation costs of training a new one from scratch has been a trending research topic in recent years [7,8]. Knowledge Distillation (KD) methods [6] train a light-weight target model (the *"student"* model) by learning from a well-trained cumbersome model

S. Gao, Y. Fu and K. Liu—Contributed equally.

L. Iliadis et al. (Eds.): ICANN 2023, LNCS 14255, pp. 192–204, 2023.
https://doi.org/10.1007/978-3-031-44210-0_16

(the *"teacher"* model), which improves the performance of students with any architectures compared to the models trained from scratch. Knowledge Amalgamation (KA) [11,13] aims to train a versatile student model by transferring knowledge from multiple pre-trained teachers. The above method requires mapping teachers and student to a common representation space. The student learn similar intermediate features through the aggregated cues from the pre-trained teachers. Further, by integrating probability knowledge from pre-trained teachers using KL divergence, student can predict the joint of teachers' label sets.

However, complex optimization designs are required for heterogeneous teachers in previous works. Besides, direct application of previous KA methods to downstream tasks causes severe performance degradation because of domain shifts, additional noise, as well as information loss in feature projections. Moreover, due to the imperfection of pre-trained teachers and absence of human annotation, the supervision signals for students are confused.

In this work, we endeavor to explore an efficient and effective KA scheme for unsupervised image classification. We aim to transfer knowledge as much as possible from pre-trained teachers who specialize in heterogeneous unsupervised image classification tasks to a compact and versatile student. For example, if one teacher classifies cars and the other classifies airplanes, the student should be able to classify both cars and airplanes. To achieve this, we first extend the contrastive learning paradigm to the knowledge fusion environment, for two reasons. Firstly, CL can effectively push positive sample pairs together and pull negative sample pairs apart without the need for manual annotations. Additionally, different teacher and student models are natural augmentation schemes, and their combination significantly increases the number of positive and negative samples for training the student. Secondly, supervised contrastive loss models have been shown to outperform traditional cross-entropy losses[9]. Thus, they can be effectively used in teacher pre-training to alleviate the incompleteness and unreliability of supervising teacher models.

We propose a novel **C**ontrastive **K**nowledge **A**malgamation, refered to as CKA, by implementing the CKA framework via DNNs for unsupervised classification. Concretely, we first construct a common representation space based on the shared multilayer perceptron (MLP), and design contrastive and alignment losses to achieve intra-class cohesion and inter-class separation of samples. As a way of unsupervised learning, the contrastive loss intra- and inter- models aims to enlarge the distance between feature representations of different sample categories and reduce the distance between feature representations of the same sample category. Besides, alignment losses are proposed to minimize the sample-level distribution difference between different models. Apart from learning the teachers' features, a soft target distillation loss finally is designed to effectively and flexibly transfer probability knowledge from pre-trained teachers to a student, enabling the student to make inferences similar to or the same as the teachers' during task-level amalgamation.

The contributions of this work are summarized as follows:

- We propose a novel model reuse paradigm to supervise the student model without annotations, named CKA, which introduces contrastive losses and an alignment loss to achieve intra-class cohesion and inter-class separation.
- We design a soft target distillation loss to effectively transfer knowledge from the pre-trained teachers to a student in the output probability space.
- Extensive experiments on standard benchmarks demonstrate that CKA provides more accurate supervision, and is generalizable for amalgamating heterogeneous teachers.

2 Related Works

2.1 Knowledge Distillation and Knowledge Amalgamation

Knowledge distillation (KD) [6,16] is a method of transferring knowledge from one model to another. However, existing approaches are still performed under a single teacher-student relationship with a sharing task, are not applicable to multiple and heterogeneous teachers. Knowledge amalgamation (KA) aims to acquire a compact student model capable of handling the comprehensive joint objective of multiple teacher models, each specialized in its own task. There are two kinds of approaches: (1) *Homogeneous* KA, where all teachers and students have identical network architectures [13]. (2) *Heterogeneous* KA, where each teacher has different architecture and specializes in its own class set [11,14]. Among these, [14] matches the outputs of students to the corresponding teachers, while [11] aligns the features of students and teachers in a shared latent space by minimizing the maximum mean discrepancy. However, when facing with the imperfect teachers with unreliable supervisions, previous studies suffer from conflicting supervisions in the student training process, which significantly harms the performance of the student model. To the best of our knowledge, it is the first time to explore the CKA paradigm for unsupervised classification tasks.

2.2 Contrastive Learning

Contrastive Learning is an unsupervised learning method where supervision is automatically generated from the data. Currently, contrastive learning (CL) has achieved state-of-the-art performance in representation learning [1,2,4]. SimCLR [1] proposes the proposal by performing data augmentation on the raw input data and mapping it to a feature space, constructing a contrastive loss (i.e., InfoNCE loss) to maximize the similarity between positive pairs and minimize the similarity between negative pairs. BYOL [4] and SimSiam [2] extend the work by designing their losses to measure the similarity between positive samples, effectively eliminating the need for negative samples. However, all of these approaches are tailored for single-model and single-task. Our method extends the concept of CL to a knowledge amalgamation environment, designing intra-and inter- model contrastive losses to explore the model-agnostic semantic similarity and further apply them to downstream unsupervised multi-classification tasks.

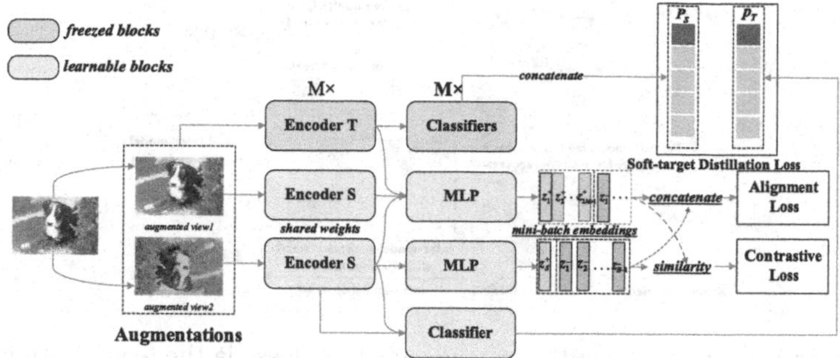

Fig. 1. The overflow of contrastive knowledge amalgamation.

3 Problem Formulation

We define the problem of knowledge amalgamation as follows. Assume that we are given $\mathcal{T} = \{\mathcal{T}_t\}_{t=1}^N$ well pre-trained teachers, where each teacher $\mathcal{T}_t$ specializes a distinct classification task, i.e., a set of full labeled classes $\mathcal{T}_t = (\mathcal{D}_t; \mathcal{Y}^t)$. Our proposal is to learn a versatile student with an unlabeled dataset $\mathcal{D} = \bigcup_{t=1}^N \mathcal{D}_t$, which is able to perform predictions over the comprehensive class set of distinct-task teachers, $\mathcal{Y} = \bigcup_{t=1}^N \mathcal{Y}^t$. In our KA setting, N tasks $\mathcal{T} = \{\mathcal{T}_t\}_{t=1}^N$ can be built for either the same or cross dataset. Without loss of generality, we assume that for any two tasks $\mathcal{T}_i, \mathcal{T}_j \in \mathcal{T}$, their specialties are totally disjoint, i.e., $\mathcal{Y}^i \cap \mathcal{Y}^j = \oslash$.

4 Approach

This work is aimed to build a contrastive knowledge amalgamation framework, and implement it by DNNs for unsupervised image classification. Knowledge amalgamation is particularly challenging when teacher-student structures are heterogeneous and data annotation is not available. To tackle the difficulty, we first leverage the distance between feature representations of the samples, and introduce contrastive and alignment losses to achieve intra-class coherence and inter-class separation of the feature representations. Additionally, we design a soft-target distillation loss to effectively transfer the soft-target probability knowledge from pre-trained teachers to the student. The overview of the proposed CKA is shown in Fig. 1, in which the knowledge of pre-trained teachers is fixed. By training the student model in downstream tasks, the student is capable of making inferences that are similar or identical to those of their teachers.

4.1 Margin-Based Intra- and Inter-model Contrast

As there are no annotated data available, we novely use contrastive learning (CL) to construct supervision for guiding the student. CL aims to maximize the similarities of positive pairs while minimizing those of negative ones [1]. The

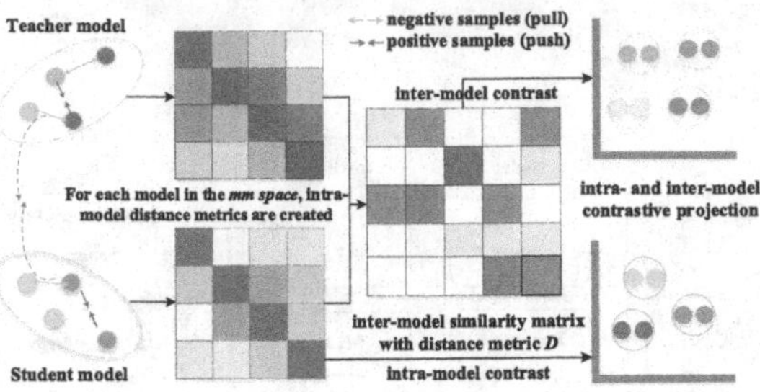

Fig. 2. Illustrations of intra- and inter-model contrast loss via the teacher-student pair.

characteristics of pairs can be defined by different criteria. Motivated by this, we develop two types of contrastive losses, including edge-based student-internal contrast (intra-model contrast) and distance-based teacher-student model contrast (inter-models contrast), to increase the distance between different sample class feature representations and decrease the distance between the same sample class feature representations. The overall schematic is shown in Fig. 2.

Margin-based Intra-model Contrast. To begin with, we describe the standard contrastive loss term, following the most popular setups of SimCLR [1], which is defined as:

$$\mathcal{L}(\tilde{x}, \hat{x}) = -\log \frac{e^{s(\tilde{z},\hat{z})/\tau}}{e^{s(\tilde{z},\hat{z})/\tau + \sum_{\bar{z}\in\Lambda^-} e^{s(\tilde{z},\bar{z}))/\tau}} \tag{1}$$

Here, by way of randomized data augmentation Aug(·), two different views $\tilde{x}$ and $\hat{x}$ for the input sample x are generated. The two images are then fed into an encoder network $\mathcal{E}(x)$, followed by a two-layer nonlinear projection head MLP $h(\cdot)$, yielding a pair of L_2-normalized positive embeddings $\hat{z} = h(\mathcal{E}(\hat{x}))$ and $\tilde{z} = h(\mathcal{E}(\tilde{x}))$. $\bar{z} \in \Lambda^-$ represents the negative sample in a mini-batch. $s(\cdot, \cdot)$ declares the *cosine similarity* for measuring the relationship between embedding pair $\tilde{z}$ and $\hat{z}$ (resp. $\tilde{x}$ and $\hat{x}$), formulated as:

$$s(\tilde{z}, \hat{z}) = \frac{(\tilde{z})(\hat{z})^\top}{\|\tilde{z}\| \cdot \|\hat{z}\|} \tag{2}$$

To prevent the loss from being dominated by easy negatives (different class samples with little similarity), a constant margin α is introduced that only negative pairs with similarity larger than α contribute to the contrastive loss in Eq. 1. Formally, the margin-based intra-model contrastive loss for training the student model is denoted as:

$$\mathcal{L}_{intra} = (1 - s(\tilde{z}, \hat{z})) + \sum_{\bar{z}\in\Lambda^-} (s(\tilde{z}, \bar{z}) - \alpha) \tag{3}$$

Distance-based Inter-model Contrast. For inter-model contrast, data across models are embedded as point distributions in high-dimensional vector spaces. To measure the inter-model distance between those two point distributions, we model two *metric measure spaces* (mm-spaces) $\mathcal{X} = (X, d_X, \mu)$ and $\mathcal{Y} = (Y, d_Y, \nu)$, where data X (resp. Y) is a complete separable set endowed with a distance d_X and a positive Borel measure $\mu \in \mathcal{M}+(X)$. Those two mm-spaces are considered up to isometry (denoted $\mathcal{X} \sim \mathcal{Y}$), meaning that there is a bijection $\psi : \text{spt}(\mu) \to \text{spt}(\nu)$ (where $\text{spt}(\mu)$ is the support of μ) such that $d_X(x, y) = d_Y(\psi(x), \psi(y))$ and $\psi_\sharp \mu = \nu$. Here $\psi_\sharp$ is the push-forward operator.

Specifically, let $\mu \in \mathcal{P}(\mathbb{R}^p)$ and $\nu \in \mathcal{P}(\mathbb{R}^q)$ with $p \neq q$ to be discrete measures on mm-spaces with $\mu = \sum_{i=1}^{n} a_i \delta_{x_i}$ (here δ_{x_i} is the mass at x_i) and $\nu = \sum_{i=1}^{n} b_j \delta_{y_j}$ of supports X and Y, where $a \in \Sigma_n$ and $b \in \Sigma_m$ are simplex histograms. The distance $\mathcal{D}$ between those points is defined as:

$$\mathcal{D}(\mathcal{X}, \mathcal{Y})^q = \sum_{i,j,k,l} \left| d_X(x_i, x_k) - d_Y(y_j, y_l) \right|^q \pi_{i,j} \pi_{k,l} \tag{4}$$

Here $d_X(x_i, x_k) : \mathbb{R}^p \times \mathbb{R}^p \to \mathbb{R}_+$, measures the euclidean distance between sample points x_i and x_k in μ. The intuition underpinning the definition of this distance is that there exists a fuzzy correspondence map $\pi \in \mathcal{P}(X \times Y)$ between the points of the distributions, which tends to associate pairs of points with similar distances within each pair: the more similar $d_X(x_i, x_k)$ is to $d_Y(y_j, y_l)$, the stronger the transport coefficients $\pi_{i,j}$ and $\pi_{k,l}$ are. From a semantic perspective, by simultaneously learning the model structures of both the teacher and student, this distance can measure the similarity between samples, reducing the distance between the feature representations of similar sample classes and increasing the distance between feature representations of dissimilar sample classes.

Given a mini-batch size B of feature maps $P \in \mathbb{R}^{B \times c \times h \times w}$ and $Q_t \in \mathbb{R}^{B \times c \times h \times w}$ extracted from the student encoder and t-th teacher encoder, where c, h, and w denote the number of channel, height and width of the feature maps respectively. For simplicity, we omit the superscripts and subscripts and denote the feature maps of two different models as P and Q. The distance metric on P and Q is designed firstly to guide the contrast across different models, i.e., inter-model contrast. To this end, we first reshape P and Q to $\mathbb{R}^{B \times m}$, i.e., $P = [p_1, p_2, \ldots, p_B]$ and $Q = [q_1, q_2, \ldots, q_B]$, where $m = c \times h \times w$ is the feature vectors. The transport map $\pi^p, \pi^q \in \mathbb{R}^{B \times B}$ for P and Q can be derived by:

$$\pi_{i,j} = \frac{e^{-d(p_i, p_j)}}{\sum_{j=1}^{N} e^{-d(p_i, p_j)}} \tag{5}$$

where $d(\cdot, \cdot)$ is the mm-space distance between two instances p_i and p_j. Unless stated otherwise, euclidean distance is used in our experiments.

As for any k-th row vector in π^p and π^q, π_k^p and π_k^q can be termed as positive pairs because they both semantically illustrate the distance of k-th sample and others in the mini-batch N, regardless of the model representation. Our distance-based inter-model contrastive loss, discovering fine-gained sample similarity matching between the student and each teacher, can be defined as:

$$\mathcal{L}_{inter} = \sum_{t=1}^{N} \left(\left(1 - s\left(\pi^{p}, \pi_{t+}^{q}\right)\right) + \sum_{\pi_{t\text{-}}^{q} \in \Lambda^{-}} s\left(\pi^{p}, \pi_{t\text{-}}^{q}\right) \right) \tag{6}$$

where $\pi_{t\text{-}}^{q}$ and π_{t+}^{q} denote the distance-based negative and positive pairs.

4.2 Common Feature Alignment

To enable a student to mimic the aggregated hints from heterogeneous teachers, a shared multilayer perceptron (MLP) is designed for mapping all features to a common latent space. Specifically, a 1×1 kernel convolution is added after the backbone network of each model separately, thereby unifying the outputs of different models into the same channel, which is taken to be the input of MLP and set to 256 in our implementation.

As represented in CFL [11], we adopt the Maximum Mean Discrepancy (MMD) to measure the discrepancy between the output features of the student and that of teachers in the unit ball of a reproducing kernel Hilbert space [3]. Take a teacher-student pair as an example, we extract the mini-batch common space features with the designed shared MLP and represent them as $f_{\mathcal{S}}, f_{\mathcal{T}} \in \mathbb{R}^{B \times d}$, of which d denotes the output dimension of the MLP and is set to 128 in our implementation. An empirical l_2 *norm* approximation to the MMD distance of $f_{\mathcal{S}}$ and $f_{\mathcal{T}}$ is computed as follow:

$$\text{MMD} = \frac{1}{B} \left\| \sum_{i=1}^{B} \phi\left(f_{\mathcal{T}}^{i}\right) - \sum_{j=1}^{B} \phi\left(f_{\mathcal{S}}^{j}\right) \right\|_{2}^{2} \tag{7}$$

where ϕ is an explicit mapping function. The extension of multi-kernel formulation of MMD can then be defined as:

$$\begin{aligned} \text{MMD}^{2}[K, f_{\mathcal{S}}, f_{\mathcal{T}}] = & K\left(f_{\mathcal{S}}, f_{\mathcal{S}}\right) - 2K\left(f_{\mathcal{T}}^{i}, f_{\mathcal{S}}^{j}\right) + \\ & K\left(f_{\mathcal{T}}, f_{\mathcal{T}}\right) \end{aligned} \tag{8}$$

K is defined as the convex combination of m PSD kernel:

$$\mathcal{K} = \left\{ K = \sum_{u=1}^{m} \sigma_{u} K_{u} : \sum_{u=1}^{m} \sigma_{u} = 1, \sigma_{u} \geq 0, \forall u \right\} \tag{9}$$

here $\mathcal{K}$ denotes the multi-prototypical kernel set. The constraints on coefficients $\{\sigma_{u}\}$ are imposed to guarantee that the derived multi-kernel K is characteristic.

The process of aligning each teacher and student is equivalent to minimizing the MMD distance between them. This can achieve intra-class cohesion of similar

Table 1. Statistics of datasets used in this paper.

Dataset	Images	Categories	Train/Test
CUB-200-2011	11,788	200	5,994/5,794
Stanford Dogs	20,580	120	12,000/8,580
Stanford Cars	16,185	196	8,144/8,041
FGVC-Aircraft	102,000	102	6,667/3,333

samples. We aggregate all such MMDs between N pairs of teachers and students, and the overall alignment loss $\mathcal{L}_{align}$ in the shared MLP can be written as:

$$\mathcal{L}_{align} = \sum_{i=1}^{N} \text{MMD}\left(f_{\mathcal{S}}, f_{\mathcal{T}_t}\right) \tag{10}$$

4.3 Soft-Target Distillation

Apart from learning the teacher's features, the student is also expected to produce identical or similar inferences as the teachers do. We thus also take the teachers' predictions by feeding unlabelled input samples to them and then supervise the student's training. As there is no annotation available for each instance x in the target dataset $\mathcal{D}_s$, the predictions of pre-trained teachers can be constructed as supervision for guiding the student, named as *soft-target distillation*.

Specifically, we first feed x into each T_i to obtain the golden label probability distribution $\Phi(x; T_i)$ in the *softmax layer*, and then concatenate them together for training the student by minimizing the KL-divergence between their probability distribution:

$$\mathcal{L}_{std} = \sum_{x \in \mathcal{D}_s} \text{KL}(\Phi(x, S) \| \Phi(x, T)) \tag{11}$$

where $\Phi(x, S)$ and $\Phi(x, T)$ denote the *softmax* probability distribution of the student and that of the concatenated teachers for input x, respectively.

Considering the weighted sum of contrastive losses (including $\mathcal{L}_{intra}$, and $\mathcal{L}_{inter}$), alignment loss $\mathcal{L}_{align}$ and soft-target distillation loss $\mathcal{L}_{std}$ together, the total training objective of our CKA can be described as:

$$\mathcal{L} = \lambda_{intra}\mathcal{L}_{intra} + \lambda_{inter}\mathcal{L}_{inter} + \lambda_a\mathcal{L}_{align} + \lambda_d\mathcal{L}_{std} \tag{12}$$

5 Experiments

In this section, we evaluate the proposed method on standard benchmarks and compare the results with the recent state of the arts. We also conduct ablation studies to validate the effect of the major components.

Table 2. Comparison of different methods on comprehensive classification tasks. Best results are shown in bold.

Method	Size	Dogs	Cars	CUB	Aircraft	Average
Supervised	163M	83.62 ± 0.00	89.64 ± 0.00	72.68 ± 0.00	82.78 ± 0.00	82.14
Teacher1	130M	66.64 ± 0.00	70.33 ± 0.00	65.37 ± 0.00	63.01 ± 0.00	66.80
Teacher2	240M	72.03 ± 0.00	87.85 ± 0.00	66.12 ± 0.00	81.12 ± 0.00	76.60
Ensemble	370M	73.90 ± 0.22	77.08 ± 0.64	68.25 ± 0.00	75.76 ± 0.00	73.38
Vanilla KD	240M	76.16 ± 0.60	80.39 ± 0.31	69.94 ± 0.79	78.00 ± 0.01	76.06
CFL	240M	76.23 ± 0.26	81.12 ± 0.21	70.67 ± 0.97	79.98 ± 0.22	76.86
CKA-Intra	240M	78.89 ± 0.59	82.33 ± 0.31	71.07 ± 0.04	79.02 ± 0.21	77.71
CKA-Inter	240M	79.72 ± 0.60	**82.95 ± 1.20**	**71.49 ± 0.25**	80.45 ± 0.51	78.46
CKA	240M	**79.76 ± 0.09**	82.88 ± 0.21	71.32 ± 0.55	**80.78 ± 0.08**	78.45

5.1 Experiments Setup

Datasets. We evaluate our proposed CKA on four widely used benchmarks, i.e., CUB-200-2011 [15], Stanford Cars [10], Stanford Dogs [9], and FGVC-Aircraft [12]. The detailed statistics are summarized in Table 1.

Implementation Details. We adopt the *resnet* family [5] including *resnet*-18, *resnet*-34, and *resnet*-50, as our model samples. Besides, all the teachers are first pre-trained as [10] and fine-tuned to heterogeneous tasks. To construct heterogeneous tasks on the given datasets, we split all the categories into non-overlapping parts of equal size to train the teachers. The trained teacher model weights are frozen during the student training process. In student training phrase, data augmentation is performed via Random ResizedCrop, Random ColorJitter, Random HorizontalFlip, and Random GaussianBlur while in testing, Center Crop is used. During training, the learning rate is set to 0.0005, and the cosine decay is used; the weight decay is set to 0.0005; Adam is used as the optimizer, and the batch size is set to 64; a total of 100 epochs are trained. All experiments are completed with GPUs of RTX 2080 Ti 11 GB and CPUs of Intel. There are several hyper-parameters involved in our method, including α in Eq. 3, set to 0.4, for alleviating the dominance of negative sample pairs; λ_{intra}, λ_{inter}, λ_a and λ_d for the final CKA loss in Eq. 12, are set to $\lambda_{intra} = \lambda_{inter} = \lambda_d = 1$ and $\lambda_a = 10$.

Compared Methods. We implement various baselines to evaluate the effectiveness of our proposal, which are categorized as: (1) *Original Teacher*: The teacher models are used independently for prediction. We set the probabilities of classes out of the teacher specialty to zeros. (2) *Ensemble*: The output logits of teachers are directly concatenated for predictions over the union label set. (3) Vanilla KD [6]: The student is trained to mimic the soft targets produced by logits combination of all teacher models, via minimizing the vanilla KL-divergence objective. (4) CFL [11]: CFL first maps the hidden representations of the student and the teachers into a common feature space. The student is trained by aligning the mapped features to that of the teachers, with supplemental supervision from the logits combination. We also include a supervised learning method, which trains

Table 3. Ablation analysis of CKA. Remove modules lead to deteriorated performance.

Method	Vanilla KD_{kd}	CFL	CKA	W/O Inter-model loss	W Inter-model loss			W/O Intra-model loss
					Euclidean	Cosine	MMD	
Cars	80.22	81.12	82.88	80.04	82.33	82.95	83.21	82.33
Aircraft	78.00	79.98	80.78	77.97	80.21	80.45	81.42	79.02

the student with labeled data for a better understanding of the performance. We compare the average accuracy of each method in three random experiments.

5.2 Quantitative Analysis

We compare our proposed method CKA with SOTA on above-mentioned classification datasets. The experiment results and corresponding model size are listed in Table 2. Our findings are: (1) Simple baselines can be seriously affected by incomplete datasets and annotations, showing that it is necessary to conduct amalgamation. (2) CFL cannot achieves consistent improvements on comprehensive tasks, demonstrating the instability of supervision based on simple feature alignments. (3) Our proposed CKA and its variants outperform the previous baseline models on all the datasets, and the average accuracy of CKA-Inter is achieves a 1.60 points gain over the best performing baseline model. On the FGVC-Aircraft dataset, the knowledge consolidation accuracy of CKA reached 80.78% without label information, approaching that of supervised learning methods. We attribute this success to the fact that CKA provides the student with natural semantic relevance estimated on the sample set based on contrastive losses, and the intra-class cohesion and inter-class separation methods effectively transfer feature-level knowledge. Furthermore, supervisory contradictions from incomplete teachers are avoided by soft labels at task-level amalgamation. These promising results indicate that our CKA framework produces better supervisions for training the student model, yields great potentials for model reusing.

5.3 Ablation Study

We conduct ablation studies to investigate the contribution of the contrastive losses and soft-target distillation loss described in our proposed approach.

For margin-based intra-model contrastive loss, we compare the performances by turning them on and off. For inter-model loss between teacher-student pairs, on the other hand, we define three different distances in Eq. 4, including euclidean distance, cosine and MMD distance. We summarize the comparative results in Table 3, where we observe that the CKA-Inter with MMD distance yields better performance than others. Moreover, CKA and its variants also improve with a large room over KD and CFL, validating the complement of contrastive losses and flexibility of soft-target loss.

Table 4. Result of merging heterogeneous teachers with different architectures is demonstrated by Stanford Dogs dataset.

Teachers		T_1: *restnet-18*	T_2: *restnet-34*		T_1: *restnet-50*		T_2: *restnet-34*
Method		Vanilla KD	CFL	CKA	Vanilla KD	CFL	CKA
Student Net	*resnet-34*	80.67	81.09	82.54	80.54	81.23	82.08
	resnet-50	82.04	82.25	83.18	82.62	84.55	85.21

Table 5. Results of merging from teacher models with different knowledge domains and in a cross-dataset scenario of Stanford Cars and FGVC-Aircraft.

Method	T_1: Stanford Cars	T_2: FGVC-Aircraft	Merge
Supervised	89.64 ± 0.00	82.78 ± 0.00	86.90 ± 0.00
Teacher1	89.64 ± 0.00	–	–
Teacher2	–	78.00 ± 0.00	–
Ensemble	–	–	82.08 ± 0.54
Vanilla KD	85.26 ± 0.25	80.31 ± 0.85	83.76 ± 0.59
CFL	87.99 ± 0.73	84.22 ± 0.48	86.76 ± 0.46
CKA-Intra	88.95 ± 0.00	84.93 ± 0.58	87.75 ± 0.60
CKA-Inter	**89.48 ± 0.31**	84.91 ± 0.59	88.11 ± 0.79
CKA	89.28 ± 0.75	**85.78 ± 0.07**	**88.21 ± 0.50**

5.4 Results in Challenging Settings

CKA with Heterogeneous Teachers. We further consider merging knowledge from heterogeneous teachers with different structures. Specifically, we random select two different *resnet* architectures as the teachers, respectively. The results are listed in Table 4. We find that while a larger student tends to perform better, indicating that the wider and larger the model, the more complete the knowledge can be learned. Our CKA achieves the best results on the Stanford Dogs, showing its effectiveness for heterogeneous teachers.

CKA with Heterogeneous Teachers For Cross-Dataset. Specifically, we pretrain distinct-task teacher models on different datasets separately and then train a student to perform classification over the union label set of both datasets. The results of merging knowledge from two combined datasets, Stanford Cars and FGVC-Aircraft are listed in Table 5. *resnet-34* is adopted for training student in the cross-dataset setting. Our CKA still outperforms previous baseline models in this settings. Interestingly, we find that the performance of CKA is superior to all baselines and even to the results of supervision. We speculate that the reason is that the correlation between classes in different datasets is weak and the data classification categories are complex, which is prone to confusion by label supervision alone. In contrast, our CKA uses contrast loss to compute the distance between samples, which is more robust and discriminative.

6 Conclusion

In this paper, we explore knowledge amalgamation for unsupervised classification tasks for promoting better model reuse. We present a principled framework CKA, in which contrastive losses and alignment loss are designed to enlarge the distance between feature representations of samples from different categories and decrease that of samples from the same categories, as a self-supervised way to guide the student to learn discriminative features. Besides, we present a soft-target distillation loss to efficiently and flexibly transfer the dark knowledge in the task-level amalgamation. Experiments on several benchmarks demonstrate our CKA can substantially outperform strong baselines. More extensive investigations show that CKA is generalizable for challenging settings, including merging knowledge from heterogeneous teachers, or even cross-dataset teachers.

References

1. Chen, T., Kornblith, S., Norouzi, M., Hinton, G.: A simple framework for contrastive learning of visual representations. In: International Conference on Machine Learning, pp. 1597–1607. PMLR, Virtual (2020)
2. Chen, X., He, K.: Exploring simple Siamese representation learning. In: Proceedings of the IEEE/CVF Conference on Computer Vision and Pattern Recognition, pp. 15750–15758. Computer Vision Foundation/IEEE, Virtual (2021)
3. Gretton, A., Borgwardt, K.M., Rasch, M.J., Schölkopf, B., Smola, A.: A kernel two-sample test. J. Mach. Learn. Res. **13**(1), 723–773 (2012)
4. Grill, J.B., et al.: Bootstrap your own latent-a new approach to self-supervised learning. Adv. Neural Inf. Process. Syst. **33**, 21271–21284 (2020)
5. He, K., Zhang, X., Ren, S., Sun, J.: Deep residual learning for image recognition. In: Proceedings of the IEEE Conference on Computer Vision and Pattern Recognition, pp. 770–778. IEEE Computer Society, Las Vegas, NV, USA (2016)
6. Hinton, G., Vinyals, O., Dean, J.: Distilling the knowledge in a neural network. arXiv preprint arXiv:1503.02531 (2015)
7. Jiang, W., et al.: PTMTorrent: a dataset for mining open-source pre-trained model packages. arXiv preprint arXiv:2303.08934 (2023)
8. Jiang, W., et al.: An empirical study of artifacts and security risks in the pre-trained model supply chain. In: Proceedings of the 2022 ACM Workshop on Software Supply Chain Offensive Research and Ecosystem Defenses, pp. 105–114. ACM, Los Angeles, U.S.A (2022)
9. Khosla, A., Jayadevaprakash, N., Yao, B., Li, F.F.: Novel dataset for fine-grained image categorization: Stanford dogs. In: Proceedings of CVPR Workshop on Fine-Grained Visual Categorization (FGVC), vol. 2. Citeseer, Colorado Springs, CO (2011)
10. Krause, J., Stark, M., Deng, J., Fei-Fei, L.: 3d object representations for fine-grained categorization. In: 2013 IEEE International Conference on Computer Vision Workshops, pp. 554–561 (2013). https://doi.org/10.1109/ICCVW.2013.77
11. Luo, S., Wang, X., Fang, G., Hu, Y., Tao, D., Song, M.: Knowledge amalgamation from heterogeneous networks by common feature learning. In: 28th Proceedings of the International Joint Conference on Artificial Intelligence. ijcai.org, Macao, China (2019)

12. Maji, S., Rahtu, E., Kannala, J., Blaschko, M., Vedaldi, A.: Fine-grained visual classification of aircraft. arXiv preprint arXiv:1306.5151 (2013)
13. Shen, C., Wang, X., Song, J., Sun, L., Song, M.: Amalgamating knowledge towards comprehensive classification. In: Proceedings of the AAAI Conference on Artificial Intelligence, pp. 3068–3075. AAAI Press, Honolulu, Hawaii, USA (2019)
14. Vongkulbhisal, J., Vinayavekhin, P., Visentini-Scarzanella, M.: Unifying heterogeneous classifiers with distillation. In: Proceedings of the IEEE/CVF Conference on Computer Vision and Pattern Recognition, pp. 3175–3184. Computer Vision Foundation/IEEE, Long Beach, CA, USA (2019)
15. Wah, C., Branson, S., Welinder, P., Perona, P., Belongie, S.: The caltech-UCSD birds-200-2011 dataset (2011)
16. Zhao, B., Cui, Q., Song, R., Qiu, Y., Liang, J.: Decoupled knowledge distillation. In: Proceedings of the IEEE/CVF Conference on Computer Vision and Pattern Recognition, pp. 11953–11962. Computer Vision Foundation/IEEE, Virtual (2022)

Cross Classroom Domain Adaptive Object Detector for Student's Heads

Chunhui Li, Haoze Yang, Kunyao Lan, and Liping Shen(✉)

Shanghai Jiao Tong University, Shanghai, China
{lch2016,yhz_ev3r,lankunyao,lpshen}@sjtu.edu.cn

Abstract. Training on a label-rich dataset and test on another label-scarce dataset usually leads to a poor performance because of the domain shift. Unsupervised domain adaptation is proved to be effective on this problem in recent researches. Unsupervised domain adaptive object detection of students' heads between different classrooms has becoming an important task with the development of Smart Classroom. However, few cross-classroom models for students' heads have been proposed despite the rapid development of domain adaptive object detection. In this paper, we propose two adaptations which focus on the challenges of domain adaptive object detection of students' heads between different classrooms, including the adaptation based on the numbers of students and the adaptation based on the locations of students. Based on Unbiased Mean Teacher framework, our Cross Classroom Domain Adaptive Object Detector achieves an average precision of 50.2% on the cross-classroom students' heads dataset called SCUT_HEAD, which outperforms the existing state-of-the-art methods.

Keywords: Unsupervised domain adaptation · Object detection · Cross-classroom · Student's heads

1 Introduction

The rapid development of deep convolutional neural networks (DCNN) such as Faster R-CNN [1], Single Shot MultiBox Detector (SSD) [2] and You Only Look Once (YOLO) [3] has achieved significant advancement in the field of object detection. Generally, DCNN models trained with annotated images [4–6] are often lack of generalization capability because of the difference between training images and real-world images. Most domain adaptation researches consider that the source domain dataset is label-rich and the target domain dataset is label-scarce [7], and the gap between source domain and target domain is called domain shift or distribution shift [8]. Considering the high cost of annotating samples from each domain, a lot of unsupervised domain adaptation methods are proposed, which aim to improve the model's performance trained on label-rich source dataset and label-scarce target dataset.

L. Iliadis et al. (Eds.): ICANN 2023, LNCS 14255, pp. 205–216, 2023.
https://doi.org/10.1007/978-3-031-44210-0_17

With the rapid development of smart classrooms, more and more tasks such as teacher behavior analysis, student expression analysis and calculation of front-row seating rate need to be undertaken by automated methods. In order to finish the above tasks, detecting the heads of students is an essential step. Detecting the heads of students in different classes can be finished by end-to-end object detection models including Faster R-CNN. However, considering the different styles, layouts and colors of different classrooms, simple object detection models are not able to adapt to all the images from different classrooms without the help of unsupervised domain adaptation methods. In fact, there are few works of unsupervised domain adaptation for object detection focus on this specific field. In this paper, we proposed Cross Classroom Domain Adaptive Object Detector (CCOD), which utilizes the adaptation based on the numbers of students and the adaptation based on the locations of students to improve the performance on cross-classroom object detection of students' heads.

The main contribution of our methods is shown as follow: first, we describe the cross-classroom task based on the SCUT_HEAD dataset [32] and analyze the reasons why existing models have a poor performance on this task. Second, we propose the adaptation based on the numbers of students and the adaptation based on the locations of students. Finally, we test CCOD with cross-classroom domain adaptation experiments, which prove our CCOD achieves better performance on cross-classroom object detection of students' heads than other models.

2 Related Work

2.1 Unsupervised Domain Adaptation

Unsupervised Domain Adaptation (UDA) aims to transfer the ability of model trained on label-rich source domain to target domain without label. Domain Adaptive Faster R-CNN [23] is the earliest model which focuses on the unsupervised domain adaptation for the task of object detection, which utilizes image-level alignment and instance-level alignment to get the invariance between source domain and target domain.

2.2 Domain Adaptive Object Detection

In recent years, many methods of unsupervised domain adaptation for object detection have been proposed. According to their principles, we can category them into the following types: adversarial learning based methods [9–12], pseudo-labels based methods [13,14], image-to-image translation based methods [15,16], domain randomization based methods [17], teacher-student model based methods [18,19] and graph reasoning based methods [20,21]. Teacher-student model based methods is applied in this paper, which utilize the teacher and student model in the field of knowledge distillation to domain adaptation. According to their frameworks, there are SSD-framework methods [13,22] and faster R-CNN based methods [23–28]. MeGA-CDA [26] combined category-wise discriminators and memory-guided attention maps to accurately align objects belonging to the same category. iFAN [27] proposed Deep Image-level Alignment, Category-Aware Instance Alignment and Category-Correlation Instance Alignment to improve the performance on unsupervised domain adaptive object detection, by accurately align the image-level and instance-level features. Unbiased Mean Teacher (UMT) [18] applied cross-domain distillation on unsupervised domain adaptive object detection, which is based on Mean Teacher [29] (MT). These existing methods are not suitable for our task because they are designed for detection of other objects such as cars instead of heads.

3 Method

3.1 Problem Definition

The goal of this paper is to address unsupervised domain adaptive object detection of students' head cross different classrooms, where we are given labeled images $D^s = \{I^s, Y^s\}$ in source domain and unlabeled images $D^t = \{I^t\}$ in target domain. We need to design a generalized model which is trained by $\{D^s, D^t\}$ and has a good performance on predicting the labels Y^t of target images.

3.2 Cross Classroom Domain Adaptive Object Detector

Our method is based on Unbiased Mean Teacher (UMT) [18] and focuses on improving the model's performance on cross-classroom object detection of students' heads. The overview of the proposed Cross Classroom Domain Adaptive Object Detector (CCOD) is shown in Fig. 1. Our model consists of two major modules: a student model and a teacher model. The student model takes source-like sample P^t, and the teacher model takes target sample I^t, target-like sample P^s and source sample I^s, where P^t and P^s are generated by image-to-image translation using CycleGAN [31]. At first, the teacher model and the student model is initialized with same parameters. Then, during the training phase, the teacher model guides the update of student model by distillation loss $\mathcal{L}_{dis}$, and the student model updates teacher model's weights by exponential moving average (EMA). Besides, a dynamic adaptation is utilized to correct the bias during the training process. In this paper, the adaptation based on students' numbers and locations are proposed to improve the performance on cross-classroom object detection of students' heads.

Image-to-Image Translation. CCOD utilizes target-like samples P^s and source-like target samples P^t to improve the performance on the cross-classroom object detection task, which are generated by CycleGAN [31] as shown in Fig. 2. Following UMT, CCOD uses the source-like target images P^t to heal the bias of teacher model, and uses target-like source samples P^s to heal the bias of student model. By using the source-like target images, the teacher model is expected to have a more accurate prediction, which can better guide the student model.

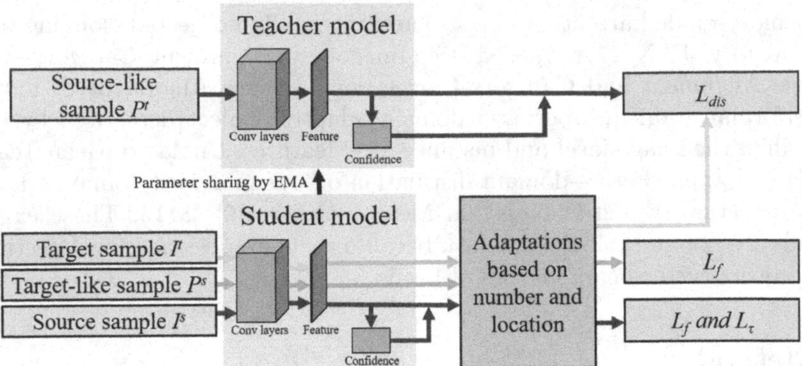

Fig. 1. Overview of the proposed Cross Classroom Domain Adaptive Object Detector. Our contribution is shown as the blue part. Adaptation based on the numbers of students encourages the model to recognize more bounding boxes when the number of bounding boxes already determined is very small or large. Adaptation based on the locations of students encourages the model to recognize more bounding boxes which are located inside the student region. (Color figure online)

By adding the target-style source samples to training, the student model will be adapted to be more suitable for target domain images. In this way, the bias of student model can be reduced.

Detection Loss. Denoting the faster-RCNN's detection loss as $\mathcal{L}_f$, the detection loss by source images and target-like images can be written as:

$$\mathcal{L}_f(I^s, Y^s) + \mathcal{L}_f(P^s, Y^s) \tag{1}$$

Distillation Loss. Following UMT [18], by applying a distillation loss between the teacher model and the student model, the student model will be guided to be more stable. The distillation loss $\mathcal{L}_{dis}(\theta)$ refers to the distance of predictions between the teacher model and the student model. Denoting the teacher model as M_{tea}, the student model as M_{stu}, the augmented P^t as $\widetilde{P}^t$, the augmented I^t as $\hat{I}^t$, the distillation loss can be also written as:

$$\mathcal{L}_{dis}[M_{tea}(\widetilde{P}^t), M_{stu}(\hat{I}^t)] = \mathbb{E}_x[\left\|M_{tea}(\widetilde{P}^t) - M_{stu}(\hat{I}^t)\right\|^2] \tag{2}$$

Dynamic Adaptation. Following UMT [18], our model utilizes a dynamic adaptation to correct the bias during the training process, by selecting the source-like images using confidences predicted by the model. Denoting the confidence score as τ, then the additional loss can be written as:

$$\mathcal{L}_\tau = -log(\tau) \tag{3}$$

Besides, the confidence scores can be used to get soft labels. After denoting the predicted class probability as $\mathcal{P}'$, the category labels as Y_{cls}, the soft labels $\mathcal{P}$ can be calculated by the equation:

$$\mathcal{P} = \tau \cdot \mathcal{P}' + (\mathbf{1} - \tau) \cdot Y_{cls} \tag{4}$$

Then, the detection loss of source images I^s can be updated from $L_f(I^s, Y^s)$ to $L_f(I^s, \mathcal{P})$.

(a) Source sample (b) Target-like sample

(c) Target sample (d) Source-like sample

Fig. 2. Samples before and after the translation of CycleGAN. (a) is a sample from source domain dataset. (c) is a sample from target domain dataset. (b) is the image by translating (a) into target style using CycleGAN. (d) is the image by translating (b) into source style using CycleGAN.

Adaptation Based on the Numbers of Students. To get a better cross-classroom model for object detection, it is important for us to find out the domain-invariance characteristics between different classrooms. There is a phenomenon that the numbers of students in most classrooms' images are either very large or very small in this classroom image set [32] as shown in Fig. 3. According to this phenomenon, we encourage the model to recognize more bounding boxes when the number of bounding boxes already determined is quite small or very large, by adjust the threshold which is used to judge the bounding boxes as shown in Fig. 4. Denoting the number of bounding boxes already determined as

n, the average number of classrooms' max capacities as $\overline{n}$, the original threshold as T, the dynamic threshold T_{n+1} for n+1-th bounding box can be calculated by:

$$T_{n+1} = max\{T - \frac{(n - \overline{n}/2)^2}{N}, 0.6\} \tag{5}$$

where T is set to 0.8.

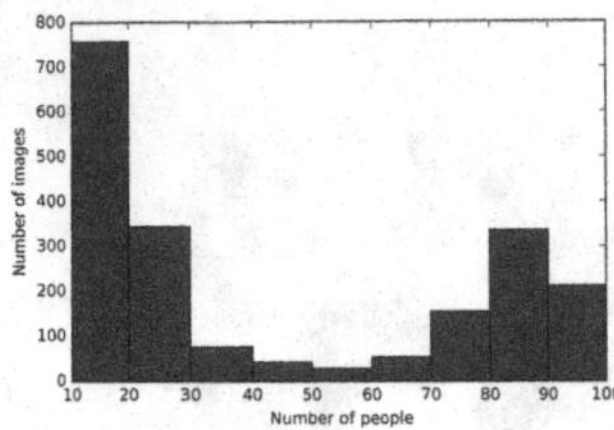

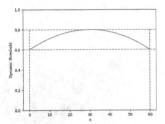

Fig. 3. The numbers of students in all the classrooms of source domain [32].

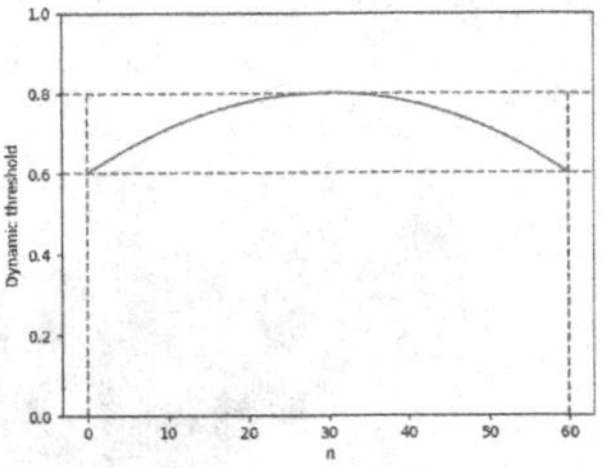

Fig. 4. The relationship between dynamic threshold and the number of bounding boxes n.

Adaptation Based on the Locations of Students. Then, there is a regional phenomenon that most of the students' heads are located in a part of the images of classrooms, because classrooms are usually divided into teach region and student region. In a traditional classroom, the student region is very clear as shown in Fig. 5. Even in the classroom with several discussion groups such as Fig. 6, we can see that locations of students' heads are still restricted in a rather small region compared with the whole image. According to this phenomenon, we encourage the model to recognize more bounding boxes which are located inside the student region. In order to simplify the calculation, we assume that the student region is a rectangle. We denote the student region as R, the upper bound of the student region is r_{upper}, the lower bound of the student region is r_{lower}, the left bound of the student region is r_{left}, the right bound of the student region is r_{right}. The student region R is initialized to R_0 using the first predicted bounding box B_0 whose upper bound is b_{upper_0}, lower bound is b_{lower_0}, left bound is b_{left_0}, right bound is b_{right_0}:

$$R_0 = B_0 \tag{6}$$

This adaptation is executed by iterative method. In the i-th iteration, our operation can be divided into three steps. Firstly, we judge whether the i-th bounding box B_i is located inside the student region R_i of the i-th iteration. The Intersection over Union (IoU) between B_i and R_i may become inaccurate when the area difference between B_i and R_i is too large. Therefore, we judge B_i is located inside the student region by $CoverRate_i$, when the $CoverRate_i$ is higher than 0.9:

$$CoverRate_i = \frac{Area\ of\ Overlap\ between\ B_i\ and\ R_i}{Area\ of\ B_i} \tag{7}$$

Secondly, we encourage the model to recognize more bounding boxes which are located inside the student region, by adjusting B_i's threshold from 0.8 to T_{loc} if B_i is located inside the student region.

Thirdly, after the adjustment of threshold, if B_i is accepted as one of the prediction results, we update the student region R_i by B_i:

$$r_{upper\_i} = min\{\alpha b_{upper\_i} + (1-\alpha) r_{upper\_i-1}, r_{upper\_i-1}\} \tag{8}$$

$$r_{lower\_i} = min\{\alpha b_{lower\_i} + (1-\alpha) r_{lower\_i-1}, r_{lower\_i-1}\} \tag{9}$$

$$r_{left\_i} = min\{\alpha b_{left\_i} + (1-\alpha) r_{left\_i-1}, r_{left\_i-1}\} \tag{10}$$

$$r_{right\_i} = min\{\alpha b_{right\_i} + (1-\alpha) r_{right\_i-1}, r_{right\_i-1}\} \tag{11}$$

where the updated student region R_i can be used for next iteration.

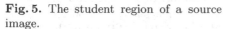

Fig. 5. The student region of a source image.

Fig. 6. The student region of a target image.

Overall Loss Function. In conclusion, the overall loss of CCOD can be written as:

$$\begin{aligned} \mathcal{L} = \mathcal{L}_f(I^s, \mathcal{P}) + \mathcal{L}_f(P^s, Y^s) + \\ \lambda \mathcal{L}_{dis}[M_{tea}(\widetilde{P}^t), M_{stu}(\hat{I}^t)] + \gamma \mathcal{L}_{\mathcal{T}} \end{aligned} \tag{12}$$

where λ and γ is a trade-off parameter.

4 Experiments

The dataset we use in this paper is SCUT_HEAD [32], which consists of two sub-dataset called SCUT_A and SCUT_B. SCUT_A contains 2000 images from several similar classrooms, which annotate 67321 students' heads. SCUT_B contains 2405 images from many different classrooms with different styles, which annotate 43940 students' heads.

Our model is inspired by original UMT [18], which is based on faster-RCNN [1] model. We use VGG16 which is pretrained on ImageNet [4] as the backbone of our model. Following UMT, we set the trade-off parameter $\lambda = 0.01$ and $\gamma = 0.1$, and confidence threshold T is set to 0.8 for all the experiments. All of the above results are tested on the VGG16 backbone pretrained with ImageNet.

5 Results and Discussion

The results of our model and previous state-of-the-art methods such as Domain Adaptive Faster-RCNN (DA) [23], Strong-Weak Faster-RCNN (SWDA) [24] and UMT [18] is shown in Table 1, which uses average precision (AP) of person as evaluation criteria. The detection which has an overlap greater than 0.5 with ground-truth is regarded as correct prediction.

5.1 Transfer from SCUT_A to SCUT_B

As shown in Table 1, the classic model DA and SWDA get APs of 20.1% and 25.5%, which outperform the source-only model's 18.5%. This proves classic unsupervised domain adaptive methods on object detection is helpful for the cross-classroom object detection of students' heads. The original UMT model achieves a significant improvement on AP (from 18.5% to 40.2%), which means that the teacher-student model framework and image-to-image translation are also useful for the task in this paper. However, as we have discussed before, the UMT model's performance is not good enough, because it is not specially designed for the unsupervised cross-classroom object detection of students' heads. By using the adaptation based on the numbers of students and the adaptation based on the locations of students, CCOD reaches an AP of 50.2%, which outperforms the original UMT model with a boost of 10.0% AP. From this table, we can observe that our proposed CCOD achieves the best performance among all compared models.

5.2 Transfer from SCUT_B to SCUT_A

In this part, CCOD reaches an AP of 26.1%, which outperforms the original UMT model with a boost of 5.1% AP. Compared with the cross-domain adaptation from SCUT_A to SCUT_B, there is a significant drop in the performances of all the models in the from SCUT_B to SCUT_A. We think the reason may be the lower quality of SCUT_B's images and annotations, which are collected on the Internet.

We also test the oracle result by training the faster-RCNN directly on the images of target domain (SCUT_A) with ground-truth labels, which achieves an AP of 40.4%. There is still a gap between the performance of CCOD and the oracle result. In order to match the oracle result, more unsupervised domain adaptation methods may need to be applied in the future, besides the adaptation based on the numbers of students and the adaptation based on the locations of students we proposed.

Table 1. The average precision (AP, in %) on person from different methods for cross-domain object detection on the SCUT dataset for SCUT_A to SCUT_B and SCUT_B to SCUT_A.

Methods	A → B	B → A
Source Only	18.5	15.1
Oracle	79.5	40.4
DA [23]	20.1	15.2
SWDA [24]	25.5	13.0
UMT [18]	40.2	21.0
CCOD	**50.2**	**26.1**

5.3 Parameter Sensitivity

In Fig. 7, we show the sensitivity of $\overline{n}$ and N, which control the adaptation based on number in Eq. (6). The experiments are conducted in the domain adaptation from SCUT_A to SCUT_B. Our model reaches the highest precision (50.2%) when n1 is 30 and n2 is 7000.

In Fig. 8, we show the sensitivity of T_{loc}, which is the new threshold of bounding boxes located inside the student region. The following experiments are also conducted in the domain adaptation from SCUT_A to SCUT_B. Our model achieves the highest precision when T_{loc} is set to 0.775.

5.4 Ablation Study

To determine the impact of the suggestions we proposed, we design the ablation study as follows in Table 2. Our model which only uses adaptation based on the numbers of students reaches an AP of 45.2%, which has a gain of 5.0%. Our model which only uses adaptation based on the locations of students reaches an AP of 47.4%, which has a gain of 7.2%. CCOD which uses both adaptation based on the numbers of students and adaptation based on the locations of students

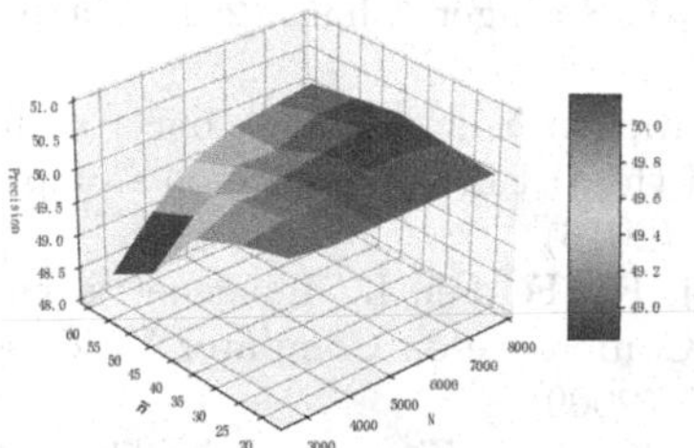

Fig. 7. Parameter sensitivity on $\overline{n}$ and N. $\overline{n}$ is the average number of classrooms' max capacities and N is a hyperparameter which limits the effect of $\overline{n}$.

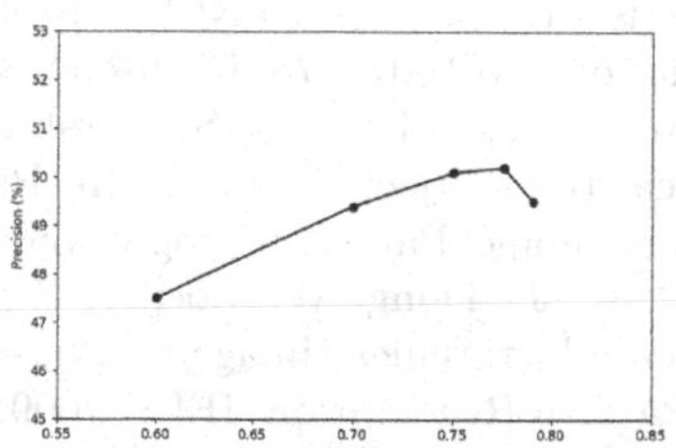

Fig. 8. Parameter sensitivity on T_{loc}, which is the new threshold of bounding boxes located inside the student region.

achieves the best performance than others, which proves our two adaptations are able to be applied on the original UMT model simultaneously.

Table 2. Ablations on SCUT_A to SCUT_B adaptation. The num and loc denote the adaptation based on the numbers of students and the adaptation based on the locations of students respectively.

	num	loc	AP	gain
UMT			40.2	-
CCOD	✓		45.2	5.0
		✓	47.4	7.2
	✓	✓	**50.2**	**10.0**

6 Conclusion

In this paper, we propose CCOD model for cross-classroom object detection of students' heads, which is a novel research direction. Our framework is based on UMT model, which is originally designed for unsupervised domain adaptation of object detection cross city scape. To solve the cross-classroom problem, we firstly propose the adaptation based on the numbers of students to encourage the model to recognize more bounding boxes when the number of bounding boxes already determined is small or large. Then we propose the adaptation based on the locations of students. Experiments prove our model have a better performance on cross-classroom unsupervised domain adaptation than other existing models.

References

1. Ren, S., He, K., Girshick, R., Sun, J.: Faster R-CNN: towards real-time object detection with region proposal networks. IEEE Trans. Pattern Anal. Mach. Intell. **39**(6), 1137–1149 (2016)
2. Liu, W., Anguelov, D., Erhan, D., Szegedy, C., Reed, S., Fu, C.-Y., Berg, A.C.: SSD: single shot MultiBox detector. In: Leibe, B., Matas, J., Sebe, N., Welling, M. (eds.) ECCV 2016. LNCS, vol. 9905, pp. 21–37. Springer, Cham (2016). https://doi.org/10.1007/978-3-319-46448-0_2
3. Redmon, J., Divvala, S., Girshick, R., Farhadi, A.: You only look once: unified, real-time object detection. In: Proceedings of the IEEE Conference on Computer Vision and Pattern Recognition, pp. 779–788 (2016)
4. Deng, J., Dong, W., Socher, R., Li, L.-J., Li, K., Fei-Fei, L.: Imagenet: a large-scale hierarchical image database. In: IEEE Conference on Computer Vision and Pattern Recognition. IEEE 2009, pp. 248–255 (2009)
5. Everingham, M., Van Gool, L., Williams, C.K., Winn, J., Zisserman, A.: The pascal visual object classes (VOC) challenge. Int. J. Comput. Vision **88**(2), 303–338 (2010)
6. Lin, T.-Y., et al.: Microsoft COCO: common objects in context. In: Fleet, D., Pajdla, T., Schiele, B., Tuytelaars, T. (eds.) ECCV 2014. LNCS, vol. 8693, pp. 740–755. Springer, Cham (2014). https://doi.org/10.1007/978-3-319-10602-1_48

7. Patel, V.M., Gopalan, R., Li, R., Chellappa, R.: Visual domain adaptation: a survey of recent advances. IEEE Signal Process. Mag. **32**(3), 53–69 (2015)
8. Ben-David, S., Blitzer, J., Crammer, K., Kulesza, A., Pereira, F., Vaughan, J.W.: A theory of learning from different domains. Mach. Learn. **79**(1), 151–175 (2010)
9. Zhu, X., Pang, J., Yang, C., Shi, J., Lin, D.: Adapting object detectors via selective cross-domain alignment. In: Proceedings of the IEEE Conference on Computer Vision and Pattern Recognition, pp. 687–696 (2019)
10. He, Z., Zhang, L.: Multi-adversarial faster-RCNN for unrestricted object detection. In: Proceedings of the IEEE International Conference on Computer Vision, pp. 6668–6677 (2019)
11. Hsu, C.-C., Tsai, Y.-H., Lin, Y.-Y., Yang, M.-H.: Every pixel matters: center-aware feature alignment for domain adaptive object detector. In: Vedaldi, A., Bischof, H., Brox, T., Frahm, J.-M. (eds.) ECCV 2020. LNCS, vol. 12354, pp. 733–748. Springer, Cham (2020). https://doi.org/10.1007/978-3-030-58545-7_42
12. Sindagi, V.A., Oza, P., Yasarla, R., Patel, V.M.: Prior-based domain adaptive object detection for hazy and rainy conditions. In: Vedaldi, A., Bischof, H., Brox, T., Frahm, J.-M. (eds.) ECCV 2020. LNCS, vol. 12359, pp. 763–780. Springer, Cham (2020). https://doi.org/10.1007/978-3-030-58568-6_45
13. Kim, S., Choi, J., Kim, T., Kim, C.: Self-training and adversarial background regularization for unsupervised domain adaptive one-stage object detection. In: Proceedings of the IEEE International Conference on Computer Vision, pp. 6092–6101 (2019)
14. Zhao, G., Li, G., Xu, R., Lin, L.: Collaborative training between region proposal localization and classification for domain adaptive object detection. In: Vedaldi, A., Bischof, H., Brox, T., Frahm, J.-M. (eds.) ECCV 2020. LNCS, vol. 12363, pp. 86–102. Springer, Cham (2020). https://doi.org/10.1007/978-3-030-58523-5_6
15. Chen, C., Zheng, Z., Ding, X., Huang, Y., Dou, Q.: Harmonizing transferability and discriminability for adapting object detectors. In: Proceedings of the IEEE/CVF Conference on Computer Vision and Pattern Recognition, pp. 8869–8878 (2020)
16. Rodriguez, A.L., Mikolajczyk, K.: Domain adaptation for object detection via style consistency. In: British Machine Vision Conference (2019)
17. Kim, T., Jeong, M., Kim, S., Choi, S., Kim, C.: Diversify and match: a domain adaptive representation learning paradigm for object detection. In: Proceedings of the IEEE Conference on Computer Vision and Pattern Recognition, pp. 12 456–12 465 (2019)
18. Deng, J., Li, W., Chen, Y., Duan, L.: Unbiased mean teacher for cross domain object detection. In: Proceedings of the IEEE Conference on Computer Vision and Pattern Recognition 2021, pp. 4091–4101 (2021)
19. Cai, Q., Pan, Y., Ngo, C.-W., Tian, X., Duan, L., Yao, T.: Exploring object relation in mean teacher for cross-domain detection. In: Proceedings of the IEEE Conference on Computer Vision and Pattern Recognition, pp. 11 457–11 466 (2019)
20. Xu, M., Wang, H., Ni, B., Tian, Q., Zhang, W.: Cross-domain detection via graph-induced prototype alignment. In: Proceedings of the IEEE/CVF Conference on Computer Vision and Pattern Recognition, pp. 12 355–12 364 (2020)
21. Wu, A., Han, Y., Zhu, L., Yang, Y.: Instance-invariant adaptive object detection via progressive disentanglement. IEEE Trans. Pattern Anal. Mach. Intell. (2021)
22. Inoue, N., Furuta, R., Yamasaki, T., Aizawa, K.: Cross-domain weakly-supervised object detection through progressive domain adaptation. In: Proceedings of the IEEE Conference on Computer Vision and Pattern Recognition, pp. 5001–5009 (2018)

23. Chen, Y., Li, W., Sakaridis, C., Dai, D., Van Gool, L.: Domain adaptive faster R-CNN for object detection in the wild. In: Proceedings of the IEEE Conference on Computer Vision and Pattern Recognition, pp. 3339–3348 (2018)
24. Saito, K., Ushiku, Y., Harada, T., Saenko, K.: Strong-weak distribution alignment for adaptive object detection. In: Proceedings of the IEEE Conference on Computer Vision and Pattern Recognition, pp. 6956–6965 (2019)
25. He, Z., Zhang, L.: Domain adaptive object detection via asymmetric tri-way faster-RCNN. In: Vedaldi, A., Bischof, H., Brox, T., Frahm, J.-M. (eds.) ECCV 2020. LNCS, vol. 12369, pp. 309–324. Springer, Cham (2020). https://doi.org/10.1007/978-3-030-58586-0_19
26. Vs, V., Gupta, V., Oza, P., Sindagi, V.A., Patel, V.M.: Mega-cda: memory guided attention for category-aware unsupervised domain adaptive object detection. In: Proceedings of the IEEE/CVF Conference on Computer Vision and Pattern Recognition 2021, pp. 4516–4526 (2021)
27. Zhuang, C., Han, X., Huang, W., Scott, M. : ifan: image-instance full alignment networks for adaptive object detection. In: Proceedings of the AAAI Conference on Artificial Intelligence, vol. 34, no. 07, pp. 13 122–13 129 (2020)
28. Xu, C.-D., Zhao, X.-R., Jin, X., Wei, X.-S.: Exploring categorical regularization for domain adaptive object detection. In: Proceedings of the IEEE/CVF Conference on Computer Vision and Pattern Recognition, pp. 11 724–11 733 (2020)
29. Tarvainen, A., Valpola, H.: Mean teachers are better role models: Weight-averaged consistency targets improve semi-supervised deep learning results. In: Advances in Neural Information Processing Systems, pp. 1195–1204 (2017)
30. Laine, S., Aila, T.: Temporal Ensembling for Semi-Supervised Learning. arXiv:1610.02242 [cs], October 2016. arXiv: 1610.02242
31. Zhu, J.-Y., Park, T., Isola, P., Efros, A.A.: Unpaired image-to-image translation using cycle-consistent adversarial networks. In: Proceedings of the IEEE International Conference on Computer Vision, pp. 2223–2232 (2017)
32. Peng, D., Sun, Z., Chen, Z., Cai, Z., Xie, L., Jin, L.: Detecting heads using feature refine net and cascaded multi-scale architecture. In: ICPR, pp. 2528–2533 (2018)

Diffusion-Adapter: Text Guided Image Manipulation with Frozen Diffusion Models

Rongting Wei(✉), Chunxiao Fan, and Yuexin Wu

Beijing University of Posts and Telecommunications, Beijing, China
{weirongting,cxfan,wuyuexin}@bupt.edu.cn

Abstract. Research on vision-language models has seen rapid development, enabling natural language-based processing for image generation and manipulation. Existing text-driven image manipulation is typically implemented by GAN inversion or fine-tuning diffusion models. The former is limited by the inversion capability of GANs, which fail to reconstruct pictures with novel poses and perspectives. The latter methods require expensive optimization for each input, and fine-tuning is still a complex process. To mitigate these problems, we propose a novel approach, dubbed Diffusion-Adapter, which performs text-driven image manipulation using frozen pre-trained diffusion models. In this work, we design an Adapter architecture to modify the target attributes without fine-tuning the pre-trained models. Our approach can be applied to diffusion models in any domain and only take a few examples to train the Adapter that could successfully edit images from unknown data. Compared with previous work, Diffusion-Adapter preserves a maximal amount of details from the original image without unintended changes to the input content. Extensive experiments demonstrate the advantages of our approach over competing baselines, and we make a novel attempt at text-driven image manipulation.

Keywords: Diffusion model · Image manipulation · Adapter · Multi-modal

1 Introduction

Applying textual information to edit real images has been an interesting task in image processing. By providing a simple text prompt, the model could modify the corresponding attributes in the image, which will significantly save the cost of manual revision. However, accomplishing this task is challenging since the model is required to carefully alter the relevant semantic attributes without changing the original content information. Many methods were proposed for text-based image editing, showing promising results and continuously improving [3,8,11,12,17,21]. However, the current leading models suffer from, to varying degrees, several drawbacks: (i) They are frequently incapable of reconstructing images with novel gestures and struggle to preserve details from the original image [3,8,17]. (ii) They need to fine-tune the large-scale pre-trained models [11,12,21], which unfortunately limits their usefulness, as fine-tuning is still a complex process that requires a skilled practitioner.

L. Iliadis et al. (Eds.): ICANN 2023, LNCS 14255, pp. 217–231, 2023.
https://doi.org/10.1007/978-3-031-44210-0_18

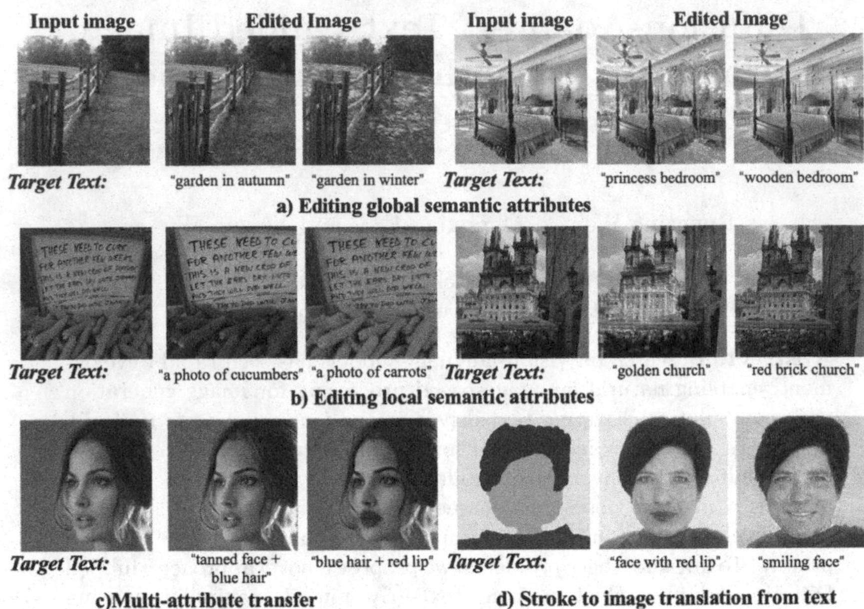

Fig. 1. Diffusion-Adapter could edit global and local semantic attributes in real images and also perform multiple manipulation tasks and stroke-conditioned synthesis.

In this paper, we propose a novel image editing approach to mitigate these problems. Our goal is to edit images in a way that satisfies the given text without changing the parameters of the pre-trained model, while preserving a maximal amount of detail from the input image. Our work is inspired by the recent success of diffusion model [9,16], which is a powerful generative model capable of synthesizing high-quality images [5]. To the best of our knowledge, we are the first to introduce an Adapter on top of the pre-trained diffusion models, aiming to modify attributes for the original image robustly. Remarkably, we do not need to fine-tune the pre-trained diffusion models for any task. Only providing several samples to train the Adapter that could be applied to different domains. Furthermore, this paper explores a strategy to speed up sampling and effectively reduce image generation time without destroying their quality. Qualitative analysis and human evaluation confirm the robust and superior manipulation performance of our method compared with the existing baselines.

Figure 1 illustrates the diverse image editing tasks that can be accomplished by our Diffusion-Adapter using only text prompts. Our approach enables to modify the global and local attributes while preserving the overall structure, composition, and background, see Fig. 1 a), b). Diffusion-Adapter can also simultaneously modify multiple attributes, such as hair color, skin tone, and red lip, with perfect preservation of the facial identity, see Fig. 1 c). By providing an intuitive textual description, such as "face with red lip" or "smiling face", our approach can translate from the stroke picture into a semantically consistent image in the corresponding domain and effectively fill in the missing information, see Fig. 1 d). It can be seen that our method produces impressive results in all tasks. The outputs resemble the input image to a high degree and align well with the target text. Moreover, we apply our model on numerous images from various domains. Experimental results show that Diffusion-Adapter significantly accomplished diverse manipulation tasks, in addition to achieving high performance close to the recent state-of-the-art baselines.

2 Related Work

2.1 Text-Driven Image Manipulation

Since images can be manipulated in various ways (*e.g.* image translation, semantic manipulation and local edits), a variety of methods have existed. Earlier work used RNNs or GANs [6] for the task of text-driven image manipulation. These approaches, however, are typically restricted to class specific image generation or generally trained on smaller datasets. Although GANs could generate high-quality images, they are usually unstable during training and are prone to mode collapse. In the recent past, several works [3,8,17] have performed this task combined with CLIP model [18] for aligning with the target texts. Specifically, a given image is first converted to a latent code by pre-trained GANs and then find the target latent code of desired attributes with the guidance of CLIP. However, limited by the capability of GAN inversion, the reconstructed results typically alter the object identity or produce unwanted image artifacts, see Fig. 6.

More recently, diffusion models were utilized for the same image manipulation tasks. Relying on the full inversion and high-quality image generation power, diffusion models showcased remarkable results. SDEdit [15] added intermediate noise to an image and denoised it using a diffusion process conditioned on the desired edit, which is only available for global edits. Blend diffusion [1] presented a solution for local image editing by combining images with a masked region in the latent space using pre-trained DDPMs and CLIP model. Gal et al. [7] proposed a textual inversion method that represents visual concepts as new pseudo-words in the embedding space of a frozen text-to-image model [19]. Relying on the robust text-to-image diffusion models, the Dream-Booth [21] and Imagic [11] enabled more challenging editing tasks by fine-tuning the Imagen model [22] with additional images.

More closely related to ours is the work of Kim et al. [12], which utilized language-vision model gradients, DDIM inversion [23], and model fine-tuning to edit images with a domain-specific diffusion model. However, due to the effect of fine-tuning, the generated images may fail to preserve the details from the original photos, and even destroy the attributes of non-target objects, see Fig. 7. In this work, we introduce an Adapter on top of the pre-trained DDIM model that modifies attributes according to the text prompt. Our approach eliminates the complex process of fine-tuning and remarkably keeps the rest of the image intact.

2.2 Diffusion Models

Denoising diffusion probabilistic models (DDPMs) [9,16,24] have recently shown high performance in image generation, and Dhariwal et al. [5] obtained superior image quality than state-of-the-art GANs models. DDPMs consist of two stages: a forward diffusion process and a reverse diffusion process. The forward process is gradually adding Gaussian noise to the original image, and the data eventually becomes an isotropic standard Gaussian distribution when the forward step is large enough. And the reverse process learns to restore the data structure from a Gaussian noise using a neural network.

The forward process of the DDPMs [9] relies on the Markov and adopts Gaussian noise to generate latent variables from X_1 to X_T. Formally: given an initial data distribution $X_0 \sim q(x_0)$, we define a forward process q that adds Gaussian noise with variance $\beta_t \in (0,1)$ at time t to generate the next sample X_{t+1}:

$$q(x_t|x_{t-1}) = \mathcal{N}(x_t; \sqrt{1-\beta_t}x_{t-1}, \beta_t\mathbf{I}) \tag{1}$$

An essential property of the forward noising process is that any step x_t can be sampled directly from x_0, without the need to generate the intermediate steps,

$$q(x_t|x_0) = \mathcal{N}(x_t; \sqrt{\overline{\alpha_t}}x_0, (1-\overline{\alpha_t})\mathbf{I}) \tag{2}$$

where $\alpha_t = 1 - \beta_t$. Following the trick of reparameterization [13], the resulting latent variable x_t can be expressed as shown in Eq. 3:

$$x_t = \sqrt{\overline{\alpha_t}}x_0 + \sqrt{1-\overline{\alpha_t}}\epsilon \tag{3}$$

where $\epsilon \in \mathcal{N}(0,1)$ and $\overline{\alpha_t} = \prod_{i=1}^{T} \alpha_i$.

The reverse process starts from a standard Gaussian noise $X_T \sim \mathcal{N}(0,\mathbf{I})$, and reconstructs the image by sampling the posterior $q(x_{t-1}|x_t)$. However, $q(x_{t-1}|x_t)$ is unknown, as it depends on the unknown data distribution $q(x_0)$. In order to approximate this function, a neural network ϵ_θ is trained to predict the mean and the covariance of x_{t-1} given x_t as input:

$$\epsilon_\theta(x_{t-1}|x_t) = \mathcal{N}(\mu_\theta(x_t,t), \Sigma_\theta(x_t,t)) \tag{4}$$

If model ϵ_θ directly predicts the mean $\mu_\theta(x_t,t)$ and variance $\Sigma_\theta(x_t,t)$, which will lead to instability in training process. Hence, Ho et al. [9] propose to predict the noise ϵ_t added from x_{t-1} to x_t for simplifying the training object. The optimized target function is as follows:

$$\min_\theta \mathbb{E}_{t,x_0,\epsilon}||\epsilon_t - \epsilon_\theta(x_t,t)||^2 \tag{5}$$

After training $\epsilon_\theta(x,t)$, the data is sampled using following reverse diffusion process:

$$x_{t-1} = \frac{1}{\sqrt{1-\beta_t}}\Big(x_t - \frac{\beta_t}{\sqrt{1-\alpha_t}}\epsilon_\theta(x_t,t)\Big) + \sigma_t^2 z) \tag{6}$$

where $z \sim \mathcal{N}(0,\mathbf{I})$.

Since DDPMs require numerous sampling steps to generate an image, which is limited in inference time compared to GANs. Song et al. [23] proposed an alternative non-Markovian noising process which has the same forward marginals as DDPMs while owning a distinct sampling process as follows:

$$x_{t-1} = \sqrt{\overline{\alpha_{t-1}}} f_\theta(x_t, t) + \sqrt{1 - \overline{\alpha_{t-1}} - \sigma_t^2} \epsilon_\theta(x_t, t) + \sigma_t^2 z \tag{7}$$

where $z \sim \mathcal{N}(0, \mathbf{I})$ and $f_\theta(x_t, t)$ is the prediction of x_0 at t given x_t:

$$f_\theta(x_t, t) = \frac{x_t - \sqrt{1 - \overline{\alpha_t}} \epsilon_\theta(x_t, t)}{\sqrt{\overline{\alpha_t}}} \tag{8}$$

In the case of Eq. 7, different sampling strategies can be obtained by changing the variance of the noise σ_t. Especially, by setting σ_t to 0, which is a DDIM sampling process [23], enabling reduce the sampling steps by means of discrete sampling. In this work, we utilize the DDIM strategy to accomplish image manipulation, while DDPM is more suitable for stroke synthesis, which will be discussed in more detail later.

3 Diffusion-Adapter

Given an image x_0, a reference text y_{ref}, and a target text y_{tar}, our goal is to generate a modified x_0' picture whose semantic information corresponds with the target text y_{tar}, while preserving the details of the original image x_0. The overall flow of the proposed Diffusion-Adapter is shown in Fig. 2. Here, the input image x_0 is first converted into a latent code x_T using the pre-trained diffusion model ϵ_θ. Then, in the reverse process, the latent code x_t is simultaneously fed into the frozen diffusion model ϵ_θ and Adapter $\epsilon_{\theta'}$, accumulating the output f, f' (see Eq. 8) as the prediction of x_0 at time t. Lastly, guided by the CLIP loss, the parameters of Adapter $\epsilon_{\theta'}$ are updated to generate samples satisfying the target text y_{tar}. The components of Diffusion-Adapter will be described in Sect. 3.1 $\sim$ 3.3, and more complex tasks accomplished by our model will be discussed in Sects. 3.4 and 3.5, respectively.

3.1 Adapter Network

The Adapter executes an interpolation operation on the output of pre-trained diffusion models so that the attributes from the original image can be modified. For 256×256 pictures in LSUN [27] and CelebA-HQ [10] datasets, we design a parameter-sharing architecture based on the U-Net network [20] as an Adapter, presented in Fig. 3. The Adapter consists of four parts: the encoder part, middle part, decoder part, and time embedding part. In the encoder part, the $8{\times}8$ feature is obtained from the $256{\times}256$ input image through 1 convolutional layer and 5 Res blocks. Each of Res blocks is composed of two convolutional blocks and introduces a self-attention module at $16{\times}16$ resolution. The middle part consists

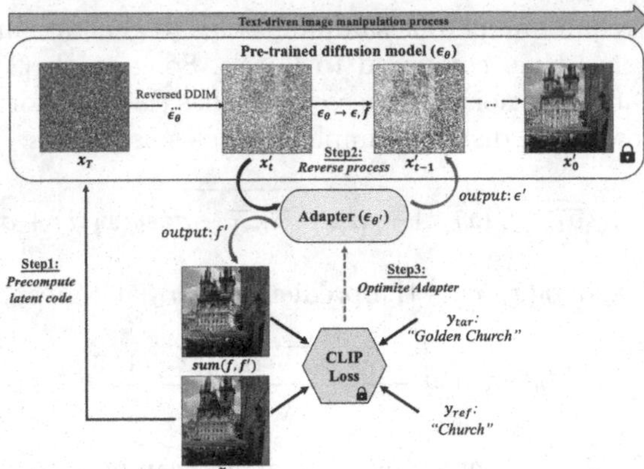

Fig. 2. Overview of Diffusion-Adapter. The input image is first converted into a latent code via diffusion models. Then, the latent code simultaneously feed into the diffusion model and Adapter in reverse process. Lastly, the Adapter is updated with the guidance of CLIP loss step by step, and generate images that align well with the target text.

of 3 Res blocks and a self-attention module is added to the second block. In the decoder part, the output whose resolution is the same as the input is generated through 5 Res blocks and 1 output convolution with skip connections from the features in the encoder part. In the time embedding part, the diffusion time t is embedded into each residual block after the Transformer sinusoidal encoding [25] to assist the model in specifying the current diffusion step. For manipulating 512×512 images from ImageNet dataset [4], we use a large-scale Adapter that adds self-attention blocks at 8×8, 16×16 and 32×32 resolution.

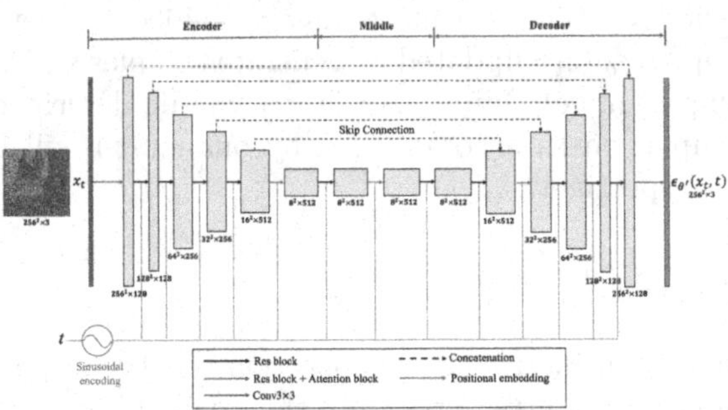

Fig. 3. The network of Adapter generates 256×256 images. The model receives x_t and t as inputs and outputs $\epsilon_{\theta'}(x_t, t)$.

3.2 CLIP Guidance for Image Manipulation

CLIP [18] was proposed to learn visual concepts with natural language supervision. In CLIP, a text encoder and an image encoder are trained to evaluate the semantic similarity between the given text and image. Consequently, we utilize the CLIP model at each sampling step to guide the latent x_t aligning with the text prompt y_{tar}. However, CLIP is pre-trained on clean images (without noise), we need a way of estimating a clean image $\hat{x_0}$ from each noisy latent x_t during the reverse process. Recall that the process estimates the noise $\epsilon_\theta(x_t, t)$ at each step that was added to x_0 to obtain x_t. Thus, x_0 could be obtained from $\epsilon_\theta(x_t, t)$ by rewriting Eq. 3:

$$\hat{x_0} = \frac{x_t}{\sqrt{\overline{\alpha_t}}} - \frac{\sqrt{1-\overline{\alpha_t}}}{\sqrt{\overline{\alpha_t}}}\epsilon_\theta(x_t, t) \tag{9}$$

Now, a global CLIP loss $\mathcal{L}_{global}$ may be defined as the cosine distance between the CLIP embedding of the target text and the embedding of the estimated clean image $\hat{x_0}$:

$$\mathcal{L}_{global}(\hat{x_0}, y_{tar}) = \mathcal{D}_{CLIP}(\hat{x_0}, y_{tar}) \tag{10}$$

where $\mathcal{D}_{CLIP}$ denotes the cosine distance in CLIP space between the image and text embeddings. However, a known problem with global CLIP loss is the adversarial attack [14], where the optimization cheats the CLIP classifier by adding pixel-level perturbations to the image. To mitigate such problem, a directional CLIP loss [8] is adopted to align the CLIP-space directions between the source and target text-image pairs, which is defined as:

$$\mathcal{L}_{direction}(\hat{x_0}, y_{tar}; x_0, y_{ref}) = 1 - \frac{<\Delta I, \Delta T>}{\|\Delta I\|\|\Delta T\|} \tag{11}$$

where $\Delta T = E_T(y_{tar}) - E_T(y_{ref})$, $\Delta I = E_I(\hat{x_0}) - E_I(x_0)$. Here, E_T and E_I are the text and image encoders of CLIP, respectively, and y_{tar}, x_0 are the target text and original image, respectively. Note that the text is generally composed of concise words. Taking church style transfer as an example, we may use "church" as the reference text y_{ref}, and "golden church" as the target text y_{tar}. Based on the above analysis, we utilize the following objective which consists the global and directional loss as the CLIP loss:

$$\mathcal{L}_{CLIP} = \mathcal{L}_{direction} + \alpha\mathcal{L}_{global} \tag{12}$$

where α denotes the weighting coefficient of the global loss.

In order to prevent unwanted changes and preserve the identity of the original object, we also utilize ℓ_2 regularization as the identity loss. Therefore, the final loss function is as follows:

$$\mathcal{L}_{total} = \mathcal{L}_{CLIP} + \lambda_{ID}\mathcal{L}_{ID} \tag{13}$$

where $\mathcal{L}_{ID} = \|x_0 - \hat{x_0}\|^2$, the hyperparameter λ_{ID} denotes a scaling factor of the identity loss.

3.3 Forward Diffusion and Generative Process

The procedure for image manipulation is similar to the diffusion approach, which requires a forward and reverse process. Differently, in the reverse process, we additionally design an Adapter to modify the image with the guidance of CLIP loss. In terms of text-driven image manipulation, the generated result should preserve the overall background and structure of the original image. However, the DDPM sampling process in Eq. 3 and Eq. 6 are stochastic by a random Gaussian noise, so the reconstruction of the original image is not guaranteed. To fully leverage the image synthesis performance of diffusion models, we adopt deterministic DDIM strategy [23] as the sampling process. In detail, a real image is first inverted to the latent code via forward DDIM processes as follows:

$$x_{t+1} = \sqrt{\overline{\alpha_{t+1}}} f_\theta(x_t, t) + \sqrt{1 - \overline{\alpha_{t+1}}} \epsilon_\theta(x_t, t) \tag{14}$$

where f denotes the prediction of x_0 at t given x_t, as described in Eq. 8.

In the generative process, the latent code simultaneously feeds into the pre-trained diffusion models θ and Adapter θ' to obtain the estimated image f and f', respectively. Then, accumulating both outputs as a predicted image $\hat{x_0}$ so that the Adapter could be updated guided by CLIP loss to generate desired images. As a result, the latent code for the next step can be obtained by rewriting Eq. 7:

$$x_{t-1} = \sqrt{\overline{\alpha_{t-1}}} [f_\theta(x_t, t) + f_{\theta'}(x_t, t)] + \sqrt{1 - \overline{\alpha_{t-1}}} [\epsilon_\theta(x_t, t) + \epsilon_{\theta'}(x_t, t)] \tag{15}$$

The reverse process is repeated times until converged, and the procedure is shown in Fig. 4.

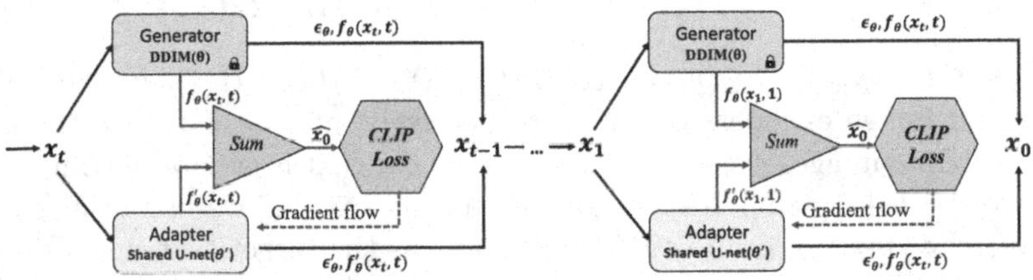

Fig. 4. Gradient flow during training the Adapter. A gradient step is proceeded at each time step t with $\hat{x_0}$, the prediction of x_0 at t.

In this work, we also explore a fast sampling strategy that effectively reduces the time of image generation. Specifically, instead of performing forward diffusion until the last time step T (T is typically set to 1000 [9,16]), we found that we may accelerate the forward diffusion by performing up to $t_{end} < T$, which called "ending step". We can further accelerate training by using fewer discretization steps between $[1, t_{end}]$, denoted as S_{for} and S_{gen} for forward diffusion and generative process, respectively.

Through qualitative and quantitative analysis, we found that the hyperparameters S_{for}, S_{gen}, and t_{end} rely on different editing subtasks. In terms of local manipulations (*e.g.* hair color transfer), whose attributes fall within a small area, and the choices of $t_{end} \in [200, 400]$ and $(S_{for}, S_{gen}) = (50, 10)$ satisfy our goal. With fewer forward steps, the latent $X_{t_{end}}$ could preserve the details of the input image, making it easier for Adapter to capture the target object and modify its attributes. For global texture manipulations (*e.g.* artistic style transfer), we need to generate images from a noisier latent that has already destroyed the contents of the original image. In response, more generative steps are required to produce the desired image, so we set $t_{end} \in [400, 600]$ and $(S_{for}, S_{gen}) = (50, 25)$. With these settings, training an image on an NVIDIA A40 machine is finished in 1~ 3 min.

3.4 Multi-attribute Manipulation

After modifying images for a single attribute, we further investigate multi-attribute manipulation. In existing work [2], users require the combination of tricky task-specific loss designs or dataset preparation with extensive manual effort. However, we do not need these extra efforts for this task. We discovered that just combined multiple Adapters that have trained on a specific attribute, there is no necessity to train a new model with a target text that defines multiple attributes. In detail, we first invert the image with a pre-trained diffusion model, then utilize various well-trained Adapters by the following sampling rule:

$$\begin{aligned} x_{t-1} = \sqrt{\overline{\alpha_{t-1}}}[f_\theta(x_t, t) + \sum_{i=1}^{M} W_i(t) \cdot f_{\theta'_i}(x_t, t)] + \\ \sqrt{1 - \overline{\alpha_{t-1}}}[\epsilon_\theta(x_t, t) + \sum_{i=1}^{M} W_i(t) \cdot \epsilon_{\theta'_i}(x_t, t)] \end{aligned} \tag{16}$$

where $W_i(t)$ is the sequence of weights for each well-trained Adapter θ'_i satisfying $\sum_{i=1}^{M} W_i(t) = 1$, which can be used for controlling the degree of each attribute.

3.5 Stroke-Conditioned Image Synthesis

The well-trained Adapters by our method can be leveraged to perform the stroke synthesis guided by texts. In the previous approach, we proposed to utilize deterministic DDIM sampling to ensure consistency with the original image. However, the latent codes produced by DDIM are without adding a random noise, which sacrifices the diversity of the outputs. When the input image lacks details, such as a stroke image, the generated results by the deterministic forward process fail to complete the missing information.

For this task, we utilize a stochastic DDPM strategy in forward process while remaining DDIM in reverse process, as shown in Fig. 5. Specifically, the image x_0 is first perturbed through the forward DDPM process in Eq. 3 until ending step t_{end}. Then, the latent code is sampled with the pre-trained diffusion models and well-trained Adapters by DDIM generative process in Eq. 15. Note that if

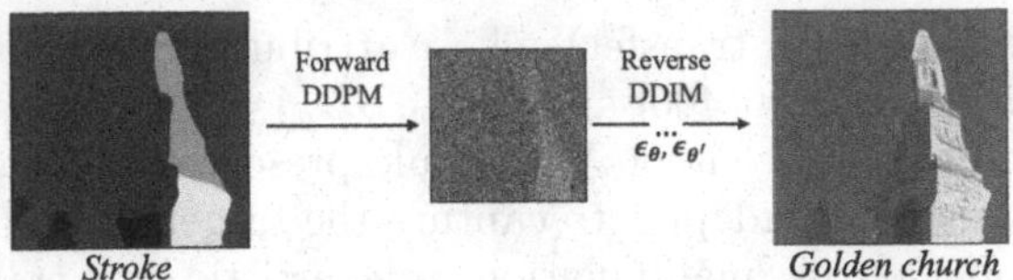

Fig. 5. Stroke-conditioned image synthesis in an unseen domain.

t_{end} is relatively small, the model will focus on the details of the stroke image and fail to generate new objects. On the contrary, a large t_{end} will destroy the reconstruction result of the Diffusion-Adapter. Through qualitative analysis, t_{end} is typically set to 500.

4 Experiments

In this work, we utilize diffusion models pretrained on CelebA-HQ [10], LSUN [27] and ImageNet [4] datasets for manipulating images in different domains, respectively. For training the Adapter, we use Adam optimizer with an initial learning rate of 5e−6 which is increased linearly by 0.8 per 50 iterations. We set the scaling factor of the global loss α and identity loss λ_{ID} to 0.2 and 0.1. To demonstrate the robust performance of the Diffusion-Adapter, we selected the methods of SOTA GAN inversion and diffusion model fine-tuning for comparison.

4.1 Comparison and Evaluation

Qualitative Comparison. For qualitative comparison with other approaches, we first selected the state-of-the-art GAN inversion methods, StyleCLIP [17], StyleGAN-NADA [8] and VQGAN-CLIP [3] where images for the target control are not similar to our method. The experimental comparison results are shown in Fig. 6.

In human face images, while StyleGAN inversion-based approaches [8,17] could manipulate semantic attributes, they struggle to reconstruct face images in atypical poses. Unexpected details in the original image, such as the microphone on the face, are completely removed or distorted in reconstruction. Because such atypical faces are barely encountered during training, StyleGAN-based model will result in a high representation error. This issue becomes even worse in the case of images from a dataset with high variance, such as church images in LSUN-Church [27]. The manipulation results may be recognized as images from different buildings, which limits its application in real-world. On the contrary, taking advantage of the full inversion in diffusion process, our reconstruction results are almost perfect with fine details and background, which enables faithful manipulation.

Furthermore, we selected DiffusionCLIP [12] for comparison, which modifies images by fine-tuning the pre-trained diffusion model, and the results are shown

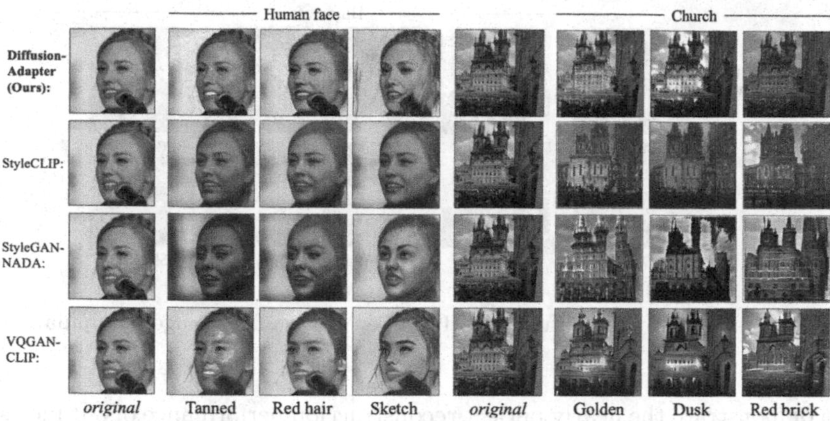

Fig. 6. Comparison with the state-of-the-art GAN inversion methods: StyleCLIP [17], StyleGAN-NADA [8] and VQGAN-CLIP [3].

in Fig. 7. Although DiffusionCLIP retains the content of the input image to a large extent, due to the impact of fine-tuning, the model fails to capture detailed information, such as clothing stripes. In addition, the fine-tuned DiffusionCLIP may destroy the attribute of non-target objects in the original image, such as the shape of the lip. In contrast, our method is able to effectively address these problems by introducing an Adapter.

Table 1. Quantitative comparison of the similarity between the generated images and the inputs.

Dataset	CelebA-HQ				LSUN-Church			
	Global		Local		Global		Local	
Metrics	LPIPS↓	SSIM↑	LPIPS↓	SSIM↑	LPIPS↓	SSIM↑	LPIPS↓	SSIM↑
StyleCLIP	0.486	0.529	0.292	0.746	0.529	0.538	0.428	0.572
StyleGAN-NADA	0.498	0.534	0.288	0.739	0.517	0.545	0.435	0.588
VQGAN-CLIP	0.468	0.578	0.304	0.724	0.466	0.551	0.377	0.604
DiffusionCLIP	0.423	0.629	0.221	0.768	0.418	0.722	0.296	0.752
Diffusion-Adapter(t_{end} = 200)	**0.415**	**0.637**	**0.198**	**0.791**	**0.406**	**0.753**	**0.254**	**0.783**
Diffusion-Adapter(t_{end} = 300)	0.436	0.615	0.215	0.762	0.421	0.731	0.261	0.761
Diffusion-Adapter(t_{end} = 400)	0.447	0.580	0.278	0.735	0.453	0.685	0.314	0.745

Quantitative Evaluation. We selected 1,000 test images from CelebA-HQ [10] and LSUN-Church [27], respectively, and conducted quantitative analysis on two kinds of tasks: local manipulation and global manipulation. The local attributes are derived from CelabA-HQ (red hair, tanned) and LSUN-Chuch (golden, red brick). The global attributes contain four transfer categories: sketch, watercolor on the human face, and snow, sunset on the church.

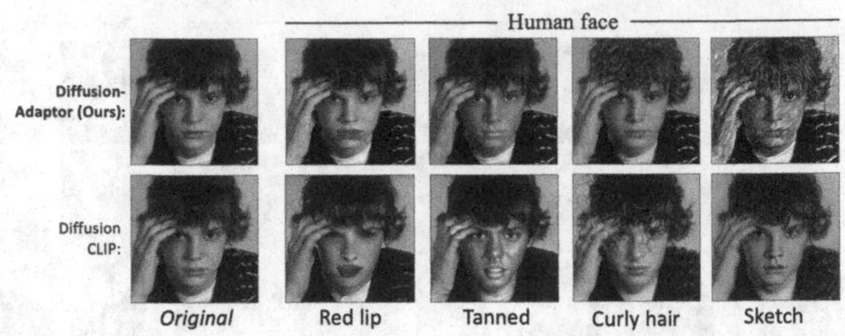

Fig. 7. Comparison with DiffusionCLIP [12] on human face image manipulation.

To demonstrate the nearly perfect reconstruction performance of our method, we use the SSIM and LPIPS metrics to assess the similarity between the modified images and the inputs. As shown in Table 1, our method performs higher reconstruction quality than all baselines in both tasks.

Additionally, we use the following metrics to evaluate the manipulation performance: global CLIP similarity ($\mathcal{S}_{glo}$) and semantic segmentation consistency (SC). To compute each metric, we use a pre-trained CLIP [18] and segmentation [26] model, respectively. $\mathcal{S}_{glo}$ represents the semantic similarity between the generated image and the target text, referred in Eq. 10. SC is used to evaluate the attribute-correspondence, denoting pixel overlap between the original image and modified image that are processed by the pre-trained segmentation model.

Table 2 shows that our model significantly preserves the details of the original image without unexpected changes and outperforms all baseline methods by a large margin on the SC metric. Furthermore, the proposed model is competitive with the state-of-the-art baselines in terms of attribute correspondence ($\mathcal{S}_{glo}$).

Table 2. Quantitative evaluation results.

Model	CelebA-HQ		LSUN-Church	
	$\mathcal{S}_{glo}$ ↑	SC ↑	$\mathcal{S}_{glo}$ ↑	SC ↑
StyleCLIP	0.296	86.8%	0.289	67.9%
StyleGAN-NADA	0.299	89.4%	**0.295**	73.2%
VQGAN-CLIP	**0.304**	70.3%	0.292	65.4%
DiffusionCLIP	0.301	93.7%	0.294	78.1%
Diffusion-Adapter	0.298	**97.6%**	0.294	**90.3%**

4.2 Multi-attribute Manipulation

Figure 8 shows that we can modify multiple attributes simultaneously just in one sampling without complex loss designs or specific data collection. Moreover,

Fig. 8. Results of multi-attribute transfer.

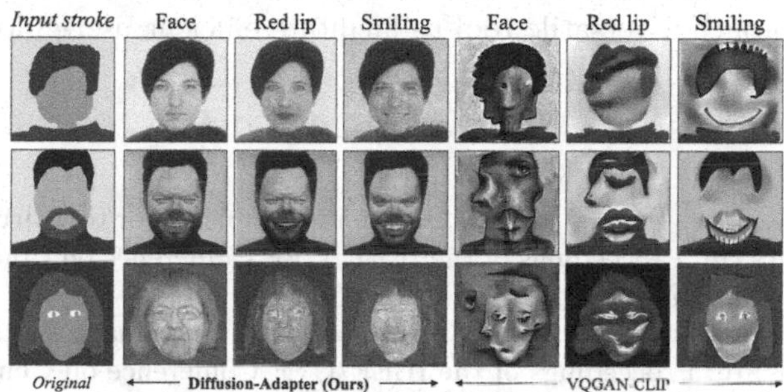

Fig. 9. Results of stroke-conditioned image synthesis.

we could control the degree of single target attributes by mixing noises from the original model and the well-trained Adapter according to w_i (see Eq. 16). The list elements in Fig. 8 denotes the degree for brown hair, red lip and tanned face, respectively. The generated images successfully control the target attributes and preserve details from the inputs.

4.3 Stroke to Image Translation from Text

In this work, our method can even translate images from unseen domains. We select several stroke images outside the datasets, which are only stitched by a few color blocks. By providing an intuitive target text prompt "face with red lip" or "smiling face", the Diffusion-Adapter can translate from stroke to a semantically consistent image in the corresponding domain, see Fig. 9. Although VQGAN-CLIP [3] could roughly modify the attributes of the input images, its performance suffers from more difficulty in completing the missing details for stoke. In contrast, our Diffusion-Adapter is able to perform these desired manipulations successfully. This application will be useful when enough images for both source and target domains are difficult to collect.

5 Conclusion

In this paper, we propose a novel image editing method called Diffusion-Adapter. Our model accepts a single image and a simple text prompt describing the desired edit, aiming to apply this edit and preserve a maximal amount of details from the original image. To that end, we introduce an Adapter on the top of pre-trained diffusion models for modifying attributes with the guidance of CLIP loss. The proposed architecture could be applied to diffusion models in almost all domains. Contrary to other editing methods, our approach eliminates the fine-tuning process for large-scale pre-trained models. Experiments demonstrated that Diffusion-Adapter accomplished diverse manipulation tasks significantly, making our approach a versatile tool to facilitate efficient user-guided editing.

References

1. Avrahami, O., Lischinski, D., Fried, O.: Blended diffusion for text-driven editing of natural images. In: Proceedings of the IEEE/CVF Conference on Computer Vision and Pattern Recognition, pp. 18208–18218 (2022)
2. Choi, Y., Uh, Y., Yoo, J., Ha, J.-W.: Stargan v2: diverse image synthesis for multiple domains. In: Proceedings of the IEEE/CVF Conference on Computer Vision and Pattern Recognition, pp. 8188–8197 (2020)
3. Crowson, K., Biderman, S., Kornis, D., Stander, D., Hallahan.: Vqgan-clip: open domain image generation and editing with natural language guidance. In: Computer Vision-ECCV 2022: 17th European Conference, Tel Aviv, Israel, 23–27 October, 2022, Proceedings, Part XXXVII, pp. 88–105. Springer, Cham (2022). https://doi.org/10.1007/978-3-031-19836-6_6
4. Deng, J., Dong, W., Socher, R., Li, L.-J., Li, K., Fei-Fei, L.: Imagenet: a large-scale hierarchical image database. In: 2009 IEEE Conference on Computer Vision and Pattern Recognition, pp. 248–255. IEEE (2009)
5. Dhariwal, P., Nichol, A.: Diffusion models beat gans on image synthesis. In: Advances in Neural Information Processing Systems 34, pp. 8780–8794 (2021)
6. Dong, H., Yu, S., Wu, C., Guo, Y.: Semantic image synthesis via adversarial learning. In: Proceedings of the IEEE International Conference on Computer Vision, pp. 5706–5714 (2017)
7. Gal, R., et al.: An image is worth one word: personalizing text-to-image generation using textual inversion. arXiv preprint arXiv:2208.01618 (2022)
8. Gal, R., Patashnik, O., Maron, H., Bermano, A.H., Chechik. Stylegan-nada: clip-guided domain adaptation of image generators. ACM Trans. Graph. (TOG) **41**(4), 1–13 (2022)
9. Ho, J., Jain, A., Abbeel, P.: Denoising diffusion probabilistic models. Adv. Neural. Inf. Process. Syst. **33**, 6840–6851 (2020)
10. Karras, T., Aila, T., Laine, S., Lehtinen, J.: Progressive growing of gans for improved quality, stability, and variation. arXiv preprint arXiv:1710.10196 (2017)
11. Kawar, B., Zada, S., Lang, O., Tov, O., Chang, H.: Imagic: text-based real image editing with diffusion models. arXiv preprint arXiv:2210.09276 (2022)
12. Kim, G., Kwon, T., Ye, J.G.: Diffusionclip: text-guided diffusion models for robust image manipulation. In: Proceedings of the IEEE/CVF Conference on Computer Vision and Pattern Recognition, pp. 2426–2435 (2022)

13. Kingma, D.P., Welling, M.: Auto-encoding variational bayes. arXiv preprint arXiv:1312.6114 (2013)
14. Liu, X., Gong, C., Wu, L., Zhang, S., Su, H., Liu, Q.: Fusedream: training-free text-to-image generation with improved clip+ gan space optimization. arXiv preprint arXiv:2112.01573 (2021)
15. Meng, C., Song, Y., Song, J., Wu, J., Zhu, J.-Y., Ermon, S.: Sdedit: image synthesis and editing with stochastic differential equations. arXiv preprint arXiv:2108.01073 (2021)
16. Nichol, A.Q., Dhariwal, P.: Improved denoising diffusion probabilistic models. In: International Conference on Machine Learning, pp. 8162–8171. PMLR (2021)
17. Patashnik, O., Wu, Z., Shechtman, E., Cohen-Or, D.: Styleclip: text-driven manipulation of stylegan imagery. In: Proceedings of the IEEE/CVF International Conference on Computer Vision, pp. 2085–2094 (2021)
18. Radford, A., Kim, J.W., Hallacy, C., Ramesh, A., Goh, G., Agarwal, S.: Learning transferable visual models from natural language supervision. In: International Conference on Machine Learning, pp. 8748–8763. PMLR (2021)
19. Rombach, R., Blattmann, A., Lorenz, D., Esser, P.: High-resolution image synthesis with latent diffusion models. In: Proceedings of the IEEE/CVF Conference on Computer Vision and Pattern Recognition, pp. 10684–10695 (2022)
20. Ronneberger, O., Fischer, P., Brox, T.: U-Net: convolutional networks for biomedical image segmentation. In: Navab, N., Hornegger, J., Wells, W.M., Frangi, A.F. (eds.) MICCAI 2015. LNCS, vol. 9351, pp. 234–241. Springer, Cham (2015). https://doi.org/10.1007/978-3-319-24574-4_28
21. Ruiz, N., Li, Y., Jampani, V.: Dreambooth: fine tuning text-to-image diffusion models for subject-driven generation. arXiv preprint arXiv:2208.12242 (2022)
22. Saharia, C., et al.: Photorealistic text-to-image diffusion models with deep language understanding. arXiv preprint arXiv:2205.11487 (2022)
23. Song, J., Meng, C., Ermon, S.: Denoising diffusion implicit models. arXiv preprint arXiv:2010.02502 (2020)
24. Song, Y., Sohl-Dickstein, J., Kingma, D.P., Kumar, A., Ermon, S.: Score-based generative modeling through stochastic differential equations. arXiv preprint arXiv:2011.13456 (2020)
25. Vaswani, A., Shazeer, N., Parmar, N., Uszkoreit. Attention is all you need. Advances in neural information processing systems, 30 (2017)
26. Xie, E., Wang, W., Yu, Z., Anandkumar, A., Alvarez, J.M., Luo., P.: Segformer: simple and efficient design for semantic segmentation with transformers. Advances in Neural Information Processing Systems, 34, pp. 12077–12090 (2021)
27. Yu, F., Seff, A., Zhang, Y., Song, S., Funkhouser, T., Xiao, J.: Lsun: construction of a large-scale image dataset using deep learning with humans in the loop. arXiv preprint arXiv:1506.03365 (2015)

DWA: Differential Wavelet Amplifier for Image Super-Resolution

Brian B. Moser[1,2(✉)], Stanislav Frolov[1,2], Federico Raue[1], Sebastian Palacio[1], and Andreas Dengel[1,2]

[1] German Research Center for Artificial Intelligence (DFKI), Kaiserslautern, Germany
{brian.moser,stanislav.frolov,federico.raue, sebastian.palacio,andreas.dengel}@dfki.de

[2] RPTU Kaiserslautern-Landau, Kaiserslautern, Germany

Abstract. This work introduces Differential Wavelet Amplifier (DWA), a drop-in module for wavelet-based image Super-Resolution (SR). DWA invigorates an approach recently receiving less attention, namely Discrete Wavelet Transformation (DWT). DWT enables an efficient image representation for SR and reduces the spatial area of its input by a factor of 4, the overall model size, and computation cost, framing it as an attractive approach for sustainable ML. Our proposed DWA model improves wavelet-based SR models by leveraging the difference between two convolutional filters to refine relevant feature extraction in the wavelet domain, emphasizing local contrasts and suppressing common noise in the input signals. We show its effectiveness by integrating it into existing SR models, e.g., DWSR and MWCNN, and demonstrate a clear improvement in classical SR tasks. Moreover, DWA enables a direct application of DWSR and MWCNN to input image space, reducing the DWT representation channel-wise since it omits traditional DWT.

Keywords: Differential Wavelet Amplifier · Image Super-Resolution

1 Introduction

Image Super-Resolution (SR) has an impressive legacy in Computer Vision (CV) yet still presents an exhilarating challenge [21,31]. SR is a task of enhancing Low-Resolution (LR) images to High Resolution (HR). It is challenging because many High Resolution (HR) images can correspond to a given Low-Resolution (LR) image, rendering the task mathematically ill-posed.

In recent years, deep learning has fueled rapid development in SR, leading to tremendous progress [6,7]. While many techniques have improved the overall quality of image reconstructions, there remains a pressing need for methods capable of producing high-frequency details, particularly when dealing with high magnification ratios [24]. Addressing this issue is crucial for the continued advancement of SR. Influenced by achievements on other CV tasks, recent research focused on trending approaches like Transformer-based networks [16,27,28], Denoising Diffusion Probabilistic Models [15,23,24] or Generative Adversarial

L. Iliadis et al. (Eds.): ICANN 2023, LNCS 14255, pp. 232–243, 2023.
https://doi.org/10.1007/978-3-031-44210-0_19

Networks [29,30]. Despite astonishing reconstruction capabilities, they often lack an explicit focus on generating high-frequency details, i.e., local variations.

This work aims to advance the field of SR by exploring wavelet-based networks. Unfortunately, this technique has received less attention despite its significant potential [21]. We seek to provide a fresh perspective and revive research by re-evaluating these approaches. Discrete Wavelet Transformation (DWT) enables an efficient image representation without losing information compared to its naïve spatial representation, i.e., traditional RGB format. It does so by separating high-frequency details in distinct channels and reducing the spatial area of input image representation by a factor of 4. Therefore, a smaller receptive field is required to capture the input during feature extraction. Using DWT like in DWSR [9] and MWCNN [17] reduces the overall model size and computational costs while performing similarly to state-of-the-art image SR architectures.

This work introduces a new Differential Wavelet Amplifier (DWA) module inspired by differential amplifiers from electrical engineering [2]. Differential amplifiers increase the difference between two input signals and suppress the common voltage shared by the two inputs, called Common Mode Rejection (CMR) [11]. In other words, it mitigates the impact of noise (e.g., electromagnetic interference, vibrations, or thermal noise) affecting both source inputs while retaining valuable information and improving the integrity of the measured input signal. Our proposed DWA layer adapts this idea to deep learning and can be used as a drop-in module to existing SR models. This work shows its effectiveness as exemplary for wavelet-based SR approaches. DWA leverages the difference between two convolutional filters with a stride difference to enhance relevant feature extraction in the wavelet domain, emphasizing local contrasts and suppressing common noise in the input signals. We demonstrate the effectiveness of DWA through extensive experiments and evaluations, showing improved performance compared to existing wavelet-based SR models without DWA: DWSR with DWA shows overall better performance w.r.t. PSNR and SSIM, and MWCNN with DWA achieves better SSIM scores with comparable PSNR values on the testing datasets Set5 [4], Set14 [32], and BSDS100 [20].

Taken together, our work makes the following key contributions:

- Introduction of Differential Wavelet Amplifier (DWA): a novel module that leverages the difference between two convolutional filters horizontally and vertically in a wavelet-based image representation, which is applicable as drop-in addition in existing network architectures.
- Comprehensive evaluation demonstrating the improved performance on popular SR datasets such as Set5 [4], Set14 [32], and BSDS100 [20] by adding DWA to existing wavelet-based SR models: DWSR [9] and MWCNN [17].
- Experimental analysis showing that DWA enables a direct application of DWSR and MWCNN to the input space by avoiding the DWT on the input image. This application reduces the input channel-wise to 3 instead of 12 channels for RGB images while keeping the spatial reduction benefit of DWT.
- Visual examinations showcasing that DWSR with the DWA module captures better distinct edges and finer details closer to the ground truth residuals.

2 Background

This chapter provides comprehensive background information on 2D Discrete Wavelet Transform (2D-DWT), how SR models (DWSR [9] and MWCNN [17]) use it, and related work to Differential Wavelet Amplifiers (DWA). Additionally, we introduce differential amplifiers from electrical engineering, which inspired our proposed method DWA.

2.1 Discrete Wavelet Transform in SR

The 2D Discrete Wavelet Transform (2D-DWT) decomposes an image into four unique sub-bands with distinct frequency components: a low-frequency approximation sub-band and three high-frequency detail sub-bands representing horizontal, vertical, and diagonal details. Let $x[n] \in \mathbb{R}^N$ be a signal. The 1D Discrete Wavelet Transformation (1D-DWT) with Haar wavelet passes the input signal first through a half-band high-filter $h[n]$ and a low-pass filter $l[n]$. Next, half of the sample is eliminated according to the Nyquist rule [9]. The wavelet coefficients are calculated by repeating the decomposition to each output coefficient iteratively [26]. In the case of images, it applies $h[n]$ and $l[n]$ in different combinations, resulting in four function applications.

The DWSR [9] SR model exploits the wavelet domain and gets the DWT representation of the interpolated LR image as input. DWSR is composed of 10 convolution layers that are applied sequentially. It adds the interpolated LR input as residual for the final reconstruction step, which results in learning only the sparse residual information between the LR and HR domains.

MWCNN [17] exploits multi-level DWT (multiple applications of DWT) and utilizes a U-Net architecture [22]. DWT replaces all downsizing steps, and the inverse operation of DWT replaces all upsampling steps. Ultimately, it uses the interpolated LR image as a residual connection for the final prediction. The standard MWCNN setup consists of 24 convolution layers.

One caveat of DWSR and MWCNN in learning the residual is that they must translate its rich information input to sparse representation, e.g., the average band. To ease the burden, we present a Differential Wavelet Amplifier, which directly transforms the input into sparse representations inspired by differential amplifiers introduced next.

2.2 Differential Amplifier

An electronic amplifier is a standard electrical engineering device to increase a signal's power [2]. One type of electronic amplifier is the differential amplifier that increases the difference between two input signals and suppresses the common voltage shared by the two inputs [14]. Given two inputs $V_{in}^{-}, V_{in}^{+} \in \mathbb{R}^N$ and the differential gain of the amplifier $A_d \in \mathbb{R}$, the output V_{out} is calculated as

$$V_{out} = A_d \left(V_{in}^{+} - V_{in}^{-} \right) \tag{1}$$

The purpose of differential amplifiers is to suppress common signals or noise sources that are present in multiple input channels while retaining valuable information. In the literature, this is called Common Mode Rejection (CMR) and is a critical property in many electrical engineering applications, particularly in systems that measure small signals in the presence of noise or interference, e.g., electromagnetic interference or thermal noise [11]. Hence, using CMR improves the signal-to-noise ratio, overall system performance, and signal integrity since the system can focus on the relevant differential signals.

2.3 Differential Convolutions

Closest to our work is Sarıgül et al. [25], which applies differential convolutions, i.e., the difference of two convolution layers, to emphasize contrasts for image classification, which is inherently different to image generation tasks such as image SR. Despite this, they do not consider a stride difference vital for capturing variations. Knutsson et al. [13] theoretically examine a normalized version of differential convolutions also with no stride difference. Due to the time of publication, they did not try it in the case of deep learning-based image SR. Newer applications like Canh et al. [5] consider learnable parameters to turn the Difference of Gaussians (DoG) [18] into a learnable framework, but has the same caveat: As Knutsson concluded, their approaches can be interpreted as a standard convolution weighted with the local energy minus the "mean" operator acting on the "mean" data, i.e., a more elaborate convolution operation.

A similarity could also be seen in the approach of residual connections of ResNets [10] when the kernel parameters have a negative sign. However, residual connections are different since they force a convolution layer to learn to extract the sparse details that are not apparent in the input. In contrast, our proposed method with Differential Wavelet Amplifier (DWA) explicitly produces sparse details by design due to the subtraction operator. Therefore, DWA does not have to learn what input information should be removed for the residual information. It can focus on relevant features that persist when the stride convolution does not detect the same feature, thereby emphasizing local contrast.

3 Differential Wavelet Amplifier (DWA)

This section presents our proposed Differential Wavelet Amplifier (DWA) module. Inspired by differential amplifiers in electrical engineering, DWA is designed to operate in the wavelet domain and exploits the difference between two input signals to improve the performance of image SR methods based on wavelet predictions. DWA is applied separately in the horizontal and vertical axis of the input image. In each direction, we perform two convolutions with a stride distance in one direction for both axis (from left to right, from top to bottom, as in MDLSTMs [8]), allowing a fine-grained feature extraction and emphasizing local contrasts while suppressing the common mode in the input, similar to CMR in electrical engineering. Figure 1 visualizes all processes involved in DWA.

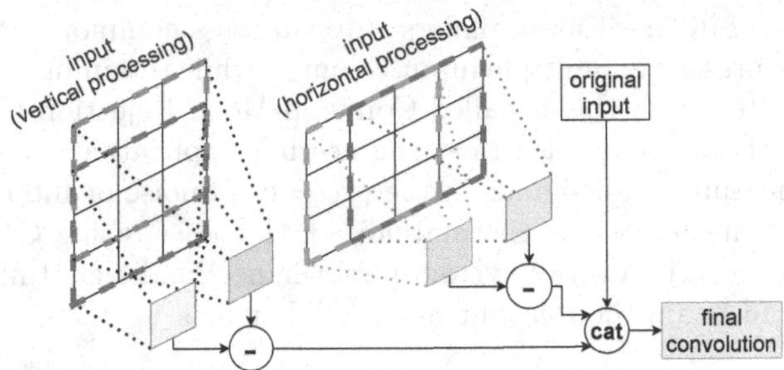

Fig. 1. Visualization of DWA. It takes the difference of two convolutional filters with a stride difference of at least 1, vertically and horizontally. Next, it concatenates the input with horizontal and vertical feature maps. In the end, it applies a final convolution.

Let $\mathbf{x} \in \mathbb{R}^{w \times h \times c_{in}}$ be an input image or feature map with c_{in} channels. We define $\psi(\mathbf{x}, (i,j)) : \mathbb{R}^{w \times h \times c_{in}} \times \mathbb{N}^2 \rightarrow \mathbb{R}^{k \cdot k \times c_{in}}$ as a function that extracts $k \cdot k$ points around a spatial position (i, j). We can then express the resulting feature maps for the horizontal $\mathbf{H}(\mathbf{x})$ and vertical $\mathbf{V}(\mathbf{x})$ axis as

$$\begin{aligned} \mathbf{H}(\mathbf{x})_{i,j} &= f(\psi(\mathbf{x}, (i,j)); \theta_1) - f(\psi(\mathbf{x}, (i+s, j)); \theta_2), \\ \mathbf{V}(\mathbf{x})_{i,j} &= f(\psi(\mathbf{x}, (i,j)); \theta_3) - f(\psi(\mathbf{x}, (i, j+s)); \theta_4), \end{aligned} \tag{2}$$

where $f : \mathbb{R}^{k \cdot k \times c_{in}} \rightarrow \mathbb{R}^{c_f}$ is a convolution operation with parameters θ_n for $0 < n < 4$, $k \times k$ the kernel size and $s \in \mathbb{N}$ a pre-defined stride difference. As a result, the local variance is captured in one direction for both axes, similar to MDLSTMs [8]: from left to right with parameters θ_1 and θ_2 and from top to bottom with parameters θ_3 and θ_4. We obtain two distinct feature maps that capture complementary input image information and provide richer feature representations for the wavelet-based SR task. The input is directly translated to sparse representations, which reduces the distance to residual target objectives in networks that use residual connections for final prediction.

We concatenate the resulting feature maps alongside the input to ensure no information is lost during the DWA processing. This combination creates a comprehensive set of feature maps that retains the original input information while incorporating the directional features obtained from both axes. More formally:

$$g(\mathbf{x}) = \mathbf{x} \odot \sigma(H(\mathbf{x}) \odot V(\mathbf{x})), \tag{3}$$

where $\odot$ is a channel-wise concatenation operator and σ is a non-linear function like sigmoid, tanh or ReLU [1]. The concatenated feature map is fed into an additional convolution layer $f_{final} : \mathbb{R}^{k \cdot k \times (c_{in} + 2 \cdot c_f)} \rightarrow \mathbb{R}^{c_{final}}$ and parameters θ_{final}, which maps the channel size after concatenation to a desired target channel size c_{final} such that our module can easily be incorporated into existing models:

$$\text{DWA}(\mathbf{x})_{i,j} = f_{final}(\psi(g(\mathbf{x}), (i,j)); \theta_{final}) \tag{4}$$

A SR model utilizing this DWA module exploits the comprehensive feature map to learn the complex relationships between LR and HR images, ultimately reconstructing the HR image with reduced noise. By employing the DWA, we aim to harness the benefits of wavelet domain processing and the difference between two convolutional filters. We demonstrate the effectiveness of our approach through extensive experiments and evaluations in the following sections.

3.1 Direct Application of DWA (DWA Direct)

One way to circumvent additional computation steps is to apply DWA directly on the image space, omitting DWT and learning the transition between image and frequency space implicitly via DWA. Thus, the interpolation of the input, which effectively adds no additional information since it generates only approximated values, can be reduced by half for networks like DWSR or MWCNN. Consequently, the network is better adapted to the given values of the LR input. In the experiments, we evaluate this alternative approach called DWA Direct and show that it further enhances the performances of DWSR and MWCNN.

4 Experiments

We evaluate our proposed DWA module by integrating it into the wavelet-based SR models DWSR and MWCNN. We begin this section by describing the experiments. Next, we discuss the results quantitatively and qualitatively. We show the effectiveness of DWA and that a direct application of wavelet-based SR models with DWA to image space is feasible without forfeiting reconstruction quality.

4.1 Experimental Setup

We applied widely-used SR datasets to evaluate our method. In addition, we utilized standard augmentation techniques such as rotation, horizontal and vertical flipping. For testing, we employed the datasets Set5 [4], Set14 [32], BSDS100 [20]. For training, we used different settings for DWSR and MWCNN to match the original works for a fair comparison, as dissected in the following. In all experiments, we train using the Adam optimizer [12] with a learning rate of 10^{-4} with $L2$ regularization of 10^{-8} on a single A100 GPU. Moreover, we use a learning rate decay schedule, which reduces the learning rate by 20% every 20 epochs.

Ablation Study: We use DIV2K [3] and follow the standard procedure by extracting sub-images of 192×192 for training. We iterate for 40 epochs over the training dataset. Since we compare with DWSR, we use $L1$-loss as the learning objective, as reported by the authors of DWSR.

DWSR-Scenario: We use DIV2K [3] like in the ablation study, but we train for 100 epochs as reported in DWSR.

MWCNN-Scenario: We collect 800 images from DIV2K [3], 200 images from BSD [20] and 4,744 images from WED [19] and train for 100 epochs. Contrary to DWSR, we adapt the $L2$-loss like the authors of MWCNN. For sub-image extraction, we use a size of 240×240 to match the training settings of MWCNN.

Table 1. Comparison of different striding settings on BSDS100 (2x and 4x scaling).

Scale	Metric	no stride	s=1	s=2	s=3
2x	**PSNR** ↑	31.8314	**31.8660**	31.8598	31.8588
	SSIM ↑	0.9058	**0.9061**	0.9060	0.9059
4x	**PSNR** ↑	27.2870	**27.3048**	27.2927	27.2872
	SSIM ↑	0.7457	**0.7471**	0.7464	0.7466

5 Results

This section presents the quantitative and qualitative analysis of this work. It shows that incorporating the DWA module into DWSR improves the performance in every dataset and for all scaling factors. Moreover, we consistently improve the SSIM scores by implementing DWA into MWCNN and achieve similar PSNR results. This section starts with an ablation study to investigate different striding settings and the effect of combining DWA with DWSR for the direct application and the regular DWT case (see Sect. 3.1). Next, we examine the performance scores of our DWA module on classical SR datasets with DWSR and MWCNN. Finally, we visually compare the quality of the reconstructions.

Ablation Study. Table 1 shows the impact of different striding settings for DWSR with DWA with 2x and 4x scaling. We observe an improvement for striding settings greater than 0, significantly for PSNR and slightly for SSIM. The differences between striding settings greater than 0 are minimal, with a slight decrease for larger striding sizes. Nonetheless, they outperform DWA with no stride difference consistently. Thus, having a stride difference to capture local variations more effectively benefits the overall performance of DWSR.

We further investigate the impact of various model configurations, DWSR with or without the DWA module, in a direct application or without (see Sect. 3.1). Figure 2 presents the results, where two graphs display the PSNR and SSIM values [21], respectively, for each method. We apply the ablation study with different model depths, ranging from 6 to 18, instead of using a standard depth of 10 for DWSR. As a result, DWSR with DWA or DWA Direct consistently outperforms the DWSR baseline across all model depths. This demonstrates the effectiveness of incorporating the DWA module as the first layer in the DWSR framework. Moreover, DWA Direct outperforms DWA applied to the DWT on the input with greater model depths. Furthermore, we observe a considerable performance drop in DWSR Direct without using the DWA module compared to all other evaluated methods. This indicates that the DWA module is crucial in enabling the Direct approach, as its absence significantly degrades performance.

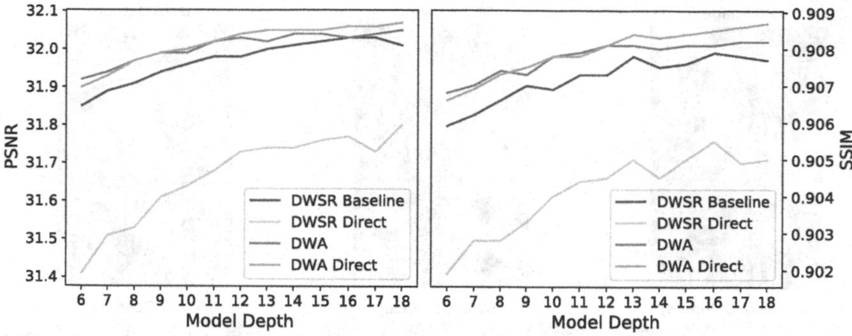

Fig. 2. Results of ablation study on BSDS100 with scaling factor 2x. We tested different configurations: Baseline, Direct (application on the image space), DWA, and DWA Direct (application on the image space).

Performance. Table 2 summarizes PSNR and SSIM scores when applying the DWA module to DWSR and MWCNN for classical SR datasets on different scaling factors for a longer training span. We observe that incorporating the DWA module into DWSR improves the performance in every dataset and for all scaling factors. For MWCNN with DWA, a similar observation can be made, especially for the SSIM scores, which show overall the best performances. However, it has slightly decreased PSNR values for some cases, e.g., for scaling factor 3. Both applications, DWSR with DWA and MWCNN with DWA, are applied directly on the input image space, omitting a DWT of the input.

Table 2. Comparison of DWSR, MWCNN, and DWA Direct with DWSR and MWCNN architecture on Set5, Set14, and BSDS100. Note that PSNR [dB] is a logarithmic scale, and SSIM reflects correlations (with values ranging from −1 to 1) [21].

Dataset	Scale	DWSR [9] PSNR/SSIM	MWCNN [17] PSNR/SSIM	DWA Direct [DWSR] PSNR/SSIM	DWA Direct [MWCNN] PSNR/SSIM
Set5 [4]	2x	37.43/0.9568	37.91/0.9600	37.79/0.9645	**37.99**/**0.9652**
	3x	33.82/0.9215	**34.18**/0.9272	33.85/0.9310	34.09/**0.9329**
	4x	31.39/0.8833	32.12/0.8941	31.76/0.8898	**32.16**/**0.9054**
Set14 [32]	2x	33.07/0.9106	**33.70**/0.9182	33.38/0.9237	**33.70**/**0.9265**
	3x	29.83/0.8308	**30.16**/0.8414	29.90/0.8504	30.12/**0.8545**
	4x	28.04/0.7669	28.41/0.7816	28.31/0.7928	**28.70**/**0.8012**
BSDS100 [20]	2x	31.80/0.8940	**32.23**/0.8999	32.01/0.9080	32.21/**0.9102**
	3x	n.a	**29.12**/0.8060	28.79/0.8174	28.93/**0.8211**
	4x	27.25/0.7240	27.62/0.7355	27.38/0.7503	**27.63**/**0.7573**

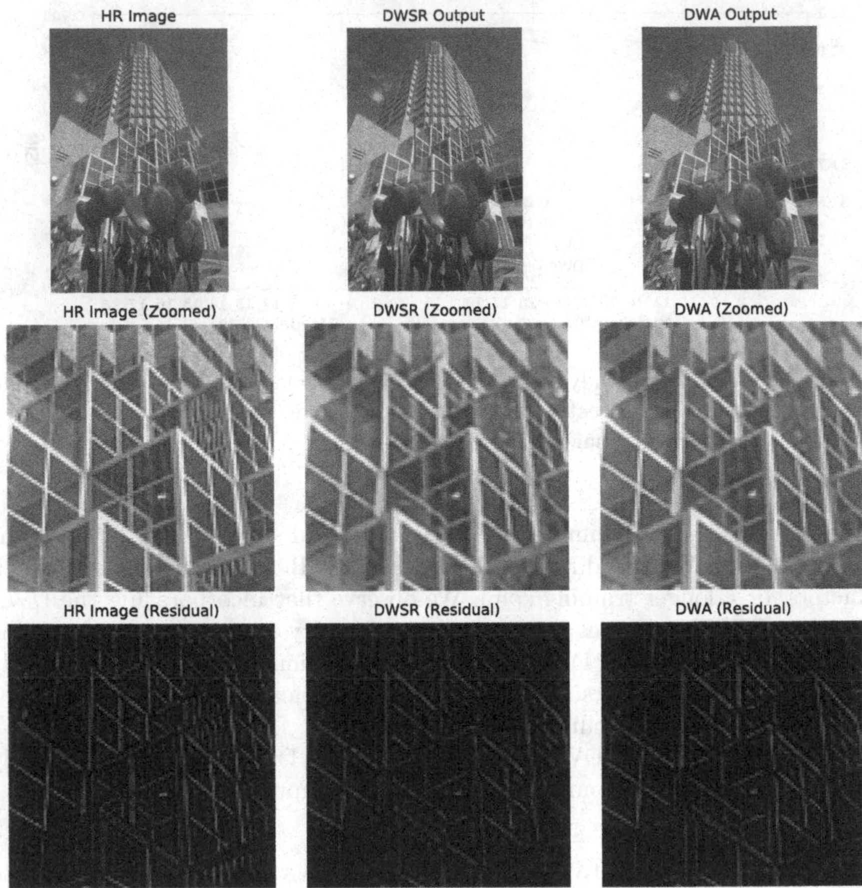

Fig. 3. Comparison of an HR ground truth image (BSDS100, 2x scaling), DWSR, and DWA. First row: the entire image space of the HR image and the corresponding reconstructions obtained by the SR models. Second row: zoomed-in regions within the images from the first row. Third row: residual image representing the difference between the LR and HR images. As a result, the DWA model captures edges and details closer to the ground truth residuals, as opposed to the DWSR model (also regarding color). (Color figure online)

Visual Comparison. Figure 3 displays the ground truth HR image alongside the DWSR and DWA reconstructions. DWSR and DWA perform reasonably well in reconstructing the images. However, the DWA reconstructions exhibit more accurate and sharp details, particularly in the zoomed-in regions. Since the added bicubic interpolation of the LR image in the reconstruction process provides a robust base prediction, we also present the residual images, which are the differences between the bicubic interpolations and the ground truth images, to highlight the performance difference between both approaches.

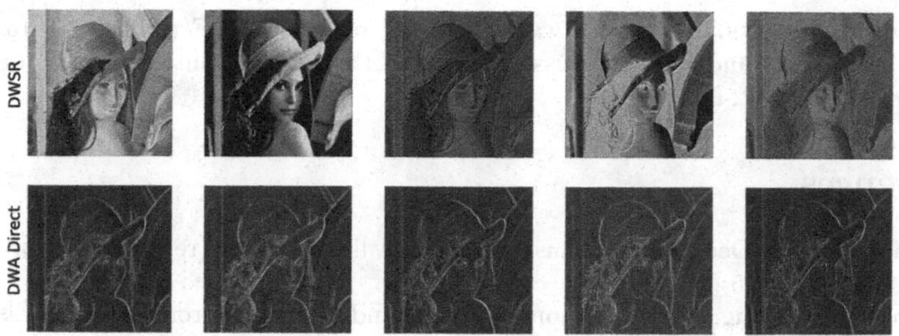

Fig. 4. Feature maps of DWSR and DWA Direct. DWA Direct extracts local contrasts and variations more effectively, closer than DWSR to the residual target.

These residual images are the learning targets of the models to improve the reconstruction quality beyond interpolation. By comparing the residual images, we can see more clearly that the DWA model captures better distinct edges and finer details, which are also closer to the ground truth residuals, as opposed to the DWSR model. It has more substantial edges and finer points in the residual images, which are also closer in color (see red colored lines of DWSR reconstruction in Fig. 3 as a comparison). This observation aligns with our quantitative results, where DWA outperforms DWSR regarding various performance metrics.

To provide deeper insights into our proposed models, Fig. 4 presents feature maps generated by the DWSR and DWA Direct models after the first layer. To ensure diversity, we selected the top five channels from each method based on the highest sum of distances between pairwise differences of all channels. Our analysis reveals that although DWSR operates on the frequency space, it still remains similar to the LR input and fails to capture the desired target residual. In contrast, DWA Direct extracts local contrasts and variations more effectively from the image space and performs better in mapping the target residual.

6 Conclusion and Future Work

In this work, we presented a novel Differential Wavelet Amplifier (DWA) module, which can be used as a drop-in module to existing wavelet-based SR models. We showed experimentally on Set5, Set14, and BSDS100 for scaling factors 2, 3, and 4 that it improves the reconstruction quality of the SR models DWSR and MWCNN while enabling an application of them to the input image space directly without harm to performance. This module captures more distinct edges and finer details, which are closer to the ground truth residuals, which wavelet-based SR models usually learn. This work is an opportunity to seek further advancements for SR based on frequency-based representations.

For future work, an exciting research avenue would be to explore ways to incorporate DWA on different DWT levels in MWCNN instead of only applying it initially.

Acknowledgements. This work was supported by the BMBF projects SustainML (Grant 101070408) and by Carl Zeiss Foundation through the Sustainable Embedded AI project (P2021-02-009).

References

1. Agarap, A.F.: Deep learning using rectified linear units (relu). arXiv preprint arXiv:1803.08375 (2018)
2. Agarwal, A., Lang, J.: Foundations of analog and digital electronic circuits. Elsevier (2005)
3. Agustsson, E., Timofte, R.: Ntire 2017 challenge on single image super-resolution: Dataset and study. In: Proceedings of the IEEE Conference on Computer Vision and Pattern Recognition Workshops, pp. 126–135 (2017)
4. Bevilacqua, M., Roumy, A., Guillemot, C., Alberi-Morel, M.L.: Low-complexity single-image super-resolution based on nonnegative neighbor embedding (2012)
5. Canh, T.N., Jeon, B.: Difference of convolution for deep compressive sensing. In: 2019 IEEE International Conference on Image Processing (ICIP), pp. 2105–2109. IEEE (2019)
6. Dong, C., Loy, C.C., He, K., Tang, X.: Image super-resolution using deep convolutional networks. IEEE Trans. Pattern Anal. Mach. Intell. **38**(2), 295–307 (2015)
7. Dong, C., Loy, C.C., Tang, X.: Accelerating the super-resolution convolutional neural network. In: Leibe, B., Matas, J., Sebe, N., Welling, M. (eds.) ECCV 2016. LNCS, vol. 9906, pp. 391–407. Springer, Cham (2016). https://doi.org/10.1007/978-3-319-46475-6_25
8. Graves, A., Schmidhuber, J.: Offline handwriting recognition with multidimensional recurrent neural networks. In: Advances in Neural Information Processing Systems 21 (2008)
9. Guo, T., Seyed Mousavi, H., Huu Vu, T., Monga, V.: Deep wavelet prediction for image super-resolution. In: Proceedings of the IEEE Conference on Computer Vision and Pattern Recognition Workshops, pp. 104–113 (2017)
10. He, K., Zhang, X., Ren, S., Sun, J.: Deep residual learning for image recognition. In: Proceedings of the IEEE Conference on Computer Vision and Pattern Recognition, pp. 770–778 (2016)
11. Horowitz, P., Hill, W., Robinson, I.: The art of electronics, vol. 2. Cambridge University Press Cambridge (1989)
12. Kingma, D.P., Ba, J.: Adam: a method for stochastic optimization. arXiv preprint arXiv:1412.6980 (2014)
13. Knutsson, H., Westin, C.F.: Normalized and differential convolution. In: Proceedings of IEEE Conference on Computer Vision and Pattern Recognition, pp. 515–523. IEEE (1993)
14. Laplante, P.A.: Comprehensive Dictionary of Electrical Engineering. CRC Press (2018)
15. Li, H., et al.: SRDIFF: single image super-resolution with diffusion probabilistic models. Neurocomputing **479**, 47–59 (2022)
16. Liang, J., Cao, J., Sun, G., Zhang, K., Van Gool, L., Timofte, R.: SWINIR: image restoration using swin transformer. In: Proceedings of the IEEE/CVF International Conference on Computer Vision, pp. 1833–1844 (2021)
17. Liu, P., Zhang, H., Zhang, K., Lin, L., Zuo, W.: Multi-level wavelet-cnn for image restoration. In: Proceedings of the IEEE conference on computer vision and pattern recognition workshops. pp. 773–782 (2018)

18. Lowe, D.G.: Distinctive image features from scale-invariant keypoints. Int. J. Comput. Vision **60**, 91–110 (2004)
19. Ma, K., et al.: Waterloo exploration database: new challenges for image quality assessment models. IEEE Trans. Image Process. **26**(2), 1004–1016 (2016)
20. Martin, D., Fowlkes, C., Tal, D., Malik, J.: A database of human segmented natural images and its application to evaluating segmentation algorithms and measuring ecological statistics. In: Proceedings Eighth IEEE International Conference on Computer Vision, ICCV 2001, vol. 2, pp. 416–423. IEEE (2001)
21. Moser, B.B., Raue, F., Frolov, S., Palacio, S., Hees, J., Dengel, A.: Hitchhiker's guide to super-resolution: Introduction and recent advances. IEEE Trans. Pattern Anal. Mach. Intell., 1–21 (2023). https://doi.org/10.1109/TPAMI.2023.3243794
22. Ronneberger, O., Fischer, P., Brox, T.: U-Net: convolutional networks for biomedical image segmentation. In: Navab, N., Hornegger, J., Wells, W.M., Frangi, A.F. (eds.) MICCAI 2015. LNCS, vol. 9351, pp. 234–241. Springer, Cham (2015). https://doi.org/10.1007/978-3-319-24574-4_28
23. Sahak, H., Watson, D., Saharia, C., Fleet, D.: Denoising diffusion probabilistic models for robust image super-resolution in the wild. arXiv preprint arXiv:2302.07864 (2023)
24. Saharia, C., Ho, J., Chan, W., Salimans, T., Fleet, D.J., Norouzi, M.: Image super-resolution via iterative refinement. IEEE Trans. Pattern Anal. Mach. Intell. (2022)
25. Sarıgül, M., Ozyildirim, B.M., Avci, M.: Differential convolutional neural network. Neural Networks **116**, 279–287 (2019)
26. Stephane, M.: A wavelet tour of signal processing (1999)
27. Sun, L., Dong, J., Tang, J., Pan, J.: Spatially-adaptive feature modulation for efficient image super-resolution. arXiv preprint arXiv:2302.13800 (2023)
28. Vaswani, A., et al.: Attention is all you need. In: Advances in Neural Information Processing Systems 30 (2017)
29. Wang, X., Xie, L., Dong, C., Shan, Y.: Real-esrgan: training real-world blind super-resolution with pure synthetic data. In: Proceedings of the IEEE/CVF International Conference on Computer Vision (ICCV) Workshops, pp. 1905–1914, October 2021
30. Wang, X., et al.: ESRGAN: enhanced super-resolution generative adversarial networks. In: Leal-Taixé, L., Roth, S. (eds.) ECCV 2018. LNCS, vol. 11133, pp. 63–79. Springer, Cham (2019). https://doi.org/10.1007/978-3-030-11021-5_5
31. Wang, Z., Chen, J., Hoi, S.C.H.: Deep learning for image super-resolution: a survey. IEEE Trans. Pattern Anal. Mach. Intell. **43**(10), 3365–3387 (2021). https://doi.org/10.1109/TPAMI.2020.2982166
32. Zeyde, R., Elad, M., Protter, M.: On single image scale-up using sparse-representations. In: Boissonnat, J.-D., et al. (eds.) Curves and Surfaces 2010. LNCS, vol. 6920, pp. 711–730. Springer, Heidelberg (2012). https://doi.org/10.1007/978-3-642-27413-8_47

Dynamic Facial Expression Recognition in Unconstrained Real-World Scenarios Leveraging Dempster-Shafer Evidence Theory

Zhenyu Liu[1], Tianyi Wang[2(✉)], Shuwang Zhou[1], and Minglei Shu[1]

[1] Shandong Artificial Intelligence Institute, Qilu University of Technology (Shandong Academy of Sciences), Jinan 250014, China
10431210674@stu.qlu.edu.cn, {zhoushw,shuml}@sdas.org

[2] The University of Hong Kong, Hong Kong, China
tywang@cs.hku.hk

Abstract. Dynamic facial expression recognition (DFER) has garnered significant attention due to its critical role in various applications, including human-computer interaction, emotion-aware systems, and mental health monitoring. Nevertheless, addressing the challenges of DFER in real-world scenarios remains a formidable task, primarily due to the severe class imbalance problem, leading to suboptimal model performance and poor recognition of minority class expressions. Recent studies in facial expression recognition (FER) for class imbalance predominantly focus on spatial features analysis, while the capacity to encode temporal features of spontaneous facial expressions remains limited. To tackle this issue, we introduce a novel dynamic facial expression recognition in real-world scenarios (RS-DFER) framework, which primarily comprises a spatiotemporal features combination (STC) module and a multi-classifier dynamic participation (MCDP) module. Our extensive experiments on two prevalent large-scale DFER datasets from real-world scenarios demonstrate that our proposed method outperforms existing state-of-the-art approaches, showcasing its efficacy and potential for practical applications.

Keywords: Dynamic facial expression recognition · Class imbalance · Real-world scenarios

1 Introduction

Emotions are effectively conveyed through critical facial cues, significantly impacting human interactions [3]. Furthermore, research on facial expressions can serve as an upstream task and provide a reference basis for current deepfake detection methods [17,21–23,27]. Facial expression recognition (FER) aims to classify images or video clips into primary emotions based on the input type,

L. Iliadis et al. (Eds.): ICANN 2023, LNCS 14255, pp. 244–258, 2023.
https://doi.org/10.1007/978-3-031-44210-0_20

which is categorized into static FER (SFER) for still images and dynamic FER (DFER) for video sequences [29]. Previous studies [13] indicate that facial events possess inherent dynamism, and expressions are more accurately represented as evolving sequences within a dynamic framework, leading to an increasing focus on DFER in contemporary research.

DFER data is classified into lab-controlled and in-the-wild categories, based on different scenarios. Lab-controlled datasets, such as CK+ [14], Oulu-CASIA [28], and MMI [16], involve participants enacting standardized emotions in controlled environments, ensuring balanced distribution across categories. However, these datasets do not accurately represent real-world expression frequencies. In contrast, in-the-wild datasets exhibit distribution inconsistencies compared to lab-based scenarios [29]. This discrepancy impacts DFER model performance in two primary ways: 1) biased learning due to overfitting on majority class expressions, resulting in poor generalization [15]; 2) the ongoing challenge of class imbalance impeding recognition of minority class expressions without a comprehensive solution [7]. Consequently, addressing dynamic facial expression recognition in real-world scenarios remains an urgent issue.

To tackle the aforementioned challenges, we propose the dynamic facial expression recognition in real-world scenarios (RS-DFER) network. RS-DFER comprises the spatiotemporal features combination (STC) module and the multi-classifier dynamic participation (MCDP) module. STC includes the spatial features extract block (SFEB), spatial attention mechanism (SAM), and temporal features extract block (TFEB). First, we input each frame to SFEB with SAM to effectively extract spatial features statically. Then, the spatial features are combined in the time direction and fed into TFEB to extract the video's temporal information. Finally, we construct the MCDP based on the Dempster-Shafer Theory of Evidence (DST) [4] and integrate it with TFEB to form a multi-classifier structure. By calculating the uncertainty and evidence for each classifier, the model dynamically adjusts each classifier's participation degree based on the difficulty of predicting different samples, ultimately achieving accurate prediction of imbalanced data. The main contributions of this paper are as follows:

1. To the best of our knowledge, we are the first to incorporate DST into DFER, resulting in the RS-DFER model, which effectively addresses the challenge of DFER under class imbalance conditions in real-world scenarios.
2. By incorporating the SAM, the STC is capable of efficiently extracting salient spatiotemporal features while utilizing minimal computational resources.
3. Our method outperforms existing state-of-the-art approaches in real-world expression recognition accuracy and effectively mitigates model bias due to class imbalance.

2 Related Works

2.1 Dynamic Facial Expression Recognition

In real-life conditions, static images alone cannot fully capture an individual's emotional state, necessitating the analysis of expression changes over time using time series information. To the best of our knowledge, existing FER approaches addressing class imbalance primarily concentrate on SFER. Therefore, we reviewed the main developments in DFER in this section. Traditional DFER methods employ hand-crafted features [2] and shallow classifiers [30] for classification. Subsequently, 3DCNN [8] and LSTM [25] are utilized for their advantages in handling temporal information for dynamic expression classification. Based on the transformer, Zhao et al. [29] proposed Former-DFER to learn the correlation between facial features, addressed issues such as non-frontal postures and head movements. All these approaches inevitably use imbalanced datasets in the wild, rendering them prone to unreliable predictions, particularly detrimental to minority classes.

2.2 Classification Under Data Imbalance

Various mainstream classification models exist to address class imbalance, but they often come with limitations. Xiang et al. [24] proposed a self-progressing knowledge distillation framework that employs multiple subsets to train a balanced model guiding a student model; however, this method may not adequately perceive the uncertainty of difficult samples. Li et al. [12] implemented a trusted long-tail classification (TLC) approach for classification and joint uncertainty estimation, identified hard samples within a multi-expert framework. While TLC achieves reliable uncertainty, the multi-expert framework increases model complexity, and dynamic expert participation introduces unpredictable computational costs.

3 Methodology

In this section, we present our method based on DS-DFER to achieve DFER in real-world scenarios. As illustrated in Fig. 1, we first segment a fixed-length facial expression sequence from the raw video as input. Subsequently, we extract the spatiotemporal features using the STC module in conjunction with the SAM. Finally, we employ the MCDP module to alleviate the impact of class imbalance on model performance, ultimately obtaining accurate recognition results.

3.1 Spatiotemporal Features Combination Module

The STC consists of N SFEBs and three TFEBs. Each SFEB comes with a separate SAM, and the structure is shown in Fig. 1.

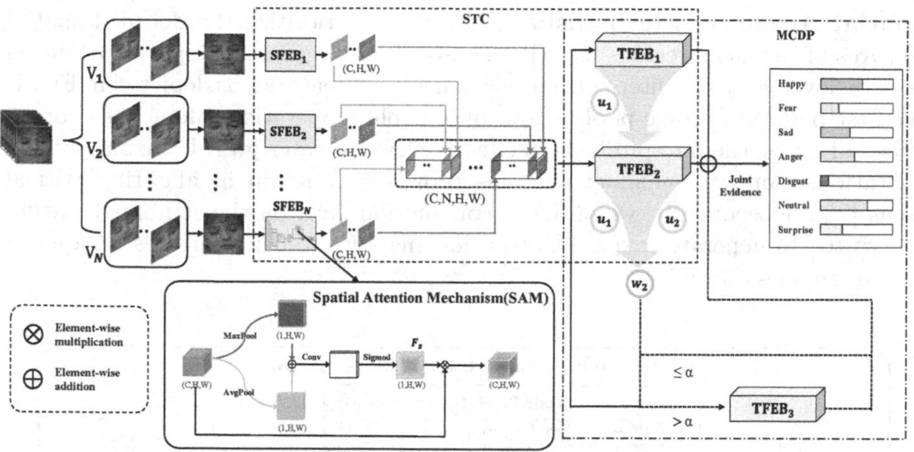

Fig. 1. The network architecture of RS-DFER. STC consists of N SFEBs and three TFEBs.

Spatial Features Extraction Block. To efficiently sample frames from the entire video, we divide each video into N equal-sized clips. We then randomly select one frame from each clip in chronological order, ensuring that the sampling of each video under a limited number of frames is neither overly dense, which would increase the computational burden, nor overly sparse, which could result in the loss of expression continuity. Next, we input the extracted video frames to their corresponding SFEB to extract spatial features. To direct the network's focus towards more crucial areas, we incorporate SAM into the last layer of the BN-Inception Basic Block. Furthermore, we introduce the concept of residual connections to mitigate the vanishing gradient problem. The detailed architecture is illustrated in Fig. 2.

We set N to the number of sampling frames, C to the number of channels, H and W to the size of the feature map, and the output of the frame i as a single tensor $M_i \in \mathbb{R}^{C\times 1\times H\times W}$. After the splicing process in Fig. 2, we get $M_\phi = [M_1, M_2, \ldots, M_N]; M_\phi \in \mathbb{R}^{C\times N\times H\times W}$.

Temporal Features Extraction Block. We feed the spatial features M_ϕ from the SFEB into the TFEB to extract temporal features. We design the TFEB to handle more complex relationships between frames and to comprehend the movements of facial muscles. For the backbone of the TFEB, we adopt the last three convolutional layers of the reliable and efficient 3D-Resnet18 architecture [8]. We believe that the TFEB is capable of addressing the intricate relationships between frames and understanding the dynamics of facial muscle movements. Finally, the spatiotemporal features of a video are obtained through the output of the fully connected layer.

Spatial Attention Mechanism. FER should prioritize the detailed spatial features of key facial regions [13]. To achieve this, we generate a spatial attention map by leveraging the inter-spatial relationships of features, as depicted in Fig. 1. We first perform average-pooling and max-pooling operations along the channel axis and merge them to produce an effective feature descriptor. Utilizing pooling operations along the channel axis has proven effective in highlighting critical areas [26]. Subsequently, we design a convolution layer on the combined feature descriptor to generate a spatial attention map F_s, which indicates regions to emphasize or suppress.

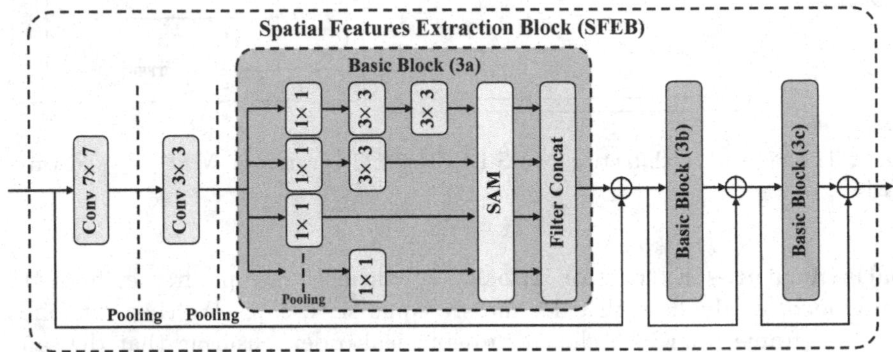

Fig. 2. The structure of SFEB.

3.2 Multi-classifier Dynamic Participation Module

For the MCDP, we first introduce how to estimate uncertainty with Dempster-Shafer Evidence Theory (DST), and then form joint uncertainty and joint evidence according to the rules of synthesis, and finally, illustrate the multi-classifier dynamic participation process.

Uncertainty Computation. The prominent advantage of DST [4] is that it can portray the uncertainty and unknown of information, which can accurately express the uncertainty of small samples, dig deeper into the intrinsic meaning of small samples, and improve recognition accuracy. For this reason, we combine the TFEB with DST to propose the MCDP, which can improve efficiency while maintaining competitive performance. For expression recognition tasks, we treat the output vectors of the TFEB in Section B as belief masses assigned to each category label, denoted by $m(\cdot)$, which can be formulated as:

$$\begin{cases} m(\emptyset) = 0, \\ m(y_k) = V_k \ for \ \sum_{k=1}^{K} m(y_k) = 1, \end{cases} \tag{1}$$

where y_k is the label corresponding to class k, V_k is the element corresponding to class k in the output vector, and K is the number of labels for the class.

Belief masses represent the level of confidence and support for the current proposition. We bring belief masses into the exp function to get evidence $e = [e_1, e_2, e_3, \ldots, e_K]$ for each class. We calculate the uncertainty u of the current sample by the evidence of each class, and the formula is as follows:

$$u = \frac{K+1}{\sum_{k=1}^{K}(e_k+1)}, \tag{2}$$

where e_k is evidence of class K. It can be seen that uncertainty is inversely proportional to evidence, which is consistent with the logic of DST.

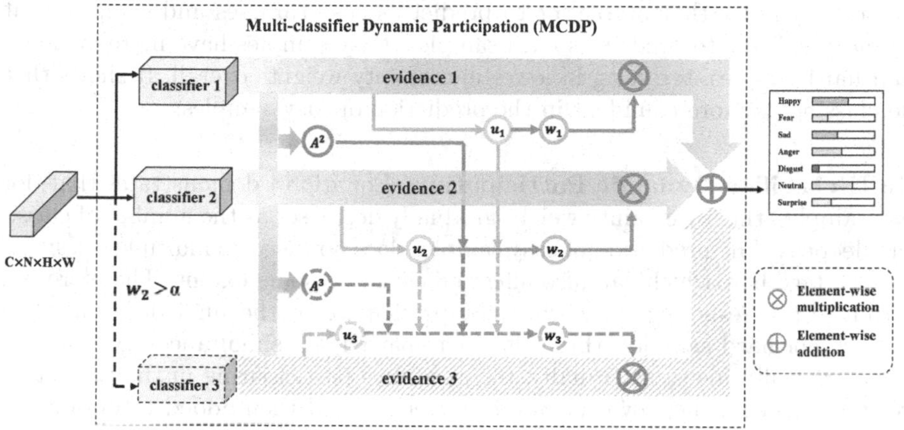

Fig. 3. The structure of the MCDP.

Synthesis Computation. The multiple classifiers can reduce the variance of the model and improve the robustness of the model [12]. Therefore, we design the multi-classifier architecture, and the network structure is shown in Fig. 3.

We find that the computational cost for expression recognition tasks increases dramatically as the number of classifiers increases. For this reason, the participation of as few experts as possible should be selected without significantly affecting the performance of the model. As shown in Fig. 3, we divide the MCDP into three branches, each consisting of the TFEB, and then calculate the uncertainty $u^{\phi} = [u^1, u^2, u^3]$ of each classifier. Based on the conflict coefficients in the synthesis rules, we assign a moderator $A^{\phi} = [A^1, A^2, A^3]$ to each uncertainty, which represents the sum of the evidence products of the two classifiers for the different parts of the classification opinions of the current sample. The formula is as follows:

$$A^m = \frac{\sum_{i \neq j} e_i^m e_j^{m-1}}{\sum_{k=1}^{K}(e_k^m+1)}, m \geq 2, \tag{3}$$

where e_j^{m-1} represents the evidence of class j of the $m-1$ classifier. Since the first classifier has no previous evidence to compare, let $A_1 = 0$. Through Eq. 2

and Eq. 3, we find that when the evidence of the two classifiers is close, the moderator is small, indicating that the uncertainty of a sample is low, and the prediction is basically consistent.

The uncertainty weight $w^{\phi} = [w^1, w^2, w^3]$ is calculated for each classifier according to the synthesis rules. The uncertainty weight reflects the overall uncertainty of the current classifier and is calculated as follows:

$$\begin{cases} w^1 = \frac{1}{1-A^1}u^1 + \alpha, \\ w^2 = \frac{1}{1-A^2}u^1u^2, \\ w^3 = w^2 \oplus u^3 = \frac{1}{1-A^3}w^2u^3. \end{cases} \tag{4}$$

We treat samples that are easier to predict as easy samples and samples that are more difficult to predict as hard samples. Easy samples have more evidence than hard samples, resulting in lower uncertainty weights overall. It shows that the classifier is more confident in the prediction of easy samples.

Multi-classifier Dynamic Participation. Equation 4 demonstrates that, for easy samples, the uncertainty weight gradually decreases as the number of classifiers deepens. The prediction of easy samples does not need to multiple classifiers to work together, which can also affect efficiency to some extent. Therefore, we introduce a threshold α that does not participate in the final decision when $w_i \leq \alpha$. For hard samples, three classifiers participate simultaneously, and evidence gradually increases. Finally, the classifiers participating in the prediction are multiplied by their own uncertainty weights and then added to obtain the overall evidence of the current sample as the output of the network.

We introduce the equation on a TFEB to derive the uncertainty of the current sample, which is simpler and more efficient than the traditional method. At the same time, we avoid the unreasonable one-vote veto problem, i.e., if there is a case where the belief masses of one piece of evidence is assigned 0, the final fusion result is also 0.

3.3 Loss Functions

Our network consists of two loss functions, namely, the uncertainty weight cross-entropy loss L_{uwce} and the Kullback-Leibler divergence [19] L_{KL}. The uncertainty weight cross-entropy loss is to balance the contribution of various samples to the loss function, which is described as follows:

$$L_{uwce} = -\frac{1}{K}\sum_{k=1}^{K}\frac{1}{w}y_k \log p_k, \tag{5}$$

where w is the overall uncertainty weight of the current sample, y_k is the unit vector converted from the label of class k, and p_k is the probability that the model predicts class k.

To make the evidence for predicting the correct category more prominent and to adjust the expectation of the difference between the probability of the data in the original distribution and the approximate distribution, we introduced the Kullback-Leibler divergence [19] L_{KL} as described below:

$$\begin{aligned} L_{KL} &= \mathrm{KL}(D(p_k \mid \alpha_k) \parallel D(p_k \mid 1)) \\ &= \log \frac{\Gamma(S)}{(\Gamma(K)\prod_{k=1}^{K}\Gamma(\alpha_k))} + \sum_{k=1}^{K}(\alpha_k - 1)(\psi(\alpha_k) - \psi(S)), \end{aligned} \tag{6}$$

where $\alpha_k = 1 + (1 - y_k) \odot e_k$, $S = \sum_{k=1}^{K} \alpha_k$, $\Gamma(\cdot)$ is a gamma function, $\psi(\cdot)$ is a Digamma function. Finally, the overall loss function for RS-DFER training is:

$$L = L_{uwce^{+}} + L_{\mathrm{KL}}. \tag{7}$$

4 Experimental Results and Analysis

4.1 Database and Processing

We evaluated our model using the publicly available Dynamic Facial Expression of Emotion in the Wild (DFEW) [9] and Acted Facial Expressions in the Wild (AFEW) [5] datasets, which encompass seven basic emotions across diverse cultures, genders, and ages. Evaluation criteria include Accuracy (ACC), Precision, Recall, and F1 Score, while model complexity is assessed through the number of parameters and FLOPs under consistent experimental conditions. Preprocessing involve using Dlib [10] to crop facial regions as 224 × 224 input images, while model training employ the Adam optimizer with a 0.01 learning rate, a 2e−4 weight decay coefficient, and the NAG momentum optimization algorithm with a 0.9 parameter momentum.

4.2 Comparative Experiment

We utilized the DFEW and AFEW datasets for training and evaluation, ensuring all models were compared under uniform experimental conditions. The results are presented in Table 1 for DFEW and Table 2 for AFEW.

Remarkably, our model surpasses existing state-of-the-art models in precision, recall, and F-1 score metrics by less than 1% in the weighted state, and by approximately 3% in the macro (unweighted mean) state for DFEW. The macro metrics are influenced by class imbalance, but our model demonstrates greater resilience to this issue, as evidenced by the larger gap between macro and weighted metrics. This indicates our approach's effectiveness in identifying true positives and minimizing false positives and false negatives.

Our proposed approach and Former-DFER outperform other models in terms of accuracy on both datasets, with over 60% on DFEW and over 45% on AFEW. These models employ 3D CNNs to extract spatiotemporal features from video frames but exhibit suboptimal performance in recognizing minority classes, resulting in low macro metrics. This inability to effectively recognize and classify minority classes contributes to a skewed distribution of predicted labels,

Table 1. The comparative results with other SOTA methods on the DFEW dataset. Best in **bold**, second best in underline.

Method	Params (M)	GFLOPs	ACC(%)	Precision (%)		Recall (%)		F-1 score (%)	
				Weighted	Macro	Weighted	Macro	Weighted	macro
C3D [20]	78.79	4.87	50.39	51.26	40.74	50.93	39.29	50.27	39.54
P3D [20]	74.43	4.83	51.37	52.44	40.88	51.83	40.72	51.32	40.18
I3D-RGB [1]	33.48	4.53	51.84	52.58	41.83	51.78	40.39	51.65	40.41
Resnet18+LSTM [8]	31.53	4.55	50.67	51.45	40.23	50.75	39.9	50.54	39.48
CAER-Net [11]	22.81	4.37	50.58	50.02	40.96	50.32	39.74	50.29	39.82
FAN [6]	34.18	4.58	56.48	58.22	47.23	56.48	47.95	56.36	47.21
Former-DFER [29]	146.78	5.13	61.43	62.76	49.94	62.09	51.51	60.76	50.46
Ours	42.52	4.78	**62.23**	**63.31**	**51.79**	**62.34**	**54.42**	**61.35**	**52.12**

negatively impacting macro metrics. Former-DFER utilizes a transformer-based architecture designed to handle long-range dependencies and global relationships between features. However, its large number of parameters and high computational cost limit its performance. These findings emphasize the importance of addressing class imbalance in emotion recognition tasks and our approach's potential to enhance minority class recognition. In summary, our proposed approach demonstrates superior performance in accuracy, precision, recall, and computational efficiency on both DFEW and AFEW datasets, achieving optimal results with limited computational resources, showcasing its effectiveness in real-world scenarios.

Table 2. The comparative results with other SOTA methods on the AFEW dataset. Best in **bold**, second best in underline.

Method	ACC (%)	Precision (%)		Recall (%)		F-1 score (%)	
		Weighted	Macro	Weighted	Macro	Weighted	macro
C3D [20]	37.46	39.85	34.15	37.66	32.19	34.79	32.23
P3D [20]	36.79	38.49	34.34	36.45	32.24	33.94	32.39
I3D-RGB [1]	37.46	39.61	35.85	37.54	33.53	35.27	33.87
Resnet18+LSTM [8]	38.78	40.54	36.34	38.78	33.86	35.96	34.05
CAER-Net [11]	41.59	43.92	39.88	41.49	37.65	39.84	37.75
FAN [6]	44.58	46.84	42.59	44.13	40.98	42.65	40.47
Former-DFER [29]	47.58	49.03	46.18	47.92	44.42	45.25	42.68
Ours	**48.23**	**49.76**	**48.88**	**48.68**	**46.91**	**46.53**	**43.94**

To thoroughly evaluate and compare our proposed approach with existing advanced methods, we analyzed the ACC for each category on the DFEW dataset and visualized the confusion matrices for both the Former-DFER and DS-DFER models applied to the AFEW dataset, as shown in Fig. 4. Our aim is

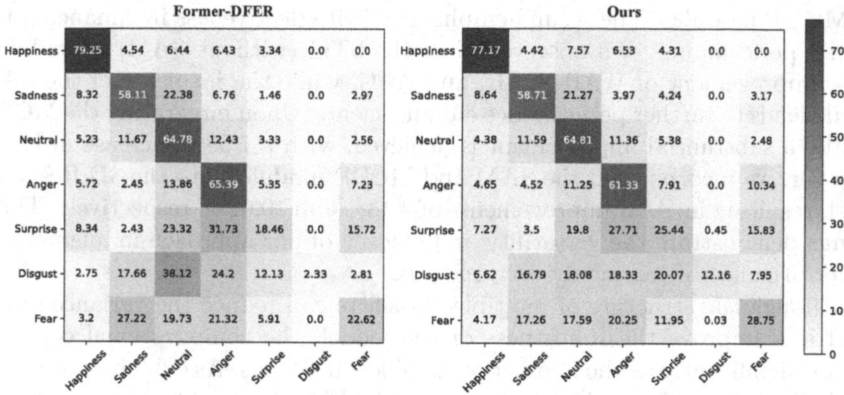

Fig. 4. Confusion matrices on AFEW.

to maximize performance with minimal computational cost, and through experimentation, we determined that using three classifiers was optimal, striking a balance between efficiency and performance. As depicted in Fig. 4, our model demonstrates comparable performance to the Former-DFER for majority classes (happy, sad, neutral, and anger), while outperforming it in minority classes (surprise, disgust, and fear). For example, our model achieves a significantly higher recall of 12.16% for the "disgust" class, nearly six times greater than the Former-DFER's 2.33%. This improvement underscores the effectiveness of our MCDP module in better learning and recognizing minority class expressions compared to existing state-of-the-art methods.

4.3 Ablation Study

Table 3. Ablation study on DFEW dataset.

Method	WAR (%)	UAR (%)	Acc (%)
3D Resnet34 [8]	45.64	35.73	45.64
3D Resnet34+SAM	49.48	39.86	49.43
3D Resnet34+SAM+MCDP	58.18	50.48	58.34
STC(w/o SAM)	53.67	42.75	53.15
STC	56.76	46.44	56.76
STC+SAM+MCDP	**62.34**	**54.42**	**62.23**

Table 3 presents the results of our ablation study conducted on the DFEW dataset, which investigates the learning ability contributions of the individual components of our RS-DFER model by incrementally incorporating the SAM and MCDP modules. The results emphasize their effectiveness in enhancing the model's performance. We observed that the STC (without SAM) contributes to the improvement of WAR, UAR, and ACC, while the inclusion of the SAM module leads to further performance enhancements. Upon integrating the MCDP module, a substantial improvement is achieved, with a 7.98% increase in UAR. Moreover, we incorporated the SAM and MCDP modules into the 3D Resnet34 model, resulting in UAR improvements of 4.13% and 10.62%, respectively. These findings demonstrate the versatility and efficacy of our approach in augmenting the performance of commonly used models.

Although the structure of multiple classifiers can reduce the variance of the model and improve the robustness of the model, the computational cost will increase significantly as the number of classifiers increases. As exhibited in Fig. 5, we calculated ACC for each category on the DFEW dataset, the number of classifiers is added from 1 to 5, and the curve represents the trend of ACC for each category as the number of classifiers increases. Our objective is to enhance model performance while minimizing computational cost. Following experimentation, we determined that utilizing three classifiers was the most appropriate configuration. This finding provides evidence that a judicious balance between computational efficiency and model performance can be achieved by carefully selecting the number of classifiers in the model architecture.

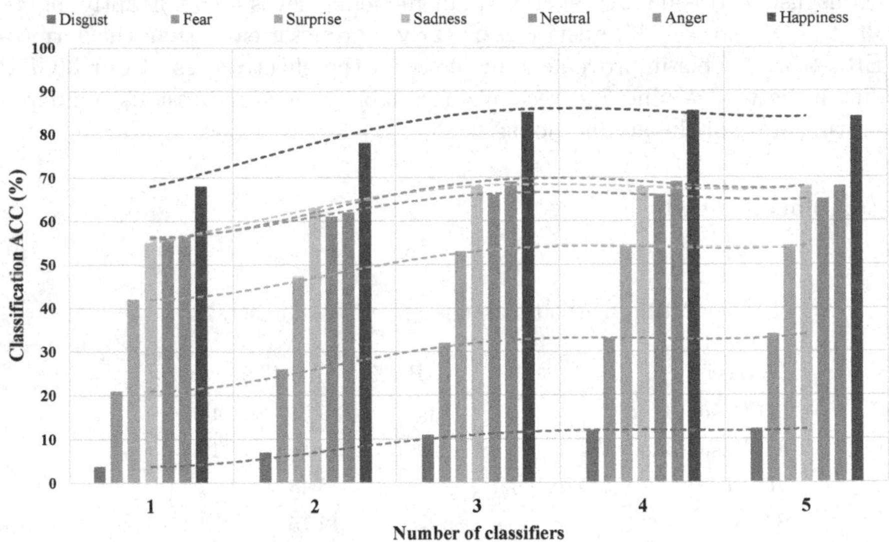

Fig. 5. Classification accuracy for the seven basic expressions with different numbers of experts.

4.4 Visualization of Heatmap

In order to investigate the areas of interest within the model during the training process, we utilized the Grad-CAM [18] technique to perform attention visualization on the AFEW dataset. Specifically, we applied Grad-CAM to our proposed RS-DFER model and compared it to RS-DFER without SAM. We calculated the Grad-CAM masks for the last convolutional outputs, and the results of the comparison were presented in Fig. 6. Our results suggest that incorporating SAM enhances the model's capacity to encompass the entire face while concentrating on critical facial regions. To achieve spatial attention features, we performed a global average pooling and maximum pooling and added the two features together. We then established the spatial correlation while maintaining the original dimension through convolutional operations. Finally, we obtained the spatial attention weight and applied it to the original feature map to extract more effective information from the input images. Our approach enables the model to focus on the most informative regions of the face, enhancing the overall recognition accuracy and improving the model's ability to generalize to new and challenging facial expressions.

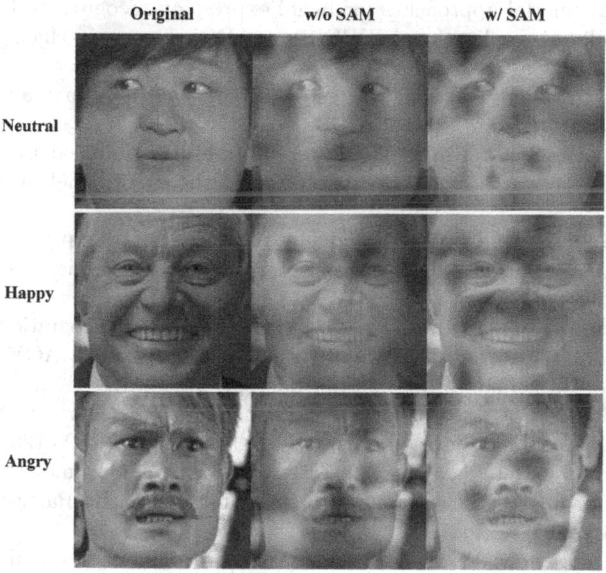

Fig. 6. The heatmap visualizations. The hotter an area is with red color, and the more feature information is adopted by the model. (Color figure online)

5 Conclusion

In this paper, we propose the RS-DFER framework for DFER in real-world scenarios. By incorporating SAM into the STC module for spatiotemporal feature extraction and dynamically combining evidence and uncertainty within the

MCDP, we effectively address the challenges encountered in real-world contexts. We evaluate the RS-DFER on multiple datasets using various metrics, and the experimental results demonstrate that our approach outperforms existing methods in real-world scenarios. Looking ahead, we anticipate further advancements in real-world DFER by exploring more robust and adaptive feature extraction techniques, as well as developing sophisticated algorithms capable of efficiently handling diverse and challenging real-world conditions.

Acknowledgements. This work was supported in part by the Taishan Scholars Program: Key R&D Plan of Shandong Province (NO. 2020CXGC010111), Distinguished Taishan Scholars in Climbing Plan (NO. tspd20181211) and Young Taishan Scholars (NO. tsqn201909137).

References

1. Carreira, J., Zisserman, A.: Quo vadis, action recognition? a new model and the kinetics dataset. In: proceedings of the IEEE Conference on Computer Vision and Pattern Recognition, pp. 6299–6308 (2017)
2. Corneanu, C.A., Simón, M.O., Cohn, J.F., Guerrero, S.E.: Survey on rgb, 3d, thermal, and multimodal approaches for facial expression recognition: history, trends, and affect-related applications. IEEE Trans. Pattern Anal. Mach. Intell. **38**(8), 1548–1568 (2016)
3. Darwin, C., Prodger, P.: The expression of the emotions in man and animals. Oxford University Press, USA (1998)
4. Dempster, A.P., et al.: Upper and lower probabilities induced by a multivalued mapping. Classic works of the Dempster-Shafer theory of belief functions **219**(2), 57–72 (2008)
5. Dhall, A., Goecke, R., Lucey, S., Gedeon, T.: Acted facial expressions in the wild database. Australian National University, Canberra, Australia, Technical Report TR-CS-11 2, 1 (2011)
6. Fan, Y., Lu, X., Li, D., Liu, Y.: Video-based emotion recognition using CNN-RNN and c3d hybrid networks. In: Proceedings of the 18th ACM International Conference on Multimodal Interaction, pp. 445–450 (2016)
7. Guerdelli, H., Ferrari, C., Barhoumi, W., Ghazouani, H., Berretti, S.: Macro-and micro-expressions facial datasets: a survey. Sensors **22**(4), 1524 (2022)
8. He, K., Zhang, X., Ren, S., Sun, J.: Deep residual learning for image recognition. In: Proceedings of the IEEE Conference on Computer Vision and Pattern Recognition, pp. 770–778 (2016)
9. Jiang, X., et al.: Dfew: a large-scale database for recognizing dynamic facial expressions in the wild. In: Proceedings of the 28th ACM International Conference on Multimedia, pp. 2881–2889 (2020)
10. King, D.E.: Dlib-ml: a machine learning toolkit. J. Mach. Learn. Res. **10**, 1755–1758 (2009)
11. Lee, J., Kim, S., Kim, S., Park, J., Sohn, K.: Context-aware emotion recognition networks. In: Proceedings of the IEEE/CVF International Conference on Computer Vision, pp. 10143–10152 (2019)
12. Li, B., Han, Z., Li, H., Fu, H., Zhang, C.: Trustworthy long-tailed classification. In: Proceedings of the IEEE/CVF Conference on Computer Vision and Pattern Recognition, pp. 6970–6979 (2022)

13. Liu, M., Shan, S., Wang, R., Chen, X.: Learning expressionlets on spatio-temporal manifold for dynamic facial expression recognition. In: Proceedings of the IEEE Conference on Computer Vision and Pattern Recognition, pp. 1749–1756 (2014)
14. Lucey, P., Cohn, J.F., Kanade, T., Saragih, J., Ambadar, Z., Matthews, I.: The extended cohn-kanade dataset (ck+): a complete dataset for action unit and emotion-specified expression. In: 2010 IEEE Computer Society Conference on Computer Vision and Pattern Recognition-Workshops, pp. 94–101. IEEE (2010)
15. Meng, D., Peng, X., Wang, K., Qiao, Y.: Frame attention networks for facial expression recognition in videos. In: 2019 IEEE International Conference on Image Processing (ICIP), pp. 3866–3870. IEEE (2019)
16. Pantic, M., Valstar, M., Rademaker, R., Maat, L.: Web-based database for facial expression analysis. In: 2005 IEEE International Conference on Multimedia and Expo, pp. 5-pp. IEEE (2005)
17. Rössler, A., Cozzolino, D., Verdoliva, L., Riess, C., Thies, J., Niessner, M.: Faceforensics++: learning to detect manipulated facial images. In: 2019 IEEE/CVF International Conference on Computer Vision (ICCV), pp. 1–11. IEEE Computer Society, Los Alamitos, November 2019. https://doi.org/10.1109/ICCV.2019.00009
18. Selvaraju, R.R., Cogswell, M., Das, A., Vedantam, R., Parikh, D., Batra, D.: Grad-cam: visual explanations from deep networks via gradient-based localization. In: Proceedings of the IEEE International Conference on Computer Vision, pp. 618–626 (2017)
19. Sensoy, M., Kaplan, L., Kandemir, M.: Evidential deep learning to quantify classification uncertainty. In: Advances in Neural Information Processing Systems 31 (2018)
20. Tran, D., Bourdev, L., Fergus, R., Torresani, L., Paluri, M.: Learning spatiotemporal features with 3D convolutional networks. In: Proceedings of the IEEE International Conference on Computer Vision, pp. 4489–4497 (2015)
21. Wang, T., Cheng, H., Chow, K.P., Nie, L.: Deep convolutional pooling transformer for deepfake detection. ACM Trans. Multimed. Comput. Commun. Appl. **19**(6) (2023). https://doi.org/10.1145/3588574
22. Wang, T., Chow, K.P.: Noise based deepfake detection via multi-head relative-interaction. Proceedings of the AAAI Conference on Artificial Intelligence **37**(12), pp. 14548–14556 (2023). https://doi.org/10.1609/aaai.v37i12.26701
23. Wang, T., Liu, M., Cao, W., Chow, K.P.: Deepfake noise investigation and detection. Forensic Sci. Int. Digital Investigation **42**, 301395 (2022). https://doi.org/10.1016/j.fsidi.2022.301395. proceedings of the Twenty-Second Annual DFRWS USA
24. Xiang, L., Ding, G., Han, J.: Learning from multiple experts: Self-paced knowledge distillation for long-tailed classification. In: Computer Vision-ECCV 2020: 16th European Conference, Glasgow, UK, August 23–28, 2020, Proceedings, Part V 16. pp. 247–263. Springer (2020)
25. Yu, Y., Si, X., Hu, C., Zhang, J.: A review of recurrent neural networks: LSTM cells and network architectures. Neural Comput. **31**(7), 1235–1270 (2019)
26. Zagoruyko, S., Komodakis, N.: Paying more attention to attention: Improving the performance of convolutional neural networks via attention transfer. arXiv preprint arXiv:1612.03928 (2016)
27. Zhang, Y., Wang, T., Shu, M., Wang, Y.: A robust lightweight deepfake detection network using transformers. In: PRICAI 2022: Trends in Artificial Intelligence: 19th Pacific Rim International Conference on Artificial Intelligence, PRICAI 2022, Shanghai, China, November 10–13, 2022, Proceedings, Part I, pp. 275–288. Springer, Heidelberg (2022). https://doi.org/10.1007/978-3-031-20862-1_20

28. Zhao, G., Huang, X., Taini, M., Li, S.Z., Pietikälnen, M.: Facial expression recognition from near-infrared videos. Image Vis. Comput. **29**(9), 607–619 (2011)
29. Zhao, Z., Liu, Q.: Former-dfer: dynamic facial expression recognition transformer. In: Proceedings of the 29th ACM International Conference on Multimedia, pp. 1553–1561 (2021)
30. Zhong, L., Liu, Q., Yang, P., Liu, B., Huang, J., Metaxas, D.N.: Learning active facial patches for expression analysis. In: 2012 IEEE Conference on Computer Vision and Pattern Recognition, pp. 2562–2569. IEEE (2012)

End-to-End Remote Sensing Change Detection of Unregistered Bi-temporal Images for Natural Disasters

Guiqin Zhao, Lianlei Shan, and Weiqiang Wang(✉)

School of Computer Science and Technology, University of Chinese Academy of Sciences, Beijing 100049, China
{zhaoguiqin20,shanlianlei18}@mails.ucas.edu.cn, wqwang@ucas.ac.cn

Abstract. Change detection based on remote sensing images has been a prominent area of interest in the field of remote sensing. Deep networks have demonstrated significant success in detecting changes in bi-temporal remote sensing images and have found applications in various fields. Given the degradation of natural environments and the frequent occurrence of natural disasters, accurately and swiftly identifying damaged buildings in disaster-stricken areas through remote sensing images holds immense significance. This paper aims to investigate change detection specifically for natural disasters. Considering that existing public datasets used in change detection research are registered, which does not align with the practical scenario where bi-temporal images are not matched, this paper introduces an unregistered end-to-end change detection synthetic dataset called xBD-E2ECD. Furthermore, we propose an end-to-end change detection network named E2ECDNet, which takes an unregistered bi-temporal image pair as input and simultaneously generates the flow field prediction result and the change detection prediction result. It is worth noting that our E2ECDNet also supports change detection for registered image pairs, as registration can be seen as a special case of non-registration. Additionally, this paper redefines the criteria for correctly predicting a positive case and introduces neighborhood-based change detection evaluation metrics. The experimental results have demonstrated significant improvements.

Keywords: Change detection · Registration · End-to-end · Synthetic dataset · Remote sensing

1 Introduction

The purpose of change detection in remote sensing images is to identify differences in objects or natural phenomena between different states. This is achieved by comparing images taken at different times but from the same geographic area, resulting in the generation of a change map. The research on change detection based on remote sensing images has been a prominent and long-standing focus

L. Iliadis et al. (Eds.): ICANN 2023, LNCS 14255, pp. 259–270, 2023.
https://doi.org/10.1007/978-3-031-44210-0_21

in the field. It plays a crucial role in providing valuable information for decision-making in various domains, such as urban expansion [13], regional changes in lake surfaces [16], and damage assessment [21].

In light of the degradation of the natural environment and the frequent occurrence of natural disasters, accurately and swiftly identifying damaged buildings in disaster areas through remote sensing images holds immense significance for analyzing the disaster situation and guiding subsequent emergency rescue efforts. However, existing change detection datasets are pre-registered using tools, which does not align with the practical scenario where images obtained at different times may not be well-matched due to variations in azimuth and shooting angles. In the event of a natural disaster, immediate change detection is desired, but separate registration would consume additional time. Furthermore, registration using tools requires specific information such as geographic coordinates and projection details, which may not always be available or may have been lost. Therefore, this paper aims to investigate end-to-end change detection for natural disasters, where bi-temporal image registration and change detection are simultaneously performed using deep networks. To the best of our knowledge, we are the first to focus on change detection of unregistered image pairs. It is important to note that registration can be considered a special case of non-registration, and our approach is also applicable to change detection for registered image pairs.

As existing public datasets for change detection are all registered, collecting unregistered bi-temporal image pairs and manually annotating them would require substantial time and effort. To address this, this paper introduces the xBD-E2ECD dataset, a synthetic dataset specifically designed for unregistered end-to-end change detection in natural disasters. Additionally, the paper proposes the E2ECDNet, an end-to-end change detection network that simultaneously predicts the flow field and change detection for unregistered bi-temporal image pairs. In contrast to single registration and single change detection approaches, the end-to-end framework in this paper considers the interplay between change detection and registration results. The presence of changing pixels increases the complexity of image registration, while the inaccuracies in image registration further complicate change detection. As image registration cannot achieve perfect accuracy, it is highly likely that pixels in the vicinity of a positive pixel are predicted as belonging to the changed class. To address this, the paper redefines the case of correctly predicting a positive and proposes neighborhood-based change detection evaluation criteria. The experimental results demonstrate significant improvements.

Deep networks have achieved significant success in both change detection and image registration. However, to the best of our knowledge, there is currently no research on integrating registration and change detection. Therefore, the objective of this paper is to investigate the end-to-end change detection of unregistered image pairs for natural disasters. The main contributions of this study are as follows:

- We construct the xBD-E2ECD dataset, a synthetic dataset specifically designed for unregistered end-to-end change detection in natural disasters. This dataset is built upon the xBD dataset [9].
- We propose the E2ECDNet, an end-to-end change detection network that takes unregistered bi-temporal image pairs as input and simultaneously predicts the flow field and change detection.
- We redefine the criteria for correctly predicting a positive case and introduce neighborhood-based change detection evaluation criteria specifically tailored for end-to-end change detection.

2 Related Work

2.1 Image Registration

Image registration aims to establish pixel-to-pixel correspondence between two images and warp the floating image to align with the reference image based on their spatial mapping. Convolutional neural networks (CNNs) have been widely used to solve the problem of image correspondence. Given an input image pair, CNNs can generate pixel-level dense correspondence known as the flow field. By rearranging the pixels of the floating image according to the flow field, it can be aligned with the reference image. Dosovitskiy et al. [7] constructed the first trainable CNN for light flow estimation, called FlowNet, which utilized a U-Net denoising autoencoder architecture [20]. PWC-Net [17,18], LiteFlowNet [11], and LiteFlowNet2 [12] employed multiple constrained correlation layers on a feature pyramid. These networks warp features at each level using the current flow estimate, resulting in a more compact and efficient architecture. GLUNet [19] combines global and local correlations to achieve more accurate dense correspondence prediction. Rocco et al. [15] improved the performance of the global correlation layer by proposing an end-to-end training neighbor consensus network, NC-Net, which filters out ambiguous matches and preserves locally and cyclically consistent matches.

2.2 Change Detection

Change detection aims to predict whether there are pixel-level changes between the input image pair. Deep networks have achieved remarkable success in bi-temporal remote sensing image change detection. Zhan et al. [22] were the first to introduce the siamese convolutional network to address the problem of bi-temporal remote sensing image change detection, achieving excellent results. Since then, several change detection methods based on siamese structures have been proposed, yielding good detection outcomes. Daudt et al. [6] designed three effective change detection architectures based on fully convolutional neural networks (FCNN): Fully Convolutional Early Fusion (FC-EF), Fully Convolutional Siamese-Concatenation (FC-Siam-conc), and Fully Convolutional Siamese-Difference (FC-Siam-diff). The main difference among these networks lies in the way they fuse bi-temporal information. Subsequently, to capture global information in space-time, some methods have addressed the limitations of convolutional operations by enlarging the receptive field (RF). For instance, [3,5] employ ResNet [10] as the backbone network, [1] replaces traditional convolution with dilated convolution, and [8,14] incorporate attention mechanisms. Moreover, BiT [4] and changeFormer [2] further introduce the transformer to enhance change detection performance.

3 Approach

3.1 End-to-End Change Detection Dataset:xBD-E2ECD

In this paper, we propose an end-to-end change detection dataset called xBD-E2ECD, which is synthesized using random affine transformations based on xBD [?], a dataset for natural disaster building detection. xBD is a large-scale dataset designed for building damage assessment and covers ten natural disaster events, including hurricane-florence, hurricane-matthew, mexico-earthquake, midwest-flooding, social-fire, santa-rosa-wildfire, hurricane-michael, hurricane harvey, palu-tsunami, and guatemala volcano. It provides pre-event and post-event satellite images with a size of 1024×1024, and each image contains at least one building. The dataset includes four damage types: no damage, minor damage, serious damage, and destructive damage. For post-event images, both the vertex coordinates and the damage type for each building polygon are recorded. For pre-event images, only the vertex coordinates for each building polygon are recorded, indicating that the buildings in the pre-event images are assumed to have no damage.

Algorithm for Establishing XBD-E2ECD. The pre-event and post-event images in xBD [9] are already well registered, but xBD only provides annotations for each building in each individual pre-event or post-event image, without directly providing change detection annotations for each pre-event and post-event image pair. Therefore, the algorithm for synthesizing xBD-E2ECD in this paper is carried out in two steps. First, we establish the change detection dataset xBD-CD by generating change detection labels for each registered pre-event and post-event image pair. Specifically, we consider the building areas that do not overlap before and after the event, as well as the building areas that overlap but have different damage types before and after the event, as the change areas. Second, based on xBD-CD, we synthesize the unregistered end-to-end change detection dataset xBD-E2ECD using random affine transformations. These transformations simulate the differences in altitude and azimuth of the aircraft when capturing images at two different times. Additionally, we record the coordinate offsets after the transformation as flow field annotations and generate masks that mark valid positions as one and invalid positions as zero. A position in the transformed image is considered valid if it corresponds to a position in the image before the transformation. The training set, test set, and hold set are divided according to the original split of xBD [9].

Furthermore, we analyze the frequency distribution of images with different numbers of positive pixels for each disaster type using histograms. We observe that there is a significant number of images with fewer than 10 or 100 positive pixels. To alleviate data imbalance, we remove the image pairs with fewer than 100 positive pixels and obtain the final dataset. The final distribution is shown in Table 1.

Table 1. Data distribution under different disaster types. I (image) represents the number of images, P (positive) represents the number of pixels belonging to the changed class in the valid area and N (negative) represents the number of pixels belonging to the unchanged class in the valid area.

event	–	train	hold	test	total
hurricane-florence	I	579	189	183	951
	P	1218960	297029	247438	1763427
	N	31161032	10355293	9934175	51450500
hurricane-matthew	I	1389	550	417	2356
	P	3146652	1591310	1029829	5767791
	N	74478688	28932865	22343437	125754990
mexico-earthquake	I	74	17	50	141
	P	153040	45563	97266	295869
	N	3959912	879175	2707642	7546729
midwest-flooding	I	187	61	68	316
	P	243350	107143	120906	471399
	N	10274063	3384751	3682900	17341714
social-fire	I	532	180	199	911
	P	3477243	1346334	999303	5822880
	N	29026719	9845793	10960984	49833496
santa-rosa-wildfire	I	994	352	250	1596
	P	803318	308667	335481	1447466
	N	51830442	18219140	12824843	82874425
hurricane-michael	I	2739	868	753	4360
	P	8820227	2824703	2272364	13917294
	N	143622411	45685385	39663651	228971447
hurricane-harvey	I	1598	544	490	2632
	P	13093228	4427544	3875806	21396578
	N	73694683	25385895	23031376	122111954
palu-tsunami	I	378	132	130	640
	P	2142905	613656	726770	3483331
	N	18601299	6676299	6560098	31837696
guatemala-volcano	I	10	12	3	25
	P	12538	36275	2904	51717
	N	551573	672670	168985	1393228
all	I	8480	2905	2543	13928
	P	33111461	11598224	9708067	54417752
	N	437200822	150037266	131878091	719116179

3.2 End-to-End Change Detection Network: E2ECDNet

Problem Definition. Let $I_s \in R^{H \times W \times 3}$ and $I_t \in R^{H \times W \times 3}$ denote the pre-event image (source image) and the post-event image (target image), respectively. For an unregistered input image pair (I_s, I_t), the goal is to output the flow field $w \in R^{H \times W \times 2}$ for image registration and the change detection probability map $p \in R^{H \times W \times 2}$ for change detection. The flow field $w \in R^{H \times W \times 2}$ represents the pixel-level two-dimensional motion vector, which allows us to warp the source image to the target image using the following equation:

$$I_t(x) \approx I_s(x + w(x)). \tag{1}$$

The change detection probability map $p \in R^{H \times W \times 2}$ indicates the probability of each pixel in the target image being classified as changed or unchanged.

Model Architecture. The overall structure of our model is illustrated in Fig. 1. Firstly, the source image I_s and the target image I_t are separately input into the backbone network with shared weights, resulting in feature maps at four scales: $\frac{1}{4}, \frac{1}{8}, \frac{1}{16}, \frac{1}{32}$. These feature maps are denoted as $F_s^1, F_s^2, F_s^3, F_s^4$ and $F_t^1, F_t^2, F_t^3, F_t^4$. Next, the lowest resolution feature maps F_s^4 and F_t^4 are passed through the global module G_module to obtain the flow prediction w^4. Then, for each scale $\{(F_s^i, F_t^i)\}|i \in \{3, 2, 1\}$, the corresponding feature maps F_s^i and F_t^i, along with the flow prediction w^{i+1} from the previous layer, are input into the local module L_module_i. This allows us to obtain the flow prediction w^i and change detection prediction p^i for the current layer. Finally, the flow prediction w^1 and change detection prediction p^1 are upsampled to w^0 and p^0 at the original resolution using bilinear interpolation.

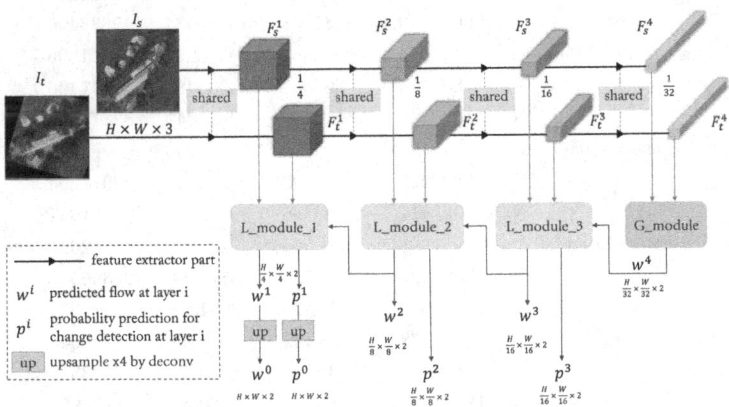

Fig. 1. The overall structure of the proposed net E2ECDNet. Multiscale feature maps are used to predict the flow field and change detection map.

The structures of the global module (G_module) and the local modules (L_modules) are depicted in Fig. 2. More details are given below.

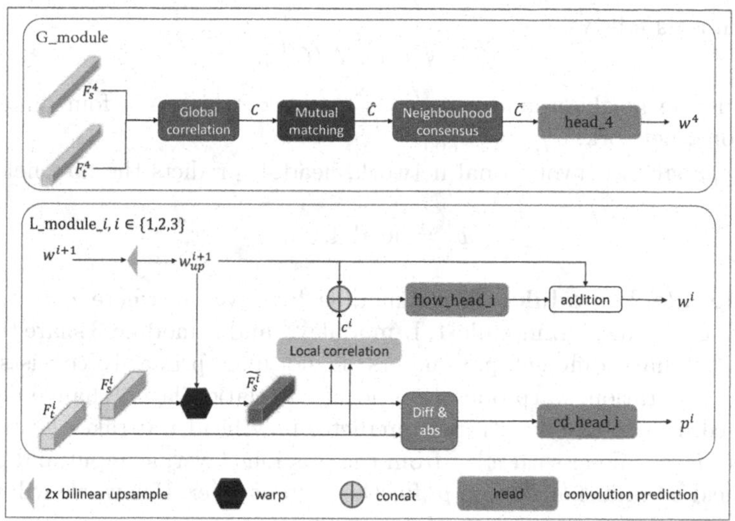

Fig. 2. G_module and L_modules: G_module predicts the flow field at scale $i = 4$. L_module takes F_s^i and F_t^i of the current layer, along with w^{i+1} of the previous layer, as input and predicts the flow field w^i and the change map p^i of the current layer.

Global Module G_module: The G_module comprises the global correlation layer, mutual matching layer, neighbourhood consensus layer, and prediction head head_4. This module is specifically applied to the lowest resolution level (F_s^4, F_t^4) due to its high computational requirements.

The global correlation layer is commonly employed to handle large displacements. It computes the similarity between the feature vectors of each position in F_t^4 and F_s^4, resulting in the global correlation map $C \in R^{\frac{H}{32} \times \frac{W}{32} \times \frac{H}{32} \times \frac{W}{32}}$. Mathematically, this can be expressed as:

$$C_{ijkl} = \frac{F_t^4(i,j)^T F_s^4(k,l)}{\|F_t^4(i,j)\| \|F_s^4(k,l)\|}. \tag{2}$$

The mutual matching layer, proposed by [15], is utilized to mitigate false matches. It suppresses the similarity scores of incorrect matches and retains only the similarity scores of the best matches for each other. Mathematically, this can be expressed as:

$$\hat{C}_{ijkl} = r_{ijkl}^s r_{ijkl}^t C_{ijkl} \tag{3}$$

$$r_{ijkl}^s = \frac{C_{ijkl}}{\max_{ab} C_{abkl}} \tag{4}$$

$$r_{ijkl}^t = \frac{C_{ijkl}}{\max_{cd} C_{ijcd}}. \tag{5}$$

The neighbourhood consensus layer is commonly employed to ensure that the prediction is independent of the order of the images in the image pair. Its calculation is as follows:

$$\tilde{C} = N(\hat{C}) + N(\hat{C}^T), \tag{6}$$

where N is the neighborhood consensus network, which is a four-dimensional convolutional network. $\hat{C}^T_{ijkl} = \hat{C}_{klij}$.

Finally, a small convolutional network, head_4, predicts the flow field w^4 as follows:

$$w^4 = \text{head\_4}(\tilde{C}). \tag{7}$$

Local Module L_module: The L_module for layer i (where $i = 1, 2, 3$) is denoted as L_module_i. L_module_1, L_module_2, and L_module_3 share the same structure but have different parameters. L_module_i primarily consists of the upsampling operation, warp operation, local correlation layer, change detection predictor cd_head_i, and registration predictor flow_head_i. It takes F^i_s and F^i_t of the current layer, along with w^{i+1} from the previous layer, as input and predicts the flow field w^i and change map p^i for the current layer. Below, we will provide a detailed description of the L_module_i module.

Firstly, the flow field prediction w^{i+1} from the previous layer is upsampled to w^{i+1}_{up}. This allows us to warp F^i_s to $\tilde{F^i_s}$ using the following equation:

$$\tilde{F^i_s}(x) = F^i_s(x + w^{i+1}_{up}(x)), \tag{8}$$

where x is a two-dimensional position vector.

Next, L_module_i branches into two paths to predict the flow field w^i and the change detection probability map p^i, respectively.

For the flow field prediction branch, the local correlation layer is employed to model correspondences under small offsets:

$$c^i(x, d) = F^i_t(x)^T \tilde{F^i_s}(x + d), \max |d| \leq r, \tag{9}$$

where x denotes the two-dimensional position coordinate, d represents the position offset from x, and r is the local search radius. In other words, the neighborhood corresponding to x is a square area centered at x with a side length of $2r + 1$. The output $c^i \in R^{\frac{H}{2^i+1} \times \frac{W}{2^i+1} \times (2r+1)^2}$.

The flow field prediction w^i is obtained using the residual mechanism:

$$w^i = w^{i+1}_{up} + \text{flow\_head\_}i(\text{Concat}(c^i, w^{i+1}_{up})), \tag{10}$$

where flow_head_i represents a small convolutional network.

For the change detection prediction branch, we calculate the absolute difference map between $\tilde{F^i_s}$ and F^i_t. This is followed by generating the change detection probability map p^i using the cd_head_i network. Mathematically, we have:

$$p^i = \text{cd\_head\_}i(|\tilde{F^i_s} - F^i_t|), \tag{11}$$

where cd_head_i represents a small convolutional network, and $|\cdot|$ denotes the absolute value operation applied to each element.

4 Results

4.1 Evaluation Metrics

In the end-to-end scenario, due to the possibility of inaccurate image registration, it is likely that pixels in the vicinity of a true positive pixel are predicted as belonging to the changed class. Therefore, we redefine the criteria for correctly predicting a positive and propose neighborhood-based change detection evaluation metrics.

For a pixel a located at (i, j) and belonging to the changed class, we define the square area with a radius of r centered on (i, j) as D. If at least one pixel in D is predicted as belonging to the changed class, we consider a to be correctly detected. Additionally, for all unchanged pixels in D, their corresponding values in the mask are set to 0, ensuring that they do not contribute to the evaluation. Thus, the neighborhood-based change detection evaluation metrics with respect to the radius r are P@r, R@r, F1@r, IoU@r, and OA@r. When r is set to 0, the above evaluation metrics are equivalent to those used in non-end-to-end change detection.

For image registration evaluation, we use the Percentage of Correct Keypoints (PCK-δ) as the metric. Here, δ represents a percentage of the image size, and we set it to 0.05.

4.2 Results: Two-Stage Method vs E2ECDNet

The results obtained from the two-stage change detection method can be considered as an upper limit for the performance of the end-to-end change detection method. Therefore, we conducted experiments using both the two-stage and end-to-end approaches to compare their results. In the two-stage method, we first trained a single registration model on xBD-E2ECD and a single change detection model on registered xBD-E2ECD. These models were then cascaded for testing. To ensure a fair comparison, both the single registration model and single change detection model adopted the same architecture as E2ECDNet.

Table 2 presents the results of the two-stage method. It can be observed that when cascading the models to perform change detection on unregistered image pairs, the performance remains consistent compared to single change detection.

Table 3 displays the results of the two-stage method compared to the end-to-end method (E2ECDNet). Our E2ECDNet achieves considerable R@5 but a lower precision rate compared to the two-stage method. This is because the registration model and change detection model in the two-stage method are trained individually and perform well on their respective tasks. However, in the end-to-end scenario, the presence of changed pixels increases the difficulty of image registration, which in turn affects the accuracy of change detection. Despite this, the two-stage method results in a more complex model and longer training time. On the other hand, our E2ECDNet can rapidly detect almost all changed areas and provide preliminary judgments for identifying damaged areas after natural disasters.

Table 2. Results (%) of the two-stage method on xBD-E2ECD.

two-stage	P	R	F1	IoU	OA	PCK-0.05
single registration	–	–	–	–	–	79.01
single change detection	34.40	79.36	47.99	31.57	88.42	–
cascade	34.37	79.40	47.97	31.56	88.41	79.01

Table 3. Results (%) of the two-stage method vs the end-to-end the two-stage method vs the end-to-end method (E2ECDNet) on xBD-E2ECD.

method	r	P@r	R@r	F1@r	IoU@r	OA@r	PCK-0.05
two-stage	0	34.37	79.40	47.97	31.56	88.41	79.01
	5	48.69	96.90	64.81	47.94	92.47	79.01
E2ECDNet	0	19.78	70.47	30.89	18.27	78.77	79.61
	5	29.22	98.25	45.04	29.07	82.83	79.61

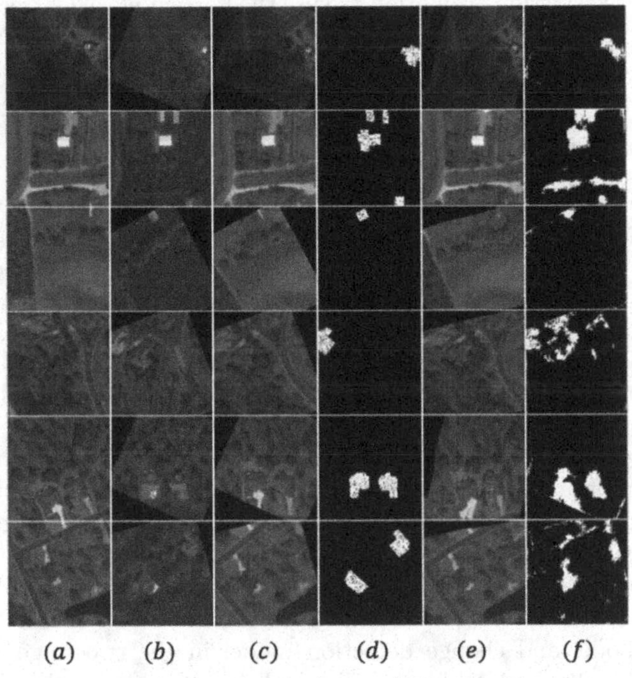

Fig. 3. End-to-end change detection results of our E2ECDNet with resnet34 and multi-scale class balance cross entropy loss on the test set. (a) is the pre-event images, (b) is the post-event images, (c) is the images obtained by warping pre-event images according to the ground truth flow field, (d) is the ground truth change detection maps, (e) is the images obtained by warping the pre-event images according to the predicted flow field, (f) is the predicted change detection maps.

Figure 3 visually presents the end-to-end change detection results obtained by our E2ECDNet on the test set. Due to the inherent limitations of warping pre-event images to their corresponding positions in post-event images, not only are pixels belonging to the changed class predicted as changed, but also the surrounding pixels are often predicted as changed. Additionally, the inaccurate registration process makes pixels belonging to the unchanged class more susceptible to being misclassified as changed.

5 Conclusions

In this study, we have addressed the challenge of incomplete matching in bi-temporal image pairs for change detection in remote sensing. To overcome the limitations of existing registered datasets and the labor-intensive process of collecting unregistered image pairs with manual annotations, we have introduced a novel synthetic dataset called xBD-E2ECD, specifically designed for unregistered end-to-end change detection. Furthermore, we have proposed a novel end-to-end change detection network, E2ECDNet, which takes unregistered bi-temporal image pairs as input and simultaneously predicts the flow field and change map. To evaluate the performance of our approach, we have introduced a neighborhood-based evaluation standard that is well-suited for end-to-end change detection. The experimental results have demonstrated the effectiveness of our proposed method. In our future work, we plan to investigate techniques to reduce the impact of pixel changes on registration and improve the precision of positive predictions.

Acknowledgements. This work is supported by NSFC Key Projects of International (Regional) Cooperation and Exchanges under Grant 61860206004, and NSFC projects under Grant 61976201.

References

1. Zhang, M., Xu, G., Chen, K., Yan, M., Sun, X.: Triplet-based semantic relation learning for aerial remote sensing image change detection. IEEE Geosci. Remote Sens. Lett. **16**(2), 266–270 (2019)
2. Bandara, W.G.C., Patel, V.M.: A transformer-based Siamese network for change detection, pp. 2–5 (2022). http://arxiv.org/abs/2201.01293
3. Chen, H., Shi, Z.: A spatial-temporal attention-based method and a new dataset for remote sensing image change detection. Remote Sens. **12**(10), 1662 (2020)
4. Chen, H., Qi, Z., Shi, Z.: Remote sensing image change detection with transformers. IEEE Trans. Geosci. Remote Sens. **60**, 1–14 (2022)
5. Chen, J., Yuan, Z., Peng, J., Chen, L., Li, H.: DASNet: dual attentive fully convolutional Siamese networks for change detection of high resolution satellite images. IEEE J. Sel. Top. Appl. Earth Obs. Remote Sens. **14**, 1194–1206 (2020)
6. Daudt, R.C., Saux, B.L., Boulch, A.: Fully convolutional siamese networks for change detection. In: 2018 25th IEEE International Conference on Image Processing (ICIP) (2018)

7. Dosovitskiy, A., et al.: FlowNet: learning optical flow with convolutional networks. In: 2015 IEEE International Conference on Computer Vision (ICCV), pp. 2758–2766 (2015). https://doi.org/10.1109/ICCV.2015.316
8. Fang, S., Li, K., Shao, J., Li, Z.: SNUNet-CD: a densely connected Siamese network for change detection of VHR images. IEEE Geosci. Remote Sens. Lett. **19**, 1–5 (2022)
9. Gupta, R., et al.: Creating XBD: a dataset for assessing building damage from satellite imagery. In: CVPR Workshops (2019)
10. He, K., Zhang, X., Ren, S., Sun, J.: Deep residual learning for image recognition. In: 2016 IEEE Conference on Computer Vision and Pattern Recognition (CVPR), pp. 770–778 (2016)
11. Hui, T.W., Tang, X., Loy, C.C.: LiteFlowNet: a lightweight convolutional neural network for optical flow estimation. In: 2018 IEEE/CVF Conference on Computer Vision and Pattern Recognition, pp. 8981–8989 (2018). https://doi.org/10.1109/CVPR.2018.00936
12. Hui, T.W., Tang, X., Loy, C.C.: A Lightweight Optical Flow CNN - Revisiting Data Fidelity and Regularization (2020). http://mmlab.ie.cuhk.edu.hk/projects/LiteFlowNet/
13. Marin, C., Bovolo, F., Bruzzone, L.: Building change detection in multitemporal very high resolution SAR images. IEEE Trans. Geosci. Remote Sens. **53**(5), 2664–2682 (2015)
14. Peng, X., Zhong, R., Li, Z., Li, Q.: Optical remote sensing image change detection based on attention mechanism and image difference. IEEE Trans. Geosci. Remote Sens. **59**(9), 7296–7307 (2021)
15. Rocco, I., Cimpoi, M., Arandjelović, R., Torii, A., Pajdla, T., Sivic, J.: NCNet: neighbourhood consensus networks for estimating image correspondences. IEEE Trans. Pattern Anal. Mach. Intell. **44**(2), 1020–1034 (2022)
16. Rokni, K., Ahmad, A., Selamat, A., Hazini, S.: Water feature extraction and change detection using multitemporal landsat imagery. Remote Sens. **6**(5), 4173–4189 (2014)
17. Sun, D., Yang, X., Liu, M.Y., Kautz, J.: PWC-Net: CNNs for optical flow using pyramid, warping, and cost volume. In: 2018 IEEE/CVF Conference on Computer Vision and Pattern Recognition, pp. 8934–8943 (2018). https://doi.org/10.1109/CVPR.2018.00931
18. Sun, D., Yang, X., Liu, M.Y., Kautz, J.: Models matter, so does training: an empirical study of CNNs for optical flow estimation. IEEE Trans. Pattern Anal. Mach. Intell. **42**(6), 1408–1423 (2020). https://doi.org/10.1109/TPAMI.2019.2894353
19. Truong, P., Danelljan, M., Timofte, R.: GLU-Net: global-local universal network for dense flow and correspondences. In: 2020 IEEE/CVF Conference on Computer Vision and Pattern Recognition (CVPR) (2020)
20. Vincent, P., Larochelle, H., Bengio, Y., Manzagol, P.A.: Extracting and composing robust features with denoising autoencoders. In: Proceedings of the 25th International Conference on Machine Learning, ICML 2008, pp. 1096–1103. Association for Computing Machinery, New York (2008). https://doi.org/10.1145/1390156.1390294
21. Xu, J.Z., Lu, W., Li, Z., Khaitan, P., Zaytseva, V.: Building damage detection in satellite imagery using convolutional neural networks. arXiv (2019)
22. Zhan, Y., Fu, K., Yan, M., Sun, X., Wang, H., Qiu, X.: Change detection based on deep Siamese convolutional network for optical aerial images. IEEE Geosci. Remote Sens. Lett. **14**(10), 1845–1849 (2017)

E-Patcher: A Patch-Based Efficient Network for Fast Whole Slide Images Segmentation

Xiaoshuang Huang[1,3], Shuo Wang[1,3], Jinze Huang[1,3], Yaoguang Wei[1,3], Xinhua Dai[2], Yang Zhao[2], Dong An[1,3], and Xiang Fang[2](✉)

[1] College of Information and Electrical Engineering, China Agricultural University, Beijing 100083, China

[2] Mass Spectrometry Engineering Technology Research Center, Center for Advanced Measurement Science, National Institute of Metrology, Beijing 102200, China
fangxiang@nim.ac.cn

[3] Beijing Engineering and Technology Research Center for Internet of Things in Agriculture, China Agricultural University, Beijing 100083, China

Abstract. UNeXt is a leading medical image segmentation method that employs convolutional and multi-layer perceptron (MLP) structure for its segmentation network. It outperforms other image recognition algorithms, such as MedT and TransUNet, in terms of faster computation speed and has shown great potential for clinical applications. However, its reliance on limited pixel neighborhood information for pixel-level segmentation of large pathological images may lead to inaccurate segmentation of the entire image and overlook important features, resulting in suboptimal segmentation results. To this end, we designed a slight and universal plug-and-play block based patch-level for fully considering local features and global features simultaneously, named "Digging" and "Filling" ViT (DF-ViT) block. Specifically, a "Digging" operation is introduced to randomly select sub-blocks from each sub-patch. Multi-Head Attention (MHA) is then applied to integrate global information into these sub-blocks. The resulting sub-blocks with global semantic features are reassembled into the original feature map, and feature fusion is performed to combine the local and global features. This approach achieves global representation while maintaining a low computational complexity of the model at 0.1424G. Compared to UNeXt, it improves mIoU by 1.07%. Moreover, it reduces the parameter count by 58.50% and the computational workload by 68.09%. Extensive experiments on PAIP 2019 WSI dataset demonstrate that the DF-ViT block significantly enhances computation efficiency while maintaining a high level of accuracy.

Keywords: Efficient Transformer · Medical Image Segmentation · Whole Slide Images

1 Introduction

Whole slide images (WSI) have transformed the field of cancer diagnosis and treatment [25] by facilitating the acquisition of high-resolution digital images of

L. Iliadis et al. (Eds.): ICANN 2023, LNCS 14255, pp. 271–282, 2023.
https://doi.org/10.1007/978-3-031-44210-0_22

tissue samples. Nonetheless, the laborious and potentially error-prone manual analysis of these images remains a critical challenge. To address this challenge, Artificial Intelligence (AI) algorithms have been successfully integrated with WSI technology [24], significantly enhancing the accuracy and efficiency of analysis, thereby allowing for more precise diagnosis and treatment planning. One major application of AI technology in WSI is image segmentation, which is essential for computer-aided diagnosis and image-guided surgery systems [4].

Pixel-Level Segmentation. Over the years, significant efforts have been made in developing efficient and robust AI-based segmentation methods for WSI analysis. UNet [14] has been a notable algorithm in this field, using a convolutional neural network (CNN) with an encoder and a decoder to extract features and map them back to the pixel-level of the original image. Since the development of UNet [14], several key extensions have been introduced, such as Unet++ [26], ResUnet++ [7], TransUNet [2], and Swin-Unet [1], with Swin-Unet [1] being the most successful in our experiments. As shown in Fig. 1, Swin-Unet [1] is a highly effective segmentation model that uses hierarchical Swin Transformer with shifted windows as the encoder to extract context features and a symmetric Swin Transformer-based decoder with patch expanding layer is designed to perform the upsampling operation to restore the spatial resolution of the feature maps. Due to the great representational ability of Swin Transformer Block, Swin-Unet [1] has excellent performance and generalization ability. Other successful image segmentation models based on transformer architecture include MedT [19], but it infers slowly. UNeXt [20] is developed as an effective alternative, combining an early convolutional stage with an MLP stage in the latent stage. Although the UNeXt [20] model can improve computational efficiency and reduce parameters, its accuracy on WSI segmentation task still needs to be improved. While pixel-level segmentation is a commonly used method, it can be computationally expensive due to the large number of high-resolution patches in each image.

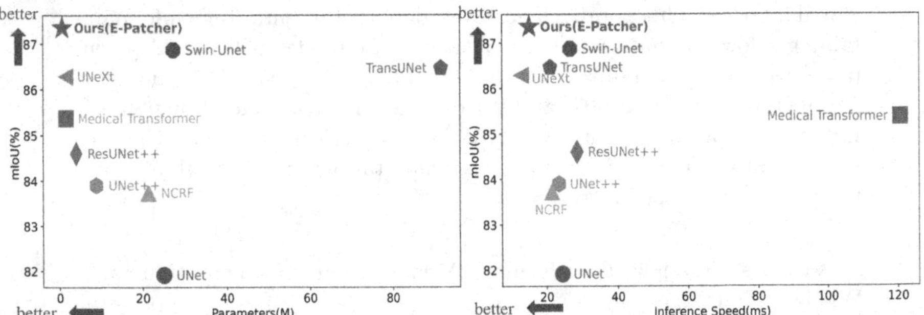

Fig. 1. Comparison of the existing medical segmentation model and ours.

Patch-Level Segmentation. Patch-level segmentation is an approach for analyzing WSI images that involves dividing large images into smaller patches and analyzing each patch individually [6,22], as an alternative to pixel-level segmentation and this method reduces computational costs and inference time. Moeskops et al. [13] extract patches of different sizes centred at the same pixel location on a separated branch of a CNN, yielding multiple-scale features which are then combined for the final prediction. Instead of extracting multiple patches at different scales, Kong et al. [9] use a CNN with a 2-dimensional long-short term (LSTM) architecture to learn spatial dependencies of image patches and their neighbours. But the existing models [9,13,17,18,23] focus on multi-scale input to improve accuracy, which is time consuming. Li et al. [10] propose a neural conditional random field (NCRF) deep learning framework to detect cancer metastasis in WSIs. NCRF considers the spatial correlations between neighboring patches through a fully connected CRF which is directly incorporated on top of a CNN feature extractor. Nevertheless, its global characterization capability is limited.

To further enhance the effectiveness of patch-level segmentation in WSI analysis, we have developed the DF-ViT block, which is a lightweight and universal plug-and-play block based patch-level model that considers both local and global features simultaneously. Our model employs a "Digging" operation to perform Multi-Head Attention (MHA) representation on randomly selected sub-blocks of each sub-patch. We then utilize a "Filling" operation to integrate the representation of sub-blocks back into the local feature map and perform feature fusion, which ensures global representation while keeping the computational complexity of the model to only 0.1424G. In this paper, our contributions can be summarized as follows:

1. We propose a new lightweight baseline model that outperforms MobileViTv1 in analyzing high-resolution images with greater efficiency;
2. We develop a new plug-and-play block, named the DF-ViT block, which ensures faster inference and requires smaller computational effort;
3. Our experiments demonstrate that the DF-ViT block exhibits superior characterization capabilities compared to original MobileViT;
4. Based on the patch-level approach, we propose an efficient WSI segmentation model and validate its performance on a publicly available dataset. Our model achieves state-of-the-art performance, confirming the effectiveness of our approach in WSI analysis.

2 Methods

The overall architecture is developed based on the MobileViT, as shown in Fig. 2. Specifically, DF-ViT block is achieved through three stages: (1) Local Representation and Digging Sub-blocks; (2) Sub-blocks Global Representation; (3) Filling and Fusion. Meanwhile, our segmentation model is based on patch level, so there is no upsampling and various fusion processes of coarse-grained and fine-grained features from the common segmentation model. We will present our novelty work detailed in the following sections.

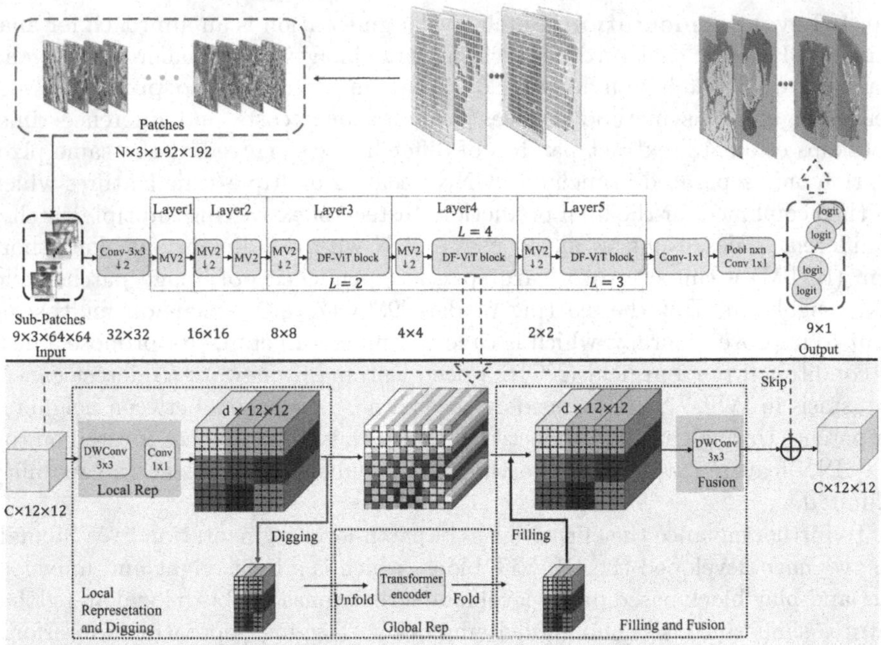

Fig. 2. Overview of the proposed model. It consists of MobileNetv2 [15] blocks and DF-ViT blocks. Note that the shape of input in the figure is shown schematically. Higher-resolution images will be applied in the model.

2.1 Local Representation and Digging

In the ordinary vision transformer encoder, the pixels correspond to tokens clearly in multi-head attention. However, the downsampling operation involves other information which makes strong redundant information between neighborhoods, damaging the performance of model and slowing down the inference efficiency. In MobileViT [11,12,21], they choose to use attention operations on the same position of different tokens, which improves the performance of the transformer in the image domain to some extent, but they still has some information redundancy for ultra-high resolution images like WSIs, which is to address issue in this section.

Specifically, the input of a DF-ViT block is defined as $X \in \mathbb{R}^{C\times H\times W}$, DF-ViT block applies depthwise 3×3 separable convolution and a point-wise convolution to produce $X_L \in \mathbb{R}^{d\times H\times W}$, where d is the dimension of the transformer and $d > C_{in}$. The depthwise 3×3 separable convolution is used to learn local spatial information of sub-patches (all sub-patches in the same DF-ViT block have same dimensions). And the point-wise convolution projects the features to a high-dimensional space by learning linear combinations of the input channels C_{in}. Then, Let $sub\_blocks = w_{i,j} * sub\_block\_rate$, where i, j is the coordinate of sub-patch and sub_block_rate is a hyper-parameter that we set it is $0.5, 0.5, 1$

at layer 3, 4, 5 respectively. Then we use the "Digging" operation on it. The representative feature map after Digging can be expressed as:

$$\hat{X}_{a,k} = X_{La,b}, 0 \leq a < h_{i,j}, 0 \leq b < w_{i,j} |\ k = idx \textbf{ mod } sub\_blocks \quad (1)$$

where $\hat{X}$ denotes the output of each sub-patch of Digging and idx is the serial number of sub-block in sub-patch. The $h_{i,j}$ and $w_{i,j}$ is the height and width of the sub-patch and a, b represent the coordinates of sub-blocks in X_L. So n sub-blocks are randomly selected for each row of each sub-patch (with the same "Digging" operation for all other sub-patches) to form a temporary feature map to represent the current sub-patch for the subsequent global characterization. It is worth noting that the sub-blocks of different sub-patches in the same batch follow the strategy of picking the same position to make up for spatial inductive biases because the transformer encoder lacks image-specific inductive bias. Briefly, if we consider the output of local representation and Digging is $\mathcal{Y}(\cdot;\phi)$, that can be expressed as:

$$\mathcal{Y}(\cdot;\phi) = \mathcal{D}(\mathcal{L}(\cdot;\phi)) \quad (2)$$

where $\mathcal{L}(\cdot;\phi)$ is local representation with parameters ϕ, and $\mathcal{D}(\cdot;)$ denotes the mapping function of "Digging".

2.2 Global Representation with Sub-blocks

As mentioned above, we get n sub-blocks at each sub-patch. The whole sub-blocks feature maps is $d \times W_{\text{sub\_blocks\_fm}} \times H_{\text{sub\_blocks\_fm}}$, where $W_{\text{sub\_blocks\_fm}} = \frac{W}{w} \times sub\_blocks$ and $H_{\text{sub\_blocks\_fm}} = H$. To learn global representations with spatial inductive bias, we unfold $\hat{X}$ into N non-overlapping flattened sub-blocks (united by sub-block) $X_U \in R^{P \times N \times d}$, where $P = sub\_blocks \times h$, $N = \frac{W}{w} \times \frac{H}{h}$ is the number of sub-blocks, Then we use transformer encoders to encode each sub-block, which can be expressed as:

$$X_G(p) = \text{Transformer}(X_U(p)), 1 \leq p \leq P \quad (3)$$

After the global representation is done, we do a fold operation on X_G to get a new feature map $\hat{X}'$, with the same shape as $\hat{X}$. Briefly, we can consider global representation is a feature extractor $\mathcal{T}(\cdot;\theta)$ with parameters θ.

2.3 Filling and Fusion

In traditional approaches, interpolation upsampling or transposed convolution are used to map shape to the shape of X_L to use concatenation. In MobileViTv1 [11] and MobileViTv3 [21], both feature fusion use concatenation first, and then use convolution. However, concatenation directly double the number of channels in the feature map, and the quantities of computation increase twice, which is not efficient enough. Therefore, we propose a way to fuse features without concatenation, named "Filling" operation, which can cleverly fuse local feature and global feature without increasing the number of channels before fusion.

Specifically, we refill $\hat{X}^{'}$ into X_L with their original position to get $X_L^{'}$. In this way, we reduce the computational effort and make $X_L^{'}$ containing the global features $\hat{X}^{'}$ and local features X_L. When Filling is done, we use depthwise 3×3 separable convolution for deep feature fusion, and then use 1×1 convolution to map the dimension back to the input number of channels to achieve skip connection followed by Resnet [5]. Briefly, if we consider the output of Filling and fusion is $\mathcal{Z}(\cdot;\xi)$, that can be expressed as:

$$\mathcal{Z}(\cdot;\xi) = \mathcal{H}(\mathcal{F}(\cdot;);\xi) \tag{4}$$

where $\mathcal{F}$ denotes the mapping function of "Filling", and $\mathcal{H}(\cdot;\xi)$ denotes the depthwise separable convolution for fusion and point-wise convolution with parameters ξ. In summary, if we consider DF-ViT block as a feature extractor $\mathcal{G}(\cdot;\phi,\theta,\xi))$, which can be expressed as:

$$\mathcal{G}(\cdot;\phi,\theta,\xi) = \mathcal{H}(\mathcal{F}(\mathcal{T}(\mathcal{D}(\mathcal{L}(\cdot;\phi));\theta));\xi). \tag{5}$$

3 Experiments

3.1 Dataset and Evaluation Protocol

PAIP 2019 [8], which was released in an MICCAI 2019 grand challenge. The PAIP 2019 challenge dataset comprises 50 de-identified whole slide images from 50 patients that underwent resection for hepatocellular carcinoma (HCC) from 2005 to June 2018. The slides have been stained by hematoxylin and eosin and digitalised using an Aperio AT2 whole-slide scanner at $\times 20$ power and 0.5021 µm/px resolution, resulting in image sizes between 35855×39407 and 64768×47009 pixels. All the images have detailed pixel-wise manual annotations provided by expert pathologists. Since the official annotation file of the test set is not publicly available, we used a five-fold cross-validation in these 50 WSIs to reasonably compare and validate the performance of our models. We split a WSI into patches that can be processed by existing computing devices. In our experiments comparing with state-of-the-art models, we used a patch size of 224×224 to ensure a fair comparison. After splitting, we used Otsu's thresholding method for tissue detection and only include patches with values greater than the threshold in training or testing. As shown in Table 1, we set five patch sizes at level 0. The evaluation metrics were uniformly chosen as mIoU, F1-score, inference time, FLOPs and model parameters.

3.2 Implementation Details

All training experiments were implemented on the PyTorch framework and conducted on NVIDIA HGX A100 GPUs with 40G memory. The optimizer used

Table 1. The numbers of patches after preprocessing.

Patch size	224 × 224	512 × 512	768 × 768	1024 × 1024	1536 × 1536
Numbers (without blank area)	1453730	285808	128777	74172	34367

Adam. Since the pre-training weights of the imagenet dataset were used, our initial learning rate was set to 0.0005. The strategy of learning rate decay used exponential decay, and we set the minimum value to 0.00005. The training epochs were set to 50. We used Swish [3] as an activation function. The cross-validation random seed on top of the PAIP2019 dataset was set to 42. We performed feed forward for 20 images to report the average inference time on GeForce RTX 2080Ti with 12G memory. All validations were based on pixel-level, including E-Patcher and other comparison of models. Moreover, we used binary cross-entropy as loss function.

3.3 Comparison with State-of-the-Art Methods

In order to validate and evaluate our model more comprehensively, we chose models based on the two latest mainstream backbones. The one was the latest mainstream CNN-based medical image segmentation models UNeXt [20], Unet++ [26], etc., and the other one was the latest mainstream transformer-based. MedT [19], Swin-Unet [1], TransUNet [2]. Although our model has obvious advantages in terms of video memory, memory, speed, accuracy for high-resolution input images, all models used 224 × 224 size patches in order to facilitate the use of pre-training weights provided by the official open source of comparison models on the imagenet dataset. As shown in Table 2, E-Patcher we proposed the mIoU and F1-score metrics are higher than all existing CNN-based and Transformer models on the PAIP 2019 dataset. Specifically, compared with the best CNN-based model UNeXt [20], E-Patcher has 58.5% less number of parameters, 68.09% less computation, and 1.07% higher mIoU metrics, although the inference speed is 1.08ms slower than that. Compared with Swin-Unet [1],

Table 2. Comparison of the latest mainstream models.

	Networks	Params (in M)↓	GFLOPs↓	Inference Speed (in ms)↓	PAIP 2019	
					mIoU↑	F1-score↑
CNN Based	UNet [14]	24.89	43.23	24.44	81.91	90.06
	Unet++ [26]	9.16	26.72	23.53	83.90	91.25
	NCRF [10]	21.29	3.68	21.53	83.73	91.14
	ResUNet++ [7]	4.06	12.11	28.63	84.60	91.66
	UNeXt [20]	1.47	0.44	**13.15**	86.29	92.64
Transformer Based	MedT [19]	1.56	1.95	180.64	85.37	92.11
	TransUNet [2]	91.67	22.33	21.04	86.46	92.74
	Swin-Unet [1]	27.17	5.92	26.75	86.87	92.97
	Ours (E-Patcher)	**0.61**	**0.14**	14.23	**87.36**	**93.25**

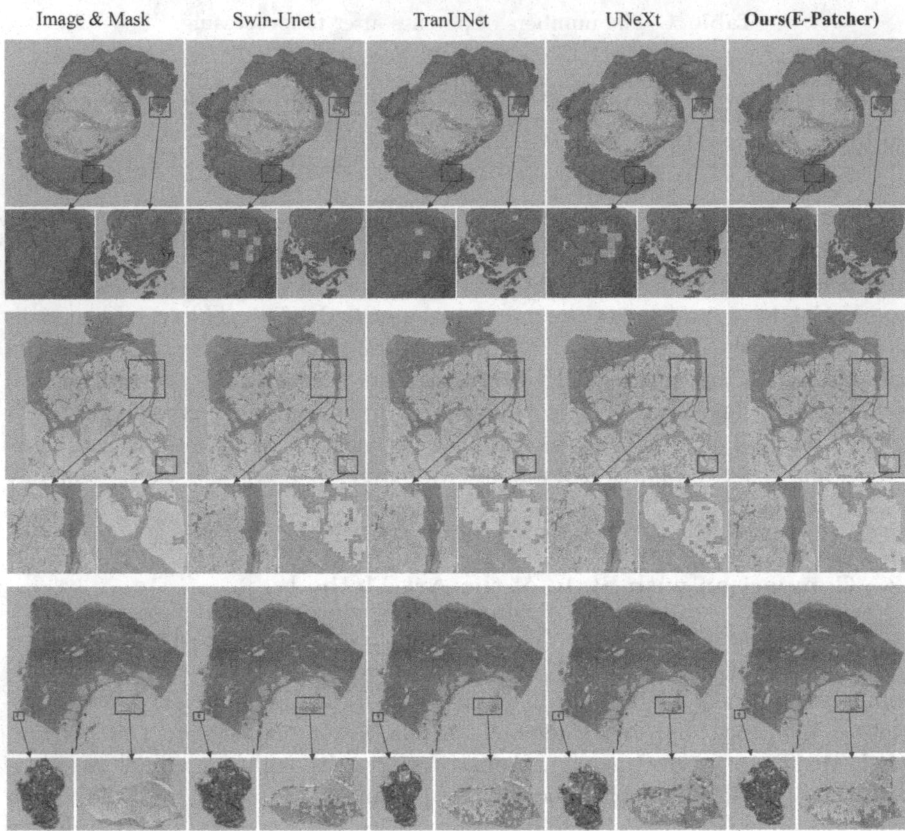

Fig. 3. Visualization of comparison of models with good performance on PAIP2019 dataset.

the best transformer-based model, the mIoU can be higher by 0.49% with 45× less number of parameters, 42× less computation, and 56.64% faster inference speed. Taken together, the E-Patcher we proposed achieves the state-of-the-art mIoU compared to the latest medical image segmentation models, while the inference speed is faster than other models except UNeXt [20], which proves that our proposed model achieves a very good balance of speed and accuracy. As shown in the Fig. 3, we made visualization of the predictions on the test set, and show that our model is able to accurately identify viable tumor regions for WSIs, although it used patch-level predictions.

3.4 Discussion

Effect of Different Block. The first and third rows of Table 3 summarize the comparison results of MobileViTv1 [11] block and DF-ViT block with replacing. The mIoU is higher 1.14% after we improving the key module than MobileViTv1 [11] block. As shown in Fig. 4, To further demonstrate the effectiveness of improved block and answer why the mIoU could be higher than baseline, we used grad-cam [16] to visualize the feature maps of the each block's output before and after the improvement. It is easy to see that the block is not only still effective in global characterization after the improvement, but also reduces risk of overfitting. Because the block we improved could pay the same attention to tumor regions in the fifth layer as the MobileViTv1 [11] block does and pay less attention to the background class in the third layer.

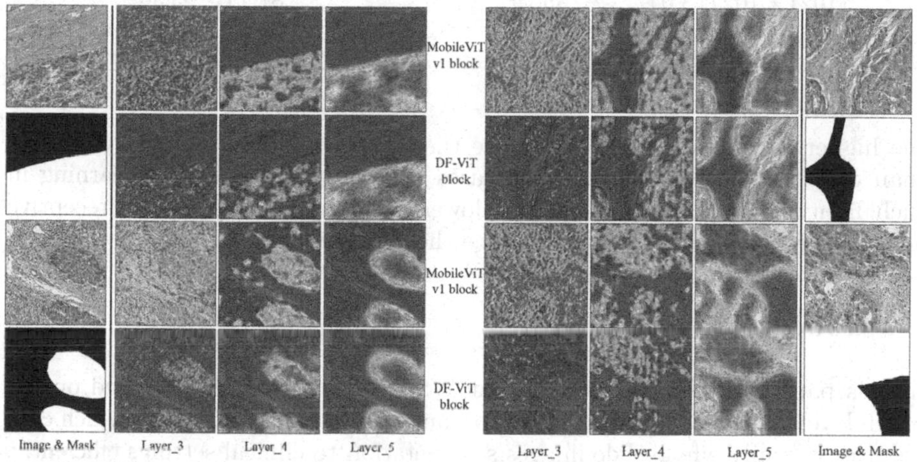

Fig. 4. Features visualization by grad-cam [16]. The first row's features is produced MobileViTv1 [11] block, and the second row's features is produced by DF-ViT block.

Effect of Fusion Way. The second and third rows of Table 3 show the comparison of the different way. It can be observed that "Filling" operation is more efficient in fusing local and global representation to perform segmentation better. Filling by replacing gives better balance than Filling by adding in local and global information.

Analysis on Resolution. Due to the number of patches, which both contains positive region and negative region, varies from different WSI, it has an impact on the performance of the model. Table 4 summarizes the performance of the different resolution. Obviously, 512 × 512 is recommended. The performance of

Table 3. Comparison of MobileViTv1 [11] block, DF-ViT block and fusion ways. All resolutions in this table were 512 × 512.

	Params (in M)↓	GFLOPs↓	Inf. Speed (in ms)↓	mIoU↑	F1-score↑
MobileViTv1 [11] block	0.9513	1.40	23.55	86.22	92.60
DF-ViT block with Adding	0.6097	0.75	21.96	86.94	93.01
DF-ViT block with Replacling	0.6097	0.75	22.18	87.36	93.25

Table 4. Analysis on Resolution.

Resolution	GFLOPs↓	Inference Speed (in ms)↓	mIoU↑	F1-score↑
224 × 224	0.14	15.15	87.36	93.25
512 × 512	0.75	23.65	88.28	93.78
768 × 768	1.69	28.69	88.07	93.66
1024 × 1024	3.04	35.79	87.45	93.30
1536 × 1536	7.09	49.56	85.15	91.98

the higher resolution is worse, because the patch containing boundary is more than others, which means the hard cases increase the difficulty of learning in such lightweight model. Instead, the lower resolution means smaller receptive field and less sub-patches, which reduce the performance.

4 Conclusion

In this paper, we proposed an efficient WSI segmentation model based on the patch level with higher mIoU and less parameters on a public dataset, which contributes to apply whole slide images segmentation to clinical settings efficiently. Compared to UNeXt [20], it improved mIoU by 1.07% and reduced the parameter count and the computational workload. We designed a slight and universal plug-and-play block based patch-level for fully considering local features and global features simultaneously, named DF-ViT block, which exhibited superior characterization capabilities. We demonstrated the DF-ViT block has excellent characterization by using grad-cam. Through our experiments, we showed that 512×512 resolution at level 0 is recommended on patch-level WSI segmentation.

Acknowledgments. This work was funded by grants from the National Key Research and Development Program of China (2022YFF0608404, 2022YFF0608401), the Research Project of the National Institute of Metrology (AKYZD2111), and was supported by the high performance computing (HPC) resources at China Agricultural University.

References

1. Cao, H., et al.: Swin-Unet: Unet-like pure transformer for medical image segmentation. In: Karlinsky, L., Michaeli, T., Nishino, K. (eds.) ECCV 2022, Part III. LNCS, vol. 13803, pp. 205–218. Springer, Cham (2023). https://doi.org/10.1007/978-3-031-25066-8_9
2. Chen, J., et al.: TransUNet: transformers make strong encoders for medical image segmentation. arXiv preprint arXiv:2102.04306 (2021)
3. Elfwing, S., Uchibe, E., Doya, K.: Sigmoid-weighted linear units for neural network function approximation in reinforcement learning. Neural Netw. **107**, 3–11 (2018)
4. Guan, Y., et al.: Node-aligned graph convolutional network for whole-slide image representation and classification. In: Proceedings of the IEEE/CVF Conference on Computer Vision and Pattern Recognition, pp. 18813–18823 (2022)
5. He, K., Zhang, X., Ren, S., Sun, J.: Deep residual learning for image recognition. In: Proceedings of the IEEE Conference on Computer Vision and Pattern Recognition, pp. 770–778 (2016)
6. Hou, L., Samaras, D., Kurc, T.M., Gao, Y., Davis, J.E., Saltz, J.H.: Patch-based convolutional neural network for whole slide tissue image classification. In: Proceedings of the IEEE Conference on Computer Vision and Pattern Recognition, pp. 2424–2433 (2016)
7. Jha, D., et al.: ResUNet++: an advanced architecture for medical image segmentation. In: 2019 IEEE International Symposium on Multimedia (ISM), pp. 225–2255. IEEE (2019)
8. Kim, Y.J., et al.: PAIP 2019: liver cancer segmentation challenge. Med. Image Anal. **67**, 101854 (2021). https://doi.org/10.1016/j.media.2020.101854. https://www.sciencedirect.com/science/article/pii/S1361841520302188
9. Kong, B., Wang, X., Li, Z., Song, Q., Zhang, S.: Cancer metastasis detection via spatially structured deep network. In: Niethammer, M., et al. (eds.) IPMI 2017. LNCS, vol. 10265, pp. 236–248. Springer, Cham (2017). https://doi.org/10.1007/978-3-319-59050-9_19
10. Li, Y., Ping, W.: Cancer metastasis detection with neural conditional random field. arXiv preprint arXiv:1806.07064 (2018)
11. Mehta, S., Rastegari, M.: MobileViT: light-weight, general-purpose, and mobile-friendly vision transformer. arXiv preprint arXiv:2110.02178 (2021)
12. Mehta, S., Rastegari, M.: Separable self-attention for mobile vision transformers. arXiv preprint arXiv:2206.02680 (2022)
13. Moeskops, P., Viergever, M.A., Mendrik, A.M., De Vries, L.S., Benders, M.J., Išgum, I.: Automatic segmentation of MR brain images with a convolutional neural network. IEEE Trans. Med. Imaging **35**(5), 1252–1261 (2016)
14. Ronneberger, O., Fischer, P., Brox, T.: U-Net: convolutional networks for biomedical image segmentation. In: Navab, N., Hornegger, J., Wells, W.M., Frangi, A.F. (eds.) MICCAI 2015, Part III. LNCS, vol. 9351, pp. 234–241. Springer, Cham (2015). https://doi.org/10.1007/978-3-319-24574-4_28
15. Sandler, M., Howard, A., Zhu, M., Zhmoginov, A., Chen, L.C.: MobileNetV2: inverted residuals and linear bottlenecks. In: Proceedings of the IEEE Conference on Computer Vision and Pattern Recognition, pp. 4510–4520 (2018)
16. Selvaraju, R.R., Cogswell, M., Das, A., Vedantam, R., Parikh, D., Batra, D.: Grad-CAM: visual explanations from deep networks via gradient-based localization. In: Proceedings of the IEEE International Conference on Computer Vision, pp. 618–626 (2017)

17. Sirinukunwattana, K., Alham, N.K., Verrill, C., Rittscher, J.: Improving whole slide segmentation through visual context - a systematic study. In: Frangi, A.F., Schnabel, J.A., Davatzikos, C., Alberola-López, C., Fichtinger, G. (eds.) MICCAI 2018, Part II. LNCS, vol. 11071, pp. 192–200. Springer, Cham (2018). https://doi.org/10.1007/978-3-030-00934-2_22
18. Tokunaga, H., Teramoto, Y., Yoshizawa, A., Bise, R.: Adaptive weighting multi-field-of-view CNN for semantic segmentation in pathology. In: Proceedings of the IEEE/CVF Conference on Computer Vision and Pattern Recognition, pp. 12597–12606 (2019)
19. Valanarasu, J.M.J., Oza, P., Hacihaliloglu, I., Patel, V.M.: Medical transformer: gated axial-attention for medical image segmentation. In: de Bruijne, M., et al. (eds.) MICCAI 2021, Part I. LNCS, vol. 12901, pp. 36–46. Springer, Cham (2021). https://doi.org/10.1007/978-3-030-87193-2_4
20. Valanarasu, J.M.J., Patel, V.M.: UNeXt: MLP-based rapid medical image segmentation network. In: Wang, L., Dou, Q., Fletcher, P.T., Speidel, S., Li, S. (eds.) MICCAI 2022, Part V. LNCS, vol. 13435, pp. 23–33. Springer, Cham (2022). https://doi.org/10.1007/978-3-031-16443-9_3
21. Wadekar, S.N., Chaurasia, A.: MobileVitV3: mobile-friendly vision transformer with simple and effective fusion of local, global and input features. arXiv preprint arXiv:2209.15159 (2022)
22. Wang, D., Khosla, A., Gargeya, R., Irshad, H., Beck, A.H.: Deep learning for identifying metastatic breast cancer. arXiv preprint arXiv:1606.05718 (2016)
23. Wetteland, R., Engan, K., Eftestøl, T., Kvikstad, V., Janssen, E.A.: A multiscale approach for whole-slide image segmentation of five tissue classes in urothelial carcinoma slides. Technol. Cancer Res. Treat. **19**, 1533033820946787 (2020)
24. Zhang, K., Zhuang, X.: CycleMix: a holistic strategy for medical image segmentation from scribble supervision. In: Proceedings of the IEEE/CVF Conference on Computer Vision and Pattern Recognition, pp. 11656–11665 (2022)
25. Zhao, Z., et al.: Deep neural network based artificial intelligence assisted diagnosis of bone scintigraphy for cancer bone metastasis. Sci. Rep. **10**(1), 17046 (2020)
26. Zhou, Z., Rahman Siddiquee, M.M., Tajbakhsh, N., Liang, J.: UNet++: a nested U-Net architecture for medical image segmentation. In: Stoyanov, D., et al. (eds.) DLMIA/ML-CDS 2018. LNCS, vol. 11045, pp. 3–11. Springer, Cham (2018). https://doi.org/10.1007/978-3-030-00889-5_1

Exploiting Multi-modal Fusion for Robust Face Representation Learning with Missing Modality

Yizhe Zhu[1,2(✉)], Xin Sun[1,2], and Xi Zhou[2]

[1] Shanghai Jiao Tong University, Shanghai, China
{zhuyizhe,huntersx}@sjtu.edu.cn
[2] CloudWalk Technology, Shanghai, China
zhouxi@cloudwalk.cn

Abstract. Current RGB-D-T face recognition methods are able to alleviate the sensitivity to facial variations, posture, occlusions, and illumination by incorporating complementary information, while they rely heavily on the availability of complete modalities. Given the likelihood of missing modalities in real-world scenarios and the fact that current multi-modal recognition models perform poorly when faced with incomplete data, robust multi-modal models for face recognition that can handle missing modalities are highly desirable. To this end, we propose a multi-modal fusion framework for robustly learning face representations in the presence of missing modalities, using a combination of RGB, depth, and thermal modalities. Our approach effectively blends these modalities together while also alleviating the semantic gap among them. Specifically, we put forward a novel modality-missing loss function to learn the modality-specific features that are robust to missing-modality data conditions. To project various modality features to the same semantic space, we exploit a joint modality-invariant representation with a central moment discrepancy (CMD) based distance constraint training strategy. We conduct extensive experiments on several benchmark datasets, such as VAP RGBD-T and Lock3DFace, and the results demonstrate the effectiveness and robustness of the proposed approach under uncertain missing-modality conditions compared with all baseline algorithms.

Keywords: multi-modal fusion · face representation learning · missing modality

1 Introduction

The utilization of multiple modalities in face recognition, such as RGB, depth, and thermal information, has been shown to improve recognition accuracy through the complementary information of the different visual modalities [1,26]. By incorporating depth or thermal information obtained from sensors or pre-trained image estimation networks, models are able to develop more resilient

Supported by organization CloudWalk.

L. Iliadis et al. (Eds.): ICANN 2023, LNCS 14255, pp. 283–294, 2023.
https://doi.org/10.1007/978-3-031-44210-0_23

and robust representations [3,22]. Previous studies on visual-modality fusion assume that all input visual modalities will be present during training and inference. However, in real-world scenarios, this may not always be the case, as sensor malfunction or failure can result in missing data. When faced with missing modal data, recognition models tend to suffer significant performance degradation [15]. Additionally, aligning the semantics of heterogeneous modalities remains a significant challenge, which plays an important role in recognition accuracy. Recent studies [7,9,13] have demonstrated the potential of using invariant features across modalities to mitigate the effects of the modality gap. However, research on multi-modal learning has primarily focused on developing efficient fusion methods [14,20] or exploring joint representation learning for specific tasks such as image synthesis [32], knowledge reasoning [29], or text-only classification [15]. To date, there has been no prior work on face recognition under missing-modality conditions.

In this paper, we propose a multi-modal fusion framework that addresses the problem of uncertain missing modalities in face recognition. Our proposed framework simultaneously performs multi-modal fusion and addresses the issue of semantic misalignment among modalities to achieve robust face recognition. Specifically, we first introduce a novel modality-missing loss function based on triplet hard loss [21] to learn individual features for RGB, depth, and thermal modalities. We then use a central moment discrepancy (CMD) [30] based distance constraint training strategy to learn joint modality-invariant representations. This approach fully leverages the characteristics of heterogeneous modalities to mitigate the modality gap, resulting in more robust multi-modal joint representations. Our key contributions are summarized as follows:

- We propose a novel multi-modal fusion framework under missing-modality conditions, utilizing the RGB, thermal, and depth modalities. Our proposed framework simultaneously performs multi-modal fusion and alleviates the semantic gap among modalities to achieve robust face recognition.
- We design a novel modality-missing loss (MML) function based on the hard triplet loss, which learns the individual modality-specific features for RGB, depth, and thermal modalities that are robust to missing-modality data. We develop a central moment discrepancy (CMD) based distance constraint strategy to learn the joint modality-invariant representations from multi-modal data.
- We conduct extensive experiments and comparative analysis on two public benchmark datasets, the VAP RGBD-T dataset [18] and Lock3DFace dataset [31], under various missing modality conditions and the results demonstrate that our proposed approach can accurately perform face recognition when some modalities are missing.

2 Related Work

Different visual modalities of information in the input, *e.g.*, RGB, depth or thermal signals, are often complementary in content while overlapping for a common

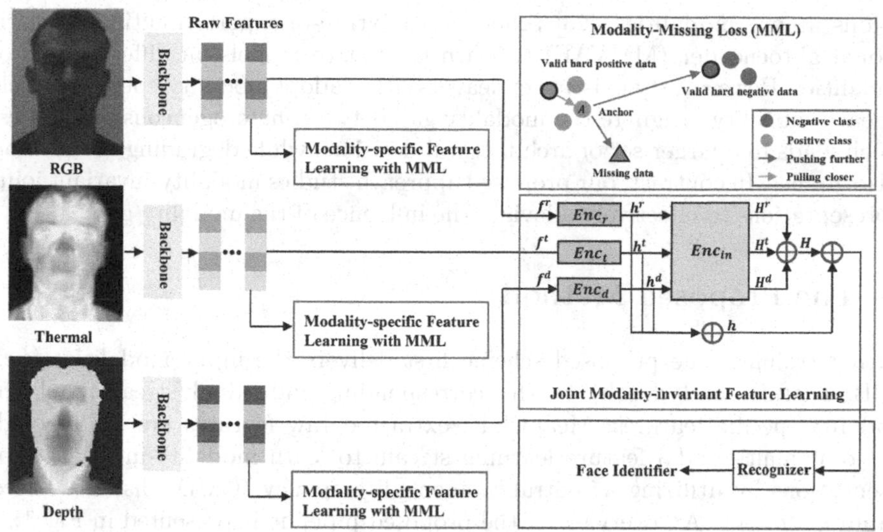

Fig. 1. The pipeline of our proposed multi-modal fusion framework for robust missing-modality face representation learning, which includes the individual modality-specific feature learning stream with the modality-missing loss, the joint modality-invariant feature learning stream and the face recognizer.

concept. It has been shown that [1] various modalities can be fused for enhanced face recognition accuracy owing to the complementary information of various visual modalities. Using proper fusion methods is one of the key issues in multi-modal face representation learning studies. Since the multimodal data collected from the real world are often imperfect due to missing modalities, the flexibility to adapt to modality-incomplete data still challenges existing multi-modal backbones. Conventional backbones [25] output the multimodal representation by simply fusing the features of each modality via concatenation [20], tensor fusion [28], low-rank fusion [14] and other mechanisms. More recently, multi-modal Transformers [4] are emerging as the dominant choice in multi-modal learning across various tasks, including classification [12], segmentation [24], and cross-model retrieval [10]. They present several advantages over conventional backbones in terms of efficiency and flexibility. Nevertheless, either these explicit fusion mechanisms or Transformer models heavily rely on the completeness of modality. They have been shown sensitive to missing modalities [15]. Therefore, the following works are proposed to build models that are robust against the missing modality cases. These solutions for the missing modality problem can be divided into three categories: 1) missing data prediction [2,5], 2) multi-modal joint representation learning [8,19], 3) cross-modal generation [23,27]. For instance, in [33], the Missing Modality Imagination Network (MMIN) is proposed for predicting missing modalities. [16] proposes an approach based on Bayesian Meta-Learning to estimate the latent feature of the modality-incomplete data. [19] proposes a translation-based method based on cycle consistency loss to learn joint representations among modalities. [23] proposes a mixture-of-experts multimodal variational autoencoder (MMVAE) to learn generative models on different sets of modalities. However, the existing endeavors either adopt modality-specific models for each modality or ignore the modality gap between heterogeneous modalities, which leads to a larger set of architectural decisions while degrading recognition performance. In contrast, our proposed approach studies modality-invariant joint representations to effectively alleviate the influence of the modality gap.

3 The Proposed Method

During training, the proposed scheme first delivers the input modalities (*i.e.*, RGB, thermal and depth) to the corresponding individual stream to learn modality-specific features. Meanwhile, extracted raw features are fed through the joint multi-modal feature learning stream to learn modality-invariant representations by utilizing a central moment discrepancy (CMD) distance-based training strategy. An overview of the proposed pipeline is presented in Fig. 1.

3.1 Individual Modality-Specific Feature Learning

Specifically, the RGB image $\mathbf{r}$, thermal image $\mathbf{t}$ and depth image $\mathbf{d}$ are delivered as input to the framework. The extracted features of RGB, thermal and depth branches are represented as $f^r = \theta_r(\mathbf{r})$, $f^t = \theta_t(\mathbf{t})$ and $f^d = \theta_d(\mathbf{d})$. The functions θ_r, θ_t, θ_d are represented using several convolutional layers. Then the three modality-specific features are learned individually using a tailored loss function based on triplet hard loss [21]. It is noteworthy that the vanilla triplet hard loss function generally uses pre-defined data to represent missing data since it assumes that the all input modalities are present. Therefore, there exists a real possibility that pre-defined data is incorrectly identified as modality-complete data(*i.e.*, an anchor, positive or negative data). Moreover, the goal of the triplet loss when considering a missing-modality triplet is to simultaneously minimize the distance between the valid anchor point and the missing positive while maximizing the distance between the valid anchor point and the missing negative points. Missing positive and negative data embedded to same point inevitably makes latent space learning unable to achieve the global optimization. To alleviate the above issues, we propose a novel modality-missing loss function, termed as MML, to explicitly account for the missing modalities. The illustration of modality-missing loss is shown by the blue block in Fig. 1. Let $d : \mathbb{C}^2 \rightarrow \mathbb{R}^+$ be the measure that calculates the distance between two data points. Each modality-missing loss $\mathcal{L}_z$, where $z \in \{r, t, d\}$ corresponds to the RGB, thermal and depth modality, is given as:

$$\mathcal{L}_z = log_e(1 + e^{\alpha}), \text{where } \alpha = d(a^v, p^v) - d(a^v, n^v) - d(a^v, e^m) \quad (1)$$

where a^v denotes the valid anchor points (*i.e.*, obtained data from available modality), p^v denotes the hard valid positive points, n^v denotes the hard valid negative points and the missing latent points is denoted as e^m.

The normalized layer output of each modality-specific raw feature is delivered as input to the modality-missing loss function (MML). We optimize each individual branch with the MML. We present the computational procedure of the modality-missing loss in $\mathcal{L}_z$ as shown in Algorithm ??. To compute the modality-missing loss in $\mathcal{L}_z$, the training dataset is partitioned into mini-batches with K samples each. Each mini-batch contains input features $X = x_{i}{}_{i=1}^{K}$, class labels, $Y = y_{i}{}_{i=1}^{Y}$, and binary validity label $B = b_{i}{}_{i=1}^{K}$. Here, $b_i = 1$ corresponds to valid features, and $b_i = 0$ corresponds to the missing features. Firstly, the pair-wise distance matrix P is computed from X, where each row in the matrix denotes the Euclidean distance vector between an anchor point and all other data points in the mini-batch. The positive matrix A_p and the valid matrix A_v are computed as Eq. 2. The missing matrix $A_m = \neg A_v$, the valid positive matrix $A_p^v = A_p \wedge A_v$, the diagonal elements are set to zero. The negative matrix $A_n = \neg A_p$, the valid negative matrix $A_n^v = A_n \wedge A_v$. $P_p^v \leftarrow P * A_p^v$, $*$, $P_n^v \leftarrow P * A_n^v$, $P_m \leftarrow P * A_m$, where $*$ corresponds to the Hadamard product between two matrices. For each of P_p^v, P_n^v, P_m, we make a row-wise maximum on the matrix and perform an element-wise multiplication with B to calculate the Euclidean distance $d\left(a^v, p^v\right)$,$d\left(a^v, n^v\right)$ and $d\left(a^v, e^m\right)$, respectively. Then We obtain each modality-missing loss $\mathcal{L}_z, z \in \{r, t, d\}$ according to Eq. 1.

$$A_p(i,j) = \begin{cases} 1, & \text{if } y_i = y_j \\ 0, & \text{otherwise} \end{cases}, A_v(i,j) = \begin{cases} 1, & \text{if } b_i = b_j = 1 \\ 0, & \text{otherwise} \end{cases} \tag{2}$$

3.2 CMD-Based Distance Joint Modality-Invariant Feature Learning

The multi-modal joint representation is learned from the high-level features of each modality as well as a concatenation of modality-specific features using the individual encoders (*i.e.*, Enc_r, Enc_t, Enc_d) and the invariance encoder Enc_{in} shown in Fig. 1. Specifically, Enc_r, Enc_t and Enc_d employs depth-guided attention [26] to extract the most prominent person-specific visual semantic features h^r, h^t, h^d from the raw feature f^r, f^t, f^d, respectively. The invariance encoder consists of the full-connected layer, the activation function, and the dropout layer. It aims to map modality-specific features $\left(h^r, h^t, h^d\right)$ into a shared subspace with CMD-based distance constraint strategy to obtain high-level semantic features $\left(H^r, H^t, H^d\right)$. Then, we concatenate the three high-level features into modality-invariant features H.

CMD [30] is an advanced distance metric, which can effectively measure the discrepancy between the two feature distributions by matching their order-wise moment differences. Inspired by this, we leverage the CMD-based distance constraint to reduce the discrepancy between the high-level features (H^a, H^v, H^t) of modalities. We ensure that modality-invariant representation can be learned by minimizing the $\mathcal{L}_{\text{cmd}}$:

$$\mathcal{L}_{\text{cmd}} = \frac{1}{3} \sum_{\substack{(m_1, m_2) \in \\ \{(r,t),(r,d)(t,d)\}}} \left(\left\|\mathbf{E}\left(H^{m_1}\right) - \mathbf{E}\left(H^{m_2}\right)\right\|_2 + \sum_{k=2}^{K} \left\|C_k\left(H^{m_1}\right) - C_k\left(H^{m_2}\right)\right\|_2\right) \tag{3}$$

where $\mathbf{E}(H)$ denotes the empirical expectation vector of the input sample H, and $C_k(H) = \mathbf{E}\left((H - \mathbf{E}(H))^k\right)$ denotes the vector of all k^{th} order sample central moments of the coordinates of H. In this way, various modality features are forced to map to the same semantic subspace under the distance constraint.

Face Recognizer. Then the obtained joint modality-invariant features and three independent modality-specific features are concatenated and given as input to the face recognizer. During the face recognizer training, the widely-used binary cross-Entropy loss $\mathcal{L}_{cls}$ is used to supervise the classification training. The total loss function of the proposed framework is represented as follows:

$$\mathcal{L} = \alpha(\mathcal{L}_r + \mathcal{L}_t + \mathcal{L}_d) + \beta(\mathcal{L}_{cmd}) + \gamma(\mathcal{L}_{cls}) \tag{4}$$

where $\mathcal{L}_r$, $\mathcal{L}_t$ and $\mathcal{L}_d$ correspond to the modality-missing losses for three modality-specific features. $\mathcal{L}_{cmd}$ corresponds to the loss for the joint modality-invariant feature representation. α, β and γ are scaling factors to control the different loss items. We set these hyper-parameters to $\alpha = 0.5$, $\beta = 0.5$ and $\gamma = 1$ empirically.

4 Experiments

4.1 Dataset

We validate the performance of the proposed approach on the *VAP* [18] RGBD-T dataset and *Lock3DFace* dataset [31]. *VAP* [18] RGBD-T dataset consists of synchronized RGB, depth, and thermal facial images with variations in pose, expression and illumination from 51 persons. Following [18], we split the available data into training, validation, and testing set with the splitting ratio $8:1:1$ according to the defined evaluation protocol. *Lock3DFace* dataset contains 5671 low-quality RGB-D face video clips from 509 subjects. The database also covers some of the most challenging test scenarios: facial expression, pose, occlusion, and time-lapse. we follow the conventional experimental setting [17] to divide *Lock3DFace* into the training and four test sets respectively.

Since Lock3DFace raw dataset only contains RGB and depth images, we utilize generative adversarial networks [6] to generate corresponding thermal infrared images from original RGB images. We then align thermal images well with RGB and depth images for evaluation.

4.2 Experiment Setting

Network Architecture. The input RGB, thermal and depth images are cropped to the size of 224×224. The raw features of RGB, thermal and depth branches are extracted using four convolution layers with the stride of 1×1 with ReLU activation. The convolutional kernel shape of first three convolution layers is $(3, 3, 128)$. The convolutional kernel shape of final convolution layer is $(1, 1, 64)$. The hidden size of individual encoders Enc_r, Enc_t and Enc_d is set to

128. The size of invariance encoder Enc_{In} output is 128. The face recognizer is consisted of two fully connected layers with 512 units, and a fully connected layer with the number of classes as the dataset. Then the layer output is batch normalized and delivered to the softmax activation function.

Training Details. We conduct all experiments, including the proposed individual modality-specific feature learning, joint modality-invariant feature learning and face recognizer training with the Adam [11] optimizer. We set the initial learning rate as 0.0002. We train the proposed model for 50 epochs with a batch size of 32 and train the face recognition model for 25 epochs with a batch size of 32. As the experiment result can vary substantially between different runs due to randomisation, each model is run for three times to avoid the one-time occasionality. We select the best model on the validation set and report its performance on the testing set. Our solution is implemented with Pytorch and is run on Nvidia 3090 GPUs.

Evaluation Metrics. Since variations in pose that is the most challenging testing scenario best reflects the discrepancy among models, we report all results in terms of Top-1 identification accuracy in the presence of pose variations (Pose) and average Top-1 identification accuracy (Acc).

Baseline Methods. We develop seven multi-modal baselines for a comparative study. These baseline approaches can be divided into four types: 1) missing data prediction. MFM [25] predicts missing modalities using the observed modalities by factorizing multimodal representations into modality-specific generative factors and multimodal discriminative factors and. SMIL [16] leverages Bayesian meta-learning in reconstructing missing-modality data. MMIN [33] predicts missing modality through the missing modality imagination network. 2) multi-modal joint representation learning. MCTN [19] learns the joint representation via a cyclic translation between missing and available modalities. 3) multimodal deep generative models such as MVAE [27] and MMVAE [23] which learn a multimodal VAE-based generative model for multimodal generation task. 4) recent multimodal Transformer (ViT) [4] and the variant robust Transformer model (Robust.) [15] applied on face recognition.

4.3 Robustness to Missing Modality

Follow a conventional setting [25], we assess the model robustness against missing-modal data on VAP RGBD-T and Lock3DFace dataset under the scenario that the training data are modality-complete, while the testing data are modality-missing data. As shown in Table 1 and Table 2, our proposed framework reports the highest identification accuracy under all missing-modality testing conditions except for conditions {T} and {D}, where it is on par with the best baseline. We attribute this to the fact that the RGB visual modality contains more semantically person-specific information than the thermal and depth

Table 1. Evaluation of our proposed method on VAP RGBD-T dataset compared with eight baselines under six missing-modality conditions (*i.e.*, testing condition {R} indicates that only RGB modality is available and both thermal and depth modalities are missing). It is noteworthy that we also provide the performance of our method on "full" evaluation setting, where all inputs are given (*i.e.*, {R,T,D}). †: missing data prediction methods. △: multi-modal joint representation learning. ○: multimodal deep generative model. □: multi-modal Transformer. Top-1 identification accuracy (%) in the presence of pose variations and average accuracy (%) are adopted as the evaluation metrics.

Method	Testing Conditions													
	{R,T,D}		{R}		{T}		{D}		{R,T}		{R,D}		{T,D}	
	Pose	Acc.	Pose	Acc.	Pose	Acc.	Pose	Acc.	Pose	Acc.	Pose	Acc.	Pose	Acc.
MFM †[25]	–	–	58.2	79.8	58.5	82.7	50.0	73.1	66.2	84.9	71.3	81.0	62.8	82.6
SMIL †[16]	–	–	62.7	86.5	61.8	84.9	54.8	78.0	68.0	87.5	77.9	88.0	70.3	89.0
MMIN †[33]	–	–	63.2	87.1	63.5	87.2	55.9	79.4	68.7	88.0	78.1	88.7	71.1	89.9
MCTN △ [19]	–	–	59.8	80.9	60.0	84.2	51.1	74.3	67.6	86.9	73.4	83.2	65.3	84.1
MVAE ○ [27]	–	–	58.9	80.7	59.4	83.5	50.8	74.0	67.1	85.6	72.0	81.7	63.5	83.3
MMVAE ○ [23]	–	–	62.0	86.1	61.5	84.4	54.2	77.6	67.3	86.8	77.2	87.3	70.0	88.6
ViT □ [4]	–	–	56.6	78.2	57.3	82.5	49.7	72.8	64.0	84.1	71.8	81.7	63.8	82.5
Robust. □ [15]	–	–	63.7	86.8	61.5	85.6	55.3	78.8	68.9	88.6	78.4	88.9	70.8	89.6
Ours	**82.6**	**94.2**	**67.4**	**90.3**	**65.2**	**89.0**	**58.1**	**81.3**	**70.2**	**89.8**	**78.9**	**89.3**	**72.8**	**90.9**

modalities. Through the vivid comparison, it is evident that our model is able to learn robust multi-modal joint representation and alleviate the modality gap by introducing modality-invariant features, hence improving the classification performance under different missing modality testing conditions.

Besides, we analyze the performance of our methods compared with advanced multi-modal Transformer model. We additionally follow a conventional setting [15] to apply masks on the attention matrix of the transformer model against missing-modal data. As Table 1 and Table 2 shows, even this robust multi-modal Transformer via multi-task learning could not perform on a par with ours on the multi-modal face dataset.

4.4 Ablation Experiments

Analysis of Effect of Each Module. Our proposed framework exploits the individual modality-specific feature learning with the modality-missing loss and utilizes the CMD-based distance training strategy to learn joint modality-invariant feature among modalities. To verify the contributions of each novel module, we develop the following variants to conduct ablation experiments: 1) *End-to-End (E2E)*. Three individual raw feature maps are directly concatenated and given as input to the recognizer. This is utilized as the baseline for multi-modal face recognition. 2) *Proposed model w/o modality-missing loss (MML)*. The modality-specific features are individually trained with cross-entropy loss. 3) *Proposed model w/o joint modality-invariant feature learning (JMIFL)* discards the CMD-based distance constraint during the model training.

Table 2. Evaluation of our proposed method on Lock3DFace RGBD-T dataset compared with eight baselines under six missing-modality conditions (*i.e.*, testing condition {R} indicates that only RGB modality is available and both thermal and depth modalities are missing). †: missing data prediction methods. △: multi-modal joint representation learning. ○: multimodal deep generative model. □: multi-modal Transformer. It is noteworthy that we also provide the performance of our method on "full" evaluation setting, where all inputs are given (*i.e.*, {R,T,D}). Top-1 identification accuracy (%) in the presence of pose variations and average accuracy (%) are adopted as the evaluation metrics.

Method	Testing Conditions													
	{R,T,D}		{R}		{T}		{D}		{R,T}		{R,D}		{T,D}	
	Pose	Acc.	Pose	Acc.	Pose	Acc.	Pose	Acc.	Pose	Acc.	Pose	Acc.	Pose	Acc.
MFM †[25]	–	–	56.3	73.0	55.3	71.6	51.0	70.5	58.3	75.2	59.8	77.0	56.2	72.1
SMIL †[16]	–	–	58.3	76.0	58.7	75.0	56.3	74.2	62.3	79.6	63.4	81.2	60.1	76.0
MMIN †[33]	–	–	60.8	78.2	60.7	79.3	58.8	76.7	63.2	80.5	65.1	82.5	60.9	77.5
MCTN △ [19]	–	–	57.5	75.2	57.8	74.1	53.4	72.0	60.6	77.5	61.2	79.1	58.5	74.3
MVAE ○ [27]	–	–	56.8	74.5	57.2	73.5	52.6	71.2	59.3	76.8	60.5	78.2	58.0	73.7
MMVAE ○ [23]	–	–	57.9	75.7	58.3	74.6	54.0	72.5	61.2	78.0	61.7	79.8	59.1	74.8
ViT □ [4]	–	–	54.5	71.2	53.1	69.4	49.8	68.5	56.0	73.1	57.6	74.8	54.0	70.0
Robust □ [15]	–	–	61.0	78.7	59.9	78.1	58.0	75.5	63.3	80.4	65.4	82.4	60.8	77.5
Ours	**91.3**	**94.2**	**62.9**	**80.8**	**63.0**	**82.1**	**60.3**	**78.9**	**65.1**	**82.2**	**67.5**	**84.5**	**62.7**	**79.4**

As shown in Table 3, we observe that adding the JMIFL module significantly outperforms the baseline (E2E) under each testing condition. This is because the invariance encoder in multi-modal joint representation learning can predict accurate modality-invariant feature under the constraints of central moment discrepancy distance. Besides, the results show that removing the MML dramatically degrades our model's performance, demonstrating the effectiveness of proposed modality-missing loss function on exploiting discriminative modality-specific features.

Analysis of Learning Joint Multi-modal Representation Ability. The goal of learning joint multi-modal representation is to retain efficient information of various modalities. Therefore, we study the joint multi-modal representation ability of the proposed model by comparing ours with the baseline model under the matched-modality testing settings. In this setting, both the training data and the test data cover the same modalities. It can be observed from Table 4 that our model significantly outperforms the baseline under both uncertain missing-modality conditions, which demonstrates the model's remarkable capabilities of learning effective and robust joint multi-modal representations.

Table 3. Framework ablation study on VAP RGBD-T dataset under six missing-modality conditions (*i.e.*, testing condition {R} indicates that only RGB modality is available and both thermal and depth modalities are missing). Average Top-1 identification accuracy (%) is adopted as the evaluation metric.

Method	Testing Conditions											
	{R}		{T}		{D}		{R,T}		{R,D}		{T,D}	
	Pose	Acc	Pose	Acc	Pose	Acc	Pose	Acc	Pose	Acc	Pose	Acc
E2E	55.2	75.5	55.3	74.0	46.4	69.2	62.0	81.4	68.1	78.0	60.2	78.8
w/o MML	63.6	87.2	62.1	86.0	55.1	78.8	69.1	88.9	78.3	88.5	70.9	89.7
w/o JMIFL	63.7	87.5	62.3	86.2	55.3	79.0	69.4	89.2	78.1	88.9	71.3	90.0
Ours	**67.4**	**90.3**	**65.2**	**89.0**	**58.1**	**81.3**	**70.2**	**89.8**	**78.9**	**89.3**	**72.8**	**90.9**

Table 4. Evaluation of the joint representation learning ability on VAP RGBD-T dataset under different train/test conditions. "Baseline" denotes the results individually trained with cross-entropy loss on modality-incomplete data. Average Top-1 identification accuracy (%) is adopted as the evaluation metric.

Method	Train/Test					
	{R}/{R}	{T}/{T}	{D}/{D}	{R,T}/{R,T}	{R,D}/{R,D}	{T,D}/{T,D}
Baseline	73.2	72.0	65.1	78.7	75.8	76.5
Ours	**87.5**	**86.8**	**78.7**	**89.4**	**89.0**	**90.1**

5 Conclusions

In this paper, we propose a novel multi-modal fusion framework for robust miss-modality face representation learning. To be specific, the proposed approach introduces the modality-missing loss function to learn the individual modality-specific features in a distinguished manner. The approach also enhances joint modality-invariant feature learning by employing the central moment discrepancy (CMD) distance-based training strategy, thus alleviating the semantic gap among modalities. Extensive experiments at uncertain missing-modality conditions on two benchmarks show intriguing capabilities of our framework at boosting modality-missing facial recognition performance.

References

1. Bebis, G., Gyaourova, A., Singh, S., Pavlidis, I.: Face recognition by fusing thermal infrared and visible imagery. Image Vision Comput. **24**(7), 727–742 (2006)
2. Cai, L., Wang, Z., Gao, H., Shen, D., Ji, S.: Deep adversarial learning for multi-modality missing data completion. In: Proceedings of the 24th ACM SIGKDD International Conference on Knowledge Discovery & Data Mining, pp. 1158–1166 (2018)

3. Cui, J., Zhang, H., Han, H., Shan, S., Chen, X.: Improving 2D face recognition via discriminative face depth estimation. In: 2018 International Conference on Biometrics (ICB), pp. 140–147. IEEE (2018)
4. Dosovitskiy, A., et al.: An image is worth 16×16 words: transformers for image recognition at scale. arXiv preprint arXiv:2010.11929 (2020)
5. Du, C., et al.: Semi-supervised deep generative modelling of incomplete multi-modality emotional data. In: Proceedings of the 26th ACM International Conference on Multimedia, pp. 108–116 (2018)
6. Goodfellow, I.: Generative adversarial networks. Commun. ACM **63**(11), 139–144 (2020)
7. Guerrero, R., Pham, H.X., Pavlovic, V.: Cross-modal retrieval and synthesis (x-mrs): Closing the modality gap in shared subspace learning. In: Proceedings of the 29th ACM International Conference on Multimedia, pp. 3192–3201 (2021)
8. Han, J., Zhang, Z., Ren, Z., Schuller, B.: Implicit fusion by joint audiovisual training for emotion recognition in mono modality. In: ICASSP 2019–2019 IEEE International Conference on Acoustics, Speech and Signal Processing (ICASSP), pp. 5861–5865. IEEE (2019)
9. Hazarika, D., Zimmermann, R., Poria, S.: Misa: modality-invariant and-specific representations for multimodal sentiment analysis. In: Proceedings of the 28th ACM International Conference on Multimedia, pp. 1122–1131 (2020)
10. Kim, W., Son, B., Kim, I.: Vilt: vision-and-language transformer without convolution or region supervision. In: Proceedings of the 38th International Conference on Machine Learning, ICML. Proceedings of Machine Learning Research, vol. 139, pp. 5583–5594 (2021)
11. Kingma, D.P., Ba, J.: Adam: a method for stochastic optimization. arXiv preprint arXiv:1412.6980 (2014)
12. Lee, S., Yu, Y., Kim, G., Breuel, T.M., Kautz, J., Song, Y.: Parameter efficient multimodal transformers for video representation learning. In: 9th International Conference on Learning Representations, ICLR (2021)
13. Liu, A.H., Jin, S., Lai, C.I.J., Rouditchenko, A., Oliva, A., Glass, J.: Cross-modal discrete representation learning. arXiv preprint arXiv:2106.05438 (2021)
14. Liu, Z., Shen, Y., Lakshminarasimhan, V.B., Liang, P.P., Zadeh, A., Morency, L.P.: Efficient low-rank multimodal fusion with modality-specific factors. arXiv preprint arXiv:1806.00064 (2018)
15. Ma, M., Ren, J., Zhao, L., Testuggine, D., Peng, X.: Are multimodal transformers robust to missing modality? In: Proceedings of the IEEE/CVF Conference on Computer Vision and Pattern Recognition, pp. 18177–18186 (2022)
16. Ma, M., Ren, J., Zhao, L., Tulyakov, S., Wu, C., Peng, X.: Smil: multimodal learning with severely missing modality. In: Proceedings of the AAAI Conference on Artificial Intelligence, vol. 35, pp. 2302–2310 (2021)
17. Mu, G., Huang, D., Hu, G., Sun, J., Wang, Y.: Led3d: a lightweight and efficient deep approach to recognizing low-quality 3D faces. In: Proceedings of the IEEE/CVF Conference on Computer Vision and Pattern Recognition, pp. 5773–5782 (2019)
18. Nikisins, O., Nasrollahi, K., Greitans, M., Moeslund, T.B.: Rgb-dt based face recognition. In: 2014 22nd International Conference on Pattern Recognition, pp. 1716–1721. IEEE (2014)
19. Pham, H., Liang, P.P., Manzini, T., Morency, L.P., Póczos, B.: Found in translation: learning robust joint representations by cyclic translations between modalities. In: Proceedings of the AAAI Conference on Artificial Intelligence, vol. 33, pp. 6892–6899 (2019)

20. Poria, S., Chaturvedi, I., Cambria, E., Hussain, A.: Convolutional mkl based multimodal emotion recognition and sentiment analysis. In: 2016 IEEE 16th International Conference on Data Mining (ICDM), pp. 439–448. IEEE (2016)
21. Schroff, F., Kalenichenko, D., Philbin, J.: Facenet: a unified embedding for face recognition and clustering. In: Proceedings of the IEEE Conference on Computer Vision and Pattern Recognition, pp. 815–823 (2015)
22. Seal, A., Bhattacharjee, D., Nasipuri, M., Gonzalo-Martin, C., Menasalvas, E.: Fusion of visible and thermal images using a directed search method for face recognition. Int. J. Pattern Recogn. Artif. Intell. **31**(04), 1756005 (2017)
23. Shi, Y., Paige, B., Torr, P., et al.: Variational mixture-of-experts autoencoders for multi-modal deep generative models. Adv. Neural Inf. Process. Syst. **32**, 1–12 (2019)
24. Strudel, R., Pinel, R.G., Laptev, I., Schmid, C.: Segmenter: transformer for semantic segmentation. In: 2021 IEEE/CVF International Conference on Computer Vision, ICCV 2021, Montreal, QC, Canada, 10–17 October 2021, pp. 7242–7252 (2021)
25. Tsai, Y.H.H., Liang, P.P., Zadeh, A., Morency, L.P., Salakhutdinov, R.: Learning factorized multimodal representations. arXiv preprint arXiv:1806.06176 (2018)
26. Uppal, H., Sepas-Moghaddam, A., Greenspan, M., Etemad, A.: Depth as attention for face representation learning. IEEE Trans. Inf. Forensics Secur. **16**, 2461–2476 (2021)
27. Wu, M., Goodman, N.: Multimodal generative models for scalable weakly-supervised learning. Adv. Neural Inf. Process. Syst. **31**, 1–11 (2018)
28. Zadeh, A., Chen, M., Poria, S., Cambria, E., Morency, L.P.: Tensor fusion network for multimodal sentiment analysis. arXiv preprint arXiv:1707.07250 (2017)
29. Zellers, R., et al.: Merlot: multimodal neural script knowledge models. Adv. Neural Inf. Process. Syst. **34**, 23634–23651 (2021)
30. Zellinger, W., Grubinger, T., Lughofer, E., Natschläger, T., Saminger-Platz, S.: Central moment discrepancy (cmd) for domain-invariant representation learning. arXiv preprint arXiv:1702.08811 (2017)
31. Zhang, J., Huang, D., Wang, Y., Sun, J.: Lock3dface: a large-scale database of low-cost kinect 3d faces. In: 2016 International Conference on Biometrics (ICB), pp. 1–8. IEEE (2016)
32. Zhang, Z., et al.: Ufc-bert: unifying multi-modal controls for conditional image synthesis. Adv. Neural Inf. Process. Syst. **34**, 27196–27208 (2021)
33. Zhao, J., Li, R., Jin, Q.: Missing modality imagination network for emotion recognition with uncertain missing modalities. In: Proceedings of the 59th Annual Meeting of the Association for Computational Linguistics and the 11th International Joint Conference on Natural Language Processing, vol. 1: Long Papers, pp. 2608–2618 (2021)

Extraction Method of Rotated Objects from High-Resolution Remote Sensing Images

Tao Sun, Kun Liu(✉), and Jiechuan Shi

University of Jinan, Jinan 250022, China
liukun@ujn.edu.cn

Abstract. In recent years, the rapid development of remote sensing technology has made intelligent interpretation possible. However, remote sensing images have arbitrary object orientation, small object size and complex background compared with natural images, and these problems cause difficulty in accomplishing accurate object detection. In this study, several classical traditional object detection methods are first used to compare the detection effects based on the self-made high-resolution remote sensing image rotation detection dataset. Then, a dual-mode rotation regression network, namely, DRRN, is designed to solve the problem of arbitrary object orientation in remote sensing images. DRRN mainly consists of two parts: dual-mode region proposal network and rotation regression network. Meanwhile, a combined regression loss with intersection over union is proposed to improve the traditional smooth L1 loss. Next, a bi-directional cross-layer connected feature pyramid network, namely, bc-FPN, is proposed to solve the problem of small objects. And a supervised hybrid attention mechanism, namely, SHAM, is proposed to solve the problem of complex background, and the two modules are portable and plug-and-play. Experiments show that the proposed methods can effectively improve the detection effects of object in remote sensing images.

Keywords: Intelligent Interpretation · Rotation Regression Network · Feature Pyramid Network · Supervised Hybrid Attention Mechanism

1 Introduction

In recent years, the rapid development of remote sensing technology has made a large number of high-resolution remote sensing images available, and they can provide very fine spatial and textural information. Recognition and analysis method based on high-resolution remote sensing image technology has been used in object detection tasks [1] to find a number of objects in a complex remote sensing image background, provide an accurate box for each object, and determine the class to which the object belongs.

At present, the development of intelligent and automatic processing technology for remote sensing images is still relatively lagging behind. Many applications, especially those in major engineering projects, still rely on manual interpretation [2]. However, the field of remote sensing has issues such as massive data volume, complex data quality, and high difficulty in data processing, which leads to high costs for manual interpretation.

L. Iliadis et al. (Eds.): ICANN 2023, LNCS 14255, pp. 295–307, 2023.
https://doi.org/10.1007/978-3-031-44210-0_24

To fully utilize remote sensing data, conducting research on remote sensing intelligent interpretation is a meaningful direction.

Although deep learning-based object detection algorithms have been widely applied in the field of natural images. However, there are still many problems that need to be solved in the field of remote sensing. In summary, the following problems exist in the field of remote sensing:

(1) The problem of small objects. Many of the objects in remote sensing images are small and only show a very small range of pixels, which leads to a lack of information about the object.
(2) The problem of arbitrary object orientation. The angle of the object varies due to overhead photography, and the direction of the object is uncertain.
(3) The problem of complex background. Remote sensing images have a relatively large field of view, and there may be various backgrounds in the scene, which can cause significant interference to object detection.

The most critical problems are arbitrary object orientation, difficulty to fit traditional rectangular boxes to the object, and a lot of additional information contained in each detection box. Moreover, the intersection over union (IoU) values between the horizontal boxes are very high, which are easily suppressed in the stage of non-maximum suppression (NMS). This condition leads to a large number of missed detections in the results. Ultimately, traditional object detection methods cannot be fully applied in the field of remote sensing.

To solve the abovementioned problems of object detection in remote sensing field, The contributions of this study can be summarized in the following four aspects:

(1) A high-resolution remote sensing image rotation detection dataset, DRD-GS, was created for the specific class of rotated objects. This dataset includes two classes, namely, greenhouse and ship, and each class includes more than 50,000 instances, and this dataset will soon be publicly available.
(2) To address the issue of arbitrary object orientation, a dual-mode rotation regression network, DRRN, was designed, and a combined regression loss with IoU was proposed to improve the traditional smooth L1 loss. According to the characteristics of different class aspect ratios in the dataset, different rotation NMS thresholds were set.
(3) To address the issue of small object size, a bi-directional cross-layer connection feature pyramid network, bc-FPN, was proposed to fully propagate bottom-level position information and top-level semantic information. This module has good portability and features plug-and-play functionality.
(4) To address the issue of complex background, a supervised hybrid attention mechanism, SHAM, was proposed to suppress image noise and enhance object information. This module has good portability and features plug-and-play functionality.

2 Related Work

The object detection methods based on deep learning mainly include one-stage methods and two-stage methods. The two-stage object detection method starts with a series of candidate boxes generated by the algorithm as samples. Then, the samples are classified by the convolutional neural network. Faster R-CNN [3] designs RPN to assist in generating samples, and this way solves the problem of slow extraction of candidate boxes by selective search. Region-based fully convolutional networks (R-FCN) [4] proposes a convolutional network with position-sensitive distribution instead of a fully connected network after the pooling layer, and this way enables feature sharing within the whole network and solving the problem of time consumption in the fully connected layer. Cascade R-CNN [5] proposes a cascaded R-CNN structure where different stages use different IoU thresholds to recalculate positive and negative samples and sampling strategies to gradually improve the bbox quality. This way solves the problem of mismatch caused by different IoU thresholds. Feature pyramid networks (FPN) [6] uses fused feature maps of different scales for object detection of different sizes, and this way solves the problem of unsatisfactory detection of small objects.

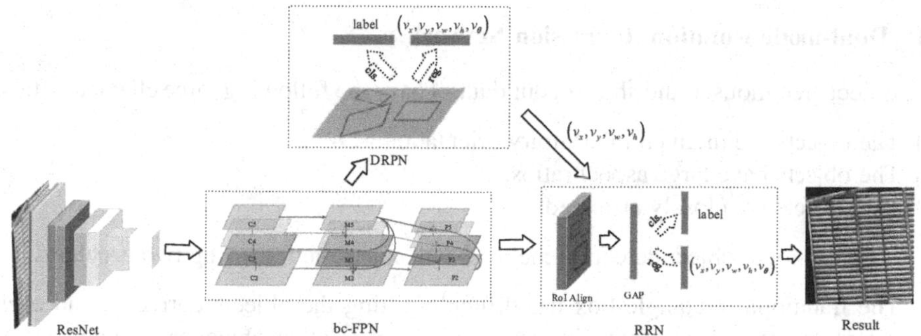

Fig. 1. Overall framework of DRRN, which consists of DRPN, RRN and bc-FPN, of which the bc-FPN is an optional module and is mainly used for the small object detection.

Different from two-stage methods, one-stage methods do not require the generation of candidate boxes, and can share features through a complete training process, greatly improving the speed of the algorithm. Single-shot object detector (SSD) [7] uses feature layers of different scales for comprehensive detection, which greatly improves the detection effect. RetinaNet [8] uses the focal loss function to suppress the loss value contributed by the large number of classes, and this way alleviates the problem of "class imbalance." Fully convolutional one-stage object detection (FCOS) [9] changes from laying anchor boxes to laying anchor points and changes the original classification and regression of anchor boxes to the classification and regression of anchor points. It is one of the most commonly used algorithms for object detection without anchor boxes.

The two types of detectors above are widely used in object detection tasks for natural images. However, these detection methods do not specifically address the problems of object in remote sensing images. Remote sensing images are taken in an overhead view and the object appears in arbitrary orientation. Fitting the object correctly for the traditional rectangular box and accomplishing accurate object detection are difficult in the field of remote sensing. Rotation detection refers to the detection method of replacing the traditional rectangular box with the inclined rectangular box. The inclined rectangular box can better fit the spatial position of the object in the remote sensing image. In this way, rotation detection can better meet the needs of object detection in the remote sensing field. At present, there are some rotation detection methods available, but most of these methods are either used in the text field [10] or used to detect fixed single class [11], and they do not pay special attention to the characteristics of objects in remote sensing images, lacking the ability to detect the generalization of multi-class objects.

3 Proposed Methods

The overall framework of DRRN is shown in Fig. 1. The detector consists of DRPN (Dual-mode Region Proposal Network), RRN (Rotation Regression Network) and bc-FPN, of which the bc-FPN is an optional module and is mainly used for the small object detection.

3.1 Dual-mode Rotation Regression Network

The object greenhouses and ships in our dataset have the following three characteristics:

(1) The objects are inclined in arbitrary orientation.
(2) The objects have large aspect ratios.
(3) The objects are closely arranged.

The traditional object detection methods will cause the following two problems:

(1) The traditional rectangle box has difficulty fitting the objects correctly, and each detection box will also contain many non-object or other object areas with a lot of extra information.
(2) The IoU values between the horizontal boxes are very high, which can easily be suppressed in the NMS stage. This condition results in a large number of missed detections in the results.

The rotation detection method replaces the traditional rectangular box with an inclined rectangular box, which can better fit the spatial position of the object in the remote sensing image. Similar to the traditional two-stage detector, our rotation detector, namely, DRRN, mainly consists of two stages: DRPN and RRN.

Dual-Mode Region Proposal Network

In the stage of DRPN, we regress anchors to provide high-quality region proposals for the next stage. We can also implement two detection modes by selecting to regress two different forms of anchor, namely, horizontal or rotational. When regressing the horizontal anchor, the anchor is represented by four parameters (x, y, w, h), and we use scale and ratio to generate the anchors. The angle is set to $\{-90\}$ by default. When regressing the rotational anchor, we use five parameters (x, y, w, h, θ) to represent the anchor. We add the angle parameter to generate the anchors. Based on the distribution of different aspect ratios of the object minimum circumscribed rectangle in the dataset, we finally use five ratios $\{1:4, 1:2, 1, 2:1, 4:1\}$. Two additional angles are added, and we set three angles $\{-90, -60, -30\}$. Finally, the anchors are regressed to the minimum circumscribed rectangle of ground truth to obtain the rotational proposals.

According to the forms of the generated anchor, DRRN is named RRN-H and RRN-R accordingly. The advantage of RRN-H is that fewer anchors can be used to match more positive samples and the model can be trained more efficiently. However, horizontal anchors will introduce a large number of irrelevant regions for objects with arbitrary orientation, large aspect ratio, and dense arrangement, and this condition can result in inaccurate prediction. RRN-R uses rotational anchors, which greatly avoid the introduction of irrelevant regions by adding the angle parameter, and it has better detection effects. However, the introduction of the angle parameter can increase the number of anchors exponentially, which reduces the efficiency of the model.

Rotation Regression Network

In the second stage of traditional object detection, the high-quality region proposals obtained in the first stage are first passed through the RoI pooling layer to obtain fixed-size RoIs. However, the objects such as greenhouses and ships have large aspect ratios and small narrow edge lengths, and the final RoIs obtained may not contain any useful information considering the feature misalignment problem existing in RoI pooling. We map the horizontal minimum circumscribed rectangle of the input to solve the narrow edge problem. We also use RoI align instead of RoI pooling to solve the problem of feature misalignment. Then, we flatten the extracted proposal features in the feature dimension and pass them through a global average pooling layer. Finally, two sibling fully connected layers are used to predict the class and the rotational bounding box of the object, respectively.

During the whole training process, we need to use NMS twice. The first time is to obtain high-quality proposals, and the second time is for post-processing of the predictions. Whether it is regressing the rotational anchors to obtain the rotational proposals, or predicting the minimum circumscribed rectangle of the object, we all use the rotational bounding box. The IoU calculation of the horizontal bounding box may lead to inaccurate IoU of the rotational bounding box. A method of calculating rotation IoU based on the idea of triangulation is proposed [10]. We use rotation NMS as a post-processing operation for the rotation IoU calculation. Meanwhile, we set different rotation NMS thresholds for different classes (greenhouse: 0.15, ship: 0.2) based on the distribution of the aspect ratios of different classes in the dataset.

Combined Regression Loss

In traditional object detection, a four-parameter tuple $v = (x, y, w, h)$ is generally used to represent the horizontal bounding box. Regression loss function can be divided into two types: one is ln-norm loss, such as the commonly used smooth L1 loss, which is defined as follows:

$$L_{reg}\left(v_i^*, v_i\right) = smooth_{L_1}\left(v_i^* - v_i\right), \tag{1}$$

$$smooth_{L_1}(x) = \begin{cases} 0.5x^2, \textit{ if } |x| < 1 \\ |x| - 0.5, \textit{ otherwise}. \end{cases} \tag{2}$$

However, the ln-norm loss has the following problems: the loss regards the four parameters as four independent objects to calculate the loss separately, which should be considered a whole. In addition, the regression loss is scale-sensitive, and the evaluation method of object detection uses IoU. Thus, IoU loss appears, which solves the abovementioned problems very well. IoU loss can be implemented in various forms. In this study, use the exponential form, which is defined as follows:

$$L_{IoU} = e^{1-IoU} - 1. \tag{3}$$

The IoU loss cannot measure the loss of two bounding boxes that are completely disjoint or have an inclusion relationship. Thus, borrowing from the practice of DIoU loss [12], a penalty term is added to the loss function, which is defined as the ratio of the square of the Euclidean distance between the central coordinates of the two bounding boxes to the square of the diagonal length of the minimum circumscribed rectangle of the two bounding boxes. The equation is as follows:

$$DIoU = IoU - \frac{\rho^2\left(b, b^{gt}\right)}{c^2}. \tag{4}$$

$$L_{cReg}\left(v_i^*, v_i\right) = |L_{RDIoU}| \frac{L_{reg}\left(v_i^*, v_i\right)}{\left|L_{reg}\left(v_i^*, v_i\right)\right|}. \tag{5}$$

For rotation object detection, the rotational bounding box is represented by a five-parameter tuple $v = (x, y, w, h, \theta)$. We can use the abovementioned calculation method of rotation IoU. However, the rotation IoU has non-differentiable points and cannot be used directly as a loss function for back propagation. Thus, we design a combined regression loss function, as shown in (5). Here, $|\cdot|$ represents the modulo length of a vector, is set to stop gradient, and does not participate in gradient backpropagation. $\frac{L_{reg}(v_i^*,v_i)}{|L_{reg}(v_i^*,v_i)|}$ is a unit vector, which represents the direction of gradient propagation. It ensures that the loss function is differentiable. $|L_{RDIoU}|$ is a scalar, which is responsible for adjusting the magnitude of the loss value to be consistent with the evaluation criteria of the detection.

3.2 Bi-directional Cross-layer Connected Feature Pyramid Network

The objects in remote sensing images generally have the characteristic of small size and our dataset also contains a large number of objects that accord with this characteristic. And the detection of greenhouses and ships can also be regarded as a small object detection task due to the large aspect ratio of greenhouses and ships. FPN significantly improves the performance of small object detection. However, FPN has the following two problems. On the one hand, the shallow features need to pass through dozens or even hundreds of network layers to reach the top layer, which leads to serious loss of feature information such as location. On the other hand, the top-down fusion focuses more on the features of adjacent layers, which leads to the loss of high-level semantic information through layer-by-layer transfer.

Bc-FPN is proposed in this study to solve the abovementioned problems, and the network implementation of bc-FPN is shown in Fig. 1. We select ResNet as the backbone and the last layer of each residual block as the reference for the feature maps, denoted as $\{C_2, C_3, C_4, C_5\}$. For the first problem, we add an additional bottom-up branch, which passes through fewer than 10 layers. This number is far fewer than the number of layers in the backbone stage and can better retain the shallow feature information and eliminate a large amount of invalid information in the process. For the second problem, we add cross-layer connections from C_5 and P_2 to the other feature maps, and low-level location and high-level semantic feature maps are built for all scales by means of cross-layer connections. The fusion between different scale feature maps is achieved by concatenating them rather than simply adding them together, which enables feature reuse and enhances feature propagation.

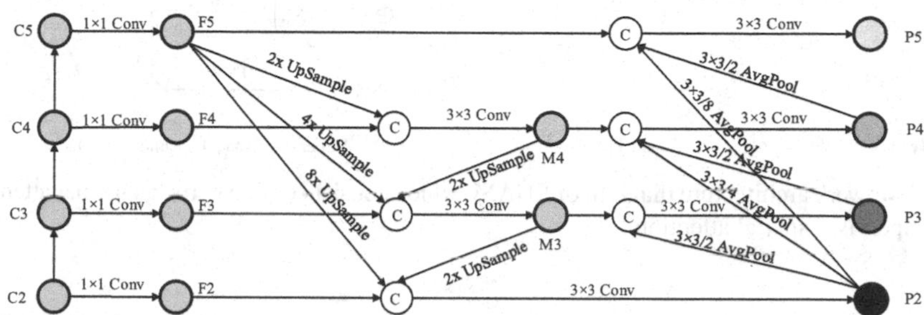

Fig. 2. Concrete implementation of bc-FPN, where C represents the concat operation.

The concrete implementation of bc-FPN is shown in Fig. 2. In the top-down branch, we first use a 1 × 1 convolutional layer to reduce the channel number. For upsampling, we use bilinear interpolation and then merge them by concatenation. Next, the 3 × 3 convolutional layer is used to eliminate the confounding effect of upsampling, reduce the channel number, and obtain the middle feature maps. In the bottom-up branch, we use average pooling downsampling and obtain the final feature maps through a 3 × 3 convolutional layer. We denote the feature maps with higher-level features obtained by bc-FPN as $\{P_2, P_3, P_4, P_5\}$. We set the number of channels to 256 for all feature maps to reduce the number of parameters and increase efficiency.

3.3 Supervised Hybrid Attention Mechanism

Remote sensing images belong to the real-world images. Due to the complexity of real-world data and the large field of view of remote sensing images, various types of background may be included in the scene, which can cause strong interference to object detection and result in high background complexity in remote sensing images. Moreover, classes such as greenhouses and ships are often closely arranged, which exacerbates this complexity.

SHAM is proposed in this study to tackle the complex background of remote sensing images and the Network architecture of SHAM is shown in Fig. 3. SHAM consists of two parts: a channel attention and a supervised spatial attention. Firstly, a channel attention module is utilized to enable the network to learn which features are meaningful. In this module, for a H × W × C input feature, a spatial global average pooling and global maximum pooling are respectively performed to obtain two parallel 1 × 1 × C channel descriptors. Then, a shared one-dimensional convolutional layer is applied to capture local cross-channel interactions. The two channel descriptors are then added together, and obtain channel weight coefficients through the sigmoid activation function. Finally, the obtained channel weight coefficients are multiplied with the original feature layer to obtain new features.

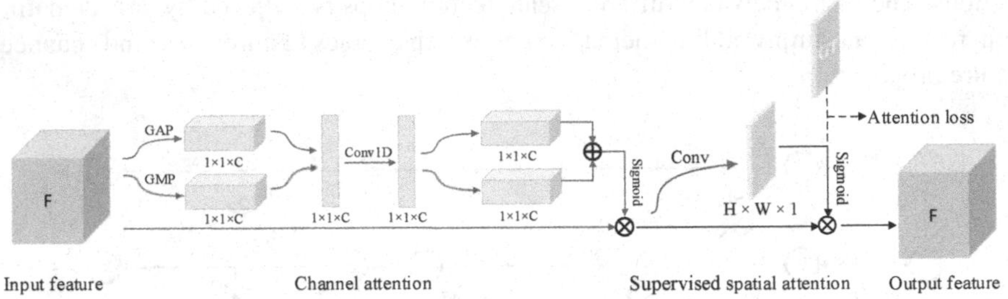

Fig. 3. Network architecture diagram of SHAM, which consists of two parts: a channel attention and a supervised spatial attention.

After the channel attention, a spatial attention is concatenated to teach the network where the meaningful features are. In the spatial attention part, a convolution structure is used to obtain a spatial description of $H \times W \times 1$. The spatial weight coefficients are obtained by sigmoid activation function, and they are multiplied with the feature layer obtained from the channel attention part to get the final features. To guide the network to learn purposefully, a supervised learning method is used where the spatial description and a binary image of the object and background obtained from ground truth are subjected to cross-entropy operation. The resulting cross-entropy loss is added to the final training as an attention loss.

The bc-FPN is organically combined with the SHAM. The rich semantic information of the feature layer F_5 is guided by the channel attention part, and the high-resolution information of the feature layer P_2 is guided by the spatial attention part.

4 Experiments

Experiments are performed on a server equipped with a NVIDIA GeForce RTX 2080ti GPU. In terms of dataset, use the self-made remote sensing image dataset, DRD-GS.

4.1 Dataset: DRD-GS

The dataset currently consists of two classes: greenhouse and ship. The greenhouses are derived from the original remote sensing images of GF-2 with a spatial resolution of 0.8 m, and they are mainly distributed in Shouguang City and Shen County in Shandong Province. The ships are mostly intercepted from Google Earth. They are mainly distributed in coastal areas. To ensure clear visibility of the objects in the image, original high-resolution remote sensing images with different time periods, different regions, and fewer cloud cover were selected.

For the images intercepted from Google Earth, we first add location information to them and then annotate them. For the original remote sensing images of GF-2, we first perform orthorectification on the multispectral images and the panchromatic images. Then, we perform the corresponding cropping operation on the two images, and we annotate the panchromatic images with high spatial resolution with the aid of the multispectral images. We use arbitrary quadrilateral to annotate instances and adopt a fine-grained annotation method that closely follows the edge shapes of various objects, so that the bounding box overlaps with the object edge as much as possible, thereby reducing interference from the background and other objects. The fine-grained annotation method can effectively improve the overall annotation quality. Finally, the panchromatic and multispectral images are fused, and the fused remote sensing images are used as our dataset. Our dataset is named as DRD-GS (Dataset of Rotation Detection of Greenhouse and Ship), which is the only remote sensing image rotation detection dataset that provides annotations for rotated class greenhouse.

To better compare the two detection methods, the annotation of arbitrary quadrilateral will be processed to ultimately provide two types of annotation styles. One is horizontal annotation, which annotates the instance by a horizontal rectangle and uses the format of $(x_{min}, y_{min}, x_{max}, y_{max})$. The other is a rotational annotation, which annotates the instance by a rotational rectangle and uses the format of $(x_1, y_1, x_2, y_2, x_3, y_3, x_4, y_4)$. Due to the large size of the cropped images, which represent the entire object area, they cannot be directly used as input images for object detection. Therefore, we split the images in the training set into 600×600 sub-images by means of a sliding window with an overlap of 150 pixels.

4.2 Traditional Object Detection Effect

Several classical one-stage and two-stage detection algorithms are selected for experiments to observe the detection effect of traditional object detection algorithms. We use ResNet-101 as backbone networks and initialize them with the corresponding pretrained models. We train a total of 22 epochs with an initial learning rate of 0.001, and then, we decay the learning rate by a factor of 10 at the 12th and 18th epochs in turn. The detection results of several object detection algorithms are shown in Table 1.

Overall, one-stage detection algorithms have a faster speed. However, two-stage algorithms have higher precision and recall. However, they have not achieved satisfactory results and cannot reach the level of practical application, especially for class, greenhouses, where neither the precision nor the recall is high, which is unacceptable in practical application. Considering the priority of meeting practical application requirements, we will focus on improving the precision and recall as key indicators and choose the two-stage algorithm for subsequent experiments.

4.3 Ablation Experiments

(1) Ablation experiments of DRRN.
Firstly, we used the rotation detector, DRRN, to conduct experiments on DRD-GS, and we compared the detection results with two-stage benchmark detection algorithm, Faster R-CNN. The detection results are shown in Table 2. By introducing the rotation

Table 1. Detection results of classical object detection algorithms. (SH: Ship, GH: Greenhouse)

Method	AP (%)		Recall (%)		mAP (%)	Time (s)
	SH	GH	SH	GH		
One-stage						
SSD	32.18	21.19	—	—	26.69	0.136
RetinaNet	74.12	52.66	75.91	53.70	63.39	0.258
FCOS	81.38	69.06	84.96	70.59	75.22	2 +
Two-stage						
Faster R-CNN	65.46	56.70	72.36	58.80	61.08	0.353
R-FCN	63.05	57.57	69.55	56.36	60.31	0.301
Cascade R-CNN	69.61	59.81	74.60	62.24	64.71	0.547
FPN	80.23	71.52	84.08	72.08	75.87	0.495

detection, the precision and recall have been improved. The improvement of the AR (average recall) is more obvious. The class greenhouse has a significant improvement in detection effect, because it is more in line with the abovementioned characteristics. RRN-R can achieve better detection effect due to the introduction of the angle parameter, but the time it requires for training also increases exponentially.

Table 2. Ablation detection results of rotation detection. (CRL: Combined Regression Loss).

Method	CRL	AP (%)		Recall (%)		mAP (%)	Time (s)
		SH	GH	SH	GH		
Faster R-CNN		65.46	56.70	72.36	58.80	61.08	0.353
RRN-H		68.40	64.15	76.31	69.02	66.27	0.371
	✓	70.69	65.93	77.98	70.57	68.31	
RRN-R		70.89	67.86	79.51	74.79	69.38	0.527
	✓	72.54	69.34	80.67	75.41	70.94	

On the basis of RRN-H and RRN-R, we added the improved method of CRL, and the detection results are shown in Table 2. By using the CRL, the detection performance has been improved. The more efficient rotation detector, RRN-H, finally achieves the mAP of 68.31% and the AR of 78.04%, and the final localization accuracy of the model has also been improved due to the introduction of the IoU parameter. The detection results of RRN-H for greenhouses and ships after using the CRL are shown in Fig. 4.

(2) Ablation experiments of bc-FPN.
On the basis of RRN-H and RRN-R, we added the improved methods such as FPN, and bc-FPN in turn, and the detection results are shown in Table 3. After adding bc-FPN, both precision and recall for object detection have been improved. The experiments show that

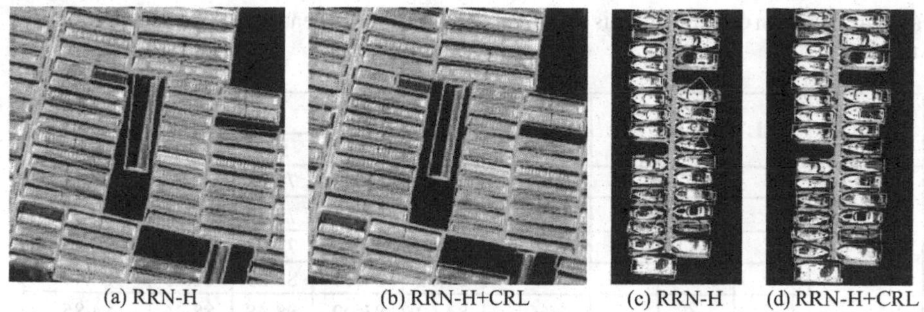

Fig. 4. Detection results before and after using CRL.

compared with adding FPN, adding the proposed bc-FPN to the detection algorithm has a more significant improvement in precision and recall, and has a stronger adaptability to small objects and objects with large aspect ratio.

Table 3. Ablation detection results of bc-FPN.

Method	CRL	FPN	bc-FPN	AP (%)		Recall (%)		mAP (%)
				SH	GH	SH	GH	
RRN-H	✓			70.69	65.93	77.98	70.57	68.31
	✓	✓		82.98	81.51	86.38	84.85	82.25
	✓		✓	84.79	84.01	88.29	87.13	84.40
RRN-R	✓			72.54	69.34	80.67	75.41	70.94
	✓	✓		82.93	84.06	88.08	86.33	83.49
	✓		✓	84.16	86.74	89.85	89.02	85.45

(3) Ablation experiments of SHAM.
On the basis of RRN-H and RRN-R, we added the improved methods of SHAM, and the detection results are shown in Table 4. The experiments show that adding SHAM to object detection algorithms improves both precision and recall by enhancing the object information while weakening the non-object information. The more efficient rotation detector, RRN-H, finally achieves the mAP of 84.85% and the AR of 88.47% on DRD-GS after adding bc-FPN and SHAM. Detection results of the improved algorithms for each class in DRD-GS are shown in Fig. 5.

Table 4. Ablation detection results of SHAM. (CA: Channel Attention, SSA: Supervised Spatial Attention).

Method	CRL	SSA	CA	bc-FPN	AP (%)		Recall (%)		mAP (%)
					SH	GH	SH	GH	
RRN-H	✓				70.69	65.93	77.98	70.57	68.31
	✓	✓			71.15	68.11	77.89	72.21	69.63
	✓	✓	✓		71.80	68.32	77.93	71.88	70.06
	✓			✓	84.79	84.01	88.29	87.13	84.40
	✓	✓	✓	✓	84.62	85.09	88.48	88.46	84.85
RRN-R	✓				72.54	69.34	80.67	75.41	70.94
	✓	✓			73.40	72.66	81.18	78.19	73.03
	✓	✓	✓		73.88	72.52	81.39	77.80	73.20
	✓			✓	84.16	86.74	89.85	89.02	85.45
	✓	✓	✓	✓	84.81	88.44	88.76	90.02	86.63

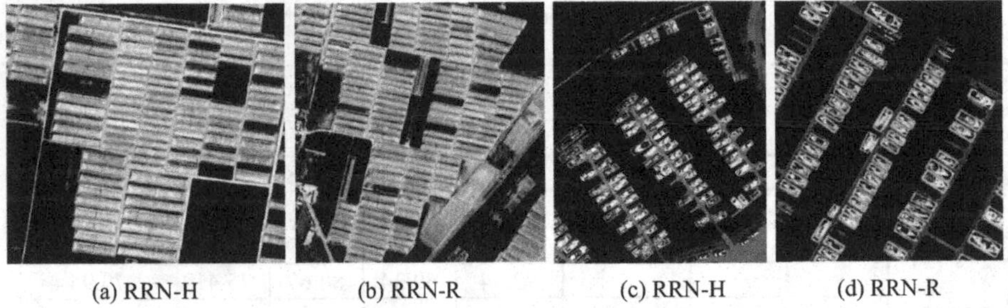

(a) RRN-H (b) RRN-R (c) RRN-H (d) RRN-R

Fig. 5. Detection results of the improved algorithms.

5 Conclusion

In this study, we first made a high-resolution remote sensing image rotation detection dataset, namely, DRD-GS, which currently consists of two classes, greenhouse and ship. We conducted the processing of cropping and slicing to solve the problem of huge size of remote sensing images. Then, we used several traditional object detection methods to compare the detection effects. We designed a rotation detector supporting multi-class, namely, DRRN, to solve the problem of arbitrary object orientation in remote sensing images. DRRN mainly consists of two parts: DRPN and RRN. Meanwhile, a combined regression loss is proposed to improve the traditional smooth L1 loss. Then, we proposed the bc-FPN to fully propagate the low-level location information and the high-level semantic information for solving the problem of small object size in remote sensing images. Finally, the SHAM is proposed to suppress image noise and enhance object information for solving the problem of complex background. Ablation experiments demonstrate that our proposed methods can effectively improve the object detection effect in remote sensing images.

References

1. Han, W., Chen, J., Wang, L., et al.: Methods for small, weak object detection in optical high-resolution remote sensing images: a survey of advances and challenges. IEEE Geosci. Remote Sens. Mag. **9**(4), 8–34 (2021)
2. Jianya, G., Yue, X.U., Xiangyun, H.U., et al.: Status analysis and research of sample database for intelligent interpretation of remote sensing image. Acta Geodaetica et Cartographica Sinica. **50**(8) (2021)
3. Ren, S., He, K., Girshick, R., et al.: Faster R-CNN: towards real-time object detection with region proposal networks. Adv. Neural Inf. Process. Syst. (2015)
4. Dai, J., Li, Y., He, K., et al.: R-FCN: object detection via region-based fully convolutional networks. Adv. Neural Inform. Process. Syst. (2016)
5. Cai, Z., Vasconcelos, N.: Cascade R-CNN: delving into high quality object detection. In: CVPR, pp. 6154–6162 (2018)
6. Lin, T.Y., Dollár, P., Girshick, R., et al.: Feature pyramid networks for object detection. In: CVPR, pp. 2117–2125 (2017)
7. Liu, W., Anguelov, D., Erhan, D., et al.: SSD: single shot multibox detector. In: ECCV, pp. 21–37 (2016)
8. Lin, T.Y., Goyal, P., Girshick, R., et al.: Focal loss for dense object detection. In: CVPR, pp. 2980–2988 2017)
9. Tian, Z., Shen, C., Chen, H., et al.: FCOS: fully convolutional one-stage object detection. In: CVPR, pp. 9627–9636 (2019)
10. Ma, J., Shao, W., Ye, H., et al.: Arbitrary-oriented scene text detection via rotation proposals. IEEE Trans. Multimedia **20**(11), 3111–3122 (2018)
11. Zhang, Z., Guo, W., Zhu, S., et al.: Toward arbitrary-oriented ship detection with rotated region proposal and discrimination networks. IEEE Geosci. Remote Sens. Lett. **15**(11), 1745–1749 (2018)
12. Zheng, Z., Wang, P., Liu, W., et al.: Distance-IoU loss: faster and better learning for bounding box regression. In: AAAI, vol. 34, pp. 12993–13000 (2020)

Few-Shot NeRF-Based View Synthesis for Viewpoint-Biased Camera Pose Estimation

Sota Ito[1(✉)], Hiroaki Aizawa[2], and Kunihito Kato[1]

[1] Faculty of Engineering, Gifu University, 1-1 Yanagido, Gifu 501-1193, Japan
ito@cv.info.gifu-u.ac.jp, kato.kunihito.k6@f.gifu-u.ac.jp

[2] Graduate School of Advanced Science and Engineering, Hiroshima University, 1-4-1 Kagamiyama, Higashi-Hiroshima City, Hiroshima 739-8527, Japan
hiroaki-aizawa@hiroshima-u.ac.jp

Abstract. Recently, several works have paid attention to view synthesis by neural radiance fields (NeRF) to improve camera pose estimation. Among them, LENS and Direct-PoseNet synthesize novel views from pre-trained NeRF and then train the pose regression convolutional network using real observations and the augmented synthetic views for better localization. Therefore, the performance depends on the three-dimensional (3D) consistency and the image quality of novel views. Especially, localization tends to fail if a diverse and high-quality training set is unavailable. To solve this issue, we tackle the problem of learning camera pose regressor from the viewpoint-biased and limited training set. We propose augmenting the regressor's training set using a few-shot NeRF instead of an original NeRF, which is employed in the previous frameworks. We can render high-quality novel views with a consistent 3D structure for stable training of the regressor. The experiments show that few-shot NeRF is an effective data augmenter for camera pose estimation under the viewpoint-biased limited training set.

Keywords: Neural Radiance Fields · Camera Pose Estimation

1 Introduction

Camera pose estimation, the task of regressing a camera's relative position and rotation to an object in a given image, is a fundamental problem in computer vision and robotics. Given RGB or RGB-D images [13], we can estimate the camera parameters by reconstructing the target scene using SfM [12], regressing the camera pose [3], or iteratively optimizing the camera parameters [6]. Recently, many researchers have paid attention to the use of view synthesis by neural radiance fields (NeRF) [8] to improve camera pose estimation. Among them, LENS [9] and Direct-PoseNet [1] are practical and sophisticated approaches that utilize novel views from pre-trained NeRF for localization. Concretely, LENS utilizes the novel view rendered from the original NeRF [8] as data augmentation

L. Iliadis et al. (Eds.): ICANN 2023, LNCS 14255, pp. 308–319, 2023.
https://doi.org/10.1007/978-3-031-44210-0_25

to train the camera pose regressor, PoseNet [3], which directly estimates camera parameters from a given single image using a convolutional neural network. Direct-PoseNet has a similar approach. However, if a diverse and abundant set of multiview images is unavailable during the training of NeRF, it may not effectively render novel views. These novel views are crucial for training the camera pose regressor. In such circumstances, the quality of novel views could degrade, leading to suboptimal performance in camera localization.

Hence, in this paper, we tackle the problem of learning the pose regressor from the viewpoint-biased and limited training set. Because the training of NeRF tends to fail in such a situation, we propose augmenting the regressor's training set using a few-shot NeRF instead of an original NeRF, which is employed in the previous frameworks. Concretely, we adopt DietNeRF [2] as a few-shot NeRF for data augmentation. Using DietNeRF, we can render high-quality novel views with a consistent 3D structure for stable training of the regressor. In the training phase of the regressor, we learn the regressor to make it more stable using actual observed data and extended views rendered from the pre-trained DietNeRF.

In the experiments, to validate the effectiveness of the proposed method, we compared DietNeRF with the original NeRF using training data with a small number of shots and viewpoint bias. Our experiments demonstrated that the novel views by the DietNeRF further improve the camera pose estimation performance compared to the original NeRF.

2 Related Work

2.1 Neural Radiance Fields

Mildenhall *et al.* proposed neural radiance fields (NeRF) [8] for learning a multilayer perceptron (MLP) that represents the three-dimensional (3D) space of a target scene from multi-view images with camera pose. The learned 3D representation can be utilized to generate an unobserved scene.

While NeRF can learn the consistent 3D structure and generate realistic novel views, training NeRFs requires multi-view images with camera parameters, which is laborious. Moreover, when the training data is small or when the viewpoints are biased, the training tends to fail the training and generate poor-quality rendering images. Therefore, several studies have been proposed to reduce the number of training data [2,4,15]. pixelNeRF [15] is a method for learning NeRFs from a single image by conditioning the color and density of the 3D coordinates on the features extracted by the trained CNN. InfoNeRF [4] learns to minimize the density of sampling points on the ray except for high-density points where an object exists, thereby suppressing the effect of noise and improving the quality of the image generation. DietNeRF [2] is a method that uses CLIP [10] for training to prevent training collapse and improve the generation quality when the amount of training data is small. This is because CLIP's image encoder can extract semantic features to make the semantic features similar between viewpoints in the 3D space during training so that unobserved regions that do not appear in the training data can be made semantically consistent. As a result, even when the training data is small or the training viewpoints are biased, it is possible to learn so that unobserved regions are complemented plausibly.

DietNeRF. In this section, we describe the training phase of DietNeRF in detail. The DietNeRF model takes 3D coordinates $\mathbf{x}$ and view direction $\mathbf{d}$ as input and outputs the density σ and color $\mathbf{c}$ of the 3D coordinates. This mapping function is modeled by a multi-layer perceptron (MLP). Next, to calculate the pixel value, we sample a ray $\mathbf{r}$ on 3D space based on camera pose, aggregate these properties $(\sigma, \mathbf{c})$ for each ray through the MLP, and then calculate the pixel value $\mathbf{C}(\mathbf{r})$ based on a volume rendering approach. The MLP's trainable parameters are optimized by minimizing the following photometric loss function,

$$\mathcal{L}_{\text{MSE}}(\mathcal{R}) = \frac{1}{N} \sum_{\mathbf{r} \in \mathcal{R}} ||\mathbf{C}(\mathbf{r}) - \hat{\mathbf{C}}(\mathbf{r})||_2^2, \tag{1}$$

where $\mathbf{C}(\mathbf{r})$ is a ground truth color and $\mathcal{R}$ is a set of N rays.

To hallucinate unseen regions, DietNeRF introduces the auxiliary semantic loss function, which aims to minimize the semantic distance between feature vectors of ground truth image $\mathbf{I}$ and synthesized image $\hat{\mathbf{I}}$. These feature vectors are extracted from CLIP's [10] image encoder ϕ. This process is formulated as

$$\mathcal{L}_{\text{sc}}(\mathbf{I}, \hat{\mathbf{I}}) = \phi(\mathbf{I})\phi(\hat{\mathbf{I}})^{\top}. \tag{2}$$

The total loss function for training DietNeRF is described as

$$\mathcal{L}_{\text{total}} = \lambda_{\text{MSE}}\mathcal{L}_{\text{MSE}} + \lambda_{\text{sc}}\mathcal{L}_{\text{sc}}, \tag{3}$$

where λ_{MSE} and λ_{sc} are hyperparameters that balance these loss function. Before training the pose regressor, we train DietNeRF according to the final loss function (Eq. (3)).

2.2 Camera Pose Estimation

Camera pose estimation is a key component for various applications. To achieve this task, several approaches have been proposed. Among them, absolute pose regression learns to regress the camera parameter from a given image by convolutional neural networks (CNN) from a pair of target scenes and the corresponding camera pose. PoseNet is one of the representative works. PoseNet regresses the parameters using MobileNet-V2 [11], enabling fast inference. However, since PoseNet is based on CNN, it easily overfits the training data and the camera distribution, resulting in poor performance. In addition, overfitting can be apparent when large-scale and diverse training data is unavailable.

For better estimation, many researchers have paid attention to the use of novel view synthesis techniques using NeRF [8]. LENS [9] augments the unseen views using NeRF-W [7] to enhance the pose regressor training. LENS generates a 3D grid based on density information obtained from NeRF-W and selects

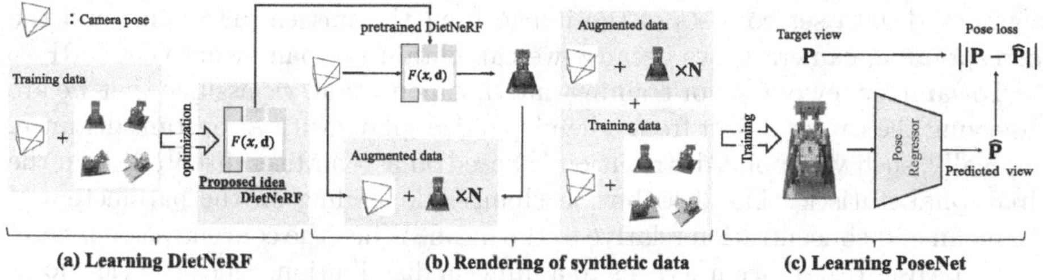

Fig. 1. Overview of the proposed method (a) Training DietNeRF from a small amount of training data. (b) Generating synthetic data for PoseNet using DietNeRF. (c) Training PoseNet using synthetic data and a small amount of real training data.

a viewpoint that is not too close to the object's location. The camera poses generated from the nearest camera pose from the selected viewpoint, and the camera pose generated from that viewpoint using NeRF-W are added to the training of the pose regressor. Direct-PoseNet [1] also uses pre-trained NeRF photometric errors for training. This has the advantage that unlabeled images can be used to train Pose Regressor.

However, the property of CNN-based regressors like PoseNet heavily depends on the view quality and the viewpoint distributions. In addition, building a training set for both the regressor and NeRF model is laborious. Therefore, in this paper, we use a few-shot NeRF, which can generate plausible unobserved views from the limited dataset, to augment training data for boosting the regressor's generalization ability.

3 Proposed Method

In this paper, we introduce an improved pipeline for few-shot and viewpoint-based camera pose estimation. As shown in the Fig. 1, the proposed method consists of three steps: training DietNeRF [2] as a view augmenter (Sect. 2.1 and Sect. 3.1), generating synthetic data for PoseNet [3] (Sect. 3.2), and training PoseNet for camera pose estimation (Sect. 3.3).

3.1 The Training of DietNeRF

To generate novel views for the pose regressor as shown in Fig. 1(a), we first train DietNeRF [2] from a given small dataset using the procedure in (Sect. 2.1).

3.2 View Synthesis for Data Augmentation

The camera pose regressor like PoseNet [3] has a problem of overfitting the training data when the limited and biased training data, results in poor performance for camera pose estimation. To solve this problem, our strategy is to utilize the novel views rendered by DietNeRF [2] as additional training data. The augmented data set consists of the image from the unseen viewpoint, and the corresponding camera poses because we can obtain the pairs from DietNeRF.

To sample viewpoints for training data augmentation, we assume that we are observing the target object from a hemispherical plane with a constant distance. Typically, such viewpoint distribution is based on a von Mises distribution in the directional statistic. The distribution changes depending on the parameters of the mean and concentration relative to the mean. When the concentration is zero, the von Mises distribution returns to a uniform distribution. Since the viewpoint of the composite data should have a viewpoint that captures a wide range of the target scene as in the uniform distribution, the azimuth and elevation angles are sampled from the von Mises distribution with mean 0 and concentration 0, and the 3D coordinates are determined. Following this sampling strategy, we sample N viewpoints consisting of azimuth and elevation angles from the von Mises distribution. Given sampled viewpoints, we generate additional view images from DietNeRF, as shown in Fig. 1(b).

3.3 The Training of Camera Pose Regressor

Finally, we train PoseNet [3] using real multi-view images with camera pose and synthetic additional images generated from DietNeRF [2] (Sect. 3.2), as shown in Fig. 1. The camera extrinsic parameters for camera pose estimation consist of the rotation and translation matrix. The following loss functions $\mathcal{L}_{\text{pose}}$ are defined based on the predicted camera pose $\hat{\mathbf{P}}$ and the ground-truth $\mathbf{P}$ of the training data.

$$\mathcal{L}_{\text{pose}} = \frac{1}{|\mathbf{P}|}||\mathbf{P} - \hat{\mathbf{P}}||_2^2. \tag{4}$$

4 Evaluation

We perform experiments from two perspectives: (i) we quantitatively and qualitatively evaluate a novel view quality of the original NeRF and DietNeRF for view augmentation in a viewpoint-biased setting, (ii) we quantitatively compare our model with previous work for camera pose estimation task.

4.1 Evaluation Setting

Dataset. We used NeRF synthetic dataset proposed in the original NeRF paper [8]. This dataset is rendered from a high-quality 3D model using Blender. Because we aim to improve the performance of the few-shot and viewpoint-biased settings in the experiments, we created subsets of 10 images as a training set from NeRF synthetic for training models. Following Sect. 3.2, we sampled augmented unseen viewpoints from a von Mises distribution with a concentration of 0. To evaluate our model in a viewpoint-based setting, we controlled the mean parameter of the von Mises distribution. The viewpoint-biased data we created are categorized into three types: `random`, `side`, and `front`. These viewpoint distributions cover the hemisphere, the target object from the side, and the

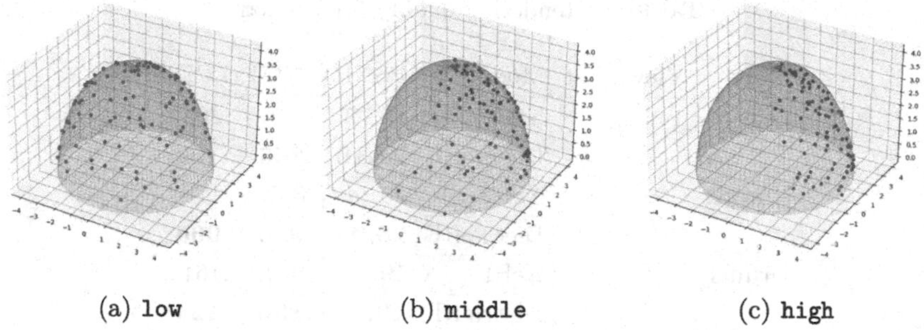

(a) `low` (b) `middle` (c) `high`

Fig. 2. `low`, `middle`, and `high`-concentrated viewpoint distribution for evaluation in the viewpoint-biased setting

Table 1. Number of training successes of `random`

Scene	Model	Successes rate
Lego	NeRF	2/5
	DietNeRF	**5/5**
Hotdog	NeRF	0/5
	DietNeRF	**5/5**
Drums	NeRF	**5/5**
	DietNeRF	**5/5**

Table 2. Number of training successes of `side`/`front`

Scene	Model	Successes rate
Lego	NeRF	1/5 / 2/5
	DietNeRF	**5/5** / **5/5**
Hotdog	NeRF	2/5 / 1/5
	DietNeRF	**5/5** / **5/5**
Drums	NeRF	**5/5** / **5/5**
	DietNeRF	**5/5** / **5/5**

target object from the front, respectively. Therefore, because `side` and `front` include largely invisible regions due to self-occlusion, we investigated variations of the `side` and `front` viewpoints. By controlling the azimuth of von Mises distribution, we additionally created `high`, `middle`, and `low` concentrated viewpoint datasets for `side` and `front` viewpoints. These `high`, `middle`, and `low` concentrated viewpoints differ in the degree of observation regions, as shown in Fig. 2.

Evaluation Metrics. We quantitatively evaluated the image completion quality in an invisible region using Peak Signal to Noise Ratio (PSNR), Structural Similarity (SSIM) [14], and Learned Perceptual Image Patch Similarity (LPIPS) [16]. To quantitatively evaluate the camera pose estimation, we used translation error and rotation error as metrics. The translation error indicates the error of the camera position and is calculated from the mean-squared error of the translation matrix between the ground truth and prediction. On the other hand, the rotation error indicates the mean-squared error of the rotation angle between the ground truth and prediction.

Network Details. We optimized the trainable parameters of DietNeRF using Adam [5], where the batch size is 1,024 and the initial learning rate is set to

Table 3. Rendering quality for `random`

Scene	Viewpoint	Model	PSNR	SSIM	LPIPS
Lego	`low`	NeRF	15.72	.688	.304
		DietNeRF	**24.10**	**.866**	**.109**
Hotdog		NeRF	20.14	.837	.179
		DietNeRF	**26.94**	**.928**	**.066**
Drums		NeRF	19.17	.812	.161
		DietNeRF	**19.66**	**.830**	**.124**

Table 4. Rendering quality for `side/front`

Scene	Viewpoint	Model	PSNR	SSIM	LPIPS
Lego	`low`	NeRF	19.23/**22.07**	.800/.837	.178/.132
		DietNeRF	**22.27**/22.02	**.836/.841**	**.114/.117**
	`middle`	NeRF	26.83/**25.45**	**.917/.903**	.064/**.073**
		DietNeRF	**27.21**/25.26	**.916**/.900	**.061**/.076
	`high`	NeRF	28.89/**27.23**	**.945/.936**	.043/**.048**
		DietNeRF	**29.33**/27.04	**.946**/.931	**.042**/.055
Hotdog	`low`	NeRF	**24.02**/23.63	**.882**/.877	**.113**/.123
		DietNeRF	20.47/**25.55**	.858/**.902**	.122/**.087**
	`middle`	NeRF	**32.18**/30.00	**.957**/.941	**.041**/.057
		DietNeRF	29.48/**30.12**	.942/**.945**	.056/**.053**
	`high`	NeRF	**35.01/32.50**	**.974/.965**	**.025/.033**
		DietNeRF	33.16/32.37	.966/**.965**	.035/.036
Drums	`low`	NeRF	18.34/18.07	.809/.811	.171/.179
		DietNeRF	**19.41/19.84**	**.827/.833**	**.124/.120**
	`middle`	NeRF	21.14/21.55	.862/.861	.115/.119
		DietNeRF	**21.62/22.02**	**.873/.871**	**.089/.090**
	`high`	NeRF	22.56/22.95	.891/.886	.088/.094
		DietNeRF	**23.13/23.14**	**.900/.892**	**.069/.076**

0.0005. For stability training, we applied an exponentially decreasing scheduler, increasing the learning rate by 0.1 over 250,000 iterations. Following the paper [2], we minimized Eq. (3) until 200,000 iterations and then minimized Eq. (1) from 200,000 to 250,000 iterations for better generalization.

4.2 The Completion Performance of DietNeRF

Quantitative Comparison. Quantitative completion results for NeRF and DietNeRF and the number of successful studies are shown in Table 1, 2, 3 and 4. From the `random` distribution results as shown in Table 3, we confirmed that

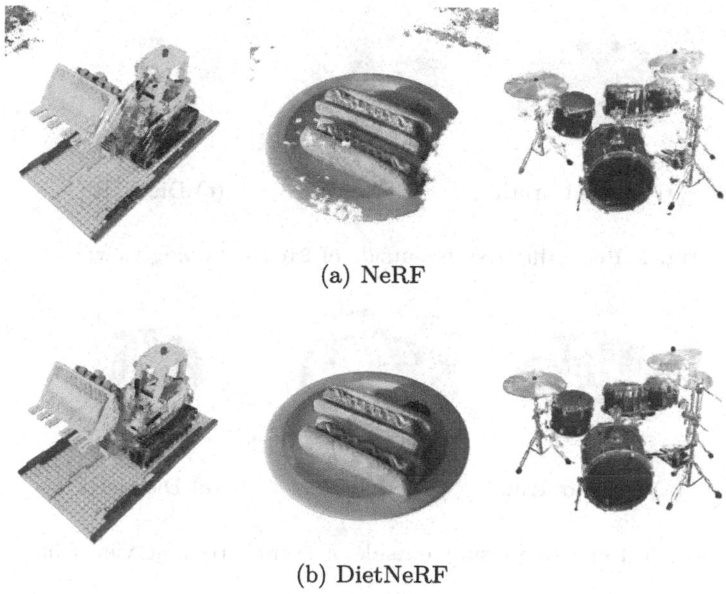

(a) NeRF

(b) DietNeRF

Fig. 3. Visual comparison between NeRF and DietNeRF. NeRF produces artifacts in an unseen viewpoint when the training dataset is small

DietNeRF did not tend to overfit training data, and the rendering quality was slightly better than that of NeRF. Especially, for the HotDog target, DietNeRF outperformed NeRF in terms of rendering quality and training stability. These results are similar to those reported in the DietNeRF paper [2] and indicate that DietNeRF's generalization ability is superior to the vanilla NeRF model. On the other hand, when the training viewpoint distribution is biased to `side`, the PSNR scores of NeRF and DietNeRF for Hotdog target were 24.02 and 20.47, respectively. In the case of `front`, the PSNR was 23.63 and 25.55, the opposite results. From these comparison results in the viewpoint-biased settings, we found that the rendering performance of DietNeRF tends to depend on the training viewpoint distribution and target object.

Visual Results of `random`. We closely looked at the rendering quality of NeRF and DietNeRF for boosting camera pose estimation performance. The rendering images of NeRF in the viewpoint-based setting are shown in Fig. 3. The figure clearly showed that while NeRF's PSNR score was partially competitive to DietNeRF, the rendering results in unseen viewpoints collapsed and had artifacts. On the other hand, DietNeRF can complete the unseen region even if the scene was not observed in the training phase. This is because CLIP's semantic feature enhances the viewpoint generalization of DietNeRF.

Visual Results of `side` and `front`. Figures 4 and 5 show the rendering results of `side` and `front` settings, respectively. Interestingly, we found that DietNeRF's completion ability depends on not only the training viewpoint distribution but

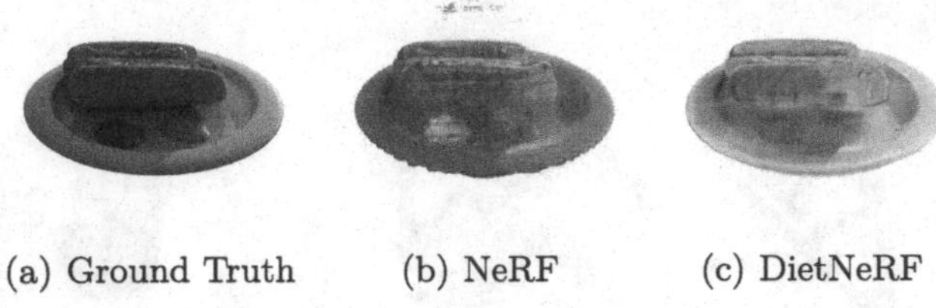

(a) Ground Truth (b) NeRF (c) DietNeRF

Fig. 4. Rendering results outside of `Side`'s training viewpoint

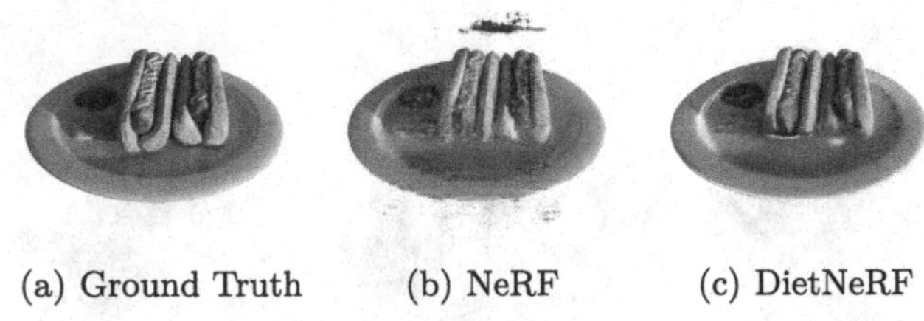

(a) Ground Truth (b) NeRF (c) DietNeRF

Fig. 5. Rendering results outside of `front`'s training viewpoint

also the **symmetric property** of the target object. Specifically, we found that DietNeRF tends to be able to complement invisible regions when the object has a symmetrical structure (Lego, Drums, and Hotdog) and the learning perspective captures one side of the symmetry.

When the training viewpoints are biased (`side` and `front`) and when DietNeRF is superior to NeRF, NeRF is sometimes superior to DietNeRF in the quality of the validation data (`middle` and `high`) for the vicinity of the training viewpoint. This indicates that while DietNeRF performs well in complementing unseen regions, it may not be as good as NeRF in producing quality for visible regions.

4.3 The Performance of Camera Pose Estimation

Quantitative Comparison. The results of camera pose estimation in the `random`, `side`, and `front` are shown in Tables 5 and 6, respectively. These scores were obtained from the PoseNet trained on real data and synthetic data by NeRF and DietNeRF. When training data was sampled from `random` distribution, DietNeRF was able to generate more high-quality novel views than NeRF, and the rendering images could enhance PoseNet's generalization, as shown in Table 5. When the training view was biased to `side` or `front`, Among NeRF and DietNeRF, higher generation quality had better camera pose estimation accuracy.

The Effect of Viewpoint Augmentation Scale. Figure 6 shows the results when changing the number of additional data generated by Blender, NeRF, and DietNeRF. From the figure, we found that the performance was significantly

Table 5. Camera pose estimation result of `random`.

Scene	Viewpoint	Synthetic data	Translation error [m]	Rotational error [°]
Lego	`low`	None	2.1019	31.34
		NeRF	1.1960	15.77
		DietNeRF	**0.3682**	**3.37**
Hotdog		None	1.9318	26.14
		NeRF	0.8784	10.15
		DietNeRF	**0.4227**	**4.04**
Drums		None	2.3129	40.71
		NeRF	0.5479	**4.46**
		DietNeRF	**0.4777**	**4.78**

Table 6. Camera pose estimation results of `side`/`front`

Scene	Viewpoint	Synthetic data	Translation error [m]	Rotational error [°]
Lego	`low`	None	3.0805/3.2724	88.07/86.82
		NeRF	1.5110/**0.7490**	33.35/**10.55**
		DietNeRF	**1.1234**/0.8608	**20.92**/13.14
	`middle`	None	1.8646/2.2959	36.59/47.11
		NeRF	**0.2384**/**0.2710**	**3.91**/**4.44**
		DietNeRF	0.2564/0.2919	4.31/5.32
	`high`	None	1.5803/1.9970	22.07/29.79
		NeRF	**0.1524**/0.2050	**2.64**/3.57
		DietNeRF	0.1795/**0.1828**	3.10/**3.18**
Hotdog	`low`	None	3.2312/2.9927	93.55/81.33
		NeRF	**1.3533**/1.3833	**15.41**/20.09
		DietNeRF	1.4252/**0.8760**	17.54/**10.28**
	`middle`	None	2.0696/1.7145	38.40/39.13
		NeRF	**0.3128**/0.4053	**3.86**/5.06
		DietNeRF	0.3399/**0.3543**	4.19/**4.32**
	`high`	None	1.8319/1.3600	24.10/21.76
		NeRF	**0.1518**/0.2698	**1.90**/3.19
		DietNeRF	0.1648/**0.2645**	2.05/**3.11**
Drums	`low`	None	2.9115/3.0163	83.87/84.22
		NeRF	1.4975/1.7794	28.62/38.94
		DietNeRF	**1.1673**/**1.2222**	**17.62**/**18.02**
	`middle`	None	2.1315/2.0425	38.18/44.91
		NeRF	0.4134/0.6202	6.00/11.24
		DietNeRF	**0.3774**/**0.5446**	**5.80**/**8.64**
	`high`	None	1.9176/1.7196	24.15/26.76
		NeRF	**0.2350**/**0.2865**	**3.06**/**4.49**
		DietNeRF	0.2480/0.3323	3.69/4.94

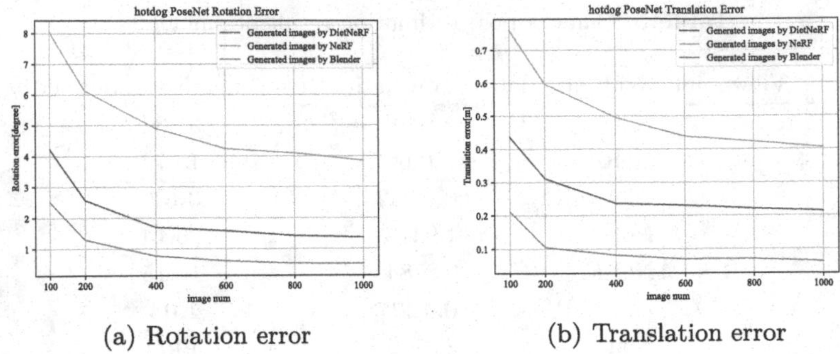

(a) Rotation error (b) Translation error

Fig. 6. Error of camera pose estimation when the scale of synthetic data is changing. Blue: camera pose estimation error of PoseNet trained on DietNeRF synthetic images, orange: NeRF synthetic images, green: ground truth images rendered by Blender. (Color figure online)

improved by DietNeRF, and increasing the number of additional data resulted in the improvement of camera pose estimation in all synthesizers (Blender, NeRF, and DietNeRF). When the number of synthetic data was set to the number of images that minimized the error of camera pose estimation using DietNeRF trained with 10 real images, we confirmed that the error of camera pose estimation was equivalent to PoseNet trained with 100 images generated by Blender for the translation error and 150 images generated by Blender for the rotation error.

5 Conclusion

In this paper, we proposed a view augmentation technique for learning a camera pose estimation model, PoseNet, from a small amount of training data. The proposed method improves the performance of camera pose estimation by generating synthetic data from DietNeRF trained with a small amount of data by generating new viewpoint images and training PoseNet using the synthetic data and a small amount of training data. In addition, we validated the improvement of camera pose estimation by increasing the number of synthetic data and confirmed that the performance improves by augmenting training data. In future work, it is necessary to verify whether the proposed method is effective in more realistic scenes.

References

1. Chen, S., Wang, Z., Prisacariu, V.: Direct-posenet: absolute pose regression with photometric consistency. In: 2021 International Conference on 3D Vision (3DV), pp. 1175–1185. IEEE (2021)

2. Jain, A., Tancik, M., Abbeel, P.: Putting nerf on a diet: semantically consistent few-shot view synthesis. In: Proceedings of the IEEE/CVF International Conference on Computer Vision, pp. 5885–5894 (2021)
3. Kendall, A., Grimes, M., Cipolla, R.: Posenet: a convolutional network for real-time 6-dof camera relocalization. In: Proceedings of the IEEE International Conference on Computer Vision, pp. 2938–2946 (2015)
4. Kim, M., Seo, S., Han, B.: Infonerf: ray entropy minimization for few-shot neural volume rendering. In: Proceedings of the IEEE/CVF Conference on Computer Vision and Pattern Recognition, pp. 12912–12921 (2022)
5. Kingma, D.P., Ba, J.: Adam: a method for stochastic optimization. arXiv preprint arXiv:1412.6980 (2014)
6. Lin, Y.C., Florence, P.R., Barron, J.T., Rodriguez, A., Isola, P., Lin, T.Y.: inerf: inverting neural radiance fields for pose estimation. 2021 IEEE/RSJ International Conference on Intelligent Robots and Systems (IROS), pp. 1323–1330 (2020)
7. Martin-Brualla, R., Radwan, N., Sajjadi, M.S., Barron, J.T., Dosovitskiy, A., Duckworth, D.: Nerf in the wild: neural radiance fields for unconstrained photo collections. In: Proceedings of the IEEE/CVF Conference on Computer Vision and Pattern Recognition, pp. 7210–7219 (2021)
8. Mildenhall, B., Srinivasan, P.P., Tancik, M., Barron, J.T., Ramamoorthi, R., Ng, R.: Nerf: representing scenes as neural radiance fields for view synthesis. Commun. ACM **65**(1), 99–106 (2021)
9. Moreau, A., Piasco, N., Tsishkou, D., Stanciulescu, B., de La Fortelle, A.: Lens: localization enhanced by nerf synthesis. In: Conference on Robot Learning, pp. 1347–1356. PMLR (2022)
10. Radford, A., et al.: Learning transferable visual models from natural language supervision. In: International Conference on Machine Learning, pp. 8748–8763. PMLR (2021)
11. Sandler, M., Howard, A., Zhu, M., Zhmoginov, A., Chen, L.C.: Mobilenetv 2: inverted residuals and linear bottlenecks. In: Proceedings of the IEEE Conference on Computer Vision and Pattern Recognition, pp. 4510–4520 (2018)
12. Sattler, T., Leibe, B., Kobbelt, L.: Fast image-based localization using direct 2D-to-3D matching. In: 2011 International Conference on Computer Vision, pp. 667–674. IEEE (2011)
13. Shotton, J., Glocker, B., Zach, C., Izadi, S., Criminisi, A., Fitzgibbon, A.: Scene coordinate regression forests for camera relocalization in rgb-d images. In: Proceedings of the IEEE Conference on Computer Vision and Pattern Recognition, pp. 2930–2937 (2013)
14. Wang, Z., Bovik, A.C., Sheikh, H.R., Simoncelli, E.P.: Image quality assessment: from error visibility to structural similarity. IEEE Trans. Image Process. **13**(4), 600–612 (2004)
15. Yu, A., Ye, V., Tancik, M., Kanazawa, A.: pixelnerf: neural radiance fields from one or few images. In: Proceedings of the IEEE/CVF Conference on Computer Vision and Pattern Recognition, pp. 4578–4587 (2021)
16. Zhang, R., Isola, P., Efros, A.A., Shechtman, E., Wang, O.: The unreasonable effectiveness of deep features as a perceptual metric. In: Proceedings of the IEEE Conference on Computer Vision and Pattern Recognition, pp. 586–595 (2018)

Ga-RFR: Recurrent Feature Reasoning with Gated Convolution for Chinese Inscriptions Image Inpainting

Long Zhao, Yuhao Lou, Zonglong Yuan, Xiangjun Dong, Xiaoqiang Ren, and Hongjiao Guan(✉)

Faculty of Computer Science and Technology, Qilu University of Technology (Shandong Academy of Sciences), Jinan 250353, China
guanhj@sdas.org

Abstract. Inscriptions were a primary means of recording historical events and literary works in ancient times, and remain an important part of Chinese ancient civilization. However, due to their large quantity and prolonged exposure to the natural environment, inscriptions have suffered significant damage. Traditional manual restoration methods are time-consuming and labor-intensive, making it necessary to explore new restoration techniques. In this study, we introduce a Ga-RFR network that uses gated convolution to replace ordinary convolution. This technique reduces feature redundancy in generated feature maps and minimizes the production of unnecessary information, thereby enhancing restoration effectiveness. We also compare our method with other advanced image restoration algorithms, and our results demonstrate that our approach outperforms other current methods.

Keywords: Image inpainting · Restoration of inscriptions · Gated convolution

1 Introduction

In Chinese culture, inscriptions on stone monuments are highly valued as precious artifacts that carry traditional Chinese characters. However, these inscriptions are often subject to irregular damage due to natural and geographical factors. The restoration of these inscriptions requires significant time and effort from researchers. Moreover, the subjective nature of personal opinions on the content and form of restoration can lead to inconsistent results and a lack of objective standards. Therefore, there is an urgent need for a more efficient and standardized method of inscription restoration [19].

Today, digital imaging technology allows for the preservation of inscriptions as images, which can then be restored using image restoration techniques. However, currently, the restoration of inscription images is predominantly carried out

Supported by the National Natural Science Foundation of China (61806105 and 62076143).

L. Iliadis et al. (Eds.): ICANN 2023, LNCS 14255, pp. 320–331, 2023.
https://doi.org/10.1007/978-3-031-44210-0_26

by universities and research institutions, and there is a lack of standardized and publicly available datasets for inscription image restoration. Many scholars use unsupervised generative adversarial networks, but these networks often generate fake characters that only resemble Chinese characters, and the restored results are not actual characters.

To improve the focus on Chinese characters in inscription image restoration, we convert inscription images into grayscale images for training. We also enhance the feature fusion module of RFR-Net by utilizing gated convolutions. Gated convolutions allow for learning to highlight mask areas and sketch information in separate channels, reducing feature redundancy and obtaining enhanced feature maps, even in deeper network layers.

Our main contributions are summarized as follows:

- Collect and organize ancient inscription text dataset, integrate the inscription text data of calligrapher Ouyang Xun, and use it as a training work for inscription image restoration.
- We improve the RFR-Net network structure using gated convolution, reduce the feature redundancy due to the deep network in the feature fusion module, improve the image quality of image inpainting, and change the input structure of the network to be used as the training of grayscale maps, thus improving the training efficiency.
- We analyze our model in terms of image restoration quality and efficiency, and compare it with advanced image restoration algorithms to demonstrate the superiority of our network.

2 Related Work

Early work on image inpainting used patches [1], exemplars [7], and diffusion-based [9] methods to draw images. In recent years, image inpainting algorithms based on deep learning have developed rapidly. Pathak et al. [13] proposed a method of adversarial training network [3,8]. Later, researchers proposed a variety of image inpainting methods such as local global discrimination method [4], partial convolution [11], gated convolution [20], RFR-Net [10] and so on.

Inscription image inpainting is a relatively new and less developed research area. Different from image restoration, restoration of inscription images requires not only accurate preservation of stroke topology, but also visual and stylistic consistency. Restoration is also a challenging task when an inscription image suffers a large area loss. Chen et al. [2] proposed a double discriminator-based image inpainting method for Yi handwritten script, which can effectively restore the structure of Yi script. However, because this method is based on obtaining the distribution probability of Yi script, it is less effective in restoring Yi script with complex strokes. Lv et al. [12] proposed a Chinese character image inpainting network based on U-Net [14], using U-Net as a generator and incorporating discriminators using generative adversarial network ideas. Song et al. [16] proposed a method to repair modern Chinese handwritten characters based on self-attention and against classification loss, which can repair handwritten

Chinese characters with partially obscured regions. Zheng et al. [18] proposed a GAN model with a dual-branch generator to improve the accuracy of recovery, but the repair effect is not good in the case of large areas missing. Wang et al. [17] proposed a semantic enhanced adversarial generative network model with global semantic supervising module.

However, due to the addition of label information in the process of font generation, the cut part was filled into the defect area, resulting in image inpainting errors. However, these methods are influenced by image inpainting and mainly pursue the visual consistency of the repaired broken regions, with little restriction on the degrees of freedom of the structure. The obtained results have many structural errors. Inscription images are not simply equivalent to traditional images; they require that the topology of the strokes in the restored image remain correct, not just visually consistent. Secondly, when significant breaks in the text contain critical locations, it is challenging to accomplish correct inpainting relying only on the edge information present. Inpainting of inscriptions requires restoring out the important radicals, not just seeking to just look like Chinese characters.

3 Proposed Method

As shown in Fig. 1, Ga-RFR is composed of three modules: pre-processing module, feature reasoning module, and adaptive gated feature fusion module. The pre-processing module is to try out the true image and the mask image to distinguish the updated position of the mask. The feature reasoning module repairs the location to be repaired to get the repaired feature map, then the feature reasoning module feeds the feature map to the pre-processing module, this operation is performed six times and saves the feature map, then the feature map obtained six times is transferred to the adaptive gated feature fusion module. We next introduce these three modules.

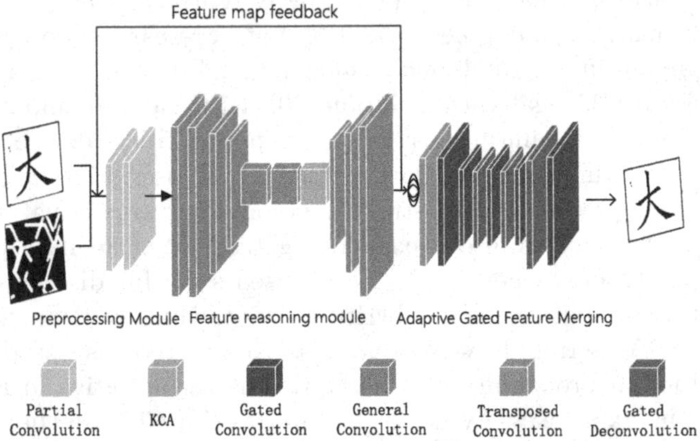

Fig. 1. Ga-RFR network structure

3.1 Model Structure

Pre-processing Module. The pre-processing module mainly accepts the feature map and the corresponding mask layer, performs partial convolution of the effective elements of the feature map based on the mask image. The mask is a randomly generated smeared picture, combined with the inscription picture to simulate the inscription damage in realistic scenarios. At each step of the training process, the model generates the next mask map based on the current output in order to progressively infer the content of the missing region. The partial convolution calculation is followed by renormalization of the feature map. The structural information of the inscription image is not affected by the color pixels, and we improve the pre-processing module by setting the input layer of the network as a single channel, which can effectively reduce the cost of updating the image and the mask. The partial convolution layer is calculated as follows:

$$f_{x,y,z}^{*} = \begin{cases} W_z^T \left[f_{x,y} \odot m_{x,y} \frac{1}{\operatorname{sum}(m_{x,y})} \right] + b, & \operatorname{sum}(m_{x,y})! = 0 \\ 0, & \text{otherwise} \end{cases} \tag{1}$$

where$f_{x,y,z}^{*}$denotes the eigenvalues of x,y in the channel z, $W_z$is the convolution kernel of channel z,$f_{x,y}$and$m_{x,y}$are the input feature blocks and mask blocks centered on x,y and of the same size as the convolution kernel, $f_{x,y,z}^{*}$ is obtained by taking a weighted sum of the eigenvalues at (x, y) on the channel z and adding a bias term.

The pre-processing module newly generates the mask map of position i,j from partial convolution with the formula:

$$m_{x,y}^{*} = \begin{cases} 1, \operatorname{sum}(m_{x,y})! = 0 \\ 0, \ \text{otherwise} \end{cases} \tag{2}$$

The pre-processing module newly generates the mask map of position i,j from partial convolution with the formula, $\operatorname{sum}(m_{x,y})$ computes the sum of the elements of the matrix $m_{x,y}$.

Feature Reasoning Module. The feature reasoning module is an encoder and decoder using a skip-long connection, and the input of the module is a feature map and a mask for the current round. The middle of the module is a KCA [10] and the output is the feature map after the current round of restoration. The KCA module generates attention masks for each local region by introducing a knowledge consistency constraint. The generated local region attention mask is further multiplied with the mask of the image to be inpainted to ensure that attention is paid only to the regions to be inpainted. The feature reasoning module is repeated six times jointly with the pre-processing module, and in each round, the output of the feature reasoning module is used as the input of the pre-processing module for the next round. Each time, the output of the feature reasoning module is recorded and used as a later fusion.

Adaptive Gated Feature Fusion Module. The feature map has passed the feature inference module several times when the feature map is fully populated or after a specific round of iterations. If the final feature map is used directly as the output, gradient disappearance may occur. To solve this problem, the intermediate feature maps must be merged. However, the convolution budget limits the number of recursions because the number of channels in the cascade is fixed. The formula for the merged feature map at position (x, y, z) is as follows:

$$\bar{f}_{x,y,z} = \frac{\sum_{i=1}^{N} f^{i}_{x,y,z}}{\sum_{i=1}^{N} m^{i}_{x,y,z}} \tag{3}$$

where N represents the total number of rounds, the output feature map of the i iteration and the effective region mask map are f^i and m^i, $\bar{f}^i$ is the feature map after the fusion result of the z channel of (x, y) at the corresponding position.

The convolutional generation of feature maps contains a large amount of redundant feature information, and different feature maps may appear similar and thus generate redundant information, which leads to poor inpainting results. Gated convolution turns the feature map into the output of the convolution layer after sigmod nonlinear activation function by adding gated convolution. It is possible to increase the perceptual field of the feature map and reduce feature redundancy in deeper networks.

As shown in Fig. 2, we use gated convolution instead of normal convolution to fuse the incoming feature maps, in order to reduce redundancy, enhance structural restoration of inscriptional text images, and improve restoration results. During the generation of feature maps, regular convolution operations may produce a significant amount of redundant information. This is because many feature maps may be similar, leading to duplicate and unnecessary information being included in the generated feature maps. This redundancy can affect the final image restoration effect, and therefore a better approach is needed to address this issue.

Currently, many existing restoration methods adopt either two-stage network structures or GAN-based network structures. These network structures consume a large amount of computational resources and require complex training to ensure their generalization capability. However, this approach may lead to network overfitting, thereby reducing its restoration effect.

Therefore, we need to explore new network structures and training methods to address these issues. Possible solutions include using more advanced convolution operations, such as using gated convolutions instead of regular convolutions to reduce the generation of redundant information.

3.2 Gated Convolution

Gated convolution is no huge difference from the original convolutional neural network, except that the gating mechanism is added to the convolutional neural network. But gated convolution is more suitable for image restoration than

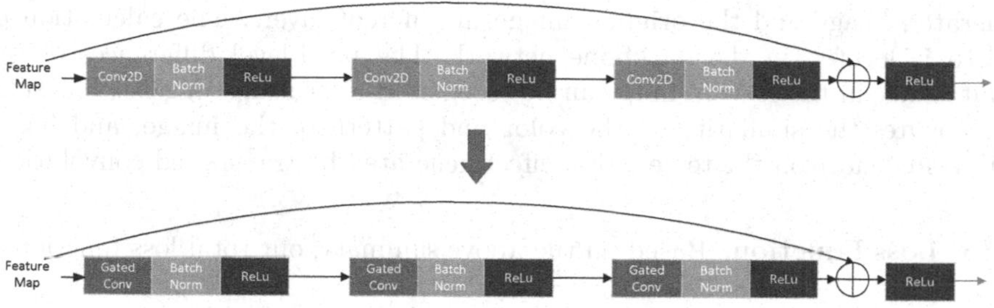

Fig. 2. Adaptive gated feature fusion module changes.

normal convolution. It is based on the improvement of partial convolution. Partial convolution improves the image restoration quality of irregularly masked images, but it also has a big problem. In terms of spatial location, partial convolution classifies all locations as valid or wireless, regardless of how many pixels are covered by the filter in the previous layer, the mask in the next layer will be set to one, and invalid pixels in partial convolution will gradually disappear in deeper network layers, with each layer of channels sharing the same mask. Gated convolution automatically learns the soft mask and dynamically identifies the location of valid pixels in the image to accomplish dynamic feature selection. The equation of gated convolution is as follows:

$$\begin{aligned} \text{Gating}_{y,x} &= \sum\sum W_g \cdot I \\ \text{Feature}_{y,x} &= \sum\sum W_f \cdot I \end{aligned} \tag{4}$$

$$O_{y,x} = \Phi(\text{Feature}_{y,x}) \odot \sigma(\text{Gating}_{y,x}) \tag{5}$$

where W_g and W_f represent two different convolutional filters, σ is the sigmoid activation function, and the output gating values are 0 and 1, Φ is the activation function. Gated convolution is the ordinary convolution followed by a sigmoid activation function as a soft gating, which weights the result of the current layer before input to the lower layer of the network. The activation function and the feature map can complete the feature extraction, and the activation function and the Gating convolution can complete the dynamic feature selection. This convolution mechanism can extract feature maps better and has better results in inpainting images with large regions missing.

3.3 Loss Function

The loss function of the recurrent feature reasoning model consists of four parts: perceptual loss $L_{perceptual}$, style loss L_{style}, L1 loss L_{mask} for the region to be filled, and L1 loss L_{unmask} for the non-filled region. $L_{unmask}$and $L_{mask}$are the L1 difference between areas with no mask and areas with a mask. The perceptual loss is calculated using the Vgg16 [15] pre-trained model at training time by comparing the Euclidean distance between the feature representations of the generated image and the original image in different layers. The calculation of Vgg16 is located in the backbone network. The pixel-level differences of the input image in the feature map can be recognized after using Vgg-16. The style loss ensures the similarity of the color and pattern of the image, and has a mitigating effect on the tessellation effect generated by transposed convolution.

Total Loss Function. Based on the above summary, our total loss function is

$$L_{\text{total}} = \lambda_{\text{mask}} L_{\text{mask}} + \lambda_{\text{unmask}} L_{\text{unmask}} + \lambda_{\text{style}} L_{\text{style}} + \lambda_{\text{perceptual}} L_{\text{perceptual}}$$

4 Experiments

4.1 Datasets

There are no available datasets of epigraph image and epigraph text, as it is complex and difficult to produce such a dataset in the Chinese language domain due to the large number of Chinese characters and the variety of written ways. The construction of training test data for deep learning is an important task for image restoration of calligraphic inscriptions. In this paper, we focus on constructing the image dataset for training test of this paper and the mask dataset for masking. We mainly used the inscriptions of Ouyang Xun, a famous Chinese calligrapher, whose calligraphy is mainly in regular script with regular structure and high recognizability, which is conducive to building a dataset for model training. The inscriptions have well-spaced and well-laid out Chinese characters, and individual Chinese characters are easy to extract. The inscriptions can be segmented by segmenting the Chinese characters, and each image after segmentation represents one Chinese character. We mainly extracted inscriptions from the Huangfujun stele and the Jiuchenggong liquan inscription. As shown in Fig. 3, we use opencv to extract the single word of the inscription into the single word picture, smooth the image of the single word with Noise Reduction technology, and then use Gauss filter technology to reduce the noise of the image background. Then, Threshold processing is used to grayscale the background and font of the inscription, and the image of the inscription with black words and white background is obtained after inverting the color. Since the damage of inscriptions is not a fixed area, weathering erosion and other ways can cause damage to indefinite areas of inscriptions. So according to the reality, the mask image is a picture of size 128 pixels to generate a randomly generated continuous smear of the interference image. The resulting training set has more than 4,000 images and the test set has more than 800 images, and the training set and the test set are mostly different fonts.

4.2 Experiment

In order to demonstrate the effectiveness of the adaptive gated feature fusion module based on gated convolution improvement proposed by the algorithm in

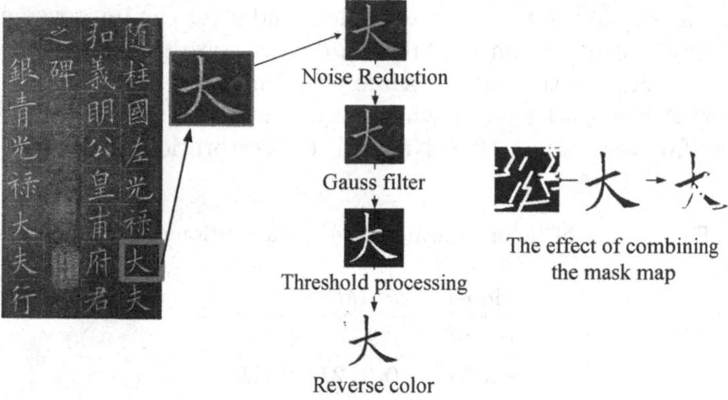

Fig. 3. Ouyang Xun's "Stele of Huangfu Jun" and the process of extracting images from the inscriptions and the effect of combining the mask map.

this paper for inscription restoration, a quantitative analysis will be performed in comparison with image inpainting model. The peak signal-to-noise ratio(PSNR), structural similarity (SSIM) [21], and Mean L1 Loss are used to compare the three objective metrics for quantitative analysis. These evaluation criteria can measure whether the image conforms to human visual perception and how similar the trained result is to the original image, which strongly proves the effectiveness of the image after restoration.

Ablation Experiment. The Adam [6] algorithm of PyTorch was used as the optimizer for training, and $2 * 10^{-4}$ was chosen at the beginning of training, and then $5 * 10^{-5}$ was used for tuning. Figure 4 shows the L1 loss in training, the horizontal axis represents the number of training sessions, and the vertical axis represents the L1 loss value.

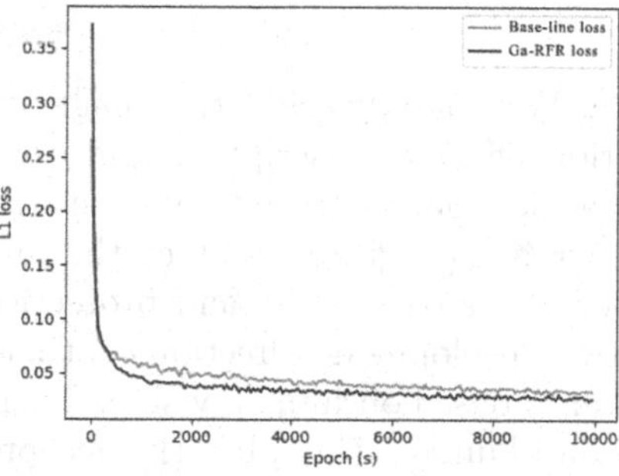

Fig. 4. L1 Loss value change chart

The comparison of the test set fixes before and after the improvement of the adaptive gating feature fusion module can demonstrate the effectiveness of the work in this paper. We trained the same effect after the work of this paper as well as the RFR-Net model, as shown in Table. 1, the values of our SSIM as well as PSNR are far better than RFR-Net, and the restoration is better.

Table 1. The Impact of Incorporating Gated Convolutions on Image Inpainting.

Model	*SSIM*	*PSNR*
Base-line	0.9533	45.71
Ga-RFR	**0.9721**	**46.16**

In order to verify the effectiveness of the work done in this paper, the experimental results of this experiment are compared separately under the same training conditions. For the text of the test set a restoration result control is performed. In this paper, we have selected the best image restoration algorithms in recent years as the control experiment, as shown in Fig. 5, we have done the experimental comparison with the best algorithms, by inputting the same mask map to get the restoration results for comparison, the results obtained from our work are superior to other models in terms of structural filling and subjective effects. The RFR-net model has redundant repair and does not repair important strokes in the font structure, and in some of the fonts there is a blurred repair effect. the Pix2Pix model [5] is not strong in general and does not show good repair effect for font repair. The Pix2Pix model is not strong in general and does not show good restoration effect for font restoration. The model in this paper can effectively repair the radicals in the inscription fonts in the restoration of the defective parts, and can The model is effective in repairing the missing parts of the inscriptions, and can effectively fill in the important stroke structures such as hooks and apostrophes in the inscriptions. The model is also effective in restoring inscriptions with large loss areas.

Qualitative Comparis. We can only select the image quality evaluation index to measure the restoration effect of inscription images. Character restoration is divided into two categories, one is to improve the accuracy of handwriting recognition, and the other is to digitally protect the ancient documents, and the purpose of this paper is the restoration and protection of inscriptions. The difference between the two development directions is that one is based on computer vision and the other is based on human vision. There are some differences between machine vision and human vision, but the accepted image quality evaluation standard is an objective means to measure the comparison of the effect of image restoration after restoration. We use PSNR and SSIM as the standards for measuring image quality. PSNR (Peak Signal to Noise Ratio) is one of the most common and widely used image objective evaluation metrics, however, it

Fig. 5. Examples of qualitative comparison

is based on the error between corresponding pixel points, i.e., it is based on error-sensitive image quality evaluation. The higher its value, the less distortion between the restored image and the real image, the better the image quality. SSIM (Structural Similarity) is a recognized metric to measure the similarity of two images. It measures the similarity of two images in terms of brightness, contrast and structure, and the higher the value, the better the image quality, as with PSNR.

Table 2. Comparison of inpainting effects of inpainting algorithms under different masks.

	Mask	Models			
		Pix2Pix	Pconv	RFR-Net	Ours
PSNR	0%–10%	38.052	46.844	52.74	**53.071**
	10%–20%	37.821	43.026	46.444	**46.644**
	20%–30%	37.638	41.059	44.235	**44.267**
	30%–40%	37.49	39.647	**42.642**	42.634
	40%–50%	37.381	38.987	41.853	**41.857**
SSIM	0%–10%	0.9564	0.9850	0.9864	**0.9913**
	10%–20%	0.9262	0.9620	0.9656	**0.9778**
	20%–30%	0.8987	0.9401	0.9435	**0.9644**
	30%–40%	0.8686	0.9140	0.9159	**0.9466**
	40%–50%	0.8491	0.8957	0.8960	**0.9348**

We are comparing with existing methods RFR-Net, Pconv and Pix2Pix image restoration algorithms using inscriptions dataset, and the experimental results are shown in Table 2. Our experiments are applied for realistic scenarios. Since the damage of inscriptions in realistic scenarios are variable in area and the size of the damaged area varies. Therefore, we select mask images with different percentages to simulate the damage of inscriptions in realistic scenarios well. And the restoration effect of different mask areas can prove the restoration effect of our model. The models perform well with a small area of mask images. Because the relatively small mask area has less occlusion for the text structure in the inscription image, there is a lot of information left in the inscription image. However, as the mask area increases, our models are more advantageous. The larger the SSIM and PSNR numbers, the better the restoration results. The method in this paper outperforms other methods and improves much in both SSIM and PSNR, and from the data in the table, we can find that our algorithm gets better results. Our model outperforms other models for different region size mask maps, especially for large region masks.

5 Conclusions

This paper presents a Ga-RFR based on adaptive gated feature fusion, which uses gated convolution to improve on the excessive feature map redundancy of deep networks. After experiments, we show that our experiments outperform existing excellent image inpainting algorithms. Inpainting of inscription images is a fledgling research direction and is not too much studied at present. Most researchers are working on the glyphs of Chinese characters. And there is no objective and accepted evaluation standard for text image inpainting, most scholars are using SSIM and PSNR. proposing a reasonable evaluation standard for text images is a future.

Acknowledgements. This paper was partly supported by the National Natural Science Foundation of China (61806105 and 62076143).

References

1. Barnes, C., Shechtman, E., Finkelstein, A., Goldman, D.B.: Patchmatch: a randomized correspondence algorithm for structural image editing. ACM Trans. Graph. **28**(3), 24 (2009)
2. Chen, S., Yang, Y., Liu, X., Zhu, S.: Dual discriminator gan: restoring ancient yi characters. Trans. Asian Low-Res. Lang. Inf. Process. **21**(4), 1–23 (2022)
3. Goodfellow, I., et al.: Generative adversarial networks. Commun. ACM **63**(11), 139–144 (2020)
4. Iizuka, S., Simo-Serra, E., Ishikawa, H.: Globally and locally consistent image completion. ACM Trans. Graph. (ToG) **36**(4), 1–14 (2017)
5. Isola, P., Zhu, J.Y., Zhou, T., Efros, A.A.: Image-to-image translation with conditional adversarial networks. In: Proceedings of the IEEE Conference on Computer Vision and Pattern Recognition, pp. 1125–1134 (2017)
6. Kingma, D.P., Ba, J.: Adam: a method for stochastic optimization. arXiv preprint arXiv:1412.6980 (2014)
7. Le Meur, O., Gautier, J., Guillemot, C.: Examplar-based inpainting based on local geometry. In: 2011 18th IEEE International Conference on Image Processing, pp. 3401–3404. IEEE (2011)

8. Ledig, C., et al.: Photo-realistic single image super-resolution using a generative adversarial network. In: Proceedings of the IEEE Conference on Computer Vision and Pattern Recognition, pp. 4681–4690 (2017)
9. Levin, A., Zomet, A., Weiss, Y.: Learning how to inpaint from global image statistics. In: ICCV, vol. 1, pp. 305–312 (2003)
10. Li, J., Wang, N., Zhang, L., Du, B., Tao, D.: Recurrent feature reasoning for image inpainting. In: Proceedings of the IEEE/CVF Conference on Computer Vision and Pattern Recognition, pp. 7760–7768 (2020)
11. Liu, G., Reda, F.A., Shih, K.J., Wang, T.C., Tao, A., Catanzaro, B.: Image inpainting for irregular holes using partial convolutions. In: Proceedings of the European Conference on Computer Vision (ECCV), pp. 85–100 (2018)
12. Lv, D., Liu, Y.: The restoration of style chinese characters based on deep learning. In: Proceedings of the 2018 International Conference on Network, Communication, Computer Engineering (NCCE 2018), pp. 426–430. Atlantis Press (2018). https://doi.org/10.2991/ncce-18.2018.67
13. Pathak, D., Krahenbuhl, P., Donahue, J., Darrell, T., Efros, A.A.: Context encoders: feature learning by inpainting. In: Proceedings of the IEEE Conference on Computer Vision and Pattern Recognition, pp. 2536–2544 (2016)
14. Ronneberger, O., Fischer, P., Brox, T.: U-Net: convolutional networks for biomedical image segmentation. In: Navab, N., Hornegger, J., Wells, W.M., Frangi, A.F. (eds.) MICCAI 2015. LNCS, vol. 9351, pp. 234–241. Springer, Cham (2015). https://doi.org/10.1007/978-3-319-24574-4_28
15. Simonyan, K., Zisserman, A.: Very deep convolutional networks for large-scale image recognition. arXiv preprint arXiv:1409.1556 (2014)
16. Song, G., Li, J., Wang, Z.: Occluded offline handwritten Chinese character inpainting via generative adversarial network and self-attention mechanism. Neurocomputing **415**, 146–156 (2020)
17. Wang, J., Pan, G., Sun, D., Zhang, J.: Chinese character inpainting with contextual semantic constraints. In: Proceedings of the 29th ACM International Conference on Multimedia, pp. 1829–1837 (2021)
18. Wenjun, Z., Benpeng, S., Ruiqi, F., Xihua, P., Shanxiong, C.: Ea-gan: restoration of text in ancient Chinese books based on an example attention generative adversarial network. Herit. Sci. **11**(1), 1–13 (2023)
19. Xu, Y., Shen, R.: Aesthetic evaluation of Chinese calligraphy: a cross-cultural comparative study. In: Current Psychology, pp. 1–14 (2022)
20. Yu, J., Lin, Z., Yang, J., Shen, X., Lu, X., Huang, T.S.: Free-form image inpainting with gated convolution. In: Proceedings of the IEEE/CVF International Conference on Computer Vision, pp. 4471–4480 (2019)
21. Zhou, W., Bovik, A.C., Sheikh, H.R., Simoncelli, E.P.: Image quality assessment: from error visibility to structural similarity. IEEE Trans. Image Process. **13**(4), 600–612 (2004)

Generalisation Approach for Banknote Authentication by Mobile Devices Trained on Incomplete Samples

Barış Gün Sürmeli[1(✉)], Eugen Gillich[2], and Helene Dörksen[1]

[1] Institute Industrial IT, OWL University of Applied Sciences and Arts, Campusallee 6, 32657 Lemgo, Germany
baris.suermeli@th-owl.de

[2] Koenig and Bauer Banknote Solutions, Westring 31, 33818 Leopoldshöhe, Germany
https://www.koenig-bauer.com/
https://www.init-owl.de/

Abstract. Reliable Banknote Authentication is critical for economic stability. Regarding everyday use, recent studies implemented successful techniques using banknote images taken by mobile phone cameras. One challenge in mobile banknote authentication is that it is impossible to collect images by all series/brands of mobile phones. In this study, classification models are implemented that are able to generalize to the samples from a wide number of mobile phone series even though they are trained with samples from a small group of series. Existing state-of-the-art banknote authentication approaches train a separate model per sub-image of a banknote, using the extracted features of that sub-image. A new approach that trains a single global model on the concatenated features of all the sub-images is presented. Furthermore, ensemble models that combine Linear Discriminant Analysis and Deep Neural Networks are employed in order to maximize the accuracy. Implemented techniques were able to reach up to F1-score of 0.99914 on a Euro banknote data set which contain images from 16 different mobile-phone series. The results also indicate that new global model approach can improve the accuracy of the existing banknote authentication techniques in case of model training with images from restricted/incomplete phone series and brands.

1 Introduction

Banknote authentication is an important area of study especially to ensure economic stability. Intaglio is a well-established printing technique that is actively in use for banknote production, as it can print characteristic patterns with very high definition. Secure identification of counterfeit banknotes is possible for people with awareness and knowledge of those characteristic patterns. However, many of the banknote users lack such information or the ability to examine

Ministry of economic affairs, industry, climate action and energy of the state of North Rhine-Westphalia.

L. Iliadis et al. (Eds.): ICANN 2023, LNCS 14255, pp. 332–343, 2023.
https://doi.org/10.1007/978-3-031-44210-0_27

them such as disabled people. Another problem is the rising quality of counterfeit banknotes, which makes it harder to do manual authentication. Some of those counterfeits even able to trick the machine-based systems that examine the infrared or magnetic markings. Even though the authentication is carried out easily by central banks, it is obvious that they cannot share information about hidden characteristic patterns with outer world as they can be used for forgeries.

Contemporary mobile phone cameras are able to take high resolution images that can capture information of very fine details. On the other hand, a well-established approach to image classification problem is to employ image processing and machine learning techniques [6,16]. Based on these facts, the idea of banknote authentication using data-driven models that are trained on images taken by mobile-phone cameras was introduced in [13]. Latest banknote authentication models that are trained with mobile-phone images are shown to be reliable in distinguishing counterfeit banknotes from genuine ones [15].

Ideally, data-driven banknote authentication models would be exposed to the labeled images taken with all available brands/models of mobile phones which it will be tested with. However, it is very hard to acquire such data since central banks only allow very limited access for collection of images of genuine and different types of counterfeit banknotes. Consequently, collecting images using all the existing cell-phone series is practically impossible and this restriction makes the task of training accurate banknote authentication models much challenging as illustrated in Fig. 1. In this study, it is aimed to train classification models that learns from sets of *incomplete samples*, namely, images of banknotes obtained using a restricted group of series of mobile-phones and using those models to accurately authenticate images taken by mobile-phones of a much larger group of mobile-phone series.

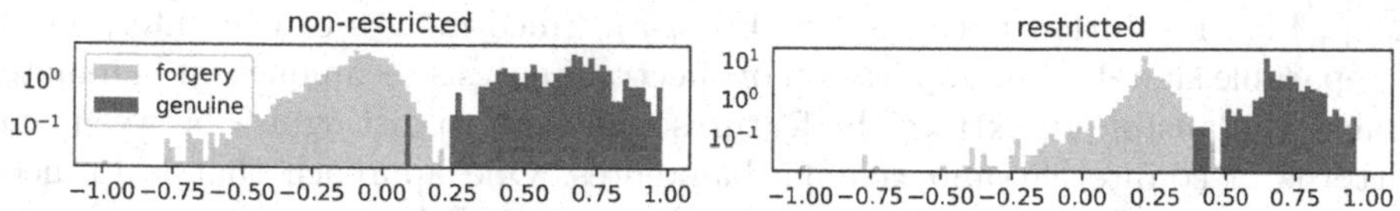

Fig. 1. The histogram of the banknote image data points which are projected on the Linear Discriminant Analysis (LDA) planes. The planes are obtained using training data that include all the available phone series (left) and using only a restricted group of most recently released series (right). It is visible that the intersection of two classes is bigger and the discrimination is more difficult for the latter plane (right).

Banknote images are conventionally divided into smaller sub-images (called Regions of Interest (ROIs)) with the aim of better local analysis. State-of-the art banknote authentication methods are based on "Sound of Intaglio" (SoI). SoI approach divides banknote images into smaller sub-images (called Regions of Interest (ROIs)) with the aim of better analysis of local patterns. From those ROIs, SoI extracts statistical features from the Wavelet transformations of ROIs in order to summarize them. Using these features, SoI usually trains separate models for each of those ROIs whose classification results are aggregated at the end to obtain a final classification decision. In this study, instead of focusing training separate models for sub-images, a global model is trained by using concatenated features of ROIs. It is investigated if this approach enables better learning by introducing additional knowledge about inter sub-image patterns. This way, a local characterization is carried out in feature extraction phase as in SoI, where a global characterization is enabled in model training phase. Furthermore, ensemble models are implemented that employ several Linear Discriminant Analysis (LDA) [2] and Deep Neural Network (DNN) [17] classifiers. With this approach, DNNs are expected to focus on well-represented patterns in the data while LDA covers the patterns that are represented in fewer data points (banknotes) which was not enough for DNN parameters to converge. Moreover, in order to optimize the hyper-parameters of the trained models, an incremental improvement based optimization method, Tree-structured Parzen Estimators [4] are employed.

Implemented techniques are evaluated on Euro banknote image data set that contain images taken by 16 different iPhone series and notably they were able reach up to F1-score of 0.99914. Based on a comparison to a baseline SoI model, results also indicate that using a global model trained on concatenated features of ROIs may perform better than the SoI approach in case of model training with images from restricted/incomplete phone series and brands.

2 Sound of Intaglio and Other Related Work

Focusing on the characteristics of the intaglio printing is one well established way to locate and make use of the intrinsic features of the banknotes for authentication. Compared to counterfeit banknotes, Intaglio printed banknotes provide sharp, high resolution patterns (see Fig. 2-a). Since images can be interpreted as separable signals [18], application of spectral analysis techniques on banknote images is plausible to extract the features that help to distinguish between the patterns of counterfeit and genuine banknotes. One approach that is formed around this idea is *Sound of Intaglio* (SoI) [14]. In SoI, images of banknotes are first divided into sub-images, which contain patterns specific to banknotes of different sums. These are called Regions of Interest (ROIs). Each ROI is analysed separately, by first applying Wavelet transform [18] where adaptive choice of Wavelets is made with respect to ROI characteristics. Given a gray-scale image matrix x with the size $m \times n$, SWT yields a matrix X with shape $2m \times 2n$:

$$X = \begin{bmatrix} A & cV \\ cH & cD \end{bmatrix} \tag{1}$$

where A contains scaling coefficients and cV, cH and cD contains vertical, horizontal and diagonal detail coefficients of x respectively. The detail coefficients are then combined in one matrix: $cG = \alpha(cV + cH + cD)$ where α is a scaling factor. Statistical features of the histograms of Wavelet coefficients (see Fig. 2) are shown to be useful in characterization of patterns in documents [12]. 3 such features; variance, curtosis and skewness are used to characterize each ROI. A ROI selection procedure follows; the contribution of each ROI to classification accuracy is assessed by statistical tests carried out on their features. The selected ROIs are consequently used to train classification models where for each ROI a separate model is trained such as a Linear Discriminant Analysis (LDA) model [15]. When a prediction is to be made for a new banknote image, majority voting is made using the class predictions of each model to get a final classification decision.

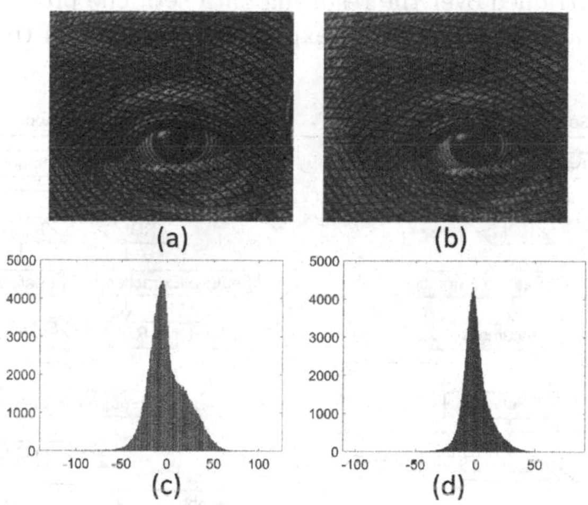

Fig. 2. Example ROIs taken from (a) a genuine and (b) a forgery banknote image. The histogram of the Wavelet coefficients of those ROIs are given in (c) and (d) respectively.

The idea of extraction of features from images of banknotes for authentication using Wavelet transform is first presented in [7]. However, the authors transformed the whole banknote image rather than working on ROIs as in SoI and used the Wavelet coefficients straightforwardly as features after a simple elimination procedure instead of using histogram statistics. Authors in [1] followed a similar feature extraction phase and trained ANN classifiers. SoI idea is first introduced and patented in [14]. With the motivation of quick and simple banknote authentication, the idea of employing mobile-phone cameras to apply SoI techniques was introduced in [13]. Recent studies used the raw images for classification without signal processing that train ANNs [11] and Convolutional Neural Networks [3]. To the best of our knowledge, a methodology that combines local ROI analysis advantages of SoI with an ANN based classifier or any approach that trains a global classifier using the concatenated features extracted with SoI approach, is yet to be implemented.

3 Methodology

A general overview of the approach is as follows. The feature extraction procedure is carried out in the scheme of SoI (see Sect. 2), so the banknote images are partitioned into ROIs, wavelet transform is applied to obtain the coefficients and three descriptive statistics, variance, curtosis and skewness of the histograms of those coefficients are obtained. However, rather than training separate models for each ROI, features of ROIs are concatenated to obtain a single vector (data point) to represent the whole image. A feature selection procedure follows to obtain the features that helps to achieve the best classification accuracy. Finally, a global model is trained over the resulting data set. The procedure is depicted in Fig. 3. The details of each step are explained in the rest of this chapter.

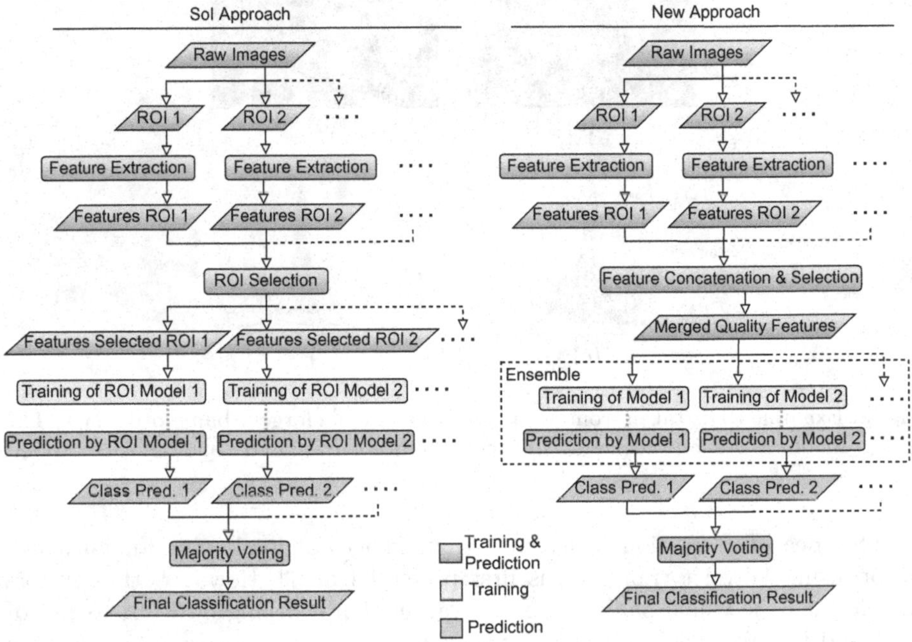

Fig. 3. Flow diagram of general SoI approach and proposed new approach.

3.1 Feature Extraction, Concatenation and Selection

In this study, feature extraction and the previous treatment of the data set is carried out in the same way as SoI (see Sect. 2). Images are divided into M ROIs and 3 wavelet coefficients are obtained per ROI; variance, curtosis and skewness, forming 3-tuples (V_r, C_r, S_r) where $r \in \{1, 2, \ldots, R\}$ and R is the total number of ROIs. As opposed to SoI which handles each ROI separately, these 3-tuples are concatenated to form one vector $x = [v_1, v_2..., v_M]$ per image and $M = R \times 3$ where M is the total number of features representing the image. A raw data matrix X_{raw} of shape $M \times N$ is obtained by stacking the image vectors, where each row corresponds to an image vector and the columns are the features representing the image. A simple feature selection method is applied on X_{raw} as following. Class labels, genuine or forgery are represented by 1 and 0 respectively form a single column target vector y, namely, $X_{raw} \implies y$. Each column in X_{raw} is evaluated for their contribution to classification accuracy by measuring their correlation with y. F-statistic was used as the metric of the evaluation. All the features are sorted with respect to their f-statistic value and k highest scoring features are taken while the remaining are removed from the matrix. Resulting data matrix X of shape $k \times N$ is used further to train classification models.

3.2 Model Training

Ensemble Learning: Ensemble techniques employ the predictions of several models to reach higher prediction accuracy in comparison to the accuracy that could be reached by one of those models alone. When using DNNs, this may help to average the impact of the randomized initialization of the parameters. This is especially helpful for network architectures with high number of parameters as the data might not be enough for the convergence of all of the parameters. LDA is a method with fewer parameters and therefore expected to be more robust to the size of the data set once the number of features is not larger than the number of data points [20]. In this study, an ensemble of 2 LDA and 3 DNN models as well as an ensemble of only 3DNN models are applied to confirm the superiority of the combination of LDA and DNN models compared to only using DNNs. The class predictions of the ensemble are obtained using majority voting on the predictions of each model. For LDA implementation, plain *vanilla* algorithm is used (see details in [2]) and detailed information of applied DNNs are given below.

Deep Neural Networks: Convolutional neural networks (CNN) are commonly employed for image processing tasks [8,10], where initial layers handle the feature extraction task as the following fully connected feed-forward (dense) layers map the features to outputs. Following a similar pattern, in this study, fully connected feed-forward (dense) DNNs [17] are employed, following feature extraction which is applied as explained in Sect. 3.1. All the used DNNs contained 3 hidden layers to fit the data well in feasible computational time. As cost function *Cross-entropy* is used, as activation function of all the nodes, *rectified linear units* are employed to tackle *learning slowdown* and *vanishing gradient problem* [17]. In order to avoid overfitting, *dropout* and *L2 regularization* [17] are applied. Another important issue with the data in hand was that the data size for forgery and genuine classes are quite imbalanced, namely, the size of the forgery class was about ten times larger, due to the fact that the data set contained images of banknotes that is produced with many different types of forgery techniques. To tackle this importance of forgery data points were decreased by introducing a class weighting parameter k to the cost function, where k was set to 1 for genuine and < 1 for forgery data points.

3.3 Hyper-Parameter Optimization

There are numerous hyper-parameters to be optimized in the models we used (see Sect. 4.2). One approach to search the space efficiently is Sequential Model-Based Optimization [9] (SMBO); after each training cycle with a specific set of values, the results obtained from all training cycles are used to determine which set of values would enable the most probable increase in the training accuracy. There are several variations of SMBO and in [4], two of those which frequently applied in hyper-parameter optimization Bayesian Optimization (BO) and Tree-structured Parzen Estimators (TPE), are explained in detail. In this study TPE is used as it was shown to have superior performance over BO on two benchmark data sets in [4]. Regarding ensemble learning using several DNNs (see Sect. 3.2), optimization of hyper-parameters becomes very costly as more DNNs are included. Therefore, for those ensembles, hyper-parameter optimization is carried out on only a single DNN following feature selection (see Sect. 3.1), and the optimized parameters for the DNN were used for all of the DNNs in the ensemble.

3.4 SoI and LDA Baseline

In order to compare and highlight the strength of the methodology of this work, a baseline solution that follows SoI (see Sect. 2) approach is implemented. Once the 3-tuples (V_r, C_r, S_r) per ROI are obtained, they are stacked to form raw data matrices X_r of size $N \times 3$, where $r \in \{1, 2, \dots, R\}$ and R is the total number of ROIs. A ROI selection procedure is implemented as following. Each column in X_r is tested for its correlation with the target variable y (see Sect. 3.1) by calculating its f-score. For each ROI, f-scores of their respective 3 columns are calculated and summed up to obtain total ROI f-score. The ROIs are then sorted with respect to their total ROI f-scores and the k highest scoring ROIs are selected. The selected ROIs are then used to train LDA models, one LDA model per ROI. Majority voting is applied for class prediction, the class that was predicted by the most of the LDA models is decided as the final class prediction.

The aim of SoI baseline is to make a comparison in fundamental level between two approaches; training a separate classifier per ROI, and training a global classifier over concatenated ROIs. Therefore for a fair comparison in basic level, a simple global LDA classifier is also implemented which takes the concatenated ROI data (see Sect. 3.1) as input.

4 Experiments

4.1 Data Set

Data set contains 2801 banknote images which were taken with 16 different models of cell phones of Apple iPhone brand. From each cell-phone model, there are 200 images that include images of approximately 10% genuine and 90% forgery banknotes that were printed using various printing techniques. However in this study, trained models are only expected to classify the banknotes as genuine or not, i.e. they are agnostic to the printing technique. The images are divided into 836 ROIs and as 3 features obtained per ROI after feature extraction, yielded data matrix had the shape 2801 × 2508.

4.2 Experimental Setup

The list of hyper-parameters and their respective ranges that were searched using TPE (see Sect. 3.3) are as follows: number of features selected (see Sect. 3.1) 10–1500, number of ROIs selected (see Sect. 3.4) 10–500, batch size 1–500, max epochs 100–500, dropout 0–1, L2 regularization 0.01–0.1, number of nodes for each layer 100–300, negative class weight 0–1.

Hyper-parameter search value ranges for the parameters are chosen with the aim of balancing between high accuracy gain and reasonable computational complexity. Empirical experiments gave worse results beyond those ranges, which will not be presented in this paper for conciseness.

The ultimate goal of this study is to obtain classification models that can do accurate banknote authentication of images taken by any phone, but were trained with images that were taken by only a restricted group of cell-phone series. Therefore for each train-test partitioning in this study, training set always formed images taken by 4 of the 16 available cell-phone series in the data set. Two different cross-validation experiment setup are implemented. In first setup, 1820 possible different train-test splits are exhausted, where for each split a different combination of 4 out of 16 series are picked for training and the remaining 12 is used for testing. In the second, the training is only done with the images of 6 most recent phone series in the data set; *11 Pro*, *11 Pro Max*, *12*, *12 Mini*, *12 Pro*, *12 Pro Max*. In each of 15 possible train-test splits, training set included images of 4 out of 6 series and remaining part of the data set (which includes older series too) is used for testing. The motivation of this setup is to investigate the impact of the camera quality of the newer phone series on the training set quality. First and second setups will be referred to as *train-all* and *train-new* respectively for the rest of the paper. For both setups, the procedure is visualized in Fig. 4.

4.3 Evaluation

Hyper-parameter optimization is done with respect to well-established F1-score, so the hyper-parameter-optimized model had the highest F1-score, compared to the models that had other hyper-parameter configurations. All four implemented models in this study; ensemble models 3DNN + 2LDA, 3DNN (see Sect. 3.2) and LDA and SoI baseline models (see Sect. 3.4) are evaluated with five different metrics. Four of these metrics are standard for binary classification problems: F1, precision, false positive rate (FPR), false negative rate (FNR). We also use another metric, *balanced accuracy* which is shown to be a better evaluator compared to the accuracy when the sizes of two classes are imbalanced. It is also *adjusted*, which means its a measure of relative accuracy compared to a random

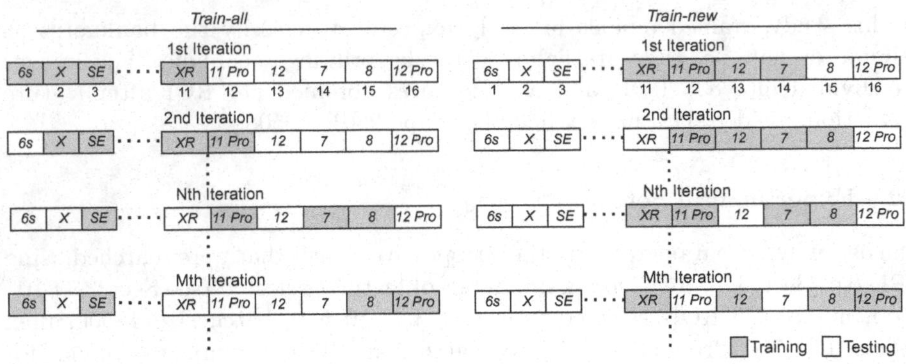

Fig. 4. Visualization of cross validation procedure for experimental setup *train-all* (above) and *train-all* (below). Each box represents banknote images taken by the series of iPhone given in them.

classifier. Interested readers can find more information including the formulation in [5].

5 Results and Discussion

Hyper-parameter optimization results of DNN training after feature selection for experimental setup *all* is visualized in the *paralel coordinates* plot in Fig. 5. The change of F1-score with respect to the hyper-parameters can be observed. A general robustness can be argued for *batch size, max epochs* and number of nodes in all the layers of the network. *dropout* values below 0.5 and *L2 regularization* below 0.05 ensures these methods are in effect and overfitting is prevented. *neg. class weight* values between 0.4 up until near 1 yields good performance, however the maximum scores were obtained when *neg. class weight* ≈0.9. Also, a balanced value for feature selection seems to be between the range 1000–1100.

The results of the experiments using hyper-parameter-optimized models for setups *train-all* and *train-new* are shown on Table 1, at top and bottom respectively. Even though state-of-the-art banknote authentication techniques that use cell-phone images obtain F1-scores of 1, none of those methods were tested on training sets that contain images of only a restricted series of cell-phones.

Regarding setup *train-all*, top part of Table 1 shows that 3DNN+2LDA ensemble model reached near 1 F1-score and outperformed other models in all evaluation metrics. Another remarkable result is that the baseline LDA which is trained on concatenated ROI data was significantly more successful than SoI baseline, which supports the argument of concatenation of ROIs might be a promising approach in banknote authentication. 3DNN+2LDA ensemble gave better results compared to 3DNN and LDA models and this suggests that DNNs and LDA might be used together to cover for each others weaknesses in banknote authentication. In banknote authentication, FPR is especially critical, namely, a

Table 1. Cross validation results of the experiment setup *train-all* on top and *train-new* at the bottom.

Setup	Model	Balanced Acc.	Precision.	F1	FPR	FNR
train-all	3DNN+2LDA	**0.99365**	**0.99213**	**0.99572**	**0.00023**	**0.00603**
	3DNN	0.99340	0.99073	0.99500	0.00037	0.00616
	LDA	0.97859	0.97583	0.98651	0.00053	0.02072
	SoI Base	0.96460	0.95523	0.97516	0.00151	0.03363
train-new	3DNN+2LDA	**0.99922**	**0.99834**	**0.99914**	**0.00010**	0.00070
	3DNN	0.99883	0.99773	0.99881	0.00014	0.00105
	LDA	0.99532	0.95561	0.97718	0.00468	**0.00000**
	SoI Base	0.98005	0.84967	0.91766	0.01823	0.00174

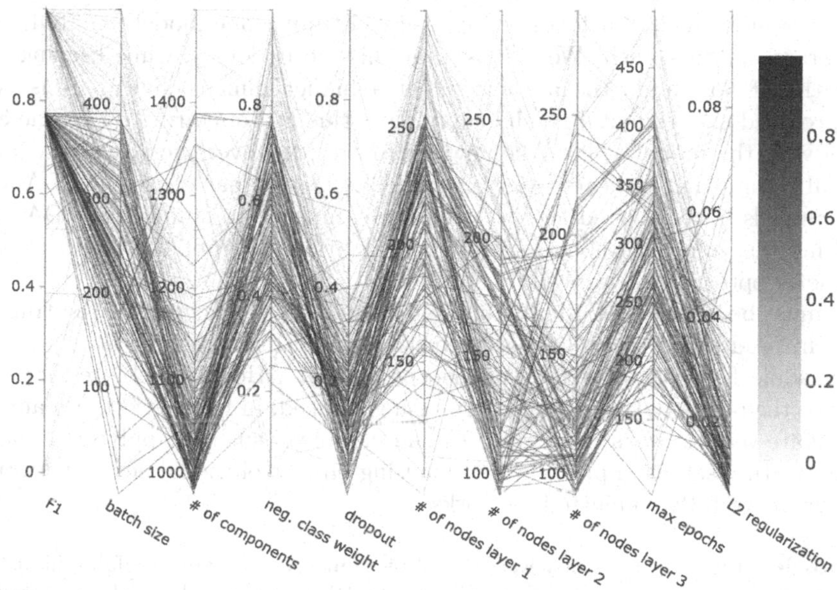

Fig. 5. Parallel coordinates plot for hyper-parameter optimization of DNNs following feature selection. The change of the F1-score with respect to the changes in each hyper-parameter is shown.

counterfeit should never be classified as a genuine banknote. Nevertheless FNR should also be close to zero as much as possible. Therefore, it is also promising especially for 3DNN+2LDA, the main source of error is rather FNR compared to FPR. For setup *train-new*, it is visible from table bottom part of Table 1 that 3DNN+2LDA again has the best overall score in terms of F1 and balanced accuracy. In fact, FPR value of 3DNN+2LDA implies that its total number of false positives that for all folds of this setup is only 2. TPR value of LDA shows that it is the most successful in terms of classifying the forgeries correctly, however the critical FPR value is drastically lower compared to 3DNN+2LDA. It might be argued that this is caused by the fact that vanilla LDA implementation is not re-balanced against imbalanced data sets, however it is shown in [19] that there is no evidence for LDA to have such a drawback. Another important outcome is the even-worse FPR of SoI base which also effected its F1-score heavily. Near 1 balanced accuracy score for both experiment setups express the overall significance of the success of the implemented models.

6 Conclusion

In this study, we developed models that even though they are trained with banknote images from a restricted series of mobile phones, they can do successful banknote authentication on images from a larger variety of series. We have also shown that a global model that is trained on the concatenation of wavelet-transformed ROI features, instead of training one model per ROI, can be a promising approach. We believe that this methodology, while keeping the strengths of SoI, adds the advantages of a higher dimensional analysis. We also provided experimental results supporting this by comparing a baseline SoI model with the models follow the new approach. Moreover, we provided experimental results that indicate using an ensemble model that consist of LDA and DNN models have boosted the performance compared to standalone LDA and DNN models. In order to obtain a robust evaluation, we applied a *clever* hyper-parameter optimization procedure.

It must be noted that the banknote authentication accuracy of the trained is not in production-ready level as industry standards dictate no false positive policy while F1-score must be aimed over 99.999%. However, the results also indicate the presented approach is promising. Indeed, in future work, we aim to investigate various ways to improve the methodology such as applying a multivariate feature selection procedure or focusing on convolutional neural networks [17] instead of fully-connected networks.

Acknowledgment. This study was funded by ministry of economic affairs, industry, climate action and energy of the state of North Rhine-Westphalia with the funding code 005-2011-0117.

References

1. Ahangaryan, F.P., Mohammadpour, T., Kianisarkaleh, A.: Persian banknote recognition using wavelet and neural network. In: 2012 International Conference on Computer Science and Electronics Engineering, vol. 3, pp. 679–684. IEEE (2012)
2. Alpaydin, E.: Introduction to Machine Learning. MIT press, Cambridge (2020)
3. Aseffa, D.T., Kalla, H., Mishra, S.: Ethiopian banknote recognition using convolutional neural network and its prototype development using embedded platform. J. Sensors **2022**, 1–18 (2022)
4. Bergstra, J., Bardenet, R., Bengio, Y., Kégl, B.: Algorithms for hyper-parameter optimization. Adv. Neural Inf. Process. Syst. **24**, 1–9 (2011)
5. Brodersen, K.H., Ong, C.S., Stephan, K.E., Buhmann, J.M.: The balanced accuracy and its posterior distribution. In: 2010 20th International Conference on Pattern Recognition, pp. 3121–3124. IEEE (2010)

6. Byerly, A., Kalganova, T., Ott, R.: The current state of the art in deep learning for image classification: a review. In: Science and Information Conference, pp. 88–105. Springer, Heidelberg (2022). https://doi.org/10.1007/978-3-031-10464-0_7
7. Choi, E., Lee, J., Yoon, J.: Feature extraction for bank note classification using wavelet transform. In: 18th International Conference on Pattern Recognition (ICPR 2006), vol. 2, pp. 934–937. IEEE (2006)
8. Farfade, S.S., Saberian, M.J., Li, L.: Multi-view face detection using deep convolutional neural networks. CoRR abs/1502.02766 (2015). http://arxiv.org/abs/1502.02766
9. Hutter, F., Hoos, H.H., Leyton-Brown, K.: Sequential model-based optimization for general algorithm configuration. In: Coello, C.A.C. (ed.) LION 2011. LNCS, vol. 6683, pp. 507–523. Springer, Heidelberg (2011). https://doi.org/10.1007/978-3-642-25566-3_40
10. Krizhevsky, A., Sutskever, I., Hinton, G.E.: Imagenet classification with deep convolutional neural networks. Commun. ACM **60**(6), 84–90 (2017)
11. Kumar, G.R., Nagamani, K.: Banknote authentication system utilizing deep neural network with pca and lda machine learning techniques. Int. J. Recent Sci. Res. **9**(12), 30036–30038 (2018)
12. Lohweg, V., Schaede, J.: Document production and verification by optimization of feature platform exploitation. In: Optical Document Security-The Conference on Optical Security and Counterfeit Detection II, pp. 1–15 (2010)
13. Lohweg, V., Dörksen, H., Gillich, E., Hildebrand, R., Hoffmann, J., Schaede, J.: Mobile devices for banknote authentication-is it possible? In: Optical Document Security-The Conference on Optical Security and Counterfeit Detection, vol. 3, pp. 1–12 (2012)
14. Lohweg, V., Gillich, E., Schaede, J.: Authentication of security documents, in particular of banknotes (2014). uS Patent 8,781,204
15. Lohweg, V., et al.: Banknote authentication with mobile devices. In: Media Watermarking, Security, and Forensics 2013, vol. 8665, pp. 47–60. SPIE (2013)
16. Lu, D., Weng, Q.: A survey of image classification methods and techniques for improving classification performance. Int. J. Remote Sensing **28**(5), 823–870 (2007)
17. Nielsen, M.A.: Neural Networks and Deep Learning, vol. 25. Determination press, San Francisco (2015)
18. Walnut, D.F.: An Introduction to Wavelet Analysis. Springer, Heidelberg (2002). https://doi.org/10.1007/978-1-4612-0001-7
19. Xue, J.H., Titterington, D.M.: Do unbalanced data have a negative effect on lda? Pattern Recogn. **41**(5), 1558–1571 (2008)
20. Zollanvari, A., James, A.P., Sameni, R.: A theoretical analysis of the peaking phenomenon in classification. J. Classif. **37**(2), 421–434 (2020)

Image Caption with Prior Knowledge Graph and Heterogeneous Attention

Junjie Wang[1(✉)] and Wenfeng Huang[2]

[1] Northeast Forestry University, Harbin 150006, China
1154311951@nefu.edu.com

[2] Shenzhen Institute of Advanced Technology, Chinese Academy of Sciences, Shenzhen, China

Abstract. Currently, most image description models are limited in their ability to generate descriptions that reflect personal experiences and subjective perspectives. This makes it difficult to produce relevant and engaging descriptions that truly capture the essence of the image. To address this issue, we propose a novel approach called Subject-awareness-driven Heterogeneous Attention (SCHA). SCHA leverages users' knowledge and expertise to generate content-adaptive image descriptions that are more human-like and reflective of personal experiences. Our approach involves a carefully designed heterogeneous cascade annotation model that captures scene information from multiple perspectives. We also incorporate a prior knowledge graph with textual information to enhance the richness and relevance of the generated descriptions. Our method has great potential for industrial production detection and can open up new possibilities for increasing the flexibility and variety of detection steps. When compared to the results of MSCOCO and Visual Genome datasets, our approach produces richer and more adaptive descriptions than widely used baseline models.

Keywords: Image Caption · Knowledge Graph · Heterogeneous Attention

1 Introduction

Neutral images and text are the most commonly encountered forms of information in our daily lives [1]. With the advancements in deep learning, automatic image captioning has become a popular and useful topic that benefits many industrial applications. Inspired by neural machine translation [2], modern image captioning tasks mostly adopt an end-to-end encoder-decoder model [3]. The encoder encodes the image into a vector representation, and the decoder decodes it into a paragraph of text.

With the advancements in CNNs and RNNs, encoders and decoders have undergone significant reforms, such as top-down [4] and bottom-up [5] visual

J. Wang and W. Huang—Contribute equally to this work.

L. Iliadis et al. (Eds.): ICANN 2023, LNCS 14255, pp. 344–356, 2023.
https://doi.org/10.1007/978-3-031-44210-0_28

attention mechanisms. The sequence decoding mechanism has introduced reinforcement learning [6] and various forms [7] of attention in the coding-decoding model. However, it remains challenging for most existing image captioning methods to generate descriptions that are both detailed and diverse. For instance, an image often contains multiple objects, and the observer's perspective and knowledge may differ. This passive subtitle generation results in monotony and tends to produce unimpressive results [8–12].

To enhance the generation of comprehensive and flexible descriptions leveraging the user's existing knowledge, we introduce the SCHA model. The SCHA model harnesses the power of a prior knowledge graph combined with a heterogeneous attention framework. By integrating these two components, we aim to produce more nuanced and adaptable descriptions. We conducted experiments on two extensively utilized image description datasets, MSCOCO [13] and Visual Genome [14], in order to establish our knowledge base. Our method demonstrated superior expressive capabilities compared to established baseline models, particularly when leveraging specific knowledge priors. Furthermore, our approach exhibits the ability to generate descriptions that are both more comprehensive and varied.

The main contributions of this paper can be summarized as follows:

1. We propose abstracting the image into a knowledge map to generate image descriptions that reflect different perspectives. This approach allows us to capture details during the generation process and take into account the user's intentions.
2. We introduce the Heterogeneous Attention Image Description Structure (SCHA), which is based on the subject's consciousness and is designed to assist in the text generation process.
3. SCHA is composed of an encoder-attention-decoder structure, which automatically identifies nodes in the knowledge graph and controls text generation to produce descriptions that reflect different perspectives on the content and its order.

2 Related Work

The neural encoder-decoder framework has significantly improved image description tasks [4,5,13,15–18]. A classic work in this field is Vinyals et al. [13], which uses the idea of machine translation to extract image features using GoogleNet and then inputting them into LSTM to generate the corresponding description. While this is a straightforward method, it attempts to handle image captioning based on both image and text. To capture the details of specific parts of the image and the generated text, Xu et al. [4] introduced hard and soft attention to calculate the weight corresponding to the generated words and image regions. The features multiplied by the weight are then fed into LSTM to generate the entire description.To address the accumulated error and mismatch problems caused by word formation dependence on antecedent words during training and assessment, Rennie et al. [6] proposed a reinforcement learning method to train the model of the backpropagation algorithm. The experiment showed that the reinforcement learning approach is better than traditional training methods. With the development of target detection technologies, recent studies tend to describe the image in a fine-grained way, i.e., describing object attributes and the relationship between them in the image, instead of simply observing the image region by region. Anderson et al. [19] proposed using target detection methods to divide the image into k areas. The attention of the LSTM input language decode LSTM moment of implicit variables is used to get the weight of k areas. The characteristics of the area weighted get to k, and this moment attention LSTM hidden variables are regarded as language decoding words LSTM input to get the final prediction. The experiment shows that this structure can greatly improve the performance of image description.

Control-based [12,20–22] image description methods aim to generate sentences that leverage specific representation information, such as emotion, style, and semantics. These methods can be divided into two control modes: content control and style control. This type of method is highly interactive, flexible, and controllable, allowing for the generation of diverse texts. The style method [10,11,22–24] is designed to control the image by using different styles to describe it. Recent work hopes to extract the corresponding style description based on the text's semantics, enabling asymmetric transformation.

In general, these models do not generate descriptions in a way that mimics the human mind. In this paper, we propose using a more detailed SCHA to simultaneously control the target object, attribute, and relationship between the target object to generate a personified description.

3 The SCHA Model

Image caption tasks use attention mechanisms to capture relationships between text entities and image regions, improving results. However, they often produce linguistically regular or picture-appropriate descriptions without a subjective human perspective. To address this, we propose SCHA, a base model for subject-aware image descriptions. SCHA simulates human cognition through a triadic structure of entity objects, relations, and attributes, generating various subject-aware image descriptions. Attention mechanisms act on content, order, and update states in generating graphs for text generation.

The task of generating a natural sentence $y = \{y_1, y_2, ..., y_T\}$, given an image I and a pre-built knowledge graph G, is the focus of this chapter. To achieve this, we propose the SCHA model, as shown in Fig. 1, which will be described in detail in various subsections.

3.1 Encoder

The encoder abstracts the image I into nodes $X = \{x_1, x_2, ..., X_{|V|}\}$, which represent objects and their roles. Nodes are encoded uniformly, but have specific

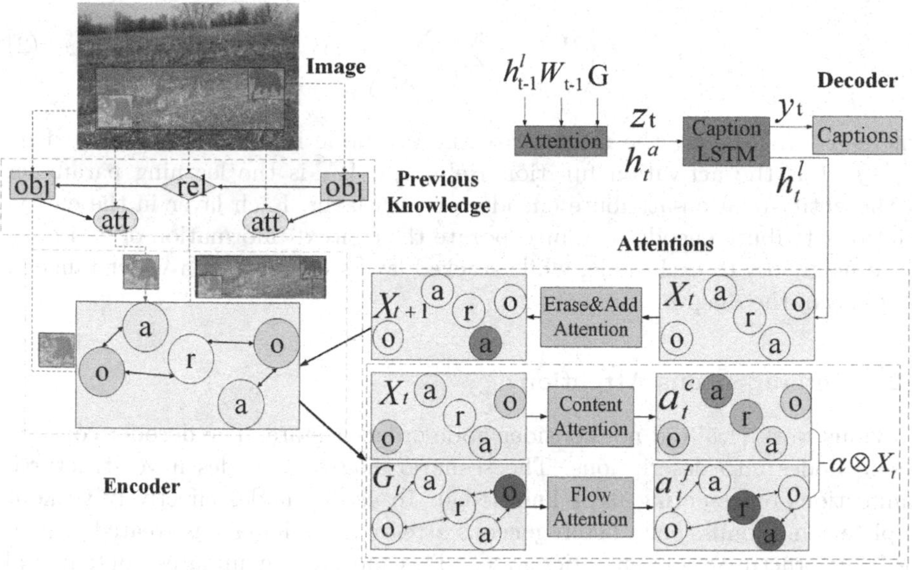

Fig. 1. SCHA model,The core consists of a priori knowledge graph and a heterogeneous stacked attention structure. The whole structure can be expressed in the form of encoder-attention-decoder.

meanings and relationships with neighboring nodes. Relationships have semantic meanings, so an encoder is needed to represent the complex network diagram of node embeddings and context encoding, as shown in Fig. 1.

Different types of nodes in the network have varying contents of communication. To account for this, we extend the one-way relationship into a two-way edge and form a complex relationship network graph with mapping context relations $\mathcal{G}_m = \{\mathcal{V}, \mathcal{E}, \mathcal{R}\}$.

We initialize the i-th node in the knowledge prior graph G as the region marked by the target detection vi. The nodes are embedded into the knowledge prior graph as nodes through special roles to represent the role of objects in the knowledge network. The formula for converting it to an embedded node $X_i^{(0)}$ i is shown below:

$$x_i^{(0)} = \begin{cases} v_i \cdot W_r(0), if \quad i \; is \; obj \\ v_i \cdot W_r(1), if \quad i \; is \; att \\ v_i \cdot W_r(2), if \quad i \; is \; rel \end{cases} \tag{1}$$

where, $W_r \in R^{3xd}$ is the role hidden vector, $d$is the attribute hidden vector dimension, $W_r[k]$ is the certain line represent object, attribute and relation respectively. As there are three different types of nodes in the network graph - entity, relationship, and attribute - the connection modes of nodes also include entity-attribute, entity-relationship, relation-object, and their reverse processes. To account for this, we propose an entity-relation-attribute encoder to encode the relationships:

$$x_i = f\left(W_i x_i + \sum_{\bar{r}\in\mathcal{R}} \sum_{j\in N_i^r} \frac{1}{|\mathcal{N}_i|} W_{\dot{r}} x_j\right) \tag{2}$$

where $\mathcal{N}_i^{r^*}$ represents the neighbor of the i-th node in relation $r^* \in \mathcal{R}$, where $i \neq j$, f is the activation function Relu, and W_* is the learning parameter of the entity-relation-attribute encoder at each layer. Each layer in the entity-relation-attribute encoder can incorporate the context information of its immediate neighbors to each node, while stacked layers can encode a wider range of contexts in the diagram.

3.2 Heterogeneous Attention

Previous work [4,5] did not consider node order or state. The decoder converts image nodes into descriptions. The scenario diagram's nodes have structured connections representing prior knowledge. To use all nodes effectively without duplication or omission, a heterogeneous attention mechanism is created to handle the structure and semantics of G. This mechanism updates content and records known/unknown parts of the description. See Fig. 1 for details.

Graph Content Attention. From an intuitive perspective of our human language generation mechanism, we must have a corresponding length or position of a sentence or paragraph in the brain during the process, but it remains unknown until we actually say it. Once the beginning discourse is triggered, we can examine the previous discourse and produce the most appropriate dialogue. The attention mechanism then requires us to consider the current description both globally and locally to generate a description more suitable for the current semantic scene. Specifically, attention uses the semantic similarity between the embedded node $\mathcal{X}$ and query vector a to generate the score h_t^a of the attention vector, as follows:

$$\alpha_t^c = softmax(w_c^T \tanh\left(f\left(x_{t,i}, h_t^a\right)\right)) \tag{3}$$

where w_c^T is the parameter to be learned. For convenience, we omit the bias part, and f is the convolution operation.

Ignoring the connection between nodes, paying attention to them is similar to transmission, as it allows for decoding time step teleportation from one node to another. Through the analysis of the embedded node and the correlation degree between the query vector sequence, we represent the semantic similarity, considering both the global information between nodes and the strength of the relationship between adjacent nodes.

Graph Access Order Attention. We use sequential attention to determine the next node based on the current node type, such as attribute to object nodes. Fig. 2 shows the modified diagram with an initial symbol and bidirectional connections. Node order is determined by language characteristics, and spin structures prevent isolated nodes. The adjacency matrix W_f represents node degree. Graph access order attention is achieved through decoding in step A. For example, in "A bird flying into the sky," sequential attention determines the next node if the current node is "bird." then $\alpha_{t,0}^{f} = \alpha_{t-1}$:

A) One degree relationship: $\alpha_{t,0}^{f} = W_0 \alpha_{t,0}^{f}$, for example, it can represent the transfer from an object node to its relationship node, such as "bird" and "fly".;
B) Two degree relationship: $\alpha_{t,1}^{f} = W_1 \alpha_{t,1}^{f}$, for example, it can represent the transfer from the object node to its attribute node, such as 'bird' and 'up';
C) Three degree of movement: $\alpha_{t,2}^{f} = W_2 \alpha_{t,2}^{f}$, for example, it can represent the transfer from an object node to another object node, such as "bird" and "sky", to strengthen the connection between target objects.

$$\begin{aligned} s_t &= \operatorname{softm ax}\left(W_s \sigma\left(W_h h_t^a + W_c c_{t-1}\right)\right) \\ \alpha_t^f &= \textstyle\sum_{k=0}^{2} s_{t,k} \alpha_{t,k}^f \end{aligned} \tag{4}$$

where W_s,W_h and W_c respectively represent the learning parameter $s_t \in R^3$ of neural network, and Fig. 2 shows the flow of access order. Therefore, the context vector used to predict words is:

$$c_t = \sum_{i=1}^{|\mathcal{V}|} \alpha_{t,i} x_{t,i} \tag{5}$$

Finally, we calculate the attention score ϖ_t of access order by calculating s_t method in similar formula 4. The difference is that the σ function replaces $softmax$. Content attention a_c^t of the graph is dynamically fused with access order attention a_f^t of the graph to represent the thinking process of generating descriptions:

$$\alpha_t = \varpi_t \alpha_t^c + \left(1 - \varpi_t\right) \alpha_t^f \tag{6}$$

The above equation is the weighted sum of image node features.

Graph Content Attention. To keep track of nodes during generation, the knowledge graph needs continuous updates. High-attention nodes are updated more often, but some high-frequency stops like "of" don't add much meaning. Frequent patterns should be suppressed for more speculative statements. Therefore, we propose an update gate to appropriately modify the intensity distribution of attention and suppress high-frequency stop words, as shown below:

$$\mu_t = \sigma(f_L[h_t^l, x_{t,i}; \theta_\mu]) \cdot \boldsymbol{\alpha}_{\mathrm{t}} \tag{7}$$

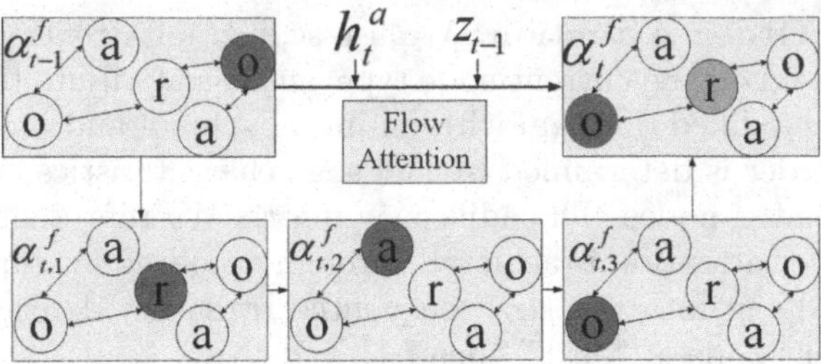

Fig. 2. Access order attention of knowledge graph. For a complete sentence, we want to establish the connection between entities as much as possible, so from the perspective of language, we often need to go through the relationship and attribute nodes, which is the third degree relationship.

where f_L is the fully connected network of parameter θ_μ, which outputs a scalar to indicate whether the node of concern is represented by the generated word. The symbol $\cdot$ is the dot product operation.

The update mechanism for a node consists of two parts, the first is an erasure, followed by a supplement operation. First, the i-th graph node represents that $x_{t,j}$ erasure for each feature dimension in a fine-grained manner according to its update intensity $x_{t,j}$:

$$\begin{aligned} e_{t,i} &= \sigma(f_L[h_t^l, x_{t,i}; \theta_e]) \\ x_{t+1,i} &= x_{t,i}\left(1 - \mu_{t,i} e_{t,i}\right) \end{aligned} \tag{8}$$

where f_L is the fully connected network of parameter θ_e.

For the above, we can interpret that if we need to deprecate a node, we can set it to a minimum. If you need to access a frequently accessed node multiple times and keep track of its status, then you need to add:

$$\begin{aligned} a_{t,i} &= (f_L([h_t^l, x_{t,i}; \theta_a])) \cdot x_{t,i} \\ x_{t+1,i} &= x_{t,i} + u_{t,i} a_{t,i} \end{aligned} \tag{9}$$

where f_L is the dot product operation of parameter θ_a .

In this way we update the x_t to x_{t+1} graph embedding process for the next decoding step, note that not every process produces erasure and addition operations.

3.3 Decoder

Our decoder is composed of two layers of LSTM stacked on top of each other, including the LSTM based on heterogeneous attention and a language-generated LSTM model. Heterogeneous attention form LSTM is globally embedded in $\bar{v}$, the previous word is embedded in w_{t-1} , and the output of LSTM generated by the previous step language h_l^{t-1} is used as input to calculate the attention score h_t^a, as shown below:

$$h_t^a = f_{\text{LSTM}}\left(\left[\bar{v}, w_{t-1}, h_{t-1}^l\right], h_{t-1}^a\right) \tag{10}$$

where f_{LSTM} represents a running unit of the LSTM, and we embed attention into each LSTM unit, and the [,] operation is vector concatenation.

4 Experimental Results and Analysis

4.1 Dataset

We used the COCO and Visual Genomedatasets as our model datasets, which are widely used. Table 1 shows their statistics. We used the Stanford sentence scene graph parser to parse image regions into a prior knowledge graph, and followed a Karpathy [25] split setting. MSCOCO images contain complex information with more logical and practical relationships and detailed text descriptions. We introduced artificially fanciful conjectures by replacing one of the textual descriptions in the training data with a subjective description. We modified approximately 10 percent of the training data, without changing the validation and test sets, and only used unmodified data equivalents for computation during validation and testing.

Table 1. Statistics of Visual Genomeand MSCOCO data sets. Including the number of images and corresponding sentences, the number of entities, relationships and attributes that appear in the entire data set, used for heterogeneous attention image descriptions with prior knowledge graphs

Dataset	Train		Validation		Test	Objects	Relation	Attributes
	Images	Sentences	Images	Sentences	Images	number	pair	number
MSCOCO	112k	47k	4k	20k	1k	151k	806k	263k
Visual Genome	97k	339k	5k	172k	2k	782k	3554k	1758k

4.2 The Experimental Setup

We evaluated the generated descriptions using five rating metrics: BLEU [26], METEOR [27], ROUGE [28], CIDER [29], and SPICE [30]. Generally, high scores are obtained if the generated sentence's semantics are reasonable and the sentence structure is more similar to the prior knowledge graph.

To evaluate the description results, we first generated the same number of statements using the model and measured the richness of generated statements from two different perspectives:

1) N-gram method: a commonly used model in language tasks, which selects the five generated descriptions with different N-grams [31,32] and the best ratio of the total word count.
2) Self-cider [29]: a new method to measure similarity between semantics. Generally, a higher score indicates a richer description.

Table 2. Comparison of results from SCHA with other baseline models

model	MSCOCO					Visual Genome				
	B4	meteor	rouge	cider	spice	B4	meteor	rouge	cider	spice
ShowTell [4]	10.5	16.7	36.1	100.8	24.5	11.1	17.1	34.4	139.9	31.8
BUTD [19]	11.5	17.9	37.9	111.5	26.9	10.8	17.0	34.5	139.4	31.4
M_ShowTell [4]	14.4	20.1	41.4	135.6	32.9	12.8	19.0	37.6	157.6	36.6
M_BUTD [19]	15.5	20.9	42.6	143.8	34.9	12.7	19.1	37.9	159.5	36.8
SCHA	**21.7**	**23.4**	**48.9**	**190.8**	**40.5**	**15.4**	**21.6**	**42.8**	**182.3**	**38.6**

We employed pretrained Faster-RCNN and ResNet152 to extract local features and global image features. For the language model, we set the word embedding and LSTM hidden size to 512. During the training step, we set the learning rate to 1e-4 with a batch size of 128 and trained for 150 epochs.

Knowledge Prior Graph Evaluation. We compared SCHA with two well-designed baseline models. The first group included a more traditional model that does not incorporate any prior knowledge of the showTell model. This model uses a trained Resnet101 model to extract image feature information and then uses LSTM to translate the image information into text. The second group included the most advanced model BottomUptopDown(BUTD), which dynamically pays different attention to different areas of the image when generating descriptions.

In contrast, SCHA focuses on the embedded node of the prior knowledge graph rather than the detected image region. M represents an optimized solution, which introduces global information or attentional filtering. Table 2 shows that SCHA effectively reconciles the relationships between objects, attributes, and relationships by leveraging the quality of the knowledge graph structure.

In addition to the corresponding description corresponding to objective facts, in Fig. 3, we show a set of examples with a priori knowledge generation description, which is a description with a progressive relationship in detail to a certain extent. ① and ②, as descriptions of objective facts, simply describe the existing objects in the image, while ④ and ⑤ not only display the object, but also further describe the relationship between the objects. Moreover, even for large complex graph structures ④ and ⑤ with bidirectional relationships, our model successfully generates corresponding descriptions. The missing attribute word 'blue' appears in ③, which is information the model learns from the data outside the tag. Slight differences in attributes can also affect the description order, such as ① and ②.

Richness Evaluation. Our proposed prior knowledge graph aims to generate image descriptions with varying emphases. Results in Table 3 show that convolutional fusion improves performance by combining local and global information. By incorporating diverse experiential knowledge, we aim to capture multiple

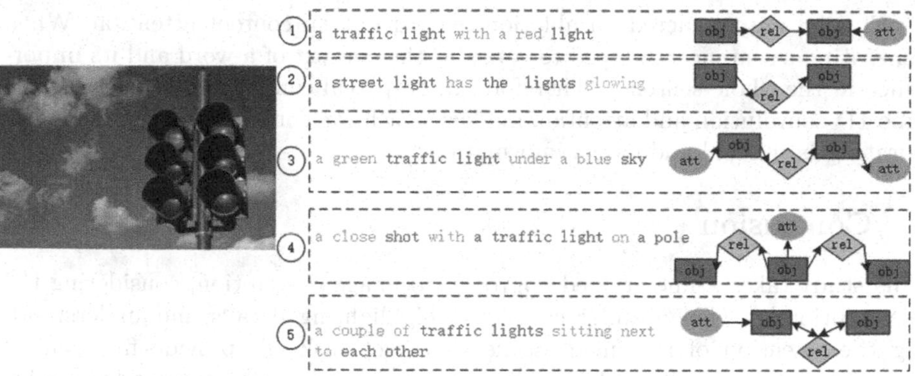

Fig. 3. Generate the details of the description

Table 3. The contribution of convolutional attention to the whole model

model	MSCOCO					Visual Genome				
	B4	meteor	rouge	cider	spice	B4	meteor	rouge	cider	spice
w Conv	20.2	22.5	47.7	188.4	39.5	15.1	20.7	42.3	177.2	37.9
w Attention	21.2	22.8	48.2	111.5	26.9	10.8	17.0	34.5	139.4	31.4
w/o Conv+Attention	**21.7**	**23.4**	**48.9**	**190.8**	**40.5**	**15.4**	**21.6**	**42.8**	**182.3**	**38.6**

perspectives and information about the image, ultimately aligning with human cognitive processes.

We manually reviewed the results and tallied the instances, where the presence of intentional speculation was observed. As shown in Table 4, we found that y-intent speculation on the target object was present in each model on both datasets. However, it is evident that the baseline models performed poorly, possibly due to the lack of a corresponding attention mechanism. Although there was some improvement after optimization, there still remained a significant gap from SCHA, which highlights the superiority of SCHA in this regard.

Table 4. Statistics on the rate of being judged as user intent descriptions

model	MSCOCO		Visual Genome	
	Quantity	Rate	Quantity	Rate
ShowTell [4]	89	8.90%	111	5.50%
BUTD [19]	195	19.50%	188	9.90%
M_ShowTell [4]	174	17.40%	223	11.30%
M_BUTD [19]	221	22.10%	247	12.70%
SCHA	423	42.30%	36.9	18.90%

Finally, we conducted an ablation experiment on content attention. When generating a sentence, we need to consider the context of a word and its importance in the whole sentence. Therefore, in graphical content attention, we combine 1D convolution and attention models to achieve content attention by incorporating both local and global information.

5 Conclusion

This study takes a fine-grained approach to image description, considering the user's prior knowledge and focusing on highlighting details and understanding the intention of the image scene or target task. To provide fine control over description details and content, we propose representing prior knowledge information using triple structures. These structures consist of three types of graph nodes: object, attribute, and relationship, corresponding to image content without semantic annotation. We then introduce a heterogeneous attention model, consisting of three layers for content, access order, and update supplement, specifically designed for text generation from knowledge graph structures without semantic labels. This approach significantly improves the fineness and richness of image captions, but the stacked attention method also brings high complexity, which is a goal for later optimization.

References

1. Baltrusaitis, T., Ahuja, C., Morency, L.P.: Multimodal machine learning: a survey and taxonomy. IEEE Trans. Pattern Anal. Mach. Intell. **41**, 423–443 (2017)
2. Cho, K., et al.: Learning phrase representations using rnn encoder-decoder for statistical machine translation. In: Computer Science (2014)
3. Mori, Y., Fukui, H., Hirakawa, T., Nishiyama, J., Fujiyoshi, H.: Attention neural baby talk: captioning of risk factors while driving. In: 2019 IEEE Intelligent Transportation Systems Conference - ITSC (2019)
4. Xu, K., et al.: Show, attend and tell: neural image caption generation with visual attention, pp. 2048–2057 (2015)
5. Lu, J., Xiong, C., Parikh, D., Socher, R.: Knowing when to look: adaptive attention via a visual sentinel for image captioning. In: 2017 IEEE Conference on Computer Vision and Pattern Recognition (CVPR) (2017)
6. Rennie, S.J., Marcheret, E., Mroueh, Y., Ross, J., Goel, V.: Self-critical sequence training for image captioning (2016)
7. Bahdanau, D., Cho, K., Bengio, Y.: Neural machine translation by jointly learning to align and translate. In: Computer Science (2014)
8. Shetty, R., Rohrbach, M., Hendricks, L.A., Fritz, M., Schiele, B.: Speaking the same language: matching machine to human captions by adversarial training. In: 2017 IEEE International Conference on Computer Vision (ICCV) (2017)
9. Wang, Q., Chan, A.B.: Describing like humans: on diversity in image captioning. In: 2019 IEEE/CVF Conference on Computer Vision and Pattern Recognition (CVPR) (2020)
10. Gan, C., Gan, Z., He, X., Gao, J., Deng, L.: Stylenet: generating attractive visual captions with styles. In: IEEE Conference on Computer Vision & Pattern Recognition (2017)

11. Guo, L., Liu, J., Yao, P., Li, J., Lu, H.: Mscap: multi-style image captioning with unpaired stylized text. In: 2019 IEEE/CVF Conference on Computer Vision and Pattern Recognition (CVPR) (2020)
12. Zhang, P., et al.: Training efficient saliency prediction models with knowledge distillation. In: Proceedings of the 27th ACM International Conference on Multimedia, pp. 512–520 (2019)
13. Vinyals, O., Toshev, A., Bengio, S., Erhan, D.: Show and tell: a neural image caption generator (2015)
14. Krishna, R., et al.: Visual genome: connecting language and vision using crowdsourced dense image annotations. Int. J. Comput. Vision **123**, 32–73 (2017)
15. Sutskever, I., Vinyals, O., Le, Q.V.: Sequence to sequence learning with neural networks. In: NIPS (2014)
16. Gan, Z., Gan, C., He, X., Pu, Y., Deng, L.: Semantic compositional networks for visual captioning. In: 2017 IEEE Conference on Computer Vision and Pattern Recognition (CVPR) (2017)
17. Wu, Q., Shen, C., Liu, L., Dick, A., Hengel, A.V.D.: What value do explicit high level concepts have in vision to language problems? In: Computer Science, pp. 203–212 (2015)
18. Zhou, Y., Wang, M., Liu, D., Hu, Z., Zhang, H.: More grounded image captioning by distilling image-text matching model. In: 2020 IEEE/CVF Conference on Computer Vision and Pattern Recognition (CVPR) (2020)
19. Anderson, P., et al.: Bottom-up and top-down attention for image captioning and visual question answering (2017)
20. Hu, Z., Yang, Z., Liang, X., Salakhutdinov, R., Xing, E.P.: Toward controlled generation of text (2017)
21. Moratelli, N., Barraco, M., Morelli, D., Cornia, M., Baraldi, L., Cucchiara, R.: Fashion-oriented image captioning with external knowledge retrieval and fully attentive gates. Sensors **23**(3), 1286 (2023)
22. Javanmardi, S., Latif, A.M., Sadeghi, M.T., Jahanbanifard, M., Bonsangue, M., Verbeek, F.J.: Caps captioning: a modern image captioning approach based on improved capsule network. Sensors **22**(21), 8376 (2022)
23. Mathews, L.X.A., He, X.: Semstyle: learning to generate stylised image captions using unaligned text. In: Proceedings of the IEEE Conference on Computer Vision and Pattern Recognition, pp. 8591–8600 (2019)
24. Xie, L., Mathews, A.P., He, X.: Senticap: generating image descriptions with sentiments. In: Thirtieth AAAI Conference on Artificial Intelligence (2016)
25. Karpathy, A., Fei-Fei, L.: Deep visual-semantic alignments for generating image descriptions. In: IEEE Conference on Computer Vision & Pattern Recognition, pp. 664–676 (2016)
26. Ward, T., Papineni, K., Roukos, S., Zhu, W.-J.: Bleu: a method for automatic evaluation of machine translation. In: Proceedings of the 40th Annual Meeting on Association for Computational Linguistics, pp. 311–318 (2002)
27. Banerjee, S., Lavie, A.: Meteor: an automatic metric for mt evaluation with improved correlation with human judgments. In: Proceedings of the ACL Workshop on Intrinsic and Extrinsic Evaluation Measures for Machine Translation and/or Summarization, pp. 65–72 (2005)
28. Webber, B., Byron, D.: Proceedings of the 2004 ACL Workshop on Discourse Annotation (2004)
29. Vedantam, R., Zitnick, C.L., Parikh, D.: Cider: consensus-based image description evaluation. In: 2015 IEEE Conference on Computer Vision and Pattern Recognition (CVPR) (2015)

30. Anderson, P., Fernando, B., Johnson, M., Gould, S.: SPICE: semantic propositional image caption evaluation. In: Leibe, B., Matas, J., Sebe, N., Welling, M. (eds.) ECCV 2016. LNCS, vol. 9909, pp. 382–398. Springer, Cham (2016). https://doi.org/10.1007/978-3-319-46454-1_24
31. Batra, D., Aneja, J., Agrawal, H., Schwing, A.: Sequential latent spaces for modeling the intention during diverse image captioning. In: Proceedings of the IEEE International Conference on Computer Vision (2019)
32. Deshpande, A., Aneja, J., Wang, L., Schwing, A.G., Forsyth, D.: Fast, diverse and accurate image captioning guided by part-of-speech. In: 2019 IEEE/CVF Conference on Computer Vision and Pattern Recognition (CVPR) (2019)

Image Captioning for Nantong Blue Calico Through Stacked Local-Global Channel Attention Network

Chenyi Guo[1], Li Zhang[1](✉), and Xiang Yu[2]

[1] School of Computer Science and Technology, Soochow University, Suzhou 215006, China
20215227095@stu.suda.edu.cn, zhangliml@suda.edu.cn

[2] Department of Computer Science and Technology, Nantong Vocational College of Science and Technology, Nantong 226007, China

Abstract. Nantong blue calico, a Chinese folk hand-made printing and dyeing craft, has become one of intangible cultural heritages (ICHs) in China. To inherite and promote the ICH of Nantong blue calico, this study applies the image captioning technology to explaining blue-calico images. For this purpose, a novel image captioning method, called the stacked local-global channel attention network (SLGCAN), is proposed. This new network focuses on extracting important features from blue-calico images so that it can generate more accurate captions for blue-calico images. SLGCAN contains three parts, residual network (ResNet), stacked local-global channel attention module (SLGCAM), and Transformer. First, the pre-trained ResNet-101 model is used to extract rough features from blue-calico images and then, SLGCAM is to obtain the fine-grained information from rough image features. Eventually, SLGCAN adopts Transformer to encode and decode the fine-grained information of blue-calico images to predict the word information for generating accurate image captions. Experiments are conducted on a collected blue-calico image dataset. In experiments, we compare our SLGCAN with baseline models and show that that the proposed model is feasible and effective.

Keywords: Intangible cultural heritage · Nantong blue calico · Image captioning · Channel attention · Transformer

1 Introduction

Blue calico has excellent artistic value and cultural connotation, which is a kind of Chinese folk handmade printing and dyeing craft. Nantong is the main production area of blue calico in China. Nantong blue calico is famous because it is one of the first batch of Chinese intangible cultural heritages (ICHs). As early as 1996, Mr. Wu Yuanxin, the representative inheritor of Nantong blue calico

L. Iliadis et al. (Eds.): ICANN 2023, LNCS 14255, pp. 357–372, 2023.
https://doi.org/10.1007/978-3-031-44210-0_29

ICH, founded the Nantong blue calico museum, which can well inherit and preserve blue calico. This museum owns tens of thousands of blue calico materials crafted during the Ming and Qing Dynasties. This museum is privately owned so it may have limited collection conditions to some extend, such as collection space. Under the limited conditions, not all blue calico can be stored very well.

Digital technology in computer science brings a new possible approach to the preservation and inheritance of all ICHs [1]. For example, Zhang et al. [2] used the geographic information system (GIS) 3D space technology to collect Longquan celadon ICH data and utilized a virtual reality technology to create the digital scenery that approximates the real environment. Dimitropoulos et al. [3] explored a novel holistic approach for conserving and developing ICHs, which can capture the high-level semantics in ICH data through an innovative multisensory technology and analyze in depth the evolution of a particular ICH and the implicit connections contained between various ICHs representations or interpretation styles. Zhu et al. [4] designed a semantic information ontology model for ICH images to extract different semantic information in ICHs, such as paper-cut handicraft and musical instrument performing arts, and established an ICH digital archive platform. For blue calico, it is urgent to use digital technology to preserve this traditional folk art and to awaken the public's appreciation and recognition of traditional crafts.

On the basis of a large number of blue calico treasures in the Nantong blue calico museum, Yu et al. [5] collected and constructed a Nantong blue-calico (NtBC) image dataset by using the digital information technology, which is the first large-scale dataset for blue calico. On a part of images from the NtBC dataset, Yu et al. [5] analyzed the classification problem of common blue-calico patterns by introducing four popular convolutional neural networks (CNNs). In addition, several researchers have utilized the deep learning technology to analyze blue calico. For instance, Jia et al. [6] used an improved CNN and optimized the parameters in the network structure to rationally classify the veined pattern elements of blue calico. Wang and Fu [7] investigated the improvement and optimization of network construction and loss function in deep convolutional generative adversarial networks (CGAN) to redesign new creative patterns of blue calico.

These studies have provided important ideas for digital research and inheritance of the blue-calico ICH. However, no study is related to captioning blue-calico images. It is well known, blue calico expresses the idea of auspicious content through specific and objective morphological characteristics. Due to the lack of interpretation of the cultural connotation of blue calico, the public cannot fully understand the artistic value and abundant connotative themes contained in blue calico. Accordingly, we thought that explaining blue-calico images is a important and pivotal step to inheriting and developing the blue-calico ICH.

By applying the technique of image captioning, we could implement the description of blue-calico images. Image captioning is a promising research direction at the intersection of natural Language processing (NLP) and computer vision (CV), which aims to automatically generate a natural language description text for a given image. Many existing image captioning algorithms follow the encoder-decoder architecture [8]. The encoder is to extract visual features of the image, whereas the decoder is to transform the extracted image features into high-level semantic information, i.e., generate a sentence that is semantically and grammatically correct. At present, image captioning technology has not been applied to the field of generating image captions for blue-calico images.

The purpose of this study is to introduce the image captioning technique for describing blue-calico images from the NtBC image dataset in language, which is the first work of generating image captions for blue-calico images. To construct a blue-calico dataset for image captioning, we tagged a part of images in nine classes from two themes of the NtBC image dataset. Images in these classes contain at least two targets. For captioning blue-calico images, a stacked local-global channel attention network (SLGCAN) is proposed, which follows the encoder-decoder structure. The encoder consists of residual network (ResNet), stacked local-global channel attention module (SLGCAM), and Transformer-based visual encoder. ResNet is used to extract rough features, whereas SLGCAM is designed here to extract underlying features for the blue-calico images. Subsequently, the encoded information is introduced into the language decoder model (Transformer) to generate the analytical description of the blue-calico patterns. By applying SLGCAN, we can easily interpret the cultural connotation of blue-calico images, so that the blue-calico ICH has been digitally continued and promoted.

2 Description of NtBC-C Image Dataset

2.1 Origin of NtBC-C Dataset

As mentioned before, the NtBC image dataset provides a large number of blue-calico images [5]. This dataset consists of 43,209 images that belong to four themes (plants, animals, myth, and compound) and 34 categories. Yu et al. [5] used the image classification methods based on deep learning to recognize blue-calico-images for a total of 10 categories of Chrysanthemum, Kylin Songzi, Lions with balls, Peony, Phoenix, Orchid, Plum, Butterfly, Peaches, and Bat. Experimental results show that classification methods based on deep learning obtain some success, but there still has a lot of room for growth.

In particular, blue-calico patterns are mostly taken from folk legends, animals, flowers, and trees, which not only express the sincere wish of pursuing auspiciousness by means of homonym, symbolism and allegories, but also send people's wishes for a better life. However, it is hard to understand the meaning contained in a blue calico image if one does not have a prior knowledge on blue calico. Thus, it is necessary to describe the original provenance and the represented ideas in blue-calico images, which is another crucial direction to inherit and prevent blue calico. This study is to investigate the image captioning of a part of blue-calico images from the NtBC image dataset by using methods based on deep learning.

The characteristics and artistic value of blue calico are embodied in the pattern features to express auspicious meaning by mixing several elements together.

We acquired blue-calico images that belong to nine classes in the compound or myth theme from the NtBC image dataset. Here, we call this new subset NtBC-C (NtBC for image captioning).

2.2 Construction of NtBC-C Dataset

First, the size of each image in NtBC-C was normalized to 256×256. Then, we performed data enhancement operations on the NtBC-C dataset, where we augmented the data samples by adopting random probability rotation, offset, and scaling techniques to increase the number and diversity of samples and reduce the dependence of the model on certain attributes. After data enhancement, the total of 7440 blue-calico images were used for image captioning. The ratio of training and test samples is about 10:1 in the NtBC-C dataset. The statistical display of the NtBC-C dataset is shown in Table 1, where we refer to the samples used for training after the data enhancement operation of the original blue calico images as "Enhanced training". "Form" is the way of forming a special cultural meaning for a given blue-calico image through two or more thematic elements. There are three forms: allegory, symbolism, and homonym. Generally, allegory is to use the auspicious meaning of specific things known in traditional Chinese life to express the wonderful thought, symbolism is the expression of the blissful meaning through the natural morphological features of the thing itself, and homonym is the use of the same or similar pronunciation between Chinese characters to replace the Chinese characters and meanings. We also note the inevitably imbalanced distribution of the NtBC-C dataset, which brings a new challenge for the image captioning of blue calico.

Figure 1 shows nine blue-calico images each of which belongs to an image class. In the following, we describe each image class in detail.

- Fig. 1(a) presents the image belonging the class of Die-lian-hua. This class depicts butterflies fluttering in flowers. In Chinese traditional culture, butterfly is a symbol of happiness and love, and flower symbolizes beauty and wealth. Thus, Die-lian-hua expresses the sweetness of love and the beauty of life.
- A blue-calico image of Feng-xi-mu-dan is shown in Fig. 1(b), which describes a phoenix flying next to a peony flower, symbolizing the harmony of the couple.
- In Chinese characters, "bat" and "bless" are pronounced as "fu"; "money" and "front" are pronounced as "qian". Thus, in the expression of blue-calico images, bats are often used to represent good fortune, and coins are used to represent the front. As shown in Fig. 1(c), a bat flying around two coins expresses the class of Fu-dao-yan-qian, implying that happiness in front of eyes.
- In Fig. 1(d), four bats form a circle and a coin in the middle. The pattern means Fu-shou-tuan-yuan that uses the homonym form to express best wishes of good fortune, long life, and family reunion.
- Fig. 1(e) shows an image with a jade chime with two fish hung under it, which belongs the class of Ji-qing-you-yu. In Chinese culture, "fish" is the harmonic of "surplus". Thus, Ji-qing-you-yu represents a desire for wealth.

Table 1. Statistical display of NtBC-C for image captioning

No.	Class	Form	#Original training	#Original test	#Enhanced training	#Enhanced test	Total
1	Die-lian-hua	Allegory	18	3	900	90	990
2	Feng-xi-mu-dan	Allegory	35	6	1750	180	1930
3	Fu-dao-yan-qian	Homonym	12	2	600	60	660
4	Fu-shou-tuan-yuan	Homonym	7	2	350	60	410
5	Ji-qing-you-yu	Homonym	12	2	600	60	660
6	Lian-nian-you-yu	Homonym	6	1	300	30	330
7	Qi-lin-song-zi	Symbolism	13	2	650	60	710
8	Shi-zi-wu-xiu-qiu	Allegory	22	3	1100	90	1190
9	Xi-shang-mei-shao	Homonym	10	2	500	60	560

- Fig. 1(f) depicts a fish swimming under a lotus flower, signifying Lian-nian-you-yu. In Chinese characters, "lotus" and "continuous" are pronounced as "Lian-hua" and "Lian-xu", respectively. The lotus flower is used to represent continuity. Thus, Lian-nian-you-yu means that inexhaustible wealth every year.
- In Fig. 1(g), a child holding a lotus flower rides on the back of a Kirin, representing Qi-lin-song-zi. Kirin is a sacred animal in Chinese folklore as a symbol of good luck. Qi-lin-song-zi is the custom of praying for children in China.
- Fig. 1(h) shows the image from Shi-zi-wu-xiu-qiu, which consists of a lion stepping on an embroidered ball. Shi-zi-wu-xiu-qiu is a Chinese custom of exorcizing evil spirits, signifying good things to come.
- In Fig. 1(i), a magpie is standing on a plum blossom on a branch, which means Xi-shang-mei-shao. In Chinese culture, "magpie" symbolizes the arrival of happy events in Chinese folklore, "plum" and "eyebrow" have the same sound. Originally, Xi-shang-mei-shao describes how people look when they are happy. In blue-calico images, Xi-shang-mei-shao represents a desire for happiness and auspiciousness.

2.3 Annotation of NtBC-C Dataset

Note that there are 6750 blue-calico images in the training set after data enhancement. We need to annotate these images for captioning. Specifically, five English sentences (captioning labels) were assigned for each training image to illustrate the meanings of blue-calico patterns, where each sentence is limited to 50 words. According to all sentences, we constructed a vocabulary of words each of which appeared at least five times in the training set. In this way, the training set is transformed into a standard format required by the model training.

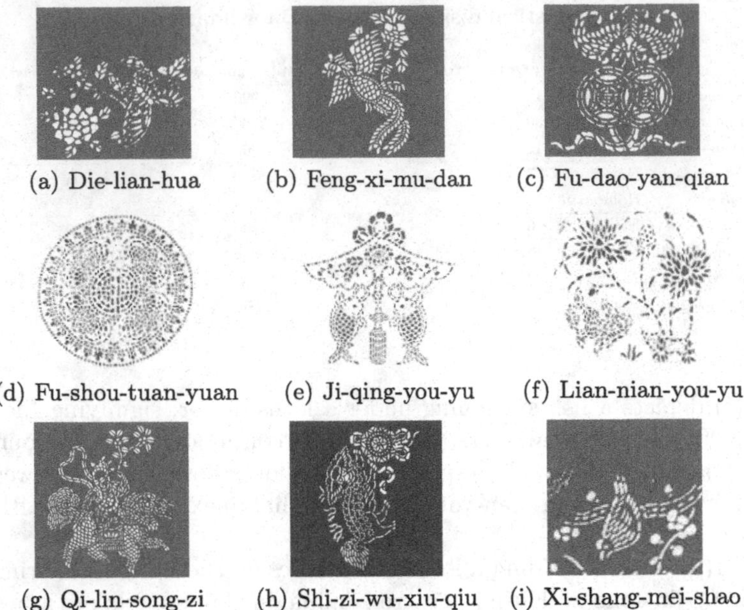

Fig. 1. Showing the content of blue-calico with the compound theme in Chinese phoneticize: (a) Die-lian-hua, (b) Feng-xi-mu-dan, (c) Fu-dao-yan-qian, (d) Fu-shou-tuan-yuan, (e) Ji-qing-you-yu, (f) Lian-nian-you-yu, (g) Qi-lin-song-zi, (h) Shi-zi-wu-xiu-qiu, and (i) Xi-shang-mei-shao

Figure 2 shows three blue-calico images from the class of Xi-shang-mei-shao. These images have the same captioning labels. Although images in the same class have the same captioning labels, they are diverse in their expression of the combination of magpie and plum blossoms. We know that blue calico is made manually, including shaping weaving, printing, and dyeing. Thus, the shapes of patterns are all influenced by the aesthetics, and knife techniques of the artisans. Consequently, even if blue calico pattern represents the same symbolic meaning, it would embody various and different pattern expressions.

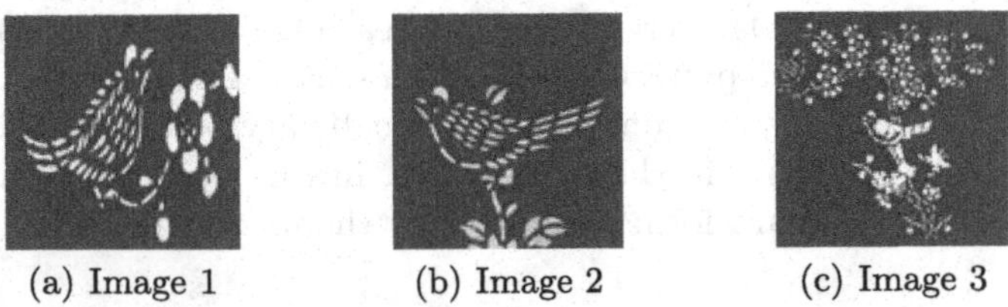

Fig. 2. Diversity of blue-calico images in the class of Xi-shang-mei-shao, (a) Image 1, (b) Image 2, and (c) Image 3

3 Method

This section presents the proposed image captioning model, SLGCAN, for blue-calico images. Figure 3 shows the architecture of the proposed model that has an encoder-decoder structure. The encoder part of SLGCAN include three modules: ResNet-101, SLGCAM, and the visual encoder of Transformer. The main role of the encoder part is to extract features from images and encode them. The decoder part of SLGCAN is the exact decoder of Transformer. In the following, we discuss SLGCAN from encoder and decoder parts.

3.1 Encoder of SLGCAN

As mentioned above, the encoder part consists of three modules. First, the pre-trained ResNet-101 is used to extract rough features from blue-calico images. Second, SLGCAM is designed to extract the fine-grained information from the outputs of ResNet-101. Third, the visual encoder of Transformer is applied to encode the outputs of SLGCAM.

ResNet. Deep convolutional neural networks (CNNs), such as VGGNet (visual geometry group network) [9] and ResNet [10], have demonstrated the powerful capability of feature extraction, which is of benefit to image tasks including image captioning. By introducing residual connection, ResNet avoids the phenomenon of gradient disappearance and gradient explosion to a certain extent.

To capture rich image information at different levels, we use ResNet-101 pre-trained on the ImageNet dataset, which is a large-scale image dataset [11]. The original ResNet-101 is a classification model; however, our goal is to captioning blue-calico images instead of classifying them. It is enough for us to use features extracted by ResNet-101. Thus, we remove the final average pooling layer and fully connected layer of the original ResNet-101, and then obtain rough features extracted from blue-calico images by using transform learning. In this way, we can reduce resource and time overhead, and improve the training speed of the proposed model to some extent.

SLGCAM. This study designs a new module, SLGCAM, for further extract fine-grained information from images by introducing channel attention mechanism. This mechanism aims to obtain the importance of each feature channel through network learning and assign different weights to each channel for modeling the correlation between channels, so as to strengthen the features that are useful for the current task and suppress the non-important features [12]. SLGCAM includes two local channel-attention blocks and a global channel-attention block, as shown in Fig. 4. Specifically, the local channel-attention block leverages a convolution kernel to change the dimension of feature channels, construct correlations between different channels, and focus on the fine-grained feature between channels; thus, this block improves the characterization capability of the network. Moreover, the global channel-attention block adopts a global

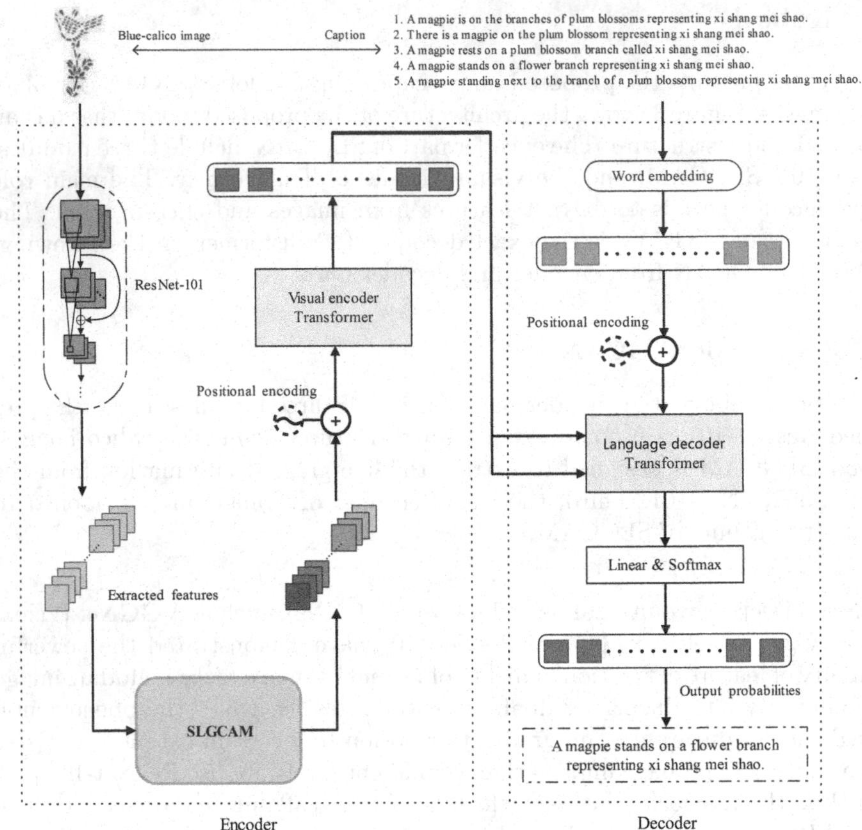

Fig. 3. Architecture of our SLGCAN

average pooling (GAP) to further fuse the features extracted from local channel-attention blocks. In addition, we stack the second part of channel attention to obtain dependency relationship between local and global features of the image as well as between channel features, which focuses more precisely on meaningful features in blue-calico images and enables the extracted local information to be further combined with the global information.

The output (feature map) of the local channel-attention block is defined as

$$\mathrm{L}\,(X) = \mathrm{BN}\,(\mathrm{conv2}\,(\mathrm{ReLU}\,(\mathrm{BN}\,(\mathrm{conv1}\,(X))))) \tag{1}$$

where X denotes the rough feature map extracted by ResNet-101; conv1 indicates a 1×1 convolution kernel that can reduce the number of channels for the input feature X to $1/r$; BN means the function of BatchNorm, which normalizes the data, so that data will not be oversized and cause network performance instability before ReLU is performed; conv2 is also a 1×1 convolution kernel that restores the number of channels to the channel number of X.

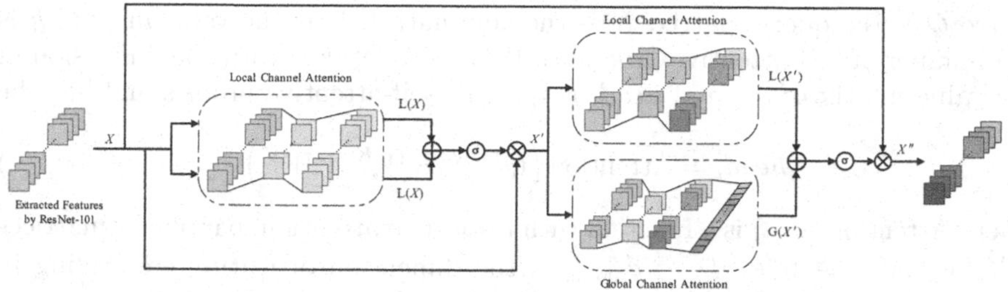

Fig. 4. Structure of SLGCAM

The output of global channel-attention block is defined as

$$\mathrm{G}\left(X'\right) = \mathrm{GAP}\left(\mathrm{BN}\left(\mathrm{conv2}\left(\mathrm{ReLU}\left(\mathrm{BN}\left(\mathrm{conv1}\left(X'\right)\right)\right)\right)\right)\right) \tag{2}$$

where GAP is the operation of global average pooling, and X' is the feature map generated by the first stage of the local channel-attention block, that is

$$X' = X \otimes \sigma(\mathrm{L}(X) \oplus \mathrm{L}(X)) \tag{3}$$

where $\sigma\left(\cdot\right)$ is the sigmoid activation function, $\oplus$ is the operation of adding up feature maps, $\otimes$ is the operation of multiplying a feature map with feature weights separately. Unlike the local channel-attention feature map $\mathrm{L}\left(X\right)$, the global channel-attention feature map $\mathrm{G}\left(X'\right)$ performs the global average pooling of X', preserving and further fusing the features extracted by the local channel-attention block.

In the process of channel attention stacking, the ultimate feature map X'' is obtained after attention enhancement of input feature X, that is

$$X'' = X \otimes \sigma\left(\mathrm{G}\left(X'\right) \oplus \mathrm{L}\left(X'\right)\right) \tag{4}$$

Visual Encoder. This study adopts two encoder layers of Transformer as our model's visual encoder. The input of visual encoder is the local features of blue-calico images extracted by SLGCAM. Thus, the visual encoder obtains global information by self-attention mechanism capturing the dependencies between its input and the output sequence.

In the encoding stage, each encoder layer consists of two sub-modules, the multi-head attention (MHA) sub-module and the fully connected feed-forward network (FFN) sub-module, in that order. In addition, residual connection and layer normalization (LayerNorm) are applied after each sub-module.

It is convenient for MHA to associate one pixel with other pixels in the input feature maps of the current sub-module, which can select the pixels focused on. Specifically, MHA maps and then divides its input into obtain the query, key, and value vectors. The attention values are obtained by self-attention mechanism, and are eventually connected into a matrix output. The MHA sub-module is defined as

$$\mathrm{MHA}(Q, K, V) = \mathrm{Concat}\left(head_1, \ldots, head_h\right) W^o \tag{5}$$

where Q is the query matrix, K is the key matrix, V is the value matrix, h is the number of self-attentive processes, $W^o \in \mathbb{R}^{hd_v \times d_{\text{model}}}$ with the dimension of the value matrix of d_v, and $head_i$ is the i-th self-attentive process and has the form

$$head_i = \text{Attention}\left(QW_i^Q, KW_i^K, VW_i^V\right) \tag{6}$$

where Attention$(\cdot,\cdot,\cdot)$ is a function with respect to attention, parameter matrices $W_i^Q, W_i^K, W_i^V \in \mathbb{R}^{d_{\text{model}} \times d_k}$, d_{model} is the dimension of feature embedding in MHA, d_k is the dimension of the key matrix and $d_k = d_{\text{model}}/h$.

In (6), the attention function is a self-attention function that is also called scaled dot-product attention. In detail, the self-attention function has the form

$$\text{Attention}(Q, K, V) = \text{softmax}\left(\frac{QK^T}{\sqrt{d_k}}\right)V \tag{7}$$

Note that SLGCAN superimposes the self-attentive process with eight times to form the MHA sub-module.

3.2 Decoder of SLGCAN

From the architecture of our model, Fig. 3, we can see that the decoder mainly uses the language decoder of Transformer. The language decoder of Transformer uses a self-attentive mechanism to weight different parts of the input sequence to different degrees, thus focusing on the important regions in the image when generating captions. In addition, it can capture the dependencies between various positions in the input sequence to a greater extent when dealing with long sequences, enabling the model to better obtain the global contextual information in the image and thus generate higher-quality description sentences. Transformer decoder takes both the output of visual encoder and the combination of positional embedding with the word embedding features.

Typically, Transformer decoder contains a masked MHA sub-module, a multi-head cross attention sub-module, and an FFN sub-module, where each sub-module is followed by residual connection and LayerNorm. The masked MHA sub-module performs masking operation with the mask matrix in which the lower-triangular matrix values are filled with zeros, and which has the same size as the attention weight matrix. This sub-module ensures that the prediction of each word depends only on the current position and previously generated words when generating words one by one, avoiding the influence of future words on the model. The multi-head cross attention sub-module takes the masked MHA sub-module output as Q, and the outputs of the encoder as K and V. This process aligns the output of the encoder with the input of the decoder, enabling the decoder to determine the sub-sequences related to the focused content of the encoder.

The output of the language decoder is predicted using a linear layer and softmax with an output dimension that is the same as the vocabulary size to predict each generated word. The model is trained using a cross-entropy loss.

Given image I_0 and a ground-truth caption $y_{1:M}$, where M is the length of the description sequence. The cross-entropy loss Loss (Θ) can be expressed as

$$\operatorname{Loss}(\Theta)=-\sum_{m=1}^{M} \log p_{\Theta}\left(y_m \mid y_{1:m-1}, I_0\right) \tag{8}$$

where $p_{\Theta}\left(y_m \mid y_{1:m-1}\right)$ denotes the probability of the word y_m given the word sequence $y_1, \ldots, y_{m-1}$ and image I_0, and Θ is the parameters of the captioning model.

4 Experiments

The goal of this section is to validate the feasibility of captioning blue-calico images and the effectiveness of the proposed model SLGCAN.

4.1 Experimental Setting

As described in Sect. 3, our SLGCAN has an encoder-decoder structure, and the encoder part includes ResNet-101, SLGCAM, and Transformer encoder. ResNet-101 has an input image size of 256×256 and an output feature map size of $8\times8\times2048$. The output feature map of SLGCAM is adjusted to a fixed size of 14×14 by applying two-dimensional adaptive average pooling, and the number of channels is changed before and after. The Transformer encoder and decoder layers are stacked 2 and 6 times, respectively. By using 8 attention heads, the feature dimension in the MHA sub-module is set to 512, and the feature dimension d_k for each *head* is 64. To avoid overfitting, the parameter in the droupout trick is set to 0.1. The model parameters are optimized by using Adam optimization algorithm [13]. The size of batch training is set to 32, and initial learning rate is set to 0.0001.

To compare the performance of the proposed model, we use the model with two CNNs (CNN-CNN) [14], the model of CNN and LSTM with soft attention (CNN-LSTM+SA) [15], the model of CNN and LSTM with adaptive attention (CNN-LSTM+AA) [16], and the model with both CNN and Transformer (CNN-Transformer) [17]. The hyper-parameter setting of these models were followed the corresponding references. All the compared models are trained by using cross-entropy loss.

In order to evaluate the model performance, the experimental evaluation metrics include BLEU (bilingual evaluation understudy) [18], METEOR [19], ROUGE-L [20], and CIDEr (consensus-based image description evaluation) [21] to evaluate the accuracy of the predicted captions generated by models. BLEU is an accuracy-based similarity measure that uses an n-gram matching rule, here $n=1,2,3,4$. That is BLEU-1, BLEU-2, BLEU-3, and BLEU-4. Totally, there are seven metrics in our experiments. Generally, the better the model performs, the higher the scores of these metric indicators.

4.2 Experimental Analysis

Table 2 shows the ultimate evaluation metric scores for compared models on the NtBC-C dataset, where the highest accuracy scores for each metric are highlighted by boldface. As can be seen that SLGCAN proposed in this paper obtains the best results compared to baseline models on all the evaluated metrics. In particular, the score of METEOR is improved by more than 8% points compared with the second best, and the scores of other evaluation metrics are also superior to baseline models, indicating the higher quality of captions generated by the method in this paper on the NtBC-C dataset. These baseline models were designed for general image captioning, and their attention mechanisms, such as spatial attention, may not be effectively able to focus on the specific characteristics of blue-calico images. By contrast, SLGCAN is tailored to blue-calico image captioning and the main module of SLGCAN, SLGCAM, can extract fine-grained feature information between various blue-calico images.

Figure 5 visualizes the attention map of our model for each word when generating captions. It can be seen that for words, such as "stands", "flower", and "branch", our model adaptively pays attention to the corresponding reasonable region.

Table 2. Performance comparison of various models.

Models	Evaluation metrics						
	BLEU-1	*BLEU-2*	*BLEU-3*	*BLEU-4*	*METEOR*	*ROUGE-L*	*CIDEr*
CNN-LSTM+SA [15]	94.05	93.44	93.18	93.05	70.83	94.21	4.72
CNN-LSTM+AA [16]	95.85	95.26	94.95	94.77	72.94	95.40	4.79
CNN-CNN [14]	93.71	93.30	92.40	93.54	62.49	92.26	4.40
CNN-Transformer [17]	94.25	94.80	94.34	94.17	65.27	94.27	4.44
SLGCAN	**98.35**	**98.24**	**98.19**	**98.18**	**81.13**	**98.37**	**5.15**

4.3 Ablation Experiments

This part verifies the effectiveness of the SLGCAM module through ablation experiments. In ablation experiments, we consider five variants of SLGCAM in SLGCAN: (1) SLGCAM is not used, called None; that is, the output of ResNet-101 is the input to the Transformer encoder; (2) SLGCAM is reduced to one local channel-attention block, called LCAB; (3) SLGCAM is reduced to two stacked local channel-attention blocks, called LLCAB; (4) SLGCAM is reduced to stacked local and global channel-attention blocks, called LGCAB; (5) SLGCAM is maintained, which is the exact form in this paper.

Table 3 shows results of the ablation experiments, where BLEU-1, BLEU-2, BLEU-3, BLEU-4, METEOR, ROUGE-L, and CIDEr are evaluation scores achieved by five models mentioned above on the test set. It can be seen that the

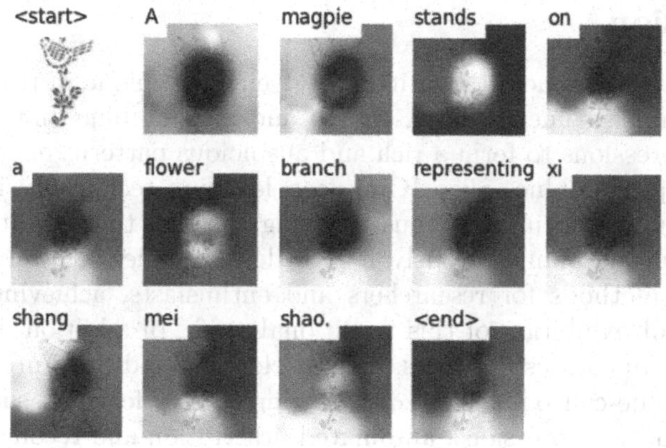

Fig. 5. Attention visualization of generated words

SLGCAM module plays an important role in improving the model performance because not only the model with SLGCAM (SLGCAN) achieves superior results in each metrics compared with None but also it significantly outperforms other variants. For example, our method improves 2.43 % on BLEU-4 and 6.38% on METEOR compared to LCAB. From using one local channel-attention block (LCAB) to two local channel-attention blocks (LLCAB), the model achieves higher scores on all evaluation metrics except BLEU-1. By comparing LLCAB and LGCAB, we has a conclusion that the global channel-attention block is helpful in extracting the association between local and global information, allowing the model to obtain a higher performance.

Consequently, the SLGCAM module in SLGCAN is effective for further extracting the detail information of blue-calico images. Because SLGCAM is the main contribution in our work, its effectiveness also validates the effectiveness of our work, SLGCAN.

Table 3. Comparison of ablation experimental results.

Method	*BLEU-1*	*BLEU-2*	*BLEU-3*	*BLEU-4*	*METEOR*	*ROUGE-L*	*CIDEr*
None	96.52	96.10	95.81	95.72	75.10	96.55	4.83
LCAB	96.63	96.13	95.87	95.75	74.75	96.40	4.89
LLCAB	96.54	96.17	95.96	95.84	75.52	96.52	4.93
LGCAB	96.70	96.22	95.99	95.90	76.03	96.93	5.01
SLGCAM	98.35	98.24	98.19	98.18	81.13	98.37	5.15

5 Conclusion

Blue calico is a time-honored printing and dyeing technique in traditional folk, which uses simple geometric lines, simple and elegant blue and white colors, and unique expressions to form a rich and auspicious patterns of calico. For the digitalized project of blue-calico ICH, deep learning technology is utilized to describe the blue-calico images, thus breaking through the limitations of blue-calico dissemination. Simultaneously, it provides convenient digital retrieval and understanding methods for researchers and enthusiasts, achieving the digital preservation and exhibition of this traditional craft. In addition, blue calico is commonly used in various products, such as clothing and furniture supplies. By describing the blue-calico images and extracting the key features, such as pattern styles and thematic expressions, automated description and recommendation of products can be achieved, further ensuring the continuity and innovation of blue calico. In order to describe more accurate sentences for the content of blue-calico images, this paper proposes an SLGCAN to generate image captioning. The architecture of the proposed model uses the encoder-decoder structure. The main contribution of this study is to design SLGCAM that further enhances the fine-grained differences in the image features extracted by the ResNet-101 model and combines the connection between local and global features to obtain the effective information of diverse blue-calico images. In addition, we tag a part of NtBC dataset and form the NtBC-C dataset for image captioning. On the basis of the NtBC-C dataset, we conduct extensive experiments to validate the feasibility and effectiveness of SLGCAN. Experimental results show that the proposed model achieves superior performance compared with the other baseline models. Especially, the the METEOR index of SLGCAN is increased by 8.19% compared to the second best method. Moreover, the ablation experiments demonstrate that SLGCAN is optimal when varying the SLGCAM module by gradually adjusting the channel attention.

Although SLGCAN performs well on the constructed NtBC dataset, there are still some limitations. First, this NtBC dataset is not large enough. More large-scale dataset on blue calico will be expected. Second, convolution operations usually require a large number of parameters to extract image features, and Transformer is a more complex structure. SLGCAN combines Transformer and CNN in series may increase the number of parameters and computational complexity of the model, which leads to a slow training speed. In future, we plan to better fuse them in a way and hence improve performance of image captioning on blue-calico images.

References

1. Severo, M., Venturini, T.: Intangible cultural heritage webs: comparing national networks with digital methods. New Media Soc. **18**(8), 1616–1635 (2016). https://doi.org/10.1177/1461444814567981
2. Zhang, Y., Han, M., Chen, W.: The strategy of digital scenic area planning from the perspective of intangible cultural heritage protection. J. Image Video Proc. **130** (2018). https://doi.org/10.1186/s13640-018-0366-7

3. Dimitropoulos, K., et al.: A multimodal approach for the safeguarding and transmission of intangible cultural heritage: the case of i-Treasures. IEEE Intell. Syst. **33**(6), 3–16 (2018). https://doi.org/10.1109/MIS.2018.111144858
4. Zhu, X.-F., Wang, R.-C.: Research on ICH image semantic information ontology construction of and its linked data storage & publication. Mod. Inf. **41**(6), 54–63 (2021). https://doi.org/10.3969/j.issn.1008-0821.2021.06.005
5. Yu, X., Zhang, L., Shen, M.: Nantong blue calico image dataset and its recognition. In: 2022 IEEE Congress on Evolutionary Computation (CEC), pp. 1–7. IEEE, Padua (2022). https://doi.org/10.1109/CEC55065.2022.9870225
6. Jia, X.-J., Deng, H.-T., Liu, Z.-H., Ye, L.-H.: Vein pattern classification based on VGGNet convolutional neural network for blue calico. J. Optoelectron. · Laser **30**(8), 867–875 (2019). https://doi.org/10.16136/j.joel.2019.08.0073
7. Wang, Y., Fu, R.: Research on the regenerated design of blue calico based on computer image processing. In: Rauterberg, M. (ed.) HCII 2020. LNCS, vol. 12215, pp. 428–438. Springer, Cham (2020). https://doi.org/10.1007/978-3-030-50267-6_32
8. Vinyals, O., Toshev, A., Bengio, S., Erhan, D.: Show and tell: a neural image caption generator. In: 2015 IEEE Conference on Computer Vision and Pattern Recognition (CVPR), pp. 3156–3164. IEEE, Boston (2015). https://doi.org/10.1109/CVPR.2015.7298935
9. Simonyan, K., Zisserman, A.: Very deep convolutional networks for large-scale image recognition. In: International Conference on Learning Representations. ICLR, Santiago (2015). https://doi.org/10.48550/arXiv.1409.1556
10. He, K., Zhang, X., Ren, S., Sun, J.: Deep residual learning for image recognition. In: 2016 IEEE Conference on Computer Vision and Pattern Recognition (CVPR), pp. 770–778. IEEE, Las Vegas (2016). https://doi.org/10.1109/CVPR.2016.90
11. Deng, J., Dong, W., Socher, R., Li, L.-J., Li, K., Li, F.-F.: ImageNet: a large-scale hierarchical image database. In: 2009 IEEE Conference on Computer Vision and Pattern Recognition, pp. 248–255. IEEE, Miami (2009). https://doi.org/10.1109/CVPR.2009.5206848
12. Hu, J., Shen, L., Albanic, S., Sun, G., Wu, E.: Squeeze-and-excitation networks. IEEE Trans. Pattern Anal. Mach. Intell. **42**(8), 2011–2023 (2020). https://doi.org/10.1109/TPAMI.2019.2913372
13. Kingma, D.-P., Ba, J.: Adam: a method for stochastic optimization. In: Proceedings of the 3rd International Conference on Learning Representations. ICLR, San Diego (2015). https://doi.org/10.48550/arXiv.1412.6980
14. Wang, Q.-Z., Chan, A.-B.: CNN+CNN: convolutional decoders for image captioning. arXiv preprint (2018). https://doi.org/10.48550/arXiv.1805.09019
15. Xu, K., et al.: Show, attend and tell: neural image caption generation with visual attention. In: Proceedings of the 32nd International Conference on Machine Learning, pp. 2048–2057. IEEE (2015)
16. Lu, J., Xiong, C., Parikh, D., Socher, R.: Knowing when to look: adaptive attention via a visual sentinel for image captioning. In: 2017 IEEE Conference on Computer Vision and Pattern Recognition (CVPR), pp. 3242–3250. IEEE, Honolulu (2017). https://doi.org/10.1109/CVPR.2017.345
17. Castro, R., Pineda, I., Lim, W., Morocho-Cayamcela, M.-E.: Deep learning approaches based on Transformer architectures for image captioning Tasks. IEEE Access **10**, 33679–33694 (2022). https://doi.org/10.1109/ACCESS.2022.3161428

18. Papineni, K., Roukos, S., Ward, T., Zhu, W.-J.: BLEU: a method for automatic evaluation of machine translation. In: Proceedings of the 40th Annual Meeting of the Association for Computational Linguistics, pp. 311–318. Association for Computational Linguistics, Philadelphia (2002). https://doi.org/10.3115/1073083.1073135
19. Banerjee, S., Lavie, A.: METEOR: an automatic metric for MT evaluation with improved correlation with human judgments. In: Proceedings of the ACL Workshop on Intrinsic and Extrinsic Evaluation Measures for Machine Translation and/or Summarization, pp. 65–72. Association for Computational Linguistics, Ann Arbor (2005). https://aclanthology.org/W05-0909
20. Lin, C.-Y.: ROUGE: a package for automatic evaluation of summaries. In: ACL 2004 Workshop, pp. 74–81. Association for Computational Linguistics (2004)
21. Vedantam, R., Zitnick, C.-L., Parikh, D.: CIDEr: consensus-based image description evaluation. In: 2015 IEEE Conference on Computer Vision and Pattern Recognition (CVPR), pp. 4566–4575. IEEE, Boston (2015). https://doi.org/10.1109/CVPR.2015.7299087

Improving Image Captioning with Feature Filtering and Injection

Menghao Guo, Qiaohong Chen(✉), Xian Fang, Jia Bao, and Shenxiang Xiang

School of Computer Science and Technology, Zhejiang Sci-Tech University, Hangzhou 310018, China
{chen_lisa,xianfang,baojia}@zstu.edu.cn

Abstract. Image captioning represents a challenging multimodal task, requiring the generation of corresponding textual descriptions for complex input images. Existing methods usually leverage object detectors to extract visual features of images, and thus utilize text generators for learning. However, the features extracted by these methods lack focus and tend to ignore the relationship between objects and background information. To solve the aforementioned problems, we exploit both region features and grid features of the image to fully leverage the information encapsulated within the images. Specifically, we first propose an Object Filter Module (OFM) to extract the primary visual objects. Furthermore, we introduce a Global Injection Cross Attention (GICA) to inject the global context of the image into the filtered primary objects. The experimental results substantiate the efficacy of our model. Our model's effectiveness and immense potential have been demonstrated through extensive experimentation on the widely-used benchmark COCO dataset. It outperforms previous methods on the image captioning task, achieving a CIDEr score of 136.1.

Keywords: Image Captioning · Region Feature · Grid Feature · Transformer

1 Introduction

As an emerging branch of multimodal tasks, image captioning has garnered raising attention in recent studies [1,2]. The purpose of the image captioning task is to generate a textual description in natural language that conveys the meaning of the corresponding image. Inspired by deep learning methods employed in machine translation [3], most image captioning models utilize encoder-decoder architecture. The encoder extracts the visual features of the image, while the decoder generates the corresponding description text using these visual features.

In early work [1,4], a CNN was used as an encoder to extract image features, while an RNN or LSTM was utilized as a generative model to generate descriptions. In order to better consider the image regions of interest, Anderson

L. Iliadis et al. (Eds.): ICANN 2023, LNCS 14255, pp. 373–384, 2023.
https://doi.org/10.1007/978-3-031-44210-0_30

et al. [5] used object detectors to extract image features, and proposed an attention mechanism that combines bottom-up and top-down approaches. Inspired by recent language research like transformer [6] and BERT [7], transformer-based models [8–10] can better capture the relationship between image features and generated sequences.

However, the current methods have the following problems: 1) The objects encoded by object detection have no priority, and there are many objects that are not semantically related. 2) The obtained target objects lack global information and relationship information between objects. The problem limits the semantic understanding of sentences, and the traditional Transformer architecture cannot effectively deal with the above problems.

For the above problem, we propose an Object Filter Module (OFM) and a novel cross-attention called Global Injection Cross Attention (GICA). The OFM learns and queries regional features through grid features, and filters out the most important objects to reduce the interference of irrelevant objects. And the GICA adaptively injects global information into the primary objects in the decoding stage and learns the global visual representation, so that it has the background information and understands the relationship between the objects.

We extensively evaluate our method using the COCO benchmark dataset [11], demonstrating the effectiveness of our model through quantitative and qualitative experiments.

All in all, this paper's contributions can be summarized as follows:

- We propose an Object Filter Module (OFM) to obtain more precise object regions by filtering region features. OFM can effectively eliminate the interference of redundant information on the description quality.
- We propose a novel cross-attention called Global Injection Cross Attention (GICA), which extracts global information through grid features and injects it into filtered objects to make visual representation more adequate.
- We incorporate the Object Filter Module and Global Injection Cross Attention to our model, outperforming the advanced approaches on the widely-used COCO benchmark dataset.

2 Related Work

2.1 Dual Visual Feature for Image Captioning

In the image captioning task, choosing an appropriate visual feature representation method is crucial to generate accurate descriptions. Many researchers have proposed methods using grid or region features to better represent images.

The grid feature splits the image into several grids and extracts features for the individual grid. The most commonly used methods, among them, are based on deep convolutional neural networks. These methods usually encode the image as a vector of fixed length. The advantage of using the grid feature is that it is easy to use and can extract global features, but the disadvantage is that it is

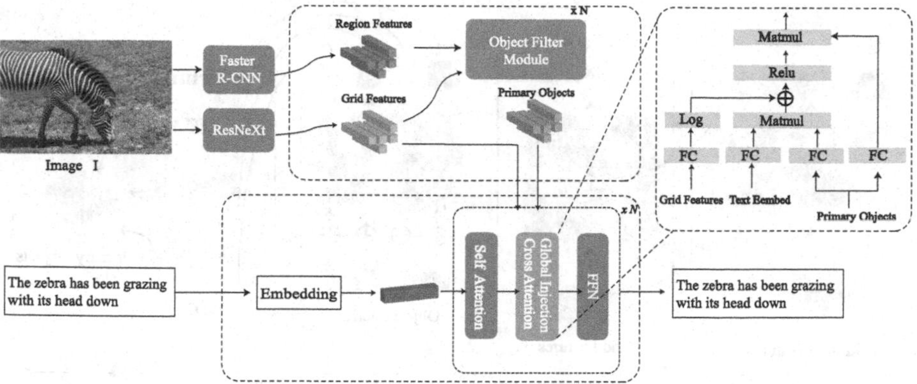

Fig. 1. Overview of our proposed network. We utilized two types of visual features and devised an Object Filter Module to extract primary objects. Then, we employed Global Injection Cross Attention to incorporate global information into the region objects.

difficult to deal with the position information of the object and the granularity is insufficient. Jiang *et al.* [12] show that grid features can perform as well as region-based methods on the VQA task, and RSTNet [13] applies these grid features to image captioning.

In contrast, region features refer to the method of treating each object in the image as an independent region and extracting features for each region. This approach usually requires the use of an object detector [14] to determine the location and size of each region. Region features can better capture the position and size information of objects, thereby generating more accurate descriptions, but its disadvantages are high computational complexity and the potential risk of not being able to represent background information and the relationship between objects.

Recently, some studies [15,16] have proposed methods that combine grid features and region features to take into account the advantages of both. However, it still fails to effectively integrate the relationship between different visual features.

2.2 Transformer for Image Captioning

In recent years, Transformer [6,7] architecture has become a fundamental paradigm in natural language processing tasks, and is increasingly being adapted to computer vision tasks, including image classification, semantic segmentation, and object detection. A recent study [17] also applies the DETR framework to vision-language task pre-training instead of using it to obtain regional features.

Meanwhile, transformer architecture is also extensively utilized in the task of image captioning, and many studies have proposed a variety of transformer variants for this domain. Specifically, Anderson *et al.* [5] based on the transformer architecture, utilizes the visual features extracted by the object detector,

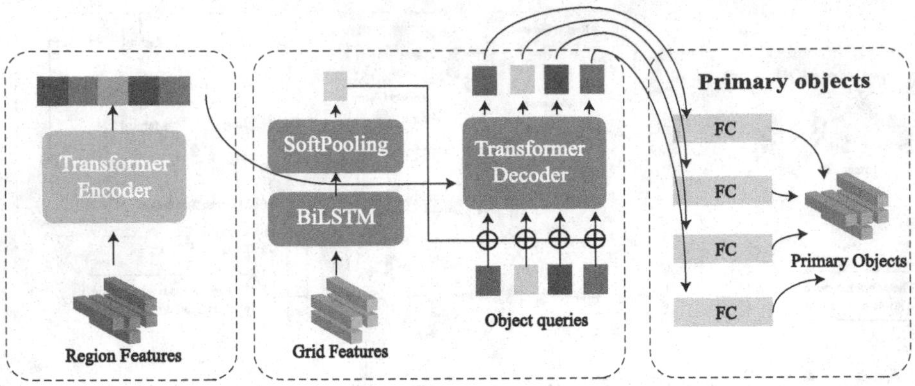

Fig. 2. Illustration of the Object Filter Module

and extends the attention module to help the model better focus on the regions related to description generation. Huang *et al.* [8] introduced a trainable prior to enhance the attention method in the transformer encoder, and introduced a network structure to construct a full connection. Cornia *et al.* [10] utilizes a multi-layer encoder and decoder with a grid structure that connects the encoding and decoding layers, leveraging both low-level and high-level features. Pan *et al.* [9] incorporated bilinear pooling into the transformer architecture, thereby leveraging the spatial and channel bilinear attention distributions.

In our work, we adopt the transformer as the basic architecture and adopt DETR's architecture to design an Object Filter Module to filter out the primary objects in the region objects.

3 Method

Figure 1 illustrates the general architecture of our model. The proposed model follows the traditional encoder-decoder paradigm, utilizing both region and grid features for complementarity. First, we employ our Object Filter Module as an encoder to output features of the primary objects. Afterward, the transformer's decoder is improved by Global Injection Cross Attention, which injects global information into the primary object during decoding to generate descriptions.

3.1 Object Filter Module

As input to an image, we initially extract its region and grid features. Similar to prior research on image captioning, our approach depends on object detectors to extract regional features via Faster R-CNN [5,14] and we denote the extracted regional features as $\mathcal{R}$. The pre-trained CNN model [12] is employed to extract the grid features of the image, denoted the grid features as $\mathcal{G}$.

Considering that only a select few of the objects within an image are utilized in the captions, we have designed an Object Filter Module that intelligently filters out the primary objects.

The general architecture of the Object Filter Module is illustrated in Fig. 2. Specifically, it is comprised of a transformer encoder and decoder. Inspired by DETR [18], DETR leverages the transformer backbone to train a pre-determined set of object queries, which can directly predict bounding boxes for objects and aid in object detection tasks. Our goal is not to simply detect objects, but to filter out important objects in the image. Building upon the concept of learning object queries, we developed our own set of queries.

First, the encoder handles the region object $\mathcal{R}$:

$$\mathcal{R}' = TransformerEncoder(\mathcal{R}) \tag{1}$$

Our decoder takes three inputs and minimizes a set-based global loss that is predicted by bipartite matching to yield the primary object features $\mathcal{O}$:

$$\mathcal{V} = SoftPool(BiLSTM(\mathcal{G})) \tag{2}$$

$$\mathcal{C}' = \mathcal{C} + \mathcal{V} \tag{3}$$

$$\mathcal{O} = TransformerDecoder(\mathcal{R}', \mathcal{G}, \mathcal{C}) \tag{4}$$

where $\mathcal{R}'$ is the encoder output, $\mathcal{G}$ is the grid feature, $\mathcal{C} = \{c_i\}_{i=1}^{N}$ are N random initialization queries parameter. We first pass $\mathcal{G}$ into BiLSTM module to generate the hidden signals, and then obtain the embedding of the identified image content through the SoftPool [19] aggregation layer, which is recorded as $\mathcal{V}$, which is used to strengthen the query parameter $\mathcal{C}$, get the final query parameter $\mathcal{C}'$.

3.2 Global Injection Cross Attention

Overall Design of Caption Decoder: The decoder of our model adopts the decoder based on transformer architecture used in previous studies [20] as the basic framework. The model generates descriptions in an autoregressive manner. At time t, we feed the preceding sequence of predicted words from time $t-1$ into the decoder to predict the upcoming word. To generate the input at time t, we combine the word embedding with the sinusoidal position embedding.

The decoder is composed of N identical layers. The initial layer accepts the predicted word sequence, and the output of the last layer is fed into a linear layer with an output dimension equal to the vocabulary size for predicting the succeeding word.

Every transformer layer consists of a masked self-attention layer on sentence words, a cross-attention layer that fuses visual features, and a feed-forward network. At the l_{th} layer, the masked self-attention layer takes an input sequence at time step t and performs self-attention on the sequence, updating the tokens through the attention mask, and preventing interactions with unpredicted words during training.

The cross-attention layer of the l_{th} layer is situated after the attention layer. Its function is to fuse the output of the self-attention layer with visual features.

Global Injection Cross Attention: In the previous section, we used the Object Filter Module (OFM) to filter the relationship between regional objects and images in order to locate more precise regions during feature fusion.

In order to query textual features more efficiently during caption generation, we propose a novel cross-attention called Global Injection Cross Attention, as illustrated in Fig. 1 's right. For enhancing the global relationship of regional features, we extract global information $\mathcal{X}$ for grid features:

$$X = Drop(FC(Norm(I))) \tag{5}$$

where $\mathcal{I}$ represents the grid feature of the image and Norm is the layer normalization layer. After extracting the global information $\mathcal{X}$, we use the regional features as keys and values, and the output of text features through self-attention as queries, and integrate them through Global Injection Intersection Attention (GICA). Our Multi-head Global Injection Cross Attention (MGICA) can be expressed as:

$$MGICA(Q, K, V) = Concat(h_1, ..., h_n)W^O \tag{6}$$

$$h_i = GICA(QW_i^Q, KW_i^K, VW_i^V, X) \tag{7}$$

$$GICA(Q, K, V, \Omega) = Relu(\frac{QK^T}{\sqrt{d_k}} + X)^2 V \tag{8}$$

3.3 Training Details

The standard practice for training image captioning models involves utilizing the cross-entropy loss (XE). The formula looks like this:

$$L_{XE}(\theta) = \sum_{t=1}^{T} log(p_\theta(y_t^* | y_{1:t-1}^*)) \tag{9}$$

where θ is the parameter in the model, and $y_{1:T}^*$ is the true sequence value of the target.

Meanwhile, in order to solve the exposure bias and target mismatch problem in the XE method, we employ continuous optimization of the non-differentiable CIDEr [21] score through the method of self-critical sequence training (SCST) [22], the formula is as follows:

$$b = \frac{1}{k}(\sum_{i}^{k} r(y_{1:T}^i)) \tag{10}$$

$$L_{RL}(\theta) = -\frac{1}{k}\sum_{t=1}^{T}((r(y_{1:T}^i) - b)logp_\theta(y_{1:T}^i)) \tag{11}$$

where k represents the batch number, r is the score function of CIDEr, and b is the average value of the reward obtained by the sampling sequence.

4 Experiments

4.1 Datasets

We use COCO [11] dataset as the benchmark dataset to experiment and compare the models studied in this paper. The COCO dataset is the most extensive public dataset for image captioning tasks. The dataset comprises 123,287 images, out of which 82,783 and 40,504 images are utilized for training and validation, respectively. Each image has five different descriptions. For evaluation, we split the dataset according to the method of Karpathy [23]. The data is subsequently divided into training, validation, and testing phases, comprising of 113,287, 5,000, and 5,000 images, respectively.

4.2 Implementation Details

Evaluation Metrics. We use conventional evaluation metrics to equitably evaluate the models. Specifically, the evaluation metrics we use are BLEU [24], METEOR [25], ROUGE [26], and CIDEr [21].

Originally developed for machine translation, BLEU is an ensemble of evaluation metrics that have gained widespread applicability in the domain of image captioning. METEOR is another evaluation metric that was originally developed for machine translation. ROUGE is an evaluation metric originally intended for automatic summary generation, which matches word sequences and their respective n-grams with ground truth captions. CIDEr is a specialized evaluation metric designed specifically for image captioning.

Feature Extraction and Text Processing. For each image, we extract region features using Faster-RCNN [14] as an object detector pre-trained on Visual Genome. Grid features are extracted using the ResNeXt backbone provided by Jiang*et al.* [12]. Before inputting into our model, all visual features will be projected into a 512-dimensional space, and the encoding dimension of visual features is also set to 512.

For subtitle processing, we removed punctuation and converted letters to lowercase, subtitles were all truncated to 20 words and tokenized using the SpaPy toolkit. We adopt the standard word representation method, which is linearly projecting the one-hot vector to a vector of dimension 512.

Other Details. Both the encoder and decoder of our target module consist of 3 transformer layers, 8 attention heads, and 512 hidden states. As mentioned before, the model is trained for 12 epochs using cross-entropy loss L_{XE}. The learning rate of our model is fixed at 10^{-5}. Subsequently, the model was fine-tuned for 8 epochs using CIDEr optimization, while setting the fixed learning rate of the whole model as 10^{-6}. The Adam optimizer is utilized with a batch size of 128. We generate captions for CIDEr optimization using beam search, employing a beam size of 5. The whole system is implemented with PyTorch, and all experiments are performed on Nvidia 3090 GPUs.

Table 1. Performance comparisons on the Karpathy test split of COCO dataset.

Model	Visual Features	BLEU-1	BLEU-4	METEOR	ROUGR	CIDEr
SCST [22]	$\mathcal{G}$	–	34.2	26.7	55.7	114.0
UpDown [5]	$\mathcal{R}$	79.8	36.3	27.7	57.3	120.1
ORT [20]	$\mathcal{R}$	80.5	38.6	28.7	58.4	128.3
AoANet [8]	$\mathcal{R}$	80.2	38.9	29.2	58.8	129.8
M2 Transformer [10]	$\mathcal{R}$	80.8	39.1	29.2	58.6	131.2
X-Transformer [9]	$\mathcal{R}$	80.9	39.7	29.5	59.1	132.8
RSTNet [13]	$\mathcal{G}$	81.8	40.1	29.8	59.5	135.6
DLCT [15]	$\mathcal{R}$&$\mathcal{G}$	81.4	39.8	29.5	59.1	133.8
Dual Global [16]	$\mathcal{R}$&$\mathcal{G}$	81.3	**40.3**	29.2	59.4	132.4
Ours	$\mathcal{R}$&$\mathcal{G}$	**82.1**	40.1	**29.9**	**59.8**	**136.1**

4.3 Performance Comparison

In Table 1, we conducted a performance evaluation of our proposed model against various SOTA image captioning models. For evaluation purposes, we employ the COCO Karpathy split. The models we compared include SCST [22], UpDown [5], ORT [20], AoANet [8], $\mathcal{M}^2$ Transformer [10], X-Transformer [9], RSTNet [13], DLCT [15], Dual Global [16]. SCST proposes the use of self-critical training strategies. UpDown proposes to use region features to improve performance. To integrate diverse CNN features, RFNet employs a cyclic fusion network. ORT uses the Transformer architecture to model the relationships between regional features. AoANet strengthens attention by computing the correlation between attention results and queries. $\mathcal{M}^2$ transformer exploits different hierarchical relationships by building connections among each encoder and decoder layer. X-Transformer improves the attention module in the transformer architecture and introduces Bilinear Pooling. RSTNet incorporates positional encodings in grid features to enhance visual representations. DLCT and Dual Global uses both region features and grid features. Experimental results demonstrate that our model is more efficient than other SOTA models.

4.4 Ablation Study

To confirm the effectiveness of our novel modules, we access the effectiveness of each module by extracting each module individually and subsequently retraining the model. Table 2 displays the results. All the proposed modules contribute significantly to the overall performance. Among them, the OFM contributes the most, followed by the GICA.

To validate the effectiveness of incorporating grid features into the OFM, we conduct an ablation study by removing the embedded grid features from the OFM. As shown in the 'Original Object' row of Table 2, the model's performance degrades significantly, indicating the crucial role of grid feature embedding in filtering out the primary objects.

Table 2. Ablation studies on COCO benchmarks. Performance with/without OFM or GICA. Original Object represents removing the embedded grid features from the OFM.

Model	BLEU-1	BLEU-4	METEOR	ROUGR	CIDEr
w/o OFM	80.5	39.0	28.9	59.1	133.4
w/o GICA	81.3	39.4	29.4	58.4	135.5
Original Object	81.2	39.1	29.7	59.3	135.2
Ours	**82.1**	**40.1**	**29.9**	**59.8**	**136.1**

Table 3. Ablation studies of our GICA module in Transformer-based methods on COCO benchmarks.

Model	BLEU-1	BLEU-4	METEOR	ROUGR	CIDEr
M2 Transformer [10]	80.8	39.1	29.2	58.6	131.2
DLCT [15]	81.4	39.8	29.5	59.1	133.8
Dual Global [16]	81.3	40.3	29.2	59.4	132.4
M2+GICA	81.2	39.4	29.3	58.8	131.8
DLCT+GICA	81.8	40.1	**29.6**	**59.6**	**134.7**
Dual Global+GICA	**81.9**	**40.5**	29.4	59.6	133.1

To validate the effectiveness of our GICA module in Transformer-based methods on the COCO benchmark dataset, we conduct ablation studies by individually extracting and retraining the models with and without the GICA module in Transformer-based methods [10,15,16]. The results are presented in Table 3, where we observe that the GICA module contributes significantly to the overall performance of the Transformer-based models. Specifically, the inclusion of the GICA module leads to a noticeable improvement in the detection accuracy, indicating the importance of the module in enhancing the model's performance.

4.5 Qualitative Analysis

In Fig. 3, we demonstrate several illustrations of image captions produced by our model. In this figure, the Transformer is the same as the network proposed by Herdade *et al.* [20].

As shown in the first and second columns of Fig. 3, the basic Transformer model failed to capture unimportant objects such as "fork" and "granite" in the images. In the third column, the caption missed the relationship between "road" and "car". In contrast, our model successfully captured the relationships between objects. In the fourth column, our model accurately captured the relationship between the background information "night" and the objects in the image.

As can be seen, the outcomes of our proposed network are adequate, and our model focuses on more primary objects and obtains more detailed contextual information to generate more accurate descriptions.

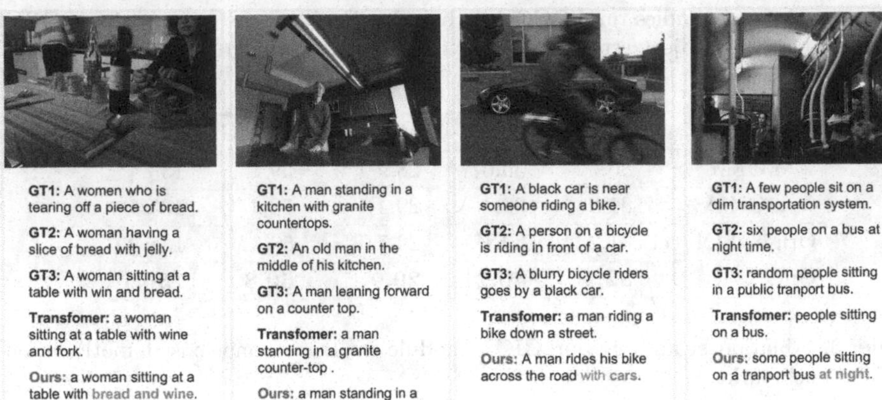

Fig. 3. Illustration of some qualitative results from the validation set using COCO

5 Conclusion

This work focuses on extracting abundant visual features and filtering and combining visual features more accurately. To this end, we propose an Object Filter Module to filter out primary target objects from source objects based on grid features via a learned query approach. Meanwhile, to compensate for the lack of spatial relationship and background information among target objects, we propose a Global Injection Cross Attention, which incorporates the global grid features into the primary target objects when computing attention. Finally, comprehensive experiments demonstrate that our model achieves superior performance to existing methods on the COCO dataset.

References

1. Vinyals, O., Toshev, A., Bengio, S., Erhan, D.: Show and tell: a neural image caption generator. In: 2015 IEEE Conference on Computer Vision and Pattern Recognition (CVPR), pp. 3156–3164 (2015). https://doi.org/10.1109/CVPR.2015.7298935
2. Xu, K., et al.: Show, attend and tell: neural image caption generation with visual attention. In: International Conference on Machine Learning, pp. 2048–2057. PMLR (2015)
3. Sutskever, I., Vinyals, O., Le, Q.V.: Sequence to sequence learning with neural networks. In: Ghahramani, Z., Welling, M., Cortes, C., Lawrence, N., Weinberger, K. (eds.) Advances in Neural Information Processing Systems, vol. 27. Curran Associates, Inc. (2014)
4. Mao, J., Xu, W., Yang, Y., Wang, J., Yuille, A.L.: Explain images with multimodal recurrent neural networks. arXiv (2014). https://doi.org/10.48550/ARXIV.1410.1090

5. Anderson, P., et al.: Bottom-up and top-down attention for image captioning and visual question answering. In: Proceedings of the IEEE Conference on Computer Vision and Pattern Recognition (CVPR) (2018)
6. Vaswani, A., et al.: Attention is all you need. In: Guyon, I., et al. (eds.) Advances in Neural Information Processing Systems, vol. 30. Curran Associates, Inc. (2017)
7. Devlin, J., Chang, M.W., Lee, K., Toutanova, K.: Bert: pre-training of deep bidirectional transformers for language understanding. arXiv (2018). https://doi.org/10.48550/ARXIV.1810.04805
8. Huang, L., Wang, W., Chen, J., Wei, X.Y.: Attention on attention for image captioning. In: 2019 IEEE/CVF International Conference on Computer Vision (ICCV), pp. 4633–4642 (2019). https://doi.org/10.1109/ICCV.2019.00473
9. Pan, Y., Yao, T., Li, Y., Mei, T.: X-linear attention networks for image captioning. In: 2020 IEEE/CVF Conference on Computer Vision and Pattern Recognition (CVPR), pp. 10968–10977 (2020). https://doi.org/10.1109/CVPR42600.2020.01098
10. Cornia, M., Stefanini, M., Baraldi, L., Cucchiara, R.: Meshed-memory transformer for image captioning. In: 2020 IEEE/CVF Conference on Computer Vision and Pattern Recognition (CVPR), pp. 10575–10584 (2020). https://doi.org/10.1109/CVPR42600.2020.01059
11. Lin, T.-Y.: Microsoft COCO: common objects in context. In: Fleet, D., Pajdla, T., Schiele, B., Tuytelaars, T. (eds.) ECCV 2014. LNCS, vol. 8693, pp. 740–755. Springer, Cham (2014). https://doi.org/10.1007/978-3-319-10602-1_48
12. Jiang, H., Misra, I., Rohrbach, M., Learned-Miller, E., Chen, X.: In defense of grid features for visual question answering. In: Proceedings of the IEEE/CVF Conference on Computer Vision and Pattern Recognition (CVPR) (2020)
13. Zhang, X., et al.: Rstnet: captioning with adaptive attention on visual and non-visual words. In: 2021 IEEE/CVF Conference on Computer Vision and Pattern Recognition (CVPR), pp. 15460–15469 (2021). https://doi.org/10.1109/CVPR46437.2021.01521
14. Ren, S., He, K., Girshick, R., Sun, J.: Faster r-cnn: towards real-time object detection with region proposal networks. IEEE Trans. Pattern Anal. Mach. Intell. **39**(6), 1137–1149 (2017). https://doi.org/10.1109/TPAMI.2016.2577031
15. Luo, Y., et al.: Dual-level collaborative transformer for image captioning. Proc. AAAI Conf. Artif. Intell. **35**(3), 2286–2293 (2021). https://doi.org/10.1609/aaai.v35i3.16328
16. Xian, T., Li, Z., Zhang, C., Ma, H.: Dual global enhanced transformer for image captioning. Neural Netw. **148**, 129–141 (2022). https://doi.org/10.1016/j.neunet.2022.01.011
17. Xu, H., et al.: E2E-VLP: end-to-end vision-language pre-training enhanced by visual learning. In: Proceedings of the 59th Annual Meeting of the Association for Computational Linguistics and the 11th International Joint Conference on Natural Language Processing, vol. 1: Long Papers, pp. 503–513. Association for Computational Linguistics, Online (2021). https://doi.org/10.18653/v1/2021.acl-long.42
18. Carion, N., Massa, F., Synnaeve, G., Usunier, N., Kirillov, A., Zagoruyko, S.: End-to-end object detection with transformers. In: Vedaldi, A., Bischof, H., Brox, T., Frahm, J.-M. (eds.) ECCV 2020. LNCS, vol. 12346, pp. 213–229. Springer, Cham (2020). https://doi.org/10.1007/978-3-030-58452-8_13
19. Stergiou, A., Poppe, R., Kalliatakis, G.: Refining activation downsampling with softpool. In: Proceedings of the IEEE/CVF International Conference on Computer Vision (ICCV), pp. 10357–10366 (2021)

20. Herdade, S., Kappeler, A., Boakye, K., Soares, J.: Image captioning: transforming objects into words. In: Wallach, H., Larochelle, H., Beygelzimer, A., d'Alché-Buc, F., Fox, E., Garnett, R. (eds.) Advances in Neural Information Processing Systems, vol. 32. Curran Associates, Inc. (2019)
21. Vedantam, R., Zitnick, C.L., Parikh, D.: Cider: consensus-based image description evaluation. In: 2015 IEEE Conference on Computer Vision and Pattern Recognition (CVPR), pp. 4566–4575 (2015). https://doi.org/10.1109/CVPR.2015.7299087
22. Rennie, S.J., Marcheret, E., Mroueh, Y., Ross, J., Goel, V.: Self-critical sequence training for image captioning. In: 2017 IEEE Conference on Computer Vision and Pattern Recognition (CVPR), pp. 1179–1195 (2017). https://doi.org/10.1109/CVPR.2017.131
23. Johnson, J., Karpathy, A., Fei-Fei, L.: Densecap: fully convolutional localization networks for dense captioning. In: 2016 IEEE Conference on Computer Vision and Pattern Recognition (CVPR), pp. 4565–4574 (2016). https://doi.org/10.1109/CVPR.2016.494
24. Papineni, K., Roukos, S., Ward, T., Zhu, W.J.: Bleu: a method for automatic evaluation of machine translation. In: Proceedings of the 40th Annual Meeting on Association for Computational Linguistics, pp. 311–318. Association for Computational Linguistics (2002)
25. Denkowski, M., Lavie, A.: Meteor 1.3: automatic metric for reliable optimization and evaluation of machine translation systems. In: Proceedings of the Sixth Workshop on Statistical Machine Translation, pp. 85–91. Association for Computational Linguistics (2011)
26. Lin, C.Y.: ROUGE: a package for automatic evaluation of summaries. In: Text Summarization Branches Out, pp. 74–81. Association for Computational Linguistics, Barcelona (2004). https://aclanthology.org/W04-1013

In Silico Study of Single Synapse Dynamics Using a Three-State Kinetic Model

Swapna Sasi and Basabdatta Sen Bhattacharya(✉)

Computer Science and Information Systems, BITS Pilani, Goa Campus, Sancoale, Goa, India
{p20190054,basabdattab}@goa.bits-pilani.ac.in
https://www.bits-pilani.ac.in/goa/

Abstract. In this study, we validate a single synapse neural mass model based on a 3-state kinetic framework. Our model implements the ligand-gated neurotransmitter receptors mediated by excitatory alpha-amino-3-hydroxy-5-methyl-4-isoxazolepropionic-acid (AMPA) and N-methyl-D-aspartate (NMDA), and inhibitory gamma-amino-butyric acid subtype A ($GABA_A$) synapses. Our results show the 3-state model equipped with desensitization state can assay the synaptic transmission processes recorded in both *in vivo* and *in silico* studies. Overall, we present a computationally light, single synapse kinetic model that can adapt as new molecular studies evolve. The fundamental behavioural study presented here also lays the foundation for building larger *in silico* models, that are computationally efficient and capable of replicating physiological and experimental observations as well as make testable predictions.

Keywords: Kinetic Models · AMPA · GABA · NMDA · Single Synapse

1 Introduction

Over the years, neural mass models (NMM) have made significant contributions in the field of neuroscience, deepening our understanding of brain dynamics. The NMM represents the interacting ensemble of neurons at macro and mesoscopic scale and rely on its mathematical framework to make brain-inspired modelling simpler and computationally light. These models have been used to elucidate the fundamental mechanisms governing both the brain functions and its dysfunctions [3]. NMM establishes itself over a rich history of several seminal works [7,17,19,20] from which evolves a popular class of conduction-based NMM. The traditional NMM's were known to be limited by the classical Rall's alpha functions which lacked the flexibility to assay the intrinsic dynamics of

Supported by the BITS Pilani K. K. Birla Goa Campus Institutional Funds and the Computer Science and Information Systems (CSIS) Departmental Funds.

L. Iliadis et al. (Eds.): ICANN 2023, LNCS 14255, pp. 385–396, 2023.
https://doi.org/10.1007/978-3-031-44210-0_31

ion channels [4]. As a replacement of alpha function, Markov kinetic models were proposed by Destexhe and colleagues [4–6] which could innate the synaptic transmission process through a set of states and related transitions between them. Their detailed mathematical framework consisting of two or more kinetic states, could reproduce bio-physically precise observations and soon gathered community attention for providing an adaptive computational framework that was flexible to evolve in light of new bio-physical and molecular findings.

Extending this flexibility of kinetic models into NMM's, we incorporated Destexhe et al's two-state (2-state) kinetic framework to replace Rall's alpha function in the traditional NMMs [13,15]. Our 2-state model consist of open (conducting) and closed (unresponsive) ion channel states and implement the neurotransmitter receptors viz. excitatory synapses based on alpha-amino-3-hydroxy-5-methyl-4-isoxazolepropionic-acid (AMPA) and inhibitory synapses by gamma-amino-butyric acid subtype A ($GABA_A$). We use this model in a series of our work to investigate the thalamocortical population dynamics underlying the visual pathway [11,12,14]. Besides providing a simple framework to simulate ensemble neuronal characteristics, it is also found to be computationally efficient than the traditional alpha functions [13,15]. However, to capture certain behavioural characteristics seen in bio-physical experimental studies for example reducing amplitudes of membrane currents for AMPA synapses [2] (see Sect. 3.1), a third desensitization state (a decrease in channel's responsiveness to neurotransmitters) is required [5]. Again, Destexhe et al [5] provides a simple three-state (3-state) kinetic model that can encompass desensitization dynamics. In this study we test the single synapse NMM based on 3-state kinetics for AMPA and GABA_A receptors and replicate the phenomena of both progressive decay and build-up of membrane currents. In addition, we replicate the N-methyl-D-aspartate (NMDA) neurotransmitter based single synapse responses as seen in physiological and model-based studies [2,5,10]. The study for GABA_B (subtype B) 3-state model will be done as future work.

We present the models mathematical framework and simulation methods in Sect. 2, followed by the presentation of observations and results of validating the single synapse model in Sect. 3. The concluding remarks with road map of future work is discussed in Sect. 4.

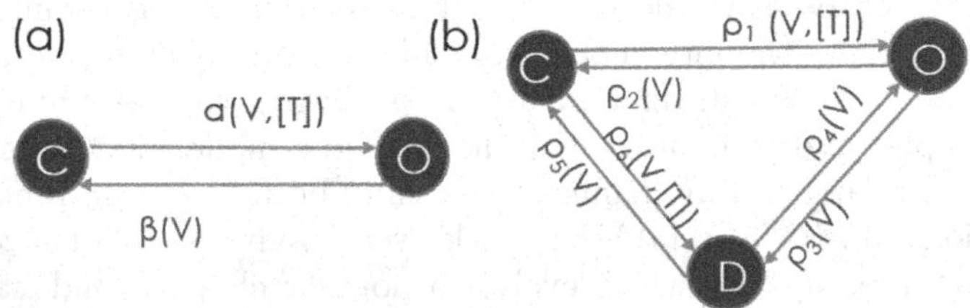

Fig. 1. The kinetic state diagrams of Markov's (a) 2-state and (b) 3-state models for the ligand-gated AMPA neurotransmitter receptor channel. α and β are forward and backward rates of reaction for the 2-state model. ρ_1 - ρ_6 are the rate constants governing transitions between the open state O, the desensitized D and the closed state C.

2 Methods

2.1 Two- and Three-State Kinetic Models

The kinetic models of chemical synapses represent the transmitter concentration in the synaptic cleft as well as the channel's state transitions involved in generating the post synaptic potential. In a series of researches, Destexhe and colleagues [5] have introduced both 2- and 3-state kinetic models to demonstrate their ability in mimicking synaptic dynamics of experimental studies. Specifically, they have demonstrated single synapse dynamics corresponding to excitatory (AMPA, NMDA) and inhibitory ($\text{GABA}_{A,B}$) synapses from hippocampal slices *in vitro*. The 2-state kinetic models consist of an open conducting state (O) and a closed unresponsive state (C) as shown in Fig. 1(a). The 3-state models consist of both the states as the 2-state models; in addition, they consist of a third state viz. desensitized (D) state that represent a decreased channel response state, and shown in Fig. 1(b). Mathematically, kinetic equations can be represented as a series of first or second order differential equations as detailed below for Eqs. 1–8.

The kinetic equations for the fraction of open channels (r_o) in a 2-state model is given in Eq. 1:

$$\frac{dr_o}{dt} = \alpha[T]\,(1 - r_o(t)) - \beta\, r_o(t) \tag{1}$$

For 3-state, the gating mechanism of the ion channels are governed by the second order Eqs. (2) and (3):

$$\frac{dr_o}{dt} = \rho_1[T]\,(1 - r_o(t) - r_d(t)) - [\rho_2 + \rho_3]\, r_o(t) + \rho_4\, r_d(t) \tag{2}$$

$$\frac{dr_d}{dt} = \rho_6[T]\,(1 - r_o(t) - r_d(t)) - [\rho_4 + \rho_5]\, r_d(t) + \rho_3\, r_o(t) \tag{3}$$

The current for AMPA and $GABA_A$ is obtained from Eq. 4:

$$I(t) = g_{max}\, r_o(t)\,(V(t) - E_{rev}) \tag{4}$$

For NMDA, due to the presence of magnesium block (Mg^{2+}), the gating function and current are given by Eqs. (5) and (6) respectively:

$$B(V(t)) = 1/(1 + exp(-0.062\, V(t))\,(Mg^{2+}/3.57)) \tag{5}$$

$$I(t) = g_{max}\, B(V(t))\, r_o(t)\,(V(t) - E_{rev}) \tag{6}$$

The leak currents and the membrane potentials for all receptors are computed using Eqs. (7) and (8) respectively:

$$I^{lk}(t) = g^{lk}(V(t) - E^{lk}_{rev}) \tag{7}$$

$$\kappa\frac{dV(t)}{dt} = -(I(t) + I^{lk}(t)) \tag{8}$$

where r_o is the proportion of open ion-channels caused by the binding of pre-synaptic neurotransmitters on the post synaptic neurotransmitter-receptors while $r_{d'}$ is the proportion of desensitized channels; $[T]$ is the neurotransmitter concentration in the synaptic cleft and is assumed to be a pulse with OFF value of 0.0001 and ON value of 1 which simulates the maximum neuronal concentration of $T_{max} \approx 1mM$ [16]; $\rho1$–$\rho6$ are the rate constants of the chemical reaction as it transitions between the three states; α and β are forward and reverse rates of chemical reaction in a 2-state model; g_{max} is the maximum conductance of the post synaptic membrane (μS); $I(t)$ is the post synaptic current due to open channels (nA); $B(V(t))$ is the magnesium block for NMDA receptors; $V(t)$ is the post synaptic membrane potential of the synapse (mV), κ is the membrane capacitance (pF), E_{rev} is the reversal potential for the neurotransmitter-receptor (mV); I^{lk} is the leak current (nA), g^{lk} is the maximum leak conductance (μS) and E^{lk}_{rev} is receptor's leak reversal potential (mV).

Table 1. The parameters (Params) used in Eqs. 1–8. Updates to original ρ parameters from [4] are highlighted in bold.

(1) Params	(2) Units	(3) AMPA	(4) NMDA	(5) GABA$_A$	(6) AMPA	(7) NMDA
ρ_1	$s^{-1}mM^{-1}$	1000	0	150***2**	1000+**100**	0+**2000**
ρ_2	s^{-1}	10	6.9	200***2**	10***50**	6.9-**5**
ρ_3	s^{-1}	180	0	22	180***5**	4
ρ_4	s^{-1}	0	160	11	0	10/**30**
ρ_5	s^{-1}	0.63	4.7	34	0.63***100**	4.7/**2**
ρ_6	$s^{-1}mM^{-1}$	0	190	190	0	10
α	$s^{-1}mM^{-1}$	1100	–	–	–	–
β	s^{-1}	190	–	–	–	–
K	pF	1	1	1	1	1
E_{rev}	mV	0	0	–80	0	0
g_{max}	μS	0.16	2.5	0.325	0.28	0.28
E_{lk}	mV	–70	–70	–70	–70	–70
g_{lk}	μS	1.5	1.5	0.5	0.35	1.5
V_{rst}	mV	–70	–70	–70	–65	–65
Mg^{2+}	mM	–	1	–	–	1

2.2 Validating 3-State Models

A single synapse is considered to be the simplest and yet, is the most fundamental way to understand the complex synaptic transmission processes of ionic channels. Our existing NMM's were based on the validation of 2-state single synapse kinetic model [15] and it was configured to generate the synaptic responses which were fitted to bio-physical studies of hippocampus neurons in [6]. Hence, we validate our 3-state single synapse model (which is again based on Destexhe et al. 3-state kinetics [4]) by reproducing the 2-state behaviour as documented in [6] (see their Fig. 4).

As the 3-state have the additional desensitization state, we used a recent work of Micheli et al. [10] to validate the desensitization characteristics. Their compartmentalized kinetic model with eight states for NMDA and seven states for AMPA were used to study the CA3-CA1 hippocampal synapse. They attempt to analyze the impact by a single disease associated variant of NMDA receptors (Observed in neurological disorders and cognitive impairments) on the whole synaptic transmission process. Initially to establish their models fundamental characteristics, single synapse response to single and burst pre-synaptic pulse inputs are studied (see Figs. 3, 4 and 5 in [10]) for both receptors. We try to replicate these synaptic dynamics using our 3-state single synapse model.

Additionally, we validate the 3-state single synapse responses of a pulse train input with an *in vivo* study conducted in [2] for AMPA and NMDA receptors. Using whole-cell recordings, Augustinaite et al. studied the synaptic responses of thalamocortical neurons to a pulse train stimulation of retinal afferents [2]. The excitatory postsynaptic potentials (EPSP) of AMPA and NMDA receptors were studied after pharmacologically isolating them and the observations show temporal summation of the EPSP's. We used the results from [2] (Fig. 3) to validate our 3-state AMPA and NMDA model's single synapse responses to a pulse train.

We further validate the ratio of the peak amplitudes of AMPA and NMDA currents which give a good estimate of the NMDA dynamics in comparison with AMPA. Both these excitatory neurotransmitter receptors are known to be co-expressed at many synapses in the brain [18], and hence their combined influence will greatly depend on their time course and strength of the individual currents. For example, the depolarization characteristics elicited by the AMPA and NMDA models when acting together are known to complement each other where the AMPA component have a stronger hold at the beginning of the input stimulus while the NMDA component takes over at the later part, resulting in longer depolarization [2]. All the results of these above validations are discussed in detail in Sect. 3.

2.3 Simulation Methods

As an initial choice of configuration, we commence our preliminary simulations by using the ρ parameter set listed in [4] for 3-state and compare the outputs with the 2-state results from [6]. The complete configurations used for these validations are listed under columns (3)–(5) in Table 1 and corresponding observations are recorded in Sect. 3.1. The 3-state model uses another updated set of parameters listed in columns (6)–(7) of Table 1 to emulate the outputs from [10]. The comparative analysis can be found Sect. 3.2. Wherever necessary, the updated parameters were obtained through trial and error to generate desired observations. Note the parameters modified from the original source [4] are highlighted in bold in Table 1.

The implementation is done on MATLAB 2023a (Mathworks Inc. ^{TM}). Differential equations are solved using forward Euler's method with simulation time-step of 1 µs. The model's outputs are represented by the rate of opening (r_o)

and desensitizing of ion channels (r_d), postsynaptic membrane potential (V) and the post synaptic current (I). The initial value of r_o and r_d in Eqs. 1 to 3 are set to 0.0002 for simulations run in Sect. 3.1 and 0.0001 for simulations in Sect. 3.2. The post synaptic voltage is initialized to the resting state membrane potential (V_{rst}) given in Table 1. The transmitter concentration is assumed to be a single or a burst of rectangular pulses with frequencies in the range of 10 Hz to 400 Hz. During the ON time of the pulse, the amplitude is set to 1 mM and ON duration is set by varying the pulse widths in the range of 0.5 ms to 1.5 s. During the pulse OFF time, amplitude is set to an arbitrary small number $\lim_{\varepsilon \to 0} \varepsilon = 1e^{-04}$. As the 3-state model is also required to be computationally efficient in order to be a good replacement candidate for our 2-state models. We run thousand iterations for 2- and 3-models, in an identical environmental setup, and record their execution times in MATLAB. The execution times are compared to arrive at the computational efficiency of the 3-state model. See Sect. 3.1 for the computational stats.

3 Results

3.1 Comparing with 2-State Models

At first, we validate the 3-state single synapse model for AMPA with the 2-state model that we have been implementing in our research [11]. Parameters in the third column of Table 1 are used for this. A burst of five input transmitter pulses of 1 ms width at a frequency of 50 Hz is fed to the model as shown in Fig. 2(a). The resulting excitatory post synaptic currents and voltages are shown in Figs. 2 (b–c). As seen in these two figures, on arrival of the first pulse, the amplitudes of the current (Fig. 2(b)) and voltage (Fig. 2(c)) responses to the first pulse are identical for both the 2-state (magenta line) and 3-state (blue line) models. The 2-state amplitude responses remain constant for the subsequent pluses while a progressive decay in amplitudes are seen for the 3-state model responses. The decreasing trait is introduced by the desensitization state [4] and mimics the *in vivo* response of thalamocortical neurons in dorsal lateral geniculate nucleus [2] on receiving retinal stimulus. This establishes a major behavioural difference between both the single synapse models.

For analysing computational efficiency, we compare the run-time of both 2-state and 3-state models after thousand simulations. The 2-state model took ≈31 s while 3-state took ≈41 s to complete the simulation runs. Thus, a negligible increase of computational time by ≈1 s is seen while using 3-state model. As the computational efficiency is maintained in the 3-state model, we can consider 3-state to be a good replacement for 2-state in large scale complex models. While extending in large models, the efficiency can be further improved by using parallel computing and higher computational resources like GPU based systems.

Next to replicate the results of the 2-state single synapse model from [6] (see their Fig. 4) with our 3-state single synapse model, inputs of single pulse (Figs. 2(d, f & h)) and a burst of four pulses at 400 Hz and 1 ms width (Figs. 2(e,

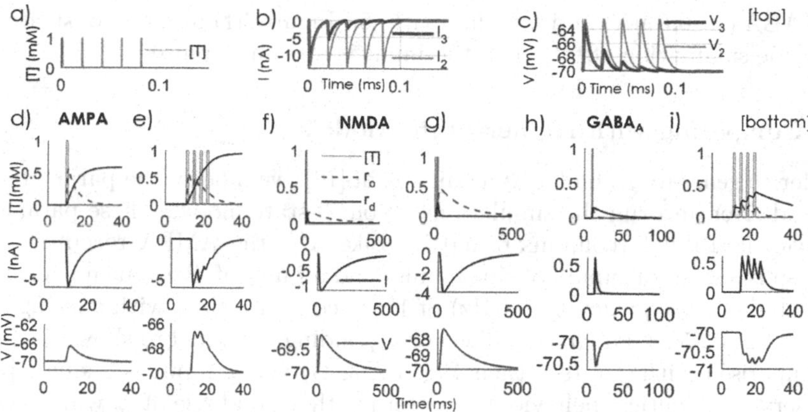

Fig. 2. (a–c) in the top panel displays the comparison of the 2-state and 3-state AMPA model's excitatory post synaptic currents (I) and voltages (V) after giving input of 5 transmitter [T] pulses of 1 ms pulse width. The magenta and blue trajectories in (b–c) correspond to the 2-state and 3-state outputs and a subscript of 2 and 3 are added in the legend for V & I to differentiate the states. One can note here the decaying amplitude behaviour of the 3-state model. In the bottom panel, the 3-state model is simulated in Figs. (d–e) AMPA (f–g) NMDA and (h–i) $GABA_A$ receptors to generate the equivalent 2-state synaptic dynamics from [6]. The behaviour of a single pre-synaptic transmitter pulse input in Figs. (d, f & h) are compared with the input of 400 Hz (4 pulses are shown in the Figs. (e, g & i) for each receptor types) burst of pulses. The outputs show proportionate scale of r, V and I as seen in [6]. (Color figure online)

g & i)) are tested separately for the 3-state AMPA, NMDA and GABA_A synaptic models. The other parameters for each of the neurotransmitter receptors are set according to columns 3–5 of Table 1.

From Fig. 2(d & f), we observe that the ratio of AMPA to NMDA peak current amplitudes is at an approximate ratio of 5:1 (the current peaks for AMPA is –6 nA and NMDA is ≈ –1.2 nA). This matches with the ratio which is computed from [6] (see their Fig. 2). We note a sharper peak for V which may be attributed to the different time constants for the 3-state parameters for r_o & r_d. We also observe that among the three neurotransmitter receptors, AMPA generates the highest amplitude membrane potential which progressively decreases for subsequent stimulus. In comparison, NMDA have the slowest decay and the train of impulses shows additive nature which causes the membrane potential to buildup. Both these observations are consistent with those noted in the *in vivo* study of thalamocortical neurons response to train of stimulus in [2]. Similar to the AMPA synapses, the inhibitory $GABA_A$ synapses are known to have fast kinetics in comparison to NMDA [21]. Looking at the Fig. 2(d & h), we note the ratio of the current peaks for AMPA and $GABA_A$ is 10:1 (AMPA = –6 nA and GABA$_A$ = 0.6 nA) and matches with [6]. Figure 2(f) also demonstrates the amplitude summation effect when the input is a train of pulses.

3.2 Comparing with Higher-State Models

In order to generate a similar dynamics as in [10], we modify the parameters by trial and error and run the simulations on our 3-state model. These parameters are given in Table 1 (columns 6 and 7). Like [10], the AMPA receptor model response is tested for inputs of single pulse and a burst of five transmitter pulses (generated at a frequency of 100 Hz) of 1 mM concentration, with varying pulse widths of 1 ms, 5 ms and 10 ms. The corresponding outputs are shown in Fig. 3. A comparison with [10] (see their Fig. 3 A & B) where input is a single pulse, we observe an identical behavioural pattern with a rapid rise of r_o which attains a peak at 1.96 ms as seen in Fig. 3(a). Our model gives the 20–80 % rise time of ≈0.35 ms. In the decay phase, we see the slower desensitization kinetics of r_d when the transmitter pulse is ON, and a much quicker deactivation kinetics when the transmitter is removed (see Fig. 3(b)). The desensitization time course is ≈3 ms and the deactivation time course (after the pulse is removed) is ≈0.7 ms which are obtained by fitting with single exponential function. These timings are observed to be well within bounds for AMPA receptors as recorded in *in vivo* experiments [1,9]. Though we find our desensitization time of ≈3 ms being much faster than those obtained in [10] (≈25 ms), the overall observation

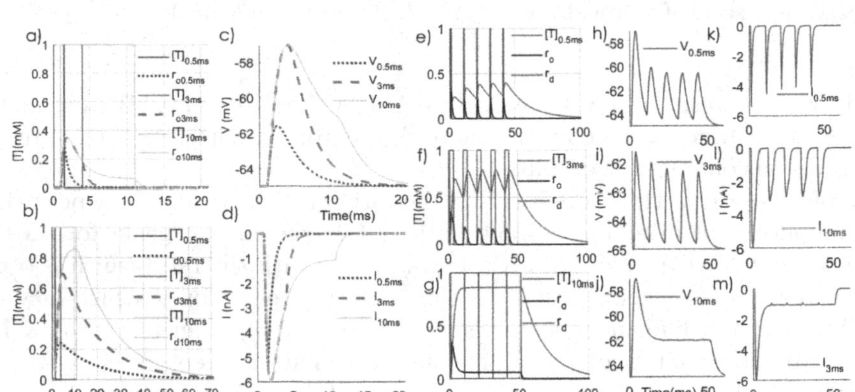

Fig. 3. Plots show the AMPA model's response to single transmitter pulse in Figs. (a–d) and a train of five transmitter pulses in Figs. (e–m). Transmitter [T] is set to 1 mM amplitude and varying pulse-widths of 1 ms, 5 ms, and 10 ms are used. For a single pulse, we can see the behaviour of (a) open receptors (r_o) (b) desensitized receptors (r_d) (c) post synaptic membrane potential (V) and (d) the corresponding current (I). For the burst input, simulations are run for the same pulse widths with an intra-burst frequency of 100 Hz. For 1 ms pulse width, we see in (e) fraction of open and desensitized receptors; (h) post synaptic membrane potential; (k) post synaptic current. Similar plots are displayed for 5 ms in (f), (i) and (l) and for 10 ms in (g), (j) and (m) respectively. In the legend, the pulse width is carried in the subscript.

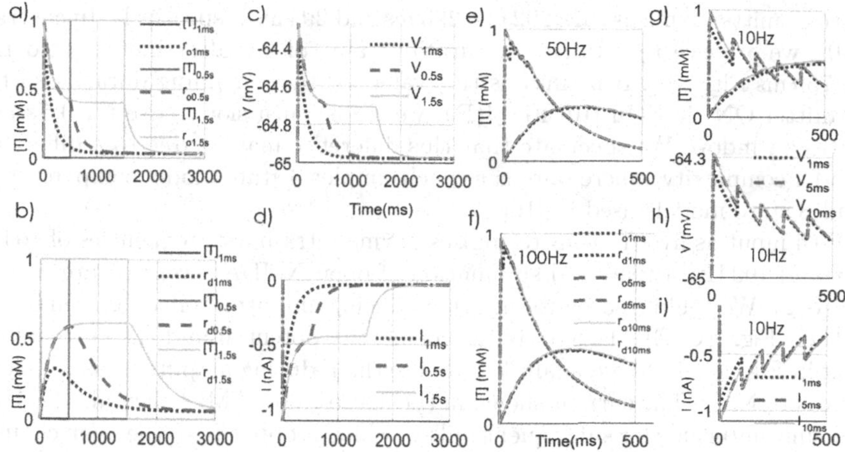

Fig. 4. Shows the NMDA models response to a (a–d) single transmitter pulse of widths 1 ms, 5 ms, and 10 ms and (e–i) burst of five transmitter pulses with widths 1 ms, 5 ms, and 10 ms. For both cases a 1 mM transmitter pulse is used. The plots display the ratio of (a) open (r_o) and (b) desensitized receptors (r_d) along with their corresponding post synaptic (c) membrane potential (V) and (d) current (I). For burst input ro and r_d are shown for various intra-burst frequency of (e) 50 Hz, (f) 100 Hz and (g) 10 Hz and the trends follow the legend listed in (f). Additionally, for 10 Hz the post synaptic membrane potential and current trends are shown in (h) and (i) respectively.

of desensitization time course being much slower than the deactivation kinetics is consistent with [10]. The 3-state model could also capture the important AMPA receptor properties of preferentially undergoing a temporal accumulation of desensitized states instead of the open states causing amplitude dampening. A stronger depolarization of the membrane potential and increased currents are seen due to updated conductance parameters g_{max} & $g_l k$ in Fig. 3(c & d). Alongside we compared the effect of varying the duration of pre-synaptic input train of five transmitter pulses at a 100 Hz intra-burst frequency. In Figs. 3(e)–(m), we could replicate the observations seen in [10] (see their Fig. 3(C–E)), where an increasing temporal summation of desensitized AMPA receptors are seen when the transmitter exposure duration is increased. The corresponding membrane potentials (Figs. 3(h)–(j) and currents (Figs. 3(k)–(m)) show the response to the first pulse is the largest, followed by a progressive decrease of amplitude for subsequent pulses in accordance with the observation in [2].

Next, we proceed to study the NMDA receptor dynamics. As NMDA is known to have a slower kinetics as compared to AMPA [8], longer duration transmitter pulses from 1 ms to 1.5 s are used as inputs. Figure 4(a–d) show the response to a single transmitter pulse, where we see the slowing of desensitization and deactivation kinetics. The 20–80% rise time is noted to be between 0.4 to 0.66 ms. Desensitization time constant is ≈150 ms (fitted with a double exponential on MATLAB) while the deactivation time constants at the end of 1 ms, 0.5 s and

1.5 s transmitter exposure are 202 ms, 293 ms and 294 ms respectively. In contrast to [10], we observe r_d attains a saturation value of 0.6 after initial rapid rise until 750 ms Fig. 4(b). It maintains this value for the remaining duration of the transmitter ON time. In [10] Fig. 4(D), we see a much slower rise for 0.5 s and 1.5 s time window. We speculate that this difference may be due to a difference in model complexity, where ours is a much simpler 3-state model compared to a 7- and 8-state models used in [10].

With input as five transmitter pulses having intra-burst frequencies of 10 Hz, 50 Hz and 100 Hz, a temporal summation of open NMDA receptors are seen in Fig. 4(e–g). We could also reproduce the reducing amplitude effect as seen in [10] (see their Fig. 4(C–E)). For 10 Hz the membrane potential and the currents are shown in Fig. 4(h–i) where again we can see the reducing amplitude as it follows r_o characteristics. The current shown in the figure 7 (B) of Micheli et al. [10] have increasing amplitude for subsequent pulses, which is opposite to the open channel dynamics where progressive reduction of amplitude is shown. This difference may be introduced by the difference in formula for NMDA gating mechanism or the due to additional states in the model. We are looking further into this in our ongoing work.

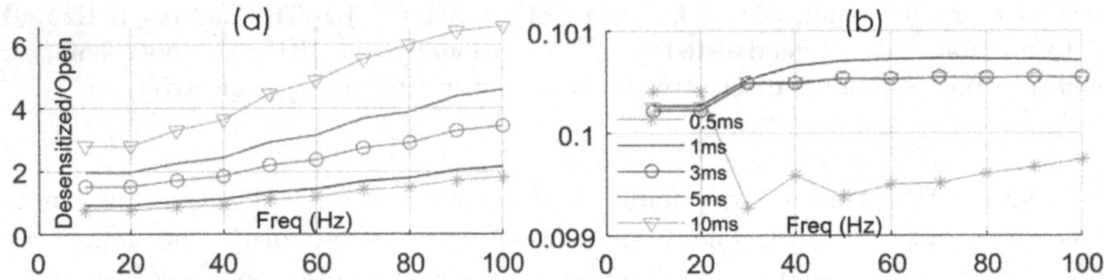

Fig. 5. The plots show the ratio of desensitized to open receptors against varied intra-burst frequencies for the pre-synaptic input of five transmitter pulses of 1 mM strength. The transmitter pulse-widths are set as 0.5 ms, 1 ms, 3 ms, 5 ms and 10 ms. (a) Represents the ratio for AMPA receptors (b) Indicates the ratio for NMDA receptors.

In [10], to further investigate the differences between AMPA and NMDA receptor kinetics, the authors simulated pre-synaptic input with 5 transmitter pulses of 1 mM amplitude having pulse widths of 1, 5 and 10 ms. The intra-burst frequency is varied between 10 to 100 Hz in steps of 10 and the ratio of desensitized/open is computed and plotted in Fig. 5 [10]. In comparison, we also simulate our model with identical input settings and pulse widths of 0.5 ms, 1 ms, 3 ms, 5 ms and 10 ms for AMPA and NMDA receptors. Figure 5(a–b) show the desensitized/open ratio where we can derive the dependence of AMPA on transmitter pulse duration and the stimulating frequencies, is more than NMDA. For NMDA, we observe that for our model, these dependencies minimizes after 1ms pulse width.

4 Conclusion

We have validated the synaptic transmission using a simple NMM based on the 3-state single synapse kinetic framework introduced in [4]. Our study here considers the receptors mediated by AMPA, $GABA_A$ and NMDA neurotransmitters and validates with physiological and model-based [2,6,10] studies that record single synaptic dynamics. The original parameters are sourced from [4], which is modified using trial and error method to reproduce the synaptic behaviours. Our results show the 3-state model is able to closely reproduce the excitatory postsynaptic voltage and current behaviour for both a single pulse input as well as for a train of transmitter pulses. A ratio of the peak current amplitudes and their time courses, demonstrate AMPA and $GABA_A$ to have much faster kinetics than NMDA. The 3-state model with its third desensitization state could replicate the temporal summation of excitatory postsynaptic currents which is known to be critical for simulating healthy and neurological conditions of the brain.

In summary, our single synapse 3-state model provides a simple NMM to innate synaptic transmission processes which is computationally light and flexible for adapting to new molecular findings through its kinetic framework. This fundamental study presented here will form the basis to evolve our larger thalamocortical model [11] which is currently based on 2-state. Thus, bringing the thalamocortical model closer to mimic experimental findings and improve its prediction capability to make biologically plausible testable predictions.

References

1. Angulo, M.C., Rossier, J., Audinat, E.: Postsynaptic glutamate receptors and integrative properties of fast-spiking interneurons in the rat neocortex. J. Neurophysiol. **82**, 1295–1302 (1993)
2. Augustinaite, S., Heggelund, P.: Changes in firing pattern of lateral geniculate neurons caused by membrane potential dependent modulation of retinal input through NMDA receptors. J. Physiol. **528**, 297–315 (2007)
3. Deschle, N., Ignacio Gossn, J., Tewarie, P., Schelter, B., Daffertshofer, A.: On the validity of neural mass models. Front. Comput. Neurosci. **14**, 581040 (2021)
4. Destexhe, A.: Synthesis of models for excitable membranes, synaptic transmission and neuromodulation using a common kinetic formalism. J. Comput. Neurosci. **1**, 195–230 (1994)
5. Destexhe, A., Mainen, Z.F., Sejnowski, T.J.: Fast kinetic models for simulating AMPA, NMDA, GABAA and GABAB receptors. In: The Neurobiology of Computation, pp. 9–14. Springer, Boston (1995). https://doi.org/10.1007/978-1-4615-2235-5_2
6. Destexhe, A., Mainen, Z., Sejnowski, T.: Kinetic models of synaptic transmission. In: Koch, C., Segev, I. (eds.) Methods in Neuronal Modelling, pp. 1–25. MIT Press, Cambridge (1998)
7. Freeman, W.J.: Mass Action in the Nervous System, 1st edn. Academic Press, New York (1975)

8. Iacobucci, G., Popescu, G.: NMDA receptors: linking physiological output to biophysical operation. Nat. Rev. Neurosci. **18**(4), 236–249 (2017)
9. Jonas, P., Major, G., Sakmann, B.: Quantal components of unitary EPSCs at the mossy fibre synapse on CA3 pyramidal cells of rat hippocampus. J. Physiol. **472**, 615–63 (1993)
10. Micheli, P., Ribeiro, R., Giorgetti, A.: A Mechanistic model of NMDA and AMPA receptor-mediated synaptic transmission in individual hippocampal CA3-CA1 synapses: a computational multiscale approach. Int. J. Mol. Sci. **22**(4), 1536 (2021)
11. Sasi, S., Sen Bhattacharya, B.: In silico effects of synaptic connections in the visual thalamocortical pathway. Front. Med. Technol. **4**, 856412 (2022)
12. Sasi, S., Sen Bhattacharya, B.: Phase entrainment by periodic stimuli in silico: a quantitative study. Neurocomputing **469**, 273–288 (2022)
13. Sen Bhattacharya, B.: Implementing the cellular mechanisms of synaptic transmission in a neural mass model of the thalamo-cortical circuitry. Front. Comput. Neurosci. **7**, 81 (2013)
14. Sen Bhattacharya, B., Bond, T.P., O'hare, L., Turner, D., Durrant, S.J.: Causal role of thalamic interneurons in brain state transitions: a study using a neural mass model implementing synaptic kinetics. Front. Comput. Neurosci. **10**, 115 (2016)
15. Bhattacharya, B.S., Coyle, D., Maguire, L.P., Stewart, J.: Kinetic modelling of synaptic functions in the alpha rhythm neural mass model. In: Villa, A.E.P., Duch, W., Érdi, P., Masulli, F., Palm, G. (eds.) ICANN 2012. LNCS, vol. 7552, pp. 645–652. Springer, Heidelberg (2012). https://doi.org/10.1007/978-3-642-33269-2_81
16. Sen Bhattacharya, B., Durrant, S.J.: A neural mass computational framework to study synaptic mechanisms underlying alpha and theta rhythms. In: Érdi, P., Sen Bhattacharya, B., Cochran, A.L. (eds.) Computational Neurology and Psychiatry. SSB, vol. 6, pp. 405–427. Springer, Cham (2017). https://doi.org/10.1007/978-3-319-49959-8_14
17. da Silva, F.L., Hoeks, A., Smits, H., Zetterberg, L.: Model of brain rhythmic activity. Kybernetic **15**, 27–37 (1974)
18. Watt, A.J., van Rossum, M.C., MacLeod, K.M., Nelson, S.B., Turrigiano, G.G.: Activity coregulates quantal AMPA and NMDA currents at neocortical synapses. Neuron **29**(3), 659–670 (2000)
19. Wendling, F., Bellanger, J.J., Bartolomei, F., Chauvel, P.: Relevance of nonlinear lumped-parameter models in the analysis of depth-EEG epileptic signals. Biol. Cybernet. **83**, 367–378 (2000)
20. Wilson, H.R., Cowan, J.D.: Excitatory and inhibitory interactions in localized populations of model neurons. Biophys. J. **12**, 1–24 (1972)
21. Wu, S.H., Ma, C.L., Kelly, J.B.: Contribution of AMPA, NMDA, and GABA(A) receptors to temporal pattern of postsynaptic responses in the inferior colliculus of the rat. J Neurosci. **24**(19), 4625–4634 (2004)

Interpretable Image Recognition by Screening Class-Specific and Class-Shared Prototypes

Xiaomeng Li, Jiaqi Wang, and Liping Jing(✉)

School of Computer and Information Technology, Beijing Key Lab of Traffic Data Analysis and Mining, Beijing, China
{22125203,19112028,lpjing}@bjtu.edu.cn

Abstract. Convolutional neural networks (CNNs) have shown impressive performance in various domains, but their lack of interpretability remains an important issue. Prototype-based methods have been proposed to address this problem. Prototype-based methods assign a fixed number of prototypes to categories. But prototype networks are limited by the non-learnable relationship between prototypes and categories, which restricts each prototype to only one category. Furthermore, the large number of prototypes used in these methods often leads to poor prototype distribution. To address these limitations, we propose a deep learning approach with an active learning concept inspired by the associative function of the human brain. We introduce the Prototype Screening Matrix (PSM). We optimize PSM by label smoothing to describe the relationship between categories and prototypes, so that it can dynamically filter prototypes and retain prototypes that are more suitable for concept learning. PSM enables similar prototypes to be shared among different classes, which significantly reduces the number of prototypes and leads to a more rational distribution of prototypes. We experimentally validate the effectiveness of our proposed method on the CUB-200-2011 and Stanford Cars datasets and show that it achieves higher accuracy than existing methods. Our method is more interpretable, uses fewer prototypes, and has a simpler structure, advancing the state-of-the-art in interpretable and efficient prototype-based image classification methods. The code is available at https://github.com/Lixiaomemg/PSMnet.

Keywords: Interpretability · Prototype screening matrix · Class-specific and class-shared prototypes

1 Introduction

Image classification tasks have been a major area of research in computer vision, with Convolutional Neural Networks (CNNs) emerging as a powerful tool in

Supported by the Fundamental Research Funds for the Central Universities (2019JBZ110); the Beijing Natural Science Foundation under Grant L211016; and Chinese Academy of Sciences (OEIP-O-202004).

L. Iliadis et al. (Eds.): ICANN 2023, LNCS 14255, pp. 397–408, 2023.
https://doi.org/10.1007/978-3-031-44210-0_32

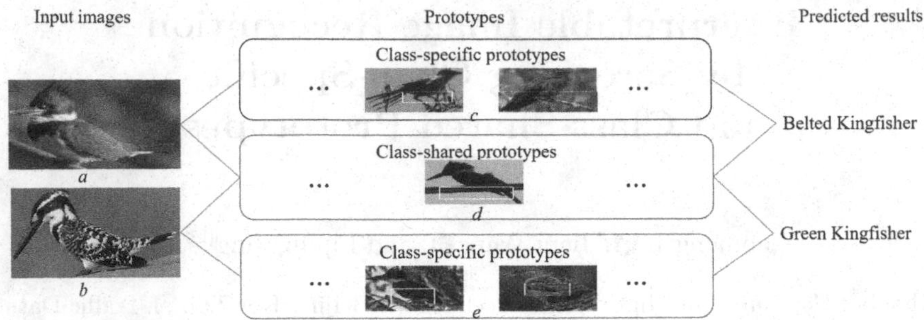

Fig. 1. For images a and b, they each have prototypes specific to their respective categories, c and e, as well as a prototype they share, d. With a prototype number of 600, the network can still correctly predict that image a is Belted Kingfisher, and image b is Green Kingfisher.

achieving outstanding results in various domains. However, the interpretability of these networks has been a major issue, particularly in cases where the filters extract mixed category concepts, making it difficult for humans to understand the network's decision-making process. This lack of transparency and interpretability poses a significant challenge in high-stakes decision-making fields such as medical diagnosis and transportation. In the current landscape of computer vision, a prototype network architecture has been proposed as a solution. However, it must be pointed out that the existing method's association of categories and prototypes is preordained, leading to a substantial demand for numerous prototypes for each category, rendering the very concept of network learning unjustifiable. Therefore, we propose a simple yet effective structure that enhances the interpretability of CNNs in image classification tasks. Our approach enables humans to better understand the underlying reasoning process of neural networks, ultimately leading to better outcomes for all.

Consider Fig. 1, for a training image b of a bird with a red beak and a white chest, how to classify the bird in this image? Humans first observe its distinguishing features, namely the red beak and white chest. The white chest feature is associated with a number of categories, and it just so happens that one of these categories has a red beak. Eventually, the category of this bird image was determined.

The above reasoning process seems to be more in line with the way humans think, which actually involves the associative function of the human brain. The associative function relies on two main mechanisms. One of them is pattern matching, which links similar things together, while the other is conditioned reflex, which links together things that repeatedly appear at the same time. The associative function is responsible for enhancing memory and enabling the learning of unknown objects from known objects. Inspired by the idea of pattern matching, we have discovered that two types of concepts are involved in the above reasoning process including class-specific concepts like red beaks and class-shared concepts like white chests. By relying on these two concepts, the image classification task is completed. The concept shared by the category uses the associative function of the brain. That is, when the concepts involved in multiple categories are similar, we can use a similar concept to associate multiple categories. This approach reduces the number of concepts to be learned and makes it easier to learn the unknown category through the use of this similar concept.

Thus, this paper puts forward the Prototype Screening Matrix (PSM), which can dynamically illustrate the relationship between prototypes and categories in a way that reflects the nuances of the network. In the PSMnet networks, the prototypes are not assigned passively, but they actively learn the category concepts, leading to a more robust and reliable network. The PSM is trained to ensure that prototypes are more similar within the same category and less similar between different categories, which promotes consistency while also allowing for sharing of similar prototypes across categories. Remarkably, this paper uses only label information for the images, and yet still provides global and local explanations. The local explanation offers insights into the entire process of how a picture is classified when it is fed into the network.

This paper has several contributions:

- By incorporating the associative function of the brain into the network, this work makes the network more compatible with human reasoning in image classification tasks, increasing interpretability.
- This paper allows multiple categories to share a similar concept, making it more reasonable for classes to own concepts.
- The relationship between prototypes and categories in this paper is continually updated, and prototypes are dynamically screened during training rather than being pruned afterward, resulting in more reasonable prototype representations.

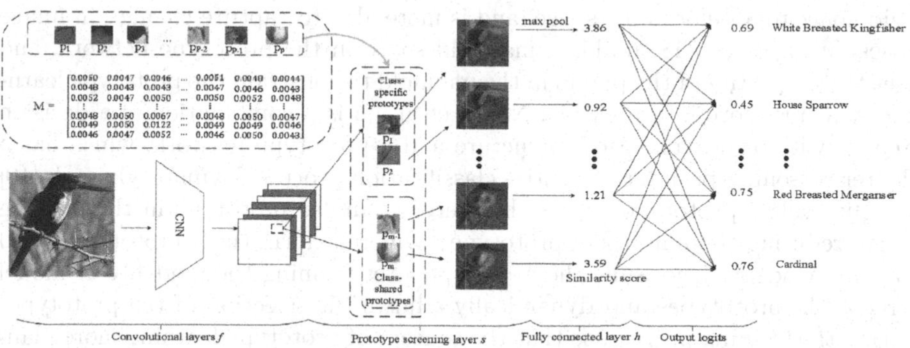

Fig. 2. Image x extracts features through convolutional layer f. Then, after the prototype screening layer s, the prototypes are divided into two types, class-specific prototypes and class-shared prototypes. Finally, through the fully connected layer h, the predicted result is White Breasted Kingfisher.

2 Related Work

The realm of concept representation learning is vast and complex, and within it, we find diverse strategies that use different semantic representation manners to achieve interpretability. Some of these strategies are based on the concepts of interpretable filters, while others are based on the concepts of interpretable activation vectors.

In based on the concepts of interpretable filters, Zhang et al. [19] adopted an addition loss function to implement each filter corresponding to an object part, but the receptive field of training process is an oval in the network. Liang et al. [20] trained a Class-Specific Gate through alternate training, so that a convolution kernel in the network corresponds to a category. Shen et al. [11] still adopted an addition loss function. It uesd spectral clustering to implement a set of filters corresponding to an object part or a background part without a specific structure. This cluster-based improvement makes filters represent concept of diversity.

Interpretable filters aim to establish a correspondence between each filter in the feature map and a specific image region, while interpretable activation vectors actively learn concepts and represent them as vectors. This is achieved by calculating the distance between the learned concept and the top-level feature map, and converting the maximum distance value into a similarity score. This score is then combined with the final classifier to obtain the classification result. A well-known example of interpretable activation vectors is the prototype-based learning method [3], which has been studied in several research works.

The prototype-based learning method is to assign a fixed number of prototypes to each category, and train a prototype network by learning a large amount of data. There are many works based on prototype network. For instance, Donnelly et al. [5] is a combination of the deformable convolutional neural network [4] and the prototype network. It transforms the prototype's receptive field from a rigid space to a deformable space, and is more able to capture changes in image poses. Wang et al. [18] builds a manifold space in the prototype network, and uses the properties of the points in the manifold to constrain the prototype learning, which is more interpretable. Nauta et al. [9] is a combination of a decision tree [1] with own explanatory structure and a prototype network, which has a clearer reasoning path for the entire classification process. Rymarczyk et al. [10] mainly realizes prototype sharing by merging similar prototype in the pruning stage, reducing the number of prototypes. Different form these prototype-based learning models, they prune the prototype after training the model. Our model screens the prototypes and dynamically adjusts the selection of the prototypes during the training process, so that the concept of prototype learning more plausible.

3 Method

CNNs have been known to be opaque and difficult to interpret. To address this issue, a new model for interpretable image classification has been proposed in

Algorithm 1: Training a PSMnet

for e in num_train **do**
  if $e < num\_warm$ **then**
    ifmask = False
    $L \leftarrow CE + \lambda_2 Clust + \lambda_3 Sep$
  else
    ifmask = True
    $L \leftarrow LSCE + CE + \lambda_1 \Phi(M) + \lambda_2 Clust + \lambda_3 Sep$
    $M \leftarrow M - \epsilon \frac{\partial(LSCE+\lambda_1 \Phi(M))}{\partial M}$
  end if
  $\theta \leftarrow \theta - \frac{\partial L}{\partial \theta}$
  if $e \in push\_epochs$ **then**
    ifmask = False
  end if
end for

this paper. By incorporating the associative function of the human brain, the network is designed to mimic the human reasoning process. The key idea is to use a matrix that dynamically reflects the relationship between prototypes and categories, allowing similar concepts to be shared across different categories. This section will delve into the process of prototype screening, which is essential in completing the image classification task using this model.

3.1 General Framework of PSMnet

In our network, in Fig. 2, given an input image x, the corresponding category of the image is y. The size of image is $H \times W \times K$, where H, W, K represent the input image height, width, number of channels respectively. The image x belongs to class t $(t = 1, 2, 3, ..., c)$. The network includes a convolutional layer f, a prototype screening layer s, and a fully connected layer h.

The convolutional layer f is any general convolutional network, and this experiment is verified in various models. The convolutional layer f is used to extract image features, and the output result Z_x is obtained after the convolutional layer f. Z_x contains the feature information of the input image. In the prototype screening layer s, in order that different categories can share similar prototypes, we initialize a matrix $M_{c \times p}$ with c representing the number of categories and p representing the number of prototypes. Each element $M_{ij}(i = 1, 2, 3, ..., c), (j = 1, 2, 3, ..., p)$ in the matrix represents the correlation between categories and prototypes. The prototype screening layer s performs prototype screening based on this correlation to enable the network to dynamically learn category concepts. In the fully connected layer h, the score is multiplied by the weight of the fully connected layer, and finally normalized by the softmax function to obtain the category prediction probability of a given image.

3.2 Problem Formulation

Let us represent the correlation between the convolutional output Z_x and the screened prototype unit by the L_2 distance.

$$d(Z_x, s_{p_i}) = \|\boldsymbol{Z}_x - \boldsymbol{s}_{p_i}\|_2^2 \tag{1}$$

The reasoning process we discussed earlier involves two types of prototypes, and regardless of the type, our minimum expectation of a prototype is to be able to accurately represent the concept. This implies that the prototype should be able to learn the concept at a minimum, and each category should have at least one prototype of its own. In order to ensure this, we utilize *Clust* and *Sep* as follows:

$$Clust = \frac{1}{n}\sum_{i=1}^{n} \min_{j:s_{p_j} \in s_{p_{y_i}}} \min_{Z_x \in patches(f(x_i))} d(Z_x, s_{p_j}) \tag{2}$$

$$Sep = \frac{1}{n}\sum_{i=1}^{n} \min_{j:s_{p_j} \notin s_{p_{y_i}}} \min_{Z_x \in patches(f(x_i))} d(Z_x, s_{p_i}) \tag{3}$$

In the typical case, when we begin our experiments, we set the matrix M using a one-hot encoding strategy, whereby we assign a probability of 1 to the target category of the prototype vector in the training data, and a probability of 0 to the non-target categories. However, this initialization scheme results in the value of the target category in the predicted logits vector to skyrocket to infinity, thereby steering the model to learn the direction of increasing the difference in logits between the correct and incorrect labels. Although this approach may seem promising, the predicted results tend to be overly rigid, and an overemphasized difference in logits can negatively affect the generalization ability of the model.

In the real world, the matrix initialization method described above may seem appealing, but it has a crucial flaw: it renders the prototypes of different categories orthogonal to one another, making it impossible for them to be shared. As a result, the network fails to accomplish the intended effect. To avoid overfitting and address this issue, we draw inspiration from the field of label smoothing [2,7,8]. We achieve this by updating each element of the matrix with a novel continuous value, which is given by the following formula:

$$y_i = \begin{cases} 1 - \alpha, & i = y \\ \frac{\alpha}{c-1}, & i \neq y \end{cases} \tag{4}$$

α is a small hyperparameter.

The label smoothing technique employs a soft label strategy to promote an increase in the distance between classes, while decreasing the distance within classes, thereby improving the generalization ability of the network. Specifically, label smoothing encourages the prototypes of the same category to be more similar, while the prototypes of different categories are more distinct. Notably, the hyperparameter α associated with label smoothing ensures that the prediction result of the optimized matrix M will not be overly absolute when compared to one-hot labeling. As such, when dealing with classification tasks involving relatively similar categories, it is possible to achieve category sharing of prototypes. To optimize the matrix M, we leverage label smoothing techniques.

$$LSCE = \sum_{i=1}^{c} \sum_{j=1}^{p} \log(M_{ij}) y_i \tag{5}$$

Finally, the network needs to optimize the following functions:

$$Loss = LSCE + CE(\hat{y_i}, y_i) + \lambda_1 \Phi(M) + \lambda_2 Clust + \lambda_3 Sep \tag{6}$$

Among them, λ_1, λ_2, λ_3 are hyperparameters, and θ represents the hyperparameters of the model. $\Phi(M)$ is the L_2 regularization term, which makes the matrix relax from discrete values to continuous values smoother. Finally, Algorithm 1 shows the whole optimization process.

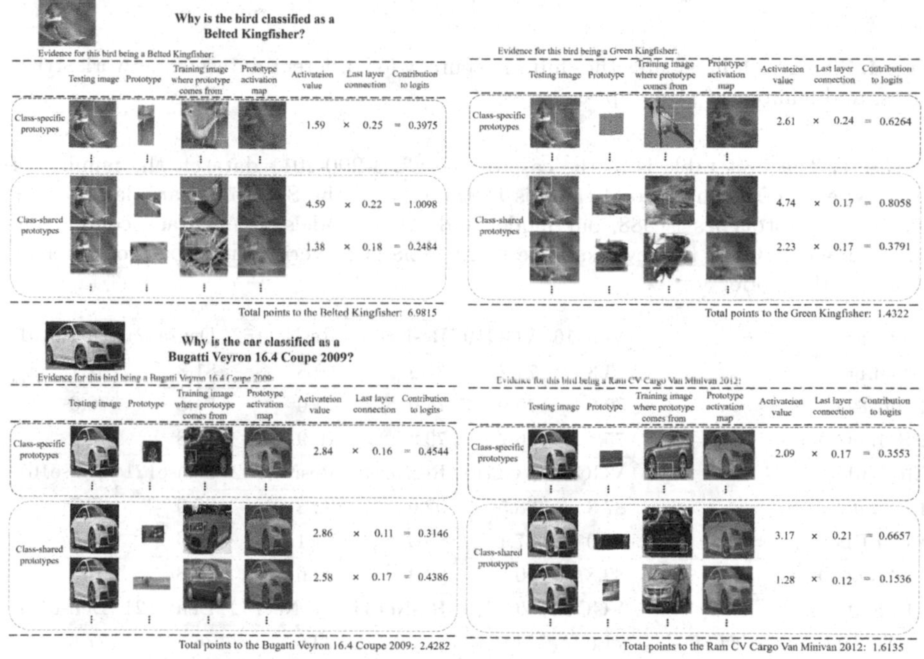

Fig. 3. The top line:the test image is Belted Kingfisher, not Green Kingfisher's entire inference process.The bottom line:the test image is Bugatti Veyron 16.4 Coupe 2009, not Ram CV Cargo Van Minivan 2012's entire inference process. (Color figure online)

4 Experiment

In this experimentation, the prototypes ought to be sifted utilizing the PSM structure. However, in order to advance the experiment's efficacy, the PSM structure was employed to screen the activation map linking the prototype $s_{p_i}(i = 1, 2, 3, ..., p)$ with the feature map Z_x. These two methods are fundamentally the same and both accomplish prototype screening. We conduct experiments on the Caltech-UCSD Birds-200-2011 (CUB-200-2011) and Stanford Cars datasets and validate our results experimentally. We compare the effects of different network architectures, different numbers of prototypes, and different models.

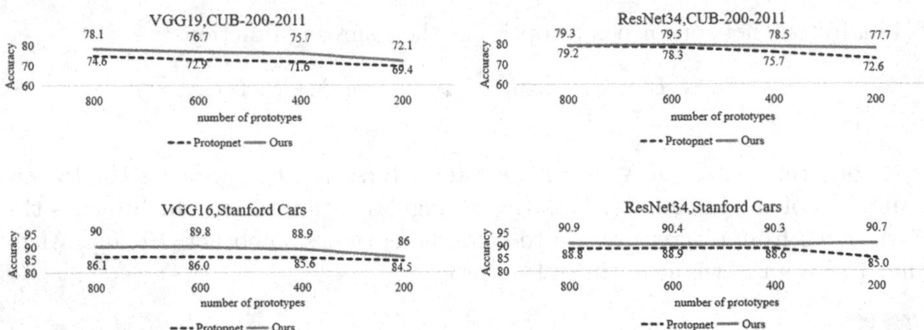

Fig. 4. This graph illustrates the shift in accuracy for different datasets, network structures, and number of prototypes.

Table 1. The first table is in the case of the CUB-200-2011 dataset, the number of prototypes is 600. The second table is in the case of the Stanford Cars dataset, the number of prototypes is 588, our model and other models in Accuracy comparison under different CNN frameworks. The third table is to verify the impact of different losses on the model.

Method	VGG16	VGG19	ResNet34	ResNet152	Dense121	Dense161
Baseline	73.3	74.7	82.2	80.8	81.8	82.1
ProtoPnet	70.9	72.9	78.0	74.0	74.5	78.0
PSMnet(Ours)	75.4	76.7	79.6	76.9	77.8	79.5
Method	VGG16	VGG19	ResNet34	ResNet152	Dense121	Dense161
Baseline	87.3	88.5	92.6	92.8	92.0	92.5
ProtoPnet	86.0	87.1	88.9	84.1	87.6	87.5
PSMnet(Ours)	89.8	90.5	90.4	90.6	90.8	91.4
Method	VGG16	VGG19	ResNet34	ResNet152	Dense121	Dense161
PSMnet($LSCE + \Phi(M)$)	71.0	74.9	76.3	72.6	76.3	77.6
PSMnet($CE + Clust + Sep$)	72.4	74.0	77.1	74.1	76.8	76.8
PSMnet(Ours)	75.4	76.7	79.6	76.9	77.8	79.5

4.1 The Caltecg-USCD Birds-200-2011 Dataset

Recognition Results. We validate our model on the CUB-200-2011 dataset with a large number of CNN frameworks, namely VGG-16, VGG-19, ResNet-34, ResNet-152, DenseNet-121 and DenseNet-161 [6]. As shown in Table 1, our model achieves higher accuracy when the number of prototypes reaches 600. Further experiments on VGG-19 and ResNet-34 are conducted to investigate the performance of our model with different numbers of prototypes (800, 600, 400 and 200) in more depth. As shown in Fig. 4, our model achieves victory, outperforming prototypal networks under different network structures and number of prototypes.

Reasoning Process. Using the CUB-200-2011 dataset as an example, our model utilizes two types of prototypes for a given test image, as illustrated in Fig. 3. We observe that the network has learned both class-specific concepts (such as the background) and class-shared concepts (such as the beak and the head). Notably, the concept of the beak is shared among three categories: Belted Kingfisher, Barn Swallow, and Philadelphia Vireo. By leveraging the prototype of class sharing, we can effectively reduce the image category to a smaller range. Moreover, the concept of class-specific background is derived from Belted Kingfisher. By combining these two prototypes, we are able to accurately determine the category of the image.

Table 2. We compare the accuracy with different models under the framework of CUB-200-2011 dataset and vgg19.

Method	Protoptype	Accuracy
Tesnet [18]/PSMnet(Ours)	200	55.2 /72.1
	400	75.3 /75.7
	600	76.8 /76.7
	800	78.7 /78.1
ProtoPshare [10]/PSMnet(Ours)	200	29.8 /72.1
	400	50.4 /75.7
	600	60.2 /76.7
	800	68.5 /78.1

4.2 The Stanford Cars Dataset

Recognition Results. In a similar fashion to validating the Stanford Cars dataset, we perform experimental validation on different network architectures. Table 1 shows our findings: When the number of prototypes is 588, the performance of our model outperforms the performance of the prototype network by at least 2% on average. Furthermore, we carefully study the performance of our model with different numbers of prototypes. As shown in Fig. 4, our model clearly outperforms the prototype network. Figure 3 shows the inference process of the network on the Stanford Cars dataset.

Reasoning Process. Using the Stanford Cars dataset as an example, our model utilizes two types of prototypes for a given test image, as illustrated in Fig. 3. We observe that the network has learned both class-specific concepts (such as tires) and class-shared concepts (such as car lights and side rear mirrors). Notably, the concept of car lights is shared among four categories: Audi S4 Sedan 2012, BMW ActiveHybrid 5 Sedan 2012, Bugatti Veyron 16.4 Coupe 2009, and Ford Edge SUV 2012. By leveraging the prototype of class sharing, we can effectively reduce the image category to a smaller range. Moreover, the concept of class-specific tires is derived from Bugatti Veyron 16.4 Coupe 2009. By combining these two prototypes, we are able to accurately determine the category of the image.

In addition, we tried to validate the power of our model with other models. For Wang et al. [18], the Since our network can implement classes with similar prototypes, the smaller the number of prototypes, the better our network compares to other models. Turning our attention to Rymarczyk et al. [10], we see that it operates significantly differently from ours. the ProtoPshare network uses an unorthodox pruning method that merges the trained prototypes afterwards. The consequence of this approach is that when the number of prototypes is critically low, the ProtosPshare network will chop off key prototypes during pruning, with deleterious effects. In contrast, our network dynamically filters prototypes during training, allowing for a more rational notion of class assignment. Our network provides class-sharing similar prototypes during training, thus facilitating accurate classification of images even when the number of prototypes is insufficient. The experimental results are shown in Table 2.

Ablation Study. In the case of the CUB-200-2011 dataset and the number of prototypes 600, we conduct ablation experiments to verify the effectiveness of PSMnet. We mainly consider two kinds of losses: the prototype loss and the optimization PSM loss. As shown in Table 1, the loss of the prototype can improve the accuracy by an average of 3% to ensure that the prototype can learn correctly. Optimizing the loss of PSM improves the accuracy by an average of 2% for classes sharing similar prototypes.

4.3 PSM Visualization

We elucidate the complex relationships between categories and prototypes via PSM. That is, we leverage the PSM to illustrate how categories share similar prototypes. As shown in Fig. 5, the rows in the graph correspond to categories,

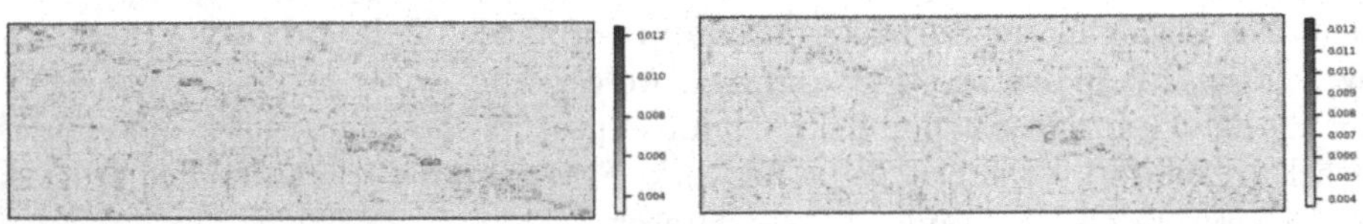

Fig. 5. The left picture: visualization of PSM on the CUB-200-2011 dataset under the vgg19 architecture. The right picture: visualization of PSM on the Stanford Cars dataset under the vgg16 architecture.

while the columns represent prototypes. A heatmap describes the probability that a particular concept is shared by a category, which we can see by looking at each column.

5 Conclusion

In this study, we have introduced a novel approach to improving the interpretability of convolutional neural networks (CNNs) in image classification tasks. Our prototype screening matrix (PSM) is inspired by the associative function of the human brain, and we have shown that optimizing the PSM through label smoothing can lead to a more reasonable and interpretable reasoning process. Our results demonstrate that the PSMnet approach outperforms existing methods in terms of both accuracy and interpretability, with fewer prototypes required to achieve comparable results. By leveraging the shared concepts between categories, we have also shown that it is possible to reduce the number of prototypes needed, making the learning process more efficient and justifiable. Overall, our study highlights the potential for incorporating insights from cognitive neuroscience into machine learning. Future research could explore further ways of incorporating cognitive principles into machine learning or natural language processing tasks [12–17], and we look forward to further developments in this exciting area of research.

Acknowledgements. This work was supported by the National Natural Science Foundation of China under Grant (62176020), the National Key Research and Development Program (2020AAA0106800), the Beijing Natural Science Foundation under Grant (Z180006, L211016), CAAI-Huawei MindSpore Open Fund and Chinese Academy of Sciences (OEIP-O-202004).

References

1. Bai, J., et al.: Rectified decision trees: towards interpretability, compression and empirical soundness. arXiv preprint arXiv:1903.05965 (2019)
2. Chen, B., et al.: An investigation of how label smoothing affects generalization. arXiv preprint arXiv:2010.12648 (2020)
3. Chen, C., et al.: This looks like that: deep learning for interpretable image recognition. Adv. Neural Inf. Process. Syst. **32**, 1–12 (2019)
4. Dai, J., et al.: Deformable convolutional networks. In: Proceedings of the IEEE International Conference on Computer Vision, pp. 764–773 (2017)
5. Donnelly, J., Barnett, A.J., Chen, C.: Deformable protopnet: an interpretable image classifier using deformable prototypes. In: Proceedings of the IEEE/CVF Conference on Computer Vision and Pattern Recognition, pp. 10265–10275 (2022)
6. Huang, G., et al.: Densely connected convolutional networks. In: Proceedings of the IEEE Conference on Computer Vision and Pattern Recognition, pp. 4700–4708 (2017)
7. Lukasik, M., et al.: Does label smoothing mitigate label noise? In: International Conference on Machine Learning, pp. 6448–6458. PMLR (2020)

8. Müller, R., Kornblith, S., Hinton, G.E.: When does label smoothing help? Adv. Neural Inf. Process. Syst. **32**, 1–10 (2019)
9. Nauta, M., Van Bree, R., Seifert, C.: Neural prototype trees for interpretable fine-grained image recognition. In: Proceedings of the IEEE/CVF Conference on Computer Vision and Pattern Recognition, pp. 14933–14943 (2021)
10. Rymarczyk, D., et al.: Protopshare: prototypical parts sharing for similarity discovery in interpretable image classification. In: Proceedings of the 27th ACM SIGKDD Conference on Knowledge Discovery & Data Mining, pp. 1420–1430 (2021)
11. Shen, W., et al.: Interpretable compositional convolutional neural networks. arXiv preprint arXiv:2107.04474 (2021)
12. Song, M., Feng, Y., Jing, L.: A preliminary exploration of extractive multi-document summarization in hyperbolic space. In: Proceedings of the 31st ACM International Conference on Information & Knowledge Management, pp. 4505–4509 (2022)
13. Song, M., Feng, Y., Jing, L.: A survey on recent advances in keyphrase extraction from pre-trained language models. Find. Assoc. Comput. Linguist. EACL **2023**, 2108–2119 (2023)
14. Song, M., Feng, Y., Jing, L.: HISum: hyperbolic interaction model for extractive multi-document summarization. In: Proceedings of the ACM Web Conference 2023, pp. 1427–1436 (2023)
15. Song, M., Feng, Y., Jing, L.: Utilizing BERT intermediate layers for unsupervised keyphrase extraction. In: Proceedings of the 5th International Conference on Natural Language and Speech Processing (ICNLSP 2022), pp. 277–281 (2022)
16. Song, M., Xiao, L., Jing, L.: Learning to extract from multiple perspectives for neural keyphrase extraction. Comput. Speech Lang. **81**, 101502 (2023)
17. Song, M., et al.: Hybrid summarization with semantic weighting reward and latent structure detector. In: Asian Conference on Machine Learning, pp. 1739–1754. PMLR (2021)
18. Wang, J., et al.: Interpretable image recognition by constructing transparent embedding space. In: Proceedings of the IEEE/CVF International Conference on Computer Vision, pp. 895–904 (2021)
19. Zhang, Q., Wu, Y.N., Zhu, S.C.: Interpretable convolutional neural networks. In: Proceedings of the IEEE Conference on Computer Vision and Pattern Recognition, pp. 8827–8836 (2018)
20. Zhang, R., et al.: Invertible concept-based explanations for cnn models with non-negative concept activation vectors. In: Proceedings of the AAAI Conference on Artificial Intelligence, vol. 35, pp. 11682–11690 (2021)

Joint Edge-Guided and Spectral Transformation Network for Self-supervised X-Ray Image Restoration

Shasha Huang[1], Wenbin Zou[1], Hongxia Gao[1,3](✉), Weipeng Yang[1], Hongsheng Chen[1], Shicheng Niu[1], Tian Qi[1], and Jianliang Ma[2]

[1] South China University of Technology, Guangzhou, China
hxgao@scut.edu.cn

[2] KUKA Robotics Guangdong Co., Ltd., Foshan, China

[3] Research Center for Brain-Computer Interface, Pazhou Laboratory, Guangzhou, China

Abstract. X-rays are widely utilized in the security inspection field due to their ability to penetrate objects and visualize intricate details and structural features. However, X-ray images often suffer from degradation issues, such as heavy noise and artifacts, which can adversely affect the accuracy of subsequent high-level tasks. Therefore, X-ray image restoration plays a critical role in the applications of X-ray images. Existing supervised restoration methods depend on numerous noisy-clean image pairs for training, which restricts their application to X-ray images. Although there have been a few attempts to train models with single noisy images, they ignored the unique prior knowledge of X-ray images. This result in poor performance with artifacts and inadequate denoising. To tackle these challenges, we propose a novel self-supervised restoration method called the Joint Edge-guided and Spectral Transformation Network (ESTNet), which integrates edge guidance and spectral transformation techniques to restore color X-ray images. Specifically, ESTNet leverages an adaptive edge guidance module to emphasize edge details. In addition, to achieve a balance between noise suppression and detail preservation in image restoration, we propose spatial spectral blocks that enable the network to capture both global and local contextual information. Extensive experiments on real-world images confirm the superiority of ESTNet over state-of-the-art methods in terms of quantitative metrics and visual quality.

Keywords: X-ray images · Image Restoration · Self-Supervised learning · Convolutional neural networks

1 Introduction

Since X-ray imaging technology has allowed for the creation of density distribution images of different objects based on their material properties, making

L. Iliadis et al. (Eds.): ICANN 2023, LNCS 14255, pp. 409–420, 2023.
https://doi.org/10.1007/978-3-031-44210-0_33

it popular in the medical imaging and security inspection fields [1–3]. However, X-ray images often suffer from degradation issues such as high levels of noise and motion blur in practical applications [4]. These degraded images not only have poor visual perception but also decrease the accuracy of high-level tasks such as automatic security inspection, and disease identification. Therefore, X-ray image restoration is a critical research area with practical applications in various fields.

Image restoration has been extensively studied and can be broadly classified into two categories: model-based and CNN-based methods. Model-based methods [5,6] convert the image restoration problem into an optimization problem to incorporate prior information constraints in the image. Although these model-based methods have strong mathematical derivations and do not require a reference image, they heavily rely on the accuracy of the modeling and iterative optimization makes them time-consuming, which limits their development on large-scale datasets.

With the rapid development of deep learning in the field of computer vision, CNN-based image restoration methods are gradually gaining popularity. These methods can be broadly classified into two categories: supervised and self-supervised learning algorithms, based on whether the dataset includes paired data or not. Supervised learning methods [7–11] use a mapping function to restore degraded images by exploiting statistical distribution differences between paired data. This approach has gained popularity due to the increasing availability of publicly accessible datasets. But acquiring paired data, especially in practical applications like normal dose X-ray images, can be challenging and sometimes even impossible. To overcome these restrictions, self-supervised learning algorithms [12–16] that applied prior knowledge of the original noisy image have gained attention. Inspired by the success of Noise2Noise [12], a new family of blind-spot networks [12–15] has emerged. The Blind-spot network (BSN) is noteworthy as it can reconstruct a pixel from its surrounding noisy pixels without a reference pixel. However, while these methods can achieve good performance on natural image data, they often face the problem of over-smoothed edges or poor noise suppression when applied to X-ray images for lacking prior knowledge information.

To address the aforementioned problems, we propose a novel self-supervised image restoration framework. Our approach fully incorporates prior information about the image. We designed an adaptive edge guidance module that can utilize edge features as prior information to guide the reconstruction network in preserving edge details and accurate texture. Furthermore, to tackle the issues of artifacts and poor denoising performance in self-supervised restoration methods, we propose a spatial spectral block to help the network capture local and global contextual information, thereby enhancing its capability to suppress noise and restore fine details. Through extensive experimentation on both real-world and synthetic datasets, our proposed ESTNet has demonstrated superior performance compared to state-of-the-art methods in both quantitative metrics and visual quality assessments. In comparison with the original noisy images, the subsequent prohibited item detection shows 1.81% mAP gains and 1.66% recall gains when applied to our restored images.

To our knowledge, it is the first attempt to combine self-supervised algorithm and convolution neural networks (CNNs) for color X-ray image restoration. The key contributions of this work are as follows:

(1) A novel self-supervised image restoration method called Joint Edge-guided and Spectral Transformation Network (ESTNet). Unlike existing self-supervised methods that only utilize spatial information to restore images, our method effectively integrates both spatial and spectral domain information to help the network capture both local and global contextual information, resulting in high-quality image restoration.
(2) A spatial spectral block to effectively incorporate information from different domains. Specifically, this module restores local and global features of the image in both spatial and spectral domains, and then aggregates the information from different domains through an efficient feature fusion method to restore accurate texture and promote denoising performance.
(3) An adaptive edge guidance module that is aware of edge features is utilized as prior information to guide the reconstruction network in maintaining edge details and accurate texture.

2 Related Work

After incorporating deep neural networks into image denoising, there has been a significant improvement in both the denoising performance and processing speed of the images. Since Zhang et al. [7] proposed DnCNN, which first introduced deep learning methods into the image denoising field and achieved superior performance against previous works [5,6]. To better incorporate the specificity of different images, a series of CNN-based methods driven by prior knowledge have been proposed. [9] addressed excessive smoothing edges problem in X-ray image restoration by proposing a trainable Sobel convolution operator as a prior. DeamNet [10] introduced a new adaptive consistency prior to help the network recover sharper edge textures. Although these studies achieved excellent image restoration performance in natural images by merging prior information, they all rely on pair data.

Obtaining pair data can be challenging, especially in practical applications like normal dose X-ray images. Thus, many self-supervised methods have been developed with only noisy images. Among these, the Noise2Noise [12] has inspired novel approaches such as Noise2Void [14] and Noise2Self [13]. These techniques employed a novel self-supervised learning strategy that leveraged a blind spot approach, where a portion of the noisy pixels in the input image are masked during training. To further enhance this concept, researchers have developed a global-aware mask mapper known as Blind2Unblind [15]. However, the design of this complex masker has led to reduced efficiency in the learning process.

Inspired by the aforementioned methods, we aim to combine CNNs and self-supervised learning. Therefore, we propose a self-supervised method that jointly uses edge guidance and spectral transformation for color X-ray image restoration.

3 Proposed Method

3.1 The Overall Architecture of ESTNet

An overview of our proposed Joint Edge-guided and Spectral Transformation Network (i.e., ESTNet) is shown in Fig. 1. The pipeline of ESTNet can be divided into two stages. In the first stage, the adaptive edge guidance module generates an adaptive edge-guided map based on the inherent edge features of the image, which serves as explicit prior information to guide the reconstruction network in retaining critical image edge details and accurate texture. Next, we concatenate the original noisy image with the adaptive edge-guided map that has a clear spatial location and uses the resulting tensor as the input for the second reconstruction stage.

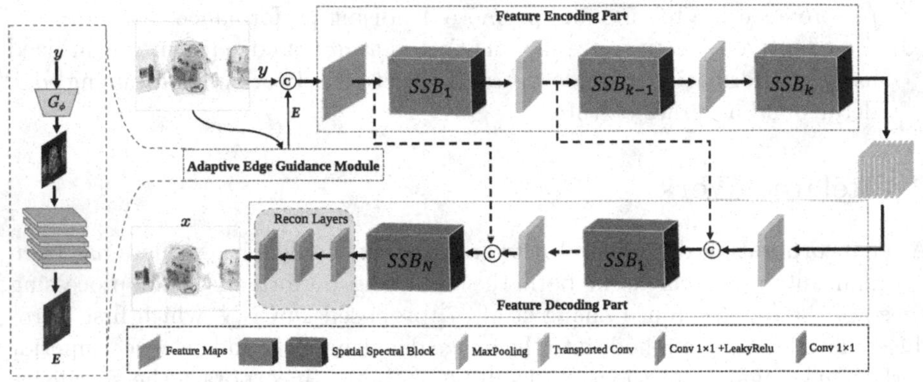

Fig. 1. Architecture of the proposed ESTNet

In the second stage, to better capture the long distant context of an image, spatial spectral blocks (SSBs) are integrated into a multi-scale feature network structure, forming an asymmetric encoder-decoder architecture. The encoder is composed of multiple SSBs and down-sampling modules. The decoder consists of a series of SSBs and up-sampling modules that effectively fuse multi-scale features from coarse to fine. To further keep the fine details, a reconstruction subnetwork is introduced that operates at the original resolution without any down-sampling operation. Our ESTNet can be expressed as:

$$x = ESTNet(y, E), \tag{1}$$

where y and x represent the original noisy image and restored image respectively. E is the adaptive edge-guided map.

3.2 Adaptive Edge Guidance Module

To address the information loss problem mentioned in self-supervised methods that may cause over-smoothed edges, we incorporate guided image filtering. Different from previous approaches, we use a neural network composed of a series of linear convolutional layers to learn the adaptive edge-guided map. Theoretically, deep linear networks have infinitely equivalent global minima [17], which allows the network to acquire the adaptive edge-guided map.

Furthermore, as illustrated in Fig. 1, to constrain the module, we employ an edge detector to initially grab the edge structure information about the image and then feed it into the neural network for further optimization so that this module can better be aware of the edge features of images. The edge detector in this work can be expressed as the following formula.

$$G_{\phi} = \sqrt{G_h^2 + G_v^2}, \tag{2}$$

where G_h and G_v represent the horizontal gradients and vertical gradients respectively.

Essentially, the output of the adaptive edge guidance module can be represented as edge weighting information with clear spatial location, which will guild the reconstruction network to focus more attention on preserving texture details. We denote the adaptive edge-guided map as E, whose values lie in [0,1]. It can be formulated as follows.

$$E = T_{\theta}(G_{\phi}(y)), \tag{3}$$

where $T_{\theta}(\cdot)$ describes the deep linear kernel parameters by θ, y is the original noisy image.

3.3 Spatial Spectral Block

Catching long-term dependencies is crucial in image restoration, while excessive convolution stacking is prone to optimization difficulties in self-supervised algorithms lacking constraints, and even causing gradient explosion problems. Considering these challenges, we design SSB that integrates information from both spatial and spectral domains to aid the network in capturing long-range contextual information across the entire image.

Theoretically, the spectral transformation has advantageous for effectively modeling the global receptive field of images [18]. As shown in Fig. 2, by regarding X_g as the global receptive field branch, X_l as the local receptive field branch, the SSB allocates features generated by a feature extractor CLR to X_g and X_l with the channel-wise allocation coefficients α_1 and α_2. The X_g with global receptive field consists of one local and one global path. In the global path, Fast Fourier Transformation (FFT) is used to transform the spatial feature domain into the spectral feature domain, generating the spectral path feature. The FFT we used can be defined as follows:

$$F(u, \nu) = \sum_{x=0}^{M-1} \sum_{y=0}^{N-1} f(x, y) e^{-j2\pi(ux/M + \nu y/N)}, \tag{4}$$

where $F(u, \nu)$ represents the complex-valued spectrum in the frequency domain. The variables u and ν correspond to the horizontal and vertical frequencies,

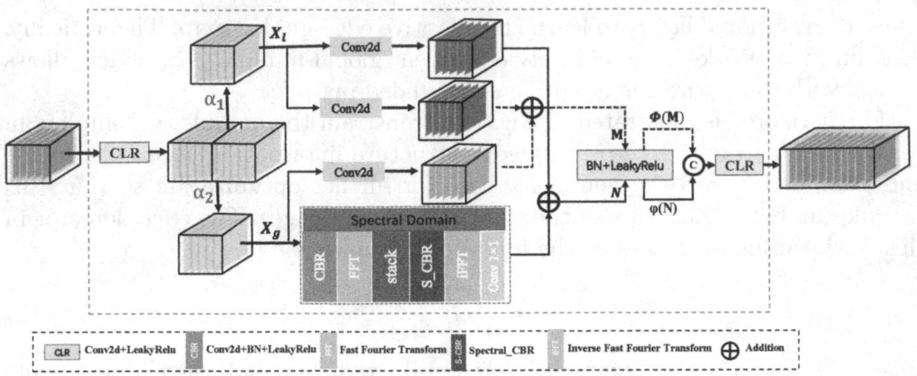

Fig. 2. Spatial Spectral Block consists by global receptive field branch X_g and local receptive field branch X_l.

respectively. $f(x, y)$ represents the pixel value in the original image at spatial coordinates x and y, with the image dimensions denoted as (M, N). The symbol j denotes the imaginary unit.

The spatial features are converted into amplitude F_A and phase F_B through FFT, representing the color texture and semantic information, respectively. These amplitude and phase components are then stacked to obtain B_g using the function $f_{stack}(F_A, F_B)$. Next, a 1×1 Conv layer κ_1 is used for efficient global updates, followed by batch normalization operation ζ_1 to avoid excessively large updates and ensure convergence. A LeakyReLU activation function η_1 is then applied to further enhance the representative ability of the spectral domain. This network is known as Spectral_CBR.

$$\Gamma_{S\_CBR}(B_g) = \eta_1(\zeta_1(\kappa_1(B_g))), \tag{5}$$

where $\Gamma_{S\_CBR}(\cdot)$ represents the spectral neutral network Spectral_CBR.

For the local path of the X_g, we use the same structure as the local receptive field branch X_l. Two parallel vanilla Conv layers are used to map the spatial features to new local features. To better capture local-global contextual information, we aggregate the information from different domains through an efficient feature fusion method to restore accurate texture and suppress noise. This fusion method can be expressed as

$$O = \eta_2(\kappa_2(c(\Phi(M), \phi(N)))), \tag{6}$$

Where M and N refer to local-local information and local-global features individually. $\Phi(\cdot)$ and $\phi(\cdot)$ respectively represent two normalization and nonlinear layers with different weights. η_2, c and κ_2 are LeakyRelu, channel concatenate and 3×3 Conv layer respectively.

3.4 Loss Function

Observing the attributes of the current color X-ray image datasets, which only include original noisy images with high resolution, we have adopted the self-supervised strategy proposed by Neighbor2Neighbor [16]. Specifically, we introduced a neighbor sub-sampler to generate pairs of noisy data $g_1(\mathbf{y})$ and $g_2(\mathbf{y})$. For this pair of sub-sampled images from the noisy image $\mathbf{y}$, we express the following regularized loss function to train our restoration network.

$$\mathbf{L} = \mathbf{L}_{rec} + \Gamma \cdot \mathbf{L}_{reg}, \tag{7}$$

where Γ is used to control the strength of the regularization term $\mathbf{L}_{reg}$. $\mathbf{L}_{rec}$ is reconstruction loss. And more specifically as

$$\mathbf{L} = ||f_\theta(g_1(\mathbf{y})) - g_2(\mathbf{y})||_2^2 + \Gamma \cdot ||f_\theta(g_1(\mathbf{y})) - g_2(\mathbf{y}) - (g_1(f_\theta(\mathbf{y})) - g_2(f_\theta(\mathbf{y})))||_2^2, \tag{8}$$

where f_θ is ESTNet, and (g_1, g_2) represents the neighbor sub-sampler.

4 Experiments and Analysis

4.1 Implementation Details

Model Setup. In this work, we give the implementation details of the proposed ESTNet. In the encoder section, we experimented with five SSBs and four downsampling modules. The input and output channel numbers for the first SSB module were 4 and 48 respectively, while the remaining encoder channels were kept constant. For the decoder section, we used five SSBs and four upsampling modules. And we adopt both α_1 and α_2 as 0.5 in SSB.

Experiment Setup. In the experiment, we set the batch size as 16 and train the network for 15 epochs in OPIXray and set the batch size as 1, and train the network for 20 epochs in PIDray. The Adam optimizer with $\beta 1$ and $\beta 2$ of default values is used to accelerate the training. The initial learning rate is set to 3×10^{-4}. and the simulated annealing method is used with an annealing interval of 4 epochs and a decay coefficient of $\eta = 0.5$. As for the hyper-parameter Γ which is used to control the strength of the regularization term, we set $\Gamma = 2$ in our experiments. Our experiments are implemented in the equipment with the Ubuntu18.04 operating system, an NVIDIA GeForce RTX3090 graphics card, and the configured PyTorch deep learning framework.

4.2 Evaluation Metrics

To evaluate color X-ray images without any clean images, we divide the images into smooth and edge areas for analysis. For the smooth areas, we use the Mean to Standard deviation Ratio (MSR) [19] to assess the denoising ability of algorithms. Generally, the larger the MSR value, the smoother the image, indicating better denoising performance. For image edge areas, we use Laplacian gradient [20] (LS) to measure the edge-preserving ability of algorithms. Additionally, the Noise Power Spectrum [21] (NPS) can visualize the frequency distribution of noise images as an auxiliary tool. To evaluate the color structure information of the restored image, we apply IL-NIQE [22] as an evaluation index. BRISQUE [23] considers factors such as image distortion, noise, and artifacts to evaluate visual quality.

4.3 Module Analysis

As shown in Table 1, we conducted ablation experiments to analyze the contribution of each component of our model. Evaluation was performed on PIDray dataset [3].

Table 1. Ablation studies of the Adaptive Edge Guidance Module(AEGM) and Spatial Spectral Block(SSB). The average MSR, LS and BRISQUE performance on the 3733 real-world images dataset PIDray.

AEGM	✗	✓	✗	✓
SSB	✗	✗	✓	✓
average MSR(↑)	9.94	9.95	10.01	**10.06**
average LS(↑)	245.31	**245.52**	244.92	244.69
average BRISQUE(↓)	33.9	35.28	25.77	**23.19**

In Table 1, the AEGM achieves the highest LS, indicating effective enhancement of edge information. Adding the SSB results in an improvement of 0.07 and 8.13 in MSR and BRISQUE respectively, demonstrating its contribution towards improving the network's denoising performance. Although LS decreased slightly, it suggests some edge loss due to the SSB module's noise smoothing effect. The proposed model effectively balances edge preservation and noise suppression by leveraging the advantages of both modules, leading to significant improvements in both MSR and BRISQUE.

4.4 Comparisons with the State-of-the-Art Methods

The Real-World Dataset. Restoring the real-world X-ray images is a challenging task due to its complexity in imaging process. We conduct experiments on a real X-ray image dataset PIDray [3], which contains 47677 images with 29,457 images in the training set and 18,220 images in the testing set. We choose 3733 hard images for evaluation.

Table 2. Quantitative comparison results of competing methods on OPIXray and PIDray dataset. The best performance is highlighted.

Dataset	OPIXray			PIDray		
Index	IL-NIQE (↓)	BRISQUE (↓)	MSR (↑)	IL-NIQE (↓)	BRISQUE (↓)	MSR (↑)
Input	39.16	161.19	10.00	44.45	64.56	9.92
CBDNet [8]	31.61	66.28	10.25	36.03	30.18	9.94
EDCNN [9]	33.11	122.56	10.21	35.55	28.14	9.99
DeamNet [10]	31.89	77.91	10.26	36.01	30.33	9.95
N2N [16]	32.83	70.32	**10.36**	34.83	33.9	9.94
NAFNet [11]	31.54	67.28	10.30	35.04	30.06	9.96
B2U [15]	33.36	73.44	**10.36**	36.99	31.3	9.98
ESTNet	**31.33**	**65.78**	10.26	**33.72**	**23.19**	**10.06**

The Synthetic Dataset. The synthetic dataset OPIXray [2] consists of 7,109 training images and 1,776 testing images. To deal with the large blank margins on the OPIXray dataset, we perform preprocessing before training. Specifically, we clip the images into 512×512 patches with a sliding window and a step size of 256. Next, we compute gradient violin plots for these image patches and discard those with thresholds less than 25, resulting in 74,400 image patches for the training set. This preprocessing is only performed on the training set, and the testing set remains unprocessed.

For comparisons, we choose six representative denoising methods: CBDNet [8], EDCNN [9], DeamNet [10], NAFNet [11], Neighbor2Neighbor (N2N) [16] and Blind2Unblind (B2U) [15]. It should be noted that the former four methods originally supervised restoration methods, and we compared their performance using our self-supervised training strategy. In addition, we also selected the latest self-supervised method, N2N [16] and B2U [15], as comparison experiments, which have its own unique training strategy. The average IL-NIQE, BRISQUE and MSR scores of the competing methods are shown in Table 2, and the perceptual comparisons are shown in Fig. 4 and Fig. 5. The NPS comparisons with B2U [15] and NAFNet [11] are shown in Fig. 3.

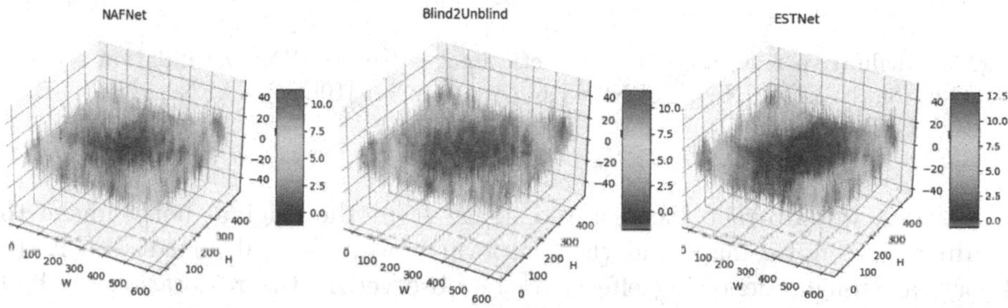

Fig. 3. NPS comparisons with NAFNet [11] and B2U [15].

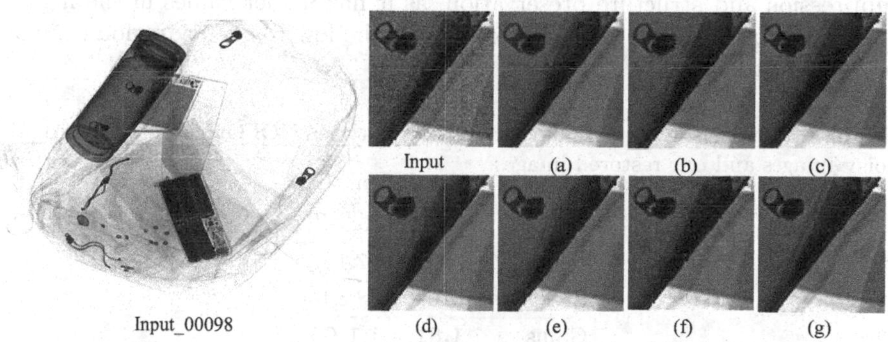

Fig. 4. Qualitative results on real-world images from PIDray validation set: (a) CBDNet [8], (b) EDCNN [9], (c) N2N [16] (d) DeamNet [10], (e) NAFNet [11], (f) B2U [15], (g) ESTNet(Ours).

We can observe that ESTNet achieved the best performance on the real-world dataset PIDray. On the OPIXray dataset, our method got the highest scores in IL-NIQE and BRISQUE. Although B2U and N2N achieve a higher MSR than ESTNet, the reason is that these two methods sacrifice image details for a better signal-to-noise ratio in smooth regions. Moreover, B2U introduces false edges in smooth regions, leading to the misclassification of those regions as edges and a higher MSR value in smooth regions. Furthermore, the visual results show that our method removes noises robustly, suppresses artifacts effectively, and preserves image edges well.

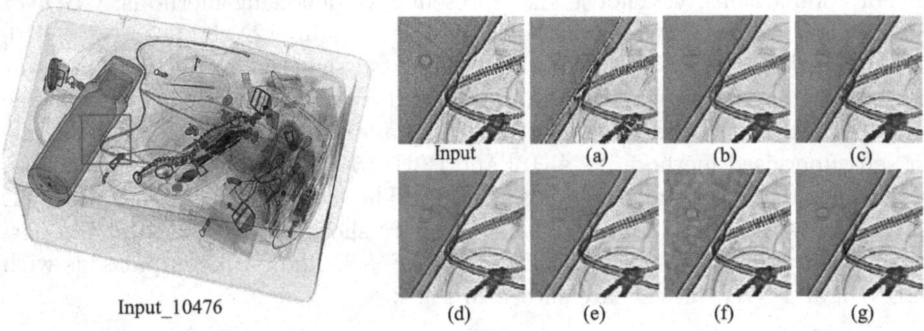

Fig. 5. Qualitative results on the synthetic images from OPIXray validation set: (a) CBDNet [8], (b) EDCNN [9], (c) N2N [16] (d) DeamNet [10], (e) NAFNet [11], (f) B2U [15], (g) ESTNet(Ours).

Besides, we subtract the restored image from the original noisy image to obtain a pure noise map, and then perform power spectral analysis on it. In theory, a stronger denoising effect can be observed in the restoration method when the high frequency part of NPS has a higher value and the low frequency part is closer to 0. It can be seen that our method demonstrates excellent noise suppression and structure preservation, as it has higher values in the high frequency region and lower values close to 0 in the low frequency region compared to other methods.

Table 3. Comparison of mAP and recall scores between YOLOv5 inputs of the original noisy images and our restored images.

Index	mAP(↑)	Recall(↑)
Input	88.89	87.14
ESTNet	90.70	88.80
Gains	↑ **1.81**	↑ **1.66**

4.5 Prohibited Item Detection Performance

According to the evaluation metric of [24], we use YOLOv5 as the detector to compare the mAP and recall metrics of the restored and original noisy images on the OPIXray dataset, validating the efficacy of our restoration approach in downstream tasks. More clearly, we adopt the "small" framework with default parameters, except for changing the input size from 300×300 to 1248×1248. Table 3 shows that our method achieves 1.81% mAP gains and 1.66% recall gains compared to the original noisy image. This confirms that X-ray image restoration is effective in improving accuracy in high-level task.

5 Conclusion

In this paper, we propose a novel self-supervised method called Joint Edge-guided and Spectral Transformation Network (ESTNet), which firstly introduces deep learning techniques into the color security X-ray image restoration. In order to prevent the loss of important edge information, we design an adaptive edge guidance module that effectively incorporates additional edge information into the input image, guiding the network to focus on and preserve edge details. Furthermore, considering that long-range contextual information is effective in avoiding images with erroneous artifacts, we design a spatial spectral block to extract and recover features using the spectral transformation. Quantitative and qualitative experiments have demonstrated the superiority of our method. In the future, we will explore the application of this idea in medical X-ray images.

Acknowledgments. This work was supported by the Science and Technology Project of Guangzhou under Grant 202103010003, Science and Technology Project in key areas of Foshan under Grant 2020001006285, Xijiang Innovation Team of Zhaoqing under Grant XJCXTD3-2019-04B.

References

1. Afshar, P., Heidarian, S., Naderkhani, F., Oikonomou, A., Plataniotis, K.N., Mohammadi, A.: Covid-caps: a capsule network-based framework for identification of covid-19 cases from x-ray images. Pattern Recognit. Lett. **138**, 638–643 (2020)
2. Wei, Y., Tao, R., Wu, Z., Ma, Y., Zhang, L., Liu, X.: Occluded prohibited items detection: an x-ray security inspection benchmark and de-occlusion attention module. In: Proceedings of the 28th ACM International Conference on Multimedia, pp. 138–146 (2020)
3. Wang, B., Zhang, L., Wen, L., Liu, X., Wu, Y.: Towards real-world prohibited item detection: a large-scale x-ray benchmark. In: Proceedings of the IEEE/CVF International Conference on Computer Vision, pp. 5412–5421 (2021)
4. Sakdinawat, A., Attwood, D.: Nanoscale x-ray imaging. Nat. Photon. **4**(12), 840–848 (2010)
5. Beck, A., Teboulle, M.: Fast gradient-based algorithms for constrained total variation image denoising and deblurring problems. IEEE Trans. Image Process. **18**(11), 2419–2434 (2009)
6. Buades, A., Coll, B., Morel, J.-M.: A non-local algorithm for image denoising. In: 2005 IEEE Computer Society Conference on Computer Vision and Pattern Recognition (CVPR 2005), vol. 2, pp. 60–65. IEEE (2005)

7. Zhang, K., Zuo, W., Chen, Y., Meng, D., Zhang, L.: Beyond a gaussian denoiser: residual learning of deep CNN for image denoising. IEEE Trans. Image Process. **26**(7), 3142–3155 (2017)
8. Guo, S., Yan, Z., Zhang, K., Zuo, W., Zhang, L.: Toward convolutional blind denoising of real photographs. In: Proceedings of the IEEE/CVF Conference on Computer Vision and Pattern Recognition, pp. 1712–1722 (2019)
9. Liang, T., Jin, Y., Li, Y., Wang, T.: EDCNN: edge enhancement-based densely connected network with compound loss for low-dose CT denoising. In: 2020 15th IEEE International Conference on Signal Processing (ICSP), vol. 1, pp. 193–198. IEEE (2020)
10. Ren, C., He, X., Wang, C., Zhao, Z.: Adaptive consistency prior based deep network for image denoising. In: Proceedings of the IEEE/CVF Conference on Computer Vision and Pattern Recognition, pp. 8596–8606 (2021)
11. Chen, L., Chu, X., Zhang, X., Sun, J.: Simple baselines for image restoration. In: Computer Vision—ECCV 2022. ECCV 2022. LNCS, vol. 13667. Springer, Cham (2022). https://doi.org/10.1007/978-3-031-20071-7_2
12. Lehtinen, J., et al.: Noise2noise: learning image restoration without clean data. arXiv preprint arXiv:1803.04189 (2018)
13. Batson, J., Royer, L.: Noise2self: blind denoising by self-supervision. In: International Conference on Machine Learning, pp. 524–533. PMLR (2019)
14. Krull, A., Buchholz, T.-O., Jug, F.: Noise2void-learning denoising from single noisy images. In: Proceedings of the IEEE/CVF Conference on Computer Vision and Pattern Recognition, pp. 2129–2137 (2019)
15. Wang, Z., Liu, J., Li, G., Han, H.: Blind2unblind: self-supervised image denoising with visible blind spots. In: Proceedings of the IEEE/CVF Conference on Computer Vision and Pattern Recognition, pp. 2027–2036 (2022)
16. Huang, T., Li, S., Jia, X., Lu, H., Liu, J.: Neighbor2neighbor: self-supervised denoising from single noisy images. In: Proceedings of the IEEE/CVF Conference on Computer Vision and Pattern Recognition, pp. 14781–14790 (2021)
17. Lv, F., Yu, L., Lu, F.: Attention guided low-light image enhancement with a large scale low-light simulation dataset. Int. J. Comput. Vis. **129**(7), 2175–2193 (2021)
18. Chi, L., Jiang, B., Yadong, M.: Fast fourier convolution. Adv. Neural Inf. Process. Syst. **33**, 4479–4488 (2020)
19. Geronimo, J.S., Hardin, D.P., Massopust, P.R.: Fractal functions and wavelet expansions based on several scaling functions. J. Approx. Theory, **78**(3), 373–401 (1994)
20. Xue, W., Mou, X., Zhang, L., Bovik, A.C., Feng, X.: Blind image quality assessment using joint statistics of gradient magnitude and laplacian features. IEEE Trans. Image Process. **23**(11), 4850–4862 (2014)
21. Kijewski, M.F., Judy, P.F.: The noise power spectrum of CT images. Phys. Med. Biol. **32**(5), 565 (1987)
22. Zhang, L., Zhang, L., Bovik, A.C.: A feature-enriched completely blind image quality evaluator. IEEE Trans. Image Process. **24**(8), 2579–2591 (2015)
23. Mittal, A., Moorthy, A.K., Bovik, A.C.: No-reference image quality assessment in the spatial domain. IEEE Trans. Image Process. **21**(12), 4695–4708 (2012)
24. Zou, Z., Chen, K., Shi, Z., Guo, Y., Ye, J.: Object detection in 20 years: a survey. In: Proceedings of the IEEE (2023)

Lightweight Human Pose Estimation Based on Densely Guided Self-Knowledge Distillation

Mingyue Wu[1,2], Zhong-Qiu Zhao[1,2,3(✉)], Jiajun Li[1,2], and Weidong Tian[1,2,3]

[1] School of Computer Science and Information Engineering, Hefei University of Technology, Hefei 230009, China
z.zhao@hfut.edu.cn

[2] Intelligent Manufacturing Institute of HFUT, Hefei, China

[3] Guangxi Academy of Sciences, Nanning, China

Abstract. The current human pose estimation network has difficulty to be deployed on lightweight devices due to its large number of parameters. An effective solution is knowledge distillation, but there still exists the problem of insufficient learning ability of the student network: (1) There is an error avalanche problem in multi-teacher distillation. (2) There exists noise in heatmaps generated by teachers, which causes model degradation. (3) The effect of self-knowledge distillation is ignored. (4) Pose estimation is considered to be a regression problem but people usually ignore that it is also a classification problem. To address the above problems, we propose a densely guided self-knowledge distillation framework named DSKD to solve the error avalanche problem, propose a binarization operation to reduce the noise of the teacher's heatmaps, and add a classification loss to the total loss to guide student's learning. Experimental results show that our method effectively improves the performance of different lightweight models.

Keywords: Pose estimation · Konwledge distillation · Binarization operation

1 Introduction

Human pose estimation [2,3] has been an increasingly active research area in computer vision with a wide range of scene applications including 3D human pose estimation [25], action and activity recognition [8]. Its purpose is to locate human keypoints in the input image, such as eyes, mouth, nose, shoulders, wrists and knees, etc. At present, deep learning [11] has been widely used in the field of human pose estimation. Especially, the methods based on deep convolutional neural networks [7,10,17,22] have rapidly accelerated the progress in this field. However, the improvement of AP performance usually leads to a substantial increase of parameters, computation and deployment overhead. Li et al. [14] successfully constructed a HRNet-based body rehabilitation system for home

L. Iliadis et al. (Eds.): ICANN 2023, LNCS 14255, pp. 421–433, 2023.
https://doi.org/10.1007/978-3-031-44210-0_34

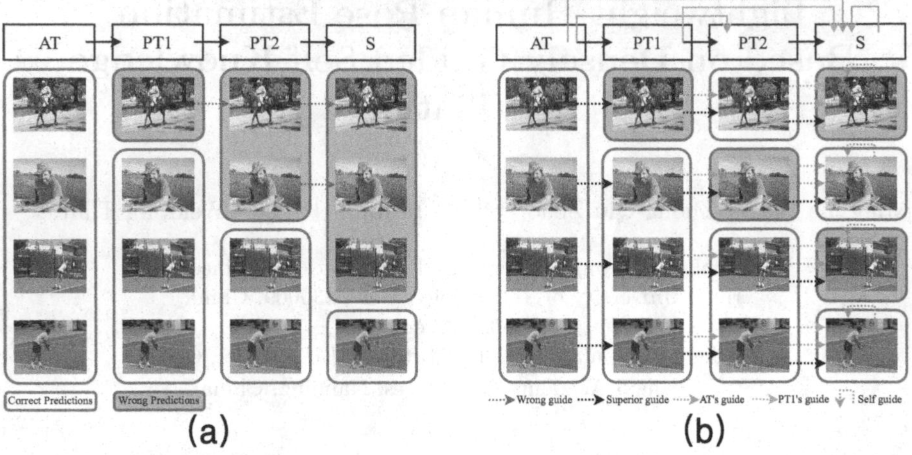

Fig. 1. Error avalanche problem (a) Assuming that a unique error occurs one by one when a higher-level teacher (AT) teaches a lower level PT. The error case continues to increase whenever teaching more PTs. Meanwhile, in (b), the proposed densely guided self-knowledge distillation can be relatively free from this error avalanche problem because it does not teach PTs at each level alone, thereby eliminating the error avalanche in terms of AP caused by one-way knowledge transfer.

use. Yu et al. [26] proposed a lightweight pose estimation network named Lite-HRNet, which introduces a lightweight conditional channel weighting to replace expensive 1×1 convolution. These works have made the task of lightweight pose estimation attract more attention, and the tradeoff between the performance and efficiency of the model has become a focus. There have been many attempts to solve the problem of lightweight model. Recent works [14,18,30] reduce the backbone network to achieve model compression [21,23].

Among these methods, knowledge distillation shows great advantages. Specifically, knowledge distillation transfers the knowledge of a teacher model to a student model with fewer parameters by means of soft label prediction [1]. However, there still exists the follow problems: Firstly, though multi-teacher knowledge distillation can alleviate the gap between teacher and student. There is an error avalanche problem in multi-teacher knowledge distillation, as shown in Fig. 1. Secondly, the heatmap predicted by the teacher usually contains noise, which is harmful to the student, causing the heatmap predicted by the student with multiple peaks. As Zhang et al. [28] found, redundant peaks add useless knowledge. Thirdly, people ignore the validity of self-knowledge distillation which can further improved student. Fourthly, pose estimation is often considered as a regression problem, but it's also a classification problem. And there should be an additional loss function design for this classification problem.

To address the above problems, we propose a densely guided self-knowledge distillation framework named DSKD, which adopts one advanced teacher(AT), two primary teachers(PT) and one student. We employ binarization operation to simplify the learning process of the student. And an appropriate threshold can eliminate redundant peaks to avoid ineffective learning and model degradation. Moreover, keypoint localization is currently regarded as a regression task, and the heatmap predicted by the model is constantly approaching the label heatmap by minimizing the MSE loss. But distinguishing keypoint pixels from background is also a classification task. So we adopt a classification loss to guide the model to learn the teacher's knowledge from multiple perspectives.

Overall, the main contributions of this paper can be summarized as follows: (1) We propose a densely guided self-knowledge distillation (DSKD) framework for lightweight human pose estimation. (2) We adopt the binarization operation to reduce the noise of teacher and to simplify the learning process of the target model. (3) We combine the regression loss with a classification loss to enable the model to distinguish between background and keypoints.

2 Related Works

2.1 Lightweight Human Pose Estimation

There have been a lot of research advances on lightweight human pose estimation in recent years. Rafi et al. [19] built an efficient convolutional network to accelerate inference without requiring quantitative experiments on model efficiency. Bulat et al. [4] adopted neural network binarization for compression. Zhang et al. [30] proposed a lightweight pose estimation network (LPN) equipped with depthwise separable convolutions [13] and an iterative training strategy. Li et al. [14] proposed a lightweight HRNet with efficient spatial pyramid (ESP)attention mechanism. All above methods can achieve a good trade-off between performance and model complexity.

2.2 Knowledge Distillation

The key of knowledge distillation [12] is to teach a student network to imitate not only the outputs of a teacher network, but also true labels of datasets. It has been widely used in many computer vision tasks, such as image classification [24], object detection [9] and soon. Chen et al. [5] suggested using peers where multiple student models train each student model assisted by auxiliary peers and one group leader. Zhang et al. [28] extended the lightweight human pose estimation network by introducing knowledge distillation. Let l_s and l_t be the logits of student and teacher, respectively. T is a temperature parameter to soften the output of student and teacher. $y_s = softmax(l_s/T)$ and $y_t = softmax(l_t/T)$ are the softened outputs of student and teacher, respectively. To encourage student to mimic the output of teacher, a KL-divergence loss L_{KD} can be designed as follows:

$$L_{KD} = T^2 KL(y_s, y_t) \tag{1}$$

To minimize the gap between the output of student softmax(l_s) and the true labels l, the cross-entropy loss L_{CE} can be defined as follows:

$$L_{CE} = F(softmax(l_s), l) \tag{2}$$

Finally, the overall loss function with a balanced factor α can be defined as follows:

$$L_{CE} = (1 - \alpha)L_{CE} + \alpha L_{KD} \tag{3}$$

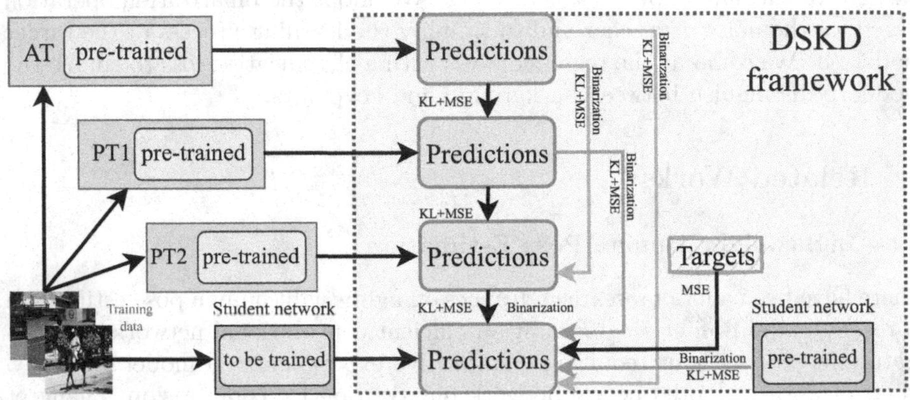

Fig. 2. Overview of our DSKD We adopt two loss functions: MSE loss and KL loss. β-Binarization denotes the binarization operation with a factor β.

3 The Proposed Work

3.1 DSKD Framework

Our proposed DSKD, as shown in Fig. 2, consists of one advanced teacher AT and two primary teachers PT. As TAKD [16] said, assistant teacher can bridge the gap between teacher and student, but there is the problem of error avalanche. So we adopt the strategy of DGKD [20], which utilizes multi-level teachers to densely guide the training of student. Thereby, student acquires knowledge from teachers with complementary knowledge and the problem of error avalanche is effectively alleviated. Several differences between our DSKD and DGKD deserve to be emphasized. Firstly, DGKD aims at classification tasks, but we aim at pose estimation tasks. Secondly, DGKD has four teacher networks of different size, which increases the training cost. For promote the efficiency, we adopt three teacher networks and achieve approximate results. Finally, DGKD ignores the effect of self-distillation, while we add self-distillation to further strengthen the guidance effect. The AT model is with the largest size and the PT models are with smaller sizes. AT is a common human pose model (e.g. HRNet-W48 [16]), while PTs are the models(e.g. HRNet-W32 or HRNet-W24) with the same network structure but fewer channels. We train two PTs by densely guided knowledge distillation during teaching, and finally combine AT, two PTs and a trained student model to train the student model. During testing, only the student model is used.

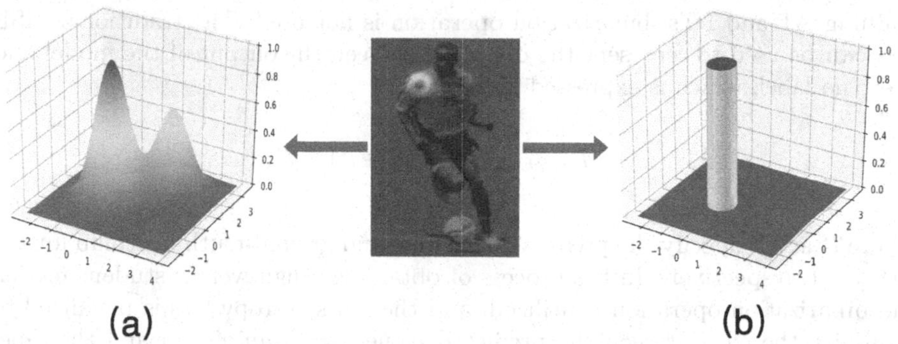

Fig. 3. Convergence analysis of our DSKD method with and without a binarization operation.

3.2 Binarization Operation

The binarization operation is designed to simplify the learning task and reduce noise in the teacher-generated heatmap. It is worth mentioning that the binarization in [6] is to transform the task so that the focal loss [15] can solve the class imbalance problem, but we use it to simplify the keypoint location and remove noise. As shown in Fig. 3(a), the predictions of the teacher model almost exhibit a 2D gaussian distribution structure, where each pixel of the heatmap ranges from 0 to 1. It's difficult for the predictions of a lightweight student model to approximate such distributions, where a solution is to convert the difficult task into an easy one. Additionally, there are multiple peaks in the heatmap generated by teacher, and the extra peaks provide worthless learning for students. Therefore, we adopt a binarization operation for a lightweight student model, which can be expressed as a threshold β as follows:

$$C(y) = \begin{cases} 1, & if\, H(y) > \beta \\ 0, & if\, H(y) \leq \beta \end{cases} \tag{4}$$

where $H(y)$ and $C(y)$ are the heatmap value and class of pixel at position y, respectively. For the ground-truth heatmaps, we empirically set β to 0.6. For the heatmaps from teachers, the threshold is chosen by the ablation experiments. After the binarization operation, we obtain the results in Fig. 3(b). The student only needs to make a simple binary classification for each pixel, and an appropriate threshold can eliminate redundant peaks.When training AT and PTs, we do not employ the binarization operation as the complexity and capacity of these two models are large enough to approximate the data distribution.

3.3 Loss Function

In addition to considering the location prediction as a regression task, we use the MSE loss function to make the student model prediction close to the teacher model prediction. We also regard the task as a classification (keypoint and background) task, and use the KL-divergence loss function to guide students. When training AT and PTs, binarization operation is not used. The traditional MSE loss can be used to represent the distance between the output of the model and the true label, which is expressed as follows:

$$L_{MSE} = \frac{1}{n}\sum_{i=1}^{n}(\hat{l^i} - l^i)^2 \tag{5}$$

where $\hat{l^i}$ and l^i specify the predicted heatmap and ground-truth heatmap for the i-th joint, respectively. In the process of obtaining a lightweight student model, the binarization operation is utilized, and the cross-entropy loss is penalized to minimize the gap between the predicted value $q = Sigmoid(l_s)$ and the label value p:

$$\begin{aligned} L_C &= -(plogq + (1-p)log(1-q)) \\ &= \begin{cases} -logp & if\, p=1 \\ -log(1-q) & if\, p=0 \end{cases} \end{aligned} \tag{6}$$

There are two PT models: $PT1$ and $PT2$ in DSKD, one AT model: AT, the pre-trained student model is represented as $Sself$. Taking Eq. 3, Eq. 5 and Eq. 6 and adding the classification loss, the student's loss is finally expressed as follows:

$$\begin{aligned} L_S &= L_{AT} \rightarrow S + L_{PT1} \rightarrow S + L_{PT2} \rightarrow S + L_{Sself} \rightarrow S \\ &= (1-\alpha)L_{MSE} + \alpha(L_{MSE}AT \rightarrow S + L_{KL}AT \rightarrow S \\ &\quad + L_{MSE}PT1 \rightarrow S + L_{KL}PT1 \rightarrow S + L_{MSE}PT2 \rightarrow S \\ &\quad + L_{KL}PT2 \rightarrow S + L_{MSE}Sself \rightarrow S + L_{KL}Sself \rightarrow S) \end{aligned} \tag{7}$$

where the right arrow at the subscript indicates the teaching direction, and α is the balance factor. In the experiments, we select HRNet-W48, HRNet-W32 and HRNet-W24 as AT, PT1 and PT2 respectively. The value of α of the loss function is set to 0.5 according to experience.

4 Experiments

4.1 Datasets

We evaluate models on the COCO dataset, which contains over $200K$ images and $250K$ person instances labeled with 17 keypoints. The images are extracted from real scenes. We train models on the train2017 set, equipped with $57K$ images and $150K$ person instances, and evaluate models on the val2017 set and test-dev2017 set, consisting of $5K$ images and $20K$ images, respectively.

Fig. 4. Qualitative results of some examples images on COCO validation set.

4.2 Evaluation Metric

We employ the evaluation metric based on Object Keypoint Similarity(OKS), which is calculated by:

$$OKS = \frac{\sum_i exp(-d_i^2/2\,s^2k_i^2)\delta(v_i > 0)}{\sum_i \delta(v_i > 0)} \tag{8}$$

where d_i is the Euclidean distance between each ground truth keypoint and the corresponding detected keypoint, v_i is the visibility flag of the ground truth, s is the object scale, k_i is a per-keypoint constant that controls falloff, and δ represents the normalization factor of the keypoint. We report standard average precision: AP (the mean of AP scores at OKS = 0.50, 0.55, ..., 0.90, 0.95).

4.3 Training

Our models are trained on one NVIDIA 2080Ti GPU. We extend the human detection boxes to a fixed ratio, namely height: width = 4 : 3, and then crop the boxes from images. Finally, we resize the cropped images to a fixed size of 256 × 192. The total epochs are set to 210, and the learning rate becomes to drop at the 170th and 200th epochs.

4.4 Testing

The top-down pipeline is adopted, first locating the human body by the person detectors and then applying the pose estimation models to acquire the detection results. For a fair comparison, we adopt the same person detectors as HRNet

[21] for both COCO validation and test-dev set. The human detection AP is 56.4 and 60.9, respectively. We compute the heatmap by averaging the heatmaps of the original and flipped images. The final keypoints are obtained by adjusting a quarter offset in the direction from the highest response to the second highest response.

4.5 Experimental Results

Table 1. Comparisons of various methods on the COCO validation set. The input size is unified to 256×192.

Method	Backbone	Pretrain	Params	FPS	AP
Large networks					
8-stage Hourglass [17]	8-stage Hourglass	N	25.1M	-	66.9
HRNet-W32 [21]	HRNet-W32	N	28.5M	140	73.4
CPN [7]	ResNet-50	Y	27.0M	77	69.4
SimpleBaseline [23]	ResNet-50	Y	34.0M	187	70.4
SimpleBaseline [23]	ResNet-101	Y	53.0M	155	71.4
SimpleBaseline [23]	ResNet-152	Y	68.6M	124	72.0
HRNet-W32 [21]	HRNet-W32	Y	28.5M	140	74.4
HRNet-W48 [21]	HRNet-W48	Y	63.6M	103	75.1
Small networks					
LPN50 [30]	ResNet-50	N	**2.7M**	**243**	64.5
+DSKD	ResNet-50	N	**2.7M**	**243**	**66.0(+1.5)**
4-stage Hourglass [29]	4-stage Hourglass	N	**3.3M**	**158**	68.3
+DSKD	4-stage Hourglass	N	**3.3M**	**158**	**69.4(+1.1)**
HRNet-W16 [21]	HRNet-W16	N	**7.5M**	**163**	68.4
+DSKD	HRNet-W16	N	**7.5M**	**163**	**71.8(+3.4)**
Lite-HRNet [26]	Lite-HRNet-18	N	**1.1M**	-	61.4
+DSKD	Lite-HRNet-18	N	**1.1M**	-	**62.0(+0.6)**
Lite-HRNet [26]	Lite-HRNet-30	N	**1.8M**	-	64.2
+DSKD	Lite-HRNet-30	N	**1.8M**	-	**65.6(+1.4)**

We report the results of our method and other state-of-the-art methods on the COCO validation set in Table 1. (1) When DSKD is applied to lightweight models such as LPN50 [30], 4-stage Hourglass [29], and HRNet-W16 [21], AP performance can be consistently improved, which demonstrates the superiority of our proposed DSKD. However, the improvements on different baseline models are discrepant. Compared to LPN50 and 4-stage Hourglass, our DSKD improves AP by 1.5 points and 1.1 points, respectively. Compared to HRNet-W16, our method achieves 3.4 gains. Compared to the latest Lite-HRNet [26], the accuracy improvement of our DSKD-based model is lower than HRNet-W16. The reason is that the gaps between the student and the teacher for different networks are different. The difference between Lite-HRNet and HRNet-W16 is that Lite-HRNet employs a depth-wise separable convolution [13] while HRNet-W16 uses regular convolutions. There are also two differences between 4-stage Hourglass and 8-stage Hourglass. One is different numbers of stages, and the other is different numbers of channels. The difference between HRNet-W16 and HRNet-W32 lies on the number of channels. The model similarity between HRNet-W16 and HRNet-W32 is higher than other pairs, and thereby yields higher performance improvements. (2) Compared to 8-stage Hourglass and CPN, LPN50 and 4-stage Hourglass based on DSKD achieve comparable performance, but with much fewer parameters. (3) HRNet-W16 trained with DSKD obtains better performance than SimpleBaseline with ResNet-50 and ResNet-101. However, in the experiment, we find that the HRNet-W16 model needs more the inference time than LPN50 due to the problem of the parallel structure. (4) Although both HRNet-W32 and HRNet-W48 achieve superior accuracy, inference time is much longer than our models. In conclusion, the proposed DSKD is a general framework and can be applied to various models to further improve the performance without changing the parameters and FPS. Figure 4 shows the qualitative results

Table 2. Comparisons of various methods on the COCO test-dev set. The input size is unified to 256×192.

Method	Backbone	Params	AP
Large networks			
CPN [7]	ResNet-50	27.0M	68.6
SimpleBaseline [23]	ResNet-50	34.0M	70.0
HRNet-W32 [21]	HRNet-W32	28.5M	73.5
HRNet-W48 [21]	HRNet-W48	63.6M	74.2
Small networks			
LPN50 [30]	ResNet-50	**2.7M**	64.2
+DSKD	ResNet-50	**2.7M**	**65.6(+1.4)**
4-stage Hourglass [29]	4-stage Hourglass	**3.3M**	67.8
+DSKD	4-stage Hourglass	**3.3M**	**69.2(+1.4)**
HRNet-W16 [21]	HRNet-W16	**7.5M**	67.6
+DSKD	HRNet-W16	**7.5M**	**71.1(+3.5)**
Lite-HRNet [26]	Lite-HRNet-18	**1.1M**	61.1
+DSKD	Lite-HRNet-18	**1.1M**	**61.8(+0.7)**
Lite-HRNet [26]	Lite-HRNet-30	**1.8M**	63.9
+DSKD	Lite-HRNet-30	**1.8M**	**65.1(+1.2)**

generated by baseline models and our DSKD improvements. We can observe that our DSKD models can work well in lots of challenging situations.

Table 2 shows the results of our method and other state-of-the-art methods on the COCO test-dev set. Our proposed DSKD can promote LPN50 and 4-stage Hourglass by 1.4 AP points. For HRNet-W16, the improvement is 3.5 AP points. Compared to the bottom-up approaches, our models achieve acceptable results with much fewer parameters. HRNet-W16 based on DSKD is significantly better than CPN and SimpleBaseline. Compared to HRNet-W32 and HRNet-W48, HRNet-W16 trained with DSKD obtains close performance without pre-training. Compared to Lite-HRNet, our models achieve better performance with similar parameters.

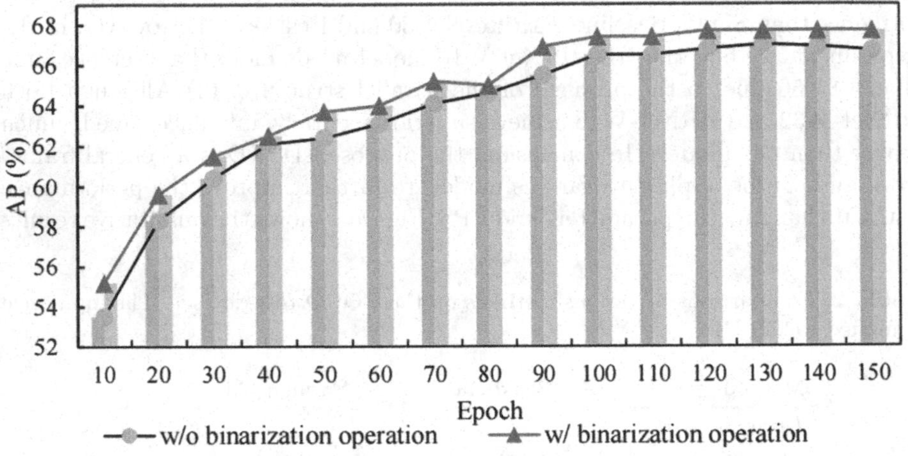

Fig. 5. Convergence analysis of our DSKD method with and without a binarization operation.

Table 3. The ablation study of the architecture of DSKD on the COCO validation set. We choose HRNet16 as baseline.

Dense-Distillation	Binarization	KL+MSE	Self-Distillation	AP
✗	✗	✗	✗	68.4
✗	✗	✓	✗	68.9
✗	✗	✗	✓	69.7
✓	✗	✗	✗	70.3
✓	✓	✗	✗	71.2
✓	✓	✓	✓	71.8

4.6 Ablation Studies

We explore the effectiveness of different components on the COCO validation set. As shown in Table 3, the first line is the baseline model, which achieve the AP of 68.4. In the second line, the AP is improved by 0.5, where the loss function KL+MSE is adopted. This verifies that the classification loss function plays an important role. In the third line, we find that the AP is improved by 1.3AP by self-distillation. As Yuan et al. [27] said, the reason why knowledge distillation is effective may be that it provides regularization for labels. This experiment also shows the importance of students' self-learning. So we add self-distillation in the framework of dense guidance Knowledge distillation. In the fourth line, we can see that Dense-Distillation can improve the accuracy of the baseline model by 1.9. Compared with the fourth line, the binarization operation can improve AP by 0.9, indicating that it can help the model to eliminate redundant learning signals. When applying all our proposed components, the model can achieve the highest AP of 71.8.

Table 4. The ablation study of the binarization threshold on the COCO validation set. The batch size is set as 24, GMU denotes GPU memory usage. We choose LPN [30] as baseline.

Models	DSKD w/o binarization	DSKD w/ binarization				
β	–	0.2	0.3	0.4	0.5	0.6
AP	65.2	65.7	**66.0**	65.7	65.4	65.1
GMU(MB)	9286	**6694**				

We empirically study the effects of the heatmaps with different binarization thresholds on the COCO validation set. As shown in Table 4, with increasing β, the AP performance first increases and then decreases. It is known that the binarization threshold represents the degree of reducing noise. The larger it is, the stronger the degree of reducing noise is. When β is set to 0.3, the model achieves the best 66.0 AP score. But when it is larger such as 0.6, part of the learning signal in heatmaps is eliminated, which leads to model degradation. So we set the β value as 0.3. Besides, we also observe that the binarization operation effectively reduces GPU memory usage (GMU), which is friendly to resource-limited devices. We also visualize the convergence process with or without the use of binarization operations, as shown in Fig. 5, and the binarization operation can effectively improve the AP performance.

5 Conclusion

In this paper, we propose a densely guided self-knowledge distillation (DSKD) human pose estimation framework that can improve the performance of lightweight models with limited computational budget. Furthermore, we reduce the noise of the teacher model and help the student model to learn effectively by adopting a binarization operation and an improved loss function. We conduct a series of experiments on the COCO dataset, and the experimental results show that DSKD can effectively improve existing lightweight human pose estimation models without changing the parameters and FPS.

Acknowledgements. This work was supported in part by the National Natural Science Foundation of China under Grants 61976079, in part by Guangxi Key Research and Development Program under Grant 2021AB20147, and in part by Anhui Key Research and Development Program under Grant 202004a05020039.

References

1. Ahn, S., Hu, S.X., Damianou, A., Lawrence, N.D., Dai, Z.: Variational information distillation for knowledge transfer. In: CVPR (2019)
2. Andriluka, M., Pishchulin, L., Gehler, P., Schiele, B.: 2d human pose estimation: new benchmark and state of the art analysis. In: CVPR (2014)
3. Belagiannis, V., Zisserman, A.: Recurrent human pose estimation. In: FG. IEEE (2017)
4. Bulat, A., Tzimiropoulos, G.: Binarized convolutional landmark localizers for human pose estimation and face alignment with limited resources. In: ICCV (2017)
5. Chen, D., Mei, J.P., Wang, C., Feng, Y., Chen, C.: Online knowledge distillation with diverse peers. In: AAAI (2020)
6. Chen, X., Yang, G.: Multi-person pose estimation with limb detection heatmaps. In: ICIP (2018)
7. Chen, Y., Wang, Z., Peng, Y., Zhang, Z., Yu, G., Sun, J.: Cascaded pyramid network for multi-person pose estimation. In: CVPR (2018)
8. Cho, S., Maqbool, M., Liu, F., Foroosh, H.: Self-attention network for skeleton-based human action recognition. In: WACV (2020)
9. Dai, X., et al.: General instance distillation for object detection. In: CVPR (2021)
10. Fang, H.S., Xie, S., Tai, Y.W., Lu, C.: Rmpe: regional multi-person pose estimation. In: ICCV (2017)
11. He, K., Gkioxari, G., Dollár, P., Girshick, R.: Mask r-cnn. In: ICCV (2017)
12. Hinton, G., Vinyals, O., Dean, J., et al.: Distilling the knowledge in a neural network. arXiv preprint arXiv:1503.02531 (2015)
13. Howard, A.G., et al.: Mobilenets: efficient convolutional neural networks for mobile vision applications. arXiv preprint arXiv:1704.04861 (2017)
14. Li, Y., Wang, C., Cao, Y., Liu, B., Tan, J., Luo, Y.: Human pose estimation based in-home lower body rehabilitation system. In: IJCNN (2020)
15. Lin, T.Y., Goyal, P., Girshick, R., He, K., Dollár, P.: Focal loss for dense object detection. In: ICCV (2017)
16. Mirzadeh, S.I., Farajtabar, M., Li, A., Levine, N., Matsukawa, A., Ghasemzadeh, H.: Improved knowledge distillation via teacher assistant. In: AAAI (2020)
17. Newell, A., Yang, K., Deng, J.: Stacked hourglass networks for human pose estimation. In: ECCV (2016)
18. Osokin, D.: Real-time 2d multi-person pose estimation on cpu: lightweight openpose. arXiv preprint arXiv:1811.12004 (2018)
19. Rafi, U., Leibe, B., Gall, J., Kostrikov, I.: An efficient convolutional network for human pose estimation. In: BMVC (2016)

20. Son, W., Na, J., Choi, J., Hwang, W.: Densely guided knowledge distillation using multiple teacher assistants. In: ICCV (2021)
21. Sun, K., Xiao, B., Liu, D., Wang, J.: Deep high-resolution representation learning for human pose estimation. In: CVPR (2019)
22. Toshev, A., Szegedy, C.: Deeppose: Human pose estimation via deep neural networks. In: CVPR (2014)
23. Xiao, B., Wu, H., Wei, Y.: Simple baselines for human pose estimation and tracking. In: ECCV (2018)
24. Xu, K., Rui, L., Li, Y., Gu, L.: Feature normalized knowledge distillation for image classification. In: ECCV (2020)
25. Xu, T., Takano, W.: Graph stacked hourglass networks for 3d human pose estimation. In: CVPR (2021)
26. Yu, C., et al.: Lite-hrnet: a lightweight high-resolution network. In: CVPR (2021)
27. Yuan, L., Tay, F.E., Li, G., Wang, T., Feng, J.: Revisiting knowledge distillation via label smoothing regularization. In: CVPR (2020)
28. Zhang, F., Zhu, X., Dai, H., Ye, M., Zhu, C.: Distribution-aware coordinate representation for human pose estimation. In: CVPR (2020)
29. Zhang, F., Zhu, X., Ye, M.: Fast human pose estimation. In: CVPR (2019)
30. Zhang, Z., Tang, J., Wu, G.: Lightweight human pose estimation under resource-limited scenes. In: ICASSP (2021)

MCAPR: Multi-modality Cross Attention for Camera Absolute Pose Regression

Qiqi Shu, Zhaoliang luan, Stefan Poslad, Marie-Luce Bourguet, and Meng Xu(✉)

Queen Mary University of London, London E1 4NS, UK
meng.xu@qmul.ac.uk

Abstract. Absolute camera pose regression typically estimates the position and orientation of a camera solely based on the captured image, trained with a convolutional backbone with multilayer perceptron heads for a single reference scene only. Recently, leading pose regression results have been achieved on multiple datasets by extending this approach to learn multiple scenes by leveraging data from different modalities, especially by fusing RGB and point cloud data. In this work, we propose to use cross-attention Transformers to learn multi-scene absolute camera pose regression, where cross-attention modules are used to aggregate activation maps with self-attention from different data modalities and convert latent features and scene index into candidate pose predictions. This mechanism allows our model to focus more on the general localization features. We evaluate our approach on the popular indoor benchmark dataset 7-scenes and compare it against both state-of-the-art (SOTA) single-scene and multiple absolute pose regression models. Our main result is the rotation accuracy is improved using our method more than slightly improved position accuracy compared to existing multi-scene methods.

Keywords: Absolute Pose Regression · Transformer · Multi-modality

1 Introduction

There are key indoor vision-based applications such as automating care and health of an increasing elderly, physically less-able population at home. Computer vision here needs to handle multiple rather than single views of the same scene, e.g., because objects may be placed in different locations and orientations after and when they are used by humans. For these, determining the position and orientation of the camera using multimodal sensors is critical. Current camera localization techniques involve various precision, runtime, and memory usage trade-offs. The most accurate visual localization method [15,20] involves hierarchical localization pipelines that generally employ a coarse-to-fine processing stream. In general, to estimate the camera's six degrees of freedom (6DoF) accurately, it is necessary to map the 2D-2D correspondences to 2D-3D, the pose

L. Iliadis et al. (Eds.): ICANN 2023, LNCS 14255, pp. 434–445, 2023.
https://doi.org/10.1007/978-3-031-44210-0_35

of the camera is then determined via the perspective n-point (PnP) algorithm and Random Sample Consensus (RANSAC). Other approaches based on visual absolute pose regressors (APRs) have been proposed, which can estimate camera pose with only the query image through a single forward pass, significantly reducing latency, albeit with significantly lower accuracy. Furthermore, because of its small memory footprint, APRs can be deployed as stand-alone applications on edge devices with limited computing resources. [23] gives an exhaustive survey of visual camera pose estimation.

Blanton et al. [9] proposed a method that extends APR from a single scene to multiple scenes. This method is similar to existing APRs that utilize a CNN backbone to generate the image's global latent descriptor. This approach trains a set of fully connected layers (FC), one for each scene, indexed by the predicted scene identifier. While providing a new generic framework that can optimize a single model for multi-scenes, this method falls short in matching the precision of SOTA APRs. Shavit et al. [17] proposed a new multi-scene absolute pose regression formula named MS-tran based on the recent successful applications of self-attention transformer in computer vision tasks such as image recognition [5] and object detection [17]. MS-tran showed the effectiveness of encoder self-attention in aggregating informative latent features for a specific task. Furthermore, this method was shown to generate multiple predictions that can correspond to independent queries based on the self-attention mechanism.

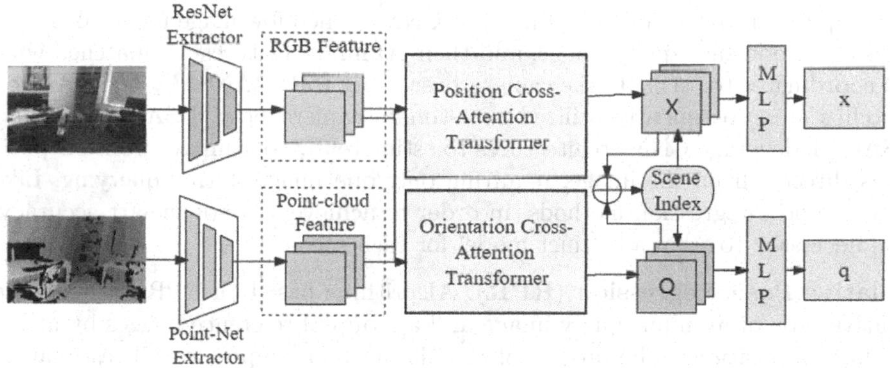

Fig. 1. Overview of the multi-modality cross attention model architecture.

In this work, drawing inspiration from the work of MS-tran, we apply the transformer module to the task of multi-scene absolute pose regression. Specifically, we fuse visual and depth information and transform the encoded scene index into a latent pose representation, as illustrated in Fig. 1. Our approach differs from general APR methods which learn using a single global image encoding to estimate the camera's 6DoF pose [21]. Instead, we propose a multi-modality sensor fusion approach based on cross-attention, as the data varies greatly from different modalities, therefore, we utilize two separate extractors for RGB and depth feature extraction. As camera pose estimation involves two distinct sub-tasks (position and orientation estimation). We use two separate cross-attention transformer modules, each dedicated to one of the sub-tasks. The outputs of the transformer are used for scene classification and selecting embedding respectively, then we regress the position and orientation feature vector. By providing an adaptive analysis of the point cloud and image feature, the proposed architecture based on dual sensor fusion and a cross-attention mechanism aims for a robust and accurate model when applied to a contemporary indoor scenes benchmark.

In summary, our main contributions are as follows:

- We propose a novel architecture for fusing multi-modality data from different sensors and performing multi-scene APR using cross-attention transformers.
- We demonstrate through experimentation that self-attention and cross-attention can aggregate position and rotation image features.
- The rotation accuracy is improved using our method more than slightly improved position accuracy compared to existing both single and multi-scene APR methods.

2 Related Work

2.1 Image Pose Retrieval

3D or Structure-Based Localization methods are recognized to have the best precision. Hierarchical pose estimation pipelines have introduced a two-stage approach to this process. Firstly, a CNN trained for image retrieval (IR) is used to encode each query image, and then 2D image features are matched with 3D coordinates to estimate the camera pose using PnP-RANSAC. The obtained matches are subsequently utilized to estimate camera pose. DSAC++ [2] and DSAC [3], leverage CNN architectures to estimate 3D coordinates from 2D positions directly from the image, requiring only one image during querying. Like absolute pose regression methods, in order to achieve state-of-the-art accuracy, it is necessary to train a distinct model for each scene.

Relative Pose Regression (RPR). Algorithms based on RPR estimate the relative pose of an input query image and a group of reference images by utilizing known positions. The process of calculating relative pose entails estimating the relative position and orientation between the reference images and the query image [1,10]. The closest neighbouring set of images is determined using image retrieval (IR) methods, and the relative translation and rotation between the query image and each retrieved image is estimated. The estimated relative pose and known position of the reference images are utilized to determine the absolute pose. Similar to 3-D and structure-based localization techniques, the RPR algorithm is a multi-step process that necessitates access to a database of annotated images during querying.

Absolute Pose Regression (APR). PoseNet by Kendall et al. [9] is the first APR method that uses a convolutional neural network backbone and multi-layer perceptron head to regress the camera's position and orientation.

This method is simple and can run in 5ms. Subsequently, several APR methods have achieved good results by modifying PoseNet's backbone and MLP architecture [11,12,16,20–22], as well as alternative loss functions and optimization strategies [15]. However, since indoor environments exhibit dynamic scenes characterized by different lighting conditions and viewpoints, relying solely on visual information from RGB cameras may limit the network's adaptability and reduce the accuracy.

2.2 Transformer

Initially developed for machine translation, the Transformer architecture has emerged as the SOTA approach in natural language processing. More recently, there have been efforts to introduce Transformer-like networks to various computer vision tasks, including object detection, image recognition, segmentation, and visual question answering (VQA) [18,19,24] . The Vision Transformer (ViT) [5] directly inputs image patches into a Transformer used for image classification, eliminating the need for any convolutional operations. Our work builds upon these studies, demonstrating the effectiveness of Transformers module in fusing multi-modality information for precise pose estimation. Specifically, to the best of our knowledge, we are the first to propose a multi-modality cross-attention Transformer that adjusts the weights of the multi-heads attention based on the input image and point cloud.

3 Method

Generating stronger representations by matching point clouds and images has been a long-standing challenge due to the inherent differences in features between RGB images and point clouds. In this research, a novel multi-modality cross-attention network is proposed that models both intra- and inter-modal relationships between image regions and point cloud data in a single deep model, allowing for image-point cloud matching and information fusion. To ensure robust cross-modality matching and fusing, two effective attention modules, namely self-attention and cross-attention modules, are designed, each of which plays a critical role in modelling the intra- and inter-modal relationships.

Self-attention and cross-attention modules are illustrated in the green solid line block and the black dashed line block in Fig. 2, respectively. Given a pair of RGB and depth images, we first extract image features by using the Resnet-50 model, and simultaneously use a pre-trained Point-net to extract point cloud features, while the point cloud was generated by depth image with intrinsic parameters. Based on these granular representations of image and point clouds, we model the intra-modal relationships using the self-attention module and model the intra-modal relationships between image and point clouds using the cross-attention module. To handle multiple different scenes, we also apply separate position and orientation transformers modules to encode the localization parameters for each scene. The architecture is based on the DETR method [4] with

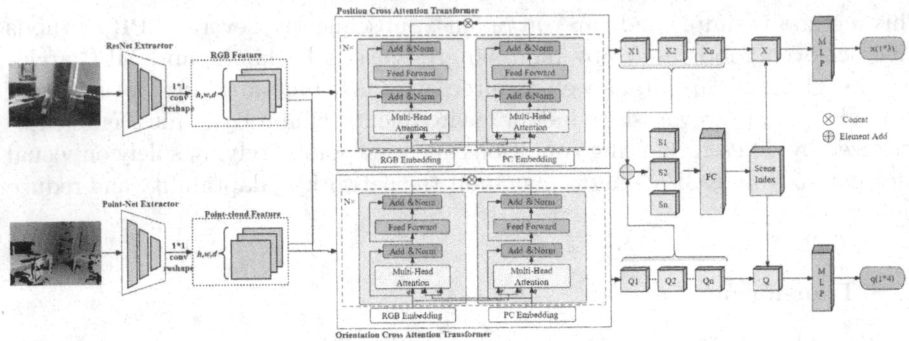

Fig. 2. Multi-modal cross-attention mechanism for absolute pose regression in multiple scenes. The proposed approach consists of two separate cross-attention transformer modules, each of which processes information from RGB and depth modalities, respectively, and outputs features for position and orientation. Afterwards, the scene encoding is integrated with the features from both modalities and softmax processing is applied to obtain a single scene index. Finally, the index and the encoded features are used to regress the position x and orientation q, respectively.

MS-tran [17]. The cross-attention Transformer architecture allows for learning multiple scenes simultaneously while attending to local information in the image and point cloud content. To obtain accurate camera poses, we classify scenes by concatenating $\{X_i\}_0^m$ and $\{Q_i\}_0^m$, then the index of the final detected scene X_i, Q_i is obtained by Soft-Max process. Finally, the final predicted x and q are obtained by separately encoding the indexed X and Q using MLP. It is worth mentioning that in the training phase, we use hard negative mining to construct the triplet loss to optimize the parameters of the model.

3.1 Overall Architecture

Our model architecture is illustrated in Fig. 2. Given a pair of RGB images and a depth map as inputs, we first convert the depth map into a corresponding point cloud by calculating the camera intrinsic and extrinsic matrices. In the feature extraction module, we employ a ResNet model to extract features $F_r \in \mathbb{R}^{D_m \times H_q \times W_q}$ of salient regions $I_r \in \mathbb{R}^{3 \times H \times W}$ in the images. Meanwhile, we use PointNet as the point cloud feature encoder to obtain point cloud features $F_p \in \mathbb{R}^{D_m \times H_q \times W_q}$ from point cloud $P_i \in \mathbb{R}^{3 \times N_i}$. We denote $\phi(F_r) \in \mathbb{R}^{D_m \times H_t \times W_t}$ and $\phi(F_p) \in \mathbb{R}^{D_m \times H_q \times W_q}$ as the feature maps extracted from RGB and point cloud. After that, we use a 1×1 convolution to compress the number of channels of $\phi(F_r), \phi(F_p)$ from 1024 to $D_m = 512$. The two features are then further aggregated using the CAT module, which incorporates a cross-attention mechanism, as defined in the following formula::

$$(F_x, F_q) = \mathrm{CAT}(\phi(F_r), \phi(F_p)), \tag{1}$$

where F_x and F_q represent the output embedding from the position transformer and orientation transformer.

Then, we independently feed the image region and point cloud feature region into different cross-attention Transformer units to model the intra-modality relationships. Subsequently, the global representation can be obtained by aggregating these fragment features. To perform index-based classification, the F_x features and the F_q features are first subjected to global average pooling (GAP) before being concatenated and used as input to the classifier ϕ_c. The classification results $P(scene_i), i = 1, 2, ..., n$ can be formulated as:

$$P\left(scene_i\right) = \Phi_c\left(\text{Concat}\left(\text{GAP}\left(\psi\left(F_i, p_i\right)\right)\right)\right) \quad (2)$$

Subsequently, the output vectors corresponding to the highest probability at the scene index are selected. These output vectors, represented as (X_i, Q_i), are then fed into their respective MLP heads with one hidden layer and Gaussian Error Linear Unit (GELU) non-linearity to perform regression on the target vectors, namely x or q.

3.2 Cross-Attention and Self-attention

The self-attention mechanism is a process that involves mapping a set of key-value pairs and a query to produce an output. The output is calculated as the weighted sum of the values, where the weight matrix is determined based on the query and its corresponding key. The multi-head self-attention is accomplished by applying different learnable linear projections to the query (Q), key (K), and value (V) h times.

Specifically, given a set of sequences$\{F_i\}_1^n$, we first compute the input Q_F, K_F, and V_F, respectively. Then, the weight matrix can be obtained through "Scaled Dot-Product Attention". The weighted sum of the values is then computed as follows:

$$\text{Attention}\left(\mathbf{Q}_F, \mathbf{K}_F, \mathbf{V}_F\right) = \text{softmax}\left(\frac{\mathbf{Q}_F \mathbf{K}_F^T}{\sqrt{d_k}}\right) \mathbf{V}_F \quad (3)$$

The Head is then calculated by the following equation:

$$\text{head}_i = \text{Attention}\left(\mathbf{F}\mathbf{W}_i^Q, \mathbf{F}\mathbf{W}_i^K, \mathbf{F}\mathbf{W}_i^V\right), \quad (4)$$

Afterwards, the values of all the heads are computed and concatenated together as follow:

$$\text{MultiHead}\left(\mathbf{F}\right) = \text{concat}\left(\text{head}_1, \ldots, \text{head}_h\right) \mathbf{W}^O, \quad (5)$$

After the MHA operation, there is a Feed-forward Network (FFN) module composed of two linear transformation layer with ReLU activation, defined as:

$$\text{FFN}(x) = \max\left(0, xW_i + b_i\right) W_j + b_j \quad (6)$$

where $W_i, W_j$and $b_i, b_j$are the weight matrices and basis vectors respectively. In order to fuse the image feature and point cloud feature, in one stream of CAT, we let $Q = F_i$and $K = V = F_p$ in equation (3), and obtain the aggregated target feature. This procedure can be summarized as:

$$\widetilde{F_t} = \text{Norm}\left(F_t + P_t + \text{MultiHead}\left(F_t + P_t, \quad F_q + P_q, F_q\right)\right) \tag{7}$$

$$Y_t = \text{Norm}\left(\widetilde{F_t} + FFN\left(\widetilde{F_t}\right)\right) \tag{8}$$

where P_t, P_q, are the spatial position encodings corresponding to Ft and Fq, respectively. In another stream, we set $Q = Fq$ and$K = V = Ft$ and generate Y_q, then aggregate the query feature. The entire computation described above represents one layer of the proposed cross-attention Transformer. The output of one layer serves as the input of the next layer in the network.

3.3 Multi-scene Camera Pose Loss

The pose estimation error is calculated by comparing the ground truth pose $p_{gt} = (x_{gt}, q_{gt})$, where $x \in R^3$ denotes the position and $q \in R^4$ encodes its direction as a quaternion, with the predicted pose $p =< x, q >$. The position error and orientation error denoted as L_x and L_q are computed as the Euclidean distance between the predicted value and ground truth. We train our model to minimize both L_x and L_q

$$\begin{aligned} L_x &= \left\|\mathbf{x}_{gt} - \mathbf{x}\right\|_2 \\ L_q &= \left\|\mathbf{q}_{gt} - \frac{\mathbf{q}}{\|\mathbf{q}\|}\right\| \|_2 \end{aligned} \tag{9}$$

We referred to the method of [8] to balance the various loss functions defined for individual objectives using different weighting schemes. The loss equation is as follows.

$$L_p = L_x \exp\left(-\alpha\right) + \alpha + L_q \exp\left(-\beta\right) + \beta, \tag{10}$$

where α, β are the learned parameters. To further improve the performance of the model, we incorporated a negative log-likelihood (NLL) loss term based on the ground truth scene index s_{gt}. Like the loss function in [17], this loss term is calculated using the estimated pose p and the predicted log probability distribution s of the scene. The overall loss function is:

$$L_{\text{multi-scene}} = L_{\mathbf{p}} + NLL\left(\mathbf{s}, \mathbf{s_{gt}}\right) \tag{11}$$

3.4 Implementation Details

The implementation of our model uses PyTorch [13]. As an encoder for RGB images, we use a pre-trained e-ResNet-50 [7], which decreases the size of the feature maps and increases the number of feature channels. And we have also used Point-Net [14] as a point cloud encoder to extract sufficient geometry information. We denote F_{rgb} and F_{pc} as RGB and point cloud feature input:$F_{rgb} \in \mathbb{R}^{3\times H_q \times W_q}$ and$F_{pc} \in \mathbb{R}^{3\times H_q \times W_q}$. We set $C = 512$ for the input dimension of the components of the cross-attention transformer. All cross-attention transformers consist of 5 layers with GELU non-linearity. For each layer, we use 4 MHA heads and a 2-layer MLP with a hidden dimension of 256. Then we regress the position and orientation vectors from the latter two MLP heads in the dimension of 1024 with only one hidden layer.

4 Experiments and Results

4.1 Dataset

Our method is evaluated on the 7Scenes datasets [6], which are commonly used for the evaluation of indoor pose regression methods. The 7Scenes dataset consists of seven small-scale scenes of indoor office environments.

4.2 Training Details

To minimize the loss function in Eq. 11, we optimize our model using the Adam optimization algorithm with the following hyperparameters: $\alpha = 0.3$, $\beta = 0.9$. The batch size is 4, and the learning rate is set to $\lambda = 10^{-6}$. We reduced the learning rate by %25 every 150 epochs, with a maximum of 900 epochs. The output of the decoder is selected during training using the ground-truth scene index, whereas the estimated scene index is used only for NLL loss evaluation. The scene index is unknown during the inference process, and we rely on the model's prediction by choosing the index with the highest (log) likelihood. All of the experiments reported were carried out on a 40Gb Nvidia-A100.

Table 1. Comparison to state-of-the-art methods: 7-Scenes. We take the median errors of position and orientation for each method.

Method	Chess	Fire	Heads	Office	Pumpkin	Kitchen	stairs
MSPN[3]	0.09/4.76	0.29/10.5	0.16/13.1	0.16/6.8	0.19/5.5	0.21/6.61	0.31/11.63
MS-tran	0.11/4.66	0.24/9.6	0.14/12.19	0.17/5.66	0.18/4.44	0.17/5.94	0.26/8.45
MCAPR(ours)	0.10/4.55	0.22/8.4	0.14/11.6	0.15/5.7	0.17/4.5	0.16/5.88	0.23/8.03

Table 2. Current APR results for the 7Scenes dataset. We take the average median errors of position and orientation of each method.

MethodAverage	position [meters]	Orientation [degrees]
Single-sceneAPRs		
PoseNet	0.44	10.4
BayesianPN	0.47	9.81
LSTM-PN	0.31	9.86
GPoseNet	0.31	9.95
PoseNet-Learnable	0.24	7.87
GeoPoseNet	0.23	8.12
MapNet	0.21	7.78
IRPNet	0.23	8.49
AttLoc	0.20	7.56
Multi-sceneAPRs		
MSPN	0.20	8.41
MS-tran	0.18	7.28
MCAPR(Ours)	0.16	7.03

4.3 Comparison with Other APRs

Our approach aims to provide a multi-modality APR paradigm that improves upon the accuracy achieved by existing APR methods. Therefore, we compare our method against MSPN and MS-tran, which are the only 2 multi-scene APR method we are aware of, as well as leading single-scene APR methods. Table 1 shows the results obtained by our approach (MCAPR) and MS-tran, as well as MSPN, on the 7Scenes dataset. It is shown that our method(MCAPR) outperforms MSPN and MS-tran in the 7Scenes dataset mostly, reducing both position and orientation errors. We further compare our results with other single-scene APR solutions. Table 2 shows the performance of different APRs, MSPN, MS-tran, and our method . We report the average position and orientation errors of all scenes. It's clear that our method achieves the smallest position and orientation errors. In the scene index classification part, our model achieves 97.5% mean cross-scene prediction accuracy, which is crucial for latter pose regression.

4.4 Ablation Study

In this section, we mainly explore the effect of different data modalities and the Cross-Attention Transformer (CAT) module with different hyper-parameters since this module is the core component of our model.

Table 3. Ablation study of different CAT layers. We take the median errors of position and orientation.

Layers	position [meters]	Orientation [degrees]
3	0.19	7.41
4	0.15	7.33
5	0.16	7.03
6	0.18	8.36

Table 4. Ablation study of different Transformer Dimensions. We take the median errors of position and orientation.

Transformer Dimensions	position [meters]	Orientation [degrees]
64	0.17	8.02
128	0.17	7.76
256	0.16	7.43
512	0.16	7.03

Transformer Architecture. We investigate the performance of a Cross-Attention Transformer with different feature dimensions and numbers of layers. As illustrated in Table 3, we test the results of the CAT module with 3 to 6 layers. The CAT that contains 4 layers achieves the best performance on position error, while on orientation the best result is obtained with 5 layers. It can be seen that only increasing the number of layers does not always improve performance, which may cause overfitting in the orientation perception. It should be noted that even using only 3 layers, our model still has better performance than many other proposed methods. In the remaining experiments, the number of CAT layers is set to 5 as we found it has the best accuracy. We also found that the performance of the model improves with the Transformer dimension, suggesting that larger models may achieve further improvement in localization accuracy (Table 4). In conclusion, regardless of the number of layers and feature dim, our model maintains SOTA position and orientation accuracy compared to other APR solutions (Table 2).

Table 5. Ablation study of different modality. We take the median errors of position and orientation.

modality	position [meters]	Orientation [degrees]
RGB	0.18	7.9
Point cloud	0.35	14.33
RGB with Point cloud	0.16	7.03

Different Modality. Table 3 shows the result with different data modalities. We investigate the performance of this cross-attention module with different data modalities. More specifically, we trained and tested our model with multi-modality(image and point cloud), image only(point cloud was filled with zero), and point cloud only(image was filled with zero) in the same network architecture. The result shows that using only point cloud is not sufficient for the camera pose location task, and only using the RGB information can also outperform many other solutions in Table 5. But above all, fusing RGB and point cloud data together through a cross-attention transformer achieves the best performance.

5 Conclusion

Unlike general methods relying solely on RGB image data for absolute scene pose estimation, this work proposes a novel multi-modal approach using cross-attention transformers for multi-scene absolute pose regression. By encoding both RGB and point cloud data and inputting them into separate transformer cross-attention modules, position and orientation information are obtained. This approach allows for the utilization of multi-modal information and aggregation of non-scene-specific features. Our method achieve state-of-the-art localization accuracy in both single-scene and multi-scene absolute regression methods on indoor datasets.

References

1. Balntas, V., Li, S., Prisacariu, V.: Relocnet: continuous metric learning relocalisation using neural nets. In: Proceedings of the European Conference on Computer Vision (ECCV), pp. 751–767 (2018)
2. Brachmann, E., et al.: Dsac-differentiable ransac for camera localization. In: Proceedings of the IEEE Conference on Computer Vision and Pattern Recognition, pp. 6684–6692 (2017)
3. Brachmann, E., Rother, C.: Learning less is more-6d camera localization via 3d surface regression. In: Proceedings of the IEEE Conference on Computer Vision and Pattern Recognition, pp. 4654–4662 (2018)
4. Carion, N., Massa, F., Synnaeve, G., Usunier, N., Kirillov, A., Zagoruyko, S.: End-to-end object detection with transformers (2020)
5. Dosovitskiy, A., et al.: An image is worth 16x16 words: transformers for image recognition at scale. arXiv preprint arXiv:2010.11929 (2020)
6. Glocker, B., Izadi, S., Shotton, J., Criminisi, A.: Real-time rgb-d camera relocalization. In: 2013 IEEE International Symposium on Mixed and Augmented Reality (ISMAR), pp. 173–179. IEEE (2013)
7. He, K., Zhang, X., Ren, S., Sun, J.: Deep residual learning for image recognition. In: Proceedings of the IEEE Conference on Computer Vision and Pattern Recognition, pp. 770–778 (2016)
8. Kendall, A., Cipolla, R.: Geometric loss functions for camera pose regression with deep learning. In: Proceedings of the IEEE Conference on Computer Vision and Pattern Recognition, pp. 5974–5983 (2017)

9. Kendall, A., Grimes, M., Cipolla, R.: Posenet: A convolutional network for real-time 6-dof camera relocalization. In: Proceedings of the IEEE International Conference on Computer Vision, pp. 2938–2946 (2015)
10. Laskar, Z., Melekhov, I., Kalia, S., Kannala, J.: Camera relocalization by computing pairwise relative poses using convolutional neural network. In: Proceedings of the IEEE International Conference on Computer Vision Workshops, pp. 929–938 (2017)
11. Melekhov, I., Ylioinas, J., Kannala, J., Rahtu, E.: Image-based localization using hourglass networks. In: Proceedings of the IEEE International Conference on Computer Vision Workshops, pp. 879–886 (2017)
12. Naseer, T., Burgard, W.: Deep regression for monocular camera-based 6-dof global localization in outdoor environments. In: 2017 IEEE/RSJ International Conference on Intelligent Robots and Systems (IROS), pp. 1525–1530. IEEE (2017)
13. Paszke, A., et al.: Pytorch: an imperative style, high-performance deep learning library. In: Advances in Neural Information Processing Systems, vol. 32, pp. 8024–8035. Curran Associates, Inc. (2019). http://papers.neurips.cc/paper/9015-pytorch-an-imperative-style-high-performance-deep-learning-library.pdf
14. Qi, C.R., Su, H., Mo, K., Guibas, L.J.: Pointnet: deep learning on point sets for 3d classification and segmentation. In: Proceedings of the IEEE Conference on Computer Vision and Pattern Recognition, pp. 652–660 (2017)
15. Sarlin, P.E., Cadena, C., Siegwart, R., Dymczyk, M.: From coarse to fine: robust hierarchical localization at large scale. In: Proceedings of the IEEE/CVF Conference on Computer Vision and Pattern Recognition, pp. 12716–12725 (2019)
16. Shavit, Y., Ferens, R.: Do we really need scene-specific pose encoders? In: 2020 25th International Conference on Pattern Recognition (ICPR), pp. 3186–3192. IEEE (2021)
17. Shavit, Y., Ferens, R., Keller, Y.: Learning multi-scene absolute pose regression with transformers. In: Proceedings of the IEEE/CVF International Conference on Computer Vision, pp. 2733–2742 (2021)
18. Su, W., et al.: Vl-bert: pre-training of generic visual-linguistic representations. arXiv preprint arXiv:1908.08530 (2019)
19. Touvron, H., Cord, M., Douze, M., Massa, F., Sablayrolles, A., Jégou, H.: Training data-efficient image transformers & distillation through attention. In: International Conference on Machine Learning, pp. 10347–10357. PMLR (2021)
20. Walch, F., Hazirbas, C., Leal-Taixe, L., Sattler, T., Hilsenbeck, S., Cremers, D.: Image-based localization using lstms for structured feature correlation. In: Proceedings of the IEEE International Conference on Computer Vision, pp. 627–637 (2017)
21. Wang, B., Chen, C., Lu, C.X., Zhao, P., Trigoni, N., Markham, A.: Atloc: attention guided camera localization. In: Proceedings of the AAAI Conference on Artificial Intelligence, vol. 34, pp. 10393–10401 (2020)
22. Wu, J., Ma, L., Hu, X.: Delving deeper into convolutional neural networks for camera relocalization. In: 2017 IEEE International Conference on Robotics and Automation (ICRA), pp. 5644–5651. IEEE (2017)
23. Xu, M., et al.: A critical analysis of image-based camera pose estimation techniques. arXiv preprint arXiv:2201.05816 (2022)
24. Zhu, X., Su, W., Lu, L., Li, B., Wang, X., Dai, J.: Deformable detr: Deformable transformers for end-to-end object detection. arXiv preprint arXiv:2010.04159 (2020)

MC-MLP: A Multiple Coordinate Frames MLP-Like Architecture for Vision

Zhimin Zhu[1], Jianguo Zhao[1], Tong Mu[1], Yuliang Yang[1(✉)], and Mengyu Zhu[2]

[1] School of Computer and Communication Engineering, University of Science and Technology Beijing, Beijing, China
yangbit@ustb.edu.cn

[2] School of Medical Technology, Beijing Institute of Technology, Beijing, China

Abstract. In deep learning, Multi-Layer Perceptrons (MLPs) have once again garnered attention from researchers. This paper introduces MC-MLP, a general MLP-like backbone for computer vision that is composed of a series of fully-connected (FC) layers. In MC-MLP, we propose that the same semantic information has varying levels of difficulty in learning, depending on the coordinate frame of features. To address this, we perform an orthogonal transform on the feature information, equivalent to changing the coordinate frame of features. Through this design, MC-MLP is equipped with multi-coordinate frame receptive fields and the ability to learn information across different coordinate frames. Experiments demonstrate that MC-MLP outperforms most MLPs in image classification tasks, achieving better performance at the same parameter level. The code will be available at: https://github.com/ZZM11/MC-MLP.

Keywords: Multiple Coordinate Frames · All-MLP Architecture · Orthogonal Transform · DCT · Hadamard Transform

1 Introduction

Recently, transformers have achieved remarkable success in various computer vision tasks [3–5, 14, 35, 43, 44, 46, 48]. The Multi-Head Self-Attention (MHSA) mechanism has powerful information learning ability and can model the long-term dependencies. Therefore, many network models based on MHSA have been proposed. However, most deep learning models focus on acquiring information from the spatial domain [10, 18, 24, 38, 39], or a single coordinate frame. Rao et al. [17, 20, 25, 32, 34, 37, 45, 47, 49] found that information can be learned through frequency transform and this method significantly improves the performance of the model. Frequency transform can also be considered as a coordinate transform.

We speculate that coordinate frames may affect the learning efficiency. Semantic information is highly abstract in Deep Neural Networks (DNN) and we cannot be sure that all information will be learned well under one coordinate frame. It is more reasonable that some semantic information may be more easily learned under one coordinate frame and some under another. One motivation is the coordinate frame. Dr. Hinton also

L. Iliadis et al. (Eds.): ICANN 2023, LNCS 14255, pp. 446–456, 2023.
https://doi.org/10.1007/978-3-031-44210-0_36

mentioned in an interview of the Wired magazine that coordinate frames play a rather important role in making visual observations perception for humans [33]. His words inspire us to use orthogonal transform to change the coordinate frame.

Orthogonal transforms mean changing the coordinate frames of features. DFT, DCT and Hadamard Transform are common orthogonal transform. In the transform domain, some information can be more effectively learned than in the spatial domain. According to this idea, we abstract the whole model into a general architecture called the multi-coordinate frame network, which does not adopt the MHSA. Our multi-coordinate mechanism is shown in Fig. 1. The proposed architecture is based on the MLP and the multi-coordinate frame transform, this layer consists of two key operations: Converts the input spatial features to the transform domain using the 2D DCT and Hadamard Transform, and concatenate the spatial features with the transform domain features. These two steps enable the proposed model to learn in both spatial and transform domain [11, 16, 27].

In this paper, we propose a new MLP block, named MC-Block, based on the multi-coordinate frame. By utilizing MC-Blocks, we construct a concise network called MC-MLP. Unlike complex MHSA structures, MC-MLP only requires a unique multiple coordinate frame structure and full connection layer to achieve the expected performance. We introduce a novel MLP in this work, where we employ Hadamard Transform and DCT to transform features from the spatial domain to the transform domain. By leveraging the concatenation and MLP operations, features can be more efficiently integrated from different domains. The transform domain features are the beneficial supplement of the spatial domain features. Such cross-domain information interaction can improve the learning ability of the model.

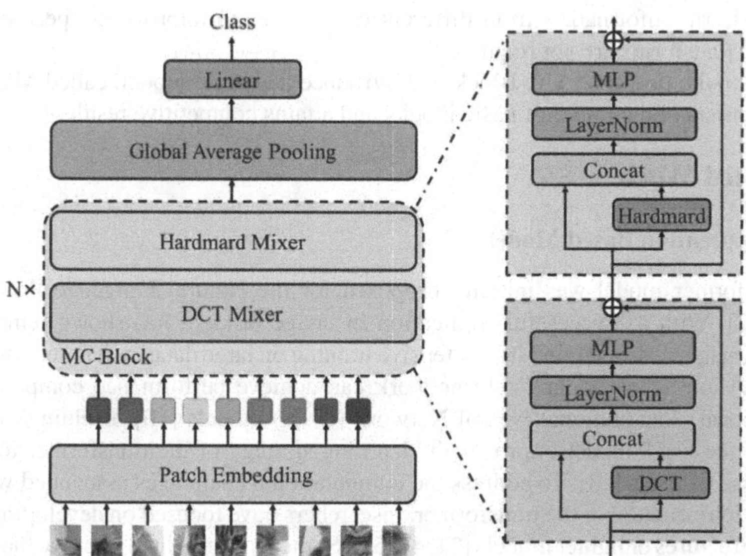

Fig. 1. The overall architecture of MC-MLP.

We use the DCT and Hadamard Transform as the method of multiple coordinate transform, and transform the spatial feature information into the transform domain. The transform domain information will not be limited by the spatial channels and can provide cross-channel information interaction. After obtaining the transform domain features, we concatenate the transform domain features and spatial domain features in the channel dimension, and feed into the full connection layer. With the joint learning and interaction of multi-domain feature information, the potential of the proposed model can be fully unleashed in the moderate parameters and complexity.

In a nutshell, we present a novel MLP-like model design approach that leverages multi-coordinate transform. This method effectively enhances the model's performance by incorporating multi-domain transform, providing more comprehensive understanding of features. By utilizing this approach, the proposed MC-MLP is able to improve its performance without introducing a complex architecture and the transform adopted in it has an efficient and fast algorithm.

Our experiments verified the MC-MLP's effectiveness on the CIFAR100 dataset [2]. The results showed that MC-MLP outperformed the recent ViT and MLP models under similar parameters and MACs. These findings indicate that MC-MLP can serve as a viable alternative to MLP models and CNNs in terms of efficiency, generalization ability, and robustness.

Our contributions are summarized as follows:

- Unlike many recent works that use self-attention to improve transformer models, we find that orthogonal transforms, along with the standard FC layer, can model various relationships in images.
- We propose a module design method that implements multi-coordinate transform. By incorporating DCT and Hadamard transforms as coordinate transforms, the proposed model learns information from different coordinates to improve the performance. Inverse transforms are not required.
- Based on the proposed MC-Block, we introduce a concise model, called MC-MLP, that consists of a number of basic blocks and attains competitive results.

2 Related Work

2.1 Self-attention Based Models

The transformer model was initially proposed for the Natural Language Processing (NLP) [42]. With its successful application in image tasks, it has shown remarkable results in image classification [40]. Extensive training on large datasets has demonstrated that the Vision Transformer (ViT) network can achieve performance comparable to the traditional Convolutional Neural Network (CNN) models [10]. Building on these advances, the DeiT model improves the learning strategy of the transformer to better handle large datasets [13]. To address the computational challenges associated with the self-attention structure of the transformer, researchers have focused on developing more efficient structures or lighter models [21, 41, 52]. Some have sought to improve the hybrid architecture by incorporating convolutional layers [9, 22, 36, 55]. Currently, scholars are exploring new token mixing mechanism to more efficiently exchange information, which could obviate the necessity for self-attention [50]. Despite transformers' achievements, their architecture can be intricate, prompting a growing interest in more streamlined models [15, 21, 29, 41, 52].

2.2 MLP-Like Models

Recently, MLP models have garnered renewed attention from researchers in the field of computer vision [6, 12, 23, 24, 37–39, 53, 54, 56]. The MLP-Mixer proposed by Google has demonstrated the potential of MLP models to become the next research paradigm, replacing the traditional CNNs and Transformers. MLP-Mixer and ResMLP both abandon the convolution and attention mechanism, relying solely on stacking two MLP layers: token-mixing MLP and channel-mixing MLP, while still achieving performance comparable to existing mainstream models [38, 39]. ViP and sMLP enhance the efficiency and functionality of MLPs by encoding feature representations along two axial dimensions [31, 56]. Another research trend involves building a complex receptive field through token mixing to improve the performance of MLP models [6, 12, 54]. For example, gMLP incorporates Spatial Gated Units (SGUs) to model attention mechanisms, resulting in competitive performance [24]. In Wave MLP, tokens are represented as wave functions with amplitude and phase, and a new token aggregation mechanism is proposed [37]. GFNet is a MLP-like architecture that leverages DFT or FFT, resulting in substantial performance gains [49]. This highlights the potential of orthogonal transform for further exploration. The proposed MC-MLP offers a novel token aggregation mechanism, which combines token mixing with the coordinate frame transform, providing a more flexible global modeling.

3 The Proposed Model

Figure 1 shows the overall architecture of MC-MLP. In summary, MC-MLP accepts a series of patch embeddings and keeps theirs feature dimension unchanged. It then applies N layers of MC-Blocks, each consisting of a Hadamard mixer block and a DCT mixer block. In this section, we introduce our design and describe each component in details.

In this paper, feature maps are represented by tensor $X \in R^{B \times N \times C}$, where B is the batch size, C is the sequence dimension, and N is the sequence length. First, we use a 2D orthogonal transform to convert the input 2D features:

$$Y = OT(X) \tag{1}$$

where OT represents a 2D orthogonal transform. In order to correctly complete the transform, it must be ensured that the sequence length (N) and sequence dimension (C) are integer powers of 2. The 2D orthogonal transform does not change the dimension of the feature vector, where the transformed vector $Y \in R^{B \times N \times C}$. Concatenating the original features and the transformed features, the new dimension is decided by the sequence Z:

$$Z = Y \oplus X \tag{2}$$

where $Z \in R^{B \times N \times 2C}$.

Finally, sequence Z feeds into a full connection layer where $LN(Z) = Z\prime$:

$$Z'' = MLP\left(Z'\right) + X \tag{3}$$

where LN is Layer Normalization, and MLP is a multi-layer perceptron. MLP can be formulated as follows:

$$MLP\left(Z'\right) = \sigma(W_2\sigma(W_1Z')) \tag{4}$$

where $W_1, W_2 \in R^{n\times(f\times n)}$. $f \times n$ means the width of the hidden layer.

Based on the aforementioned analysis, we propose two fundamental modules, namely the DCT Mixer and the Hadamard Mixer. These design paradigms are intended to improve the feature extraction and token aggregation capabilities of MLP models, thereby leading to the enhanced performance. By applying either a DCT or Hadamard transform to the input features, the transformed features can be concatenated and further processed via an MLP. The combination of orthogonal transform and MLP can efficiently extract and utilize feature information. The design of the proposed MC-MLP holds significant potential to substantially enhance the performance of MLP models and can serve as a crucial component in future MLP-based models.

3.1 DCT Mixer

The DCT Mixer is a critical component of the MC-Block. It utilizes the 2D DCT to convert the input features into another coordinate frame, effectively highlighting diverse and complementary information. The transformed features are then concatenated with those in the original domain and processed through a MLP for learning. This approach allows the MLP learning features represented from multiple coordinate frames, leading to improved performance. The implementation of the 2D DCT is achieved through two sequential one-dimensional DCT.

The 1D DCT can be perceived as the DFT of the input signal treated as a real even function. To convert the input signal to a real even function, it extends any input signal to a real even signal before applying DFT.

The formula for 1D DCT is as follows [51]:

$$F(k) = C(k)\sqrt{\frac{2}{N}}\sum\nolimits_{n=0}^{N-1} f(n)cos\frac{\pi(2n+1)k}{2N} \tag{5}$$

$$C(k) = \begin{cases} \frac{1}{\sqrt{2}}, k = 0 \\ 1, 1 \le k \le N-1 \end{cases} \tag{6}$$

where $f(n)$ is a discrete signal sequence and $0 \le n < N$. $C(k)$ is a constant determined by k.

For 2D discrete sequences such as images, let $f(i,j)$ be the image matrix of $M \times N$, and its 2D DCT formula is as follows [57]:

$$F(u,v) = c(u)c(v)\sum_{i=0}^{N-1}\sum_{j=0}^{M-1} f(i,j)cos\left[\frac{(i+0.5)\pi}{N}u\right]cos\left[\frac{(j+0.5)\pi}{M}v\right] \tag{7}$$

$$c(u) = \begin{cases} \sqrt{\frac{1}{N}}, u = 0 \\ \sqrt{\frac{2}{N}}, u \neq 0 \end{cases} \tag{8}$$

where $f(i,j)$ is a 2D discrete signal matrix and $0 \leq i < N, 0 \leq j < M$. $c(u)$ is a constant determined by u.

The specific calculation amount varies slightly depending on the specific algorithms, and the magnitude of the computation is $O(MNlog(MN))$ [8]. The specific process is illustrated in the figure below:

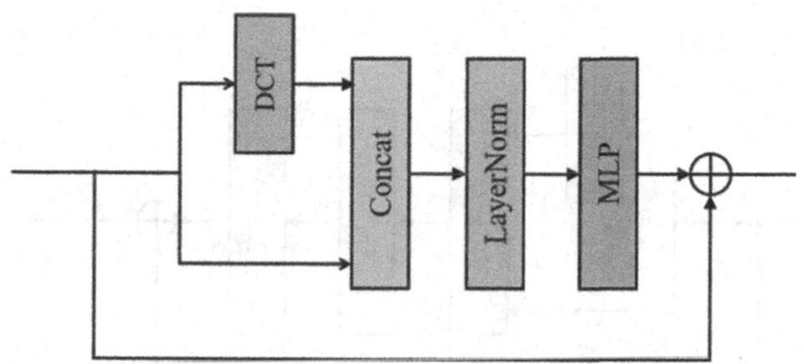

Fig. 2. The structure of DCT Mixer.

3.2 Hadamard Mixer

The Hadamard [1] mixer can be used as a complementary module to the DCT mixer, and it further enhances the overall performance of the model. This module embodies the multi coordinate frame learning principle introduced in this study. In principle, the 2D Hadamard transform is achieved by applying two separate 2D Hadamard matrices to the original feature matrix, one as a left-multiplication and the other as a right-multiplication. The fast Hadamard algorithm can significantly reduce the amount of computation.

The Hadamard transform is a non-sinusoidal transform that utilizes the Hadamard matrix as its transform formula. It concentrates information on the characteristic corners after transform. The Hadamard transform only requires addition or subtraction, without multiplication, resulting in low computational cost. The Hadamard matrix is an orthogonal matrix that consists of +1 and −1 elements. Its first-order Hadamard matrix is defined as:

$$H_1 = [1] \tag{9}$$

The second order Hadamard matrix is defined as

$$H_2 = \begin{bmatrix} 1 & 1 \\ 1 & -1 \end{bmatrix} \tag{10}$$

Higher order Hadamard matrix can be derived from lower order, namely:

$$H_N = H_{2^n} = H_2 \otimes H_{2^{n-1}} = \begin{bmatrix} H_{2^{n-1}} & H_{2^{n-1}} \\ H_{2^{n-1}} & -H_{2^{n-1}} \end{bmatrix} = \begin{bmatrix} H_{\frac{N}{2}} & H_{\frac{N}{2}} \\ H_{\frac{N}{2}} & -H_{\frac{N}{2}} \end{bmatrix} \tag{11}$$

The 2D Hadamard transform involves left-multiplying the original matrix by a Hadamard matrix of corresponding order and right-multiplying it by another Hadamard matrix of the same order, followed by division by the square of the order. The process is illustrated below:

$$W = \frac{H_n \otimes X \otimes H_n}{n^2} \tag{12}$$

Assuming that the dimensions of the input 2D data are $M \times N$, where M and N are both integer powers of 2, the computation of the Hadamard Fast Algorithm is $O(MNlog(MN))$. The specific process is shown in the figure below:

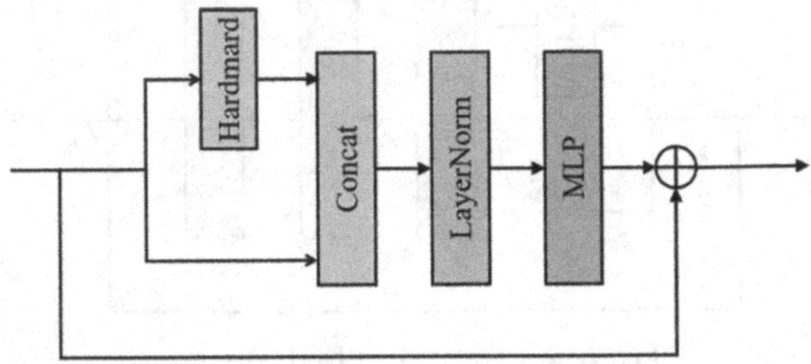

Fig. 3. The structure of Hadamard-Mixer.

4 Experiments

In this section, we present the experimental results and analysis. First, we will give the experimental configurations of the proposed MC-MLP. Then the results on the CIFAR-100 dataset are provided. At last, the ablation studies are presented to provide a deep understanding of the designs in it.

4.1 Experimental Configurations of MC-MLP

We utilized the PyTorch and TIMM code base to implement the proposed model and trained it on two NVIDIA Titan XP graphics cards [7]. The training was conducted for 400 epochs from scratch on the CIFAR-100 [2] dataset. We employed the AdamW optimizer [26] and set the initial learning rate to 0.01. The learning rate attenuation strategy employed was cosine attenuation with linear preheating. Throughout the training and testing phases, the input model image size remained fixed at 224 × 224.

The CIFAR-100 dataset comprises 60,000 32 × 32 color images containing 600 images each category. Each category includes 500 training images and 100 test images. During model training, we employed the Mixup and Cutmix data enhancement techniques. The specific super parameters for training are presented in the following Table 1:

Table 1. Hyperparameters for Image classification on CIFAR-100.

Hyperparameters	Settings
Learning Rate Scheduler	Cosine
Epochs	400
Warmup Epochs	3
Learning Rate	0.01
Optimizer	AdamW
Weight Decay	$1 \times e^{-5}$
Cutmix	0.4
Mixup	0.2

4.2 Results on CIFAR-100

The accuracy of Top-1 trained from scratch on CIFAR-100. The model parameters and calculation amount are as follows:

Table 2. Top-1 accuracy on CIFAR-100 without pre-training.

Architecture	Models	Parameters(M)	MACs(G)	Top-1(%)
CNN	ResNet-50 [19]	25.6	4.10	75.10
Transformer	ViT [10]	22.1	4.60	66.45
CNN-ViT	Conformer [30]	23.5	5.20	75.43
MLP	MLP-Mixer [38]	18.5	3.78	73.06
	ViP [28]	25.0	8.50	70.51
	AS-MLP [28]	28.0	4.40	65.16
	gMLP	24.5	5.56	64.80
	MC-MLP(ours)	24.1	6.00	77.60

As shown in Table 2 on CIFAR100 datasets. The result of ViP and AS-MLP was from the corresponding paper [28]. Other model results come from the training results of our GPU equipment. MC-MLP achieves the best accuracy of 77.6%, among all CNN, Transformer, CNN-ViT and MLP-like models on CIFAR100 with the 24.1M parameters and 6G MACs. In the case of MC-MLP, the configuration is determined experimentally. The hidden dimension is set to 256, the depth is set to 15, the dilation factor is set to 4 and the patch size is set to 14.

4.3 Ablation Study

In this subsection, we present ablation study results with MC-MLP to provide a deeper understanding of the proposed methods.

Table 3. The effects of different coordinate transforms.

Model	MC-Block	Top-1(%)
MC-MLP-D	DCT Mixer + DCT Mixer	76.40
MC-MLP-H	Hadamard Mixer + Hadamard Mixer	75.51
MC-MLP	DCT Mixer + Hadamard Mixer	77.60

In order to analyze the effect of different coordinate transforms, we construct different models composed of different MC-Blocks. MC-Blocks of MC-MLP-D are each consisting of two DCT Mixers. MC-Blocks of MC-MLP-H are each consisting of two Hadamard Mixers. MC-Blocks of MC-MLP are each consisting of a Hadamard mixer block and a DCT mixer block. As shown in the Table 3, We find MC-MLP is 1.2% and 2.09% higher than MC-MLP-D and MC-MLP-H at the same settings. By incorporating DCT and Hadamard transforms as coordinate transforms, the proposed model learns information from different coordinates better than single transform domain.

5 Conclusion

This paper introduces the MC-MLP architecture, which is a computationally efficient image classification model for vision tasks. Our proposed MC-Block replaces the self-attention sublayer with a combination of DCT and Hadamard transform. Transform completes the transformation of the coordinate frame of features, where the difficulty in learning features can vary across domains. Moreover, the computational cost of DCT and Hadamard transform is low, as fast algorithms exist.

Our architecture is highly efficient, benefiting from the multi-coordinate transform. Our experimental results demonstrate that MC-MLP is a competitive alternative to visual transformers, MLP-like models, and CNNs in terms of the accuracy/complexity trade-off. In the future, we will investigate the potential of MLP-like structures in different tasks further.

References

1. Ahmed, N., Rao, K.R., Bars, R., et al.: Orthogonal transform for digital signal processing. In: ICASSP (1976)
2. Krizhevsky, A., Hinton, G., et al.: Learning multiple layers of features from tiny images (2009)
3. Dosovitskiy, A., et al.: An image is Worth 16×16 words: transformers for image recognition at scale. arXiv:2010.11929 (2020)
4. Wu, B., et al.: Visual transformers: token-based image representation and processing for computer vision. arXiv:2006.03677 (2020)
5. Cheng, B., Schwing, A.G., Kirillov, A.: Per-pixel classification is not all you need for semantic segmentation. In: NIPS (2021)
6. Chen, S., (The University of Hong Kong, Hong Kong), Xie, E., Ge, C., Chen, R., Liang, D., Luo: CYCLEMLP: a MLP-like architecture for dense prediction. In: ICLR (2022)

7. Hendrycks, D., Gimpel, K.: Gaussian Error Linear Units (GELUs). arXiv:1606.08415 (2016)
8. Reisis, D., Vlassopoulos, N.: Conflict-free parallel memory accessing techniques for FFT architectures. In: IEEE Transactions on Circuits and Systems I: Regular Papers, pp. 3438–3447 (2008)
9. d'Ascoli, S., Touvron, H., Leavitt, M.L., Morcos, A.S., Biroli, G., Sagun: ConViT: improving vision transformers with soft convolutional inductive biases. Department of Physics, Ecole Normale Supérieure, Paris, France; arXiv:2103.10697 (2021)
10. Dosovitskiy, L., et al.: An image is worth 16 × 16 words: transformers for Image recognition at scale. In: ICLR (2021)
11. Baxes, G.A.: Digital Image Processing: Principles and Applications. John Wiley & Sons, Inc. (1994)
12. Guo, J., (Huawei Noah's Ark Lab.) et al.: Hire-MLP: vision MLP via hierarchical rearrangement. In: CVPR (2022)
13. Touvron, H., Cord, M., Douze, M., Massa, F., Sablayrolles, A., Jégou, H.: Training data-efficient image transformers and distillation through attention. In: PMLR pp. 10347–10357 (2021)
14. Touvron, H., Cord, M., Douze, M., Massa, F., Sablayrolles, A., Jégou, H.: Training data-efficient image transformers and distillation through attention. arXiv:2012.12877 (2020)
15. Radosavovic, I., Kosaraju, R.P., Girshick, R., He, K., Dollar, P.: Designing network design spaces. In: CVPR, pp. 10428–10436 (2020)
16. Pitas, I.: Digital Image Processing Algorithms and Applications. John Wiley & Sons (2000)
17. Lee, J.-H., Heo, M., Kim, K.-R., Kim, C.-S.: Single-image depth estimation based on fourier domain analysis. In: CVPR, pp. 330–339 (2018)
18. Yang, J., et al.: Focal self-attention for local-global interactions in vision transformers. arXiv: 2107.00641 (2021)
19. He, K., Zhang, X., Ren, S., Sun, J.: Deep residual learning for image recognition. In: CVPR, pp. 770–778 (2016)
20. Lee-Thorp, J., Ainslie, J., Eckstein, I., Ontañón, S.: FNet: mixing tokens with fourier transforms. In: NAACL 2021–2022 Conference of the North American Chapter of the Association for Computational Linguistics: Human Language Technologies, pp. 4296–4313 (2022)
21. Li, Y., et al.: MViTv2: improved multiscale vision transformers for classification and detection. In: CVPR (2022)
22. Li, Y., (Computer Vision Lab, ETH Zurich, Switzerland), Zhang, K., Cao, J., Timofte, R., van Gool, L.: LocalViT: bringing locality to vision transformers. arXiv:2104.05707 (2021)
23. Lian, D., (ShanghaiTech University, China), Yu, Z., Sun, X., Gao, S.: AS-MLP: an axial shifted MLP architecture for vision. In: ICLR (2022)
24. Liu, H., Dai, Z., So, D., Le, Q.: Pay attention to MLPs. In: NIPS (2021)
25. Liu, P., Zhang, H., Lian, W., Zuo, W.: Multi-level wavelet convolutional neural networks. In: IEEE Access, pp. 74973–74985 (2019)
26. Loshchilov, I., Hutter, F.: Decoupled weight decay regularization. arXiv:1711.05101 (2017)
27. Chi, L., Jiang, B., Mu, Y.: Fast fourier convolution. In: NIPS (2020)
28. Lv, T., Bai, C., Wang, C.: MDMLP: image classification from scratch on small datasets with MLP. arXiv:2205.14477 (2022)
29. Mehta, S., Ghazvininejad, M., Iyer, S., et al.: Delight: deep and light-weight transformer. arXiv:2008.00623 (2020)
30. Peng, Z., (University of Chinese, Academy of Sciences, Beijing, China), et al.: Conformer: local features coupling global representations for visual recognition. In: ICCV (2021)
31. Hou, Q., Jiang, Z., Yuan, L., Cheng, M.-M., Yan, S., Feng, J.: Vision permutator: a permutable MLP-like architecture for visual recognition. arXiv:2106.12368 (2021)
32. Qin, Z., Zhang, P., Wu, F., Li, X.: FcaNet: frequency channel attention networks. Source: In: The IEEE International Conference on Computer Vision, pp. 763–772 (2021)

33. Sabour, S., Frosst, N., Hinton, G.E.: Dynamic routing between capsules. In: NIPS, pp. 3857–3867 (2017)
34. Li, S., et al.: FALCON: a fourier transform based approach for fast and secure convolutional neural network predictions. In: CVPR, pp. 8705–8714 (2020)
35. Zheng, S., et al.: Rethinking semantic segmentation from a sequence-to-sequence perspective with transformers. arXiv:2012.15840 (2020)
36. Srinivas, A., (UC Berkeley), Lin, T.-Y., Parmar, N., Shlens, J., Abbeel, P., Vaswani, A.: Bottleneck transformers for visual recognition. In: CVPR (2021)
37. Tang, Y., et al.: An image patch is a wave: phase-aware vision MLP. In: CVPR, pp. 10925–10934 (2022)
38. Tolstikhin, I.O., et al.: MLP-mixer: an all-MLP architecture for vision. In: NIPS (2021)
39. Touvron, H., et al.: ResMLP: feedforward networks for image classification with data-efficient training. arXiv:2105.03404 (2021)
40. Vaswani, A., (Google Brain), et al.: Attention is all you need. arXiv:1706.03762 (2017)
41. Wang, W., et al.: Pyramid vision transformer: a versatile backbone for dense prediction without convolutions. In: ICCV, pp. 568–578 (2021)
42. Wolf, T., Debut, L., Sanh, V., et al.: HuggingFace's transformers: state-of-the-art natural language processing. arXiv:1910.03771 (2019)
43. Dong, X., et al.: CSWin transformer: a general vision transformer backbone with cross-shaped windows. arXiv:2107.00652 (2021)
44. Chen, X., Yan, B., Zhu, J., Wang, D., Yang, X., Lu, H.: Transformer tracking. In: CVPR (2021)
45. Xu, K., Qin, M., Sun, F., Wang, Y., Chen, Y.-K., Ren, F.: Learning in the frequency domain. In: CVPR, pp. 1737–1746 (2020)
46. Yu, X., Rao, Y., Wang, Z., Liu, Z., Lu, J., Zhou, J.: PoinTr: diverse point cloud completion with geometry-aware transformers. In: ICCV (2021)
47. Yang, Y., Soatto, S.: FDA: fourier domain adaptation for semantic segmentation. In: CVPR, pp. 4085–4095 (2020)
48. Rao, Y., Zhao, W., Liu, B., Lu, J., Zhou, J., Hsieh, C.-J.: DynamicViT: efficient vision transformers with dynamic token sparsification. In: NIPS (2021)
49. Rao, Y., Zhao, W., Zhu, Z., Lu, J., Zhou, J.: Global filter networks for image classification. arXiv:2107.00645 (2021)
50. Yu, W., Luo, M., Zhou, P., ct al.: MetaFormer is actually what you need for vision. In: CVPR (2022)
51. Rao, K.R., Yip, P.: Discrete Cosine Transform: Algorithms, Advantages, Applications. Academic press (2014)
52. Liu, Y.L., et al.: Swin transformer: hierarchical vision transformer using shifted windows. In: ICCV, pp. 10012–10022 (2021)
53. Zhang, W., Yin, Z., Sheng, Z., et al.: Graph attention multi-layer perceptron. arXiv:2206.04355 (2022)
54. Zhang, D.J., et al.: MorphMLP: an efficient MLP-like backbone for spatial-temporal representation learning. In: ECCV. National University of Singapore, Singapore, Singapore (2022)
55. Zhang, J., (Youtu Lab, Tencent, China) et al.: Rethinking mobile block for efficient neural models. arXiv:2301.01146 (2023)
56. Zhao, Y., Wang, G., Luo, C., Xie, W., Zeng, W., Tang, C., (Microsoft Research Asia, Beijing, China) et al.: Sparse MLP for image recognition: is self-attention really necessary? In: AAAI (2022)
57. Gonzalez, R.C., Woods, R.E.: Digital image Processing. N.J Prentice Hall, Upper Saddle River (2008)

Medical Image Segmentation and Saliency Detection Through a Novel Color Contextual Extractor

Xiaogen Zhou, Zhiqiang Li, and Tong Tong(✉)

College of Physics and Information Engineering,
Fuzhou University, Fuzhou, People's Republic of China
ttraveltong@gmail.com

Abstract. Image segmentation is a critical step in computer-aided system diagnosis. However, many existing segmentation methods are designed for single-task driven segmentation, ignoring the potential benefits of incorporating multi-task methods, such as salient object detection (SOD) and image segmentation. In this paper, we propose a novel dual-task framework for the detection and segmentation of white blood cells and skin lesions. Our method comprises three main components: hair removal preprocessing for skin lesion images, a novel color contextual extractor (CCE) module for the SOD task, and an improved adaptive threshold (AT) paradigm for the image segmentation task. We evaluate the effectiveness of our proposed method on three medical image datasets, demonstrating superior performance compared to representative approaches.

Keywords: Saliency detection · Medical image segmentation · Skin lesion segmentation · WBC segmentation

1 Introduction

Salient object detection (SOD) aims to localize the most visually attractive regions in images and videos, and it finds wide applications in various fields such as image segmentation [9,12,20,24,27]. SOD methods can be classified into bottom-up models that use hand-crafted features [8,11], top-down models that train on a large number of samples to capture high-level features, or a combination of both hand-crafted and high-level features.

Hand-crafted feature-based saliency detection approaches are commonly used for the SOD task to generate binary foreground regions, indicating the saliency likelihood of each pixel. For instance, contrast-based methods [8,11] utilize image contrast information for saliency detection. Although these methods improve SOD performance and effectively extract low-level features such as image color, contrast, edge, and texture from input images, they have limitations that they may miss small salient objects, introduce additional outliers, and fail to capture high-level semantic features. To address these issues, various deep convolutional

L. Iliadis et al. (Eds.): ICANN 2023, LNCS 14255, pp. 457–468, 2023.
https://doi.org/10.1007/978-3-031-44210-0_37

neural networks (DCNNs) for SOD have been proposed [22,25], which can encode more high-level feature representations compared to hand-crafted feature-based methods. DCNN-based saliency detection models mainly capture and integrate contextual information and high-level semantic features through spatial relations. While these DCNN-based methods achieve notable performance, they often require a large number of annotated images for training, which is a costly and labor-intensive procedure.

Furthermore, the saliency-based strategy has found extensive applications in various fields, including medical image processing and computer vision. Particularly, researchers have widely employed this strategy in conjunction with other methods for image segmentation tasks [3,6,10,14,15,19,23,26]. During the image segmentation stage, the saliency-based strategy is first applied to generate a saliency map, which highlights a target object or pixel relative to its neighbors. The resulting saliency map then provides localization information to enhance image segmentation performance. Moreover, the combination of visual saliency and active contour models was implemented in [13] to improve segmentation performance. However, these saliency-based methods may not accurately segment image objects with weak edges caused by color inhomogeneity. Additionally, hand-crafted feature-based biomedical image segmentation methods, such as saliency-based [8,9,11,12] and thresholding-based [3,6] methods, have limitations in producing fine-grained features and smoothed edges. Furthermore, they often rely on a fixed threshold to generate a binary image as the final result, considering only grayscale values above the threshold. While this strategy ensures that only high-quality feature maps are subject to the pre-defined thresholds, it overlooks other feature maps, especially those at adjacent threshold values.

Recently, with the advancement of DCNNs in medical image diagnosis, various DCNN-based medical image segmentation approaches have been proposed [1,21,22,25]. Although these DCNN-based segmentation models have achieved remarkable performance in image segmentation, they require a large amount of labeled images for training, which is a time-consuming and labor-intensive process. Moreover, these methods are usually designed to segment target objects in a single-task manner, neglecting the potential benefits of multi-task approaches that simultaneously address salient object detection (SOD) and image segmentation tasks.

To address the aforementioned issues, we propose a novel dual-task framework for medical image saliency detection and segmentation. The framework comprises a preprocessing step for hair removal in skin lesion images, a novel color contextual extractor module for the SOD task, and an improved adaptive threshold (AT) strategy for the image segmentation task. In the SOD stage, we introduce a novel color contextual extractor (CCE) module to extract hand-crafted features. The CCE module is composed of a novel color channel volume (CCV) block and a refined salient map (RSM) block. Firstly, the CCV block is applied to extract the region of interest (ROI) corresponding to the target object. Next, the RSM block generates a refined salient map from the extracted ROI. Finally, we propose a novel adaptive threshold (AT) strategy to automatically segment the target object from the refined salient map during the image segmentation stage. Our approach combines the benefits of the CCE module, which extracts hand-crafted features to enhance saliency detection, with the utilization of the refined salient map to provide localization information for effective segmentation of white blood cells (WBC) and skin lesions.

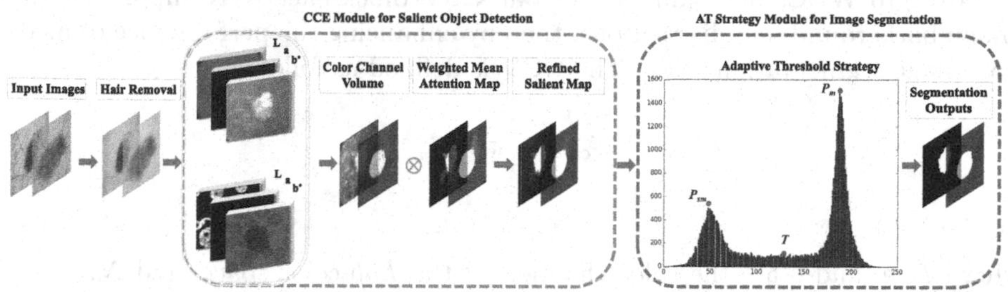

Fig. 1. Illustration of the proposed method, which consists of three main modules: hair removal preprocessing, color contextual extractor (CCE) module for the saliency object detection (SOD) task, and adaptive threshold (AT) strategy module for the segmentation task. Firstly, the CCE module is applied to generate a refined salient map (RSM). Subsequently, the AT strategy is employed to segment the target object based on the obtained salient map. Within the AT strategy module, the optimal threshold (T) is determined adaptively, the highest peak of the grey-level histogram is denoted as P_m, and the second highest peak of the grey-level histogram is denoted as P_{sm}. (Color figure online)

2 The Proposed Method

Figure 1 illustrates the architecture of our proposed method, which consists of three main modules: preprocessing for hair removal in skin lesion images, a color context extractor (CCE) module for the salient object detection (SOD) task, and an adaptive threshold (AT) strategy for the segmentation task. In the following sections, we provide detailed explanations of each module.

2.1 Preprocessing

To ensure accurate performance in skin lesion saliency detection and segmentation tasks, it is essential to address visual artifacts such as skin hairs. Therefore, in our proposed method, we incorporate a preprocessing step for hair removal using a dedicated hair removal algorithm [5].

2.2 CCE Module for Salient Object Detection

Color Channel Volume: We introduce a color context extractor (CCE) module, comprising a novel color channel volume (CCV) block and a refined salient map (RSM) block. The CCV block serves as a hand-crafted color feature extractor based on the *Lab* color space transformation, enabling effective extraction of features from the *Lab* color space. Our CCV block builds upon the color volume [11] and color space volume [8] techniques. It specifically addresses the localization and recognition challenges associated with white blood cells (WBCs) and skin lesions. By explicitly highlighting the regions of interest (ROIs) corresponding to WBCs and skin lesions, our CCV block effectively suppresses the image background and distractions, thereby enhancing the performance of medical image segmentation tasks. The CCV is defined as follows:

$$C_{cv} = \frac{2}{3}\pi Lab^*, \tag{1}$$

$$b^* = N_a + b, \tag{2}$$

where L, a, and b are the color channels of the *Lab* color space, and N_a has a range of values[0, 255] normalized by the color channel a.

Refined Salient Map Block: In order to obtain the region of interest (ROI) corresponding to the target object, we employ the CCV block. Additionally, we enhance the saliency map by incorporating a weighted mean attention map in conjunction with the CCV block, resulting in a refined salient map (RSM) extracted from the ROI. Our RSM block is an improvement over the work of Lou et al. [12], who proposed a novel color name space for the salient object detection (SOD) task by linearly combining a set of sequential attention maps.

To elaborate, we initially utilize the **im2c** function provided by [18] to generate a color name volume (CNV), denoted as $C = \{C_1, C_2, C_3, ..., C_{11}\}$. Each channel of the CNV, denoted as C_i (where $i \in [1, 11]$), represents a probabilistic 11-dimensional vector that maps the color representation of each pixel in an RGB image I. Each C_i is normalized to the range [0, 255] for subsequent thresholding operations. Subsequently, we binarize each C_i into n ($n \in [1, 11]$) boolean maps (BM) using the following function:

$$BM_i^j = Threshold(C_i, T_j), |T_j \in [0, 255] \tag{3}$$

Here, BM_i^j represents a boolean map obtained by applying the threshold T_j, which is determined using the Otsu method [16].

Following the generation of the boolean maps, we perform several morphological operations on BM_i^j, including closing, hole-filling, and connecting foreground regions, to derive an attention map A_i^j. Similar processing steps are also applied to the complement map of A_i^j, denoted as $\bar{A}_i^j$. Moreover, we compute the mean attention map $A_m(i)$ by averaging A_i^j and $\bar{A}_i^j$ [12]. All attention maps, including A_i^j and $\bar{A}_i^j$, contribute equally and are combined to form the weighted mean attention map $A_w(i)$, as proposed by Lou et al. [12].

Finally, we integrate the weighted mean attention map A_w with the color channel volume CCV to generate the refined salient map (RSM). The mean attention map $A_m(i)$, the weighted mean attention map A_w, and the refined salient map (RSM) can be computed using the following equations:

$$A_m(i) = \frac{1}{2n}\sum_{j=1}^{n}(A_i^j + \bar{A_i^j}), \tag{4}$$

$$A_w = \frac{1}{11}\sum_{i=1}^{11} A_m(i), \tag{5}$$

$$RSM = A_w \times C_{cv}. \tag{6}$$

2.3 AT Strategy for Image Segmentation

We can obtain the final salient map by performing the color context extractor (CCE) module. Subsequently, we employ an adaptive threshold (AT) strategy to segment the target object from the final salient map. Our AT strategy is an improvement upon Otsu's method [16], a nonparametric automatic threshold selection method for image segmentation. It utilizes only the zeroth- and first-order cumulative moments of the gray-level histogram. The segmentation result generated by the AT strategy effectively preserves edge and contour information.

The salient regions in the final salient map, produced by the CCE module, are highlighted while suppressing image background and distractions, thereby facilitating image thresholding segmentation. Furthermore, the AT strategy automatically selects an optimal threshold for image segmentation from the refined salient map. The detailed processes of the AT strategy are as follows:

Step 1: Calculate a gray-level histogram H from the refined salient map (RSM), and identify its peaks $\{P_1, P_2, ..., P_n\}$, where n represents the number of peaks in histogram H.

Step 2: Determine P_m and P_{sm} of the gray-level histogram H, corresponding to the gray-level of the highest and second highest peaks, respectively. P_m and P_{sm} are defined as follows:

$$P_m = \max_{1 \leq i \leq n} P_i, \tag{7}$$

$$P_{sm} = \max_{1 \leq i \leq n} P_i, (P_i \neq P_m) \tag{8}$$

- Step 3: Obtain an adaptive threshold T by the following formula:

$$T = \min_{P_{sm} \leq i \leq P_m} H(i), \tag{9}$$

where T denotes an adaptive threshold. T is a float value between 0 and 1.

- Step 4: Generate the final segmentation result through the obtained threshold T as follows:

$$AT_{seg}(x, y) = \begin{cases} 1, & \textit{if}\ RSM(x, y) > T \\ 0, & \textit{otherwise} \end{cases} \tag{10}$$

where AT_{seg} is the final segmentation results.

3 Experiment Results

3.1 Datasets

We utilized three medical image datasets to evaluate the performance of the proposed method in salient object detection and medical image segmentation.

ISIC-2016 Dataset: The ISIC-2016 dataset is sourced from the international skin imaging collaboration (ISIC) archive, and it comprises 900 dermoscopy images for training and 379 images for testing. Each image in the dataset has been labeled by experts to provide corresponding ground truth.

ISIC-2017 Dataset: The ISIC-2017 dataset is associated with a specific disease type and provides manual lesion segmentation for each image. It consists of 2000 training, 150 validation, and 600 testing dermoscopy images. The ground truth for each image is provided by expert manual segmentation.

SCISC Dataset: In addition to the above, we employed the publicly available SCISC dataset for our experiments. This dataset comprises 268 single WBC (white blood cell) images from human blood smears, including 51 neutrophils, 54 eosinophils, 56 basophils, 54 monocytes, and 53 lymphocytes. The dataset is divided into 185 training, 53 validation, and 30 testing images. Each image is paired with expert manual segmentation as the ground truth, which has been labeled by pathologists.

Implementation Details: In our experimental studies, we validated both the saliency object detection (SOD) and medical image segmentation tasks using two datasets: the ISIC-2017 dataset and the SCISC dataset. The proposed method was implemented using MATLAB R2018a. During the testing phase, the average processing time for the proposed method on a typical image was approximately 7 s. The testing was conducted on a PC equipped with an Intel i7 CPU running at 2.260 Hz.

Evaluation Metrics: To evaluate the effectiveness of our proposed method and other methods in saliency detection and image segmentation, we conducted experiments using several metrics, including F-measure, Precision, Recall, AUC, Dice, mIoU, F1-score, and pixel accuracy (PA).

Table 1. Quantitative saliency detection results of our method and other methods on the SCISC and the ISIC-2017 datasets.

Method	SCISC Dataset				ISIC-2017 Dataset			
	Fmeasure	Precision	Recall	AUC	Fmeasure	Precision	Recall	AUC
CNS [12]	0.888	0.878	**0.916**	0.892	0.709	0.741	0.787	0.843
FCB [11]	0.821	0.952	0.611	0.849	0.638	0.755	0.537	0.716
SPCA [3]	0.832	0.942	0.661	0.804	0.735	0.836	0.645	0.806
MSER [13]	0.812	0.832	0.633	0.784	0.638	0.831	0.694	0.631
SRIS [6]	0.811	0.812	0.631	0.752	0.714	0.728	0.759	0.703
STR [9]	0.867	0.946	0.723	0.797	0.619	0.681	0.754	0.748
Ours	**0.904**	**0.972**	0.781	**0.918**	**0.739**	**0.841**	**0.791**	**0.846**

Table 2. Quantitative segmentation results of our method and other methods on the SCISC and the ISIC-2017 datasets.

Methods	SCISC Dataset				ISIC-2017 Dataset			
	Dice	mIoU	F1-score	PA	Dice	mIoU	F1-score	PA
CNS [12]	**0.801**	0.711	0.666	0.888	0.794	0.7126	0.661	0.897
FCB [11]	0.783	0.702	0.663	0.831	0.807	0.803	0.741	0.805
SPCA [3]	0.767	0.691	0.651	0.861	0.756	0.659	0.594	0.875
MSER [13]	0.615	0.558	0.334	0.837	0.626	0.536	0.345	0.841
SRIS [6]	0.597	0.512	0.414	0.722	0.566	0.431	0.376	0.654
STR [9]	0.696	0.606	0.579	0.773	0.802	0.712	0.663	0.901
Ours	0.799	**0.717**	**0.672**	**0.895**	**0.878**	**0.809**	**0.789**	**0.944**

WBC Salient Object Detection Results: We compared our proposed method with other salient object detection (SOD) approaches, namely CNS [12], FCB [11], SPCA [3], MSER [13], SRIS [6], and STR [9]. We evaluated the SOD performance of these methods using four metrics: F-measure, Precision, Recall, and AUC. The quantitative comparison is presented in Table 1. Our proposed method achieves the best performance in terms of F-measure, Precision, and AUC on both datasets. For the SOD task on the SCISC dataset, our proposed method achieves F-measure, Precision, and AUC scores of 0.904, 0.972, and 0.918, respectively, outperforming other SOD methods. However, our proposed method falls slightly behind CNS [12] in terms of Recall, which achieves a score of 0.781. When compared to FCB [11], our proposed method demonstrates significant improvements, with an 8.3% increase in F-measure (from 0.821 to 0.904), a 2.0% increase in Precision (from 0.952 to 0.972), a 17.0% increase in Recall (from 0.611 to 0.781), and a 6.9% increase in AUC (from 0.849 to 0.918). These results demonstrate the effectiveness of our proposed CCE module for the WBC SOD task in blood smear images.

Skin Lesion Salient Object Detection (SOD) Results: On the ISIC-2017 dataset, our proposed method achieves superior results compared to other methods in skin lesion SOD. We obtain F-measure, Precision, Recall, and AUC scores of 0.7385, 0.8402, 0.791, and 0.846, respectively. When compared to FCB [11], our proposed method shows notable improvements, with a 10.04% increase in F-measure (from 0.6381 to 0.7385), an 8.6% increase in Precision (from 0.755 to 0.841), a 5.4% increase in Recall (from 0.737 to 0.791), and a 3.0% increase in AUC (from 0.816 to 0.846). These results indicate that the proposed CCV block and RSM block are beneficial for the skin lesion SOD task. Additionally, these outcomes are reasonable since the introduced CCV block enables the RSM block to focus more on target regions rather than the background.

WBC Segmentation Results: We further compared our proposed method with several segmentation approaches, including CNS [12], FCB [11], SPCA [3], MSER [13], SRIS [6], STR [9], FSD [7], SCOT [4], SLSS [1], SBLS [2], and SCS

[17]. We evaluated the segmentation performance of these methods using four metrics: Dice, mIoU, F1-score, Recall, and PA. The quantitative comparison is presented in Table 2. Our proposed method achieves the best segmentation performance on both medical image datasets in terms of mIoU, F1-score, and PA, demonstrating its competitive segmentation ability. On the SCISC dataset, our proposed method achieves Dice, mIoU, F1-score, and PA scores of 0.7988, 0.7167, 0.6722, and 0.8951, respectively, outperforming other medical image segmentation methods. However, our proposed method falls slightly behind CNS [12] in terms of Dice, achieving a score of 0.799. Compared to SPCA [3], our proposed method demonstrates improvements, with a 3.2% increase in Dice (from 0.767 to 0.799), a 2.6% increase in mIoU (from 0.691 to 0.717), a 2.1% increase in F1-score (from 0.651 to 0.672), and a 3.4% increase in PA (from 0.861 to 0.895). These results indicate that our AT strategy benefits WBC segmentation.

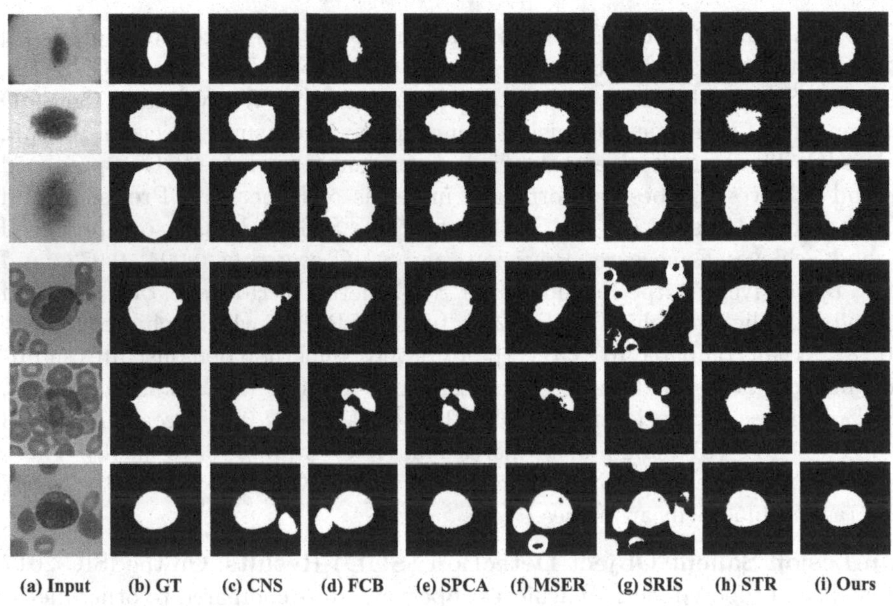

Fig. 2. Visual comparison of WBC and skin lesion segmentation results generated from several state-of-the-art methods, including our proposed method.

Skin Lesion Segmentation Results: On the ISIC-2017 dataset, our proposed method achieves higher accuracy in Dice (0.878), mIoU (0.809), F1-score (0.789), and PA (0.944) compared to other medical image segmentation methods. When compared with the SPCA method ch37b56, our method demonstrates significant improvement. Specifically, the Dice score increases from 0.756 to 0.878, representing a 12.2% increase; the mIoU improves from 0.659 to 0.809, a 15.0% increase; the F1-score improves from 0.594 to 0.789, a 19.5% increase; and the PA improves from 0.875 to 0.944, a 6.9% increase. These results clearly demonstrate the effectiveness of our proposed AT strategy for skin lesion segmentation.

Table 3. Quantitative skin lesion segmentation results of our proposed method with other methods on the ISIC-2016 dataset.

Methods	Dice	mIoU	F1-score	Recall
CNS [12]	0.851	0.601	**0.799**	0.734
FCB [11]	0.838	0.648	0.756	0.661
SRIS [6]	0.769	0.597	0.615	0.622
STR [9]	0.757	0.586	0.639	0.629
FSD [7]	0.856	–	–	0.799
SCOT [4]	0.818	–	–	0.747
SLSS [1]	0.74	–	–	0.628
SBLS [2]	0.839	–	–	–
SCS [17]	0.843	–	–	0.832
Ours (w/o hair remove)	0.853	0.653	0.778	0.842
Ours (w/ hair remove)	**0.883**	**0.678**	0.786	**0.853**

Additionally, on the ISIC-2016 dataset, our method achieves higher accuracy in Dice (0.883), mIoU (0.678), and Recall (0.786) compared to other comparison methods, except for the F-score, which is slightly lower than that of the CNS method [12] (0.786 vs 0.799). The results are summarized in Table 1. Notably, the incorporation of our hair removal strategy enhances the performance of skin lesion segmentation, improving the Dice, mIoU, F1-score, and Recall compared to the method without hair removal. This finding underscores the effectiveness of the hair removal strategy in enhancing the segmentation of skin lesions. Furthermore, these improvements can be attributed to the enhanced attention mechanism, which allows our proposed AT strategy to focus more on target regions rather than background and distractions in medical images.

Overall, the experimental results on both the ISIC-2017 and ISIC-2016 datasets demonstrate the superior performance of our proposed method for skin lesion segmentation. The significant improvements in accuracy metrics and the interpretability of the generated RSM highlight the effectiveness of our approach.

Visualization of WBC and Skin Lesion Segmentation Results: In our experiments, we presented visualizations of the segmentation results for skin lesions and WBC. Figure 2 illustrates a visual comparison of the segmentation results obtained from several state-of-the-art methods, including our proposed method. It is evident from the figure that our proposed method achieves the most favorable segmentation performance on the three biomedical image datasets, demonstrating its competitive ability in segmentation.

Visualization of WBC and Skin Lesion Salient Object Detection Results: We also provided visualizations of skin lesion and WBC salient object detection (SOD) results in our experiments. Figure 3 presents a visual comparison of the salient object detection results generated by our proposed method and other comparative methods. The figure demonstrates that our proposed method outperforms the other six methods in terms of SOD performance, as the salient region identified by our method closely aligns with the ground truth. However, there was a slight under-detection issue observed in row 5 of Fig. 3 (i).

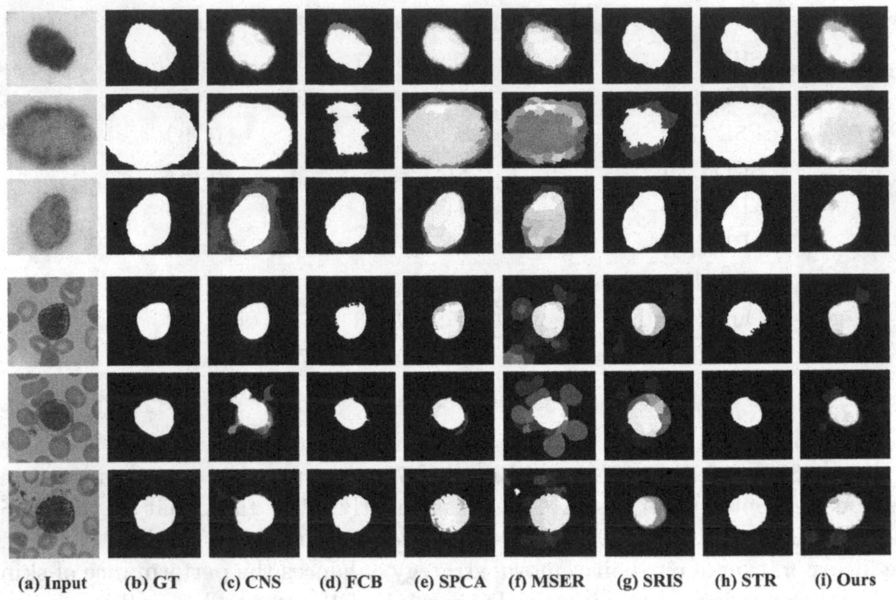

Fig. 3. Visual comparison of salient object detection results generated from several state-of-the-art methods, including our proposed method.

4 Conclusions

In this study, we propose a novel dual-task hand-crafted feature-based framework for WBC and skin lesion saliency detection and segmentation in medical images. Our framework consists of a novel color contextual extractor (CCE) module for the saliency object detection (SOD) task and a novel adaptive threshold (AT) strategy for image segmentation. The CCE module extracts hand-crafted features to significantly improve the SOD performance. Additionally, the salient map obtained from the SOD task provides valuable localization information for the subsequent segmentation task, facilitating the accurate segmentation of WBC and skin lesions. Experimental results demonstrate that our proposed method outperforms several state-of-the-art SOD and medical segmentation approaches. In this paper, we validate our proposed method using three public 2D medical image datasets, and we suggest the extension of this method to 3D data as a possible avenue for future research.

Acknowledgements. This work was supported by National Natural Science Foundation of China under Grant 62171133.

References

1. Ahn, E., et al.: Automated saliency-based lesion segmentation in dermoscopic images. In: 2015 37th Annual International Conference of the IEEE Engineering in Medicine and Biology Society (EMBC), pp. 3009–3012. IEEE (2015)
2. Ahn, E., et al.: Saliency-based lesion segmentation via background detection in dermoscopic images. IEEE J. Biomed. Health Inf. **21**(6), 1685–1693 (2017)
3. Bi, L., Kim, J., Ahn, E., Feng, D., Fulham, M.: Automated skin lesion segmentation via image-wise supervised learning and multi-scale superpixel based cellular automata. In: 2016 IEEE 13th International Symposium on Biomedical Imaging (ISBI), pp. 1059–1062. IEEE (2016)
4. Fan, H., Xie, F., Li, Y., Jiang, Z., Liu, J.: Automatic segmentation of dermoscopy images using saliency combined with OTSU threshold. Comput. Biol. Med. **85**, 75–85 (2017)
5. Huang, A., Kwan, S.Y., Chang, W.Y., Liu, M.Y., Chi, M.H., Chen, G.S.: A robust hair segmentation and removal approach for clinical images of skin lesions. In: 2013 35th Annual International Conference of the IEEE Engineering in Medicine and Biology Society (EMBC), pp. 3315–3318. IEEE (2013)
6. Joshi, A., Khan, M.S., Soomro, S., Niaz, A., Han, B.S., Choi, K.N.: Sris: saliency-based region detection and image segmentation of covid-19 infected cases. IEEE Access **8**, 190487–190503 (2020)
7. Khan, Z.N.: Frequency and spatial domain based saliency for pigmented skin lesion segmentation. arXiv preprint arXiv:2010.04022 (2020)
8. Li, Z., Lai, T., Zhou, X.: Saliency detection based on weighted saliency probability. In: 2019 IEEE Intl Conf on Parallel & Distributed Processing with Applications, Big Data & Cloud Computing, Sustainable Computing & Communications, Social Computing & Networking (ISPA/BDCloud/SocialCom/SustainCom), pp. 1550–1555. IEEE (2019)
9. Li, Z., Liu, G., Zhang, D., Xu, Y.: Robust single-object image segmentation based on salient transition region. Pattern Recogn. **52**, 317–331 (2016)
10. Lin, X., Zhou, X., Tong, T., Nie, X., Li, Z.: Sg-net: a super-resolution guided network for improving thyroid nodule segmentation. In: 2022 IEEE 24th International Conference on High Performance Computing & Communications; 8th Internatiional Conference on Data Science & Systems; 20th International Conference on Smart City; 8th International Conference on Dependability in Sensor, Cloud & Big Data Systems & Application (HPCC/DSS/SmartCity/DependSys), pp. 1770–1775. IEEE (2022)
11. Liu, G.H., Yang, J.Y.: Exploiting color volume and color difference for salient region detection. IEEE Trans. Image Process. **28**(1), 6–16 (2019)
12. Lou, J., et al.: Exploiting color name space for salient object detection. Multim. Tools Appl. **79**(15), 10873–10897 (2020)
13. Lou, J., Zhu, W., Wang, H., Ren, M.: Small target detection combining regional stability and saliency in a color image. Multim. Tools Appl. **76**(13), 14781–14798 (2017)
14. Nie, X., Zhou, X., Li, Z., Wang, L., Lin, X., Tong, T.: Logtrans: providing efficient local-global fusion with transformer and CNN parallel network for biomedical image segmentation. In: 2022 IEEE 24th International Conference on High Performance Computing & Communications; 8th International Conference on Data Science & Systems; 20th International Conference on Smart City; 8th International Conference on Dependability in Sensor, Cloud & Big Data Systems & Application (HPCC/DSS/SmartCity/DependSys), pp. 769–776. IEEE (2022)

15. Nie, X., et al.: N-net: a novel dense fully convolutional neural network for thyroid nodule segmentation. Front. Neurosci. **16**, 872601 (2022)
16. Otsu, N.: A threshold selection method from gray-level histograms. IEEE Trans. Syst. Man Cybern. **9**(1), 62–66 (1979)
17. Ramella, G.: Saliency-based segmentation of dermoscopic images using colour information. Comput. Methods Biomech. Biomed. Eng. Imag. Vis. **10**(2), 172–186 (2022)
18. Van De Weijer, J., Schmid, C., Verbeek, J.: Learning color names from real-world images. In: 2007 IEEE Conference on Computer Vision and Pattern Recognition, pp. 1–8. IEEE (2007)
19. Wang, L., et al.: A multi-scale densely connected convolutional neural network for automated thyroid nodule classification. Front. Neurosci. **16**, 878718 (2022)
20. Zheng, H., Zhou, X., Li, J., Gao, Q., Tong, T.: White blood cell segmentation based on visual attention mechanism and model fitting. In: 2020 International Conference on Computer Engineering and Intelligent Control (ICCEIC), pp. 47–50. IEEE (2020)
21. Zhou, X., Li, Z., Tong, T.: DM-net: a dual-model network for automated biomedical image diagnosis. In: Research in Computational Molecular Biology: 27th Annual International Conference, RECOMB 2023, Istanbul, 16–19 April 2023, Proceedings, LNCS, pp. 74–84. Springer, Cham (2023). https://doi.org/10.1007/978-3-031-29119-7_5
22. Zhou, X., et al.: Cuss-net: a cascaded unsupervised-based strategy and supervised network for biomedical image diagnosis and segmentation. IEEE J. Biomed. Health Inf. **27**(5), 2444–2455 (2023)
23. Zhou, X., Li, Z., Wang, C.: Color space volume and superpixel based leukocyte image segmentation. In: 2019 10th International Conference on Information Technology in Medicine and Education (ITME), pp. 84–88. IEEE (2019)
24. Zhou, X., et al.: Leukocyte image segmentation based on adaptive histogram thresholding and contour detection. Curr. Bioinf. **15**(3), 187–195 (2020)
25. Zhou, X., et al.: H-net: a dual-decoder enhanced FCNN for automated biomedical image diagnosis. Inf. Sci. **613**, 575–590 (2022)
26. Zhou, X., Tong, T., Zhong, Z., Fan, H., Li, Z.: Saliency-CCE: exploiting colour contextual extractor and saliency-based biomedical image segmentation. Comput. Biol. Med. **154**, 106551 (2023)
27. Zhou, X., Wang, C., Li, Z., Zhang, F.: Adaptive histogram thresholding-based leukocyte image segmentation. In: Advances in Intelligent Information Hiding and Multimedia Signal Processing: Proceedings of the 15th International Conference on IIH-MSP in conjunction with the 12th International Conference on FITAT, 18–20 July 2020, Jilin, vol. 2, pp. 451–459. Springer, Singapore (2020). https://doi.org/10.1007/978-981-13-9710-3_47

MedNet: A Dual-Copy Mechanism for Medical Report Generation from Images

Peng Nie[1] and Xinbo Liu[2](✉)

[1] Guangdong University of Science and Technology, Dongguan, China
[2] College of Information and Intelligence, Hunan Agricultural University, Changsha, China
xinbo_liu@hnu.edu.cn

Abstract. Generating medical reports from images is a complex task in the healthcare domain. Existing approaches often rely on predefined templates to retrieve sentences and do not take into account the hierarchical structure of medical reports. Additionally, they overlook the selective copying of input sequences to output sequences.

To address these challenges, we propose MedNet, a generation-based model that employs a dual-copy mechanism to automatically generate medical reports from images. Our methodology involves first extracting features from images using an image encoder. Next, we use a dual-copy mechanism as the sequence encoder for retrieved reports to combine word generation in the decoder with bi-copying subsequences from the input sequence and placing them appropriately. Finally, a language decoder generates coherent and informative reports.

We evaluate our MedNet on two public datasets, Open-I and MIMIC-CXR, and demonstrate that it outperforms current state-of-the-art methods. Our approach not only improves the quality of the generated reports but also allows for flexible generation, making it well-suited for a variety of healthcare applications. The proposed dual-copy mechanism in our approach enables the utilization of both integral tokens and sub-tokens, enhancing the accuracy and relevance of generated reports. Our work represents a significant step forward in the field of automated medical report generation from images.

1 Introduction

The generation of medical reports from pathology images is a crucial and demanding task that requires considerable time and expertise from physicians. Writing reports manually can be a tedious and error-prone process, leading to potential inaccuracies in patient diagnoses and treatment. To address these challenges, researchers have developed advanced machine learning techniques to automate the report generation process. These methods help physicians save time by eliminating the need for manual report writing and improve the accuracy of medical reports by leveraging the vast amounts of data available in pathology

L. Iliadis et al. (Eds.): ICANN 2023, LNCS 14255, pp. 469–481, 2023.
https://doi.org/10.1007/978-3-031-44210-0_38

images. Furthermore, the integration of machine learning-based report generation systems into clinical practice can enhance patient care and lead to more efficient diagnosis and treatment planning. With the continued development and refinement of these systems, physicians can expect to see increased efficiency and accuracy in their daily workflow, ultimately benefiting patients and healthcare systems alike.

Previous studies have investigated two distinct types of techniques for automatic medical report generation: generation-based and retrieval-based. Retrieval-based methods, which can be seen in HRGR-Agent [7] and KEPP [6], employ pre-existing templates to create standard reports from a predetermined database. However, the quality of the reports produced is highly dependent on the template database's manual curation. With the successful use of deep learning in various fields, including text representation, signal processing, and image analysis [3,14,17], medical researchers have recently begun to explore the application of these techniques in report generation. Models such as LRCN [4], CoAtt [5], MvH+AttL [21], and MedWriter [20] utilize image encoders to extract features from medical images and text decoders to generate reports. However, these methods struggle to generate diverse descriptions and accurately depict rare but significant medical findings. On the other hand, retrieval-based techniques such as HRGR-Agent and KEPP still rely on memorized templates, limiting their accuracy due to a reliance on manually curated databases and the lack of coarse-to-fine retrieval learning.

We present a solution to address the aforementioned challenges by introducing a new framework called `MedNet`, which utilizes a Dual-Copy generation approach and hierarchical retrieval to automatically generate medical reports for given medical images. The proposed framework, illustrated in Fig. 1, is inspired by how physicians generate medical reports in real life. Our approach involves keeping rare names and templates with retrieved medical reports and placing them in the correct positions in the generated reports.

To fuse the semantics between medical images and retrieved medical reports, we introduce the image report attention mechanism. The `MedNet` framework retrieves report-level reports from the NNGen module, and to ensure the accuracy of rare medical nouns, we propose a Dual-copy mechanism (DCM) module that can generate tokens from the vocabulary and copy both integral tokens and sub-tokens from the input. Finally, we use two-level transformer decoders to fuse the DCM module for generating diverse medical reports accurately.

Our contributions can be summarized as follows:

- We propose a coarse-to-fine retrieved report representation that captures relevant reports for given medical images and facilitates medical image description generation.
- We design a novel decoder model for medical image report generation that employs transformer with a dual copy mechanism to exploit both whole tokens and sub-tokens.
- We conduct an extensive experiment that compares our approach with state-of-the-art methods on two large-scale medical report generation datasets,

namely Open-I and MIMIC-CXR. Our approach outperforms state-of-the-art methods on ROUGE-L, BLUEs, and CIDEr metrics.

In conclusion, our proposed MedNet framework provides an effective and efficient solution to automatically generate medical reports from medical images, and our experimental results demonstrate its superiority over existing state-of-the-art methods.

2 Approach

As shown in Fig. 1, we propose a new framework called MedNet, which consists of two main parts. The **Nearest Neighbour Report Retrieval Generator (NNGen)** module works on retrieving similar medical report for given images. The **Dual Copy** module works on retrieving a series of candidates that are most likely to be predicted or copied. Finally, MedNet generates accurate, diverse, and disease-specified medical reports by a dual copy mechanism medical report decoder that fuses the visual, linguistics and pathological information by NNGen and FAG modules.

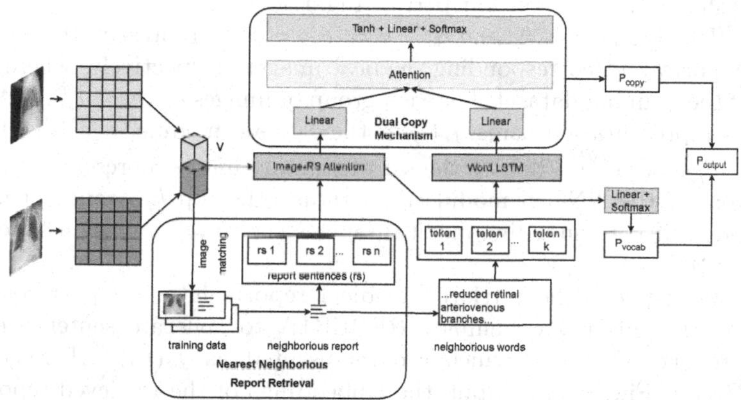

Fig. 1. Architecture of proposed MedNet for medical report generation. There are two main parts in the architecture, one is a module for retrieving the nearest neighbours' report and the other is a dual copy mechanism module for generating rare professional medical words.

2.1 Initial Image Embedder

The input of the NNGen module is a series of pairs of medical images and corresponding report $(\{I_i\}_{i=1}^b, r)$ where $\{I_i\}_{i=1}^b$ consists of b images and r represents medical report. We leverage a Convolution Neural Network (CNN) $f_v(\cdot)$ as the image encoder to obtain the feature of a given medical image I_i, i.e., $v_i = f_v(I_i)$, where v_i is the representation for the *i-th* image I_i.

Given a pair of images and one report $(\{I_i\}_{i=1}^{b}, r)$, we obtain virtual features $\{I_i\}_{i=1}^{b}$, then we add them together as the input of MedNet, which is added and fused by Eq. 1:

$$Avg_{(\{\mathbf{I}_i\}_{i=1}^{b}} = W\left(\sum_{i=1}^{b} v_i/b + bias\right) \tag{1}$$

where W and $bias$ are the weight and bias in a full connected layer.

2.2 NNGen: Nearest Neighbours Generator

Nearest Report. We discovered that the medical images in the majority of good reports exhibit lexical similarity to one or more images in the training dataset. Building on this finding, we propose an approach that is faster and more direct, called the Nearest Neighbor Generator (NNGen), for automatically generating medical reports from medical images. Our methodology is based on the nearest neighbor algorithm and does not require a training phase. To generate a medical report for a new image, NNGen finds the image in the training set with the closest embeddings to the new image, i.e., the nearest neighbor. It then outputs the medical report of the nearest neighbor as the generated medical report, as shown in the lower-left part of Fig. 1.

Let $\mathcal{D}^{(tr)}r = r_j j = 1^{N_{tr}}$ and $\mathcal{I}^{(tr)}c = c_j j = 1^{N_{tr}}$ represent the set of all training reports and corresponding medical images, respectively, where N_{tr} is the size of the training dataset. For each group of images c_j $(c_j = I_{i\,i=1}^{\;b})$, MedNet obtains its representation using $f_v(\cdot)$ in the NNGen module, which is denoted as $c_j = f_v(c_j)$. Let $\mathcal{C}^{N_{j=1}^{tr}}$ denote the set of training image representations.

The goal of the NNGen module is to return the top k_r groups of medical images and their corresponding medical reports $(\hat{r}j^{k_r}j = 1)$, given a set of medical images $\mathbf{I}i^b i = 1$.

Next, we segment the retrieved medical reports into n report sentences, denoted as rs. Initially, we employ REBERTA to generate sentence embeddings of report sentences, which are represented as $f_r(rs)$, where $f_r(\cdot) = REBERTA(\cdot)$. Finally, we obtain the embeddings of the retrieved report sentences, denoted as $\boldsymbol{rs}$=$\boldsymbol{rs_1}$, $\boldsymbol{rs_2}$,$\cdots$,$\boldsymbol{rs_n}$.

Image Report Sentence Attention (IRSA). After computing the embeddings for images, $\boldsymbol{v}$, and the vector representation for report sentences, $\boldsymbol{rs_1}$, $\boldsymbol{rs_2}$,$\cdots$,$\boldsymbol{rs_n}$, using f_v and f_r, respectively, we concatenate them to obtain the image-report-sentence representation, $\boldsymbol{VRS}$=$\boldsymbol{v}$, $\boldsymbol{rs}$ =$\boldsymbol{v}$, $\boldsymbol{rs_1}$, $\boldsymbol{rs_2}$,$\cdots$,$\boldsymbol{rs_n}$.

The self-attention (SA) mechanism, introduced in the basic module in Transformers [15], uses three projected matrices $\boldsymbol{Q} \in \mathbb{R}^{d_q \times d_q}$, $\boldsymbol{K} \in \mathbb{R}^{d_k \times d_k}$, and $\boldsymbol{V} \in \mathbb{R}^{d_v \times d_v}$ to compute an output that is the weighted sum of the input by attention score:

$$SA(\boldsymbol{Q},\boldsymbol{K},\boldsymbol{V}) = softmax(\frac{\boldsymbol{Q}\boldsymbol{K}^{\mathrm{T}}}{\sqrt{d}})\boldsymbol{V}$$
$$s.t. \quad \begin{bmatrix}\boldsymbol{Q}\\ \boldsymbol{K}\\ \boldsymbol{V}\end{bmatrix} = \boldsymbol{VRS}\begin{bmatrix}\boldsymbol{W}^{Q}\\ \boldsymbol{W}^{K}\\ \boldsymbol{W}^{V}\end{bmatrix} \tag{2}$$

The input sequence for the self-attention module is $\boldsymbol{VRS} = \boldsymbol{v}, \boldsymbol{rs_1}, \boldsymbol{rs_2}, \cdots,$ $\boldsymbol{rs_n}$, where $\boldsymbol{rs}_i \in \mathbb{R}^d$, and d represents the dimension of the hidden state. The matrices $\boldsymbol{W}^Q \in \mathbb{R}^{d\times d_q}$, $\boldsymbol{W}^K \in \mathbb{R}^{d\times d_k}$, and $\boldsymbol{W}^V \in \mathbb{R}^{d\times d_v}$ are the learnable parameter matrices of the self-attention component. We set $d_q = d_k = d_v = d$ following previous works [12,15,22]. Thus, the previous equation can be rephrased as:

$$\boldsymbol{z}_i = \sum_{j=1}^{n} \frac{\exp(\alpha_{ij})}{\sum_{k=1}^{n}\exp(\alpha_{ik})}((\boldsymbol{rs}_j \ or \ v)\boldsymbol{W}^V)$$
$$s.t. \quad \alpha_{ij} = \frac{(\boldsymbol{x}_i\boldsymbol{W}^Q)(\boldsymbol{x}_j\boldsymbol{W}^K)^{\mathrm{T}}}{\sqrt{d}} \tag{3}$$

where $\boldsymbol{z}_i$ is the output of $\boldsymbol{rs}_i$ and $\boldsymbol{v}$ calculated by self-attention operation.

Then, we obtain updated embeddings for $\boldsymbol{VRS}$. After that, we utilize $\boldsymbol{Avg}$ operation to obtain the average embedding of $\boldsymbol{VRS}$ as the output of this module.

2.3 Decoder

The decoder is built on the top of a transformer architecture with a novel dual copy mechanism for both integral tokens and sub-tokens.

Transformer Layer. To generate the output sequence of retrieved reports, we use the decoder component of the transformer architecture [17],?. The decoder consists of multi-head self-attention, multi-head attention over the encoder output, and a fully-connected feed-forward network.

We denote the output of the encoder as X_e, where $X_e = X^L$ for better illustration. The decoder determines each token in the retrieved reports iteratively, taking into account both the output of the encoder X_e and the tokens generated so far. At each step of generating the k-th token, we denote the output of the decoder as x_d^k (i.e., $x_d^k \in \mathcal{R}^{d_x}$), which can be computed using Eq. 3. To represent the output generated by the decoder up to the $k-1$-th token, we use X_d^{k-1}.

$$x_d^k = Transformer(X_e, X_d^{k-1}) \tag{4}$$

We introduce the detailed computation process of the transformer. First, the transformer computes multi-head self-attention (a_d^k), which is the concatenation of multiple single attentions $a_d^k(i)$, representing the weighted sum of the previously generated output X_d^{k-1}, as shown in Eq. 5. The projection parameters are denoted by $W_Q(i) \in \mathcal{R}^{d_x\times d_x}$, $W_K(i) \in \mathcal{R}^{d_x\times d_x}$, $W_V(i) \in \mathcal{R}^{d_x\times d_x}$, and $W_O(i) \in \mathcal{R}^{d_x\times hd_x}$, where h represents the number of heads.

$$a_d^{k(i)} = W_{V(i)} X_d^{k-1} \cdot SF$$
$$SF = softmax(\frac{(X_d^{k-1})^T W_{K(i)}^T \cdot W_{Q(i)} x_d^{k-1}}{\sqrt{d_x}}) \tag{5}$$
$$a_d^k = W_O [a_{d(1)}^k; a_{d(2)}^k; \cdots ; a_{d(h)}^k]$$

Third, a_e^k passes a fully connected feed-forward network to get the output x_d^k, as shown in the following equation. $W_1 \in \mathcal{R}^{d_x} \times d_x$, $W_2 \in \mathcal{R}^{d_x} \times d_x$, $b_1 \in \mathcal{R}^{d_x}$, $b_2 \in \mathcal{R}^{d_x}$ are trainable parameters.

$$x_d^k = W_2 \cdot max(0, W_1 a_e^k + b_1) + b_2 \tag{6}$$

x_d^k is then fed to a linear layer and transformed into a $|V|$-dimension vector o_v^k in shown in following equation. $|V|$ denotes the size of the vocabulary and $W_v \in \mathcal{R}^{|V| \times d_x}$ is a trainable parameter.

$$o_v^k = W_v x_d^k \tag{7}$$

Finally, the decoder computes the probability of each token in the vocabulary being chosen as the next token by using a softmax layer on o_v^k. The probability distribution across the vocabulary is denoted by p_v^k, where $p_v^k(i)$ represents the probability of selecting the i-th token. This can be computed as follows:

$$p_v^k(i) = \frac{exp\{o_v^k(i)\}}{\Sigma_{j=1}^{|V|} exp\{o_v^k(i)\}} \tag{8}$$

2.4 Dual Copy Mechanism (DCM)

To effectively use both whole tokens and sub-tokens during the generation of commit messages, we propose a dual copy mechanism and incorporate it into the decoder. With this mechanism, when generating each token in the commit message, candidate tokens can be selected not only from the vocabulary but also from the whole tokens or sub-tokens in the input.

Specifically, in the k-th iteration, we compute the probability of each input token being copied based on the current decoder output (x_d^k). In `MedNet`, we select the input token that is most similar to x_d^k with the highest probability of being copied. The similarity between x_d^k and an input token (i.e., a token in the retrieved words from the nearest medical report) can be computed as the sum of its embedding vector x_e^j and the output of the decoder x_d^k, as shown in Eq. 9. The parameters $W_1 \in \mathcal{R}^{d_x \times d_x}$, $W_2 \in \mathcal{R}^{d_x \times d_x}$, and $v \in \mathcal{R}^{d_x}$ are learnable.

$$s_k(j) = v^T \tanh(W_1 x_d^k + W_w x_e^j) \tag{9}$$

The similarity of the k-th token (s_k) is then fed into a softmax layer, which generates the probability of each input token being copied, i.e., $p_c^k = softmax(s_k)$.

At the end of the iteration, we combine the probability distribution across the vocabulary tokens (i.e., p_v^k) and the probability distribution across input tokens (i.e., p_c^k) as shown in Eq. 11. The parameters g are learned according to the output of the decoder, as shown in Eq. 10. Here, $w \in \mathcal{R}^{1 \times d_x}$ is the learnable parameter. In this way, the k-th token selected in the commit message can be a token from the vocabulary or copied from the input.

$$g = \frac{1}{1 + exp\{wx_d^k\}} \tag{10}$$

$$p^k = [g * p_v^k; (1 - g) * p_c^k] \tag{11}$$

3 Related Work

Generation-based Report Generation. Visual captioning is the process of generating a textual description given an image or a video. The dominant neural network architecture of the captioning task is based on the encoder-decoder framework [1,10,16], with attention mechanism [5,7,9,18]. As a sub-task in the medical domain, early studies directly apply state-of-the-art encoder-decoder models as CNN-RNN [4], LRCN [4] and AdaAtt [5]to medical report generation task. To further improve long text generation with domain-specific knowledge, later generation-based methods introduce hierarchical LSTM with co-attention [5] or use the medical concept features [6] to attentively guide the report generation. On the other hand, the concept of reinforcement learning [8] is utilized to ensure the generated radiology reports correctly describe the clinical findings.

To avoid generating clinically non-informative reports, external domain knowledge like knowledge graphs [8,21] and anchor words [2] are utilized to promote the medical values of diagnostic reports. CLARA [2] also provides an interactive solution that integrates the doctors' judgment into the generation process.

Retrieval-based Report Generation. Retrieval-based approaches are usually hybridized with generation-based ones to improve the readability of generated medical reports. For example, KERP [6] uses abnormality graphs to retrieve most related sentence templates during the generation. HRGR-Agent [7] incorporates retrieved sentences in a reinforcement learning framework for medical report generation. However, they all require a template database as the model input. Different from these models, MedWriter is able to automatically learn both report-level and sentence-level templates from the data, which significantly enhances the model's applicability.

4 Experimental Design

We discuss the research questions (cf. Sect. 4.1), and present the baselines (cf. Sect. 4.3), the datasets (cf. Sect. 4.2), and the metrics (cf. Sect. 4.4).

Table 1. Automatic evaluation on the Open-i and MIMIC-CXR datasets.

Dataset	Type	Model	CIDEr (%)	Rouge-L (%)	BLEU-1 (%)	BLEU-2 (%)	BLEU-3 (%)	BLEU-4 (%)	AUC (%)
Open-i	Generation	CNN-RNN [4]	29.4	30.7	21.6	12.4	8.7	6.6	42.6
		LRCN [4]	28.5	30.7	22.3	12.8	8.9	6.8	–
		Tie-Net [19]	27.9	22.6	28.6	16.0	10.4	7.4	–
		CoAtt [5]	27.7	36.9	45.5	28.8	20.5	15.4	70.7
		MvH+AttL [21]	22.9	35.1	45.2	31.1	22.3	16.2	6.8
	Retrieval	V-L Retrieval	14.4	31.9	39.0	23.7	15.4	10.5	63.4
		HRGR-Agent [7]	34.3	32.2	43.8	29.8	20.8	15.1	–
		KERP [6]	28.0	33.9	48.2	32.5	22.6	16.2	–
		MedWriter [20]	34.5	38.2	47.1	33.6	23.8	16.6	81.4
		MedNet	**38.3**	**42.6**	**49.1**	**34.9**	**25.5**	**19.8**	**85.3**
MIMIC-CXR	Generation	CNN-RNN [4]	24.5	31.4	24.7	16.5	12.4	9.8	47.2
		CoAtt [5]	23.4	27.4	41.0	26.7	18.8	14.4	74.5
		MvH+AttL [21]	26.4	30.9	42.4	28.2	20.3	15.3	73.8
	Retrieval	V-L Retrieval	18.6	23.2	30.6	17.9	11.6	7.6	57.9
		MedWriter [20]	30.6	33.2	43.8	29.7	21.6	16.4	83.3
		MedNet	**42.3**	**36.5**	**50.2**	**34.9**	**27.5**	**21.3**	**87.8**

Table 2. User study conducted by two domain experts

Method	Realistic Score	Relevant Score
Ground Truth	3.85	3.82
MedWriter	3.68	3.44
MedNet	3.76	3.71

Table 3. Automatic evaluation on the Open-i and MIMIC-CXR datasets.

Dataset	Model	CIDEr (%)	Rouge-L (%)	BLEU-1 (%)	BLEU-2 (%)	BLEU-3 (%)	BLEU-4 (%)
Open-i	MedNet w/o ISRA	30.25	33.5	32.6	17.3	12.4	9.8
	MedNet w/o DCM	34.7	35.6	31.9	19.8	19.7	15.5
	MedNet	**38.3**	**42.6**	**49.1**	**34.9**	**25.5**	**19.8**
MIMIC-CXR	MedNet w/o ISRA	32.2	30.1	39.6	21.4	20.5	16.5
	MedNet w/o DCM	38.2	33.3	43.2	30.5	23.1	19.3
	MedNet	**42.3**	**36.5**	**50.2**	**34.9**	**27.5**	**21.3**

4.1 Research Questions

- **RQ-1**: *How effective is* MedNet *in generating medical reports?*
- **RQ-2**: *What is the impact of the key design choices on the performance of* MedNet*?*

4.2 Datasets

The **Open-i** dataset contains 7,470 chest X-rays along with 3,955 reports. However, only samples with both frontal and lateral views and complete findings/impression sections in reports, totaling 2,902 cases and 5,804 images, were used in the experiments.

On the other hand, the **MIMIC-CXR** dataset has a much larger scale, with 377,110 chest X-rays linked to 227,827 radiology reports, which are further

Table 4. Examples of ground-truth and generated reports by MedWriter and `MedNet`. bold phrases are medical abnormality terms that generated and ground-truth reports have in common. Bold terms are common descriptions of normal tissues. The text in italics is the opposite meaning of the generated report and the actual report.

Frontal Image - Lateral Image	Ground Truth	MedWriter	MedNet
	emphysematous changes. resolution of prior **right midlung** infiltrate. previous h UNKi is normal in size and contour. lungs are clear. **no focal consolidation pneumothorax or pleural effusion**. interval h UNKi of previously described right midlung opacity suggesting resolved h UNKi process. **lungs are hyperexpanded** with flattened diaphragms. h UNKi and soft tissue are unremarkable.	hyperexpanded lungs. UNK right upper lobe h UNKi . no focal pneumonia. the cardiome diastinal silhouette is normal in size and contour. **negative for focal consolidation pneumothorax or large pleural effusion**. negative for acute bone abnormality	The **lungs are hyperexpanded** with UNK in the right upper lobe and **right midlung**. **No focal pneumonia is present**. The cardiovascular silhouette is normal in size and contour. No focal consolidation, pneumothorax, or large pleural effusion is present. No acute bone abnormality is detected.
	chest. **large nodule at the right lung base** that probably represents a granuloma although not it is not h UNKi calcified. **there is a <UNK> mm nodule in the right lower** lobe that is relatively dense but not <UNK> calci-fied on the corresponding rib series. there are probably right hilar calcified lymph <UNK> . lungs otherwise are clear. **there is no pleural effusion**. left ribs. no fracture or focal bony destruction.	right upper lobe pneumonia.consideration may be given for primary or <UNK> . **recommend ct of the chest may be helpful for further diagnosis**. in the interval a 3 cm <UNK> mass has developedin the right lower lobe. **nopneumothorax or pleural effusion**. the mediastinal contours are normal	**There is a large nodule at the base of the right lung** which is likely to be a granuloma, however, it is not highly calcified. There is a dense nodule in the **right lower lobe measuring <UNK> mm**, which is not significantly calcified on the corresponding rib series. There are probably calcified lymph nodes in the right hilum. The lungs are otherwise clear **with no pleural effusion**. No fractures or focal bony destruction is noted in the left ribs.

divided into subsets. By applying the same sample selection criteria, we are left with 71,386 reports and 142,772 images to work with.

4.3 Baselines

We compare four state-of-the-art image captioning models (CNN-RNN [4], CoAttn [5], MvH+AttL [21], and V-L Retrieval) on two datasets.

4.4 Metrics

We use CIDEr, ROUGE-L, BLUE, and AUC scores as evaluation metrics to evaluate performance achieved by different methods on the test sets of Open-i and MIMIC-CXR.

CIDEr is a metric used to evaluate the quality of image captions by computing the similarity between the generated caption and the reference captions provided by human annotators. It takes into account the consensus among the reference captions and uses TF-IDF scores of the n-grams to form a consensus vector representing the relevance of each n-gram to the reference captions. The similarity between the consensus vector of the generated caption and that of the reference captions is computed using cosine similarity.

$$\text{CIDEr} = \frac{\text{CIDEr}_{\text{gen}}}{\text{CIDEr}_{\text{ref}}},$$
$$\text{where} \quad \text{CIDEr}_{\text{gen}} = \frac{1}{M}\sum_{i=1}^{M}\frac{1}{n_i^2}\sum_{j=1}^{n_i}\text{TF-IDF}_{i,j}\gamma_{i,j}, \tag{12}$$
$$\text{CIDEr}_{\text{ref}} = \frac{1}{M}\sum_{i=1}^{M}\text{TF-IDF}_i^{\max}$$

Here, M is the number of images, n_i is the number of n-grams in the generated caption for image i, TF-IDFi, j is the TF-IDF score of the j-th n-gram in the generated caption for image i, $\gamma i, j$ is a function that measures the consensus between the reference captions for the j-th n-gram in the generated caption for image i, and $\text{TF-IDF}_i^{\max}$ is the maximum TF-IDF score among all reference captions for image i.

ROUGE [13] is one set of metrics for comparing automatic generated text against the reference (human-produced) ones. We focus on ROUGE-L which computes the Longest Common Subsequence.

$$ROUGE - n = \frac{\sum_{n-grams \in Ref} Count_{match}(n - gram)}{\sum_{n-grams \in Ref} Count(n - gram)} \tag{13}$$

BLEU [11] is a classical metric to evaluate the quality of machine translations. It measures how many word sequences from the reference text occur in the generated text and uses a (slightly modified) n-gram precision to generate a score.

$$BP = \begin{cases} 1, & if\ len_{pred} > len_{ref} \\ e^{1-len_{ref}len_{pred}} & if\ len_{pred} \le len_{ref} \end{cases} \tag{14}$$

where len_{pred} is the length of the predicted sentence, and len_{ref} is the length of reference sentence, each n-gram w_n is set to $\frac{1}{N}$. ROUGE

5 Experiment Result

5.1 RQ1: Overall Performance and Comparison with SOTAs

As shown in Table 1, we make the following observations. First, compared with Generation-based model, Retrieval-based model that uses the template reports as results has set up a relatively strong baseline for medical report generation. Second, compared with V-L retrieval, other Retrieval-based approaches perform much better in terms of all the metrics. This again shows that that by integrating the information retrieval method into the deep sequence generation framework, we can not only use the retrieved language information as templates to help generate long sentences, but also overcome the monotony of only using the templates as the generations. Finally, we see that the proposed `MedNet` achieves the highest language scores on 6/6 metrics on Open-i datasets and all metrics on MIMIC-CXR among all methods. MedNet not only improves current SOTA model MedWriter on Open-i in average and significantly improves the performance, even without using manually curated template databases. This illustrates the effectiveness of automatically learning templates and adopting hierarchical retrieval in writing medical reports.

Human Evaluation. We evaluated the quality of the generated reports through a user study. 50 samples from the Open-i test set were selected and evaluated by two experienced radiologists on the realism and relevance of the generated reports compared to ground-truth reports and MvH+AttL. Ratings were given on a scale of 1 to 5, with higher scores indicating better performance. Table 2 shows the average results of the human evaluation of MedNet, Ground Truth reports, and MedWriter, evaluated in terms of realism and relevance. The results show that MedNet outperforms the baseline model and approaches the performance of Ground Truth reports written by experienced radiologists, indicating that MedNet can generate accurate and comparable clinical reports to domain experts.

5.2 RQ2: Ablation Study

Removing the ISRA Module. ISRA is short for "Image Report Sentence Attention". As shown in Table 3, the performance of MedNet w/o ISRA reduce a lot on all metrics on both Open-i and MIMIC-CXR datasets. Specially, with ISRA, MedNet improve 21.14%, 21.36% on metric CIDEr and Rouge-L on Open-i, respectively. This demonstrates that "Image Report Sentence Attention" is capable in sketching out the semantic between images and medical reports. The rest of the report generation is largely influenced by semantic interaction of images and medical reports.

Removing the DCM Module. DCM is short for "Dual Copy Mechanism". Similar to MedNet w/o ISRA, without using dual copy mechanism (DCM), MedNet w/o leads a great decease of average evaluation scores more than 20% compare with the full model, which is indicated in Table 3. This verifies that the DCM module plays an essential role in generating long and coherent clinical reports.

6 Qualitative Analysis

The results of MedNet and the baseline models on the Open-i dataset are displayed in Table 4. Compared to MedWriter, tool not only generates longer reports but also accurately identifies the medical findings in the images (highlighted in red and bold). Additionally, tool offers supplementary suggestions and descriptions that are not present in the original report but have diagnostic significance. This is due to the memory retrieval mechanism that integrates prior medical knowledge to enhance the generation process.

7 Conclusion

The problem of generating reports from medical images is a challenging task in the healthcare field. In this work, we introduce a new tool, called `MedNet`, which integrates a dual-copy mechanism with a generation-based architecture for medical report generation. `MedNet` uses an image encoder to extract features from medical images, a dual-copy mechanism as the sequence encoder for retrieved reports, and a language decoder to generate meaningful medical reports. The experiments conducted on Open-I and MIMIC-CXR datasets show that `MedNet` outperforms the state-of-the-art methods.

Acknowledgement. This work was supported in part by the Hunan Provincial Department of Education Scientific Research Outstanding Youth Project (Grant NO: 21B0200), in part by the Hunan Provincial Natural Science Foundation Youth Fund Project (Grant NO: 2023JJ40333), in part by the General Project of the Natural Science Foundation of Hunan Province (Grant NO: 2022JJ30308).

References

1. Bahdanau, D., Cho, K., Bengio, Y.: Neural machine translation by jointly learning to align and translate. arXiv preprint arXiv:1409.0473 (2014)
2. Biswal, S., Xiao, C., Glass, L.M., Westover, B., Sun, J.: Clara: clinical report auto-completion. In: Proceedings of The Web Conference 2020, pp. 541–550 (2020)
3. Devlin, J., Chang, M.W., Lee, K., Toutanova, K.: Bert: pre-training of deep bidirectional transformers for language understanding. arXiv preprint arXiv:1810.04805 (2018)
4. Donahue, J., et al.: Long-term recurrent convolutional networks for visual recognition and description. In: Proceedings of the IEEE Conference on Computer Vision and Pattern Recognition, pp. 2625–2634 (2015)
5. Jing, B., Xie, P., Xing, E.: On the automatic generation of medical imaging reports. arXiv preprint arXiv:1711.08195 (2017)
6. Li, C.Y., Liang, X., Hu, Z., Xing, E.P.: Knowledge-driven encode, retrieve, paraphrase for medical image report generation. In: Proceedings of the AAAI Conference on Artificial Intelligence, vol. 33, pp. 6666–6673 (2019)
7. Li, Y., Liang, X., Hu, Z., Xing, E.P.: Hybrid retrieval-generation reinforced agent for medical image report generation. In: Advances in Neural Information Processing Systems, vol. 31 (2018)
8. Liu, G., et al.: Clinically accurate chest x-ray report generation. In: Machine Learning for Healthcare Conference, pp. 249–269. PMLR (2019)
9. Lu, J., Xiong, C., Parikh, D., Socher, R.: Knowing when to look: adaptive attention via a visual sentinel for image captioning. In: Proceedings of the IEEE Conference on Computer Vision and Pattern Recognition, pp. 375–383 (2017)
10. Mao, J., Xu, W., Yang, Y., Wang, J., Huang, Z., Yuille, A.: Deep captioning with multimodal recurrent neural networks (M-RNN). arXiv preprint arXiv:1412.6632 (2014)
11. Papineni, K., Roukos, S., Ward, T., Zhu, W.J.: Bleu: a method for automatic evaluation of machine translation. In: Proceedings of the 40th Annual Meeting of the Association for Computational Linguistics, pp. 311–318 (2002)

12. Peng, H., Li, G., Wang, W., Zhao, Y., Jin, Z.: Integrating tree path in transformer for code representation. In: Advances in Neural Information Processing Systems, vol. 34 (2021)
13. Rouge, L.C.: A package for automatic evaluation of summaries. In: Proceedings of Workshop on Text Summarization of ACL, Spain (2004)
14. Tang, X., Zhu, R., Sun, T., Wang, S.: Moto: Enhancing embedding with multiple joint factors for Chinese text classification. In: 2020 25th International Conference on Pattern Recognition (ICPR), pp. 2882–2888. IEEE (2021)
15. Vaswani, A., et al.: Attention is all you need. In: Advances in Neural Information Processing Systems, vol. 30 (2017)
16. Vinyals, O., Toshev, A., Bengio, S., Erhan, D.: Show and tell: a neural image caption generator. In: Proceedings of the IEEE Conference on Computer Vision and Pattern Recognition, pp. 3156–3164 (2015)
17. Wang, S., Tang, D., Zhang, L., Li, H., Han, D.: Hienet: bidirectional hierarchy framework for automated ICD coding. In: Bhattacharya, A., et al. (eds.) Database Systems for Advanced Applications - 27th International Conference, DASFAA 2022, Virtual Event, 11–14 April 2022, Proceedings, Part II. LNCS, vol. 13246, pp. 523–539. Springer, Cham (2022). https://doi.org/10.1007/978-3-031-00126-0_38
18. Wang, W., Chen, Z., Hu, H.: Hierarchical attention network for image captioning. In: Proceedings of the AAAI Conference on Artificial Intelligence, vol. 33, pp. 8957–8964 (2019)
19. Wang, X., Peng, Y., Lu, L., Lu, Z., Summers, R.M.: Tienet: text-image embedding network for common thorax disease classification and reporting in chest x-rays. In: Proceedings of the IEEE Conference on Computer Vision and Pattern Recognition, pp. 9049–9058 (2018)
20. Yang, X., Ye, M., You, Q., Ma, F.: Writing by memorizing: hierarchical retrieval-based medical report generation. arXiv preprint arXiv:2106.06471 (2021)
21. Yuan, J., Liao, H., Luo, R., Luo, J.: Automatic radiology report generation based on multi-view image fusion and medical concept enrichment. In: Shen, D., et al. (eds.) MICCAI 2019, Part VI. LNCS, vol. 11769, pp. 721–729. Springer, Cham (2019). https://doi.org/10.1007/978-3-030-32226-7_80
22. Zügner, D., Kirschstein, T., Catasta, M., Leskovec, J., Günnemann, S.: Language-agnostic representation learning of source code from structure and context. In: 9th International Conference on Learning Representations, ICLR 2021, Virtual Event, Austria, 3–7 May 2021 (2021)

Ms-AMPool: Down-Sampling Method for Dense Prediction Tasks

Shukai Yang[1], Xiaoqian Zhang[1,2](✉), Yufeng Chen[1], and Lei Pu[1]

[1] School of Information Engineering, Southwest University of Science and Technology, Mianyang 621010, China
zhxq0528@163.com

[2] Tianfu Institute of Research and Innovation, Southwest University of Science and Technology, Mianyang 621010, China

Abstract. In recent years, CNN-based neural networks have continuously proven to have good performance in the field of computer vision. Dense prediction tasks (object detection and image segmentation), as fundamental tasks in the field of computer vision, the CNN models currently designed for them rely mainly on the construction of multi-scale information. Pooling layer, as a low-cost down-sampling component for building such models, effectively saves the number of model parameters and computational effort. The existing mainstream pooling methods not only lose a lot of effective feature information during down-sampling, but also do not perform multi-scale fusion of feature information during down-sampling, which greatly affects the final performance of the network. To this end, we propose an adaptive mixed pooling method. It is designed to allow the network to achieve adaptive mixing of pooling methods by learning the relevant weight parameters, so that the network can retain as much valid feature information as possible when down-sampling. Further, we construct a multi-scale adaptive mixed pooling method that can ensure that the network performs adaptive fusion of multi-scale feature information when down-sampling. We have conducted related experiments in yolo series object detection network as well as UNet and UNeXt image segmentation networks, and the results show the superiority of our method compared to other mainstream pooling methods for performance and parametric balance in dense prediction tasks.

Keywords: Neural networks · Object detection · Image segmentation · Down-sampling · Pooling

1 Introduction

Dense prediction tasks are fundamental tasks in computer vision, which mainly include Object Detection [7,17,25] and image segmentation [5,18,20], etc. These tasks require a characteristic representation for pixel-level complex scene understanding. In recent years, models based on deep convolutional neural networks have shown good performance in these tasks.

L. Iliadis et al. (Eds.): ICANN 2023, LNCS 14255, pp. 482–494, 2023.
https://doi.org/10.1007/978-3-031-44210-0_39

The mainstream object detection network model [12,13,24]. Its structure is to extract the feature information to the original image by a generic feature extractor, and then to identify the object location as well as the object class by combining the corresponding region suggestions or feeding directly to the corresponding detection head. Since the detected objects are not uniform in size, the multi-scale information of the images is extremely important for the object detection task. For example, SSD [17] directly uses feature maps of different sizes in the feature extractor to detect objects of different sizes, respectively. YOLO [23] used the FPN [15] structure to construct a multi-scale feature network. Distinct from the top-down structure of FPN, PANET [16] introduces a bottom-up path, which makes it easier for the bottom information to be transmitted to the top of the higher levels. Mainstream image segmentation models, such as UNet [20], and its variants [9,10,28], mostly use an encoder-decoder structure for multi-scale model construction. The original image is reduced by the encoder to obtain feature information at different scales, and then the feature map size is up-sampled to the original image size by the decoder to obtain the final segmentation result.

Most of the above mentioned models have to take multiple down-sampling modules as the basic components of the multi-scale feature extractor. Their down-sampling serves to reduce the feature map size to reduce the number of model parameters and to increase the perceptual field. It is well known that the perceptual field is very important for dense prediction tasks, which enables the network to establish more distant dependencies when detecting and segmenting a certain object. The commonly used down-sampling methods generally include convolutional down-sampling with a step number greater than 1 and pooled down-sampling. Specifically, [7,13] taking convolution with steps larger than 1 as the down-sampling method, which not only increases the number of network parameters significantly, but also causes over-fitting to some extent. In contrast, using pooling as a down-sampling method to reduce the feature dimension of the convolutional layer output can effectively reduce the network parameters while also preventing over-fitting, and also suppressing noise and reducing information redundancy.

The mainstream pooling methods [14,19] use the same pooling operation for all feature regions in the feature map. unfortunately, such methods ignore the variability of different regions of the feature map. The pooling methods [26,27] using some randomness parameter can be used as a network regularization term, and this type of method can optimize the over-fitting problem but somehow reduces the robustness of the network. To address these shortcomings, pooling methods [4,6] using learnable parameters have been proposed successively. [6] proposed a new pooling method from the perspective of local importance, which can learn adaptive and discriminative feature maps to summarize down-sampled features. [4] adjusts the pooling tendency of the network by learning parameter p and performing power operation on each value in the feature region. For the dense prediction task, all the pooling methods described above do not perform the fusion between multi-scale information at the time of down-sampling, thus losing multi-scale information to a large extent. Although [8,11] designed pooling methods for object detection networks, the role of these pooling methods is limited to improving network efficiency and solving problems such as inconsistent input image resolutions, and they have not been used for downsampling.

To comprehensively address the shortcomings of existing methods, we first propose an adaptive mixed pooling method, which can adaptively focus on the importance of different pooling operations on different feature channels by fusing multiple pooling operations. Based on this, we design a multi-scale adaptive mixed pooling down-sampling module for object detection and image segmentation tasks that rely on multi-scale information. It mainly allows the network to perform adaptive fusion of adaptive mixed pooling operations for different kernel sizes during down-sampling, so as to reduce the loss of feature information and increase the multi-scale information fusion capability of the network during down-sampling. In summary, the main contributions of this work are:

- We design an adaptive mixed pooling method to reduce the loss of feature information in the network during down-sampling by mixing the filtering characteristics of different pooling methods.
- We design a multi-scale adaptive mixed pooling down-sampling method based on adaptive mixed pooling. It simultaneously mixes filtering characteristics of different pooling and feature information of different scales, and this fusion can be performed adaptively.
- We perform multiple sets of ablation experiments on several generic detection and segmentation networks to demonstrate the effectiveness of our method.

2 The Proposed Method

2.1 Adaptive Mixed Pooling (AMPool)

According to existing research, different pooling methods have different contributions when downsampling the same feature region. For example, max pooling can generally reduce the offset of the estimated mean caused by the parameter error of the convolutional layer, and mainly extract the edge texture information of the object. Average pooling can suppress the increase of the variance of the estimate caused by the limited neighborhood size, and retain more background information of the image. For the same feature map, if only one filtering method is used, the same filtering operation will act on each feature channel indiscriminately. And each feature channel contains different feature information, such indiscriminate filtering will lead to some useful feature information loss. Therefore, the main idea of this work is to make each feature channel have a filter that adapts to its channel characteristics when downsampling. We first propose a multi-branch adaptive hybrid pooling method AMxPool, where 'x' represents the combination of different pooling methods. Its formula is as follows:

$$MF(z) = \lambda z + b \tag{1}$$

$$Y_n = \sum_{k=1}^{s} MF_{kn}(P_k(C_n)) \tag{2}$$

where $P_k(.)$ denotes the kth pooling operation performed, and these pooling methods can be selected for any combination of max pooling, average pooling, median pooling, etc. s is the number of combined pooling methods selected, and C_n denotes the nth feature channel in the input feature map. $MF_{kn}(.)$ represents applying the mixing factor of the nth feature channel corresponding to the kth pooling filter to that feature channel, where λ and b are the mixing factors, which will adaptively change with the training of the network. After adding the multi-channel features after the action of the mixing factor, we get the adaptive mixed output Y_n of the nth feature channel. In general, when downsampling, for each feature channel, we let it adaptively adjust the importance of different characteristic filters.

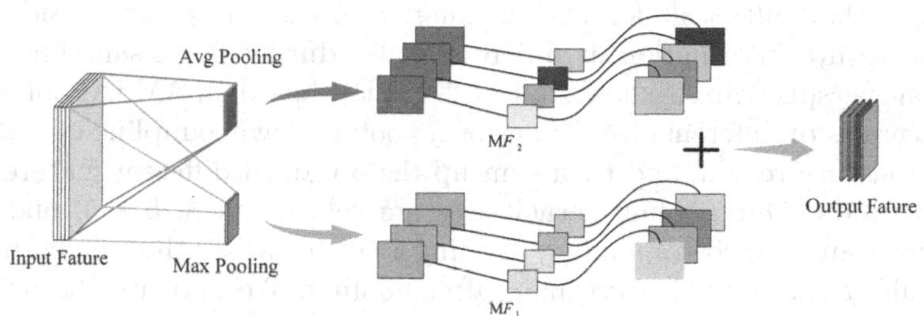

Fig. 1. Structure of AMmaPool.

We have found through some experiments (we will perform these experiments in Sect. 3.3 of this paper) that when different pooling methods are combined in different ways, and when the number of pooling branches is too large, it does not necessarily lead to performance improvements, but rather makes the network hard to train, depending mainly on the sexual performance of the individual pooling itself that is combined. So the approach in this paper is to combine pooling methods that perform relatively well: max pooling and average pooling. These are then used as the two basic building blocks of our adaptive mixed pooling, which we call AMmaPool(replacing the 'x' in AMxPool with 'ma', where 'm' stands for max pooling and 'a' stands for average pooling), its structure is shown in Fig. 1. Its formulation can be obtained by setting s in Eq. (2) to 2, and $P_1(.)$ and $P_2(.)$ to $max(.)$ and $avg(.)$, respectively:

$$Y_n = MF_{1n}(max(C_n)) + MF_{2n}(avg(C_n)) \tag{3}$$

where $max(C_n)$ and $avg(C_n)$ denote the max value calculation and the average value calculation for the feature channel C_n, respectively.

For the specific implementation of this pooling module, we first pass the input feature maps through both parallel Max-Pooling and Avg-Pooling, and then perform DW (Depth-Wise) convolution [2] operation with a convolution kernel size of 1 for each pooled feature map separately. This process takes advantage of the fact that only one channel of the input feature map is acted upon by one convolution kernel when the DW convolution operation is performed, which enables each channel of the feature map to generate its own learning parameters (one convolution kernel parameter and one bias parameter). Finally, each DW convolved feature map is linearly summed. In particular, since this pooling uses a DW convolution with a kernel size of 1 to learn the weight parameters and does not perform feature fusion between feature channels, its additional number of parameters and computation is minimal, and the increased number of parameters and computation that are replaced into the actual network model are acceptable.

2.2 Multi-scale Adaptive Mixed Pooling (Ms-AMPool)

Since the performance of object detection as well as image segmentation tasks depends on the multi-scale feature information of the image, we considered the fusion of feature information at different scales during down-sampling from a multi-scale perspective. As shown in Fig. 2. Firstly, based on AMmaPool, we take pooling kernels of different sizes to perform pooling down-sampling operation on the same feature region, and then sum up the obtained different feature values after activation. Our pooling kernel sizes are set to 3×3, 5×5, and 7×7, respectively, and the corresponding padding is set to satisfy that its feature map size is half of the input feature map after pooling. We activate the output of each mixed pooling module with the rlue function to increase its nonlinearity. The module computation process can be summarized as follows:

$$AMmaP_k(X) = DWConv(MaxP_k(X)) + DWConv(AvgP_k(X)) \tag{4}$$

$$Y = Relu(AMmaP_3(X)) + Relu(AMmaP_5(X)) + Relu(AMmaP_7(X)) \tag{5}$$

where X represents the input feature map, $DWConv(.)$ represents DW convolution, $MaxP_k(.)$ and $AvgP_k(.)$ represent max pooling and average pooling with a pooling kernel of k, respectively, $AMmaP(.)$ represents our AMmaPool, $Relu(.)$ is the activation function, and Y is the filtered feature map. We have used 3 different scales of pooling module for fusion, so the module will enhance the multi-scale feature information of the network to a great extent. So that some small objects as well as large objects in the original image have different pooling operations when pooling down-sampling, the pooling operation with small pooling kernels can retain the finer details, while the increased perceptual field with large pooling kernels is also important to retain the contour information of the objects in a large range. The pooling module at each scale uses our proposed adaptive mixed pooling as its most basic unit, which has learnable parameters and the model is trained to adjust the contribution of each pooling module to the network performance. This preserves to a large extent the feature information lost during down-sampling.

In summary, we simultaneously fuse the filtering characteristics of different pooling as well as feature information at different scales, and this fusion proceeds in an adaptive manner.

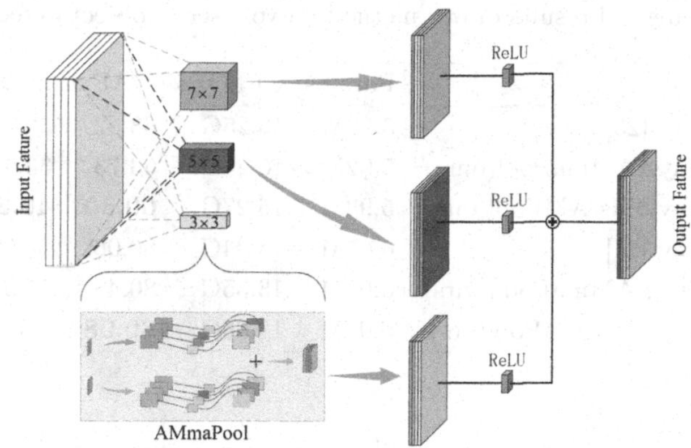

Fig. 2. The figure shows the structure of the Ms-AMPool module, where the input feature maps are summed after three AMmaPool modules with different pooling kernel sizes (k = 3, k = 5, k = 7) and then after nonlinear activation to obtain the output feature maps.

3 Experiments and Analysis

Next, we conduct related experiments on more advanced detection and segmentation networks that use pooled down-sampling, such as the object detection network architectures yolov4-tiny [23] and yolov7-tiny [24]; and the image segmentation network architectures UNet [20] and UNeXt [21]. This is used to evaluate the performance of our proposed AMmaPool and Ms-AMPool on PASCAL-VOC [22] object detection and performance on BUSI [1], ISIC 2018 [3] image segmentation. To ensure the fairness of the experiments, all of our experiments do not use pre-training weights and are trained from scratch on the corresponding datasets.

3.1 Object Detection

Datasets. Our method was first evaluated on the PASCAL-VOC [22] dataset, which consists of PASCAL VOC 2007 and PASCAL VOC 2012, the former with a total of 9963 images containing 24640 labeled objects and the latter with 11540 images containing a total of 27450 labeled objects. We used train+val from PASCAL VOC 2007 and train+val from PASCAL VOC 2012 as the training set, with a total of 16,551 images, and test from PASCAL VOC 2007 as the test set, with a total of 4,952 images.

Implementation Details. The number of training rounds is fixed at 300 epochs, the input image size is uniformly set to 640 × 640, and other hyperparameters are kept the same as in the original paper. We counted Params and GFLOPs to evaluate the additional number of parameters added by our method,

Table 1. Experimental results of our method on yolo series object detection network.

Network	Params	GFLOPs	MAP.5	mAP.5:.95
yolov4-tiny [23]	5.92M	16.25G	63.02	32.90
yolov4-tiny+AMmaPool(ours)	5.92M	16.25G	63.73	33.45
yolov4-tiny+Ms-AMPool(ours)	5.93M	16.27G	**69.50**	**40.36**
yolov7-tiny [24]	6.07M	13.34G	80.06	55.02
yolov7-tiny+AMmaPool(ours)	6.07M	13.35G	80.48	55.35
yolov7-tiny+Ms-AMPool(ours)	6.07M	13.36G	**80.98**	**56.14**

and evaluated its performance using the average precision (mAP.5) (AP at IoU = 0.50) and (mAP.5 : .95) (AP at IoU = 0.50:0.05:0.95).

Performance Comparison. We experimentally validate the performance of our proposed AMmaPool and Ms-AMPool on the advanced object detectors yolov4-tiny and yolov7-tiny, and our experimental results are shown in Table 1. It can be seen that our AMmaPool method is able to improve the performance of the network with almost no increase in the number of parameters relative to the original network. In particular, the performance of the yolov4-tiny network increases by almost 6.48% for mAP.5 and 7.46% for mAP.5:.95 metrics, with a very small increase in the number of parameters and computational effort. And its correctness rate also increases when added to yolov7-tiny. This experimental result also demonstrates the effectiveness of our method for the object detection task. This is due to the fact that our method retains more useful feature information when down-sampling and the Ms-AMPool module incorporates the multi-scale information in the image to a great extent. This is shown in Fig. 3, shows the prediction plots of the baseline network with our method, and we can see that the accuracy of the predicted object boundaries improves after adding our pooling method.

3.2 Image Segmentation

Datasets. We use the Breast Ultrasound Images(BUSI) [1], International Skin Imaging Collaboration(ISIC 2018) [3] medical image segmentation dataset to evaluate the effectiveness of our AMmaPool and Ms-AMPool in the image segmentation task. the BUSI dataset contains ultrasound images of normal, benign and malignant breast cancer cases and the corresponding segmentation maps. We used 647 benign and mailgnant images and used 80% of them as training set and 20% as test set. ISIC 2018 contains camera-acquired skin images and corresponding segmentation maps of skin lesion areas, with a total of 2594 images, again 80% of them as training set and 20% as test set.

Fig. 3. (a) Baseline Network (The top two rows are yolov4-tiny and the bottom two rows are yolov7-tiny), (b) Baseline+AMmaPool, (c) Baseline+Ms-AMPool.

Table 2. Experimental results of our method on UNet and UNeXt image segmentation networks.

Network	Params	GFLOPs	BUSI [1]		ISIC2018 [3]	
			IoU	Dice	IoU	Dice
UNet [20]	7.77M	13.75G	59.10	74.03	78.79	87.97
UNet+AMmaPool(ours)	7.77M	13.76G	60.86	75.49	79.27	88.28
UNet+Ms-AMPool(ours)	7.78M	13.79G	**64.04**	**77.75**	**80.31**	**88.91**
UNeXt [21]	1.47M	0.57G	59.37	74.20	81.12	89.44
UNeXt+AMmaPool(ours)	1.47M	0.57G	61.18	75.63	81.73	89.84
UNeXt+Ms-AMPool(ours)	1.47M	0.59G	**63.60**	**77.53**	**82.03**	**90.00**

Implementation Details. We modified the classical image segmentation network architecture UNet, as well as the more advanced network architecture UNeXt (replacing the pooling layer in the network with our pooling down-sampling module). We used BCEDiceLoss as the loss function for training, Adam was chosen as the optimizer, CosineAnnealingLR was used for learning rate decay, the initial learning rate was set to 0.0002, and the momentum was set to 0.9. According to the variability of the dataset, we set the BUSI dataset image resolution to 256 × 256, batch size to 32, 150 epochs per training, and the learning rate decayed to 0.00003. set the ISIC 2018 dataset image resolution to 512 × 512, batch size to 16, 100 epochs per training epoch, the learning rate decays to 0.00001. To prevent the effect of randomness, we assigned the training and test sets with the same random number seeds and tested them on the same device. We also counted the Params and GFLOPs of the models and used IoU and Dice as performance evaluation metrics.

Performance Comparison. As shown in Table 2. Regardless of the network, using our AMmaPool and Ms-AMPool modules are able to increase the performance of the network to a large extent with a very small increase in computational cost. In particular, the Ms-AMPool module is able to increase the performance of the network to a greater extent, increasing the IoU value of the UNet network by 4.94% on the BUSI dataset and increasing the IoU value of the UNeXt network by 4.23% on the BUSI dataset. This illustrates that our proposed method can also show excellent performance in the image segmentation task, and further demonstrates the effectiveness of our method for the mixing of pooling filtering features and the fusion of multi-scale feature information during down-sampling. We show the prediction performance of our method compared with the baseline network in Fig. 4, and we can see that the performance of our method is superior to that of the baseline network.

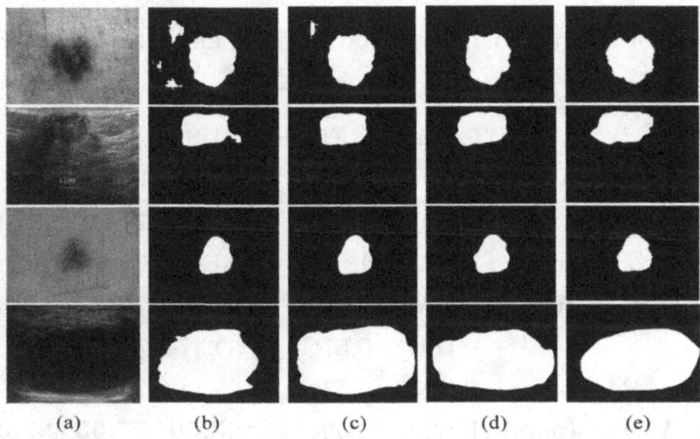

Fig. 4. Rows 1 and 3 are ISIC 2018 dataset images, rows 2 and 4 are BUSI dataset images. (a) Input Image, (b) Baseline Network (the top two rows are UNet and the bottom two rows are UNeXt), (c) Baseline + AMmaPool, (d) Baseline + Ms-AMPool, (e) Ground Truth.

3.3 Ablation Research

Next, we conducted ablation experiments on the object detection model YOLOv7-tiny and the image segmentation model UNeXt, respectively, in order to better understand the parameter settings of the AMPool and Ms-AMPool modules. The object detection experiments used the PASCAL-VOC dataset, and the image segmentation experiments used the BUSI dataset. Other experimental settings were the same as those in Sects. 3.1 and 3.2 of this chapter.

The pooling methods in the baseline network were replaced with MaxPool (Max Pooling), AvgPool (Average Pooling), MedianPool (Median Pooling), AMmmPool (Adaptive Mixed max Pooling with median Pooling), AMmaPool

Table 3. Ablation of AMPool and MS-AMPool configurations

Dataset/Baseline	VOC [22]/yolov7-tiny [24]			BUSI [1]/UNeXt [24]		
Method	Params	GFLOPs	mAP.5	Params	GFLOPs	IoU
MaxPool	6.07M	13.34G	80.06	1.47M	0.57G	59.37
AvgPool	6.07M	13.34G	80.06	1.47M	0.57G	58.95
MedianPool	6.07M	13.34G	77.96	1.47M	0.57G	58.35
AMmmPool	6.07M	13.35G	79.78	1.47M	0.57G	60.29
AMmaPool	6.07M	13.35G	**80.48**	1.47M	0.57G	**61.18**
AMmamPool	6.07M	13.35G	79.90	1.47M	0.58G	60.88
Ms-AMPool(k=2, 3, 5)	6.07M	13.36G	80.61	1.47M	0.59G	61.94
Ms-AMPool(k=2, 5, 7)	6.07M	13.36G	80.74	1.47M	0.59G	62.65
Ms-AMPool(k=3, 5, 7)	6.07M	13.36G	**80.98**	1.47M	0.59G	**63.60**
Ms-AMPool(k=3, 5, 9)	6.07M	13.36G	80.93	1.47M	0.59G	63.05

(Adaptive Mixed max Pooling with average Pooling), and AMmamPool (adaptive mixed all three Pooling) in that order. The experimental results are shown in Table 3. It can be found that not all pooling combinations result in improved network performance, especially the addition of median pooling deteriorates the performance instead. This indicates that the method is limited by the performance of the combined pooling method itself. The AMmaPool with a combination of max pooling and average pooling performs best in terms of performance, which is the best combination of pooling chosen for the method in this paper.

We next performed parametric ablation experiments on the Ms-AMPool module designed based on AMmaPool, by gradually increasing the size of the kernels we pooled, to explore the optimal kernel size. So we conducted experiments for Ms-AMPool modules with pooling kernel size combinations set to (2, 3, 5), (2, 5, 7), (3, 5, 7), and (3, 5, 9), respectively, and it can be seen from Table 3 that the performance increase is small when we set a smaller pooling kernel size. And as the pooling kernel size increases, its performance also increases gradually. However, when we set the pooling kernel size to (3, 5, 9), we find that the performance does not continue to increase, and the large pooling kernel may lose the detail information at this time and does not contribute much to the performance improvement. So we choose (3, 5, 7) as the pooling core size setting for our Ms-AMPool module.

4 Conclusions

In this paper, for dense prediction tasks such as object detection and image segmentation, we first design an adaptive mixed pooling method, AMPool, to allow each feature channel in the feature map to learn the appropriate filtering characteristics, so as to reduce the loss of feature information when down-sampling the network model. Based on this, the multi-scale adaptive mixed pooling (MsAMPool) down-sampling method is proposed from the perspective of multi-scale information fusion. By applying different-scale feature filtering to each pooling branch during downsampling and then performing multi-scale information fusion, our approach enables the network to consider feature filtering from multiple scales during downsampling. Compared to other pooling methods, our approach not only allows adaptive learning of pooling weight parameters suitable for each channel in the feature map but also adaptively integrates filtering feature information from multiple scales. In particular, the method can be arbitrarily substituted into a baseline network using pooled down-sampling, which can improve the performance of the network model to a large extent with little increase in the number of parameters and computational effort. In the future, we will make more attempts and hope to explore new down-sampling methods from other perspectives on top of this one.

Acknowledgements. This work was supported by the National Natural Science Foundation of China under Grant 62102331, the Natural Science Foundation of Sichuan Province under Grant 2022NSFSC0839 and the Doctoral Research Fund Project of Southwest University of science and Technology 22zx7110.

References

1. Al-Dhabyani, W., Gomaa, M., Khaled, H., Fahmy, A.: Dataset of breast ultrasound images. Data Brief **28**, 104863 (2020)
2. Chollet, F.: Xception: deep learning with depthwise separable convolutions. In: Proceedings of the IEEE Conference on Computer Vision and Pattern Recognition, pp. 1251–1258 (2017)
3. Codella, N.C., et al.: Skin lesion analysis toward melanoma detection: a challenge at the 2017 international symposium on biomedical imaging (ISBI), hosted by the international skin imaging collaboration (ISIC). In: 2018 IEEE 15th International Symposium on Biomedical Imaging (ISBI 2018), pp. 168–172. IEEE (2018)
4. Estrach, J.B., Szlam, A., LeCun, Y.: Signal recovery from pooling representations. In: International Conference on Machine Learning, pp. 307–315. PMLR (2014)
5. Fan, Z., Dan, T., Liu, B., Sheng, X., Yu, H., Cai, H.: SGUNet: Style-guided UNet for adversely conditioned fundus image super-resolution. Neurocomputing **465**, 238–247 (2021)
6. Gao, Z., Wang, L., Wu, G.: Lip: local importance-based pooling. In: Proceedings of the IEEE/CVF International Conference on Computer Vision, pp. 3355–3364 (2019)
7. Ge, Z., Liu, S., Wang, F., Li, Z., Sun, J.: Yolox: exceeding yolo series in 2021. arXiv preprint arXiv:2107.08430 (2021)
8. Girshick, R.: Fast R-CNN. In: Proceedings of the IEEE International Conference on Computer Vision, pp. 1440–1448 (2015)
9. Han, Z., Jian, M., Wang, G.G.: Convunext: an efficient convolution neural network for medical image segmentation. Knowl.-Based Syst. **253**, 109512 (2022)
10. Huang, H., et al.: Unet 3+: a full-scale connected UNet for medical image segmentation. In: ICASSP 2020–2020 IEEE International Conference on Acoustics, Speech and Signal Processing (ICASSP), pp. 1055–1059. IEEE (2020)

11. Huang, Z., Wang, J., Fu, X., Yu, T., Guo, Y., Wang, R.: DC-SPP-YOLO: dense connection and spatial pyramid pooling based yolo for object detection. Inf. Sci. **522**, 241–258 (2020)
12. Ke, X., Zhang, Y.: Fine-grained vehicle type detection and recognition based on dense attention network. Neurocomputing **399**, 247–257 (2020)
13. Kuang, H., Liu, C., Chan, L.L.H., Yan, H.: Multi-class fruit detection based on image region selection and improved object proposals. Neurocomputing **283**, 241–255 (2018)
14. LeCun, Y., et al.: Handwritten digit recognition with a back-propagation network. In: Advances in Neural Information Processing Systems, vol. 2 (1989)
15. Lin, T.Y., Dollár, P., Girshick, R., He, K., Hariharan, B., Belongie, S.: Feature pyramid networks for object detection. In: Proceedings of the IEEE Conference on Computer Vision and Pattern Recognition, pp. 2117–2125 (2017)
16. Liu, S., Qi, L., Qin, H., Shi, J., Jia, J.: Path aggregation network for instance segmentation. In: Proceedings of the IEEE Conference on Computer Vision and Pattern Recognition, pp. 8759–8768 (2018)
17. Liu, W., et al.: SSD: single shot multibox detector. In: Leibe, B., Matas, J., Sebe, N., Welling, M. (eds.) ECCV 2016. LNCS, vol. 9905, pp. 21–37. Springer, Cham (2016). https://doi.org/10.1007/978-3-319-46448-0_2
18. Mubashar, M., Ali, H., Grönlund, C., Azmat, S.: R2u++: a multiscale recurrent residual u-net with dense skip connections for medical image segmentation. Neural Comput. Appl. **34**, 17723–17739 (2022). https://doi.org/10.1007/s00521-022-07419-7
19. Ranzato, M., Boureau, Y.L., Cun, Y., et al.: Sparse feature learning for deep belief networks. In: Advances in Neural Information Processing Systems, vol. 20 (2007)
20. Ronneberger, O., Fischer, P., Brox, T.: U-net: convolutional networks for biomedical image segmentation. In: Navab, N., Hornegger, J., Wells, W.M., Frangi, A.F. (eds.) MICCAI 2015. LNCS, vol. 9351, pp. 234–241. Springer, Cham (2015). https://doi.org/10.1007/978-3-319-24574-4_28
21. Valanarasu, J.M.J., Patel, V.M.: UNeXt: MLP-based rapid medical image segmentation network. arXiv preprint arXiv:2203.04967 (2022)
22. Vicente, S., Carreira, J., Agapito, L., Batista, J.: Reconstructing pascal voc. In: Proceedings of the IEEE Conference on Computer Vision and Pattern Recognition, pp. 41–48 (2014)
23. Wang, C.Y., Bochkovskiy, A., Liao, H.Y.M.: Scaled-yolov4: scaling cross stage partial network. In: Proceedings of the IEEE/CVF Conference on Computer Vision and Pattern Recognition, pp. 13029–13038 (2021)
24. Wang, C.Y., Bochkovskiy, A., Liao, H.Y.M.: Yolov7: trainable bag-of-freebies sets new state-of-the-art for real-time object detectors. arXiv preprint arXiv:2207.02696 (2022)
25. Wang, Q., Zhang, S., Qian, Y., Zhang, G., Wang, H.: Enhancing representation learning by exploiting effective receptive fields for object detection. Neurocomputing **481**, 22–32 (2022)
26. Yu, D., Wang, H., Chen, P., Wei, Z.: Mixed pooling for convolutional neural networks. In: Miao, D., Pedrycz, W., Ślęzak, D., Peters, G., Hu, Q., Wang, R. (eds.) RSKT 2014. LNCS (LNAI), vol. 8818, pp. 364–375. Springer, Cham (2014). https://doi.org/10.1007/978-3-319-11740-9_34

27. Zeiler, M.D., Fergus, R.: Stochastic pooling for regularization of deep convolutional neural networks. arXiv preprint arXiv:1301.3557 (2013)
28. Zhou, Z., Rahman Siddiquee, M.M., Tajbakhsh, N., Liang, J.: UNet++: a nested u-net architecture for medical image segmentation. In: Stoyanov, D., et al. (eds.) DLMIA/ML-CDS -2018. LNCS, vol. 11045, pp. 3–11. Springer, Cham (2018). https://doi.org/10.1007/978-3-030-00889-5_1

Multi-frame Tilt-angle Face Recognition Using Fusion Re-ranking

Wenqin Song, Zhen Han(✉), Kangli Zeng, and Zhongyuan Wang

National Engineering Research Center for Multimedia Software,
School of Computer Science, Wuhan University, Wuhan, China
hanzhen_1980@163.com

Abstract. Tilt-angle face recognition is a common problem in public video surveillance. Based on the complementarity among multi-frame tilt-angle faces from far to near, it is a possible way to improve recognition performance by fusing them. However, the feature fusion in the existing multi-frame frontal face recognition methods is unsuitable for tilt-angle faces with large changes in resolution and angle. To solve this issue, a multi-frame tilt-angle face recognition approach based on fusion re-ranking is proposed, which can obtain a more accurate final similarity list by weighted fusion of initial similarity lists given by different tilt-angle faces. In order to get the person-specific and angle-specific fusion weights, an angle-guided adaptive weight prediction network is designed. Moreover, we propose a weighted ranking loss to train the network, which can make the gallery face with the same identity as the probe face rank higher in the fused list. Experimental results on the tilt-angle face datasets demonstrate the effectiveness of our method.

Keywords: Multi-frame face recognition · tilt-angle face · fusion re-ranking · weight prediction

1 Introduction

Tilt-angle face recognition is a common problem in public video surveillance due to the high location of cameras. Generally, the far tilt-angle faces show complete facial structure but lack facial texture information. In contrast, the near tilt-angle faces have better clearness but lack holistic facial profiles. Due to the incompatibility between structural integrity and resolution, the single-frame tilt-angle face recognition performance is unsatisfactory. Hence, it is necessary to improve the recognition performance by fusing far-near-sighted multi-frame tilt-angle faces based on the complementarity among them.

Most of the existing multi-frame face recognition approaches mainly adopt the fusion strategy at the feature level to utilize the cross-frame complementarity. Yang et al. [20] aligned faces with the LBF [15] method and proposed two attention blocks to obtain a feature representing the whole video. Some other studies [4,10,13] employed MTCNN [21] to detect and align faces before aggregating features. All of these approaches need to detect and align the faces with

L. Iliadis et al. (Eds.): ICANN 2023, LNCS 14255, pp. 495–507, 2023.
https://doi.org/10.1007/978-3-031-44210-0_40

small changes in angle and resolution before feature extraction. However, the detected key points of the tilt-angle faces with large changes in angle and resolution are incomplete and inaccurate. Therefore, it is difficult to align the tilt-angle faces, which leads to the existing multi-frame face recognition approaches being unsuitable for tilt-angle face recognition.

To avoid the alignment of the tilt-angle faces, we adopt the fusion strategy at the ranking level instead of the feature level to improve face recognition performance. We first get the similarity lists given by different tilt-angle faces separately and then fuse them based on their complementarity. The ranking fusion is essentially a sort of re-ranking technique which serves as a post-processing procedure of recognition or retrieval to optimize the initial ranking list for improving the ranking of the target images. Existing re-ranking approaches can be roughly categorized into two types: the single list based and the multiple lists based. The single list based re-ranking methods [12,25] only optimize a single ranking list which is unsuitable for multiple tilt-angle face recognition. The multiple lists based re-ranking methods [9,18] fuse multiple ranking lists using a fixed-weight approach to obtain a more accurate list. However, due to personalized facial features, the optimal fusion weight of lists given by different people should not be fixed. Therefore, we propose an adaptive weight prediction network to obtain the person-specific fusion weights. In order to reduce the number of predicted weights, pairwise fusion processes are adopted to progressively fuse the initial similarity lists of tilt-angle faces and only one weight is needed to be predicted for each fusion. Since the pairwise fusion processes are related to tilt-angle faces, we adopt an angle-guided block in the weight prediction network to get an angle-specific weight for each fusion. Moreover, we propose a weighted ranking loss which can make the gallery face with the same identity as the probe rank higher in the final similarity list to optimize the angle-guided adaptive weight prediction network.

The main contributions of this paper are summarized as follows:

(1) To the best of our knowledge, it is the first exploration to use the fusion re-ranking technique for multiple tilt-angle face recognition, which could exploit coupled complementarity among far and near face images of the same person to improve the recognition performance.
(2) We propose an angle-guided adaptive weight prediction network to predict the person-specific and angle-specific fusion weight between similarity lists given by different tilt-angle faces and present a weighted ranking loss to train the network.
(3) Extensive experimental results on the real-world tilt-angle face datasets demonstrate the effectiveness of our method.

2 Related Work

2.1 Multi-frame Face Recognition

Multi-frame face recognition methods can be divided into two categories according to the level of aggregation.

Image aggregation. These methods aggregate multi-frame faces directly and obtain a single representative face for recognition. Rao et al. [14] combined metric learning and adversarial learning to produce synthesized face images. Stefan et al. [7] used U-Net to aggregate an arbitrary number of faces.

Feature aggregation. The feature aggregation approaches first extract features from every frame separately and aggregate them into a single feature for recognition. Yang et al. [20] proposed an aggregation module consisting of two attention blocks to adaptively weigh the features. Zhong et al. [24] reduced the contribution of features given by low quality frames using a modified NetVLAD [1] layer. Jacinto et al. [16] proposed a novel adaptive feature aggregation method based on ordered weighted average (OWA) operators. Zhang et al. [23] proposed a context aware feature aggregation scheme to aggregate complementary information among different features. Zhang et al. [22] proposed a Feature Map Aggregation Network (FMAN) to aggregate image features from image groups at the feature map level.

These multi-frame face recognition approaches all need to align the faces before face aggregation or feature extraction. However, it is difficult for existing face detection methods to align the tilt-angle faces with large changes in angle and resolution. As a result, the existing multi-frame face recognition methods are unsuitable for tilt-angle face recognition.

2.2 Re-ranking Approaches

Re-ranking approaches can be divided into two categories based on the number of lists.

Single List Based. Compared with the traditional re-ranking methods based on artificial distance metric, the re-ranking methods based on deep learning show a better performance in recent years. Ouyang et al. [11] designed a lightweight CNN model to learn the semantic relevance among images for re-ranking. Hai et al. [12] proposed a re-ranking approach that compares query and gallery faces according to the Earth Mover's Distance (EMD). Zhou et al. [26] introduced a contextual memory cell in re-ranking network to predict the correlations between probe and gallery images.

Multiple Lists Based. The multiple lists based re-ranking is a new research direction in recent years. Sivaram et al. [18] designed a re-ranking approach by analyzing similar, dissimilar, and neutral gallery images of two initial ranking lists given by different algorithms and combined them using fixed weight to improve the recognition performance. Liu et al. [9] introduced a novel iterative local re-ranking (ILR) method for multiple ranking lists given by attribute guided synthetic faces using a fixed aggregation weight.

However, single list based re-ranking approaches are unsuitable for multiple tilt-angle face recognition. Multiple lists based re-ranking approaches used a fixed-weight strategy but the fusion weights should be person-specific and angle-specific actually, which prompts us to seek a better solution in this paper.

3 Methods

3.1 Architecture

As shown in Fig. 1, the proposed method consists of three modules: single list calculation, fusion weight prediction and multiple lists fusion.

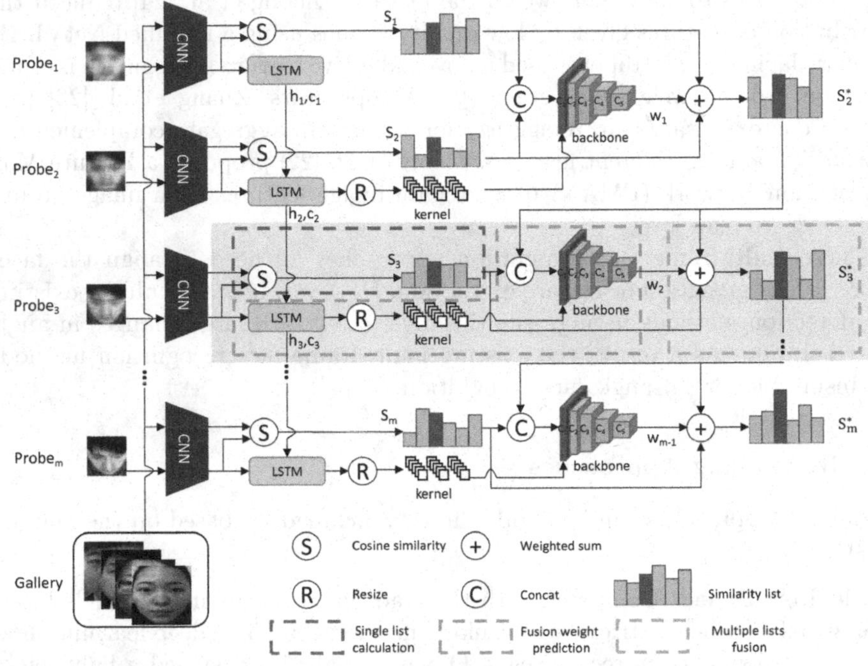

Fig. 1. The framework of our method. One of the fusion branches is highlighted.

Single List Calculation. Given m tilt-angle probe faces of the same person, we use a pre-trained ArcFace model [3] to generate feature vectors $\{f_1, f_2, ..., f_m\}$. Then the initial similarity lists $\{S_1, S_2, ..., S_m\}$ are calculated separately using cosine similarity. The list element $S_{i,j}$ denotes the similarity between the i_{th} tilt-angle probe face p_i $(i = 1, 2, ..., m)$ and the j_{th} frontal gallery face g_j $(j = 1, 2, ..., N)$.

Fusion Weight Prediction. Two initial similarity lists are fed into the angle-guided adaptive weight prediction network in this module to obtain the corresponding person-specific fusion weight between these two lists. Due to the progressive pairwise fusion strategy used in our method, this module is executed $m-1$ times for different tilt-angle faces as shown in Fig. 1, The backbone of this network is a newly trained ResNet-50 [6] which consists of 5 blocks, i.e., C_1, C_2, C_3, C_4, and C_5. Since the weight of each fusion is related to the tilt-angle, we aim to adjust the predicted weight based on the tilt-angle face image. Motivated by [8], we use a dynamic convolutional layer to regulate our network. The conventional convolutional layer uses a fixed convolutional kernel that is learned during training and is held constant during testing. In contrast, the dynamic convolutional layer uses a convolutional kernel that will vary from input to input during testing. Therefore, the first block of backbone can be regulated as follows:

$$F_1 = C_1^k(concat(S_{i-1}^*, S_i)), \tag{1}$$

where *concat* refers to concatenation operation and C_1^k denotes the C_1 block with k as the dynamic convolution kernel generated by current and previous tilt-angle face images. After that, we extract the deep features $F_j (j = 2, 3, 4, 5)$ as:

$$F_j = C_j(F_{j-1}), \tag{2}$$

where C_j denotes the C_j block shown in fig.1. Finally, the fusion weight w_i which is a concrete real number between 0 and 1 can be obtained as follows:

$$w_i = fc(F_5), \tag{3}$$

where fc denotes a fully connected layer.

In order to obtain the dynamic convolution kernel k in Eq. 1, we use an angle-guided block in our angle-guided adaptive weight prediction network. This block can generate different convolution kernels according to different tilt-angle face images so as to adjust the predicted weight. Due to the progressive pairwise fusion strategy used in our method, a newly trained single-layer LSTM [17] is adopted to generate the kernel in this angle-guided block. In addition, the structure of LSTM allows our angle-guided adaptive weight prediction network to fuse an arbitrary number of similarity lists. Specifically, we input the face feature f_i into LSTM to obtain a feature vector o_i containing the current and previous tilt-angle face information as follows:

$$o_i, h_i, c_i = LSTM(f_i, h_{i-1}, c_{i-1}), \tag{4}$$

where h_i, c_i denotes the hidden state and cell output of LSTM. Since the size of the dynamic convolution kernel k we need is $64 \times 1 \times 3 \times 3$, we set the size of o_i to 576. Therefore, the dynamic convolution kernel k can be obtained as:

$$k = Resize(o_i), \tag{5}$$

where *Resize* refers to resize operation.

Multiple Lists Fusion. Finally, the fused similarity list can be obtained as follows:

$$S_i^* = \begin{cases} S_i, & i = 1 \\ w_{i-1}S_{i-1}^* + (1 - w_{i-1})S_i, & i = 2, 3... , \end{cases} \tag{6}$$

where w_{i-1} and S_i^* are the results of the $(i-1)_{th}$ prediction and fusion respectively. As shown in Fig. 1, the final similarity list can be obtained after $m - 1$ fusions in which the gallery face with the same identity as the probe has a higher ranking.

3.2 Weighted Ranking Loss

In order to train the angle-guided adaptive weight prediction network, we design a weighted ranking loss. The objective of this loss is to make the ranking of the gallery face g_n with the same identity as the probe faces higher by optimizing w_i. And it means that the number of gallery faces which have higher similarity than g_n should be as few as possible in the fused similarity list. The above objective can be expressed as:

$$\begin{aligned} &\arg\min_{w_i} Rank(w_i S^*_{i,n} + (1-w_i) S_{i+1,n}) \\ &= \arg\min_{w_i} \sum_{j=1}^{N} Indicator_n(j, w_i), \end{aligned} \tag{7}$$

where $Rank(w_i S^*_{i,n} + (1-w_i) S_{i+1,n})$ is the ranking of g_n in the fused similarity list and S^*_i, S_{i+1} denote the two input similarity lists. $Indicator_n(j, w_i)(j = 1, 2, ..., N)$ is an indicator function and it is defined as:

$$Indicator_n(j, w_i) = \begin{cases} 0, & S^*_{i+1,n} > S^*_{i+1,j} \\ 1, & S^*_{i+1,n} \leq S^*_{i+1,j}, \end{cases} \tag{8}$$

where S^*_{i+1} denotes the fused similarity list of S^*_i and S_{i+1} according to Eq. 6. The value of the indicator function is 0 if g_n ranks higher than g_j in S_{i+1}, otherwise the value is 1.

According to Eq. 7, the optimal weight w_i should try to make the value of $Indicator_n(j, w_i)$ be 0 for minimizing $\sum_{j=1}^{N} Indicator_n(j, w_i)$. In order to achieve this objective, w_j should satisfy the following formula according to Eq. 6, Eq. 7 and Eq. 8:

$$\begin{cases} w_i > Jump_n(j), & S^*_{i,n} - S^*_{i,j} + S_{i+1,j} - S_{i+1,n} > 0 \\ w_i < Jump_n(j), & S^*_{i,n} - S^*_{i,j} + S_{i+1,j} - S_{i+1,n} \leq 0, \end{cases} \tag{9}$$

$$Jump_n(j) = \frac{S_{i+1,j} - S_{i+1,n}}{S^*_{i,n} - S^*_{i,j} + S_{i+1,j} - S_{i+1,n}}. \tag{10}$$

Equation 9 gives the value range of w_i when the value of $Indicator_n(j, w_i)$ is 0 in two cases. $Jump_n(j)$ in Eq. 10 is the value boundary of w_i and determines whether the value of $Indicator_n(j, w_i)$ is 1 or 0, therefore it is essentially the only jump discontinuity of $Indicator_n(j, w_i)$.

Figure 2, shows an example of the relationship between $Indicator_n(j, w_i)$, w_i and $jump_n(j)$. In this figure, the horizontal coordinate is w_i and the vertical coordinate is $\sum_{j=1}^{N} Indicator_n(j, w_i)$, because $\sum_{j=1}^{N} Indicator_n(j, w_i)$ only depends on w_i according to Eq. 10. Since we can get the jump discontinuity $jump_n(j)$ of $Indicator_n(j, w_i)$ for each j, $\sum_{j=1}^{N} Indicator_n(j, w_i)$ has N jump discontinuities $\{Jump_n(1), Jump_n(2), ..., Jump_n(N)\}$. As shown in fig.2, these N jump discontinuities divide the value of w_i into $N+1$

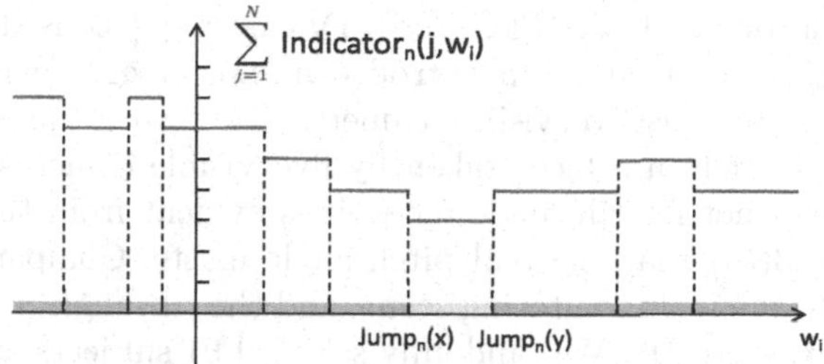

Fig. 2. An example graph of the relationship among $\sum_{j=1}^{N} Indicator_n(j, w_i)$, w_i and $jump_n(j)(N = 9)$. The red part is the optimal interval.

intervals and $\sum_{j=1}^{N} Indicator_n(j, w_i)$ has the same value in each interval. With the traversing of the $N + 1$ intervals, we can get an optimal interval $(Jump_n(x), Jump_n(y))(x, y \in \{1, 2, ..., N\})$ of w_i in which $\sum_{j=1}^{N} Indicator_n(j, w_i)$ has the minimum value and g_n has the highest ranking. Considering that the fusion weight in the actual process should be in the range of 0–1, we only consider the part of the interval between 0 and 1. After obtaining the optimal interval, loss function is defined as follows:

$$Loss = max(0, (w_i - Jump_n(x)) * (w_i - Jump_n(y))). \tag{11}$$

When w_i lies in the optimal interval, the loss value is 0. Moreover, the farther away from this interval, the greater the loss value is. Therefore, the ranking of g_n can be optimized by the weighted ranking loss.

4 Experiments

4.1 Dataset and Training Details

In our experiments, the recognition performance of the proposed method is evaluated on two datasets which are collected under real-world scenarios. The sample face images are shown in Fig. 3.

Tilt-Angle Face Dataset (TFD [19]**).** is an open-source large-scale multiple tilt-angle face dataset. It includes 8394 face images from 1399 people, each with 6 angles (0°, 15°, 30°, 45°, 60°, 75° in the pitch direction). According to the ratio of 7:3, we randomly selected 979 people as the training set and the remaining 420 people as the testing set. We employ RetinaFace [2] to detect and crop out face images. In the actual monitoring scenario, the face resolution will be higher with the increase of the tilt-angle. In order to simulate the characteristics of the tilt-angle face, we down-scaled probe faces (15°, 30°, 45°, 60°, 75°) to a lower resolution (16 × 16, 20 × 20, 24 × 24, 28 × 28, 32 × 32 pixels) separately and gallery faces (0°) to a higher resolution (112 × 112).

Surveillance Cameras Face (SCface) Dataset. [5] consists of 4160 still images of 130 subjects taken in uncontrolled indoor environments using seven video surveillance cameras(five visible cameras and two infrared cameras). In our experiment, we only use faces taken by five visible cameras (cam1-cam5). Although SCface is not for tilt-angle faces, it is evident from the face samples (as shown in Fig. 3(b)) that the real pitch angle exists. Compared with TFD, SCface is closer to the real monitoring scene, and the tilt-angle of the face at the same distance varies greatly. We randomly selected 91 subjects as a training set and 39 subjects as a testing set. In addition, we down-scaled probe faces (1m, 2.6m, 4.2m) to a lower resolution ($16 \times 16, 20 \times 20, 24 \times 24$) separately.

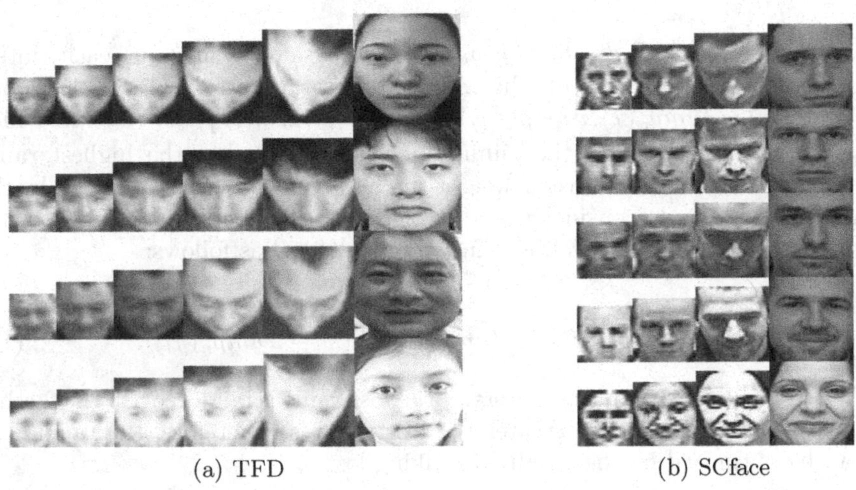

(a) TFD (b) SCface

Fig. 3. Examples from TFD and SCface. (a) From the first to the fifth column, it shows face images with different tilt-angle (T_1, T_2, T_3, T_4, T_5). The last column shows the frontal faces. (b) The first three columns show faces taken at three different distances(T_1, T_2, T_3), and the first to fifth rows are faces taken by cam1 to cam5. The last column shows the frontal faces.

During the training, we set the initial parameters as follows. Batch size is set to 16. The trained model is updated by Adam optimizer and the learning rate is set to 0.0001. The related codes run on Ubuntu of 16.04 from a PC, which consists of a CPU of Inter Core i7-7800, a RAM of 16G and three GPUs of Nvidia GeForce GTX 2080Ti in this paper. The three GPUs can be accelerated by Nvidia CUDA of 10.0 and CuDNN of 7.5.

4.2 Ablation Study

We evaluate the impact of tilt-angle face images and verify the effectiveness of the main components in our method with ablation studies on TFD and SCface.

Table 1. Ablation study of tilt-angle face images(Rank-1%).

Tilt-angle face images	TFD	SCface					
		cam1	cam2	cam3	cam4	cam5	avg
T_1	38.81	42.31	30.77	29.23	37.69	36.92	35.38
T_2	61.69	63.08	56.15	54.62	67.69	58.46	60.00
T_3	63.54	65.38	66.92	62.31	75.38	72.31	68.48
T_4	56.18	–	–	–	–	–	–
T_5	36.03	–	–	–	–	–	–
$T_1 + T_2$	64.76	68.21	65.13	65.64	75.13	71.03	69.03
$T_1 + T_2 + T_3$	77.62	79.48	82.05	80.00	93.33	82.05	83.38
$T_1 + T_2 + T_3 + T_4$	78.57	–	–	–	–	–	–
$T_1 + T_2 + T_3 + T_4 + T_5$	79.05	–	–	–	–	–	–

Table 2. Ablation study of components(Rank-1%).

Method	TFD	SCface					
		cam1	cam2	cam3	cam4	cam5	avg
w/o weight prediction	71.36	73.59	75.13	74.36	79.23	76.15	75.68
w/o dynamic kernel	74.76	76.41	77.18	77.69	85.13	78.21	78.92
Full algorithm	79.05	79.48	82.05	80.00	93.33	82.05	83.38

Ablation Study of Tilt-Angle Face Images. Table 1 shows the recognition accuracy of single frame and multiple frames tilt-angle faces. As seen in the table, the recognition performance of all tilt-angle faces is the best, which indicates that our method makes full use of the complementary information among different tilt-angle faces. Further analysis shows that T_2 and T_3 bring greater gain because these two faces have a better balance between the tilt-angle and resolution.

Ablation Study of Components. Table 2 shows the impact of different components in our method. It can be seen that the removal of dynamic kernel generation block results in a 4.29% reduction on TFD and a 4.46% reduction on SCface, which proves that this block is conducive to obtaining more accurate fusion weight for different tilt-angle faces. While we further remove the whole adaptive weight prediction network and fuse the similarity lists using the weighted average strategy, the recognition accuracy at Rank-1 is reduced by 7.69% on TFD and 7.7% on SCface which demonstrates that adaptive weight prediction is crucial for multi-frame tilt-angle face recognition using fusion re-ranking.

4.3 Comparison with Other Methods

Table 3, Table 4 and Fig. 4 show the quantitative comparison between our method and the three competing methods on TFD and SCface respectively: multiple

Table 3. Comparison of the proposed method with other methods on TFD.

Method	Rank-1(%)	Rank-5(%)	Rank-10(%)
DAlign [18]	69.76	82.14	85.24
ILR [9]	67.86	81.19	84.52
CIRL [11]	71.43	85.48	91.43
EMD [12]	71.67	85.71	91.67
ACP [26]	72.86	86.67	92.62
NAN [20]	73.98	88.21	91.49
OWANet [16]	74.91	89.78	93.85
FMAN [22]	74.17	89.23	92.51
Ours	79.05	91.90	95.24

Table 4. Face identification rates(rank-1%) comparison on SCface.

Method	cam1	cam2	cam3	cam4	cam5	avg
DAlign [18]	63.33	58.71	63.84	73.33	77.17	67.28
ILR [9]	61.79	61.28	61.53	71.79	74.10	66.10
CIRL [11]	65.12	62.56	66.41	76.92	77.43	69.69
EMD [12]	67.94	63.07	70.76	79.48	79.48	72.15
ACP [26]	67.17	62.82	68.46	77.43	78.46	70.87
NAN [20]	69.48	69.23	71.53	83.33	80.51	74.82
OWANet [16]	73.33	79.74	75.38	87.69	81.02	79.43
FMAN [22]	73.58	76.92	77.43	86.15	79.74	78.76
Ours	79.48	82.05	80.00	93.33	82.05	83.38

lists based re-ranking methods (DAlign [18] and ILR [9]), single list based re-ranking methods(EMD [12], ACP [26] and CIRL [11]), multi-frame face recognition methods(NAN [20], OWANet [16] and FMAN [22]). In particular, the single list based re-ranking methods cannot be applied to multiple tilt-angle face recognition directly, so we first optimize the single similarity list based on those methods and then fuse them using the weighted average strategy.

Multiple Lists Based Re-ranking Methods. As shown in Table 3 and Table 4, our method outperforms these methods [9,18] by a margin of up to 9.29%–11.19% at Rank-1 on TFD and 16.1%–17.28% at Rank-1 on SCface, which indicates that the person-specific and angle-specific weights in our method can contribute to more accurate fusion of multiple similarity lists compared with fixed weights in these methods.

Single List Based Re-ranking Methods. Compared with these methods, our method is improved by 6.19%–7.62% at Rank-1 on TFD and 11.23%–13.69% at Rank-1 on SCface. This is because these methods do not consider fusion and it is difficult to effectively utilize complementarity among similarity lists using the weighted average strategy.

Multi-frame Face Recognition Methods. It can be found from Table 3 and Table 4 that our method achieves an improvement of 4.14%–5.07% at Rank-1 on TFD and 3.95%–8.56% at Rank-1 on SCface compared with these methods [16, 20]. This demonstrates that our method is more suitable for faces with large changes in resolution and tilt-angle.

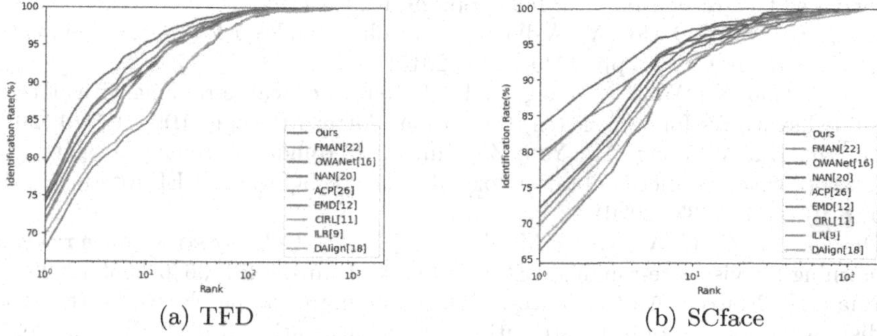

Fig. 4. CMC curves of different methods on TFD and SCface.

5 Conclusion

Multi-frame tilt-angle face images captured by real surveillance cameras show complementarity between structural integrity and resolution. In this paper, we propose an angle-guided adaptive weight prediction network to obtain the fusion weights between the similarity lists of tilt-angle faces and make full use of the complementarity among them to boost recognition performance. Experimental results on the existing tilt-angle face datasets demonstrate the effectiveness of the proposed method.

Acknowledgements. This work was supported in part by the National Natural Science Foundation of China (U1903214, 62072347), Guangdong-Macau Joint Laboratory for Advanced and Intelligent Computing(2020B1212030003), and Guangdong High-Level Innovation Research Institute(2019B0909005).

References

1. Arandjelovic, R., Gronat, P., Torii, A., Pajdla, T., Sivic, J.: NetVLAD: CNN architecture for weakly supervised place recognition. In: CVPR, pp. 5297–5307 (2016)
2. Deng, J., Guo, J., Ververas, E., Kotsia, I., Zafeiriou, S.: RetinaFace: single-shot multi-level face localisation in the wild. In: CVPR, pp. 5203–5212 (2020)

3. Deng, J., Guo, J., Xue, N., Zafeiriou, S.: ArcFace: additive angular margin loss for deep face recognition. In: CVPR, pp. 4690–4699 (2019)
4. Gong, S., Shi, Y., Kalka, N.D., Jain, A.K.: Video face recognition: Component-wise feature aggregation network (c-fan). In: ICB, pp. 1–8. IEEE (2019)
5. Grgic, M., Delac, K., Grgic, S.: SCface-surveillance cameras face database. Multimedia Tools Appl. **51**, 863–879 (2011). https://doi.org/10.1007/s11042-009-0417-2
6. He, K., Zhang, X., Ren, S., Sun, J.: Deep residual learning for image recognition. In: CVPR, pp. 770–778 (2016)
7. Hörmann, S., Cao, Z., Knoche, M., Herzog, F., Rigoll, G.: Face aggregation network for video face recognition. In: ICIP, pp. 2973–2977 (2021)
8. Klein, B., Wolf, L., Afek, Y.: A dynamic convolutional layer for short range weather prediction. In: CVPR, pp. 4840–4848 (2015)
9. Liu, D., Gao, X., Wang, N., Peng, C., Li, J.: Iterative local re-ranking with attribute guided synthesis for face sketch recognition. Pattern Recogn. **109**, 107579 (2021)
10. Ou, Z., Hu, Y., Song, M., Yan, Z., Hui, P.: Redundancy removing aggregation network with distance calibration for video face recognition. IEEE Internet Things J. **8**(9), 7279–7287 (2020)
11. Ouyang, J., Zhou, W., Wang, M., Tian, Q., Li, H.: Collaborative image relevance learning for visual re-ranking. IEEE Trans. Multimedia **23**, 3646–3656 (2020)
12. Phan, H., Nguyen, A.: DeepFace-EMD: re-ranking using patch-wise earth mover's distance improves out-of-distribution face identification. In: CVPR, pp. 20259–20269 (2022)
13. Rao, Y., Lu, J., Zhou, J.: Attention-aware deep reinforcement learning for video face recognition. In: CVPR, pp. 3931–3940 (2017)
14. Rao, Y., Lu, J., Zhou, J.: Learning discriminative aggregation network for video-based face recognition and person re-identification. Int. J. Comput. Vis. **127**(6), 701–718 (2019)
15. Ren, S., Cao, X., Wei, Y., Sun, J.: Face alignment at 3000 fps via regressing local binary features. In: CVPR, pp. 1685–1692 (2014)
16. Rivero-Hernández, J., Morales-González, A., Denis, L.G., Méndez-Vázquez, H.: Ordered weighted aggregation networks for video face recognition. Pattern Recogn. Lett. **146**, 237–243 (2021)
17. Shi, X., et al.: Convolutional LSTM network: a machine learning approach for precipitation nowcasting. In: Advances in Neural Information Processing Systems, pp. 802–810 (2015)
18. Sivaram, P.: Mudunuri, Shashanka, Venkataramanan, Soma, Biswas: dictionary alignment with re-ranking for low-resolution NIR-VIS face recognition. IEEE Trans. Inf. Forensics Secur. **4**, 886–896 (2019)
19. Wang, N., Wang, Z., He, Z., Huang, B., Zhou, L., Han, Z.: A tilt-angle face dataset and its validation. In: ICIP, pp. 894–898. IEEE (2021)
20. Yang, J., et al.: Neural aggregation network for video face recognition. In: CVPR, pp. 4362–4371 (2017)
21. Zhang, K., Zhang, Z., Li, Z., Qiao, Y.: Joint face detection and alignment using multitask cascaded convolutional networks. IEEE Sig. Process. Lett. **23**(10), 1499–1503 (2016)
22. Zhang, L., Wang, H., Wang, H.: A feature map aggregation network for unconstrained video face recognition. J. Intell. Fuzzy Syst. **44**, 2413–2425 (2023)
23. Zhang, M., Liu, R., Deguchi, D., Murase, H.: Context-aware contribution estimation for feature aggregation in video face recognition. IEEE Access **10**, 79301–79310 (2022)

24. Zhong, Y., Arandjelović, R., Zisserman, A.: GhostVLAD for set-based face recognition. In: Jawahar, C.V., Li, H., Mori, G., Schindler, K. (eds.) ACCV 2018. LNCS, vol. 11362, pp. 35–50. Springer, Cham (2019). https://doi.org/10.1007/978-3-030-20890-5_3
25. Zhong, Z., Zheng, L., Cao, D., Li, S.: Re-ranking person re-identification with k-reciprocal encoding. In: CVPR, pp. 1318–1327 (2017)
26. Zhou, Y., Wang, Y., Chau, L.P.: Moving towards centers: re-ranking with attention and memory for re-identification. IEEE Trans. Multimedia **25**, 3456–3468 (2022)

Multi-scale Field Distillation for Multi-task Semantic Segmentation

Aimei Dong(✉) and Sidi Liu

Qilu University of Technology (Shandong Academy of Sciences), Jinan, China
amdong@qlu.edu.cn, 10431200602@stu.qlu.edu.cn

Abstract. Semantic segmentation tasks in the field of computer vision have developed rapidly in recent years, because the development of autonomous driving technology requires more accurate semantic segmentation models. However, with the increasing demand, the use of deep models to solve semantic segmentation has reached a bottleneck. This is because the utilization of image information and correlations between images are not fully mined during model operation, and segmentation accuracy can only be achieved by deepening the model depth. To this end, we propose a multi-task semantic segmentation model based on multi-scale feature fusion and distillation to fully mine complementary information between related tasks. When building the multi-task learn framework, we firstly extracted multi-scale image information from the network layer at different depths, using feature fusion and jumping connection at different scales to make up for the loss of too much spatial information in the downsampling process, using distillation module to construct intermediate auxiliary tasks to roughly process features, and high-quality features can be obtained in the middle of training, thus alleviating the calculation pressure of the decoder and improving the accuracy of its own task. The proposed method uses three task-specific decoders to train for segmentation and two estimation tasks. Experiments on NYUv2 and Cityscapes data sets show that adding multi-scale information improves the efficiency of semantic segmentation and two estimation tasks, which shows the effectiveness of the proposed method.

Keywords: multi-task learning · semantic segmentation · Distillation · feature fusion

1 Introduction

In recent years, multi-task learning methods [1] have been applied in image prediction and classification, image segmentation, emotion pattern recognition and other fields due to their fast, simple and wide application scenarios, which can improve the accuracy of multiple tasks simultaneously by exploiting the relevance of multiple related tasks [2]. Intensive task prediction [3] method is often used in multi-task learning because it can deeply explore the high relationship between

L. Iliadis et al. (Eds.): ICANN 2023, LNCS 14255, pp. 508–519, 2023.
https://doi.org/10.1007/978-3-031-44210-0_41

tasks. Compared with single-task learning, it uses a common network header and a single task decoder, which can save half of the number of parameters, and has better efficiency when processing multiple tasks in parallel.

Since multi-task learning uses different loss functions for processing multiple tasks at the same time, which leads to an extremely complex overall network architecture, it may become extremely difficult and less robust in processing tasks, sometimes even worse than single-task learning on some tasks, as this problem was found in UberNet [4]. To cope with this problem, inspired in [5], we use meta-learning gradient method to assign a corresponding weight to each task, the weight allocation principle is not to let one task dominate, so that the performance of all tasks can be improved.

The proposed network architecture consists of a shared layer and task-specific decoders. In the sharing layer, we use SegNet as the backbone network and the method of hard parameter sharing [6] as the parameter passing rule in the sharing layer, compared with soft parameter sharing [6,7], it uses fewer network parameters. In the encoder, Atrous Spatial Pyramid Pooling (ASPP) is connected after each pooling layer to get features with different receptive field and concatenate them, then put the processed features into the feature extraction module and adjust the size of the feature to keep same with the last layer features of the encoder and connected. After distillation module presented in reference [8], which generate the intermediate auxiliary task (semantic segmentation, depth estimation, surface normals estimation) features corresponding to the prediction task by deconvolution, after pass characteristics to distillation module, and the characteristics of the merged into the decoder, all features are then fused using the distillate module and passed into a task specific decoder. Finally, we use residual connections and scale feature attention module (SFAM) to predict the final task. We optimize the training process to achieve optimal results for each task by propagating the loss function and auto weight adjustment.

The first contribution of this paper is to get clearer features through different receptive fields and retain more detailed information in the downsampling process. The second is using intermediate auxiliary task features to improve the accuracy of the prediction tasks. We run our proposed method on NYuV2 datasets [9] and Cityscapes datasets [10] and obtain the accuracy of three tasks: semantic segmentation, depth estimation and surface normal estimation, and demonstrate the feasibility of our method.

2 Related Work

Multi-task learning methods have developed rapidly in recent years, especially in image processing and speech recognition tasks, where they are most used. In multi-task learning methods, the weight of tasks impacts the accuracy of prediction tasks when the weights are too big or small. The Dynamically Weighted Average (DWA) [11] method uses the loss value in multiple epoch to measure the learning speed of a task and obtains the task weights by normalization. Inspired by the Pareto optimal solution, PE-LRT [12] seeks a set of values to satisfy the

KKT condition to balance the gradient of each task in the shared parameter part, to reduce the global loss of all tasks. PCGrad [13] method solves three problems in multi-task learning, firstly different gradients of tasks lead to longer training time, secondly large gradient tasks dominate, thirdly excessive curvature of gradients leads to overfitting. The weight function used in our method is borrowed from [5], which is a gradient-based meta-learning method and optimizes the weights of all tasks by meta loss.

JERT [14] was using an attention module to get features of each task, and iterate the experience learned by assistant tasks into the main task to improve the accuracy of the main task. PAD-Net [8] proposed a task distillation module that obtains intermediate tasks by processing underlying features and recursively applies the results of intermediate tasks to predict tasks. MTI-Net [15] first uses multiscale feature maps to predict tasks, and finally uses spatial attention to refine all tasks recursively. Inspired by the PAD-Net network, we use multi-scale features to obtain intermediate state tasks for a more efficient distillation module.

Multi-task learning methods have had a mature effect in the field of semantic segmentation. There are three main ways to solve semantically split tasks: patch-based methods, multilevel methods, and multiscale methods. [16] et al. applied dilated convolution to the last layer of the decoder to extract contextual information and aggregated them in a self-cascading manner. [17] et al. found the advantage of low-level texture features and introduced Texture Enhancement Module (TEM) to enhance texture details. MagNet [18] is a multi-scale segmentation network model that can generate high-resolution segmentation output without increasing the GPU memory usage, and it can alleviate the details of down sampling loss. Our method also uses a multi-scale approach, using the features of multiple receptive fields to strengthen the local and global features, and transfers more accurate features to the decoder to improve the accuracy of prediction tasks.

3 Network Model

The method proposed in this paper first fuses the features from different receptive fields, next inputs the fused features into the deconvolution layer to get the intermediate state task, then inputs all the intermediate state tasks into the distillation module, using the meta-learning gradient method to balance the weights of the tasks, and finally obtains the performance of each task through an independent decoder.

3.1 Network Architecture

Figure 1 shows our proposed network architecture. In our method, we use SegNet as the backbone architecture, which has a moderate number of layers and better performs compared to other architectures, and using fewer network parameters. We first obtain rough feature information from the encoder, and then we put the

Atrous Spatial Pyramid Pooling (ASPP) module after the encoder, which uses different receptive fields to locate the position and edge information of the object, so as to compensates for missing information in the encoder convolution layer. After that, using Scale-Layer Attention Module (SLAM) to extract and fuse the features of different receptive fields, the size of the fused features is adjusted to be the same as that of the last layer of the encoder, all features are fused and output, thus completing the first stage of feature extraction. Before the feature is fed into the decoder, we use deconvolution to obtain three intermediate state tasks (semantic segmentation, depth estimation, and surface normal estimation), the intermediate state tasks are passed through a multimodal distillation module to fuse the information from the intermediate predictions for each specific final task, this module aims to efficiently utilize intermediate prediction information for the task in question, accelerate and improve the final task accuracy. In the second stage, the decoder receives the features of the distillation module to predict all tasks. In order to improve the accuracy of the task and prevent the gradient vanishing problem of the network too deep, we use the Scale-Feature Attention Module (SFAM) to connect the encoder and decoder corresponding layers to make the final prediction for each task.

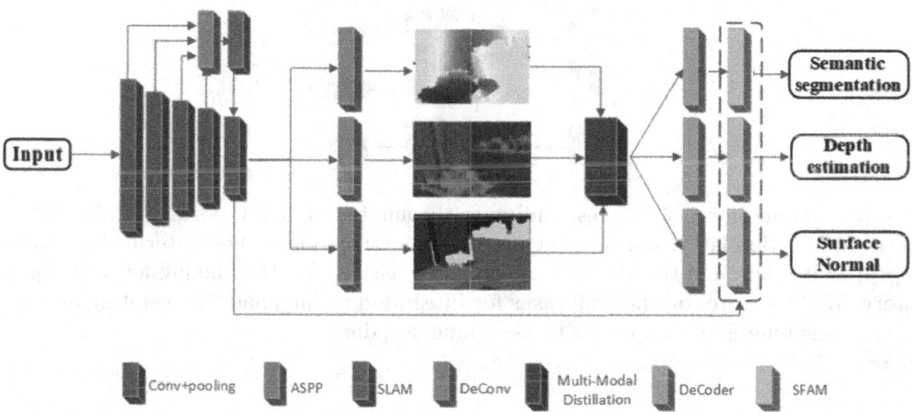

Fig. 1. The network structure Mul-CD proposed in this paper has encoder and decoder as the main architecture, supplemented by multimodal distillation as well as feature extraction and multi-level feature fusion methods, and the final prediction is generated by processing the fused features with a decoder based on independent tasks.

Figure 2 shows the feature fusion module we used. Since multitask networks do not recognize challenging objectives well because of lack of sufficient context information, the ASPP module can be used to obtain different layers of feature mappings with different receptive fields, and its effectiveness was verified in [19]. By size-matching the different perceptual field feature maps output by the ASPP module, enter the processed features into the SLAM module, and the input feature weight maps are obtained by 1 * 1 convolution, batch normalization,

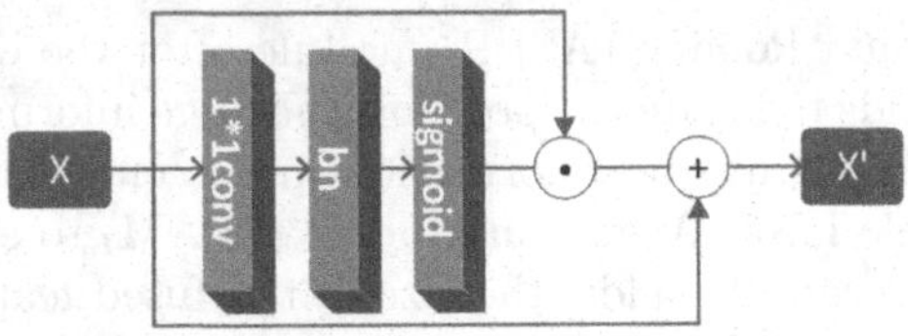

Fig. 2. The SLAM module can accept the feature maps obtained from different perceptual fields and fuse them.

and sigmoid activation functions, the weight maps are multiplied with the input features and later added with the input features in order to prevent gradient disappearance. The output of this module is represented in Eq. (1) as follows:

$$F' = F \oplus (F \odot Sigmoid(bn(conv(F)))) \tag{1}$$

3.2 Distillation Module

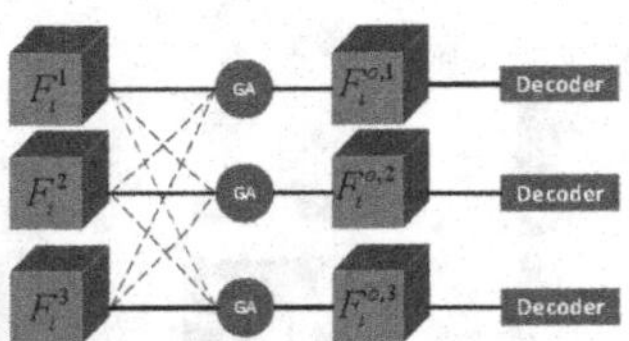

Fig. 3. Intermediate tasks corresponding to the number of final tasks are obtained after the deconvolution layer, and then the prediction information of these intermediate tasks is propagated through the attention mechanism (GA) to control the influence factor of intermediate features on the final tasks for integrated coding, and the resulting average feature mapping is passed to the task-specific decoder.

Task prediction distillation is the first approach proposed by PAD-Net, each task is initially predicted by setting intermediate state tasks, then further refines the output of each task by distillation modules. This module aims to provide complementary information to the final task by utilizing intermediate predictions of related tasks. In PAD-Net, the best performance module is "Module C", due to the use of attention-guided mechanism in the feature delivery process. The advantage of using attention mechanism is that the attention mechanism generates a mask for the feature map, which allows the network to automatically focus on or ignore information which is useful or not for its own task. This distillation module is robust and transferable and can be used in most deep learning networks, and can effectively improve the accuracy of all tasks. Equations (2) and (3) are used to calculate the output of the distillation module:

$$G_i^k \leftarrow \sigma(W_g^k | \otimes F_i^k) \quad (2)$$

$$F_i^{o,k} \leftarrow F_i^k + \sum_{t=1(\neq k)}^{T} G_i^k \odot (W_t \otimes F_i^t) \quad (3)$$

When we pass message to the k-th task, an attention map G_i^k is first produced from the corresponding set of feature maps F_i^k. Where W_g^k is the convolution parameter and σ is a sigmoid function for normalizing the attention map, $\odot$ denotes element-wise multiplication (Fig. 3).

3.3 SFAM Module

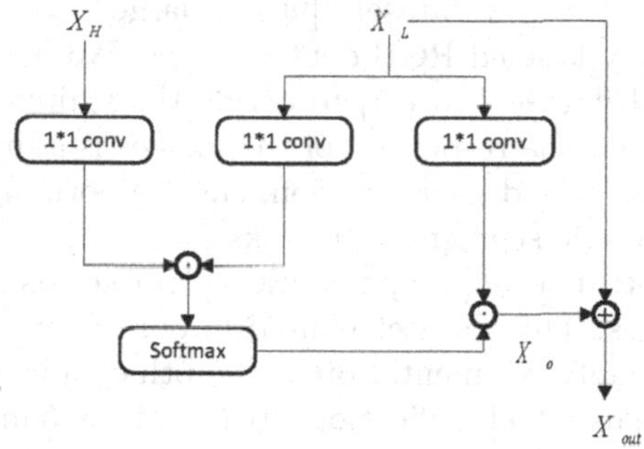

Fig. 4. The SFAM module used is able to be inserted between any layer of deep learning and is used to fuse the feature mapping of the different levels, avoiding the disappearance of gradients.

Figure 4 shows the feature fusion module we use, by fusing the low-scale features from the encoder with the high-scale features from the decoder, recycle the ignored low-scale features to improve the information richness of the output features and prevent the gradients from disappearing due to too deep network. This module is explained as follows, x_l is the feature vector on the low-level feature map, x_h is the feature vector from the high-level feature map, x_l and x_h should keep the same feature array dimension without feature map dimension adjustment. Using Eq. (4) to express:

$$x_o = soft\max(\theta(x_l) \odot \Phi(x_h) \odot g(x_l)) \quad (4)$$

The x_o is the output of the fusion process, the θ, Φ and g functions are simple point-by-point convolutions, and $\odot$ is the hadamard multiplier to calculate the feature map. In order to avoid gradient vanishing, the residual network is used for the connection and the final result $x_{out} = x_o + x_l$.

We connect the SFAM module after the decoder to prevent information loss in the deep learning process. Making the underlying features play an auxiliary role in the final prediction task. We use global information as the dominant and local information as the auxiliary to fully utilize the extracted features and refine and improve the accuracy for each task.

4 Experiment

We evaluate our proposed model on the NYUv2 dataset and the Cityscapes dataset. In this section, I will first present the datasets we used, followed by the evaluation metrics. After that, we explain the feasibility of our approach by comparing it with more advanced multi-task learning methods.

4.1 Datasets

NYUv2 datasets: The NYUv2 datasets [9] is a large dataset of indoor scenes, containing 1449 densely labeled RGB depth images. We use the data after processing of the original datasets in [11] to divide the training and test sets into 795 and 654 images, and the resolution of the images is adjusted to [288 * 384]. These datasets are used for deep regression, surface normal estimation, and 13 classifications for semantic segmentation tasks.

Cityscapes dataset: The cityscapes dataset [10] consists of high-resolution rate street view images. This dataset is used in our experiments to accomplish two related tasks: semantic segmentation and depth estimation. In the semantic segmentation task, we use 19 classification labels with 2975 images in the training set and 1525 images in the test set, and adjust the image resolution to [128 * 256].

4.2 Task Overview

Semantic Segmentation. The principle of the semantic segmentation task is to assign a class label to each pixel in the image, and we use the Mean Intersection over Union (MIoU) as the semantic segmentation criterion, which is calculated by Eq. (5) as follows:

$$MIoU = \frac{1}{k+1} \sum_{1}^{k} \frac{TP}{FN + FP + TP} \tag{5}$$

The training objective of this task is to minimize the depth cross-entropy loss between the predicted and true labels with a loss function as in Eq. (6), where N_S represents all pixel points:

$$L_{Semantic} = -\frac{1}{N_S} \sum_{n \in N_S} y_n \log(\hat{y}_n) \tag{6}$$

Depth Estimation. Depth estimation involves assigning a continuous depth value at each pixel, and we use the absolute error as the calculation for the depth estimation task, which will be represented by Eq. (7), where d_n is the true depth value, $\hat{d}_n$ is the network prediction, and N_D denotes all pixels:

$$Error_{rel} = \sum_{n} \in N_D \frac{\| d_n - \hat{d}_n \|}{d_n} \tag{7}$$

The objective of this task is to minimize the absolute error between the predicted depth and the true depth for all N_D pixels, whose loss function we express in Eq. (8):

$$L_{Depth} = \sum_{n \in N_D} \| d_n - \hat{d}_n \| \tag{8}$$

Surface Normal Estimation. Surface normal estimation is the prediction of the surface orientation of an object in an image. In the prediction of this task, we use the average angular distance as a criterion to calculate the angular distance, which is the arccosine of the sum of the products of the normalized prediction vector and the ground truth vector, which we calculate using Eq. (9), where y_n and $\hat{y}_n$ are the predicted and ground truth labels, respectively, and N_N is all pixel points:

$$D_\theta = \arccos(\sum_{n \in N_N} \hat{y}_n \cdot y_n) \tag{9}$$

The objective of this task is to minimize the element-wise dot product between the predicted and true values of all pixels N_N. The loss function is expressed in Eq. (10):

$$L_{Normals} = -\frac{1}{N_N} \sum_{n \in N_N} y_n \cdot \hat{y}_n \tag{10}$$

4.3 Results

The multi-task learning method proposed in this paper is designed based on feed-forward neural networks to solve the related tasks of semantic segmentation, depth estimation and surface normal estimation. In order to demonstrate the advantages of our model, we compare our model with single-task models and classic multi-task models, and set the trunk network of all models to SegNet network. When compared with the control group multi-task model, our proposed multi-scale feature and task distillation method can achieve better experimental results, which demonstrates the feasibility of our proposed method.

In the experiment designed in this paper, we set up seven groups of control experiments, including one group of single-task learning models and six groups of multi-task learning models. The model designed by the single-task learning method is: Single, Segnet is used as the backbone network to train a single network to solve semantic segmentation and its related tasks respectively. The multi-task learning comparative experimental methods is as follows: (1) PAD-Net [8], which uses a multi-task oriented predictive distillation network structure to assist the calculation of the final task by predicting a series of intermediate auxiliary tasks; (2) Auto [5], based on PAD-Net model, changes the weight update function into a meta-learning based dynamic weight update method; (3) ASPP [20], SegNet is used as the backbone network, and dilated convolution under different receptive fields is used to extract target features and obtain feature maps of different scales. (4) SLAM [21], which uses a module that focuses on context information and can adaptively weight feature maps; (5) SFAM [21], the fusion method improved by deconvolution does not model the pixel correspondence on the hierarchical feature map, and the fusion model with excellent effect; (6) ATI-Net [22], a new model that introduces knowledge distillation and attention into multi-task network based on PAD-Net.

Table 1 shows our experimental results on the NYUv2 dataset. From the comparative experimental results, all the multi-task learning models perform better than single-task learning models, indicating that multi-task learning shows stronger performance than single-task learning when dealing with multiple related tasks at the same time. Our method also achieves good results in comparative experiments on multi-task learning. In the semantic segmentation task, the MIoU index of our model Mul-CD is 1% higher than that of the second ranked method ATI-Net. In the depth estimation task, the absolute error is reduced by 2% compared with the second ranked method. In the surface normal estimation task, the average angular distance error is significantly reduced compared to the second ranked method.

Table 1. Semantic segmentation, depth estimation and surface normal estimation tasks performed on the NYUv2 datasets.

	Sem mIoU↑	Depth aErr↓	Normal mDist↓
single	35.96	0.6577	30.2554
PAD-Net	37.99	0.6033	29.7668
Auto	37.65	0.5553	28.7194
ASPP	42.17	0.4968	27.2290
SLAM	42.88	0.5037	26.4566
SFAM	41.93	0.5268	27.3847
ATI-Net	42.95	0.5012	26.2535
Mul-CD	**43.75**	**0.4779**	**25.9056**

Table 2 shows our experimental results on the Cityscapes dataset, and three tasks are performed on this dataset: semantic segmentation, depth estimation, and surface normal estimation. Through the experimental data, it can be seen that all the multi-task models perform better than the single-task model on the three tasks of semantic segmentation, depth estimation and surface normal estimation, and our method is also better than the control multi-task learning model. The mIoU of semantic segmentation task is about 1.5% higher than the second best method SFAM. The absolute error of the depth estimation task is also reduced compared to the second method SLAM, and the average angular distance error of the surface normal also achieves the best results.

Table 2. Experimental results on the Cityscapes dataset.

	Sem mIoU↑	Depth aErr↓	Normal mDist↓
single	43.15	0.0321	25.6354
PAD-Net	45.55	0.0255	24.8462
Auto	46.85	0.0202	23.1543
ASPP	47.08	0.0199	23.5629
SLAM	47.02	0.0195	22.0934
SFAM	47.21	0.0197	21.9556
ATI-Net	47.11	0.0199	21.5362
Mul-CD	**48.58**	**0.0188**	**21.0658**

Figure 5 shows the visualization of our model on the NYUv2 dataset. We can clearly see that the predicted map generated by the Mul-CD model has a high similarity with the ground-truth map. In the presence of noise in the label graph, a better result is obtained through the transfer of information between multi-tasks.

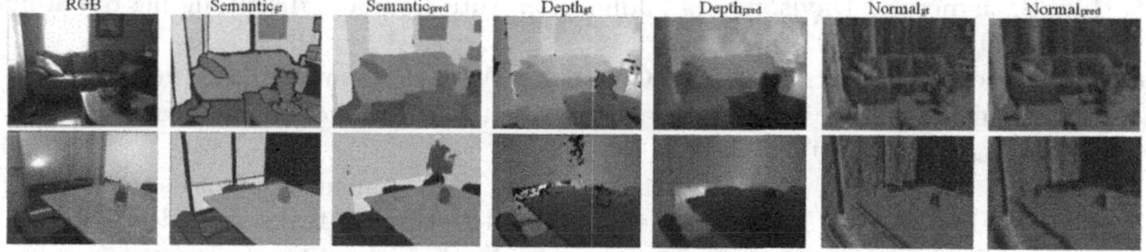

Fig. 5. Visualization of the NYUv2 dataset, where the subscripts "gt" and "pred" denote the groud truth and predicted, respectively.

The excellent results of our proposed method among all the compared methods are attributed to the following: (1) We integrate feature maps from different receptive fields to make the network more fully exploit contextual information; (2) In order to prevent the gradient from disappearing, we use residual network to connect the high-level features with the low-level features, preserving some details. (3) By adding the intermediate state task, the features are first coarsely processed, which in turn facilitates the optimization of the final task.

5 Conclusions

In this paper, we propose a multi-task learning method named Mul-CD. The method combines the task distillation method and feature fusion module whit multiple receptive fields, using meta-learning gradient to update the tasks weight. Unlike other models, our method uses feature extraction modules with residual links to preserve details in the underlying features and distillation modules to refine the intermediate state information for each task. Our method is tested on the challenging NYUv2 dataset and Cityscapes dataset and all metrics are improved, this method learns automatically end-to-end without human intervention and is very robust.

Acknowledgements. This study was supported by the Shandong Provincial Natural Science Foundation project(Nos. ZR2022MF237, Nos. ZR2020MF041) and the Youth Fund of National Natural Science Foundation of China (Nos. 11901325).

References

1. Caruana, R.: Multitask learning. Mach. Learn. **1**, 41–75 (1997)
2. Kendall, A., Gal, Y., Cipolla, R.: Multi-task learning using uncertainty to weigh losses for scene geometry and semantics. In: 2018 IEEE/CVF Conference on Computer Vision and Pattern Recognition (CVPR) (2018)
3. Tao, R., Zhang, Y., Wang, L., Liu, Q., Wang, J.: U-High resolution network (U-HRNet): cloud detection with high-resolution representations for geostationary satellite imagery. Int. J. Remote Sens. **9**, 3511–3533 (2021)
4. Kokkinos, I.: UberNet: training a 'universal' convolutional neural network for low-, mid-, and high-level vision using diverse datasets and limited memory. In: 30th IEEE/CVF Conference on Computer Vision and Pattern Recognition (CVPR) (2017)
5. Liu, S., James, S., Davison, A.J., Johns, E.: Auto-Lambda: disentangling dynamic task relationships (2022)
6. Vandenhende, S., Georgoulis, S., Gansbeke, W.V., Proesmans, M., Dai, D., Gool, L.V.: Multi-task learning for dense prediction tasks: a survey. IEEE Trans. Pattern Anal. Mach. Intell. (01) (2021)
7. Ruder, S.: An overview of multi-task learning in deep neural networks (2017)
8. Xu, D., Ouyang, W., Wang, X., Sebe, N.: Pad-Net: multi-tasks guided prediction-and-distillation network for simultaneous depth estimation and scene parsing (2018)
9. Silberman, N., Hoiem, D., Kohli, P., Fergus, R.: Indoor segmentation and support inference from RGBD images. In: Fitzgibbon, A., Lazebnik, S., Perona, P., Sato, Y., Schmid, C. (eds.) ECCV 2012. LNCS, vol. 7576, pp. 746–760. Springer, Heidelberg (2012). https://doi.org/10.1007/978-3-642-33715-4_54
10. Cordts, M., Omran, M., Ramos, S., Rehfeld, T., Schiele, B.: The cityscapes dataset for semantic urban scene understanding (2016)
11. Liu, S., Johns, E., Davison, A.J.: End-to-end multi-task learning with attention (2018)
12. Lin, X., Chen, H., Pei, C., Sun, F., Jiang, P.: A pareto-efficient algorithm for multiple objective optimization in e-commerce recommendation. In: The 13th ACM Conference (2019)

13. Yu, T., Kumar, S., Gupta, A., Levine, S., Finn, C.: Gradient surgery for multi-task learning (2020)
14. Zhang, Z., Cui, Z., Xu, C., Jie, Z., Li, X., Yang, J.: Joint task-recursive learning for semantic segmentation and depth estimation. In: Ferrari, V., Hebert, M., Sminchisescu, C., Weiss, Y. (eds.) ECCV 2018. LNCS, vol. 11214, pp. 238–255. Springer, Cham (2018). https://doi.org/10.1007/978-3-030-01249-6_15
15. Vandenhende, S., Georgoulis, S., Van Gool, L.: MTI-Net: multi-scale task interaction networks for multi-task learning. In: Vedaldi, A., Bischof, H., Brox, T., Frahm, J.-M. (eds.) ECCV 2020. LNCS, vol. 12349, pp. 527–543. Springer, Cham (2020). https://doi.org/10.1007/978-3-030-58548-8_31
16. Liu, Y., Fan, B., Wang, L., Bai, J., Xiang, S., Pan, C.: Semantic labeling in very high resolution images via a self-cascaded convolutional neural network. ISPRS J. Photogramm. Remote Sens. **145**, 78–95 (2018)
17. Zhu, L., Ji, D., Zhu, S., Gan, W., Yan, J.: Learning statistical texture for semantic segmentation (2021)
18. Huynh, C., Tran, A., Luu, K., Hoai, M.: Progressive semantic segmentation (2021)
19. Mi, L., Chen, Z.: Superpixel-enhanced deep neural forest for remote sensing image semantic segmentation. ISPRS J. Photogramm. Remote Sens. **159**, 140–152 (2020)
20. Tian, Y., Chen, F., Wang, H., Zhang, S.: Real-time semantic segmentation network based on lite reduced atrous spatial pyramid pooling module group. In: 2020 5th International Conference on Control, Robotics and Cybernetics (CRC) (2020)
21. Liu, R., Mi, L., Chen, Z.: AFNet: adaptive fusion network for remote sensing image semantic segmentation. IEEE Trans. Geosci. Remote Sens. **99**, 1–16 (2020)
22. Sinodinos, D., Armanfard, N.: Attentive task interaction network for multi-task learning (2022)

Neural Field Conditioning Strategies for 2D Semantic Segmentation

Martin Gromniak[1,2(✉)], Sven Magg[3], and Stefan Wermter[1]

[1] Knowledge Technology, Department of Informatics, University of Hamburg, Hamburg, Germany
martin.gromniak@uni-hamburg.de
[2] ZAL Center of Applied Aeronautical Research, Hamburg, Germany
[3] Hamburger Informatik Technologie-Center e.V. (HITeC), Hamburg, Germany

Abstract. Neural fields are neural networks which map coordinates to a desired signal. When a neural field should jointly model multiple signals, and not memorize only one, it needs to be conditioned on a latent code which describes the signal at hand. Despite being an important aspect, there has been little research on conditioning strategies for neural fields. In this work, we explore the use of neural fields as decoders for 2D semantic segmentation. For this task, we compare three conditioning methods, simple concatenation of the latent code, Feature-wise Linear Modulation (FiLM), and Cross-Attention, in conjunction with latent codes which either describe the full image or only a local region of the image. Our results show a considerable difference in performance between the examined conditioning strategies. Furthermore, we show that conditioning via Cross-Attention achieves the best results and is competitive with a CNN-based decoder for semantic segmentation.

Keywords: neural fields · conditioning · semantic segmentation

1 Introduction

Lately, neural networks for semantic segmentation have been mostly based on the fully convolutional network (FCN) [11] paradigm. FCN models typically consist of an encoder and a decoder which are both built with stacked convolution layers. The purpose of the encoder is to extract features from the image. With increasing depth of the encoder, the features get more abstract and the resolution of the feature maps is progressively reduced. The decoder on the other hand takes the low-resolution feature maps from the encoder as an input and upscales them to the resolution of the original image so that pixel-level classification can be performed.

While encoders in the form of convolutional neural networks (CNN) have been rigorously studied, considerably less research has been conducted on the decoder side of semantic segmentation networks. The main challenge for the decoder is to upscale the feature maps to the original resolution of the image and simultaneously produce accurate region borders. In CNN-based decoders,

L. Iliadis et al. (Eds.): ICANN 2023, LNCS 14255, pp. 520–532, 2023.
https://doi.org/10.1007/978-3-031-44210-0_42

upsampling or transposed convolution operators are typically used to progressively increase the spatial resolution of the feature maps. These operations introduce a particular kind of inductive bias. For example, transposed convolutions can create spectral artifacts in the upscaled feature maps [5]. Another apparent disadvantage of CNN decoders is that they struggle to capture long-range dependencies between different parts of the image due to their locally connected structure.

In the last few years, neural fields, aka implicit neural representations or coordinate-based networks, have received much attention for learning a variety of different signals, for example, 1D audio signals [22], 2D images [4,26] and 3D geometries [12,24]. A neural field takes (spatial) coordinates $x \in \mathbb{R}^d$ as input and maps them to a task-dependent signal $y = \Phi(x)$ through a neural network. For example, a neural field representing an RGB image takes 2D image coordinates as input and produces three RGB values at each location. One interesting property of neural fields is that they represent signals as continuous functions on their respective spatial domain.

Inspired by the recent success of neural fields, we explore the use of neural fields as decoders in semantic segmentation networks. In this regard, we hypothesize that (continuous) neural fields provide an inductive bias which can be better suited for reconstructing high-resolution semantic maps compared with (discrete) CNN-based decoders. In our work, we examine multiple conditioning strategies which enable the neural field decoder to make use of the information in the latent feature maps produced by the encoder. Through our comparative study, we aim to provide more insights into conditioning methods of neural fields, as research has been extremely sparse in this regard. Furthermore, we believe that 2D semantic segmentation provides a well-defined task for studying conditioning methods, as it has comprehensive metrics and the possibility for insightful visualizations of the learned geometries.

2 Related Work

Semantic Segmentation. Encoder-decoder fully convolutional networks [11] have become the predominant approach for semantic segmentation. They share the challenge how to encode high-level features in typically low-resolution feature maps and subsequently upscale these feature maps to retrieve pixel-accurate semantic predictions. One drawback of CNNs is that, because of their locally connected structure, they struggle to combine information which is spatially distributed across the feature maps. Research attempting to mitigate this drawback has proposed attention mechanisms over feature maps to selectively capture and combine information on a global scale [6]. Extending the concept of attention further, neural network architectures based fully on transformers have been proposed recently for semantic segmentation [25]. In our work, we utilize a CNN, which is more efficient than transformers, for extracting features and use attention in one of our conditioning methods.

CNN Decoders. Research on decoders has been more sparse than research on neural network encoders, i.e. CNN backbones. Wojna et al. [28] compare different CNN-based decoders for several pixel-wise prediction tasks and observe significant variance in results between different types of decoders. Multiple works [5,14] provide evidence that upscaling using transposed convolution operators introduces artifacts in the feature maps and therefore the decoder's output. We aim to avoid any explicit or implicit discretization artifacts by using a continuous neural field decoder.

Neural Fields. Neural fields were introduced in 2019 as a representation for learning 3D shapes [12,15]. Following works extended neural fields by learning colored appearances of scenes and objects [13,24]. Particularly NeRF [13] has attracted a lot of attention, as it is able to generate very realistic novel views of a scene, learning from images and associated poses. NeRF effectively overfits a neural network for one individual scene. This limits the usability as the neural field needs to be re-trained for every new scene. Some works have explored the use of neural fields for semantic segmentation. Vora et al. [27] built a 3D segmentation on top of the NeRF approach. Hu et al. [9] used neural fields in conjunction with CNNs for upsampling and aligning feature maps in the decoder of a semantic segmentation network.

Neural Field Conditioning. When a neural field should share knowledge between different signals, it needs to be conditioned on a latent code which describes the signal at hand. Several conditioning approaches have been explored in the literature. Methods based on global conditional codes use one code to describe the whole signal [12,23]. Methods based on local conditional codes [4,29] use a different code for each spatial area in the signal. On top of these, there exist multiple methods how a neural field can actually consume a conditional code, which we describe in detail in Sect. 3.3. Rebain et al. [18] compare different methods for conditioning neural fields for 2D and 3D tasks, but did not consider global and local conditional codes. In the neural field community, there is a lack of comparative research on what conditioning strategies work well for which task. We attempt to shed more light on this by comparing different conditioning strategies for the well-defined task of 2D semantic segmentation.

3 Method

3.1 Neural Network Architecture and Training Procedure

Our high-level architecture involves a CNN encoder and a neural field decoder (see Fig. 1). We use a CNN to efficiently encode an image into a feature volume with size $c \times h \times w$, where c is the number of channels, w is the spatial width and h is the spatial height. From this feature volume, we calculate the conditional code for the neural field decoder in different ways, depending on the conditioning strategy. During training, for every image, we sample S random points within the

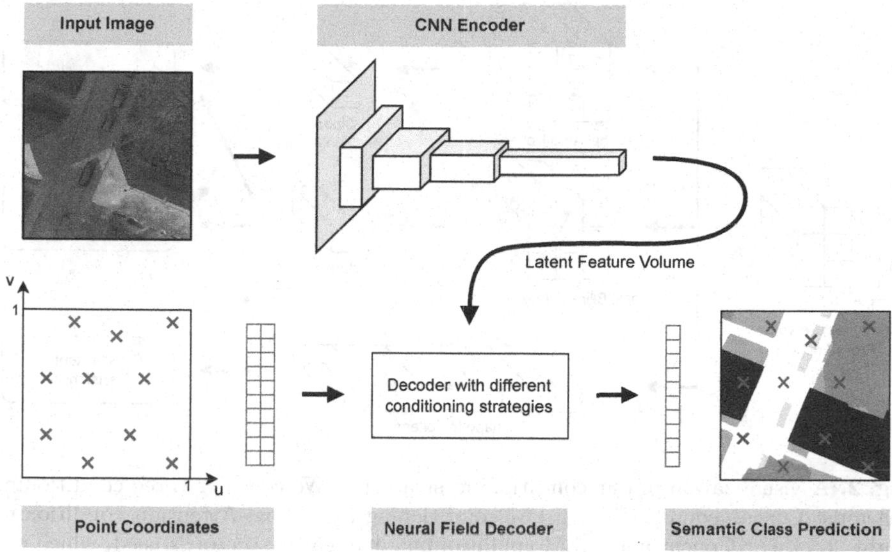

Fig. 1. Our high-level neural network architecture. A CNN encoder encodes an image into a feature volume consisting of multiple feature maps. During training, S points per image are sampled within the image (red) and fed into the decoder. The decoder is a conditional neural field for which we use different conditioning strategies. For every point the decoder outputs a prediction of the semantic class at this position (purple). (Color figure online)

image. At test time, the points are densely sampled so that there exists one point for each pixel. The point coordinates are normalized to the [0,1] range, stacked, and fed to the neural field decoder as input. For every point, the decoder predicts the semantic class at that position in the image. We use a cross-entropy loss to train the whole setup in an end-to-end fashion. At test time, the class predictions per point are arranged into an image. Thereby, we can compare the predictions with the class labels using standard image segmentation metrics, such as the Intersection over Union (IoU).

3.2 Latent Code Source: Global vs. Local

First, we differentiate how the conditional code is calculated based on the feature volume from the encoder. We consider a *global* code and a *local* code. The global code represents the content of the complete image. Naturally, it can capture the global context in the image well. However, due to its limited capacity, it might not be able to capture fine, local geometries. On the other hand, the local code represents a spatially limited area in the image. It can utilize its full capacity for modeling the geometry in one area with high fidelity, however, it might lack global context. For example, the probability of detecting a car rises when a street is detected somewhere in the image.

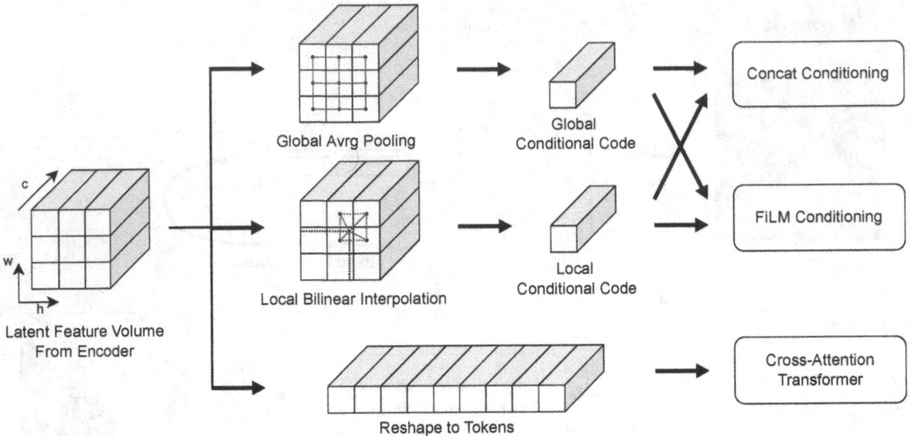

Fig. 2. A visualization of our conditioning strategies. We consider three conditioning methods: Concat conditioning, FiLM conditioning and Cross-Attention conditioning (right side). For Concat and FiLM conditioning, one feature vector is used, which can be calculated from global features (top path) or local features (mid path). The input to the Cross-Attention Transformer is the whole feature volume, which is reshaped and treated as tokens (bottom path).

We calculate the global code vector by applying a global average pooling operation. It averages all the entries in the feature maps across the spatial dimensions (see the top path in Fig. 2). This is a standard operation which is used, for example, in the ResNet classification head [8]. Through this procedure, we calculate one global code per image. For calculating the local code, we utilize the point coordinates, in addition to the feature volume. For every point, we "look up" the value of the feature maps at this position. For this purpose, we normalize the feature maps' spatial dimensions to the [0,1] range, and therefore effectively align the feature volume with the input image. We then perform a bilinear interpolation within the feature maps based on the point coordinate to calculate the local code vector (see the middle path in Fig. 2). As a result, we have S local codes per image, one for every point. In addition to using either a global or a local code, we also consider the combination of both to jointly exploit their individual advantages. We do this by concatenating both codes.

3.3 Conditioning the Neural Field Decoder

Conditioning a neural field enables it to effectively adapt the knowledge which is shared across all signals to the signal at hand.

Conditioning by Concatenation. In the simplest conditioning method, the conditional code is concatenated to the point coordinates and is jointly used as input to the neural field. We re-concatenate the conditional code to other hidden layers using skip connections. This approach is used by HyperNeRF [16]. It has the advantage of being conceptually simple, however, it is computationally inefficient [18], because it requires $O(k(c+k))$ parameters for the fully connected layers in the neural field, where k is the hidden layer width and c is the size of the conditioning vector.

Feature-Wise Linear Modulation. Another way to condition a neural field is to use the latent code together with an MLP to regress the parameters of the neural field. When all parameters of the neural field are calculated in this way, the approach is known as hyper-networks [7]. Feature-wise Linear Modulation (FiLM) [17] is a more constraint subtype of hyper-networks where, instead of predicting all weights, feature-wise modulations of activations in the neural field are predicted. This approach is used in Occupancy Networks [12] and piGAN [2].

Cross-Attention. Conditioning by Cross-Attention has been introduced by Jiang et al. [10] and was extended in the Scene Representation Transformer [21]. The core idea is to selectively attend to features at different spatial positions, based on the point coordinates. A transformer architecture with Cross-Attention layers is used where the queries are derived from the point coordinates and the feature volume serves as a set of tokens. This approach does have an interesting connection with using local codes, as both approaches calculate a feature vector by weighting entries in the feature maps based on the current point coordinate. However, in difference to the spatial "look up" of local codes, which can be performed for free, the Cross-Attention operation can flexibly query both local and global information as needed at the cost of more computation [18].

4 Experiments

We evaluate seven conditioning strategies on a public dataset for semantic segmentation. Concat conditioning and FiLM conditioning are used in conjunction with global, local and combined conditional codes each. The Cross-Attention Transformer uses the reshaped feature volume as input (see Fig. 2).

4.1 Dataset

For our experiments, we used the Potsdam dataset[1] which is part of the ISPRS semantic labeling contest [20]. It consists of satellite images of the German city Potsdam together with dense label masks for six classes: `Impervious surfaces`, `Building`, `Low vegetation`, `Tree`, `Car` and `Clutter/background`. The orthographic images have a sampling distance of 0.05 m/px. The total dataset consists of 38 tiles with a size of 6000×6000 px from which we use the same 24 tiles for training as in the original contest. From the remaining tiles, we use 7 for validation and 7 for testing. From the tiles, we randomly crop patches of 256×256 or 512×512 pixels.

[1] https://www.isprs.org/education/benchmarks/UrbanSemLab/2d-sem-label-potsdam.aspx.

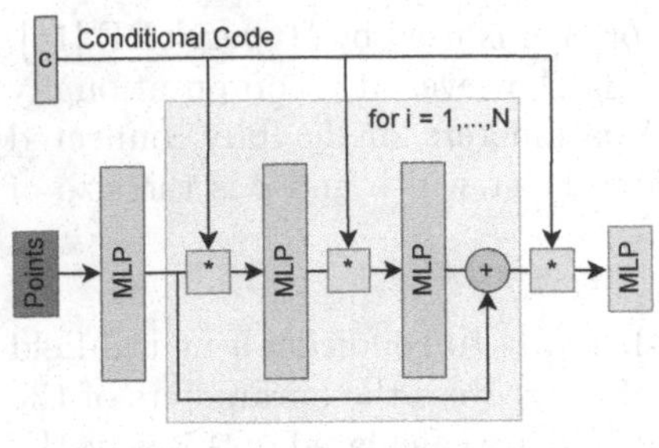

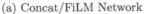

(a) Concat/FiLM Network

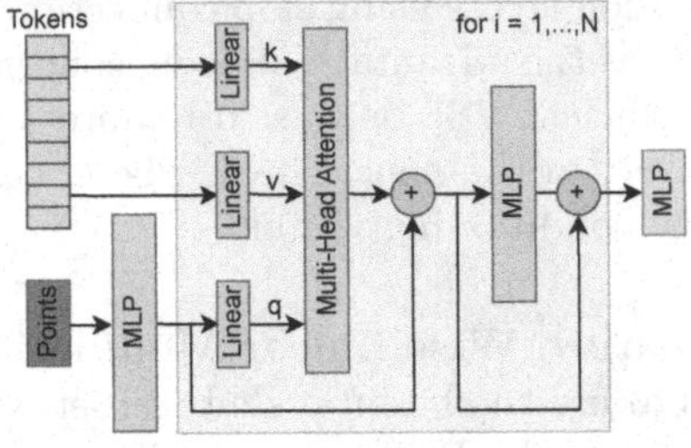

(b) Cross-Attention Transformer

Fig. 3. Our neural network architectures used for the Concat and FiLM conditioning (left) and for the Cross-Attention Transformer (right). The yellow block can be repeated N times. For the Concat approach, the orange block denoted with an asterisk represents a concatination followed by a batchnorm layer. For FiLM, the same block denotes a conditional batchnorm layer. Other batchnorm and layernorm layers have been omitted for clarity. (Color figure online)

4.2 Encoder and Decoder Implementations

For the Concat and the FiLM decoder, we use a similar neural network architecture, which is based on Occupancy networks [12] (see Fig. 3a). We use either concatenation plus conventional batchnorm or conditional batchnorm at the designated places in the neural network architecture. For the Cross-Attention conditioning, we use a transformer architecture based on the Scene Representation Transformer [21] (see Fig. 3b). It uses one multi-head attention module per block. Keys and values are calculated from the feature tokens while the queries are calculated from the point coordinates. We can scale both neural network architectures by repeating the yellow blocks N times or increasing the width of the MLP layers. For all experiments we use a ResNet34 [8] backbone as the encoder, pre-trained on ImageNet. Its output feature volume has a size of $512 \times 8 \times 8$ for input images with size 256×256 pixels and $512 \times 16 \times 16$ for input images with size 512×512 pixels respectively.

4.3 Points Embedding

It has been shown that when coordinates are directly used as inputs, neural fields have a bias towards learning low-frequency signals. To counter this, we embed both image coordinates independently into a higher dimensional space by using Fourier features as it is commonly done with neural fields [26]:

$$\gamma(x) = (sin(2^0 \pi x), sin(2^1 \pi x), ..., sin(2^l \pi x), cos(2^0 \pi x), cos(2^1 \pi x), ..., cos(2^l \pi x)), \tag{1}$$

where x is an image coordinate and l controls the embedding size.

Table 1. Results for all examined decoder architectures.

Decoder conditioning	Conditional Code Source	Image Size				Params
		256		512		
		IoU	F-score	IoU	F-score	
Concatenation	global	0.689	0.816	0.659	0.794	2.1M
	local	0.725	0.840	0.666	0.799	2.1M
	global + local	0.728	0.842	0.712	0.832	4.0M
FiLM	global	0.695	0.820	0.660	0.795	2.1M
	local	0.729	0.843	0.650	0.788	2.1M
	global + local	0.729	0.843	0.707	0.829	3.7M
Cross-Attention	feature tokens	0.758	0.862	0.754	0.860	2.6M
DeepLabV3+ [3]	–	0.760	0.863	0.763	0.866	5.4M

4.4 Training Parameters

The influence of the parameters used in our experiments was evaluated in preliminary runs, based on the validation performance. For all experiments, we choose a fixed learning rate of 1×10^{-4} for the Adam Optimizer and a batch size of 64. We use horizontal and vertical flipping as data augmentation and perform early stopping based on the IoU metric on the validation set. For all neural field architectures, 512 points are sampled per image and we choose $l = 4$ as the size of the points embedding. Empirically, we have found that the results are not sensitive to both these parameters. We have explored scaling the neural field architectures by increasing the number of blocks and the MLP layers' width. With that approach, we use a hidden size of 512 for all MLP layers. One block is used within the Concat and FiLM conditioning network and two blocks are used within the Cross-Attention Transformer. For all architectures, we try to have approximately the same amount of parameters to make a fair comparison.

5 Results

In Table 1, we show the Intersection over Union (IoU), F-Score and the number of parameters for all seven conditioning strategies and two different image sizes on the test set. We also compare our neural field decoder with the DeepLabV3+ [3] FCN for semantic segmentation which also uses a ResNet34 backbone. In Fig. 4 we show the predictions of all decoder architectures for three example images. From the results, we can make multiple key observations.

First, the Concat and FiLM decoders perform very similarly in all aspects, regardless of the conditional code source and the image size.

Second, conditioning via Cross-Attention works best amongst all neural field approaches. Furthermore, it performs similarly to the DeepLabV3+ FCN. Notably, the Cross-Attention decoder has half as much parameters and no access to the intermediate feature maps of the encoder.

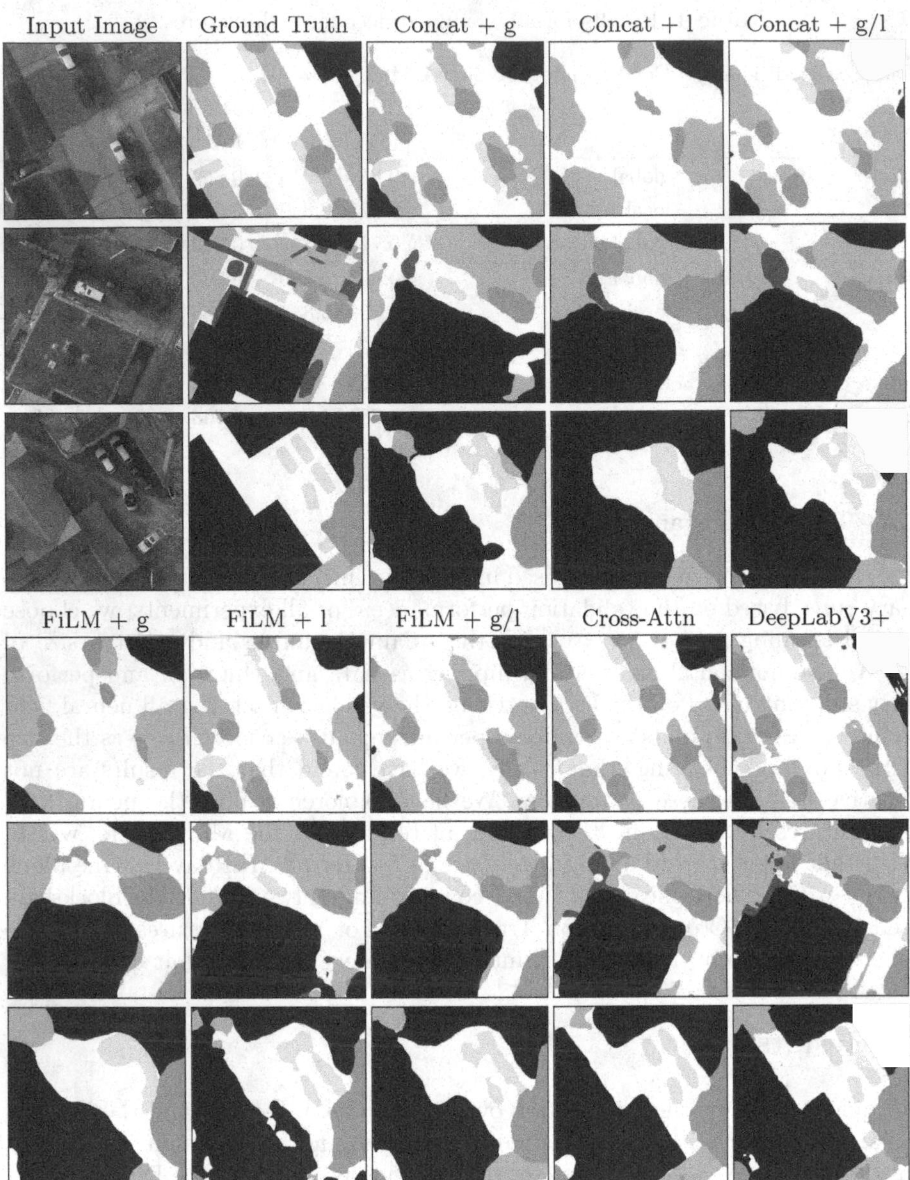

Fig. 4. The predictions of all examined decoder architectures on three example images (512×512 px) from the test set. For Concat and FiLM conditioning, g denotes a global code source, l denotes a local code source and g/l denotes a concatenation of global and local code. The class color code is: white = `Impervious surfaces`, blue = `Building`, cyan = `Low vegetation`, green = `Tree`, yellow = `Car`, red = `Clutter/background`. By comparing the predictions with the ground truth segmentation masks, it can be observed that the ability to represent details, e.g. distinct objects or angular corners, varies greatly between the approaches. Only the Cross-Attention and the DeepLabV3+ decoders are able to faithfully represent the segmentation masks, while the Concat and FiLm approaches tend to produce overly smooth geometries. (Color figure online)

Third, the performance of the Concat and FiLM approaches can be improved by using a combination of global and local features, particularly for larger images. In that case, the performance of both approaches is not much lower compared with the Cross-Attention decoder.

Fourth, the performance of the Concat and FiLM conditioning decreases with larger input images when using global codes. This can be expected, as it is harder to model more geometries in larger images with the same code length.

Fifth, when using local codes, the performance is also degraded when dealing with larger images. This is unexpected, as the sampling distance (meters per pixel) remains the same and therefore the size of the features should also remain the same. This could be an indication that the individual vectors in the feature volume produced by the CNN encoder do not model purely local features, as stated by methods using this approach [4,29]. This is further supported by the fact that modern CNN architectures have very large receptive fields so that one feature vector in the output feature volume receives input from the complete input image. In our case, the ResNet34 encoder has a receptive field of 899 pixels which fully covers both our image sizes.

6 Conclusion

In this work, we performed a comparative study of neural field conditioning strategies and explored the idea of a neural field-based decoder for 2D semantic segmentation. Our results show that neural fields can have a competitive performance when compared with a classic CNN decoder while requiring even fewer parameters. In the future, we can imagine a further increase in performance of the presented approach by making the neural field decoder utilize information from the intermediate layers of the encoder via skip connections. We also showed that the performance of the neural field is considerably affected by the conditioning strategy. The best conditioning strategy likely depends on the task. For the task of 2D semantic segmentation, a Cross-Attention-based Transformer is superior to Concat and FiLM conditioning. However, also the combination of local and global conditional codes is a promising approach, as the performance is not much lower. Lastly, for local features, we showed an unexpected degradation in performance when increasing the image size. Further research is required to explain this observation and deduce consequences for local conditioning methods.

Acknowledgements. The authors gratefully acknowledge support from the DFG (CML, MoReSpace, LeCAREbot), BMWK (SIDIMO, VERIKAS), and the European Commission (TRAIL, TERAIS).

References

1. Badrinarayanan, V., Kendall, A., Cipolla, R.: SegNet: a deep convolutional encoder-decoder architecture for image segmentation (2016). https://arxiv.org/abs/1511.00561

2. Chan, E.R., Monteiro, M., Kellnhofer, P., Wu, J., Wetzstein, G.: Pi-GAN: periodic implicit generative adversarial networks for 3D-aware image synthesis (2021). https://arxiv.org/abs/2012.00926
3. Chen, L.C., Zhu, Y., Papandreou, G., Schroff, F., Adam, H.: Encoder-decoder with atrous separable convolution for semantic image segmentation. In: Ferrari, V., Hebert, M., Sminchisescu, C., Weiss, Y. (eds.) Computer Vision - ECCV 2018, vol. 11211, pp. 833–851. Springer, Cham (2018). https://doi.org/10.1007/978-3-030-01234-2_49, https://link.springer.com/10.1007/978-3-030-01234-2_49
4. Chen, Y., Liu, S., Wang, X.: Learning continuous image representation with local implicit image function. In: 2021 IEEE/CVF Conference on Computer Vision and Pattern Recognition (CVPR), pp. 8624–8634. IEEE (2021). https://doi.org/10.1109/CVPR46437.2021.00852, https://ieeexplore.ieee.org/document/9578246/
5. Durall, R., Keuper, M., Keuper, J.: Watch your up-convolution: CNN based generative deep neural networks are failing to reproduce spectral distributions (2020). https://arxiv.org/abs/2003.01826
6. Fu, J., Liu, J., Tian, H., Li, Y.: Dual attention network for scene segmentation. In: 2019 IEEE/CVF Conference on Computer Vision and Pattern Recognition (CVPR), pp. 3146–3154. IEEE (2019)
7. Ha, D., Dai, A., Le, Q.V.: HyperNetworks (2016). https://arxiv.org/abs/1609.09106
8. He, K., Zhang, X., Ren, S., Sun, J.: Deep residual learning for image recognition. In: 2016 IEEE Conference on Computer Vision and Pattern Recognition (CVPR), pp. 770–778. IEEE (2016). https://doi.org/10.1109/CVPR.2016.90, https://ieeexplore.ieee.org/document/7780459/
9. Hu, H., et al.: Learning implicit feature alignment function for semantic segmentation. In: Avidan, S., Brostow, G., Cissé, M., Farinella, G.M., Hassner, T. (eds.) Computer Vision - ECCV 2022, vol. 13689, pp. 487–505. Springer, Cham (2022). https://doi.org/10.1007/978-3-031-19818-2_28, https://link.springer.com/10.1007/978-3-031-19818-2_28
10. Jiang, W., Trulls, E., Hosang, J., Tagliasacchi, A., Yi, K.M.: COTR: correspondence transformer for matching across images. In: 2021 IEEE/CVF International Conference on Computer Vision (ICCV), pp. 6187–6197. IEEE (2021). https://doi.org/10.1109/ICCV48922.2021.00615, https://ieeexplore.ieee.org/document/9711001/
11. Long, J., Shelhamer, E., Darrell, T.: Fully convolutional networks for semantic segmentation (2015). https://arxiv.org/abs/1411.4038
12. Mescheder, L., Oechsle, M., Niemeyer, M., Nowozin, S., Geiger, A.: Occupancy networks: learning 3D reconstruction in function space. In: 2019 IEEE/CVF Conference on Computer Vision and Pattern Recognition (CVPR), pp. 4455–4465. IEEE (2019). https://doi.org/10.1109/CVPR.2019.00459, https://ieeexplore.ieee.org/document/8953655/
13. Mildenhall, B., Srinivasan, P.P., Tancik, M., Barron, J.T., Ramamoorthi, R., Ng, R.: NeRF: representing scenes as neural radiance fields for view synthesis (2020). https://arxiv.org/abs/2003.08934
14. Odena, A., Dumoulin, V., Olah, C.: Deconvolution and checkerboard artifacts (2016). https://doi.org/10.23915/distill.00003, https://distill.pub/2016/deconv-checkerboard

15. Park, J.J., Florence, P., Straub, J., Newcombe, R., Lovegrove, S.: DeepSDF: learning continuous signed distance functions for shape representation. In: 2019 IEEE/CVF Conference on Computer Vision and Pattern Recognition (CVPR), pp. 165–174. IEEE (2019). https://doi.org/10.1109/CVPR.2019.00025, https://ieeexplore.ieee.org/document/8954065/
16. Park, K., et al.: HyperNeRF: a higher-dimensional representation for topologically varying neural radiance fields (2021). https://arxiv.org/abs/2106.13228
17. Perez, E., Strub, F., De Vries, H., Dumoulin, V., Courville, A.: FiLM: visual reasoning with a general conditioning layer. In: Proceedings of the AAAI Conference on Artificial Intelligence, vol. 32 (2018). https://doi.org/10.1609/aaai.v32i1.11671, https://ojs.aaai.org/index.php/AAAI/article/view/11671
18. Rebain, D., Matthews, M.J., Yi, K.M., Sharma, G., Lagun, D., Tagliasacchi, A.: Attention beats concatenation for conditioning neural fields (2022). https://arxiv.org/abs/2209.10684
19. Ronneberger, O., Fischer, P., Brox, T.: U-Net: convolutional networks for biomedical image segmentation (2015). https://arxiv.org/abs/1505.04597
20. Rottensteiner, F., et al.: The ISPRS benchmark on urban object classification and 3D building reconstruction I-3 (2012). https://doi.org/10.5194/isprsannals-I-3-293-2012
21. Sajjadi, M.S.M., et al.: Scene representation transformer: geometry-free novel view synthesis through set-latent scene representations (2022). https://arxiv.org/abs/2111.13152
22. Sitzmann, V., Martel, J.N.P., Bergman, A.W., Lindell, D.B., Wetzstein, G.: Implicit neural representations with periodic activation functions (2020). https://arxiv.org/abs/2006.09661
23. Sitzmann, V., Rezchikov, S., Freeman, W.T., Tenenbaum, J.B., Durand, F.: Light field networks: neural scene representations with single-evaluation rendering (2022). https://arxiv.org/abs/2106.02634
24. Sitzmann, V., Zollhöfer, M., Wetzstein, G.: Scene representation networks: continuous 3D-structure-aware neural scene representations (2020). https://arxiv.org/abs/1906.01618
25. Strudel, R., Garcia, R., Laptev, I., Schmid, C.: Segmenter: transformer for semantic segmentation (2021). https://arxiv.org/abs/2105.05633
26. Tancik, M., et al.: Fourier features let networks learn high frequency functions in low dimensional domains. In: 2020 NeurIPS (2020)
27. Vora, S., et al.: NeSF: neural semantic fields for generalizable semantic segmentation of 3D scenes (2021). https://arxiv.org/abs/2111.13260
28. Wojna, Z., et al.: The devil is in the decoder. In: Proceedings of the British Machine Vision Conference 2017, p. 10. British Machine Vision Association (2017). https://doi.org/10.5244/C.31.10, https://www.bmva.org/bmvc/2017/papers/paper010/index.html
29. Yu, A., Ye, V., Tancik, M., Kanazawa, A.: pixelNeRF: neural radiance fields from one or few images (2021). https://arxiv.org/abs/2012.02190

Neurodynamical Model of the Visual Recognition of Dynamic Bodily Actions from Silhouettes

Prerana Kumar[1,2(✉)], Nick Taubert[1], Rajani Raman[3], Anna Bognár[3], Ghazaleh Ghamkhari Nejad[3], Rufin Vogels[3], and Martin A. Giese[1]

[1] Section for Computational Sensomotorics, Centre for Integrative Neuroscience and Hertie Institute for Clinical Brain Research, University Clinic Tübingen, Tübingen, Germany
{prerana.kumar,martin.giese}@uni-tuebingen.de

[2] International Max Planck Research School for Intelligent Systems, Tübingen, Germany

[3] Laboratory of Neuro- and Psychophysiology, Department of Neurosciences, KU Leuven, Leuven, Belgium

Abstract. For social species, including primates, the recognition of dynamic body actions is crucial for survival. However, the detailed neural circuitry underlying this process is currently not well understood. In monkeys, body-selective patches in the visual temporal cortex may contribute to this processing. We propose a physiologically-inspired neural model of the visual recognition of body movements, which combines an existing image-computable model ('ShapeComp') that produces high-dimensional shape vectors of object silhouettes, with a neurodynamical model that encodes dynamic image sequences exploiting sequence-selective neural fields. The model successfully classifies videos of body silhouettes performing different actions. At the population level, the model reproduces characteristics of macaque single-unit responses from the rostral dorsal bank of the Superior Temporal Sulcus (Anterior Medial Upper Body (AMUB) patch). In the presence of time gaps in the stimulus videos, the predictions made by the model match the data from real neurons. The underlying neurodynamics can be analyzed by exploiting the framework of neural field dynamics.

Keywords: Action recognition · Silhouettes · Neurodynamical model · Neural field · Visual cortex

1 Introduction

Electrophysiological and neuroimaging studies have uncovered the presence of body-selective neurons and regions in the visual cortex. Body-selective regions in the occipitotemporal cortex (OTC), the extrastriate body area (EBA) [3] and the fusiform body area (FBA) [8,17] have been discovered in human functional magnetic resonance imaging (fMRI) studies. fMRI studies in monkeys have

L. Iliadis et al. (Eds.): ICANN 2023, LNCS 14255, pp. 533–544, 2023.
https://doi.org/10.1007/978-3-031-44210-0_43

demonstrated the presence of numerous body-selective patches [2,18,21,23] in the visual temporal cortex, including the Superior Temporal Sulcus (STS). In these regions, work on fMRI and single-unit responses has demonstrated stronger responses to bodies than to faces and other categories of objects.

However, the focus of most of these studies has been on static bodies. The detailed neural computations underlying the visual recognition of dynamic body actions are not yet well understood. While there have been some single-cell studies investigating the responses of neurons, especially in the STS, to biological motion and body motion [14,15,22], detailed physiologically-inspired neural models of the processing of dynamic bodies are required to clarify the underlying neural computations.

Biologically-inspired models have previously been proposed for the recognition of dynamic bodies [6,9,12]. Older models largely used hierarchies of primitive detectors, such as Gabor filters, for modeling the initial layers of the visual pathway. More recent studies predominantly model the visual pathway using feedforward convolutional neural networks (CNNs) [25] and other studies use different hierarchical neural network architectures [16], but these models do not make use of physiologically-plausible dynamical neural circuits. Our model combines approaches from deep learning in the form of a front-end CNN architecture (ShapeComp network [13]) which has been trained to produce perceptually relevant shape features of objects, with a neurodynamical model based on neural fields that reproduces the dynamic properties of action-selective neurons in the STS and premotor cortex [4,6].

In this paper, we aim to present, as a proof of concept, a physiologically-inspired model of the neural circuitry involved in the visual recognition of static body poses and dynamic body movements. The purpose of our model is to reproduce the invariance properties of cortical neurons, and not primarily to achieve maximum classification performance on large data sets. In its present form, the model can learn to classify actions from body silhouettes and reproduces activation dynamics of a population of body-responsive neurons in the macaque STS. Previous studies [10,19] have shown strong and selective responses in STS body patches to silhouettes comparable to those to shaded images, which is in agreement with the well-known shape-bias of human vision [11]. We present some initial comparisons with macaque electrophysiological data recorded from the AMUB body patch [2] of the rostral dorsal bank of the STS using dynamic silhouettes extracted from videos of real macaques. This work provides a starting point for the development of a detailed model of the shape selectivity and dynamic properties of body-selective neurons in the macaque STS. The model also makes predictions about the output dynamics for stimulus videos, including the responses to stimuli with time gaps of different durations, which qualitatively match the data from real neurons.

In the following sections of the paper, we will first present the architecture of the model. We will then describe the results of the recognition of dynamic human silhouettes performing actions, after training the model on only a few exemplars. Following this, we will compare our simulations with macaque electrophysiological data. After briefly explaining the behavior of the model for stimuli with time gaps by analyzing the underlying neurodynamics, we will finally discuss the implications of this work.

2 Architecture of the Model

The model combines an image-computable model ('ShapeComp' [13]) that produces high-dimensional vectors describing the shapes of objects, with an existing neurodynamical model [6] which has previously replicated the neural dynamics in higher areas of the visual and premotor cortex. The model takes videos (image sequences) of silhouettes performing various actions as input, and the output layer consists of neurons that classify the various learned body actions. The shape features extracted from the ShapeComp network are used to train radial basis function networks whose outputs feed into sequence selective neural fields (recurrent neural networks) that encode temporal sequences of keyframes (dynamic stimuli). The outputs of individual neural fields representing the different body actions or movements are temporally summated by motion pattern neurons that comprise the highest (readout) level of the model.

An overview of the model architecture is shown in Fig. 1. Sections 2.1 and 2.2 will describe the components of the model in more detail.

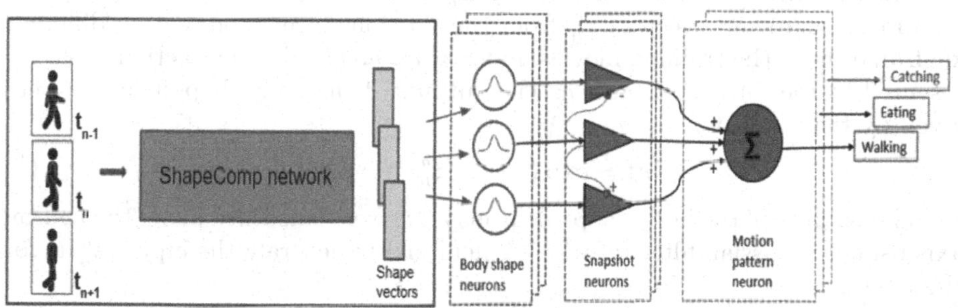

Fig. 1. Overview of model architecture: A CNN architecture (ShapeComp) is combined with a recurrent network of snapshot neurons that integrate information over time.

2.1 Extraction of Mid-Level Shape Features

The initial layers of the visual pathway that detect mid-level features are modeled by a CNN. We initially tested some standard CNNs from the computer vision literature as alternative front-ends of our model. For the detection of body postures across different individuals, we found that these networks did not facilitate robust recognition of key poses with invariance across different individuals when the model was only trained on moderately-sized data sets. A more robust recognition of body pose could be realized using the ShapeComp model [13]. This psychophysically-validated model uses the shape boundaries of objects to produce high-dimensional vectors that represent the shapes of objects. As the shape vectors produced by the ShapeComp model predict human shape similarity judgments better than features output by standard CNN architectures, we used this architecture as the front-end of our model [13].

The version of the ShapeComp architecture used in the model is a multi-layer feedforward CNN called KerNet1, pre-trained on 800,000 shapes produced by a Generative Adversarial Network (GAN), spanning the high-dimensional shape space. The network takes silhouettes of objects as input and produces 22-dimensional feature vectors as output, that describe the objects' shapes in a compact manner. These 22 dimensions are weighted linear combinations of the original 109 image-computable shape features from the ShapeComp model [13]. The architecture generates shape vectors for every keyframe, which form the input to the dynamic layers of the network that are described in the following section.

2.2 Dynamic Recognition Network

Body Shape Neurons. The mid-level feature output from the ShapeComp network was used as input for body shape detectors, which were modeled by Gaussian Radial Basis functions (RBFs), which we refer to as body shape neurons in the following text. The centers $\boldsymbol{z}_n^a$ of these RBFs were defined by the 22-dimensional shape vectors $\boldsymbol{z}_n^a$ from the previous layer representing different keyframes from the training movies, indexed by n. The different actions are represented by the integer variable a. The outputs of the body shape neurons were given by the equation:

$$r_n^a = \exp\left(-|\boldsymbol{z} - \boldsymbol{z}_n^a|^2/2\sigma^2\right). \tag{1}$$

The outputs of the body shape neurons $r_n^a(t)$ were smoothed along the neuron axis using a Gaussian filter (of width 2 neurons) to generate the inputs $s_n^a(t)$ for the next layer.

Snapshot Neurons. The smoothed output of the body shape neurons $s_n^a(t)$ provides input to sequence-selective snapshot neurons that encode temporal sequences of keyframes. Asymmetric lateral connections between these snapshot neurons encoding the image keyframes result in recurrent neural networks that show sequence selectivity i.e. the network only responds strongly if the learned keyframes occur in the correct temporal order. The underlying network dynamics can be interpreted as a dynamic neural field [1]. Each learned action is encoded by such a network. The dynamics of the discretely approximated neural field [1] is given by the following equation ($[u]_+ = u$ for $u > 0$, and 0 otherwise):

$$\begin{aligned}\tau\dot{u}_n^a(t) =& -u_n^a(t) + \sum_m w(n-m)\,[u_m^a(t)]_+ + s_n^a(t) - h - w_c I_c^a(t),\\ w(n) =& A\,\exp\left(-(n-C)^2/2\sigma_{ker}^2\right) - B,\end{aligned} \tag{2}$$

where $u_n^a(t)$ denotes the activity of the neuron in the neural field that encodes the keyframe n of the body action category a, and where the index m runs over all neurons. The resting level of the neurons is determined by the positive parameter h (= 1), and τ (= 28 ms) defines the time constant of the dynamics. The function w is an asymmetric interaction kernel. The neural sub-networks encoding different actions compete with each other. This is accomplished by the cross-inhibition term $I_c^a(t)$ that is given by the equation $I_c^a(t) = \sum_{m,a' \neq a} [u_m^{a'}(t)]_+$. The parameter w_c (= 1.5) determines the strength of the cross-field inhibition.

The snapshot neurons are keyframe-selective as well as action-selective, and exhibit phasic activity during the temporal progression of the presented action stimuli.

Motion Pattern Neurons. The responses of the snapshot neurons encoding the same action are temporally smoothed and summated by *motion pattern neurons* that form the next layer of the model. The response of these neurons is dependent on the sum of the (thresholded) activity of the snapshot neurons encoding the corresponding actions and given by the equation:

$$\tau_v \dot{v}_a(t) = -v_a(t) + \sum_n [u_n^a(t)]_+ . \tag{3}$$

In the above equation, $v_a(t)$ denotes the activity of the motion pattern neurons, and τ_v (= 28 ms) denotes the time constant of their dynamics.

Each motion pattern neuron encodes a particular action and is active during the corresponding action. It is at this level of the hierarchy that the model classifies the different types of actions. The responses of these motion pattern neurons have been compared (at the population level) with single-unit responses recorded from the macaque STS in Sect. 3.2.

3 Results

3.1 Testing the Model on Sequences of Human Silhouettes

Videos of silhouettes of 9 human subjects performing 5 types of actions that were clearly distinguishable from silhouettes were used to test the model's ability to learn actions. The selected action sequences, chosen from the publicly available Weizmann Human Action Dataset [7], were: walking, running, jumping jacks, waving with one arm, and waving with two arms. The Weizmann Human Action Dataset includes videos of the silhouettes of the subjects performing the actions, which were used for training and testing the model.

Image sequences of 25 black-and-white silhouette keyframes per action were extracted from the longer video sequences (deinterlaced 50 frames/s). The image sequences from the various subjects were coarsely time-normalized by visual inspection, such that the first and last images of the sequences of a particular action contained the corresponding poses across all subjects. The available silhouette images were already aligned/centered to a reference point, removing any effects of translation of the subject within the image. The silhouettes contained multiple "leaks" and "intrusions", which served as a test of the model's robustness. The images, which were of different sizes, were resized to uniform dimensions of 224 × 224 pixels.

Averaged across all action types, we achieved a performance of 97.77% correct classifications on the test set, determined by cross-validation (leave-one-out analysis on 9 videos per action type). The classification accuracy of the neurodynamical model using ShapeComp as its front-end was compared with that using a CNN architecture, ResNet-101, coupled with different unsupervised dimensionality reduction algorithms. ResNet-101 has been shown to predict human shape similarity better than other standard CNNs [13] and was used to produce mid-level features. The network (pre-trained on ImageNet) was read out just before the fully connected layer (at layer "Pool5"). Only output features showing high variance over time were retained (feature selection), and 3 types of unsupervised dimensionality reduction methods were applied to construct a lower-dimensional mid-level feature space (of 15 dimensions) - Principal Component Analysis (PCA), Non-negative Matrix Factorization (NNMF) and Independent Component Analysis (ICA). Increasing the number of dimensions of these mid-level feature vectors beyond 15 was found to decrease classification accuracy, probably due to overfitting to the training data.

As shown in Table 1 below, our model outperforms the CNN architecture combined with any of the three unsupervised dimensionality reduction algorithms. As another test of performance, we also added Gaussian random noise to all the models at 2 dynamic neural levels during the simulations: at the level of the snapshot neuron responses and at the level of the motion pattern neuron responses. We then re-computed the accuracy values, shown in Table 2, and performed this analysis for 3 levels ($\sigma = 2$, $\sigma = 6$, $\sigma = 10$) of noise. The model with the ShapeComp front-end shows the highest classification accuracy even in the presence of added noise.

Table 1. Accuracy of our model compared with a CNN model and different dimension reduction methods.

Model Front-End	Accuracy
ShapeComp	**97.8%**
ResNet-101 + PCA	68.8%
ResNet-101 + NNMF	75.6%
ResNet-101 + ICA	55.6%

Table 2. Accuracy of our model compared with the other models for different levels of added noise

Model Front-End	$\sigma = 2$	$\sigma = 6$	$\sigma = 10$
ShapeComp	**86.7%**	**82.2%**	**80%**
ResNet-101 + PCA	66.7%	48.9%	48.9%
ResNet-101 + NNMF	71.1%	51.1%	51.1%
ResNet-101 + ICA	53.3%	55.6%	60%

3.2 Simulations in Comparison with Macaque Electrophysiological Data

A stimulus set of 20 videos of silhouettes of rhesus monkeys performing different dynamic body movements was created for use in the experiments and modeling.

The silhouettes were centered in the videos, removing any effects of translation of the macaque within the images. Image sequences of 60 grayscale keyframes (1 s) were extracted from the videos (480 $\times$ 480 pixel images, 60 frames/s). A set of different stimulus conditions per video were used for both the experiments and modeling: Image sequences taken in the correct temporal order ("forward" condition), temporally inverted image sequences ("reverse" condition), and videos with different lengths of time gaps, during which frames of the video were replaced by blank frames for both forward and reverse conditions. The time gaps used were of 2, 4, 6, 8, 10, and 13 frames (approximately 33, 67, 100, 133, 167, and 217 ms respectively). The positions of the rest of the frames containing the macaque were unaltered in the image sequences.

For this analysis, from the responses of 32 cells recorded from the AMUB body patch, the response (averaged across 5 trials) to the video that produced the highest response over time ("best" stimulus) was chosen for each cell. There were 16 different best stimuli in total for the population. The responses of each cell were recorded for the different stimulus conditions for each video. The baseline-subtracted activity of each cell was normalized by dividing by the maximum firing rate value (bin-width = 20 ms) of the net response of that cell across all the stimulus conditions under consideration. All the cell responses were then averaged to produce the population response. Finally, the neural response curves were smoothed over time by Gaussian filtering. Likewise, the model was tested on the 16 best stimulus videos of the neurons for the same stimulus conditions. The responses of each of the motion pattern neurons to its preferred stimulus video were normalized in the same manner as in the data. The individual motion pattern neuron responses were averaged to obtain the population activity.

The model successfully reproduces the sequence selectivity of the population response of the real neurons (Fig. 2A and Fig. 2B). Interestingly, the model predicts that the difference in the population activity for the forward and reverse-ordered sequences should significantly decrease in the presence of large time gaps in the stimuli, which is actually found to be the case in the data from the experiments (Fig. 2C and Fig. 2D). In the model, this behavior can be explained by the recurrent network dynamics. If the input activity is not sufficiently continuous, a self-organized solution, which corresponds to a traveling pulse in the neural field [24], cannot emerge. In this case, the direction selectivity of the model disappears. This is systematically tested in the simulations shown in (Fig. 2E) showing the population responses of the motion pattern neurons, averaged over all time points, for different lengths of stimulus time gaps, for both the forward and reverse conditions. For larger durations, the strong sequence selectivity present for continuous stimuli disappears, while the output neurons are still significantly active. Figure 2F shows the corresponding plot for the population responses from the neural data averaged during the stimulus period (accounting for the 60 ms response latency period of the neurons), which corresponds well with the model's prediction.

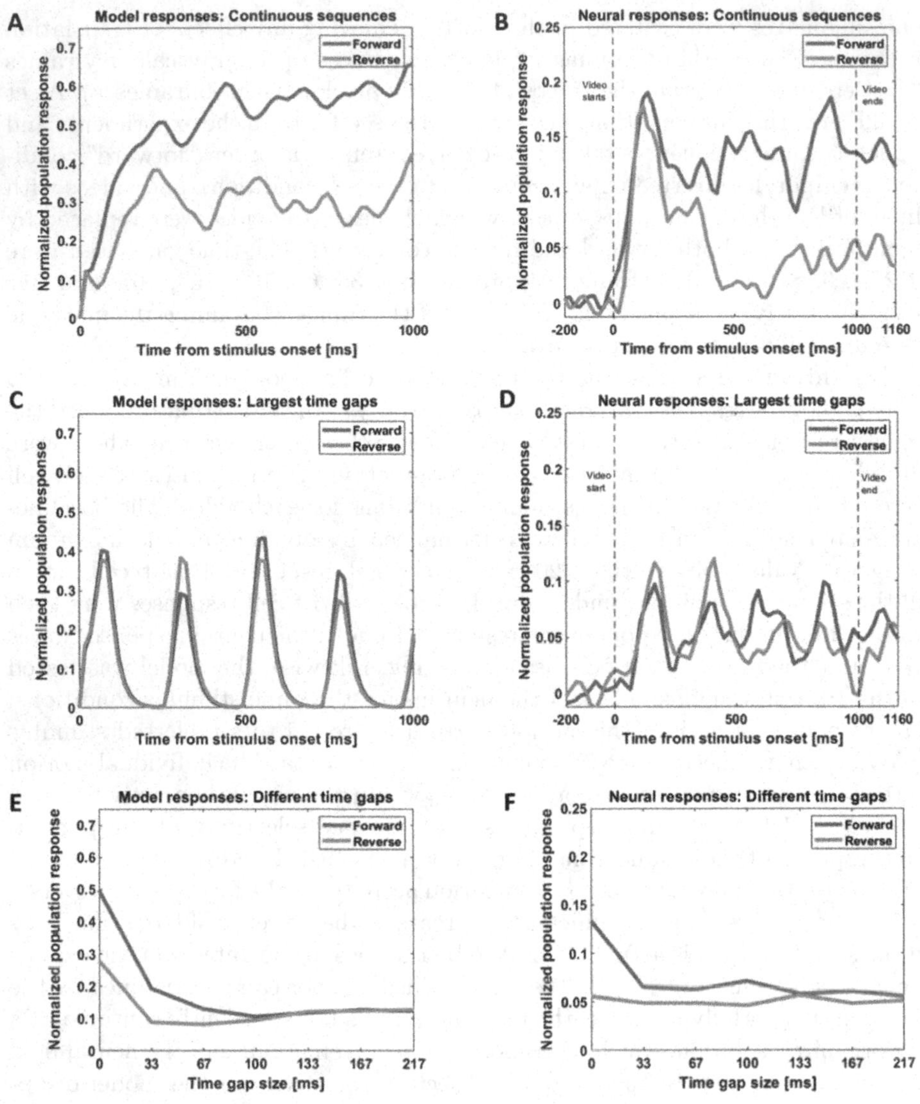

Fig. 2. Simulation results: **A** Simulated population response for forward and reverse ordered continuous sequences. **B** Population response from AMUB body patch neurons for the same continuous stimuli. **C** Simulated population response for the largest time gap (217 ms) condition of the forward and reverse-ordered stimuli. **D** Population response from AMUB body patch neurons for the same time gap length. **E** Predicted responses from the model for forward and reverse-ordered sequences containing different lengths of time gaps. **F** Population response from AMUB body patch for the same time gap stimuli.

3.3 Mathematical Analysis of the Dependence of Sequence Selectivity on Gap Duration

The core module of our model that integrates information over time is the recurrent neural network (2). Sequence selectivity and its dependence on the time gaps in the stimulus are most easy to analyze by describing the recurrent neural network in a continuum limit, resulting in the following neural field (ignoring the cross-field inhibition):

$$\tau \frac{\partial u(x,t)}{\partial t} + u(x,t) = \int w(x-x')\, \theta(u(x',t))\, \mathrm{d}x' + s(x,t). \tag{4}$$

Here, we integrate the resting level parameter h into the input signal $s(x,t)$ for simplicity. The function $\theta(\cdot)$ defines the output threshold characteristics of the neurons. For $\theta(u) \equiv u$, one obtains a linear neural field that is particularly easy to analyze. We treat this case here, and the analysis of nonlinear threshold functions will be treated in future publications. The input signal is assumed to be a traveling Gaussian peak of the form $s(x,t) = \exp(-(x-vt)^2/(2\eta^2)) \cdot \Xi(t)$, where the function $\Xi(t)$ is one while stimulus frames are present and zero during the time gaps. The traveling speed v of the input is determined by the frame rate of the stimulus video.

The analysis of the dynamics becomes easier in a traveling coordinate system, exploiting the identities $U(y,t) = u(x,t)$ and $S(y,t) = s(x,t) = \exp(-y^2/(2\eta^2)) \cdot \Xi(t)$, where $y = x - vt$. The resulting transformed dynamics are given by:

$$\tau \frac{\partial U(y,t)}{\partial t} - \tau v \frac{\partial U(y,t)}{\partial y} + U(y,t) = \int w(y-y')\, \theta(U(y',t))\, \mathrm{d}y' + S(y,t). \tag{5}$$

For the case of $\theta(u) \equiv u$, the last equation can be solved by Fourier transformation in the space-time frequency domain. The 2D Fourier transformation of the solution is given by the following product $\tilde{U}(k,\omega) = \tilde{S}(k,\omega)\tilde{H}(k,\omega)$, where $\tilde{S}(k,\omega)$ is the Fourier transformation of the input signal. The function $\tilde{H}(k,\omega) = 1/(1 + i\omega\tau - i\tau v k - \tilde{w}(k))$ is the impulse response of the dynamics. The amplitude of this function is illustrated in Fig. 3 (panels A and D). It changes for opposite signs of the velocity v, modeling the forward and reverse temporal orders of the stimulus video frames. $\tilde{w}(k)$ is the Fourier Transform of $w(x)$.

In this analytically solvable linear neural field, we also observe a dependence of the temporal order selectivity on the presence and duration of stimulus gaps. This is illustrated in Fig. 3B and Fig. 3C that show the computed solutions $u(x,t)$ for forward vs. reverse presentation of the stimulus frames without time gaps, which show different maximum (and average) amplitudes. Contrasting with this observation, the computed solutions for the stimulus with time gaps (shown in Fig. 3E vs. Figure 3F) show only a minimal amplitude difference between the forward and reverse presentation orders.

This dependence of the amplitude difference on the presence of gaps in the stimulus signal is caused by the fact that the stimulus with gaps activates high-frequency components along the ω axis in the (k,ω)-frequency space. For these components, the denominator of $\tilde{H}(k, \omega)$ is effectively less sensitive to the parameter v, and thus to the presentation order of the stimulus.

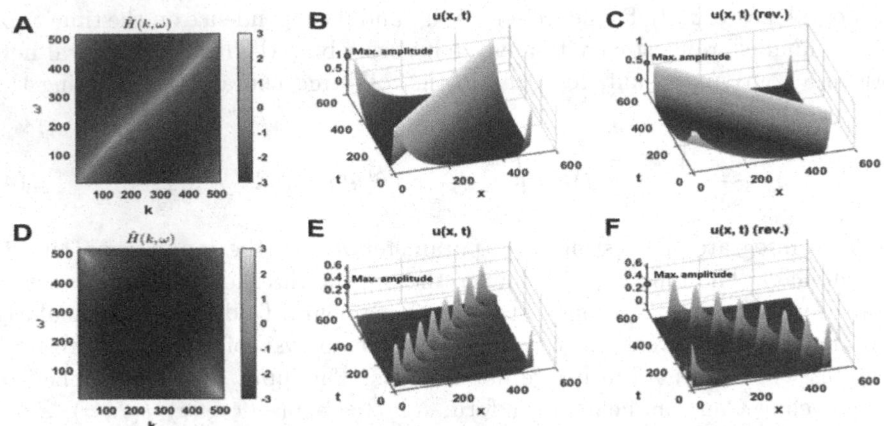

Fig. 3. Linear neural field: Fourier Spectra of the impulse response $\tilde{H}(k, \omega)$: **A** for ($v > 0$) (forward temporal order), and **D** for ($v < 0$) (reverse temporal order). Panels **B** and **C** show the computed solutions $u(x, t)$ for forward vs. reverse temporal orders for a stimulus without time gaps. Panels **E** and **F** show the computed solution with time gaps of a duration of 7 stimulus frames. Amplitude difference between the solutions is lower for the stimulus with gaps.

An important observation is that for the linear neural field it is critical to sum up *thresholded* output amplitudes, as assumed in Eq. (3) of our model. Just integrating the signal $u(x, t)$ over x turns out to be equivalent to computing the Fourier back-transformation (in time) of the function $\tilde{H}(0, \omega)$. This function does not depend on the velocity v and therefore fails to imply sequence selectivity.

4 Conclusions

In this paper, we have presented a neurodynamical model for the recognition of dynamic bodily actions performed by silhouettes, as a proof of concept. Despite the simple architecture of the model, even when trained with relatively few training examples, it accomplishes robust recognition of body poses and actions across different individuals. Using a standard CNN architecture, ResNet-101, combined with different unsupervised learning techniques, we were not able to reproduce the same robustness in body shape recognition. We think that this lack of performance could be related to the tendency of standard CNNs to overemphasize shape differences that are not relevant for keyframe pose recognition. Using modified standard CNN architectures as potential front-ends of the model with further optimization of the feature selection procedure may possibly yield higher accuracy values, but this was outside the scope of the current study.

Our model also reproduces signatures of the activity dynamics of populations of body-responsive neurons in the AMUB body patch of the STS. We could reproduce the sequence selectivity of this response, and also the fact that introducing large time gaps in the stimuli destroys this sequence selectivity. In our model, this is a consequence of the recurrent network dynamics. We mathematically analyzed this dependence of sequence selectivity on gap duration using analysis methods from linear neural field dynamics.

A major limitation of the model is that it works only on silhouettes. In future work we will try to extend the front-end of our model for more natural stimuli, where a key problem is to overcome the texture bias that is present in standard CNN architectures [5]. Furthermore, it is likely that the shape descriptors produced by the ShapeComp architecture do not exactly match those used in the brain for shape recognition. Nevertheless, we have used the ShapeComp CNN architecture to model to realize a front-end of our model that reproduces invariance properties of human shape perception better than other standard CNN networks. Another limitation of the model is the absence of neurons exhibiting both phasic and tonic responses to continuous dynamic sequences, which is an oversimplification. Finally, it is likely that neurons in the AMUB body patch are also selective for motion or optical flow features. Our model cannot account for the selectivity for local motion features. Building two pathway architectures that can reproduce these properties remains an important challenge in the modeling of the detailed properties of cortical body action-selective neurons [6,20].

Acknowledgements. This work was supported by ERC 2019-SyG-RELEVANCE-856495; SSTeP-KiZ BMG:ZMWI1-2520DAT700.

References

1. Amari, S.: Dynamics of pattern formation in lateral-inhibition type neural fields. Biol. Cybern. **27**(2), 77–87 (1977)
2. Bognár, A., et al.: The contribution of dynamics to macaque body and face patch responses. Neuroimage **269**, 119907 (2023)
3. Downing, P.E.: A cortical area selective for visual processing of the human body. Science **293**, 2470–2473 (2001). https://doi.org/10.1126/science.1063414
4. Fleischer, F., Caggiano, V., Thier, P., Giese, M.A.: Physiologically inspired model for the visual recognition of transitive hand actions. J. Neurosci. **33**(15), 6563–6580 (2013)
5. Geirhos, R., Rubisch, P., Michaelis, C., Bethge, M., Wichmann, F.A., Brendel, W.: ImageNet-trained CNNs are biased towards texture; increasing shape bias improves accuracy and robustness. In: International Conference on Learning Representations (2019)
6. Giese, M.A., Poggio, T.: Neural mechanisms for the recognition of biological movements. Nat. Rev. Neurosci. **4**(3), 179–192 (2003)
7. Gorelick, L., Blank, M., Shechtman, E., Irani, M., Basri, R.: Actions as space-time shapes. IEEE Trans. Pattern Anal. Mach. Intell. **29**(12), 2247–2253 (2007)
8. Hadjikhani, N., de Gelder, B.: Seeing fearful body expressions activates the fusiform cortex and amygdala. Curr. Biol. **13**, 2201–2205 (2003). https://doi.org/10.1016/j.cub.2003.11.049

9. Jhuang, H., Serre, T., Wolf, L., Poggio, T.: A biologically inspired system for action recognition. In: 2007 IEEE 11th International Conference on Computer Vision, pp. 1–8. IEEE (2007)
10. Kalfas, I., Kumar, S., Vogels, R.: Shape selectivity of middle superior temporal sulcus body patch neurons. ENeuro **4**(3) (2017)
11. Landau, B., Smith, L.B., Jones, S.S.: The importance of shape in early lexical learning. Cogn. Dev. **3**(3), 299–321 (1988)
12. Lange, J., Lappe, M.: A model of biological motion perception from configural form cues. J. Neurosci. **26**(11), 2894–2906 (2006)
13. Morgenstern, Y., et al.: An image-computable model of human visual shape similarity. PLoS Comput. Biol. **17**(6), e1008981 (2021)
14. Oram, M., Perrett, D.: Responses of anterior superior temporal polysensory (STPa) neurons to "Biological Motion" stimuli. J. Cogn. Neurosci. **6**(2), 99–116 (1994)
15. Oram, M., Perrett, D.: Integration of form and motion in the anterior superior temporal polysensory area (STPa) of the Macaque monkey. J. Neurophysiol. **76**(1), 109–129 (1996)
16. Parisi, G.I., Tani, J., Weber, C., Wermter, S.: Emergence of multimodal action representations from neural network self-organization. Cogn. Syst. Res. **43**, 208–221 (2017)
17. Peelen, M.V., Downing, P.E.: Selectivity for the human body in the fusiform gyrus. J. Neurophysiol. **93**, 603–608 (2005). https://doi.org/10.1152/jn.00513.2004
18. Popivanov, I.D., Jastorff, J., Vanduffel, W., Vogels, R.: Stimulus representations in body-selective regions of the Macaque cortex assessed with event-related fMRI. Neuroimage **63**(2), 723–741 (2012)
19. Popivanov, I.D., Jastorff, J., Vanduffel, W., Vogels, R.: Tolerance of Macaque middle STS body patch neurons to shape-preserving stimulus transformations. J. Cogn. Neurosci. **27**(5), 1001–1016 (2015)
20. Simonyan, K., Zisserman, A.: Two-stream convolutional networks for action recognition in videos. In: Advances in Neural Information Processing Systems, vol. 27 (2014)
21. Tsao, D.Y., Freiwald, W.A., Knutsen, T.A., Mandeville, J.B., Tootell, R.B.H.: Faces and objects in Macaque cerebral cortex. Nat. Neurosci. **6**, 989–995 (2003). https://doi.org/10.1038/nn1111
22. Vangeneugden, J., De Maziere, P.A., Van Hulle, M.M., Jaeggli, T., Van Gool, L., Vogels, R.: Distinct mechanisms for coding of visual actions in Macaque temporal cortex. J. Neurosci. **31**(2), 385–401 (2011)
23. Vogels, R.: More than the face: representations of bodies in the inferior temporal cortex. Annu. Rev. Vis. Sci. **8**, 383–405 (2022)
24. Xie, X., Giese, M.A.: Nonlinear dynamics of direction-selective recurrent neural media. Phys. Rev. E **65**(5), 051904 (2002)
25. Yamins, D.L., Hong, H., Cadieu, C.F., Solomon, E.A., Seibert, D., DiCarlo, J.J.: Performance-optimized hierarchical models predict neural responses in higher visual cortex. Proc. Natl. Acad. Sci. **111**(23), 8619–8624 (2014)

PACE: Point Annotation-Based Cell Segmentation for Efficient Microscopic Image Analysis

Nabeel Khalid[1(✉)], Tiago Comassetto Froes[1], Maria Caroprese[5], Gillian Lovell[4], Johan Trygg[3,6], Andreas Dengel[1,2], and Sheraz Ahmed[1]

[1] German Research Center for Artificial Intelligence (DFKI) GmbH, Kaiserslautern 67663, Germany
{nabeel.khalid,tiago.froes,andreas.dengel,sheraz.ahmed}@dfki.de
[2] RPTU Kaiserslautern–Landau, Kaiserslautern 67663, Germany
[3] Sartorius Corporate Research, Umeå, Sweden
[4] Sartorius, Corporate Research, Royston, UK
[5] Sartorius, BioAnalytics, Royston, UK
maria.caroprese@sartorius.com
[6] Computational Life Science Cluster (CLiC), Umeå University, Umeå, Sweden

Abstract. Cells are essential to life because they provide the functional, genetic, and communication mechanisms essential for the proper functioning of living organisms. Cell segmentation is pivotal for any biological hypothesis validation/analysis i.e., to get valuable insights into cell behavior, function, diagnosis, and treatment. Deep learning-based segmentation methods have high segmentation precision, however, need fully annotated segmentation masks for each cell annotated manually by the experts, which is very laborious and costly. Many approaches have been developed in the past to reduce the effort required to annotate the data manually and even though these approaches produce good results, there is still a noticeable difference in performance when compared to fully supervised methods. To fill that gap, a weakly supervised approach, PACE, is presented, which uses only the point annotations and the bounding box for each cell to perform cell instance segmentation. The proposed approach not only achieves 99.8% of the fully supervised performance, but it also surpasses the previous state-of-the-art by a margin of more than 4%.

Keywords: cell segmentation · weakly supervised · point annotation · deep learning

1 Introduction

Cells are the building blocks that make up all living organisms, from uncomplicated single-celled bacteria to complex multi-cellular organisms like humans. They provide the functional, genetic, and communication mechanisms essential

L. Iliadis et al. (Eds.): ICANN 2023, LNCS 14255, pp. 545–557, 2023.
https://doi.org/10.1007/978-3-031-44210-0_44

for the proper functioning of living organisms. Cell segmentation is a key tool for studying numerous aspects of cellular biology, and it allows researchers to study cell migration, cell differentiation, cell proliferation, cell physiology, gene expression patterns, and cell-cell communication in detail. Over the last decade, significant progress in deep learning-based (DL) approaches [4,7–9,14–16] for cell segmentation has been achieved. In a fully supervised setting, DL approaches require fully annotated data for training, with the boundary of each cell defined by the field experts. Manually defining the boundary of each cell in the microscopic images is very laborious and costly. In the natural image datasets like COCO [12], it takes an average of 79.2 s to draw a full mask for each object whereas the bounding box for each object takes only 7 s, which makes it 11 times faster than annotating the boundary of each object [13].

In the microscopic image analysis domain, the LIVECell dataset [4] is among the largest and most comprehensive datasets in cell biology research. It contains more than 1.6 million cells with an average cell density per image higher than any other publically available datasets in the cell biology research domain i.e., 313, which is almost 55 times more than the EVICAN [14] dataset. Annotating cells in microscopic images is more challenging than annotating objects in natural images due to the smaller scale, higher complexity, greater variability, and higher degree of noise in the images. Manually annotating the boundary of each cell in the image in the LIVECell dataset takes 46 s on average. Mask annotation time and complexity depend on cell culture morphology and density. Cell culture BV2 contains up to three thousand cells in some images, packed densely together, which makes it very hard for even the experts to identify the boundaries of the cells.

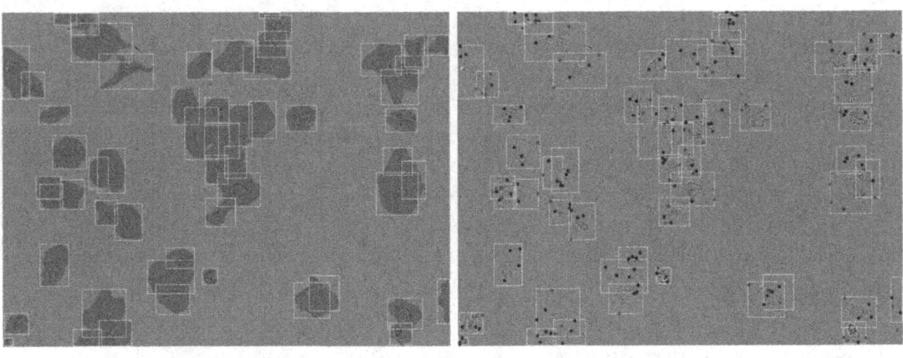

(a) Fully Supervised (b) Weakly Supervised (4-point)

Fig. 1. Fully supervised (a) vs. weakly supervised (b) example. The fully supervised method needs a full mask, whereas the presented weakly supervised approach, PACE, needs only the bounding box and the point annotations. The blue and red points represent whether the point lies on the cell or outside, respectively.

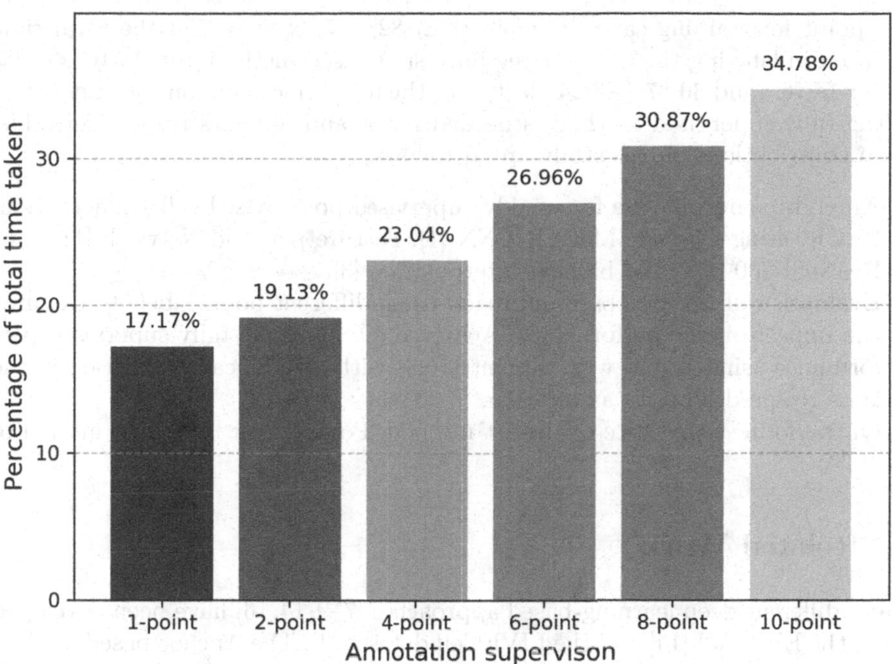

Fig. 2. Annotation time for different point-supervision on the LIVECell dataset. Labeling as many as 4 points per cell instance instead of the fully supervised (segmentation mask) annotation takes 23.04% of the total time spent on annotating the full mask for each cell and is 4.34x faster.

There is a significant amount of unlabeled cellular data available in the cell biology domain that has not been annotated for cell instance segmentation. Without annotations, this data cannot be used to train supervised DL models for cell instance segmentation. This means that the full potential of the data cannot be realized, as it is not being used to improve the accuracy and efficiency of cell segmentation algorithms. That is the reason why there is a need for a weakly supervised approach to perform cell segmentation and minimize the time and expert knowledge required in the annotation of data for the fully supervised methods. To address this issue, this paper presents a weakly supervised approach for cell segmentation, PACE, which requires only the bounding box and point annotations inside the bounding box for each cell to perform the task of cell segmentation. Figure 1 demonstrates the difference in the annotation required for the fully supervised methods 1a and the proposed weakly supervised method 1b. For the proposed weakly supervised, the first step is drawing the bounding boxes which take around $\sim$ 7 seconds per cell. After that random points are generated automatically inside the bounding boxes and the annotator only has to identify whether the point lies on the cell or outside, which takes $\sim$ 0.9 seconds. Figure 2 provides insights into the annotation time required for different point supervision methods compared to the fully supervised method. Considering just one point for training saves us more than 82% (5.2x faster) of the total time required in labeling the data for the fully supervised method. Similarly, 23.04% (4.34x faster) and 30.87% (3.24x faster) of the total time spent on the annotation of the fully supervised method is needed for 4- and 8-points respectively. The main contributions of this study are as follows:

1. An end-to-end pipeline for weakly supervised point-based cell segmentation, PACE, using Cascade Mask R-CNN [1], Feature pyramid Network [11] with ResNeSt-200 [17], and bilinear interpolation [3].
2. Evaluation of the proposed approach using different point labels to examine the impact on the performance. Achieved 99.8% of the fully supervised performance using PACE with 8-point labels with a significant reduction in the time required for data annotation.
3. Outperformed the state-of-the-art method, Point2Mask [10], by a margin of 4.3%.

2 Related Work

Many different deep learning-based approaches [7–9,14,16] have been developed using the EVICAN [14] and the LIVECell dataset [4]. The Anchor-based method reported in the LIVECell paper achieved 47.89% mask mAP. However, the annotations required for training deep learning models are often time-consuming and challenging to obtain. To address this issue, weakly supervised or semi-supervised learning approaches have been proposed to reduce the annotation burden. Weakly supervised approaches like image tags [18], points [2], and missing annotations [5] have been proposed.

Khalid et al. (2022) [10] proposed Point2Mask, an approach for cell segmentation using the bounding box and the points instead of the full mask. Point2Mask achieved 99.2% (43.53%) of the fully supervised performance (43.90%) using just 6-point labels, saving more than 70% of the time required in annotating the full masks for the cells in the LIVECell dataset. Point2Mask used Mask R-CNN with ResNet-50.

3 PACE: The Proposed Approach

Figure 3 provides a system overview of PACE. The proposed method is based on Cascade Mask R-CNN [1], Feature Pyramid Network [12], ResNeSt-200 [17] and Deformable Convolution. The proposed pipeline is composed of three blocks.

3.1 Backbone

The purpose of the backbone in the proposed method is to extract feature maps from the input image at different scales. The backbone is composed of Feature Pyramid Network (FPN) [11] along with ResNeSt-200 [17]. FPN consists of a bottom-up pathway and a top-down pathway. The bottom-up pathway extracts

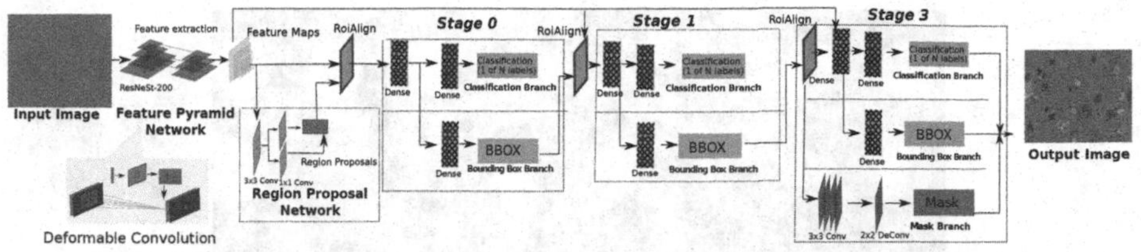

Fig. 3. System overview of the PACE pipeline for weakly supervised cell segmentation. The input image is passed to the proposed pipeline and the output image with cell detection and segmentation is produced.

feature maps from the input image at different scales using a series of convolutional layers. ResNeSt-200 with deformable convolution is used as a feed-forward CNN architecture in the bottom-up pathway of the proposed approach. The top-down pathway merges feature from the bottom-up pathway using lateral connections and upsampling with features from higher-resolution layers to create a feature pyramid.

3.2 Region Proposal Network

Multi-scale features from the FPN are further processed by the Region Proposal Network (RPN), which detects the regions that contain cells and match them to the groundtruth. The matching is done by generating anchors on the input image. After the generation of anchor boxes, the next step is to associate the groundtruth bounding boxes with the generated anchors. The anchors generated are then matched to the groundtruth by taking Intersection over Union (IoU) between anchors and groundtruth. If IoU is larger than the defined threshold of 0.7, the anchor is linked to one of the groundtruth boxes and assigned to the foreground. If the IoU is greater than 0.3 and smaller than 0.7, it is considered background and otherwise ignored.

3.3 Prediction Head

At the prediction head, we have groundtruth boxes, proposal boxes from RPN, and feature maps from FPN. The job of the prediction head is to predict the class, bounding box, and binary mask for each region of interest. We are using a 3-stage Cascade Mask R-CNN [1] as the prediction head, which is an extension of Mask R-CNN [6] with the addition of cascade stages to further improve the segmentation performance. Cascade Mask R-CNN addresses the problem of making predictions that are more accurate on a pixel level. The architectures like Mask R-CNN usually malfunction while accurately detecting objects of variable quality and size in an image. This is mainly because the models are trained using a single IoU threshold i.e., 0.5, meaning that the prediction which has over 50% match with the groundtruth will be regarded as positive samples. This can cause the model to create inaccurate proposals. To address this problem, Cascade

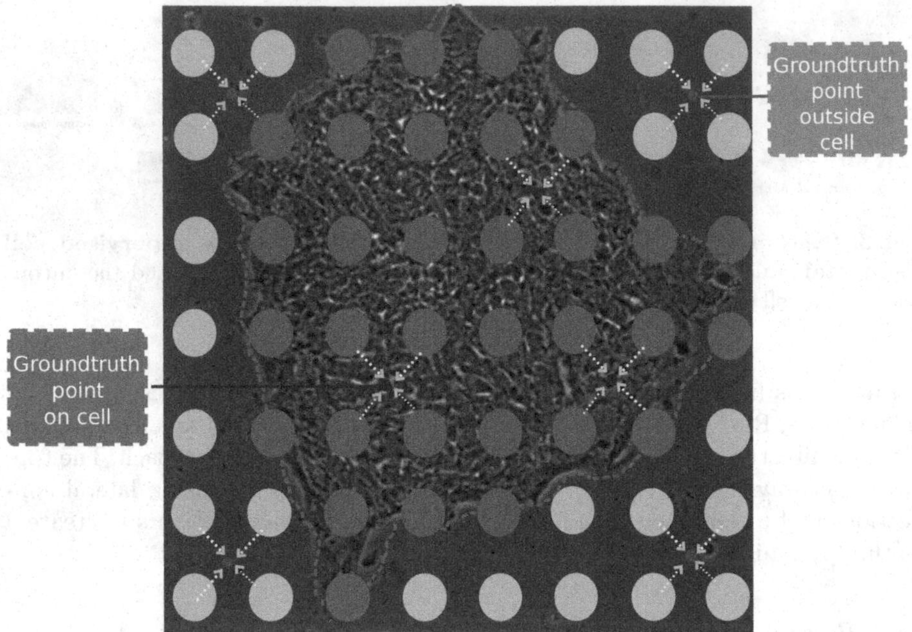

Fig. 4. PACE weak segmentation supervision illustration. For a 7×7 prediction mask on the regular grid (green color indicates foreground cell prediction), the predictions are obtained at the exact location of the groundtruth points with bilinear interpolation. Blue and red points indicate cell and background groundtruth points, respectively. The cell contour line is for illustration only. (Color figure online)

Mask R-CNN presents a multi-stage network with the IoU threshold increasing for each stage i.e., 0.5, 0.6, and 0.7 to refine the predictions. A mask branch is added in the final stage parallel to the box branch, which is composed of a small Fully Convolutional Network (FCN) to predict a segmentation mask for each RoI in a pixel-to-pixel manner to achieve the task of instance segmentation.

In fully-supervised training, the full mask for each cell is available as the ground-truth; whereas in the proposed approach only the point labels are available as the groundtruth for training. The fully supervised method is trained by extracting a matching regular grid of labels from the groundtruth full mask. In contrast, the proposed approach uses point supervision instead of mask supervision. Predictions are approximated in the locations of the groundtruth points from the predictions on the grid using bilinear interpolation (see Fig. 4) [3]. When the prediction and the groundtruth labels are on the same point, the loss can be calculated similarly to the full supervision.

4 Dataset

In the cell biology domain, there exist numerous publically available datasets to facilitate cellular research. Among these datasets, LIVECell [4] dataset has been chosen for this study due to its size and quality. The LIVECell dataset is among the largest and most comprehensive datasets in cell biology research, comprising more than 1.6 million cells in 5,239 images. LIVECell dataset consists of eight morphologically distinct cell cultures, which makes it diverse and challenging. The average cell density in the LIVECell dataset is also very high i.e., 313 cells per image, which is almost 55 times more than the EVICAN [14] dataset.

For the training of the proposed pipeline, the full masks are discarded and replaced with different point labels. In order to analyze the impact of different point labels on the segmentation performance, six different point labels (1, 2, 4, 6, 8, 10) are generated automatically and randomly for each cell of the training data. The point can either be on the cell ('1') or anywhere inside or on the edge of the bounding box ('0').

5 Evaluation Metrics

Standard COCO evaluation protocol [12] is adapted to evaluate the performance of the proposed weakly supervised method with the same modification of the area ranges and the maximum number of detections as reported in [4]. For the evaluation, the mean average precision for both object detection and segmentation tasks at different IoU thresholds of 0.5 (mAP50), 0.75 (mAP75), and 0.5:0.95 in the steps of 0.05 (mAP) is reported. To identify the performance of the model on objects of varied sizes, we have also included mAP for different area ranges.

6 Experimental Setup

The performance of the proposed weakly supervised approach, PACE, and the state-of-the-art (SotA) method, Point2Mask [10], have been reported along with their fully supervised counterparts using the LIVECell dataset. For point-supervised weak cell segmentation, six different training experiments are reported for PACE and Point2Mask with 1-,2-,4-,6-,8-, and 10-point labels.

Training for both methods use the same settings with a learning rate of 0.02, and a momentum of 0.9 using a stochastic gradient descent-based solver. A 3x training schedule is used for the training of both methods. Anchor sizes and aspect ratios were set to 8, 16, 32, 64, 128, and 0.5, 1, 2, 3, 4 for all the settings. For data augmentation, images are flipped horizontally on a random basis to reduce the risk of over-fitting. All training used multi-scale data augmentation, meaning that image sizes were randomly changed from the original 520 × 704 pixels to size with the same ratios, but the shortest side was set to one of (440, 480, 520, 580, 620) pixels.

The checkpoints selection for each training was based on the validation average precision, with 4,000 being chosen for 1-, 6-, and 10-point training, 4,500 for 2-point, 3,000 for 4-point, and 5,000 for 8-point training.

Table 1. Detection and segmentation average precision scores on different IoU thresholds and area range for full mask supervision and $\mathcal{N}$-point supervision using different weak supervision methods i.e., **Point2Mask** [10] and the proposed method, **PACE**. The best and the second-best results for each method are represented in green and blue color, respectively.

Method	Supervision	AP		AP50		AP75		APs		APm		APl	
		Det.	Seg.	Det.	Seg.	Det.	Seg.	Det.	Seg.	Det.	Seg.	Det.	Seg.
Point 2Mask [10]	**Full mask**	43.12	43.90	78.94	78.07	43.26	45.75	44.31	42.30	43.01	43.33	47.01	51.92
	1-point	42.67	42.37	78.71	77.58	42.46	42.96	43.91	41.33	42.16	41.37	46.19	48.64
	2-points	42.75	42.86	78.49	77.62	42.81	43.79	43.95	41.53	42.81	42.30	46.61	50.38
	4-points	**43.01**	43.17	**79.50**	77.91	42.96	44.60	43.97	41.68	**43.07**	42.77	47.24	51.40
	6-points	43.32	43.53	79.69	**78.18**	43.31	44.93	44.54	42.06	43.31	43.31	46.97	**51.52**
	8-points	42.97	**43.41**	78.86	**78.00**	**43.18**	**44.83**	43.95	**41.83**	42.54	42.77	46.94	51.44
	10-points	42.93	43.40	78.71	77.97	43.10	44.81	**44.12**	41.80	42.81	**43.04**	**47.01**	51.65
PACE	**Full mask**	48.43	47.89	81.44	80.80	51.41	51.64	48.50	45.75	49.49	48.33	54.18	56.94
	1-point	48.87	47.54	81.55	80.71	52.11	51.07	48.73	**45.48**	48.98	48.00	53.47	55.72
	2-points	48.54	47.45	**81.65**	81.03	51.67	50.87	**48.66**	45.55	**48.74**	47.88	53.26	55.54
	4-points	**48.56**	47.73	81.58	80.89	**51.83**	51.21	48.26	45.28	49.86	48.60	54.75	57.33
	6-points	47.81	47.24	81.21	80.60	50.33	50.65	47.47	44.50	48.70	48.18	**54.48**	**56.86**
	8-points	48.51	47.81	81.69	**80.88**	51.86	51.74	48.40	45.47	48.66	**48.39**	54.02	56.68
	10-points	48.18	**47.68**	81.26	80.76	51.27	**51.53**	48.12	45.40	48.68	48.22	53.59	56.77

Results. Table 1 shows the overall detection and segmentation average precision scores for Point2Mask [10] and PACE on the LIVECell dataset. For the full mask supervision setting, segmentation AP scores of 43.90% and 47.89% for Point2Mask and PACE, respectively. In the case of 1-point supervision, the proposed approach, PACE, achieves an improvement of over 5% compared to Point2Mask. The performance of PACE also surpasses Point2Mask for higher levels of supervision. Specifically, for 2-, 4-, 6-, 8-, and 10-points, PACE outperforms Point2Mask by margins of 4.5%, 4.6%, 3.7%, 4.4%, and 4.3%, respectively.

7 Analysis and Discussion

In this section, we present and discuss the results of our proposed point-supervised pipeline for cell segmentation and compare it with the state-of-the-art method, Point2Mask [10]. Results in Table 1 and Fig. 5 suggest that for 6 different point labels used for training, we have achieved 98.6% to 99.8% of the fully supervised performance. Even with just 1-point label per cell instance ($\mathcal{P}_1$), we were able to achieve 99.3% of the fully supervised performance, which shows that by saving almost 83% of the time spent on full mask annotations, we can still achieve the segmentation result close to the fully supervised training. For 4-, and 10-point labels, 99.7% and 99.6% of the fully supervised performance are achieved. The best performance is observed for the 8-point label with a segmentation mAP score of 47.81%, which is 99.8% of the fully supervised performance.

In comparison to the SotA i.e., Point2Mask, PACE outperforms the best performing 6-point supervision ($\mathcal{P}_6$) with just 1-point supervision ($\mathcal{P}_1$) by a margin of 4%. Point2Mask achieved 99.16% of the fully supervised performance with 6-point labels, whereas, PACE achieves 99.83% of the LIVECell Anchor-based [4] fully supervised method with 8-point labels. It shows that with only a 0.17% loss in performance, we can save almost 70% of the time spent on full mask annotations. With just a 1-point label ($\mathcal{P}_1$), Point2Mask achieved 96.51% of the fully supervised performance, whereas, the proposed method achieves 99.27%.

Figure 6 displays the comparison results of inference using the Point2Mask and PACE models on test images. These models were trained using different numbers of point annotations. Point2Mask results are depicted in the left column, while the PACE results are represented in the right column. The solid yellow lines indicate the groundtruth mask for each cell, while the dotted red lines represent the predictions made by the model. The rows colored in red, gray, and blue represent the inference results obtained from models trained with 2, 6, and 8 points, respectively. The label "AP50" displayed on top of each prediction sub-image denotes the segmentation average precision score at the IoU threshold of 0.5. The top row represents the results for the models trained with 2-point labels. The inference result of the Point2Mask model reveals some instances of false positives and splitting of a large cell into two. In contrast, the proposed approach, PACE, exhibits better performance in such cases. To provide a clearer picture of the results, specific parts of the images where the SotA Point2Mask model failed to segment cells accurately were zoomed in. It can be observed that PACE is able to segment these specific parts of the images with more precision. The middle row (colored in gray) shows the results obtained from the models trained with 6-point labels. It is evident that the proposed weak cell supervision approach performs relatively well with an AP50 score of 86.8. The last row depicts the inference results for the model trained with 8-point labels. PACE outperforms Point2Mask, as the latter segments two cells as one in one instance, while PACE correctly identifies them as two separate cells. Both methods exhibit some false positives, and in a few cases, the groundtruth is unavailable for certain cells.

The proposed approach has enabled us to achieve performance that is close to full supervision while significantly reducing the time required to annotate the data compared to full mask annotation. Results indicate that even with 1-point supervision during training, we can achieve over 99.3% of the performance achieved with full supervision. Moreover, the proposed approach can also reduce the level of expertise required from biologists to establish cell boundaries. By reducing the time and effort required for data annotation, the proposed method allows for the analysis of more data in a shorter amount of time. The proposed approach can be scaled up to larger and more complex datasets without a corresponding increase in the amount of manual labor and expertise required for data annotation. This increased efficiency in data analysis could lead to a better understanding of biological and medical phenomena, potentially leading to the development of new treatments and diagnostic tools.

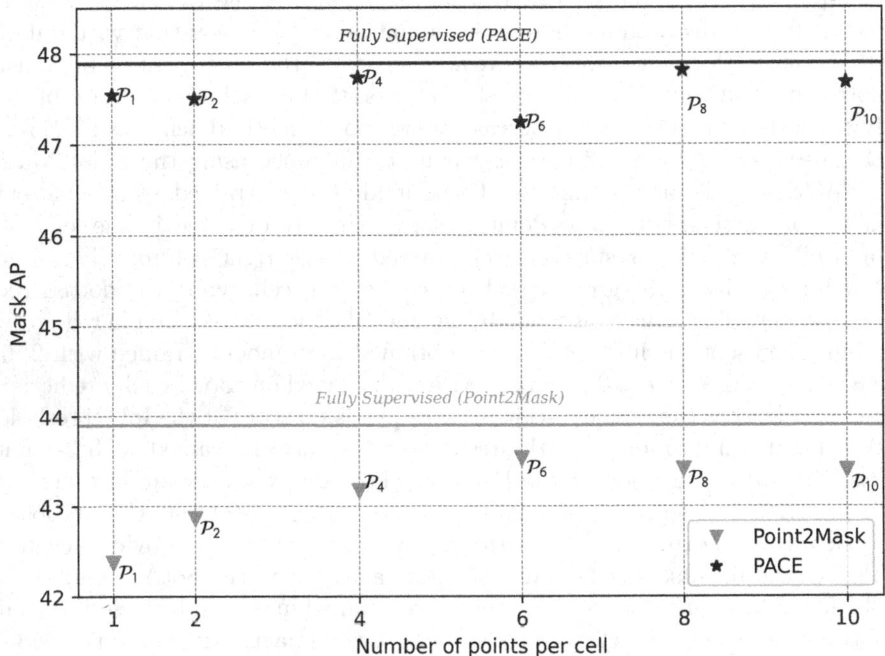

Fig. 5. Training with different numbers of points and full mask for Point2Mask [10] and PACE. Point2Mask results are shown in orange triangles and PACE results are shown in blue stars. PACE trained on LIVECell with as few as 1 labeled point per cell instance ($\mathcal{P}_1$) outperforms the best result of Point2Mask trained with 6 points ($\mathcal{P}_1$) by a margin of 4%. The best performance of PACE is seen for ($\mathcal{P}_8$) with Mask AP score of 47.81%.

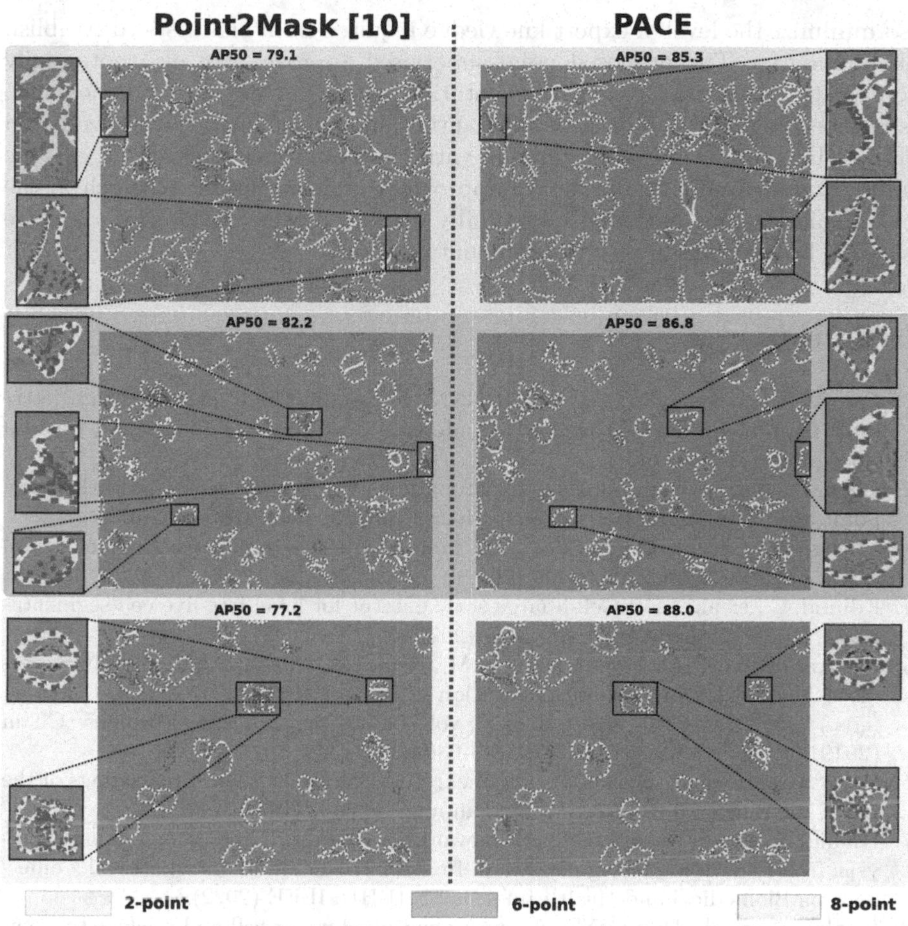

Fig. 6. Inference results using different point labels for **Point2Mask** [10] and the proposed approach, **PACE**. The Point2Mask and PACE results are shown in the left and right columns, respectively. Groundtruth masks are represented by solid yellow lines while dotted red lines show the predictions made by the models. The red, gray, and blue rows represent the inference results obtained from the models trained on 2, 6, and 8-point annotations, respectively. Some cell instances where Point2Mask failed and PACE achieved better segmentation results are also highlighted. (Color figure online)

8 Conclusion

PACE provides an improved approach for weakly supervised cell segmentation using point labels for training instead of the full mask. With just a 1-point label, more than 80% of the time spent on full mask annotations can be saved with just a 0.7% loss in performance compared to the fully supervised method. By utilizing the results of this study, we have demonstrated that it is possible to decrease the time and costs associated with fully annotating the data. In addition, we can also minimize the level of expert knowledge required from biologists to establish cell boundaries. The proposed point-supervised approach can also potentially increase the scalability of cell segmentation studies in biology and medicine. Using the proposed approach, a substantial amount of unlabeled image-based cellular data can be utilized, which in turn can help in conducting larger-scale studies and analyses. The proposed approach could further the research in the field of biology and medicine, potentially leading to new discoveries, as more data can be analyzed in a shorter amount of time.

References

1. Cai, Z., Vasconcelos, N.: Cascade R-CNN: delving into high quality object detection. In: Proceedings of the IEEE Conference on Computer Vision and Pattern Recognition (2018)
2. Chen, Z., et al.: Weakly supervised histopathology image segmentation with sparse point annotations. IEEE J. Biomed. Health Inf. **25**, 1673–1685 (2020)
3. Cheng, B., Parkhi, O., Kirillov, A.: Pointly-supervised instance segmentation. arXiv preprint arXiv:2104.06404 (2021)
4. Edlund, C., et al.: LIVECell-a large-scale dataset for label-free live cell segmentation. Nature Methods **18**, 1038–1045 (2021)
5. Guerrero-Peña, F.A., Fernandez, P.D.M., Ren, T.I., Cunha, A.: A Weakly Supervised Method for Instance Segmentation of Biological Cells. In: Wang, Q., et al. (eds.) DART/MIL3ID -2019. LNCS, vol. 11795, pp. 216–224. Springer, Cham (2019). https://doi.org/10.1007/978-3-030-33391-1_25
6. He, K., Gkioxari, G., Dollár, P., Girshick, R.: Mask R-CNN. In: Proceedings of the IEEE International Conference on Computer Vision (2017)
7. Khalid, N., et al.: DeepMuCS: a framework for co-culture microscopic image analysis: from generation to segmentation. In: 2022 IEEE-EMBS International Conference on Biomedical and Health Informatics (BHI). IEEE (2022)
8. Khalid, N., et al.: DeepCeNS: an end-to-end pipeline for cell and nucleus segmentation in microscopic images. In: 2021 International Joint Conference on Neural Networks (IJCNN). IEEE (2021)
9. Khalid, N., et al.: DeepCIS: an end-to-end pipeline for cell-type aware instance segmentation in microscopic images. In: 2021 IEEE EMBS International Conference on Biomedical and Health Informatics (BHI). IEEE (2021)
10. Khalid, N., et al.: Point2mask: a weakly supervised approach for cell segmentation using point annotation. In: Medical Image Understanding and Analysis: 26th Annual Conference, MIUA 2022, Cambridge, UK, July 27–29, 2022, Proceedings. Springer (2022). https://doi.org/10.1007/978-3-031-12053-4_11
11. Lin, T.Y., Dollár, P., Girshick, R., He, K., Hariharan, B., Belongie, S.: Feature pyramid networks for object detection. In: Proceedings of the IEEE Conference on Computer Vision and Pattern Recognition (2017)
12. Lin, T.-Y., et al.: Microsoft COCO: Common Objects in Context. In: Fleet, D., Pajdla, T., Schiele, B., Tuytelaars, T. (eds.) ECCV 2014. LNCS, vol. 8693, pp. 740–755. Springer, Cham (2014). https://doi.org/10.1007/978-3-319-10602-1_48
13. Papadopoulos, D.P., Uijlings, J.R., Keller, F., Ferrari, V.: Extreme clicking for efficient object annotation. In: Proceedings of the IEEE International Conference on Computer Vision (2017)

14. Schwendy, M., Unger, R.E., Parekh, S.H.: EVICAN-a balanced dataset for algorithm development in cell and nucleus segmentation. Bioinformatics **4**, 3863–3870 (2020)
15. Stringer, C., Wang, T., Michaelos, M., Pachitariu, M.: Cellpose: a generalist algorithm for cellular segmentation. Nature Methods **18**, 100–106 (2020)
16. Tsai, H.F., Gajda, J., Sloan, T.F., Rares, A., Shen, A.Q.: Usiigaci: instance-aware cell tracking in stain-free phase contrast microscopy enabled by machine learning. SoftwareX **9**, 230–237 (2019)
17. Zhang, H., et al.: Resnest: split-attention networks. In: Proceedings of the IEEE/CVF Conference on Computer Vision and Pattern Recognition (2022)
18. Zhou, Y., Zhu, Y., Ye, Q., Qiu, Q., Jiao, J.: Weakly supervised instance segmentation using class peak response. In: Proceedings of the IEEE Conference on Computer Vision and Pattern Recognition (2018)

Pie-UNet: A Novel Parallel Interaction Encoder for Medical Image Segmentation

Youtao Jiang[1], Xiaoqian Zhang[1,2(✉)], Yufeng Chen[1], Shukai Yang[1], and Feng Sun[3]

[1] School of Information Engineering, Southwest University of Science and Technology, Mianyang 621010, China
[2] Tianfu Institute of Research and Innovation, Southwest University of Science and Technology, Mianyang 621010, China
zhxq0528@163.com
[3] Radiology department, Mianyang Central Hospital, Mianyang 621010, China

Abstract. Most of the initial medical image segmentation methods based on deep learning adopt a full convolutional structure, while the fixed size of the convolutional window limits the modeling of long-range dependencies. ViT has powerful global modelling capabilities, but low-level feature detail is poorly represented. To address the above problems, we propose a novel encoder structure and design a new U-shaped network for medical image segmentation, called Pie-UNet. Firstly, facing the problem of lack of localization in ViT and lack of global perception in CNN, we complement each other by encoding global and local information separately and implementing both in a parallel interaction manner; meanwhile, we propose a network with local structure-aware ViT, called Rwin Transformer, to enhance the local detail representation of ViT itself; in addition, to further refine the local representation, we construct a focal modulator based on large kernels; finally, we propose a pre-fusion approach to optimize the information interaction between heterogeneous structures. The experimental results demonstrate that our proposed Pie-UNet can achieve optimal and accurate segmentation results compared with several existing medical image segmentation methods.

Keywords: ViT · CNN · Image segmentation · Large kernel · Shifted Window

1 Introduction

With the continuous development and advancement of deep learning, many problems can be solved with the help of deep learning methods. Under this wave, medical image segmentation methods based on deep learning have been further developed as an important technical tool in medical image analysis. And image segmentation as an important part of medical image analysis, especially accurate segmentation, is regarded as the basic prerequisite for subsequent pathological analysis and treatment formulation.

L. Iliadis et al. (Eds.): ICANN 2023, LNCS 14255, pp. 558–569, 2023.
https://doi.org/10.1007/978-3-031-44210-0_45

Most of the existing medical image segmentation methods use a fully convolutional U-shaped network structure, of which UNet [11], UNet++ [22] and others [9,21] are the typical. The reasons for this are the inherent inductive bias of convolutional neural networks and the sharing of convolutional kernel parameters, which make them well suited to a wide variety of image tasks, especially in pixel-level dense prediction tasks where sliding local windows are able to extract local feature details well. However, the perceptual field of a single local window is too limited, which restricts the explicit modeling of global contextual information by convolutional neural networks, and some solutions have been proposed to face such problems, among which the representative ones are VGGNet [12]and ResNet series [4,5], etc. In order to aggregate responses with large fields of perception, most of these methods build the entire model by stacking multiple modules and adopting a feature pyramid architecture [6].

However, this method of stacking convolutions to increase the perceptual field has its own shortcomings, for example, local information that is particularly important for intensive prediction tasks, especially in pixel-level segmentation tasks, is inevitably discarded as the resolution of the convolutional feature map shrinks, resulting in a lack of ability to accurately model contextual information.

After the Transformer came out of nowhere, it swept the entire field of natural language processing and continued its long reign in the following years. In order to exploit its global attention in the field of computer vision, the ViT [3] model was proposed and its stand-alone framework was applied to various visual tasks [2,13,23], with good results. However ViT has an inherent flaw in its representation of local detail. Swin Transformer's local window-based attention computation [7] provides a solution for ViT, based on the principle of extracting local interaction correlations between tokens before proceeding with global modelling. While UNeXt [14] introduces this shifted window into the MLP, making the MLP focus on local regions, the segmentation method constructed from this improved MLP and convolution achieves better results. Inspired by both of the above, we embed a shifted window mechanism in front of the ViT, and thus propose a ViT with local structure awareness, termed the Rwin Transformer.

The success of the Swin Transformer has attracted a number of workers into imitative learning of ViT, where ConvNeXt [8] has implemented a mapping of the Swin Transformer macro-architecture in pure convolution, allowing it to achieve significant methodological results in detection and segmentation tasks. But this direct processing of feature maps by large kernel convolution will inevitably overlook the interaction modelling of tokens. To further enhance local intra-feature correlation, we borrowed this SA-like token interaction and we proposed our own Large Kernel Adjuster (LKA).

In recent years, combinations between CNN and ViT have been proposed. One of them, Conformer [10], combines the advantages of both structures in an intuitive way, using CNN and ViT to build a two-channel network, based on its proposed feature coupling unit (FCU), which achieves the fusion of local features and global representations at different resolutions. In the field of medical image segmentation, TransFuse [20] combines ViT and CNN in a two-way parallel manner (the whole network is structured in parallel) to effectively capture global dependencies and low-level spatial details, and based on its proposed BiFusion module, it effectively fuses multi-level features from both branches with a new fusion technique. As can be seen, the above approach focuses on the fusion between features and lacks thinking about further optimisation of the structure. Contribution of this paper:

- We propose a novel dual encoder structure for ViT and CNN parallel interaction, which is dedicated to achieving effective aggregation of local and global feature information and improving the accuracy of segmentation.
- We also propose a local structure-aware ViT, called the Rwin Transformer, which actively adapts to input features of different resolutions, enabling the embedding of locality before global modelling.
- In this study, we build a convolutional adjuster based on large kernel convolutions to model input-dependent tokens interactions, which further refine the representation in a self-adjusting manner.

2 The Proposed Method

In this work, in addition to the proposed encoder scheme for the parallel structure, we complete more structural optimisations, which will be described in detail in this sections.

2.1 Parallel Interaction Encoder Consisting of Self-adjust CNN and Rwin Transformer

Pie-UNet constructs both as encoders in a parallel interactive manner to encode local and global information separately, and continuously performs interactive fusion of feature information between them, improving the control of global response by local regions and the detailed representation of global contextual information.

In Fig. 1, the input image is first processed by STEM. After that, the output features are fed into ViT and CNN for processing respectively to obtain the tokens sequence and feature map to be input to the encoder. Figure 2 shows the structure of the encoder on the left. As can be seen from the diagram, the convolutional layer in the CNN pathway reduces the number of channels of the input features to 1/4 of the original number to obtain X_1, which is fed into the LKA along the CNN pathway for further processing to obtain X_2.

$$X_1 = Conv_{3\times3}(Conv_{1\times1}(X_{input})), X_2 = LKA(X_1) \quad (1)$$

where X_1 is fed into the Rwin Transformer together with T^l, and the output sequence is used as input T^{l+1} for the ViT path of the next (l+*1st*) encoder unit block. T^{l+1} is also transformed by Up (the implementation principle is shown

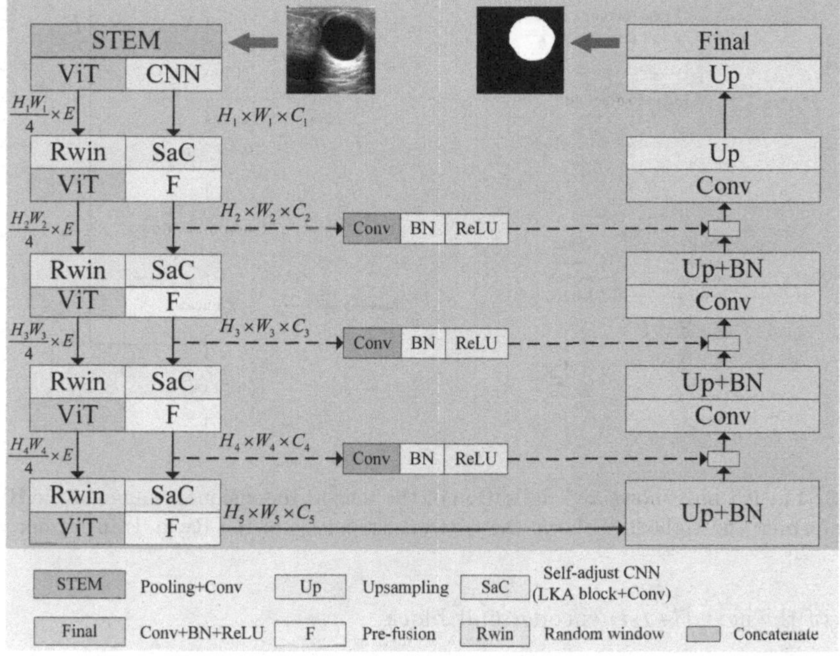

Fig. 1. Overview of the proposed Pie-UNet.

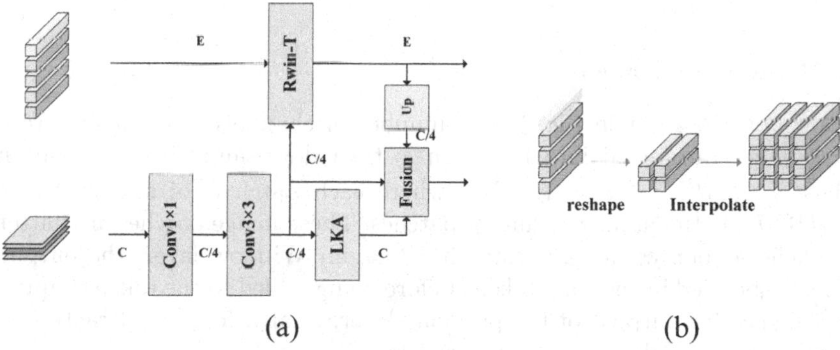

Fig. 2. (a) The unit module of the parallel interaction encoder; (b) Visualization of the tensor change process of the Up block.

on the right) into the feature map X_3, which is fed into the Pre-fusion block for feature fusion.

$$T^{l+1} = Rwin - T(T^l, X_1), X_3 = Up(T^{l+1}) \quad (2)$$

Finally, Fusion block fully fuses the feature information from the above three places, and the output X^l_{output} is used as the input feature X^{l+1}_{input} of the CNN

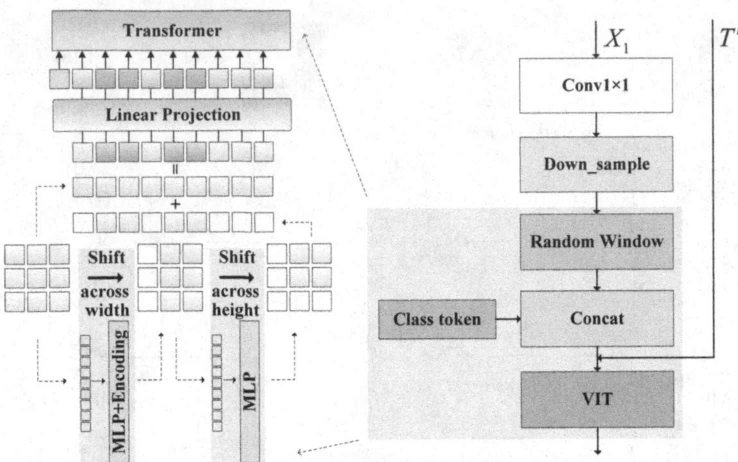

Fig. 3. The left half shows a visualisation of the tensor dimensional change of the Rwin Transformer; the right half shows the network structure of the Rwin Transformer.

path of the next (*l+1st*) encoder unit block.

$$X_{input}^{l+1} = X_{output}^{l} = Fusion(X_1, X_2, X_3) \tag{3}$$

2.2 Rwin Transformer

As shown on the right in Fig. 3, The number of channels of input feature (X_1 in Eq.(1)) is transferred into E, which is then downsampled to be split into patches$\{X_p^i \in R^{P^2 \cdot E} \mid i = 1,..,N\}$, where each patch is of size $P \times P$ and $N = HW/P^2$ is the number of image patches. These image patches are flattened into tokens sequences and fed into the Random Window layer, the output of which is embedded in the class tokens before being added to the tokens sequences from the encoder outputs of the previous layer, finally, feature extraction with a global receptive field is carried out in the ViT.

As shown on the left half of Fig. 3, the feature map experiences two channel-axis shift [16] of the feature channel before being input to the ViT, one on the width axis and the other performed on the height axis. Prior to the shifts, we expand the feature map with an equal number of padding of zeros around the feature map, so that after the shifts, areas outside of the feature map are labelled with meaningless zeros (patches of uncoloured fills that appear after each Shift operation), allowing the MLP to focus only on certain meaningful local positional features. This random windowing mechanism is similar to Swin Transformer windowing attention, which introduces local focus prior to the global information interaction. It is worth noting that we embedded a positional information encoding after the first shift on the feature width axis, and in order to lighten that

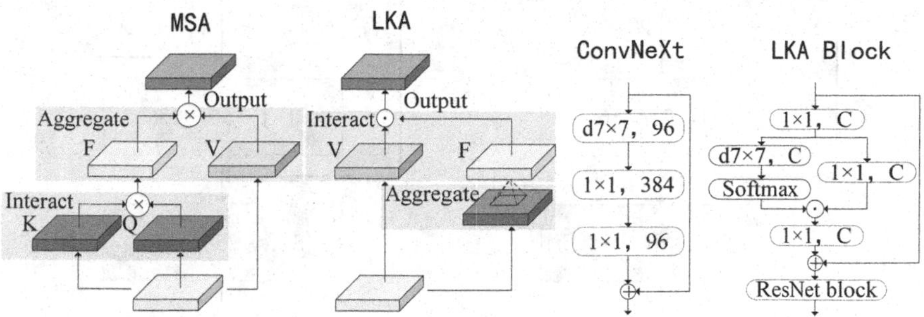

Fig. 4. (a) Self-attention module; (b) Large kernel adjuster; (c) Structure of the main block of ConvNeXt; (d) Structure of the large kernel adjuster block.

operation, we again recovered the tokens sequence as a feature map and then encoded the positional information using DWConv. [17].

2.3 Large Kernel Adjuster

Inspired by SA, we propose a convolutional structure for implementing interaction modelling between tokens similar to that in SA. The multiplication of the weight matrix with V in SA and the application of convolution can be thought of as a way of aggregating information, and the multiplication between tokens of different features (QK^T and $F \bigodot V$ in LKA) can be thought of as a process of information interaction. As shown in Fig. 4(a), SA can be further described as a process of interaction followed by aggregation. In contrast to SA, the interaction modelling process between tokens in LKA can be described as an attention-free way of aggregation followed by interaction. This inverse operation [19] is better to be memory friendly and achieve lightweight tokens interaction.

The LKA uses a depth convolution with a kernel size of 7 × 7 to aggregate feature information within a square region in space.

$$Z = DConv_{7\times7}(GELU(Conv_{1\times1}(X))) \tag{4}$$

We regard the output as weights containing local correlations, and in order to make the weights more distinguishable from each other, we perform softmax on this convolutional feature weight Z to obtain the final weight value F.

$$F = Softmax(Z) \tag{5}$$

We encode features by 1 × 1 convolution to obtain V containing fine-grained spatial information, and V performs a Hadamard product with F that contains convolutional coarse-grained spatial information to generate a refined representation, a process that can be described as:

$$V = Conv_{1\times1}(X), LKA(X) = Conv_{1\times1}(F \odot V) \tag{6}$$

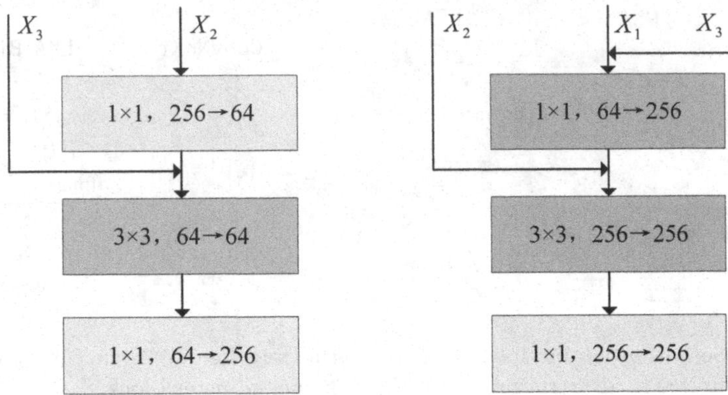

Fig. 5. Comparison of the fusion blocks. (a) ResNeXt Block structure of the fusion module; (b) the proposed Pre-fusion block; where X1, X2, X3 are explained by equations (1), (2), respectively.

In Fig. 4 we show a comparison between the structure of the LKA block and ConvNeXt [8] block. Since the weight map of the convolutional modulation is generated based on the input feature map, our convolutional modulation feature approach introduces more input dependence compared to ConvNeXt, and we refer to the implementation of this dependency as self-regulation.

2.4 Pre-fusion Block

We believe that the design of the information fusion module in a parallel dual path network greatly affects the performance of the entire network, so we have built a feature fusion module that can accommodate more features by increasing the width of the network. Unlike the bottleneck structure-based fusion module of ResNeXt block [18], its reduction in network width during feature fusion may result in loss of useful information. So we move the feature mixing structure in the middle of the ResNeXt block one layer up, and increase the number of channels to four times the input, thus providing enough network capacity for the fused feature information and reducing the loss of feature information (Fig. 5).

3 Experiments and Analysis

3.1 Experimental Settings

Dataset. In the segmentation experiments, we chose two different datasets as the objects of the segmentation task. The first is ISIC 2018, a dataset containing medical images of dermatological diseases acquired from camera shots and their corresponding lesion areas in segments, a total of 2594 images, in which we set the input resolution size of all images to 512×512 and the batch size to 4 in our experiments. Then comes BUSI, a dataset consisting of ultrasound images

Table 1. Experimental results on BUSI and ISIC dataset.(%)

Method	BUSI				ISIC			
	IoU	F1-Score	Recall	Precision	IoU	F1-Score	Recall	Precision
UNet	61.10	74.25	68.20	79.66	80.14	88.73	86.50	89.03
UNet++	61.68	74.94	71.96	66.01	77.87	86.82	84.30	88.10
Attention UNet	62.27	76,04	70.85	**82.55**	77.10	86.23	86.23	85.66
UNeXt	57.39	71.34	65.77	79.12	82.26	89.76	89.44	88.67
UNeXt-L	58.22	72.11	67.29	75.92	82.89	90.13	88.91	**90.71**
TransUNet	61.12	74.91	73.57	73.92	82.88	90.30	90.38	89.94
UCTransNet	63.02	76.36	**73.62**	76.80	81.63	89.27	88.17	89.08
Pie-UNet	**63.63**	**76.90**	72.76	80.97	**83.22**	**90.43**	**90.52**	89.10

of normal, benign and malignant cases of breast cancer and the corresponding segmentation maps of the lesions. We selected images of benign and malignant cases among them, with a total of 647 images. The input image resolution for this dataset in the experiment was 256×256 and the batch size was set to 8.

Implementation Details. Pie-UNet was implemented based on Python 3.9 and Pytorch 1.13.0. The models were trained on an Nvidia 3060 graphics card with 12GB of RAM. In our experiments, F1-score, IoU (Intersection over Union), Recall and Precision were used as accuracy metrics for the experiments, and the models were trained with the Adam optimizer in e^{-4} weight decay for 100 epochs in the BUSI dataset and 150 epochs in the ISIC dataset respectively. We combined Binary Cross Entropy loss and Dice loss as the loss function in the training. For data expansion, we have used the usual options, including random resizing, horizontal flipping and vertical flipping.

3.2 Experimental Results

Tables 1 and 2 compare the segmentation accuracy of UNet [11], Attention UNet [9], UNet++ [22], UCTransNet [15], TransUnet [1], UNeXt [14], and Pie-UNet on different datasets, and the performance of the segmentation accuracy metrics (IoU, F1-score, Recall, Precision) of the compared methods on the same dataset partition is presented in the table. IoU refers to the prediction accuracy of each class(Objects to be segmented); Recall indicates how many of the total samples(The set of pixels used to describe the object) in that class were found; Precision indicates how many of the samples judged to be in that class were correct; F1-score represents the summed average of Recall and Precision, and F1 performs well only when both are high. Therefore we focus on the performance of the IoU and F1-score, and the experimental comparisons will be analysed in the following sections (Fig. 6).

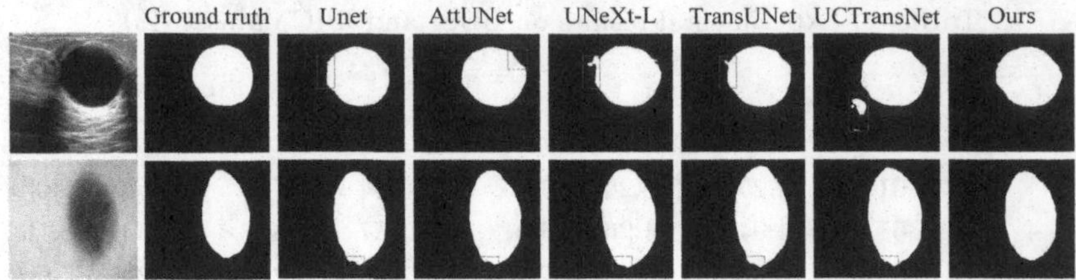

Fig. 6. UNet, Attention UNet, UNeXt, TransUnet, UCTransNet, Pie-UNet on BUSI, ISIC dataset for visual segmentation comparison.

Performance of Different Models in Different Datasets. UNet [11], a classic medical image segmentation network, still performs well in two different dataset segmentation tasks, and its segmentation accuracy has become a benchmark for judging the excellence of the latter network. Attention UNet [9] introduces the attention model into UNet, which has greatly improved the segmentation accuracy in the BUSI medical image dataset, but the performance on the ISIC dataset is weak. UNet++ [22] adds a dense structure-like convolutional layer to UNet in order to enable the skip connection structure to learn useful feature information, which gives it a significant improvement in segmentation performance relative to UNet on the BUSI dataset, but inferior to UNet on the ISIC dataset. TransUNet [1] introduces the Transformer into encoder, which effectively improves the encoder's modeling of long-distance dependent information, and its experimental results on two datasets also prove that the encoder structure composed of CNN and Transformer can indeed provide a better training effect. UCTransNet [15] rethinks skip connections in U-Net from the perspective of the Transformer's channel, which allows it to perform well on two different datasets. UNeXt [14] has improved the MLP by adapting the swin transformer shifted window mechanism and applying this useful component to the decoder and encoder, effectively enhancing the role of the MLP layer in medical image segmentation tasks and enabling it to outperform other comparison networks (except Pie-UNet) in the ISIC dataset. The experimental results demonstrate that Pie-UNet achieves better performance than the other comparison methods in both datasets.

3.3 Ablation Studies

Analysis on Main Module. We chose to conduct ablation experiments on the BUSI dataset and adopted an ablation strategy of random removal or combination of main modules. As can be seen in Table 3, the improvement in effect from the embedding of the Random window is most pronounced when the model retains only one of the three modular structures, demonstrating the superiority of the Rwin Transformer structure.

It is worth mentioning that the embedding of Pre-fusion can also achieve better method results. From Table 3, we can see that the segmentation perfor-

Table 2. Ablation Study on BUSI.

Method	BUSI				
	LKA	Pre-fusion	Rwin	IoU(%)	F1-Score(%)
Pie-UNet	-	-	-	59.08	73.32
	√	-	-	59.37	72.99
	-	√	-	60.05	74.10
	-	-	√	62.06	75.70
	√	√	-	61.73	75.34
	√	-	√	62.54	76.03
	-	√	√	62.79	76.09
	√	√	√	**63.63**	**76.90**

Table 3. Single and multiple structure encoder experiments.

Method	BUSI			
	IoU(%)	F1-Score(%)	Recall(%)	Precision(%)
CNN structure	53.36	68.57	64.07	72.75
Vit structure	54.73	69.44	63.56	**76.94**
Dual structure	**59.08**	**73.32**	**69.76**	76.43

mance of the method model is further improved whenever Pre-fusion is added to it, so the strategy of increasing the network width at the network structure of the fused features can indeed improve the segmentation accuracy of the method. This ablation experiment demonstrates that the embedding of the LKA block can also have a good impact, and can achieve better segmentation results. As can be seen from Table 3, the complete model can achieve optimal segmentation performance in this ablation experiment.

Analysis on Encoder Structure. In order to verify the superiority of this parallel structure, we split the initial model's two-path encoder into two single-path structures, each forming a U-shaped segmentation network, and perform segmentation experiments on the BUSI dataset one by one.

It is worth noting that the encoder with ViT structure has the best performance in the Precision metric, even surpassing the parallel structure. We believe that this is due to the superiority of global attention, where the network model can consider the relationship between pixels in a global perspective. It cannot be denied that the segmentation method using the CNN and ViT parallel interaction structure as the encoder does achieve better segmentation results, with optimal performance in the three segmentation accuracy metrics of IoU, F1-score and Recall.

4 Conclusions

In this work, we propose Pie-UNet, for implementing medical image segmentation. Its encoder is a parallel structure, with the ViT and CNN doing their own encoding work separately as well as interacting with each other for information. In particular, we propose a local structure-aware ViT structure that enhances local details in the global representation; moreover, experiments show that both our proposed large kernel adjuster and Pre-fusion methods can further enhance the segmentation performance of the method. Comparative experiments further demonstrating the potential of this parallel structure to achieve comprehensive and efficient information encoding.

Acknowledgements. This work was supported by the National Natural Science Foundation of China under Grant 62102331, the Natural Science Foundation of Sichuan Province under Grant 2022NSFSC0839 and the Doctoral Research Fund Project of Southwest University of science and Technology 22zx7110.

References

1. Chen, J., et al.: TransuNet: transformers make strong encoders for medical image segmentation. arXiv preprint arXiv:2102.04306 (2021)
2. Chen, M., et al.: Generative pretraining from pixels. In: International Conference on Machine Learning, pp. 1691–1703. PMLR (2020)
3. Dosovitskiy, A., et al.: An image is worth 16×16 words: transformers for image recognition at scale. arXiv preprint arXiv:2010.11929 (2020)
4. Gao, S.H., Cheng, M.M., Zhao, K., Zhang, X.Y., Yang, M.H., Torr, P.: Res2Net: a new multi-scale backbone architecture. IEEE Trans. Pattern Anal. Mach. Intell. **43**(2), 652–662 (2019)
5. He, K., Zhang, X., Ren, S., Sun, J.: Deep residual learning for image recognition. In: Proceedings of the IEEE Conference on Computer Vision and Pattern Recognition, pp. 770–778 (2016)
6. Lin, T.Y., Dollár, P., Girshick, R., He, K., Hariharan, B., Belongie, S.: Feature pyramid networks for object detection. In: Proceedings of the IEEE conference on computer vision and pattern recognition. pp. 2117–2125 (2017)
7. Liu, Z., et al.: Swin transformer: hierarchical vision transformer using shifted windows. In: Proceedings of the IEEE/CVF International Conference on Computer Vision, pp. 10012–10022 (2021)
8. Liu, Z., Mao, H., Wu, C.Y.: Christoph feichtenhofer trevor darrell and saining xie. a convnet for the 2020s. CoRR (2022)
9. Oktay, O., et al.: Attention u-net: learning where to look for the pancreas. arXiv preprint arXiv:1804.03999 10 (2018)
10. Peng, Z., et al.: Conformer: local features coupling global representations for visual recognition. In: Proceedings of the IEEE/CVF International Conference on Computer Vision, pp. 367–376 (2021)
11. Ronneberger, O., Fischer, P., Brox, T.: U-Net: convolutional networks for biomedical image segmentation. In: Navab, N., Hornegger, J., Wells, W.M., Frangi, A.F. (eds.) MICCAI 2015. LNCS, vol. 9351, pp. 234–241. Springer, Cham (2015). https://doi.org/10.1007/978-3-319-24574-4_28

12. Simonyan, K., Zisserman, A.: Very deep convolutional networks for large-scale image recognition. arXiv preprint arXiv:1409.1556 (2014)
13. Touvron, H., Cord, M., Douze, M., Massa, F., Sablayrolles, A., Jégou, H.: Training data-efficient image transformers and distillation through attention. In: International Conference on Machine Learning, pp. 10347–10357. PMLR (2021)
14. Valanarasu, J.M.J., Patel, V.M.: UNeXt: MLP-Based Rapid Medical Image Segmentation Network. In: Wang, L., Dou, Q., Fletcher, P.T., Speidel, S., Li, S. (eds) Medical Image Computing and Computer Assisted Intervention–MICCAI 2022. MICCAI 2022. Lecture Notes in Computer Science, vol. 13435, pp. 23–33. Springer, Cham (2022). https://doi.org/10.1007/978-3-031-16443-9_3
15. Wang, H., Cao, P., Wang, J., Zaiane, O.R.: UcTransNet: rethinking the skip connections in U-NET from a channel-wise perspective with transformer. In: Proceedings of the AAAI Conference on Artificial Intelligence, vol. 36, pp. 2441–2449 (2022)
16. Wang, H., Zhu, Y., Green, B., Adam, H., Yuille, A., Chen, L.-C.: Axial-DeepLab: stand-alone axial-attention for panoptic segmentation. In: Vedaldi, A., Bischof, H., Brox, T., Frahm, J.-M. (eds.) ECCV 2020. LNCS, vol. 12349, pp. 108–126. Springer, Cham (2020). https://doi.org/10.1007/978-3-030-58548-8_7
17. Xie, E., Wang, W., Yu, Z., Anandkumar, A., Alvarez, J.M., Luo, P.: Segformer: simple and efficient design for semantic segmentation with transformers. Adv. Neural. Inf. Process. Syst. **34**, 12077–12090 (2021)
18. Xie, S., Girshick, R., Dollár, P., Tu, Z., He, K.: Aggregated residual transformations for deep neural networks. In: Proceedings of the IEEE Conference on Computer Vision and Pattern Recognition, pp. 1492–1500 (2017)
19. Yang, J., Li, C., Dai, X., Gao, J.: Focal modulation networks. Adv. Neural. Inf. Process. Syst. **35**, 4203–4217 (2022)
20. Zhang, Y., Liu, H., Hu, Q.: TransFuse: fusing transformers and CNNs for medical image segmentation. In: de Bruijne, M., et al. (eds.) MICCAI 2021. LNCS, vol. 12901, pp. 14–24. Springer, Cham (2021). https://doi.org/10.1007/978-3-030-87193-2_2
21. Zhang, Z., Liu, Q., Wang, Y.: Road extraction by deep residual U-NET. IEEE Geosci. Remote Sens. Lett. **15**(5), 749–753 (2018)
22. Zhou, Z., Rahman Siddiquee, M.M., Tajbakhsh, N., Liang, J.: UNet++: a nested U-Net architecture for medical image segmentation. In: Stoyanov, D., et al. (eds.) DLMIA/ML-CDS -2018. LNCS, vol. 11045, pp. 3–11. Springer, Cham (2018). https://doi.org/10.1007/978-3-030-00889-5_1
23. Zhu, X., Su, W., Lu, L., Li, B., Wang, X., Dai, J.: Deformable DETR: deformable transformers for end-to-end object detection. arXiv preprint arXiv:2010.04159 (2020)

Prior-SSL: A Thickness Distribution Prior and Uncertainty Guided Semi-supervised Learning Method for Choroidal Segmentation in OCT Images

Huihong Zhang[1,2], Xiaoqing Zhang[2], Yinlin Zhang[2,7], Risa Higashita[2,3], and Jiang Liu[2,4,5,6(✉)]

[1] Harbin Institute of Technology, Harbin, China
12149031@mail.sustech.edu.cn

[2] Department of Computer Science and Engineering, Southern University of Science and Technology, Shenzhen 518055, China

[3] TOMEY Corporation, Nagoya 4510051, Japan

[4] Research Institute of Trustworthy Autonomous Systems, Southern University of Science and Technology, Shenzhen 518055, China

[5] Guangdong Provincial Key Laboratory of Brain-Inspired Intelligent Computation, Southern University of Science and Technology, Shenzhen 518055, China

[6] Singapore Eye Research Institute, Singapore 169856, Singapore
liuj@sustech.edu.cn

[7] School of Computer Science, University of Nottingham Ningbo China, Ningbo 315100, China

Abstract. Choroid structure is crucial for the diagnosis of ocular diseases, and deep supervised learning (SL) techniques have been widely applied to segment the choroidal structure based on OCT images. However, SL requires massive annotated data, which is difficult to obtain. Researchers have explored semi-supervised learning (SSL) methods based on consistency regularization and achieved strong performance. However, these methods suffer from heavy computational burdens and introduce noise that hinders the training process. To address these issues, we propose a thickness distribution prior and uncertainty aware pseudo-label selection SSL framework (Prior-SSL) for OCT choroidal segmentation. Specifically, we compute the instance-level uncertainty of the pseudo-label candidate, which significantly reduces the computational burden of uncertainty estimation. In addition, we consider the physiological characteristics of the choroid, explore the choroidal thickness distribution as prior knowledge in the pseudo-label selection procedure, and thereby obtain more reliable and accurate pseudo-labels. Finally, these two branches are combined via a Modified AND-Gate (MAG) to

This work was supported in part by General Program of National Natural Science Foundation of China (Grant No. 82272086), and Shenzhen Natural Science Fund (JCYJ20200109140820699 and the Stable Support Plan Program 20200925174052004).

L. Iliadis et al. (Eds.): ICANN 2023, LNCS 14255, pp. 570–581, 2023.
https://doi.org/10.1007/978-3-031-44210-0_46

assign confidence levels to pseudo-label candidates. We achieve state-of-the-art performance for the choroidal segmentation task on the GOALS and NIDEK OCT datasets. Ablation studies verify the effectiveness of the Prior-SSL in selecting high-quality pseudo-labels.

Keywords: OCT image · choroidal segmentation · semi-supervised learning (SSL) · pseudo-label · prior knowledge

1 Introduction

The choroid is a vascular tissue between the retina and the sclera [15]. In particular, the quantification of a choroidal thickness (ChT) in Optical Coherence Tomography (OCT) images is clinical evidence for diagnosing ocular diseases, including age-related macular degeneration (AMD), polypoidal choroidal vasculopathy (PCV), and pathological myopia (PM) [19]. Accurate choroid segmentation is an indispensable step in estimating ChT. With the powerful feature extraction ability of deep neural networks, deep supervised learning (SL) methods have achieved remarkable progress in choroid segmentation on OCT images [11,12,21]. However, collecting the massive annotated data to learn the informative feature representation is challenging for SL methods. To relieve this problem, researchers in the recent have used the semi-supervised learning (SSL) methods for automatic OCT segmentation [8,13,14,18]. For example, Sedai et al. [18] introduced an uncertainty aware semi-supervised method for OCT retinal layer segmentation with Bayesian student-teacher learning. Lu et. al. [14] designed a semi-supervised OCT segmentation framework by applying consistency regularization to the decode branches' predictions of unlabeled data. These methods have achieved promising results in OCT segmentation by introducing uncertainty/consistency into the training process to obtain "confident" predictions. However, there are still two major challenges: (1) They often require a heavy computational burden for pixel-level uncertainty estimation [22]. (2) We have found empirically that for some difficult samples, multiple predictions can have very similar errors, leading to high confidence for incorrect predictions. In this case, a lot of noise is introduced and hinders the training process.

Inspired by [17], the uncertainty-aware pseudo-labeling method can inherit the benefit from consistency regularization while reducing computational cost, but additional efforts are demanded to obtain reliable pseudo-labels. In this paper, we propose a thickness distribution prior and uncertainty-aware semi-supervised learning (Prior-SSL) framework for OCT choroidal segmentation. Our contribution can be described in three aspects:

(1) We establish a set of procedures to exploit prior knowledge of the ChT distribution into patterns. These patterns are used to query prior consistency for pseudo-label candidates. We initialize these patterns from limited labels and store them in a memory bank (MB). When high-confidence pseudo-labels are obtained, we can adopt them to update the patterns to be more accurate and diverse.

(2) We use a single forward pass to generate a set of pseudo-labels and corresponding instance-level uncertainty values, which requires much less training time and computation than consistency regularization methods.
(3) We introduce a Modified AND-Gate (MAG) operator to select high-quality pseudo-labels by integrating uncertainty and prior consistency information. Experimental results show that Prior-SSL efficiently mitigates the case of high confidence error and achieves comparable segmentation performance to full supervision while using only 20% labels in the NIDEK and GOALS datasets.

2 Methodology

Inspired by the fact that prior knowledge learning can exploit the underlying information of unlabeled samples, providing extra domain information to facilitate the clinical segmentation [8], we elaborately integrate unique prior information into pseudo label filtering by exploiting distribution characteristic of the choroidal thickness (ChT). Then, we denote the dataset as $X = \{X^L, X^U\}$, where the labeled subset X^L has m samples, and the unlabeled subset X^U has n samples. Each sample in X^L has a corresponding label in Y^L. Therefore, the proposed Prior-SSL model can achieve the OCT choroidal segmentation by SSL learning, incorporating the uncertainty and anatomical prior. As shown in Fig. 1, the whole flowchart of the proposed Prior-SSL consists of preprocessing, pseudo labeling, and SSL training, and the detailed implementation is described below.

2.1 Preprocessing

Segmentation Model Pretraining. Driven by the achievements for ResUNet in medical image segmentation [6], we employ ResUNet as the primary segmentation model. Specifically, we input the objective image X^L and take the labeled data Y^L as the ground truth for ResUNet training, and the classical cross-entropy function is adopted as $\mathcal{L}_{seg}$:

$$\mathcal{L}_{seg}(y, p) = -y \log(p) - (1 - y) \log(1 - p) \tag{1}$$

where y and p denotes the ground truth and model prediction, respectively.

Choroidal Thickness Prior Memory Bank Construction. Memory bank (MB) refers to storage of representations, which can be updated during training [2]. In our study, a MB containing prior anatomical knowledge is employed to maintain consistency between labeled and unlabeled data. The MB consists of three sets of elements: (1) pattern, which facilitates pseudo-label query for a prior consistency, (2) statistical information, which is used to filter out pseudo-label candidates with low confidence, and (3) V^L_{ChT}, which participates in computing statistics while renewing the MB.

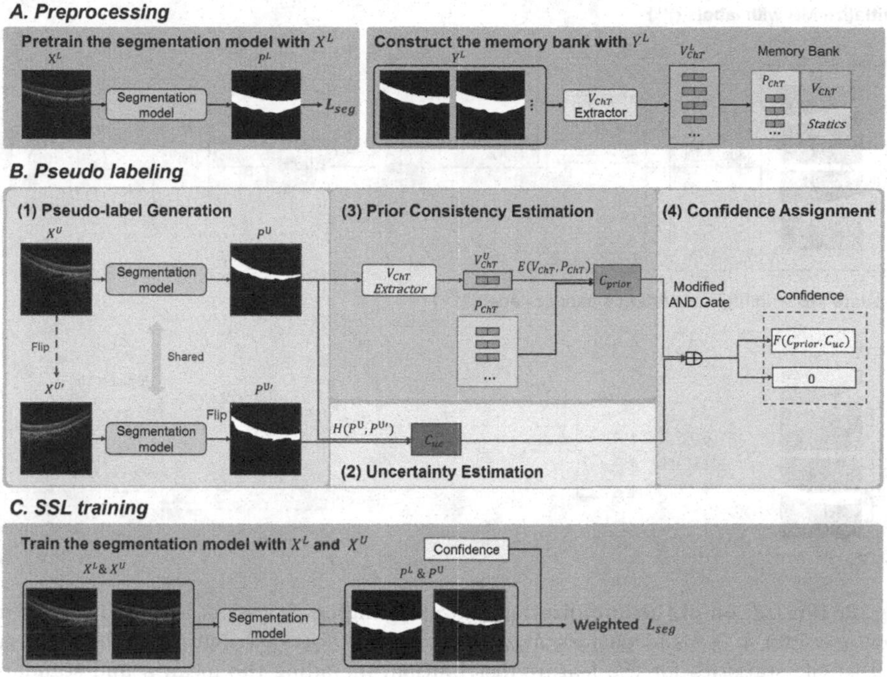

Fig. 1. Overview of the proposed Prior-SSL framework. X, Y and P denote the original image, label and model prediction, respectively. The function $H(\cdot)$ represents cross-entropy, and $E(\cdot)$ calculates represents Euclidean distance. The modified AND Gate (MAG) operates as follows: the confidence level is calculated by $F(.)$ (Eq. 5) only if both C_{prior} and C_{un} are within the specified feasible region; otherwise, the value is 0.

The initialization and updating processes of the MB are detailed in Fig. 2. The construction process of the memory bank involves (1) inputting the binarized choroidal label M and summing it up column by column to obtain the thickness map M_{ChT}; (2) performing principal component analysis (PCA) dimensionality reduction [1] on M_{ChT} to obtain the thickness distribution features V_{ChT}, with two components preserved according to Occam's razor principle since two principal components can capture over 94% of the variance contribution, and adding more principal components does not significantly improve it; (3) clustering V_{ChT} using the K-Means++ algorithm [3] to obtain k clustering centers as the pattern P_{ChT} of the thickness distribution; and (4) computing the intra-class distance using Euclidean distance, followed by the calculation of its mean μ and standard deviation σ.

2.2 Pseudo Labeling

As shown in Fig. 1, a set of pseudo-labels with corresponding confidence levels is generated in this step. To obtain the pseudo-labels, the unlabeled data is processed through a pre-trained segmentation model. The confidence level assigned

Initialize MB with labels (Y^L)

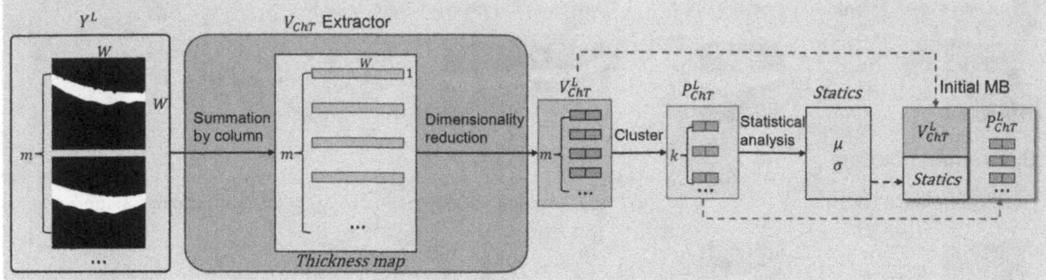

Update MB with high-confidence pseudo-labels ($\widehat{Y^U}$)

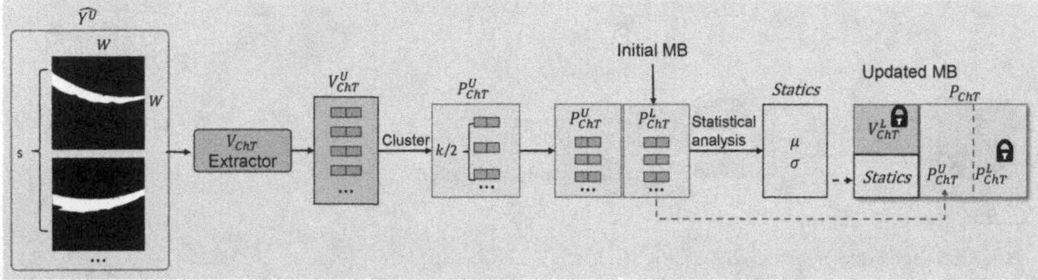

Fig. 2. Illustration of the initialization and updatinging process of MB. MB stores the feature vector V_{ChT} and pattern P_{ChT} for the thickness distribution of the label, as well as the statistics for the feature distribution, including the mean μ and standard deviation σ of the intra-class distance. The initial MB is constructed using labeled data Y^L, followed by incremental updates using high-confidence pseudo-labels $\tilde{Y^U}$. The update process entails identifying new patterns and integrating them with the existing ones, followed by updating the statistics to replace the prior data.

to each pseudo-label candidate is based on both the uncertainty of the model and the consistency of the prior information. The resulting set of pseudo-labels is then utilized for semi-supervised learning, where the confidence scores are employed to adjust the loss weights. The highest scoring pseudo-labels are chosen to update the memory bank, thereby enhancing its representation of data distribution.

The procedures to calculate the confidence of the pseudo-label includes: (1) uncertainty estimation, (2) prior consistency estimation, and (3) using the modified AND-gate (MAG) to integrate uncertainty and prior consistency to obtain the confidence level.

Uncertainty Estimation. Two sets of prediction maps, P^U and $P^{U'}$, are generated from the model by inputting X^U and its flipped one $X^{U'}$. The uncertainty D_{uc} is obtained by calculating the cross-entropy between the pair of prediction maps:

$$D_{uc} = -P^U \log P^{U'} - (1 - P^U)\log(1 - P^{U'}) \tag{2}$$

And the uncertainty-based confidence component C_{uc} is:

$$C_{uc} = \begin{cases} 1 - (D_{uc}/T)^{\beta} & D_{uc} \leq T \\ 0 & D_{uc} > T \end{cases} \quad (3)$$

where T is the upper-bound for uncertainty D_{uc}, and β is parameter to adjust the mapping function. Next, we binarize the prediction map P^U to $\tilde{Y}^U$ as a pseudo label candidate.

Prior Consistency Estimation. To estimate the prior consistency C_{prior}, we first extract $\tilde{V}^U_{ChT}$ from $\tilde{Y}^U$ (see Fig. 2). For any sample i, we use $\tilde{v}^U_{ChT_i}$ to query patterns in memory bank and compute the prior disagreement D_{prior} by measuring the Euclidean distance. The prior consistency based confidence component C_{prior} is calculated by:

$$C_{prior} = \begin{cases} \exp(-D_{prior}) & D_{prior} \leq \mu + 3\sigma \\ 0 & D_{prior} > \mu + 3\sigma \end{cases} \quad (4)$$

where μ and σ are statistics stored in MB, and $\mu + 3\sigma$ is the upper-bound for prior disagreement D_{prior}. We have also applied the inverse exponential function ($\exp(-z)$) to transform the feasible values of C_{prior} to the interval of $[0, 1]$, as suggested in [9].

Confidence Assignment by Modified AND-Gate (MAG). We design a MAG to incorporate the uncertainty-based confidence C_{uc} and prior consistency-based confidence C_{prior}. The MAG method assigns high confidence to pseudo-labels with low uncertainty and high prior consistency. Conversely, pseudo-labels with excessive uncertainty or significant deviations from the prior are assigned zero confidence and filtered out. The following equation represents the confidence calculation:

$$C = \begin{cases} \lambda * C_{uc} + (1 - \lambda) * C_{prior} & C_{uc} > 0 \& D_{prior} > 0 \\ 0 & \text{else} \end{cases} \quad (5)$$

where λ is a trade-off hyper-parameter.

2.3 SSL Training

In semi-supervised training, we utilize pseudo-labels to expand the label set and take confidence levels to balance the contributions of true labels and pseudo-labels in the loss function optimization:

$$\mathcal{L}_{SSL} = \sum_{i=1}^{m} \mathcal{L}_{ce}(y_i^L, \tilde{y}_i^L) + \sum_{i=j}^{n} c_j * \mathcal{L}_{ce}(y_j^U, \tilde{y}_j^U) \quad (6)$$

3 Experiment

3.1 Datasets

We applied the Prior-SSL methods to segment the choroid layer using two OCT datasets: GOALS [7] and NIDEK [4].

GOALS [7]: The dataset is a publicly available dataset from Glaucoma OCT Analysis and Layer Segmentation (GOALS) Challenge in conjunction with MICCAI 2022. The images were acquired using a TOPCON DRI Swept Source OCT and corresponded to a circular scan around the optic nerve head. We conducted the choroidal segmentation task in the layer segmentation dataset, which contains 100 OCT B-scans with a resolution of 1000 × 800.

NIDEK [4]: The dataset was acquired using a NIDEK OCT device from 28 normal eye subjects, each volume consisting of 4 to 5 labeled OCT B-scans centered around the macula. It consists of 119 labeled OCT B-scans with 512 × 1024 resolution.

On the GOALS dataset, we randomly split 20% (20) samples as a test set. On the NIDEK dataset, due to the high similarity of samples from the same volume, we randomly selected 20% volumes (5 volumes with 19 samples) as an independent test set. In the training set, according to the experimental setting, about 10% or 20% of the labeled data is used as X^L subset; and the rest is used as X^U subset in training, that is, only images are used without labels. We also use the X^U subset as the validation set for model selection.

3.2 Implementation Details

We implemented the network in Python with Pytorch [16] on an NVIDIA RTX A6000 GPU. The model is trained with Adam [10] optimizer with a base learning rate of 10^{-4}. The mini-batch size was 12, with 6 samples from X^L and 6 from X^U. All input images and segmentation labels were resized to a common scale (512 × 512).

3.3 Metrics

We take the common evaluation metric Dice coefficient to evaluate the segmentation quality. The Dice coefficient is defined as:

$$Dice = \frac{2 A \cap B|}{|A| + |B|},$$

where A and B are two areas.

3.4 Comparison Results and Discussion

To measure the performance of our method on OCT choroidal segmentation, we compared it with four current state-of-the-art SSL methods: MT [20], CPS

Table 1. Dice coefficient (%) comparison of the different methods on GOALS and NIDEK datasets when the ratio of X^L reaches 10%/20%.

	GOALS [7]		NIDEK [4]	
	10% (8 labels)	20% (16 labels)	10% (9 labels)	20% (19 labels)
Baseline	90.76	92.64	88.34	90.12
MT [20]	92.64	93.86	90.09	92.70
CPS [5]	93.12	93.84	90.62	91.55
MCS [14]	93.21	93.96	90.55	92.37
SGNet [13]	93.16	94.01	90.47	92.76
Ours	**93.59**	**94.12**	**91.47**	**93.50**
Oracle	94.53		93.64	

[5], SGNet [13] and MCS [14]. We also provide the result of baseline (ResUNet trained with a limited number of X^L in a supervised manner) and oracle (fully supervised with correct labels for the unlabeled samples). For a fair comparison, all methods adopt ResUNet [6] pretrained on the X^L subset as the backbone, and all models are trained and tested on the same split datasets.

As shown in Table 1, When X^L accounts for 10% of the total training set, our method outperforms the best SSL Dice by 0.52% on the GOALS dataset and 1% on NIDEK. The proposed method achieves better performance owing to the additional prior knowledge integrated into the training phase, then the network can select more reliable pseudo-labels to improve SSL when the data of X^L is very limited. Moreover, all SSL methods can achieve the best results at the 20% ratio, and our method still surpasses other SOTAs.

Table 2. Ablation study of different filtering strategy in Prior-SSL over NIDEK dataset. The results are reported when the ratio of X^L reaches 20%.

Method	Pseudo-labels filtering strategy	Dice (%)
Baseline	NO filtering	91.96
Ours	By prior consitency (C_{prior})	92.18
	By uncertainty (C_{uc})	92.87
	Mean(C_{prior},C_{uc})	92.16
	MAG(C_{prior},C_{uc})	**93.50**

3.5 Ablation Study

We compare the quality of pseudo-label sets selected by each component of our selection strategy and their impact on model generalization performance in ablation experiments.

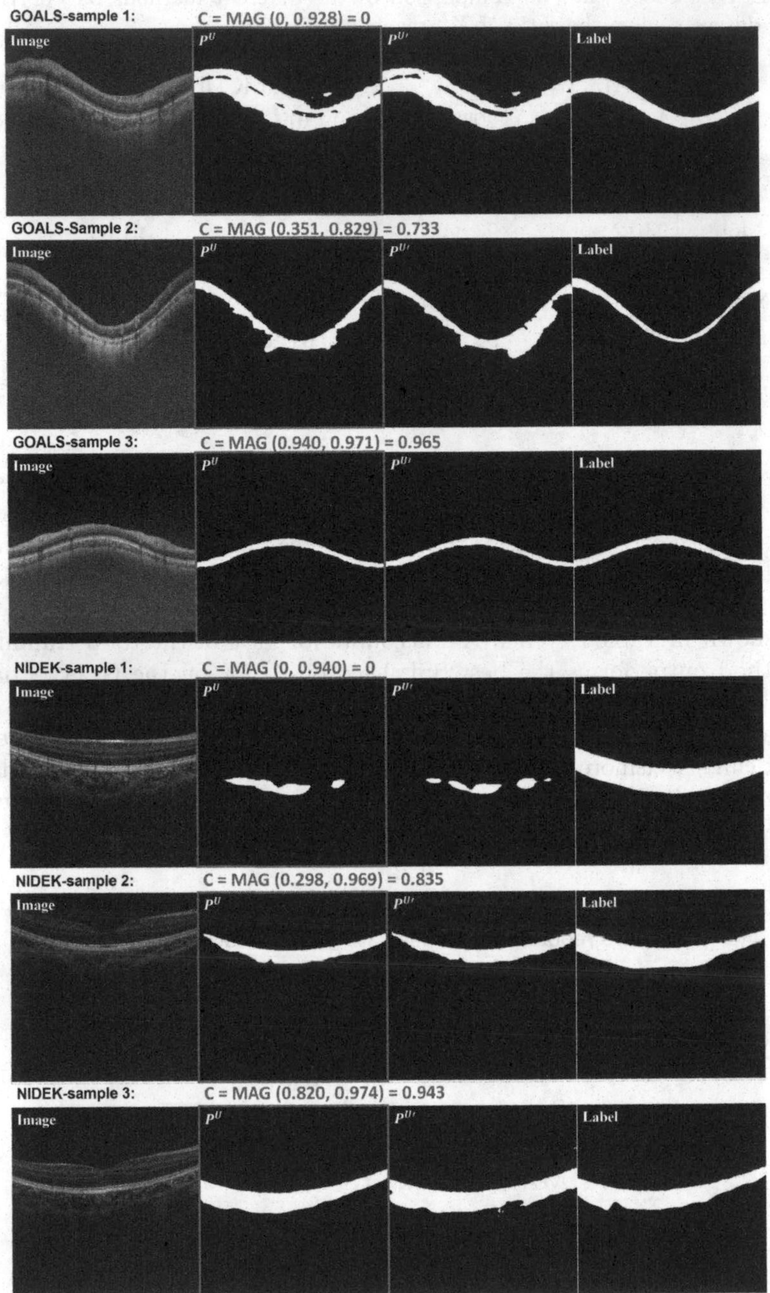

Fig. 3. Visual examples of pseudo-label selection. From left to right are: input images, pseudo-label candidates (P^U), auxiliary prediction ($P^{U'}$), and label (label is only used in evaluation). The confidence of each P^U is calculated by $C = MAG(C_{prior}, C_{uc})$.

As shown in Fig. 3, incorporating prior consistency information into the filtering strategy benefits the reduction of noisy pseudo-labels by filtering out or reducing the weight of poor candidates.

Table 2 shows that the baseline without any filtering strategy achieves inadequate performance on the test set (Dice coefficient of 91.96%). We argue that this may be because the model learns the noise pseudo-labels indiscriminately. For filtering strategies that use a single uncertainty or prior as a judgment condition, they remove low-quality pseudo-label candidates that do not meet the conditions and assign a confidence level to each instance of the selected pseudo-labels; both achieved better performance in the test set (92.18% and 92.87%, respectively).

However, the intuitive way that directly combines the two values by calculating the average seems to result in negative effects. We argue that some pseudo-label candidates originally judged to be of poor quality by a single condition can be reserved in this way. The proposed MAG, however, can avoid the recycling of noisy pseudo-labels, resulting in better performance (93.50%).

4 Conclusion and Future Work

In this paper, we proposed a novelty scheme for choroidal layer segmentation by semi-supervised learning with prior information (Proir-SSL) in OCT images. Specifically, the proposed Prior-SSL adequately considers the pathological characteristics of the choroidal layer and incorporates the thickness distribution to exploit prior knowledge information from a limited annotation and unlabelled subset. The quantitatively and qualitatively experimental results on GOALS [7] and NIDEK [4] datasets validate the effectiveness of the proposed Prior-SSL. It achieves performance comparable to full supervision while significantly reducing annotation costs.

Furthermore, we found the proposed pseudo-label selection framework can be easily combined with other backbone networks and semi-supervised training strategies to improve the performance. On the other hand, pseudo-labels that differ significantly from the prior may indicate more valuable to be annotated from an active learning perspective, as they may contain new patterns or anomalies. We will explore these insights in our future work.

References

1. Abdi, H., Williams, L.J.: Principal component analysis. WIREs Comput. Statistics **2**(4), 433–459 (2010). https://doi.org/10.1002/wics.101
2. Alonso, I., Sabater, A., Ferstl, D., Montesano, L., Murillo, A.C.: Semi-supervised semantic segmentation with pixel-level contrastive learning from a class-wise memory bank. In: 2021 IEEE/CVF International Conference on Computer Vision, ICCV 2021, Montreal, QC, Canada, October 10–17, 2021, pp. 8199–8208. IEEE (2021). https://doi.org/10.1109/ICCV48922.2021.00811
3. Arthur, D., Vassilvitskii, S.: k-means++: the advantages of careful seeding. In: ACM-SIAM Symposium on Discrete Algorithms (2007)

4. Chai, Z., et al.: Perceptual-assisted adversarial adaptation for choroid segmentation in optical coherence tomography. In: 2020 IEEE 17th International Symposium on Biomedical Imaging (ISBI), pp. 1966–1970 (2020). https://doi.org/10.1109/ISBI45749.2020.9098346
5. Chen, X., Yuan, Y., Zeng, G., Wang, J.: Semi-supervised semantic segmentation with cross pseudo supervision. In: IEEE Conference on Computer Vision and Pattern Recognition, CVPR 2021, virtual, June 19–25, 2021, pp. 2613–2622. Computer Vision Foundation / IEEE (2021). https://doi.org/10.1109/CVPR46437.2021.00264
6. Diakogiannis, F.I., Waldner, F., Caccetta, P., Wu, C.: ResUNet-a: a deep learning framework for semantic segmentation of remotely sensed data. ISPRS J. Photogrammetry Remote Sens. **162**, 94–114 (2020)
7. Fang, H., Li, F., Fu, H., Wu, J., Zhang, X., Xu, Y.: Dataset and evaluation algorithm design for GOALS challenge. In: Antony, B.J., Fu, H., Lee, C.S., MacGillivray, T.J., Xu, Y., Zheng, Y. (eds.) Ophthalmic Medical Image Analysis - 9th International Workshop, OMIA 2022, Held in Conjunction with MICCAI 2022, Singapore, September 22, 2022, Proceedings. Lecture Notes in Computer Science, vol. 13576, pp. 135–142. Springer (2022). https://doi.org/10.1007/978-3-031-16525-2_14
8. Fazekas, B., et al.: SD-LayerNet: semi-supervised retinal layer segmentation in OCT using disentangled representation with anatomical priors. In: Wang, L., Dou, Q., Fletcher, P.T., Speidel, S., Li, S. (eds.) Medical Image Computing and Computer Assisted Intervention - MICCAI 2022–25th International Conference, Singapore, September 18–22, 2022, Proceedings, Part VIII. Lecture Notes in Computer Science, vol. 13438, pp. 320–329. Springer (2022). https://doi.org/10.1007/978-3-031-16452-1_31
9. Kendall, A., Gal, Y., Cipolla, R.: Multi-task learning using uncertainty to weigh losses for scene geometry and semantics. In: 2018 IEEE/CVF Conference on Computer Vision and Pattern Recognition, pp. 7482–7491 (2017)
10. Kingma, D., Ba, J.: Adam: a method for stochastic optimization. arXiv:1412.6980 (2014)
11. Kugelman, J., et al.: Automatic choroidal segmentation in oct images using supervised deep learning methods. Sci. Rep. **9**, 13298 (2019)
12. Kugelman, J., Alonso-Caneiro, D., Read, S.A., Vincent, S.J., Collins, M.J.: Oct chorio-retinal segmentation with adversarial loss. In: 2021 Digital Image Computing: Techniques and Applications (DICTA), pp. 01–08 (2021). https://doi.org/10.1109/DICTA52665.2021.9647099
13. Liu, X., et al.: Semi-supervised automatic segmentation of layer and fluid region in retinal optical coherence tomography images using adversarial learning. IEEE Access **7**, 3046–3061 (2019). https://doi.org/10.1109/ACCESS.2018.2889321
14. Lu, Y., Shen, Y., Xing, X., Meng, M.Q.: Multiple consistency supervision based semi-supervised OCT segmentation using very limited annotations. In: 2022 International Conference on Robotics and Automation, ICRA 2022, Philadelphia, PA, USA, May 23–27, 2022, pp. 8483–8489. IEEE (2022). https://doi.org/10.1109/ICRA46639.2022.9812447
15. Nickla, D.L., Wallman, J.: The multifunctional choroid. Prog. Retin. Eye Res. **29**, 144–168 (2010)
16. Paszke, A., et al.: PyTorch: an imperative style, high-performance deep learning library. In: Advances in Neural Information Processing Systems, vol. 32(NeurIPS) (2019)

17. Rizve, M.N., Duarte, K., Rawat, Y.S., Shah, M.: In defense of pseudo-labeling: an uncertainty-aware pseudo-label selection framework for semi-supervised learning. In: 9th International Conference on Learning Representations, ICLR 2021, Virtual Event, Austria, May 3–7, 2021. OpenReview.net (2021), https://openreview.net/forum?id=-ODN6SbiUU
18. Sedai, S., et al.: Uncertainty guided semi-supervised segmentation of retinal layers in OCT images. In: Shen, D., et al. (eds.) Medical Image Computing and Computer Assisted Intervention - MICCAI 2019–22nd International Conference, Shenzhen, China, October 13–17, 2019, Proceedings, Part I. Lecture Notes in Computer Science, vol. 11764, pp. 282–290. Springer (2019). https://doi.org/10.1007/978-3-030-32239-7_32
19. Singh, S.R., Vupparaboina, K.K., Goud, A., Dansingani, K.K., Chhablani, J.: Choroidal imaging biomarkers. Surv. Ophthalmol. **64**(3), 312–333 (2019)
20. Tarvainen, A., Valpola, H.: Mean teachers are better role models: weight-averaged consistency targets improve semi-supervised deep learning results. In: Advances in Neural Information Processing Systems 30: Annual Conference on Neural Information Processing Systems 2017, December 4–9, 2017, Long Beach, CA, USA, pp. 1195–1204 (2017)
21. Zhang, H., et al.: Automatic segmentation and visualization of choroid in oct with knowledge infused deep learning. IEEE J. Biomed. Health Inform. **24**, 3408–3420 (2020)
22. Zou, K., Chen, Z., Yuan, X., Shen, X., Wang, M., Fu, H.: A review of uncertainty estimation and its application in medical imaging. CoRR abs/2302.08119. https://doi.org/10.48550/arXiv.2302.08119 (2023)

PSR-Net: A Dual-Branch Pyramid Semantic Reasoning Network for Segmentation of Remote Sensing Images

Lijun Wang[1], Bicao Li[1(✉)], Bei Wang[2], Chunlei Li[1], Jie Huang[1], and Mengxing Song[1]

[1] School of Electronic and Information Engineering, Zhongyuan University of Technology, Zhengzhou 450007, China
lbc@zut.edu.cn

[2] University Infirmary, Zhongyuan University of Technology, Zhengzhou 450007, China

Abstract. The long-range context information in the semantic segmentation network for remote sensing images (RSIs) plays an important role in the improvement of segmentation performance. However, in large RSIs, the interaction between local information and global information is limited. In order to solve the problem, we propose a dual-branch pyramid semantic reasoning segmentation network. Our dual-branch network consists of a global and local branch. The traditional CNN network is employed on the global branch, and a lightweight multi-scale hierarchical feature aggregation (MHFA) module is introduced into the local branch. In addition, the Feature Semantic Reasoning (FSR) module is proposed to enhance the valuable features and weaken the useless features to improve the semantic representation of RSIs, and then the double branch transformer is embedded. The ablation experiment on the Beijing Land-Use (BLU) dataset illustrates the effectiveness of the added modules, and the results presented by comparison with other traditional networks also confirm the superiority of our proposed network. The proposed network can achieve better segmentation accuracy on large-scale RSI datasets.

Keywords: Remote Sensing Images · Semantic Segmentation · Multi-scale Hierarchical Feature Aggregation · Feature Semantic Reasoning

1 Introduction

In the field of remote sensing, the emergence of semantic segmentation is a new demand for the development of intelligent maps and smart cities. The distinction between certain types of individuals is a prerequisite for building more refined models. Especially with the rise of high-resolution video communication satellites, the application channels and scenes have been greatly expanded. With the rapid development of neural networks, automatic semantic segmentation has been applied to high-resolution RSIs.

The shortcoming of convolution computational is one of the limitations of neural networks. The receptive field (RF) of the CNN unit is a value in the feature map obtained

L. Iliadis et al. (Eds.): ICANN 2023, LNCS 14255, pp. 582–592, 2023.
https://doi.org/10.1007/978-3-031-44210-0_47

from each layer, which is calculated from the range of pixels in the original image [1]. Due to the sparse activation of CNN, its unit effective RF is relatively small, which indicates that the traditional CNN structure only models the local image mode without considering the context information. Although some methods are presented to enlarge the RF of CNN, the long-term correlation between different regions is not considered. The remarkable feature in different scenarios can be obtained through the attention mechanism, however, the semantic relevance of different scene areas is not further modeled [2].

The technology of feature extraction pyramid has been developing continuously, and its application scope in computer vision has also expanded [3]. However, in the current image preprocessing, the operations of resize and crop cause a certain degree of image distortion, thus affecting the final accuracy. Feature pyramid network (FPN) applied different steps for convolution kernel to obtain Feature Pyramid (FP). Although these FP based methods perform well in the field of computer vision, they have a large number of parameters, which consume a lot of computing resources.

In this research, we propose the FSR and the MHFA to achieve the extraction of local feature information. In FP, a large number of parameters are used to represent multi-scale features [4], which are widely used in the deep learning model of computer vision tasks. In order to reduce the number of parameters, the multi-scale pyramid module is proposed to connect the output of the convolution module by using the jump connection method and treat each channel as a sub-pyramid. These sub-pyramids are connected by hierarchical feature aggregation (HFA) to obtain the overall FP. The main contributions of this study can be summarized as follows:

(1) A dual-branch pyramid semantic inference network for RSI segmentation is proposed, which consists of two branches, namely the global branch and the local branch, which extract global information and local information, respectively.
(2) It is proposed to enhance the ability of feature extraction in the local branch of RSIs, reduce the amount of computation, and enhance valuable features through MHFA. The FSR is proposed to improve the semantic performance of remote sensing images and extract local feature information.
(2) The experiments are implemented in a benchmark data set, namely the Beijing Land Use (BLU) dataset, and the RSIs are segmented. Experimental results demonstrate that PSRNet is superior to most existing models.

2 Related Work

2.1 Semantic Segmentation of Images

With the improvement of computing power, researchers began to consider the problem of image semantic segmentation. The appearance of FCN means that deep learning has officially entered the field of image semantic segmentation [5]. Image semantic segmentation is used to automatically segment and recognize the content of an image. The appearance of CNN also plays an important role in image feature extraction, such as in the application of multi-branch encoders in HRNet [6] and RefineNet [7].

The principle of the self-attention mechanism is to let the machine notice the correlation between different parts of the entire input, which has been applied to a variety of visual tasks. In order to achieve biased focusing for different scenes, the Squeeze-and-Excitation Networks (SE-Net) [8] are proposed to be able to aggregate the global information of images well. Channel attention was combined with nonlocal attention mechanisms in a parallel way in DANet [9]. By introducing channel attention to determine the focus position, DANet proposed to determine the focus position [9].Remote sensing segmentation requires high spatial accuracy. In order to improve spatial positioning accuracy, previous studies proposed ResUNet [10], DeepUNet [11], and MPResUNet [12]. In addition to spatial accuracy, boundary feature preservation is also very important for RSIs. The boundary feature is preserved by using MLP to correct the uncertain region predicted by CNN [13–15].

2.2 Application of Multi-scale Pyramid Network in Visual Tasks

Multi-scale pyramids can improve the performance of deep models, so they are widely used in object detection, semantic segmentation, and behavior recognition [16, 17]. A semantic generation gap is yielded after the input image is down-sampled, resulting in low accuracy for small target detection. Because Multi-scale pyramids can show appropriate features for images of different sizes at corresponding scales, and image targets of different sizes can be predicted at different scales through multi-scale information fusion, thus solving the problem of low accuracy for small targets. FPN can improve the accuracy of small target detection by fusing multi-scale information. In addition, such networks as ResNet [18] or DenseNet [19] were exploited in many common networks.

The features at different scales can obtain rich semantic information in Multi- scale pyramids by connecting the high-level features of low resolution and high semantic information and the low-level features of high resolution and low semantic information from top to bottom, so they are widely used in the deep learning of computer vision tasks. Different steps on the convolution kernel are leveraged in the multi-scale pyramid to obtain the FP. For example, PSPNet [20] obtains the multi-scale features through pooling layer pyramid blocks with different sizes.

3 Proposed Dual Branch Network

In this section, the motivation for our established large-scale segmentation model for RSIs is first introduced, and the architecture of the proposed network is expatiated. Then, we describe the multi-scale pyramid module and feature the semantic reasoning module in the local branch. Finally, we report the implementation details.

3.1 Network Architecture

A dual-branch feature extraction attention network is proposed that can well represent the long-range correlation between large images in remote sensing images, as shown in Fig. 1. Our dual branch feature extraction attention network has two coding branches, namely the global branch and the local branch. In the global branch, the commonly used CNN encoder is used to learn the global information, and the local feature information is obtained in the local branch through the clipping operation. The novelty of our network design is to introduce a lightweight multi-scale pyramid module after the local branch encoder and a feature semantic reasoning module before the patch embedding to better extract the useful features in the image. Finally, the global branch A2 is embedded into the local branch A1 through a dual branch transformer, and the final result is yielded by the local branch A1.

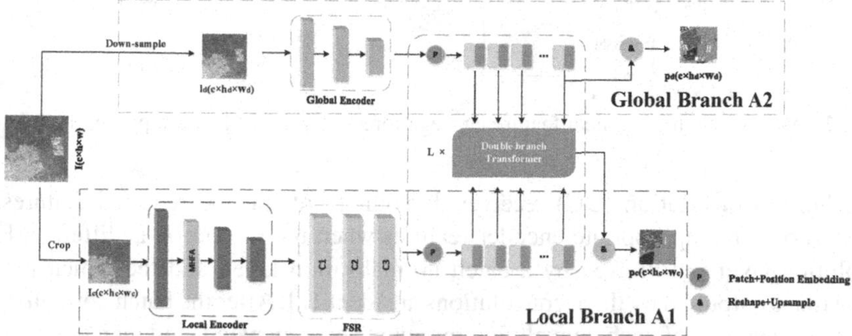

Fig. 1. The architecture of dual-branch pyramid semantic reasoning network.

3.2 Multi-scale Hierarchical Feature Aggregation

Multi-scale feature representation is very important for computer vision tasks. Feature pyramids are widely used in computer vision tasks because they can represent multi-scale features well. Previous research introduced the lightweight Channel-wise Feature Pyramid (CFP) module to remote sensing image and medical image segmentation and achieved good results. On this basis, we propose a MHFA module, which can improve the segmentation performance of small objects. The architecture is shown in Fig. 2.

It includes K channels, and each channel has a corresponding expansion rate rn (n = 1,2,3,4,5). We set the channel number K = 5, and the dilation rates for each channel {r1, r2, r3, r4, r5} = {1,2,4,8,8}. From this, it can be concluded that the dimensions of each channel are the same as M/5 (M denotes the number of scales). Then the outputs of each channel are integrated by HFA. The structure of the FP module in Fig. 2 is shown in Fig. 3, in which three 3 × 3 Convolution blocks are concatenated to obtain the output. So, a FP channel is considered a sub-pyramid. Then the general features of the FP channel are obtained through HFA. The final output FP includes five levels of feature stacks. The calculation formula is as follows:

$$\{L_1 = out_{FP1}, L_2 = L_1 + out_{FP2}, L_3 = L_2 + out_{FP3}, L_4 = L_3 + out_{FP4}, L_5 = L_4 + out_{FP5}\} \tag{1}$$

3.3 Feature Semantic Reasoning

The module is composed of three different convolutions, as shown in Fig. 4. We choose three different convolutions of Pointwise Convolution (PC), Ordinary Convolution (OC),

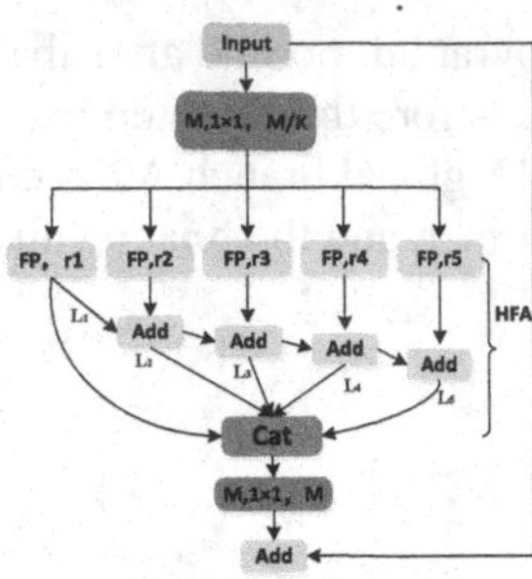

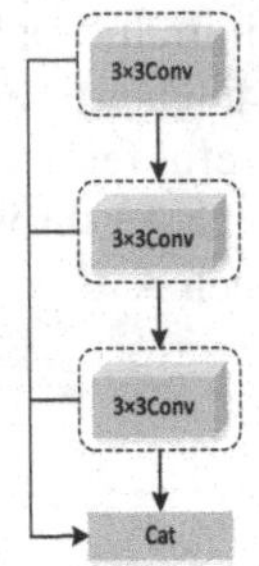

Fig. 2. Multi-scale hierarchical feature aggregation. **Fig. 3.** Feature pyramid module.

and Dilation Convolution (DC) receiver domains to obtain the required features, so we can choose the appropriate encoder features when the resolution is different. Each convolution layer is followed by a batch normalization layer, and the dimensions of feature maps outputted by three convolutions are identical. After the batch normalization layer, these features of each convolution output are concatenated, and then the valuable features are further selected through a PC. The calculation method can be represented as follows:

$$F_{concat} = \sigma_2\left(Concat\left\{ \begin{array}{l} BN\{PointwiseConv(F)\}, \\ BN\{OrdinaryConv(F)\}, \\ BN\{DilationConv(F)\} \end{array} \right\} \right) \quad (2)$$

$$F_s = F \times \sigma_3(\text{Pointwise}Conv(F_{concat})) + F \quad (3)$$

F is the encoding feature, σ_2 and σ_3 are Relu and Sigmoid activation, respectively, F_{concat} are concatenation features, and F_s are output features of multi-scale attention gate and decoder splicing. The module has the same weight as two standard non-local cells. The feature F_s is projected to three vectors q, k, and v, then the attention matrix T is obtained by multiplying q with k and the softmax function (as shown in Fig. 4) and its definition is given by:

$$T = \Phi(q \times k) \quad (4)$$

Φ is expressed as the softmax normalization function along the row dimension. Fs represents the correlation between each pair of spatial positions. Then the enhanced features x are obtained:

$$X = F_s + v \times T \quad (5)$$

4 Experimental Results and Analysis

For assessing our segmentation framework, one publicly available dataset is employed to carry out segmentation experiments. Firstly, the data set used in our experiment is elaborated. Then, the evaluation metrics are described in detail. Also, experimental settings are depicted. Finally, the effects of the ablation study on the results and comparative experiments are described in detail.

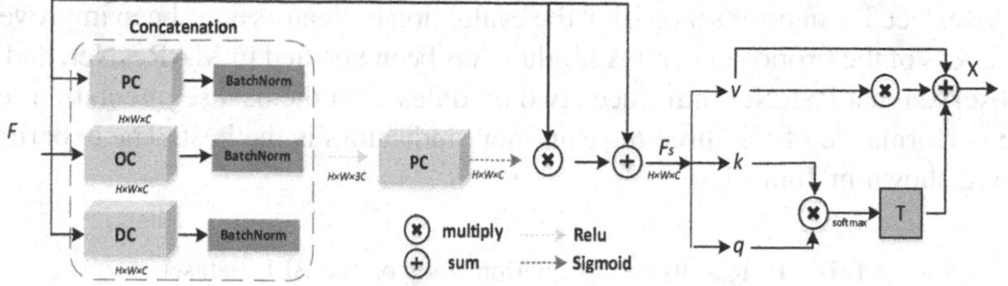

Fig. 4. Feature semantic reasoning module.

4.1 Beijing Land Use Data Set

A new benchmark BLU dataset was used for our experiment. The data is in the form of RGB optical images, which were collected and produced by the Beijing No. 2 satellite of 21st Century Aerospace Science and Technology Co., Ltd. in Beijing in June 2018. On the images collected in this data set, fine grained annotations are constructed based on six land-use (LU) categories, including background, buildings, vegetation, water, agriculture and roads.

4.2 Evaluating Metrics

In this study, three evaluation metrics are leveraged to evaluate the segmentation performance, including overall accuracy (OA), F1, and combined average intersection (mIoU). OA represents the ratio of pixels that can be correctly classified to the sum of all pixels in RSI. The F1 value of each category reveals the harmonic average between accuracy and recall. Taking the BLU dataset as an example, it contains six categories, and each category is evaluated for IoU.

4.3 Experimental Setup

The proposed network and experiments are implemented in the Pytorch framework. The hardware environment used in this study is a server configured with an NVIDIA Quadro T100 GPU. The training period of the data set is 50, the batch size is 32, the learning rate is dynamic, and the initial learning rate is 0.1. Stochastic Gradient Descent is exploited for optimization, and the momentum value is 0.9. Random clipping and random flipping are adopted in each iteration to augment the data. The validation set is evaluated, and the best OA model file is saved when the training is completed.

4.4 Experimental Results

Ablation Study

The innovation of our approach is to embed the MHFA module into the local branch and introduce the FSR module before entering the dual-branch transformer for feature fusion. In order to verify the function of the MHFA module, the proposed MHFA is introduced into MAResNet. It can be observed that the evaluation indicators have been improved, the effectiveness of the proposed MHFA module has been verified in MAResNet, and it has been observed that PSRNet introduces two modules with the best segmentation results, and the performance of the three measurement indicators is the best. The experimental results are shown in Table 1.

Table 1. Results of the ablation study on the BLU dataset.

Dataset	Method	MHFA	FSR	OA (%)	F1(%)	mIoU (%)
BLU	MAResUNet			86.83	81.82	70.03
	MAResUNet	√		86.69	81.93	70.13
	MAResUNet	√	√	87.05	82.40	70.81
	PSRNet(ours)	√	√	87.51	83.02	71.64

Experimental results on the BLU dataset show that PSRNet improves the three evaluation indicators by introducing MHFA and FSR modules. The visualization results are shown in Fig. 5. The figure shows the results of classification segmentation for some sample areas in the BLU dataset. It can be observed that the error between the segmentation categories is reduced, the segmentation boundary is clearer, and the boundary of the square, gray land, is yellow. Therefore, by introducing the MHFA module and the FSR module into the local branch, we can extract the required features and further improve the network segmentation results.

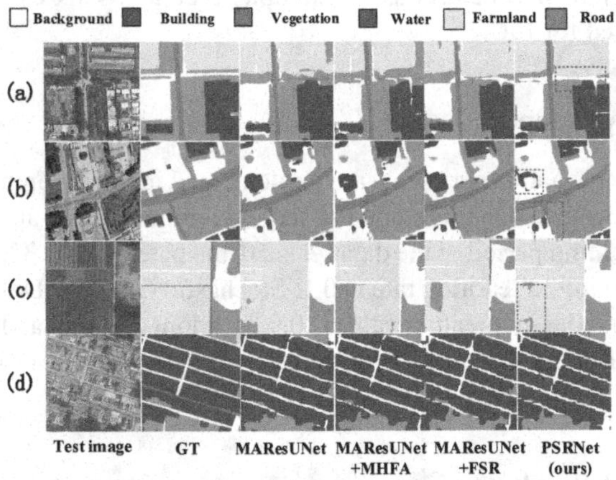

Fig. 5. Ablation study on the BLU datasets. The selected challenging scenes include: (a) occluded Background, (b) clear road surface, (c) yellow farmland, and (d) the background in the middle of the building. (Color figure online)

In order to test the effect of the size of the clipping window on the network segmentation performance, three randomly selected clipping window sizes were used in the experiment: 64, 128, and 256. Observe the changes in the three evaluation results. The experimental results are shown in Table 2. The experimental results show that the size of the clipping window has a certain impact on the evaluation metric. The number of three evaluation metrics of segmentation results presented in a large window of 256 is the best. According to Table 2, when the cropped area is 64 or 128, the segmentation accuracy decreases some compared to 256. The optimal clipping window size is 256, and its segmentation results are about 2% higher than the previous two on mIoU and F1, and about 1% higher on mIoU.

Table 2. The effects of context modeling range on the segmentation accuracy.

Dataset	Metrics	Size of local windows		
		64 × 64	128 × 128	256 × 256
BLU	OA (%) Mean F1 (%) mIoU (%)	84.08 78.12 65.05	86.43 81.53 69.66	**87.51** **83.02** **71.64**

The change in the evaluation index can be seen more intuitively from Fig. 6. We can see more intuitively that the three evaluation metrics are the best when the clipping window size is 256 × 256. The percentage of mIoU increases most significantly. The segmentation results in the 256 cases will increase by about 2% in mIoU and F1, and by about 1% in mIoU.

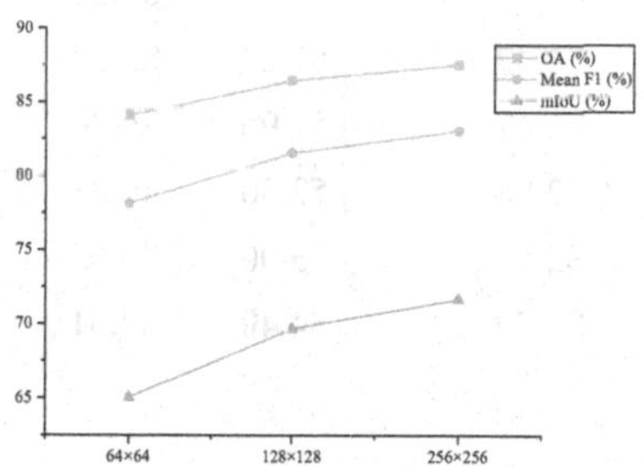

Fig. 6. Changes of three evaluation indicators under different sizes of local windows.

Comparative Experiments

In order to better assess the effectiveness of PSRNet work, the commonly used segmentation models were selected to implement the comparative experiment. These models consist of MPResNet, MAResUNet, and the commonly used IncFCN, UNet, A2FPN, and MSFCN. The experimental results are obtained by using the experimental environment on the server and indicate three different test index sizes obtained from seven experiments in total in Table 3. Analyzing the experimental results in Tables 3 and 4, PSRNet has the best results on F1 and mIoU for the random three land types and has the best results in three evaluation metrics of the overall results. Compared with MPResNet, the test results of PSRNet on F1 and mIoU proposed by us are improved by about 1%.

Table 3. F1 provided by different methods on BLU dataset.

Method	Three-class F1(%)					
	Water	Agricultural	Road	OA(%)	F1(%)	mIoU(%)
IncFCN	82.88	84.52	67.99	85.45	80.19	67.72
UNet	81.99	86.48	69.77	86.56	81.26	69.19
A2FPN	82.11	86.52	67.44	86.33	81.50	68.93
MSFCN	82.44	86.71	68.99	86.36	81.09	68.94
MAResUNet	84.33	87.22	68.88	86.83	81.28	70.03
MPResNet	85.88	86.19	69.88	86.65	82.09	70.34
PSRNet(ours)	**86.00**	**87.98**	**70.77**	**87.51**	**83.02**	**71.64**

Table 4. MIoU provided by different methods on BLU dataset.

Method	Three-class F1(%)					
	Built-up	Vegetation	Road	OA(%)	F1(%)	mIoU(%)
IncFCN	76.01	81.74	50.48	85.45	80.19	67.72
UNet	78.63	82.68	52.76	86.56	81.26	69.19
A2FPN	76.88	82.42	51.22	86.33	81.50	68.93
MSFCN	76.27	82.47	51.96	86.36	81.09	68.94
MAResUNet	78.11	82.88	52.30	86.83	81.28	70.03
MPResNet	78.56	82.51	53.00	86.65	82.09	70.34
PSRNet(ours)	**79.18**	**83.59**	**54.40**	**87.51**	**83.02**	**71.64**

In particular, the results of the three measures of MPResNet on the BLU data set are suboptimal, second only to PSRNet. Introducing MSHA and FSR into local branches can better extract features from images, enhance the semantic performance of required features, and obtain the best test results on BLU data sets. The results indicate that accurate feature extraction is very important for image segmentation. The results are shown in Fig. 7. This paper compares the segmentation and visualization results of some land categories in remote sensing images by our PSRNet and some traditional networks. Compared with other traditional networks, the segmentation results of our proposed network are more accurate, the fragmentation of segmentation categories is reduced, and the boundary is clearer.

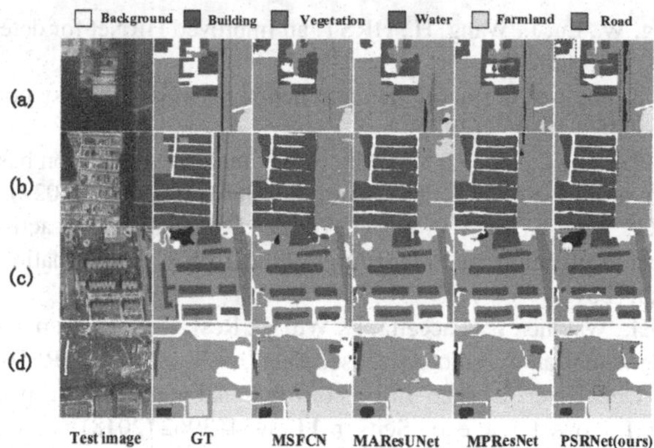

Fig. 7. Comparative experiments on the BLU datasets. The selected challenging scenes include: (a) red building emerging water, (b) background around buildings, (c) blue water and (d) the red building by the background on the right. (Color figure online)

5 Conclusion

The long-range context information in the semantic segmentation network for RSIs plays an important role in the improvement of segmentation performance. Therefore, we propose a dual-branch semantic segmentation network, PSRNet, in which a global and a local branch extract the global information and local information of a remote sensing image, respectively. Because the CNN in the global branch has local restrictions, a dual branch transformer is employed to interact the information between the global branch and the local branch, projecting the information of the global branch to the local branch, which can solve the problem of local restrictions. In addition, in order to better extract local feature information, we proposed a MHFA and FSR for the local branch to further obtain the required local feature information. Experiments are carried out on the BLU dataset, and the results indicate the effectiveness and accuracy of our proposed module. Also, we compare our network with other advanced approaches, and the results demonstrate that our method can improve the segmentation accuracy of RSIs.

References

1. Koutini, K., Eghbal-zadeh, H., Widmer, G: Receptive-field-regularized CNN variants for acoustic scene classification. J. a. p. a. (2019)
2. Niu, Z., Zhong, G., Yu, H.: A review on the attention mechanism of deep learning. J. N. **452**, 48–62 (2021)
3. Yaman, O., Tuncer, T.: Exemplar pyramid deep feature extraction based cervical cancer image classification model using pap-smear images. J. Biomed. Signal Process Control **73**, 103428 (2022)
4. Zeng, N., Wu, P., Wang, Z., Li, H., Liu, W., Liu, X.: A small-sized object detection oriented multi-scale feature fusion approach with application to defect detection. IEEE Trans. Instrument. Measure. **71**, 1–14 (2022)
5. Wang, Z., Gao, X., Wu, R., Kang, J., Zhang, Y.: Fully automatic image segmentation based on FCN and graph cuts. J. M. S **28**, 1753–1765 (2022)

6. Wang, X., Wang, W., Lu, J., Wang, H.: HRST: an Improved HRNet for detecting joint points of pigs. J. S. **22**, 7215 (2022)
7. Zhou, H.,et al.: Refine-net: normal refinement neural network for noisy point clouds. J. I. T. o. P. A. Intell. M. **45**, 946–963 (2022)
8. Yang, Z., Chen, L., Fu, T., Yin, Z., Yang, F.: Spine image segmentation based on U-Net and Atrous spatial pyramid pooling. J. Phys. Conf. Ser. IOP Publishing (2022)
9. Xue, H., Liu, C., Wan, F., Jiao, J., Ji, X., Ye, Q.: Danet: divergent activation for weakly supervised object localization. In: Proceedings of the IEEE/CVF International Conference on Computer Vision (2019)
10. Diakogiannis, F.I., Waldner, F., Caccetta, P., Wu, C.: ResUNet-a: a deep learning framework for semantic segmentation of remotely sensed data. J. I. J. o. P. Sens. R. **162**, 94–114 (2020)
11. Li, R., et al.: DeepUNet: a deep fully convolutional network for pixel-level sea-land segmentation. J. I. j. o. s. t. i. a. e. o., Sens. r. **11**, 3954–3962 (2018)
12. Maji, D., Sigedar, P., Singh, M.: Attention Res-UNet with guided decoder for semantic segmentation of brain tumors. J. B. S. P., Control **71**, 103077 (2022)
13. Tolstikhin, I.O., et al.: MLP-mixer: an all-MLP architecture for vision. J. A. i. n. i. p. s. **34**, 24261–24272 (2021)
14. Pinkus, A.: Approximation theory of the MLP model in neural networks. J. A. n. **8**, 143–195 (1999)
15. Tu, Z., et al.: Maxim: multi-axis MLP for image processing. In: Proceedings of the IEEE/CVF Conference on Computer Vision and Pattern Recognition (2022)
16. Nie, D., Lan, R., Wang, L., Ren, X.: Pyramid architecture for multi-scale processing in point cloud segmentation. In: Proceedings of the IEEE/CVF Conference on Computer Vision and Pattern Recognition (2022)
17. Rajabi, S., Roozkhosh, P., Farimani, N.M.: MLP-based learnable window size for bitcoin price prediction. J. A. S. C. **129**, 109584 (2022)
18. Fan, Z., Lin, H., Li, C., Su, J., Bruno, S., Loprencipe, G.: Use of parallel ResNet for high-performance pavement crack detection and measurement. J. S. **14**, 1825 (2022)
19. Wang, S., et al.: Improved single shot detection using DenseNet for tiny target detection. J. C., Practice, C., Exp. **35**, e7491 (2023)
20. Wang, X., Guo, Y., Wang, S., Cheng, G., Wang, X., He, L.: Rapid detection of incomplete coal and gangue based on improved PSPNet. J. M. **201**, 111646 (2022)

Author Index

L. Iliadis et al. (Eds.): ICANN 2023, LNCS 14255, pp. 593–595, 2023.
https://doi.org/10.1007/978-3-031-44210-0

Printed in the United States
by Baker & Taylor Publisher Services